THE
TEA CLIPPERS
THEIR HISTORY AND DEVELOPMENT 1833-1875

THE
TEA CLIPPERS
THEIR HISTORY AND DEVELOPMENT 1833-1875

David R MacGregor
MA, FSA, FRHistS

CONWAY MARITIME PRESS

FRONTISPIECE:
The lovely *Titania* in dry-dock for repairs to her stem. The date of the photograph is not known but must have been later in her life. (*MacGregor Collection*)

By the same author

The Tea Clippers (1952; reprinted 1972)
The China Bird (1961)
Fast Sailing Ships 1775-1875 (1973)
Square Rigged Sailing Ships (1977)
Clipper Ships (1979)
Merchant Sailing Ships 1775-1815 (1980)

Plans drawn by the author
Additional drawings by J Henderson, F A Claydon and others

© David R MacGregor 1952, 1972 and 1983

First impression 1952. New revised impression 1972. Second Edition, revised and expanded, published 1983 by Conway Maritime Press Ltd, 24 Bride Lane, Fleet Street, London EC4Y 8DR.

ISBN 0 85177 256 0

Designed by Geoff Hunt
Typesetting by Sunset Phototype, Barnet
Page make-up by Letterspace, Barnet
Printed and bound in the United Kingdom by
The Pitman Press, Bath

CONTENTS

To my wife

PREFACE TO NEW EDITION

The first edition of this work appeared thiry years ago under the imprint of Percival Marshall & Co; in 1972 there was a reprint made by Conway Maritime Press Ltd in which some minor corrections were made to the text. In addition, sail plans of *Ariel* and *Challenger* appeared for the first time and there was a new dust jacket. But the book has remained in short supply for some time and as much new material had been discovered in the past three decades, it seemed a good idea, not merely to make a further reprint, but actually to revise the book from cover to cover. This has been done. All the previous text has been carefully scrutinised and over half has been re-written. In addition, a mass of new material has been inserted and in particular many new ship biographies have been added, making 208 of these now against the original total of 88. Two of the original chapters have been split in two, three new ones written, and there are some new appendices. All the new ships have had their passage times incorporated in Appendix II, which was a major undertaking.

Of the people whose assistance I acknowledged in the original Preface, many are no more. But James Henderson has continued as a good friend over the years, supplying me with data about Aberdeen ships, and I should like to thank him for drawing the plans of *Stornoway* and *Chrysolite* especially for this edition. Frederick Claydon has allowed me to make use of his plans of *Taitsing*, *The Caliph* and *Spindrift* which is most generous of him; he has also drawn other plans for this edition, all of which makes a most valuable contribution. I am likewise grateful to Ralph Bird for drawing up the plans of *Lord of the Isles* from material supplied to him

For their comments on the first edition and their subsequent interest I should like to acknowledge the assistance of the late Howard I Chapelle and to thank Cyril L Hume, Roderick W Glassford, Robert S Craig and William Salisbury.

The late Captain Harry Daniel, who was second mate of the four-masted barque *Wanderer* at the age of nineteen, read through the first edition after it was published and found only a few minor errors, with the exception of the fact that I had confused the iron *Vanguard* of 1852 with Kelso's wooden ship of five years later. This is now rectified and each ship has a separate biography.

Some years ago I was able to spend considerable time studying the plans and records of the Clyde-side shipbuilder Alexander Stephen & Sons, and I should like to acknowledge the kindness of the directors at that time for making this possible. Also to the chief draughtsman, Robert W McGregor who, 'for the sake of the Clan', allowed me free access to the plan store.

Another important source of plan material has been that of T & J Brocklebank, and I am grateful to Michael Stammers of the Merseyside Maritime Museum, Liverpool, for allowing me access to their records. Basil W Bathe, when he was Curator of Shipping at the Science Museum, London, provided facilities for research and for measuring half-models.

At the National Maritime Museum, Greenwich, I have received great help and assistance over many years. Basil Greenhill, whose stimulating interest I acknowledged in my first Preface, has been Director of the Museum since 1967. His two-volume history, *The Merchant Schooners* has become a classic and has gone through several editions. He has also written a large number of books on allied subjects. I should also like to acknowledge the assistance of the late George P B Naish and the late Arthur Tucker, and to thank Arthur H Waite, now retired, Dr Alan McGowan and David J Lyon. All these were concerned with plans and models. More recently, George A Osbon, Bernard Carter, and Edward Archibald have helped with photographs and paintings.

Others who have provided material for this new edition include Benjamin E Nicholson, who let me take lines off his half-models of the Annan clippers; Bertram Newbury of the Parker Gallery; Dr and Mrs Donald; the directors of Baring Brothers and their archivist, T Ingram; Christopher Bull for loaning the Ryrie letters to me; Paul Mason of the Paul Mason Gallery; and Malcolm Darch. Denys W Godin, formerly senior partner at Killick, Martin & Co, and latterly David W Gravell, the present managing director, have provided great stimulus to research into the China trade and allowed me to use material on their ships.

In the matter of illustrations of American ships, I am most grateful to John S Carter, Curator of Maritime History at the Peabody Museum, Salem. Andrew Nesdall not only helped with photographs but also gave me a copy of Symondson's *Two Years Abaft the Mast* which has provided such graphic contemporary descriptions. Over the years, Mrs C S Bird has generously given me books and illustrations of American ships and their artists which have been a good source of information.

For help in copying illustrations, I am grateful to Kingston Photographic and to John Mayes of Kingprint; also to Jon Broad for copying the text.

Finally, I am grateful to my wife who has made so much of it possible.

For myself, it is hard to realize that three decades have slipped by since the first edition was undertaken, during which time my interests have certainly broadened to include vessels of many rigs as well as all classes of sailing ships in the last two centuries. But it has been a real pleasure to work exclusively on tea clippers once again.

David R MacGregor
Barnes, London, 1982

LARGER SCALE COPIES OF THE PLANS
REPRODUCED IN THIS BOOK CAN BE
OBTAINED ON APPLICATION TO THE
AUTHOR AT 99 LONSDALE ROAD, LONDON
SW13, ENGLAND

1

HISTORY OF THE TRADE
AND THE BUSINESS OF HANDLING TEA

The story of the British trade with China falls into three parts: the monopoly of the East India Company when all trade was centred at Canton; the days of free trade at Treaty Ports when the sailing ship was still supreme; and thirdly, the rapid expansion of trade in the age of steamers. This book is concerned with the second heading and especially with the carriage of tea during the period between the repeal of the Navigation Laws in 1849 and the opening of the Suez Canal twenty years later, when an influx of steamers the following year quite altered the general aspect of the China trade. But before examining the conditions affecting the running of the tea trade in the 1850s and 1860s, a brief survey of events leading up to the unique position occupied by Great Britain and other countries in their commercial relations with China may prove of interest.

The first Europeans to reach China by sea were the Portuguese who in 1557 were allowed to settle on a small promontory where they founded the town of Macao. They were followed by the Spaniards and then by the Dutch. Great Britain was the next country to send ships into these waters, but their efforts to trade, firstly by means of the Honourable East India Company's ship *London* in 1635 and then through Captain John Weddell two years later, met with little success. Although tea was not obtained on these two occasions, by the 1660s it was fast becoming a fashionable drink at the Restoration Court of Charles II, when the first import duty on it was levied.

In 1685 the Manchu Emperor opened all his ports to foreign trade, but later closed them, permitting the 'foreign devils' merely to trade at Canton. Here the European merchants established their houses or 'factories', and under the intolerable 'Eight Regulations' were allowed to do business through the medium of the Co-Hong or group of Chinese merchants. The authorities wished to subject foreign merchants to every indignity, but not to discourage them altogether, as enormous benefit was derived from the vast customs duties that were levied. Although the East India Company yearly grew more powerful, the Chinese always considered its members as mere barbarians who naturally wished to bring tribute to the Celestial Empire.

This state of affairs could not last after the East India Company lost its China monopoly in 1834 (it had lost its complete Asiatic monopoly in 1813) since the merchants, now their own masters, believed that only the opening of Chinese ports to free trade could put their business on a sound commercial basis.

The *Canton Register* of 4 February 1834 recorded that the notice about the beginning of free trade was first received

on 27 January with the arrival of the East Indiaman *Elizabeth*. On 28 October 1834 the same paper stated that the new Act permitted tea to be imported into the United Kingdom from any port to the east of the Cape of Good Hope meridian. Accordingly some English merchant, studying his map of Europe, found that Dantzic (now Gdansk) was 15 miles east of this meridian and so imported 2200 chests of tea into Liverpool consigned to Rathbone Bros. This proved to be the first tea ever unloaded by ship at this port. Of course, it was not the intention of the Act to qualify any European country as a tea exporting nation.

The East India Company in China, who could only find a limited market for a few English manufactured goods, had never been able to balance their shipments of tea with the import of metals, cotton and woollen goods, without the additional import of silver. But by increasing the growing of opium in India, they encouraged the 'country' firms to smuggle the drug into China at such a huge profit that the firms were willing to give the Company the use of the silver, for which opium was always sold, to help pay for the tea, accepting bills on London in exchange. The merchants argued that if other ports besides Canton were opened to trade, then the markets for foreign goods would be unlimited, and their import would amply repay for the tea.

Led by the house of Jardine, Matheson & Co, who were the successors in 1828 to the old firm of Magniac & Co, the merchants requested the authorities in London to back up their just demands with a show of force. A series of complications then arose which finally reached a climax when most of the opium for the 1839 season was surrendered at the demand of the Chinese Imperial Commissioner at Canton. War by then was inevitable and, after a somewhat dilatory campaign, the Treaty of Nanking was signed in 1842, in which Hong Kong was ceded absolutely to Great Britain, whilst the ports of Canton, Amoy, Foochow, Ningpo and Shanghai were opened to free trade, with Consuls at each, where the merchants could buy and sell without the offices of the Co-Hong.

Of these 'Treaty Ports', Canton remained the most important as far as the export of tea was concerned until the early 1850s. Ships loaded at Whampoa, which was situated on an island in the Pearl river, 10 miles below Canton and 60 above Macao. Shanghai, which was already an important native port, became another centre for the loading of tea, until, with the increasing desire for speed in the transaction of business, tea was found to be available for shipment at Foochow earlier than at any other port. Here the first tea was probably loaded into the *Foam* in the 1853–54

Above: Tea bushes being cultivated on a small farm in the Bohea hills (From *Illustrations of China and its People*, 1873)

Opposite: Weighing tea in front of a foreign merchant. (From *Illustrations of China and its People*, 1873)

season, and the next year quite a number of ships sailed crammed full of tea. From then on Foochow was the most popular loading port for the crack ships. The anchorage was off Pagoda Island, on the Min river, 11 miles below the town and 22 from the outer bar. Shanghai, where the foreign concessions had to be built on what at one time were mud banks, was rather nearer to the open water, being 12 miles up the Whangpoo river from Woosung, which was situated on the estuary of the great Yangtze Kiang. Ningpo shipped no tea until steamers engulfed the trade, while occasional ships loaded at Amoy at the end of the season. The only tea shipped at Hong Kong was brought there by schooner from Amoy and ports along the coast. But ships sailing for home might occasionally call there while half the outward-bound ships would terminate their passages there. Most of the ports had ample dock facilities and repair yards, which were necessary to deal with frequent accidents owing to the dangerous navigation between the ports and the sea and along the coast, though Foochow was notable in not possessing a dry-dock until early in the 1860s.

Prior to the Treaty of Nanking in 1842, each country maintained its own 'factory' at Canton which formed a sort of consular post to which the captains, agents and merchants could repair and perhaps find mutual support in their negotiations. The East India Company employed a staff of twenty and the establishment cost £100,000 annually. The sale price of tea in London had to cover such costs as this. The merchant houses, soon after 1842, were busy building their own offices at Hong Kong and other Treaty Ports although floating hulks acted as 'receiving ships' at the ports for many years, giving a merchant a cheap form of storage which was strictly under the control of his own servants.

The Tientsin Treaty of 1858 after the second Anglo-Chinese War – in which Canton was blockaded so that no tea was loaded there in 1857 and none until late in 1858 – opened up ports on the Yangtze as from April 1861, of which the most important was Hankow, 586 miles above Shanghai. The first ship to load tea there appears to have been the *Challenger*. Hankow was in the centre of a vast network of canals extending throughout the Empire, which made the place an excellent base from which to open new markets. The facility with which goods could be taken anywhere on the inland waterways brought similar prosperity to Shanghai, since the port was able to handle a mass of varied cargoes, never depending solely on the export of tea. Indeed ships loading tea at Shanghai always made up their cargo with up to 4000 or 5000 baleq of raw silk.

The system of inland waterways which the Chinese had highly developed, provided a very easy though slow means of transporting marketable goods to the ports, in spite of the fact that many of the canals were in decay through lack of attention. On these canals sampans brought down the teas from inland to the waiting ships.

There were said to be four crops obtained from the tea bushes, which were cultivated on small holdings as opposed to the large plantations in India or Ceylon. Of these four, only the first two were for export, the others being reserved for home consumption. The first picking, known as 'show-chun', or 'first spring', began about the middle of April, yielding only a small quantity, but of the highest quality. This was made up of 'two leaves and a bud'; but the second crop was of leaves and was picked at the beginning of June. The other two pickings occurred first in July and then late in the season, producing only common teas. The tea would be manufactured locally and then taken by sampans to the Treaty Ports.

Teas were either black or green according to the method of drying them before they were packed up. England principally imported black tea, the green going chiefly to America. The first picking was limited in quantity and yielded the best flavoured tea and thus the most valuable. Pekoe was one of the most expensive of the black teas to be picked in the first crop. Kaisow, named after various tea districts inland, was another. The best black teas were grown in the province of Fukien for which Foochow was the chief port, and to which fact it owed its rapid growth to become the most important loading port. In 1863 out of a total export figure of 128,000,000lbs of tea, Foochow exported 69,000,000lbs at a value of £4 million. Of the green teas, Gunpowder was from the first crop and the most expensive.

Congou and Souchong teas belonged to the second and later crops. The former was by far the most widely sold tea in England being one of the cheapest types and much of it

was loaded at Canton. Various types of Hyson were green teas of the second crop.

In the days of the Company's monopoly the term 'new season's tea' did not strictly exist. Tea as bought in London from a retailer was never less than from 18 to 24 months old. To begin with, the Indiamen always sailed from China during the strength of the favourable monsoon, between November and March, and then, when the teas did arrive home, perhaps four, five or six months later, they were stored in bonded warehouses for about a year, since a large reserve was necessary in case the China fleet failed to arrive. After the Treaty of Nanking this large reserve became a burden since the new teas were disposed of as soon as they arrived and with the import figure gradually rising, the reserve tea was put on the market only to be replaced by a larger quantity. In the early 1860s, almost 100,000,000lbs were in store at the end of the season, much to the merchants' distress, especially since some of it had been bought at prices which had become impossible to realize. Generally speaking the longer teas were kept in store the richer the flavour they assumed.

The quantity imported never varied much from year to year prior to 1834, the total for 1819 being 24,000,000lbs. Tea had become a national drink by the beginning of the nineteenth century, and it was so popular that although the duty charged on the wholesale price rose to 100 per cent the demand for tea remained constant. With wholesale prices ranging from less than 2s 6d to almost 7s some of the retail prices were up to 18s per lb.

It is true that the influence and policy of the Company was not cast aside immediately, yet the Treaty of Nanking swept away all traces of the long monopoly extending over two centuries so that free trade and competition had by the end of the 1840s created a market in England for the delicate and fragrant new season's tea. Whereas before 1834 the crop did not reach Canton before October, the bulk coming down in the next three months, by 1848 a few ships were leaving Whampoa at the end of July.

It is interesting how changes in legislation, by which trade was made freer, materially increased the import of tea into Great Britain. For instance, in 1834, 33,600,000lbs of tea were imported – the figures being taken to the nearest 100,000 – but a year later had increased to 44,300,000lbs as a result of the monopoly ending. The Navigation Laws were repealed in 1849; in the following year the imports were 50,500,000lbs; but for 1851, when American ships first began affecting the British tea trade, imports rose to 71,400,000lbs of which almost four-fifths was black tea. Of this total, some was re-exported to Europe from England since only seven or eight ships of varying nationalities took tea home direct from China.

The demand was now for tea which had been gathered at the first picking and merchants had no difficulty in selling it as soon as it arrived in the docks. Not only did it become fashionable to drink the freshest tea but also the tea which had been in the first ship to arrive. If one vessel could outdistance the others and by some good fortune arrive a week ahead, then the merchants concerned were sure of securing a good price. A certain writer of the 1920s, recounting his experiences at sea in the last century, recalled having drunk 'Belted Will' Tea' before ever he went to sea. The glamour attached to tea carried by a well-known ship might procure a higher price for it than if it had gone by an outsider. With this incentive of high prices for the first teas to arrive, shippers in China did their utmost to get the teas away as early as possible. During the 1850s, tea was shipped at Foochow from about 10 June, Shanghai and Canton being sometimes five or six weeks later. In the next decade a few ships used to get away from Foochow at the end of May and at about the same time from Hankow, which was in the centre of some of the other tea districts. By about 1869, the bulk of the season's tea had been shipped by the end of November, the total of 63,000,000lbs in 1853 having been doubled in ten years and trebled immediately steamers entered the trade on a large scale. The steady lowering of tea duties gradually encouraged a larger import. The rate during the 1840s and until 1853 was 2s 1d per lb. It then fell to 1s 6d, rose again, and in 1863 was reduced from 1s 5d to 1s. Two years later this was cut by half and remained so until 1889.

After the new teas had come down to the ports and a number of small lots had been collected together and bought by native firms, the long process of valuing the teas began. Merchants in London to whom teas were consigned would have notified firms such as Jardine, Matheson or

Dent & Co, who acted as their agents in China, that they wanted to buy teas of such and such a quality, price and description, whilst many firms resident in China besides acting as agents would decide to buy on their own account. Agents for the owners would also be in touch at the various ports with the consignees' agents, and between them they would probably have decided which ships were to load first. Many considerations had to be taken into account, but usually the vessels judged to be capable of making the shortest passages were preferred. In most of the business relations with the Chinese, foreign firms employed a native manager known as the 'compradore' (derived from the Portuguese word *compra* to buy), whose astuteness frequently gave his employer a fortune or else saved him from disaster. But though the compradore was a good buyer, he failed as a salesman of foreign goods, and as soon as members of native firms became acquainted with the manners and manufactured articles of Western civilization, he gradually faded from the scene.

When sufficient quantities of the new crop had accumulated for its merits to be judged, the tea men or 'chaa-szes' employed by the consignees' agents would commence to value the new crop and make offers to the native brokers, and after much haggling, which might last a week, a price was agreed upon.

Dramatic scenery in a gorge on the Pei-kiang river which flows into the Canton river. Such craft might have brought tea down to the clippers. (*Central Office of Information*)

This price would be reported, for instance, as from '36.50 taels to 38.25 taels per picul in 7 chops' as was the case at Hankow in July 1864. A 'tael' was worth about 6s 6d at this time and a 'picul' consisted of just over 133lbs. A 'chop' was a variable measure referring to a collection or 'parcel' of chests of tea, all of the same kind. The seven chops referred to here were therefore each composed of a separate kind of tea, the number of chests perhaps varying from a few hundred to a thousand. The word chop also occurs in the term 'chop-boat', which, with a capacity of 600 chests, used to take tea out to the waiting ships.

The prices cited above must be considered to be amongst some of the highest paid, and with freights so steep at Hankow the corresponding sale on arrival must have been high to give any profit. Unfortunately, about this time buyers were being sent out from England who had had little or no experience and were unused to intricate bargaining, but only wished to secure parcels of the new crop as speedily as possible in order to lose no time in dispatching them to England. Black tea of itself required careful preparation which meant that the best teas did not come down till the very end of May and probably remained in store in the 'godowns' or warehouses for at least two weeks until a price was agreed upon. Yet so great was the desire to get the ships loaded and away for home that poor tea was rushed on to the market merely to dispatch a clipper. In many cases, what new tea there was, was adulterated with the remains of the previous season's crop, with disastrous results.

In 1867 for instance, when up to 34 taels per picul was paid at Foochow (considered a high price there) for the new teas, which must have been bought without proper sampling and inspection, it was found on their arrival home that the new Kaisows had been badly adulterated with old leaves, thereby destroying their richness and flavour, whilst the later ships brought teas of finer quality. The consignees of the first teas to arrive can hardly have made much profit on the transaction, since whereas the usual wholesale price for Kaisows was from 2s 6d to 3s per lb, these teas went at only 1s 5d to 2s 2d per lb.

Two years earlier the duty on tea had been lowered again, thereby nominally cutting the retail price. Yet the astute dealers at once raised their wholesale prices by 6d per lb as the public were by then well accustomed to paying high prices, while the native firms in China demanded one tael per picul more. At this time the native firms worked together and so frequently could hold out against the disunited efforts of the chaa-szes. If any house was so eager to make purchases that they did not mind paying a high price, then all the other firms were bound to accept this figure for the particular chops on the market and make their purchases accordingly.

It was not until after 1869 when communications and travel speeded up considerably in the East that telegrams would occasionally be sent by the head office in London to the chaa-szes, saying 'do not buy' or 'buy at your discretion'. Writing home from Hong Kong in March 1872, Phineas Ryrie who was with Turner & Co referred to his 'regular work' as 'daily steamers and hourly telegrams – I am very tired of it.' This was in quite a different vein from his earlier letters of the 1850s, one of which is quoted later.

Before the steamers came the buyers made purchases as they thought fit, making selections themselves. At the close of the nineteenth century instructions were sent out from London and samples sent home for approval by fast mail steamer and later by air. The establishment of several reputable banking firms in China during the 1860s helped to produce modern methods of financing the trade.

As public demand for the new crop increased as from 1860, so the trade gradually became unable to maintain consistently the quality of tea and at the same time supply the early demands. So great was the interest centred on the rapid carriage of tea that it seemed as if the complex machinery of the China trade existed merely to organize a race between clippers in which tea was the cargo carried.

After a price was agreed upon for the tea, one of the next things to fix was the loading freight for the first ships. This had to be determined at the beginning of each season.

Before the days of free trade in China, the East India Company chartered most of their tea ships, paying the owners high rates of freight for their use. When Canton was the only port open for trade with a regular supply of tea and ships, freight rates maintained an average of £5 per ton of 50 cubic feet, sometimes sinking to £3 and at times of crisis rising to £12. This would be only a nominal rate, for example in the Anglo-Chinese War when there were no vessels at Whampoa. With the opening of the Treaty Ports and trade finding its feet, freight depended chiefly on the amount of tonnage available. At the beginning of the 1850s with many ships waiting for the teas to come down, freights would range from £3 10s to £5 10s for tea, with those for silk higher by £1 per ton of 50 cubic feet. 1854 seems to have been the last year in which, with tonnage scarce in December, freights rose to £7. After this year, freights only rose to that height at the commencement of the season when a ship noted for making a fast passage was engaged to load the new teas. American ships loaded at 40 cubic feet per ton.

From the 1850s onwards the day of the large commercial house which owned its own ships was beginning to fade, and even the chartering of ships by firms for their own tea which their own people had bought was starting to become unusual, as the desire to get tea home as fast as possible became the ruling factor. The case of the *Oriental* provides one of the earliest instances of a ship with a name receiving a freight of £2 10s per ton higher than any other vessel. Clippers always loaded at 10s higher than others and small ships were sometimes offered £1 more. During the 1860s ships could get up to £8 at Hankow due to the risks involved, but freights usually started at from £3 10s to £5 10s elsewhere, falling to £1 10s by the end of the year. In 1861 a premium of 10s per ton was offered by the consignees to the owner of the first ship in dock, whilst individual ships at different times often had their bills of lading signed at £1 per ton extra if first home, the *Vision* in 1854 being probably the first British ship to be so treated. In 1867, because of the dead heat the previous year, the premium was removed, but an owner who had got a high rate frequently gave a bonus of £100 or more to his captain and crew.

On one occasion the owners of the *Robin Hood* gave her master, John Mann, a present of £100 for bringing his ship safely home after damaging the rudder and after having to steer with a makeshift tiller. His grandson had the story from his father who was a young boy at the time, and who had gone with his mother and brother to greet his father's arrival. The bag of sovereigns was left on the table of the hotel

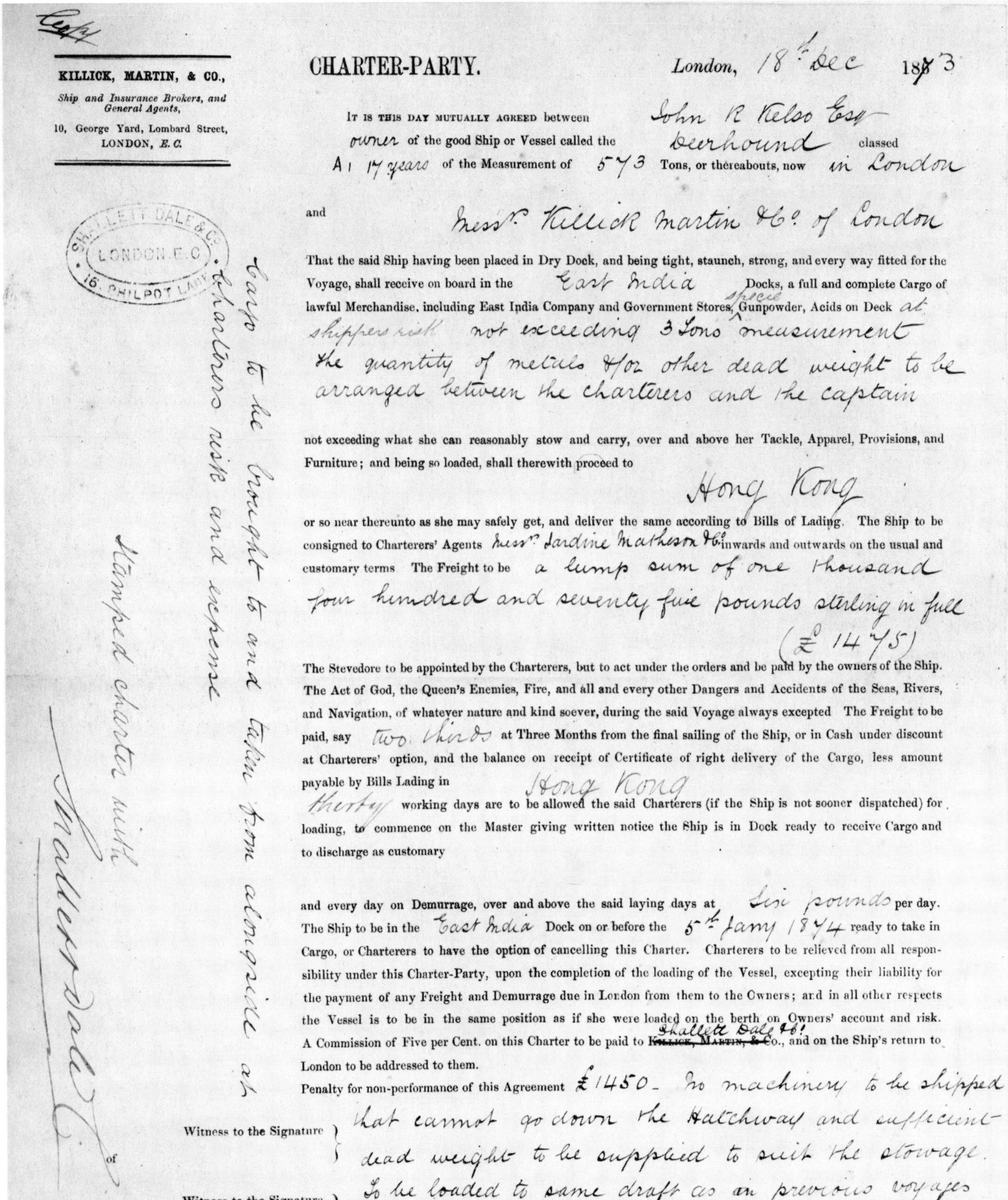

Copy

KILLICK, MARTIN, & CO.,
Ship and Insurance Brokers, and General Agents,
10, George Yard, Lombard Street,
LONDON, E.C.

[stamp: SHALLETT DALE & Co. LONDON. E.C. 16. PHILPOT LANE]

CHARTER-PARTY.

London, 18ᵗʰ Dec 18*7*3

IT IS THIS DAY MUTUALLY AGREED between *owner* of the good Ship or Vessel called the A 1 *17 years* of the Measurement of *573* Tons, or thereabouts, now *in London*

John R Kelso Esq *Deerhound* classed

and *Messʳˢ Killick Martin &Cᵒ of London*

That the said Ship having been placed in Dry Dock, and being tight, staunch, strong, and every way fitted for the Voyage, shall receive on board in the *East India* Docks, a full and complete Cargo of lawful Merchandise, including East India Company and Government Stores, *specie* Gunpowder, Acids on Deck *at shippers risk not exceeding 3 Tons measurement the quantity of metals &/or other dead weight to be arranged between the charterers and the captain*

not exceeding what she can reasonably stow and carry, over and above her Tackle, Apparel, Provisions, and Furniture; and being so loaded, shall therewith proceed to

Hong Kong

or so near thereunto as she may safely get, and deliver the same according to Bills of Lading. The Ship to be consigned to Charterers' Agents *Messʳˢ Jardine Matheson &Cᵒ* inwards and outwards on the usual and customary terms The Freight to be *a lump sum of one thousand four hundred and seventy five pounds sterling in full*

(£ *1475*)

The Stevedore to be appointed by the Charterers, but to act under the orders and be paid by the owners of the Ship. The Act of God, the Queen's Enemies, Fire, and all and every other Dangers and Accidents of the Seas, Rivers, and Navigation, of whatever nature and kind soever, during the said Voyage always excepted The Freight to be paid, say *two thirds* at Three Months from the final sailing of the Ship, or in Cash under discount at Charterers' option, and the balance on receipt of Certificate of right delivery of the Cargo, less amount payable by Bills Lading in *Hong Kong* *thirty* working days are to be allowed the said Charterers (if the Ship is not sooner dispatched) for loading, to commence on the Master giving written notice the Ship is in Dock ready to receive Cargo and to discharge as customary

and every day on Demurrage, over and above the said laying days at *Six pounds* per day. The Ship to be in the *East India* Dock on or before the *5ᵗʰ Janʸ 1874* ready to take in Cargo, or Charterers to have the option of cancelling this Charter. Charterers to be relieved from all responsibility under this Charter-Party, upon the completion of the loading of the Vessel, excepting their liability for the payment of any Freight and Demurrage due in London from them to the Owners; and in all other respects the Vessel is to be in the same position as if she were loaded on the berth on Owners' account and risk. A Commission of Five per Cent. on this Charter to be paid to ~~Killick, Martin, & Co.~~, *Shallett Dale &Cᵒ* and on the Ship's return to London to be addressed to them.

Penalty for non-performance of this Agreement £*1450* *No machinery to be shipped that cannot go down the Hatchway and sufficient dead weight to be supplied to suit the stowage. To be loaded to same draft as in previous voyages*

Witness to the Signature)
)
of

Witness to the Signature)
)
of *Killick Martin &Cᵒ*)
signed Thomas Walton

(signed) John R Kelso
" Killick Martin &Cᵒ
20/12/73

[left margin, vertical handwriting] *Cargo to be brought to and taken from alongside at charterers risk and expense* *Stamped charter with* *Shallett Dale* *of* *Demurrage £6* ...

Above: Unloading tea from ships in the East India Docks, London. *(MacGregor Collection)*

Left: Charter Party document between John R Kelso, owner of *Deerhound,* and Killick, Martin & Co, for a passage out to Hong Kong in early 1874. *(Jardine, Matheson Archives)*

bedroom where they were staying in London and whilst the parents were out of the room, the two children opened it and stuffed most of the golden sovereigns into the cracks in the floorboards. What consternation there was when the parents returned! They were obliged to take up the boards to recover the money.

As regards the actual settlement of freight, the owner's agents or captain would probably demand a certain price per ton and the agents for the consignees would have to make a decision, considering the price paid for the tea and the profit obtainable in London, the number of ships offering their services, and the possibility of one ship being far superior to the rest. Such a vessel might get a higher freight or be offered a higher premium if she could arrive home before any other.

On some occasions a vessel would offer her services at, say, 10s per ton less than the freight reigning, simply to get a cargo if there was not much demand for tonnage. In that case every ship loading would be obliged to adopt the new rate, while the tea already shipped and for which bills of lading had been signed, possibly by then on their way to London for insurance by the consignee, would have to be considered to have been loaded at this reduced freight. Sometimes ships would arrive unexpectedly and the captain or supercargo would do his best to find a tea cargo. Captains would always play an important part, perhaps acting for their owners without the use of agents, and frequently would not load if the freights were too low. The alternative would be one or more voyages up and down the coast, or to India, to fill in the time until the next season commenced. Some ships, principally those registering about 900 tons or more, might be chartered by the Government on some expedition. The usual rate was 22s 6d per ton, but when many vessels were disengaged, as was the case at Hong Kong in April 1860, the rate fell to 17s 6d. Quite often ships whose names do not appear in the sailing lists in Appendix II were so employed.

F H W Symondson, who was an apprentice on the ship *Inverness* during a voyage to Australia, China, New York and home to London in 1872–74, wrote of his experiences in 1876 in a book entitled *Two Years Abaft the Mast,* and referred to this difficulty of procuring a freight from Foochow at the end of August 1873:

Over five weeks had passed since our arrival, and we still remained without a freight; and, sailor-like, we began to speculate freely upon our destination, aided by the customary unfathomable rumours. One day it was reported that we were going to Formosa to load coals for Borneo; then that the captain had accepted a charter of tea back to Sydney. At last it transpired that he had arranged to take a native cargo of 'poles' (trunks of trees) to Shanghai, in the hopes of securing a tea-freight there for London. The owners had written to him, attacking him severely for his want of success; and being a thoroughly conscientous [sic] man, he seemed to feel it.

The master was Ferguson and his wife accompanied him.

With communication not so very much ahead of the ships actually carrying the tea, there tended to be little buying and selling of cargoes before their arrival home. When it was known that the first ships had been reported in the Channel, there was great excitement and a good deal of tension. One of the leading brokers actually had a wind indicator in their sale room operated from a vane on the roof, and this was eagerly watched for any change which might make a difference in getting tea on the market first, although one can hardly credit them with expecting winds in the Channel to be exactly similar to those whistling around their chimney pots. The brokers acting for the various consignees, who were either merchants in London or China, would be down at the docks when the first ships arrived, ready to break out a few chests from which samples were rapidly taken. These would be sent to dealers whom the brokers considered would be likely to buy. If the dealers' offers were accepted, the financial transaction would take place through the broker who would take his commission or brokerage of 1 per cent from the merchant and also half that from the dealer. The dealer would then offer his purchases at auction to the wholesaler. Most of the tea buyers and brokers had their offices in Mincing Lane. To show the speed with which ships were unloaded, the *Fiery Cross* docked in St Katherine's Dock at 4 am on 20 September 1864, and by 10 am next day had discharged her cargo of 14,000 chests.

Of all goods imported into Great Britain, tea was one of the few in which vessels raced each other in their attempts to get it on the market. During the 1850s, commercial papers concerned with wholesale prices and the state of trade mentioned that the new teas were being auctioned, but nothing more. By the middle of the next decade the names of the ships arriving with certain kinds of tea appeared in print, and soon even accounts of the contest were noted down – the one piece of print calling for a shade of imagination amongst lists of commodities and columns of monetary transactions.

But while the prospects for homeward-bound ships were good, outward passages were never so profitable with freights only a third or a quarter of those ruling in China. Insurance of outward cargoes was admittedly less – from £2 5s per ton to Hong Kong and from £3 5s to Shanghai – but then tea was considered more valuable than a general cargo and the risk worth 15s extra. In times of crisis or when there was special competition to get goods out of the country freights did indeed rise. For instance in 1853, after gold had been discovered in Australia, the iron tea clipper *Gauntlet*, an untried ship, left on her maiden voyage for Hobson's Bay to race out against the American *Sovereign of the Seas*, and at an early date brokers refused to load goods at less than £6 10s per ton. Her freight list thus amounted to £7000.

Outward-bound ships were laid on the berth with the sailing date advertised and merchants desiring to send goods on board would contact the loading brokers. In the China trade, Killick, Martin & Co of Lombard Street, and Robert-son & Co of Cornhill, were the leading brokers. Woollen cotton and linen goods ('Manchester goods') and metal were exported, as was also coal and heavy gear such a railway iron or parts of a patent slip. All ships went either to Hong Kong or Shanghai, and with so many ships seeking cargoes, freights were nearly always lower a these two ports than at Foochow, to which the majority o ships only went in ballast in order to load tea.

Loading the tea was performed entirely by Chinese steve-dores of which there were no better in the world. Before the tea came alongside, the ballast had to be very carefully arranged. Clippers employed regularly in the trade carried some 100 tons of iron kentledge built in between the floors, with perhaps 150 to 250 tons of clean shingle in addition, o which three-quarters was laid on top of the floors and the rest used for dunnage at the sides. The best position for the permanent iron kentledge was on each side of the keelson Frequently some ballast was kept in reserve in order to trim the ship, as this factor was of the utmost importance in order to maintain the ship's sailing powers at the highest level. On occasions, vessels out of trim by some eight or nine inches were known to be a knot slower than usual over the whole passage. Most ships trimmed best from an even keel to six inches by the stern, and after getting to sea there was often much shifting of provisions, coal, spare anchors, etc, in order to gain the best trim. *Ariel* was well known for using a 12ft long box filled with heavy objects for this purpose, and with her flush deck the box could easily be dragged to the most suitable position.

After the ballast had been laid, the ironwork in the hold painted, and the woodwork scraped clean, loading was ready to begin. The first sampan alongside would bring a flooring chop of either green or old tea to be laid immediately on top of the ballast as a protection to the rest of the cargo at a freight of 10s per ton less than the accepted rate. The tea chests were hove up on platforms from the sampans and lowered into the hold.

Captain R Little RNR, as quoted in *The Stowage of Ship and their Cargoes* by Robert W Stevens (1869 edition) admirably describes the entire method of ballasting and loading, and the following is his account of the process Captain Little commanded the *John Temperley* (1856) whe she loaded tea at Foochow on three occasions in the 1860s.

> The usual way of dunnaging a tea cargo in China, is to level th ballast even with the upper part of the keelson – in some cases little higher, according to the form of the ship. The depth i further regulated by taking into consideration the distance from the under part of the lower deck to the surface of the ballast s that a calculated number of tiers of chests may come in exactly after the ballast is *carefully* levelled and rounded down toward the wings; this rounding is done to give the tiers the exact curv of the deck and beams. The distance is measured very precise' with rods, as the ballast is being levelled, and the Chine stevedores will thus detect the projection of the smallest ston which is immediately removed. The ballast is covered wit half-inch boards, supplied for the purpose by the stevedores at moderate rate. The ground tier, or 'flooring chop' as it is calle in China, is then laid; the lower corners of the wing chest being kept 14 to 18 inches from the bilges of the ship. The wing are then filled in with ballast, which is levelled for the secon tier and covered with planks where that tier overlaps the firs the same as under the ground tier. The second tier is laid on th first, and the lower corners of the wing chests are carried out t about 8, 10, or 12 inches from the side, according to the form o

the ship and the quantity of ballast required to be stowed away. It is then levelled as before, and the third tier laid; the wing chests are brought to within three or four inches of the sides, the intervening space being filled in with small ballast kept especially for that purpose. When this tier is completed, the hold, in the estimation of a practical and intelligent seaman, has an appearance worthy of being admired – the surface looks like a splendid deck, flush from stem to stern. Above this tier the dunnage used is split bamboo interwoven trellis-fashion, say from two to four inches thick. There is no dunnage of any kind between the sides or ends of the three lower tiers of tea chests and the ballast, which is always very hard stone or shingle – porous sandstone or anything approaching to it being inadmissible. [The heat of a dry tea cargo will draw dampness from any porous stone previously in contact with water, and render the tea out of condition and flat.] The pump-well, chain lockers, masts, etc, were dunnaged with half-inch boards the same as on the ballast under the ground tier chop. The lower deck was dunnaged with one-inch stuff; sides with split bamboo interwoven, same as below. No matting of any kind was used on the cargo in the main hold or in the 'tween decks. In stowing the tiers they are begun from the sides, and finished in the middle. When fairly entered two Chinamen get on and jamb them down in their places, after which the tier is beaten even at the edges with a heavy wooden mallet about one foot square, and the chests are squeezed in so tight that the wing (or end) chests take the shape of the sides of the ship without injury to the packages, when properly stowed.

A first-hand account of how tea was loaded aboard the *Inverness* at Foochow in September and October 1873 is given by F W H Symondson in *Two Years Abaft the Mast:*

We had now been in port a week, and the native cargo from Shanghai was all discharged. We had cleared up the hold, levelled the ballast, and already had some two hundred half-chests of Oolongs stowed away, I being made tallyman. As the chests leave the lighter or 'chop', a small bamboo stick is wedged in between the cane lashings. This the tallyman withdraws just before they slide into the hold, and when he has collected one hundred he makes an entry in his tally-book, and returns the bamboos from whence they came . . .
The tea came down but slowly. One day would see perhaps 200 to 250 half-chests stowed away in the hold, while the following day and the next to that would pass away without any 'chop' coming alongside. Each tea 'chop' carries the flag of its shipping house, so that whenever one hove in sight with its huge mat sail, we could tell at once to what vessel she was bound. The time occupied in loading a ship with tea in Foo-chow ranges from a fortnight to two months and even more. Fortunately we were in no great hurry, as the later we sailed the weather would be less severe for New York.

Everyone is familiar with tea chests, which have changed little in their appearance since the middle of the last century. At that time the sizes were various, each tea being packed in its own particular size of chest. Congou and Souchong chests were the largest, measuring 23 inches broad, 17 inches long, and 21 inches deep, with an average weight when full of 1 cwt. Besides chests, there were also half chests weighing from a half to three-quarters of 1 cwt. Smaller still, there were catty boxes about 12 inches cube weighing up to 27lbs. The chests were made of local wood where the tea was prepared inland, lined with a loose lead case and inside that with paper. Externally they were covered with paper and then with figured transparent paper, pasted on and

Section through a tea-laden ship, showing the method of stowage and the shape taken up by the tea chests. (*Author*)

thoroughly oiled. Tea chests have always been so popular and useful that there has never been any loss on the packing, whilst the lead lining used to be so hard that it was usually sold to printers for the making of type. The varied assortment of chests and boxes was extremely useful in packing in the maximum amount of cargo, especially in the space immediately under the decks. If raw silk was carried, as was normal at Shanghai, it was packed into bales covered with matting which weighed about 1 cwt each. The driest place in the 'tween decks was selected for it, usually between the fore and main hatches, where it was stowed on a ground tier of tea in an area enclosed by tea chests.

Great care was also taken to keep the tea as dry as possible. Bamboo strips and canvas were used to cover the chests top and side, and so drain off sideways any water leaking through. In 1889 iron ships were still considered liable to injure their tea cargoes through condensation which occurred internally, due to sudden and considerable changes of temperature – 'sweating' as it was called. The effluvia from the bilge water of tight ships was another cause of injury to the tea, which was very susceptible to fumes. It was even recommended that clean water should in such cases be let down weekly and then pumped up again to keep the bilges fresh. Great care had to be taken in composite ships where bilge water came into contact with oak, iron and perhaps copper.

But though great care was taken in stowage, the operation was frequently performed very rapidly. For instance, an English ship at Shanghai in the 1850s loaded 8000 chests of tea and 1141 bales of silk in 17 hours, taking 2 days to do it.

Tea cargoes were usually measured in pounds, but because every type of tea varied in weight, it is impossible to convert this into tons, unless the exact type and quantity of each tea carried is known. For this reason it is rarely possible to compare a tea cargo with a vessel's register tonnage. Most ships stowed 50 to 60 per cent above this tonnage figure, and with an assortment of small catty boxes crammed into every available space including the poop, the figure might reach 75 per cent. The sharper the vessel, the less tea she carried. Some of the extreme American clippers barely carried their own register tonnage; whilst the *Leander*, one of the finest-lined ships in the trade, was ballasted so heavily in 1869 in order to make her stiff, that she was down to her marks before full of tea.

When freights were high, the fact that the fastest ship got the pick of them amply compensated for a small cargo capacity. But with freights gradually falling for sailing ships after 1865, economy was as important as speed. Yet although tea freights were probably more remunerative than in any other trade, running expenses were high. In China the principal items of expenditure consisted of tonnage dues in port and towage rates. The *John Temperley* of 975 tons, already mentioned, paid £160 in tonnage dues at Foochow in 1864. In this year, towage rates in the river Min for tea-laden vessels of under 1000 tons were just under 2s 2d per ton from Pagoda Anchorage to Outside Knoll or the White Dogs, the rate to Sharp Peak being 6d less. Over 1000 tons, the rates were 3d less in each case. River pilotage as performed by Chinamen cost 7s 1½d per foot of the vessel's length and sea pilotage by Europeans or Americans 19s per foot. The total expenses at Foochow for a 1000-ton ship would therefore amount to from £620 to £710. Generally speaking tonnage dues in China worked out at 2s 4d per ton, whilst total expenses averaged 22s per ton on wooden ships but 32s per ton on iron ones. The currency used was chiefly dollars and cents, the exchange rate at the end of the 1860s, being 4s 9d per dollar.

A year or two before 1849, Money Wigram assessed the expenses that his East India trader *Minerva* of 691 tons old measurement would incur in twelve months: interest at 5 per cent, £829; depreciation at 10 per cent, £1658; premium of insurance and policy due, £1029, victualling at 1s per day for crew of 39, £712; wages, £1224: total £5452. This excluded primage, pilotage, light dues and repairs. He reckoned that if his ship delivered 1000 tons of homeward cargo, his expenses for twelve months would be covered at a freight of £5 9s per ton.

There are few records in existence to show the sort of profits obtained by the tea clippers. In my study of ships owned by Killick, Martin & Co, published under the title *The China Bird*, I calculated that *Lothair's* expenses for a voyage from London to China and back in 1873–74 were: disbursements at start of voyage including provisions £650; insurance of ship and freight £720; loading and dispatch in London £150; disbursements at Anjer, Hong Kong, Whampoa and Macao, including provisions £542; unloading and docking in London £175; crew's wages £750. Total, say, £3000. Outward freight £2000; homeward freight at £3 per ton £3300. Total £5300. Profit £2300. No allowance made for interest or depreciation. This gives the gross earnings per net register ton (794 tons net) as £6 13s 6d. During the same two years the *Elizabeth Nicholson* earned £9 11s and the *Osaka* £10 (estimated) per net register ton (*The China Bird*, pp 123 and 168).

Some idea of what life was like for an Englishman working in China can be obtained from this letter written by Phineas Ryrie to his mother and sisters in Liverpool. His elder brother, John, was master of the clippers *Cairngorm* and *Flying Spur*, and his brother Alick commanded one of Jardine, Matheson's schooners on the coast, the *Audax*, having earlier served on the *John o'Gaunt* under Robertson in 1843–44. He himself worked in China from 1852, with Turner & Co, for at least twenty years. Some punctuation has been added but the capitalization is his.

Canton 26th December 1854

Dear Mamma and Girls,

I received Maggie's welcome letter of the 19th October also the Photograph of Mamma. I am delighted with it, it is so like [her]. I stuck it up before me on my desk the day it arrived and did almost nothing else the whole day but look at it. I have set old Lenqua to work copying it on Ivory for the Brooches, but the old man has been rather sick for the last few days otherwise I might have had one to send by this mail; for the same reason I cannot get Alick's likeness finished in time to send this month. I received the receipt for the Boxes on board the *Tinto*; many thanks for the Preserves & Cake, they will be duly appreciated when they arrive. Thanks also for the information about a Highland dress. I will see how the funds are at the end of the year & what the prospects are for next and then I'll make up my mind about getting one.

[next paragraph about his brother William omitted]

I had a letter from John dated Sydney 30th October. He wrote in excellent spirits. He had been there 6 days but none of his crew had then left; however he seemed to have made up his mind that they would leave him. He was not certain whether he would come to China or Ceylon: if he comes here he will do very well as there is a demand for ships now. He would get a cargo for London @ £3 almost immediately, or a charter for San Francisco at a good sum, but I am afraid Shand's will put their foot in it again. The[y] seem to hamper him with orders just when he has a chance of doing some good with the vessel.

I have not seen Alick since I last wrote. I had a note from him three days ago, however. If he is not confirmed in the command of the *Mazeppa* already, I think he is pretty sure of it. In fact I had it from Mr Percival, one of the partners, in J, M & Co with strict injunctions however not to tell Alick until Mr Jardine thought proper to announce it to him officially.

As I predicted in my last letter, the past month has been an eventful one in Canton. St Andrew's night went off well except my speech which would not go off at-all. In fact with the excitement & flurry (principally caused by my having to carve a big Turkey of which everybody at the table seemed to want a slice) & having no time to eat anything & drinking a good deal, when I came to give my speech I found that I had forgotten every word of it.

At the Regatta I was successful; *La Sylphide* shewed herself worthy of the name, coming in about 20 lengths ahead of her opponents. The Ball was very well got up but there was a dreadful scarcity of Ladies, and there being an immense crowd of officers from the British vessels of war & a Swedish Frigate lying at Whampoa (whose band played at the Ball) I did not get any dancing; in fact as one of the givers of the entertainment, I sacrificed myself to our guests.

I must conclude as it is within a few minutes of closing, so wishing you all a merry Christmas and a happy New Year,
I remain,
Your Affectionate Son & Brother,
P Ryrie.

(John Ryrie commanded the *Marian* owned by Shand of Liverpool until 1856.)

Through his connections in the shipping world, Phineas Ryrie provides a commentary on both the social and business communities on the China coast in the clipper ship era, where everyone was utterly dependent on ships, and their doings formed a basic topic of conversation.

Many of the Hong Kong artists were high-speed copyists, but ship portraits were more original works of art. (From *Illustrations of China and Its People*, 1873)

2

THE CHINA SEA
AND SAILING DIRECTIONS

Business negotiations on the opposite side of the world amongst a people of courteous manners but with a civilization far different from that found in Britain or America gave problems in itself, but another obstacle to overcome was the navigation of the China Sea which was a most hazardous area and disasters of all kinds were the accepted life on the 'Coast'. A ship might be damaged or come to grief either by means of a typhoon or through ill judgment or lack of experience amongst the numerous hazards of the almost uncharted China Sea. Shoals, reefs and currents abounded in vast numbers, and only the main rocks and islands were surveyed. Captains were continually reporting half-submerged rocks, and it was only by years of experience that a thorough working knowledge could be obtained of these dangerous seas. The Dutch were the first to attempt a proper survey, soon after they established themselves in eastern waters, but their charts were kept in great secrecy. We even read of Captain Shewan finding his way with the use of Dutch charts, and that as late as 1870. Yet in spite of all these unknown factors there was one thing on which all could rely, namely the direction and duration of the prevailing winds.

These winds, or monsoons, occurred fairly regularly over an expanse of land and ocean extending from the Red Sea to eastward of the Philippines, and from the Equator to the Bay of Bengal and coasts of Japan. In the Indian Ocean they ran on much the same course as those which existed on the other side of the Malayan Archipelago and around the coasts of China. Incidentally no apology is made here for spelling place names as they were in clipper ship days.

The China Sea is bounded on the west by the coasts of Sumatra, Malaya, Siam, Annam (later called Indo-China and then Viet Nam) and China itself as far north as Foochow; and on the east by Formosa, the Philippines and Borneo. Above Formosa the Tunghai or Eastern Sea extends up to the mouth of the Yangtze, and from then on there is the Hwang Hai or Yellow Sea, although to the seaman the China Sea extends as far north as the Yangtze. The monsoons are felt over the full extent of the China Sea, to the eastward of Luzon and north to the mouth of the Yangtze, whilst their influence extends over a still wider field. During the winter months the monsoon blows from the north-east but during the summer from the south-west. The north-east monsoon is by far the stronger so that the south-west monsoon seems light in comparison.

In the China Sea the south-west monsoon begins in the middle or end of April and extends to the beginning or middle of October, being at its greatest strength in June, July and August and varying from SSW to SSE in June and July.

North-east of Formosa the monsoon is usually a gentle southerly breeze from June to September, with occasional light summer gales under blue skies, but in the Eastern Sea July brings westerly winds, and August and early September southerly ones.

The north-east monsoon commences in early October in the northern part of the China Sea, but not till November does it blow steadily in the southern half. Usually the change of the monsooon is forecast by a ten-day gale. In December and January the monsoon blows at great strength accompanied by rain and a turbulent sea, though by March it has moderated. April is usually regarded as the finest month of the China coast. In the Eastern Sea the north-east monsoon blows for virtually nine months, from the middle of September to the middle of June. In each type of monsoon heavy weather is experienced at times with sudden and severe squalls and torrential rain.

But the severest weather is met in fierce revolving storms – 'typhoons' (great winds) as the Chinese call them. They chiefly occur between May and October or November and are most frequent in the vicinity of Luzon, Hainan Island, and the south-west corner of Japan. Only a few find their way up Formosa Strait. The average number for the worst four months is: July–4; August–8; September–12; October–7.

There were several routes that could be followed by ships leaving or approaching China, the chief deciding factor being the time of year, though the vessel's capabilities had also to be taken into account. Ships built especially for the China trade on fine lines would always lay a course right down the China Sea when homeward-bound, regardless of the season, unless they had a timid or inexperienced captain, or else met with strong south-westerly winds immediately they left, say, Foochow, in which case they would probably stand out into the Pacific, go down the eastern coast of Formosa and, if the wind was still south-westerly, continue down the east side of the Philippines and then via Gillolo Strait, Pitt Passage, and Ombai Strait, into the Indian Ocean past the island of Timor. Such a route was termed the 'Eastern passage'. *Sir Lancelot* under Richard Robinson did this in 1867, and took only 99 days on the homeward passage. Other masters might have occupied a week or more extra spent in beating down the China Sea against the

Opposite: Map of the China Sea showing the homeward-bound route of *Thermopylae* in July 1869 and the outward-bound track of *Cutty Sark* in February 1871, both made against their respective monsoons. The place names are those used in clipper ship days. (*Author*)

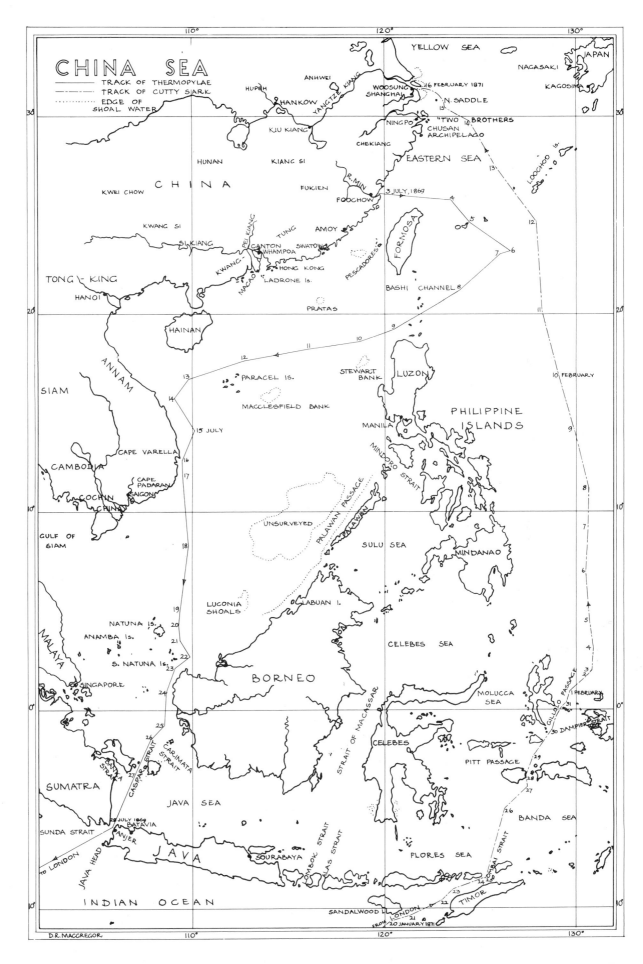

CHINA SEA

TRACK OF THERMOPYLAE
TRACK OF CUTTY SARK
EDGE OF
SHOAL WATER

south-westerlies. With a shift of wind to the south or south-east, ships could get ahead, but perhaps some masters prided themselves in never being beaten by the China Sea passage. Many ships used to make for the coast of Cochin China since land breezes were experienced there at night which enabled the ship to make good progress south. A third homeward route was down the west coast of Luzon and then into the Sulu Sea past Mindoro and from there into the Celebes Sea, Strait of Macassar and thence into the Indian Ocean through Lombok Strait. Ships going down the China Sea would pass into the Indian Ocean by way of Sunda Strait, separating Sumatra from Java, calling at Anjer on the way. The sea between Borneo and Sumatra was studded with islands, there being three passages known as Banca, Gaspar and Carimata Straits. The first was frequently used, though it would appear to be a tortuous and hazardous channel.

In *Two Years Abaft the Mast*, Symondson describes how the *Inverness* went ashore in Banca Strait in November 1873 when only some 200 yards from the shore:

As the day closed in, we were sailing smoothly along, almost due south, the island of Sumatra on our right, and Banca on our left; but so soon as the sun had gone down, squalls took possession of the night, coming in sudden gusts. If the wind had been fair, the captain would no doubt have chanced the narrow channel and moonless nights, and run before them with square yards. Although during the day it kept about a point free, at night-time it chopped round dead ahead. We were obliged to drop anchor, furl all the sails, and wait till morning. Lightning, thunder, and rain varied the monotony of our rest; the peals of thunder were so terrific that the ship trembled under the concussion.

Tuesday, the 25th – Head wind all day, and tacking ship every ten minutes. Between five and six o'clock in the evening, nearing the low-lying shore of Sumatra, we once more ran to our respective places at the mate's order, 'Stations!' (all night in: all hands on deck). Helm-a-lee! Jib-sheets and fore-sheet are let go, tacks and sheets raised, and we stand by the crossjack braces, ready to haul round the after-yards directly she gets near enough to the wind. The wind has died away to a light breeze, and she comes up but slowly. Presently the captains sings out, 'Flatten in jib-sheets!' followed by 'Board fore-tack and haul aft your fore-sheet!' She doesn't seem to move either way. We ease off the spanker-sheet, but to no purpose; there she remains. Mr Turner heaves the lead for'ard, and the cause is plain to all. We are aground; the ship is a foot and a half in the mud by the bows,

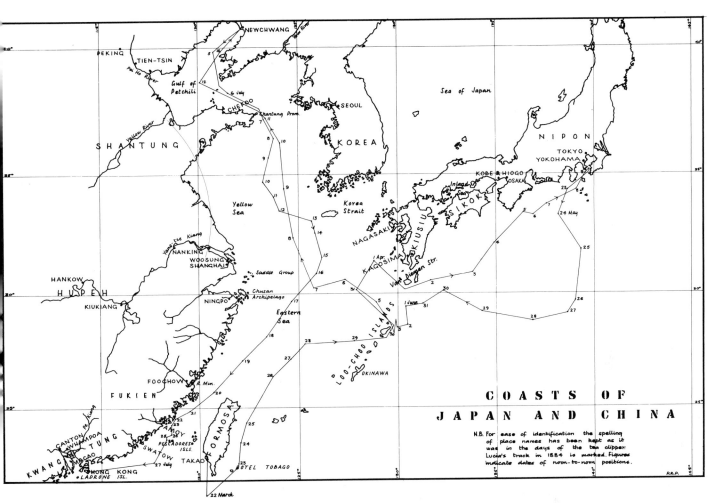

Above: Map of the coasts of Japan and China with three coasting passages of *Lucia's* plotted. She made these in May, June and July 1884. (*Author*)

Left: The *Inverness*, photographed by Gould off Gravesend in November 1872, in which F W H Symondson made a voyage to China and back in 1873–74, and extracts from his book are quoted here. (*Nautical Photo Agency*)

but apparently afloat aft. It was a couple of hours past flood. 'Clew up the royals!' and as I spring up at the fore, the quarter-boat is being lowered with the kedge-anchor. From the fore-royal-yard I obtained an extensive view of the land, which was covered with dense woods and jungle. A few birds could be discerned hurrying to their night quarters. The scene was strikingly wild and solitary as the sun sank beneath the distant tree-tops. Our distance from the shore might have been 200 yards, and the trees and bushes grew down to the water's edge so densely that any attempt at landing and moving in any direction would have been an impossibility. A few large birds could be seen hovering about the shore, while the hum and clatter of the smaller ones retiring to rest for the night was plainly audible.

Getting on deck again, I found the hands manning the capstan on the quarter-deck, heaving on the warp. We got a couple of turns in, but the ship never moved; it was the anchor dragging home. At eight o'clock anchor-watch was set, the warp being secured round the bitts, waiting for the morning's tide. Having to turn out for an hour at 10 pm, I soon went below, and rolling into my bunk, fell asleep. When I came on deck, the ship was lying over nearly on her beam-ends, from the tide receding, and everything looked dispiriting enough. The captain anxiously hove the lead over the tafferel every quarter

of an hour with 'Chips' and the mate, but the ship did not change her position. Our position was novel and unexpected, if nothing else, and nobody seemed to know how long we should remain in this helpless condition. At half past ten, one of the customary night squalls swept over us, and as the topsails and courses had not been stowed, they slatted furiously to and fro. However, by bracing the yards to the wind no damage was incurred. Before doing so, the captain had ordered the yards to be braced square to the wind, in the hopes of driving us off, but without effect.

At high water next morning we once more manned the capstan, and we put our utmost strength and weight on the bars. 'Come lads,' said 'Chips', who was next to me, 'heave – heave and paul!' 'Surge handsomely, Johnson'. In a few minutes we are walking steadily round. This time we are not heaving the 'kedge' home – we ourselves are moving; the good ship glides once more into her briny element. A smile simultaneously shines on the captain's face, and before the order is well delivered, we are up aloft loosing the top-gallant sails and royals. By a stroke of luck we got off without the slightest damage; and although the wind was still ahead, we did our best by beating against it – tacking every quarter of an hour. As night closed in we let go the anchor, and as the sky looked threatening, all the sails were furled. We were having enough of the Straits; what with dropping anchor and stowing sails, weighing in the morning and loosing them again, and beating down against a head wind, growling was plentiful.

On this passage the *Inverness* has sailed from Foochow on 8 November 1873 and after leaving Banca Strait it took her another four days to beat through Sunda Strait from which she did not get clear until 2 December, bound for New York.

23

During the south-west monsoon, August was probably the most difficult month in which to leave China as both the Pacific and Celebes Sea routes were impracticable, and although the passage from Shanghai down to off Hong Kong could be performed by ships of only moderate sailing capabilities in spite of a strong adverse current, because the south-west monsoon was not so permanent in its direction over this stretch and land breezes occurred, yet in the south China Sea the adverse monsoon was very fierce, most vessels making for the Cochin China coast. During the north-east monsoon the China Sea presented no difficulties, and even as late as May a ship might hold an easterly wind all the way down especially if she went through the Palawan Passage.

Ships bound to China during the south-west monsoon had nothing to contend with and sailed straight up the China Sea, but during the north-east monsoon four courses were open. Either a ship beat up the China Sea from Sunda Strait, or else she proceeded by way of Macassar Strait, Celebes and Sulu Seas into the China Sea. Or she might make for Ombai Strait, Pitt Passage and enter the Pacific either by Dampier or Gillolo Straits. A fourth method was to steer south of Australia and up the eastern seaboard westward of New Caledonia, crossing the equator in 156°E, and thence straight to port. *Norman Court* followed this route to Shanghai in 1871 and covered the course of approximately 21,000 miles in just over 102 days – a fine piece of work.

Homeward-bound passages are probably more rewarding of study, especially if a race amongst several ships was in progress, since accounts of typically daring navigation are more fully recorded. It is doubtful whether ships were driven to such an extent when outward-bound since there was not the same financial or sporting interest at stake. Yet very fine passages were made: witness *Cairngorm*'s 72 days to Hong Kong from Lisbon, and *Ariel*'s 83 from Gravesend to the same port, but against the north-east monsoon. Far more ships used to make their way through the Gillolo Passage and out into the Pacific when outward-bound than ever did when sailing for home, since a beat down the China Sea was

not attended with so many difficulties as was one made up it against the north-east monsoon.

In the *Oriental Voyager*, J Johnson describes a voyage to India and China aboard HMS *Caroline*, and when approaching the Canton river in 1804 he comments on how many small Chinese craft liked to seek protection from the numerous pirates, called 'ladrones', by attaching themselves to any British vessel or sailing in close convoy. At this date, only Macao and Canton were open for trade, but almost seventy years later Hong Kong was in its hey-day and Symondson describes how the Aberdeen-built clipper *Inverness* came to anchor in the harbour:

When Sunday morning dawned we were sailing steadily up the winding waters to Hong Kong, overshadowed by lofty islands, steep and barren; and owing to the clear atmosphere, their distance was very deceptive. The fishing-boats, with their two large butterfly-looking sails, had a very picturesque effect. Rounding Green Island, the town of Hong Kong presented itself to our view. Quite a flotilla of sampans had fastened on to us by this time, and it was amusing to watch the state of excitement they were all in, for what purpose I don't know. We came to anchor at sunset, furled the sails neatly, and went below to tea. Our decks were thronged with natives selling fruit, cigars, and all sorts of wares, from a bottle of curry to oilskin suits and sea-boots. The Chinese have a curious religious custom of lighting small red tapers at sunset, which they fix to various parts of their boats; I have frequently seen little children just able to walk performing this duty. The harbour was full of shipping; amongst it the *Windsor Castle*, which had arrived the previous day. The weather was very hot, forbidding us sleep on any less airy place than the forecastle-head, where we took up our blankets as a mattress every night.

Hong Kong looks very stately from the water, with its large, white, tastefully-decorated buildings, almost palaces, lining the quays and extending up the slopes of Victoria Mount into pretty suburban mansions.

Hong Kong (fragrant streams) island is one of a group called by the Portuguese Ladrónes (thieves), from the character of the old inhabitants, and is situated near the mouth of the Canton

river. Its length is about nine miles, breadth two to five miles, and area a little over twenty-nine square miles. The Ly-ee-moon Pass, a narrow channel separating the island from the mainland, is not more than half a mile in width. The opposite peninsula of Kowloon was ceded to Great Britain in 1861, and now forms part of Hong Kong. It possesses one of the best harbours in the world, surrounded by quaint red sandy hills rising between 2000 and 3000 feet high. The city of Victoria extends for four miles at the foot of the hills on the south side of the harbour, and contains 6000 houses, amongst which are the residences of the European merchants – magnificent mansions.

Owing to ships lying here at anchor away from the quays, we experienced some difficulty in getting ashore, as sampans are dear at Hong Kong in comparison with Foo-chow or Shanghai. The first time I went ashore was to post the ship's letter. As I walked through the crowded narrow streets, I was greatly struck with the quaint native dress and shops; everything told of an Eastern town, the absence of vehicles and horses especially.

The crack ships liked to be at their respective loading ports in time to take on the very first of the new crop, but dismastings on the outward passage or a long series of coasting trips might not bring them to their ports until the first ships had sailed. The 'intermediate passages', as these coasting trips were called, ranged from Yokohama to Rangoon, but normally were made with rice cargoes from Bangkok or

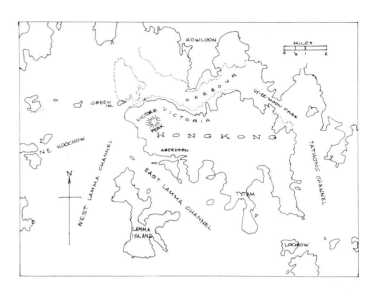

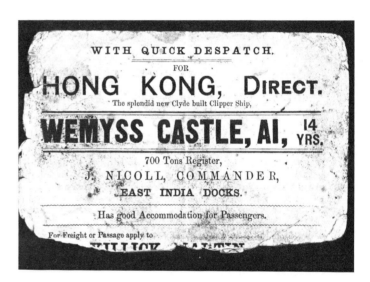

Top: Map of Hong Kong copied from a plan in *Treaty Ports of China and Japan* by N B Dennys (1867). *(Author)*

Right: A sailing card for the *Wemyss Castle* which Killick, Martin & Co loaded in October 1868. *(Killick, Martin & Co Ltd)*

Below: Looking south from Kowloon across to Hong Kong in 1857, showing Lord Elgin's expeditionary force assembled before the capture of Canton. *(Royal Geographical Society)*

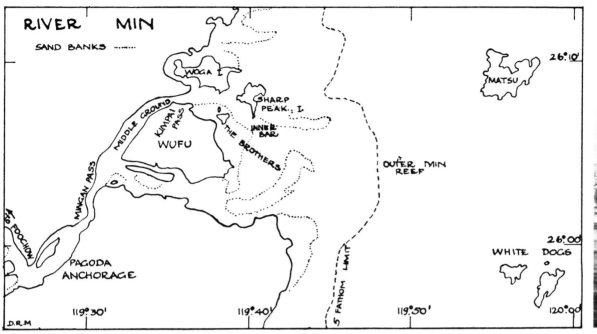

Saigon to Chinese ports, the beat up the China Sea against the monsoon being very tedious and hard on a ship that wished to be in good shape for the run home. It would not take many days to run down to Bangkok but perhaps twenty or more to get back to Hong Kong.

From Hong Kong the *Inverness* sailed up to Foochow where she hoped to get a cargo of tea. Symondson describes the approach to the coast, the passage up the Min river and lastly Pagoda Anchorage where so many clippers used to lie at anchor waiting for the tea to arrive.

Friday evening we sighted a lighthouse, which the captain had been looking out for; and as soon as it became dark we dropped anchor, stowed the sails, 'chalked' for watches, and turned in for the night. At daybreak we loosed sail, weighed anchor, and proceeded under small canvas on our course to the mouth of the river Min, leading up to Foo-chow. We shortly after signalled a pilot-boat, and took a pilot (European) aboard. The sea-pilots are all Europeans, in Yankee cutters, manned by half-a-dozen natives. The native pilots, as a rule, only ply on the rivers, and then only for ridiculous distances, as will be seen hereafter. Propelled by a gentle breeze on a smooth sea, the coast steadily developed before us, sandy and burning to the eyes. As we entered the river the breeze somewhat freshened, carrying us along at about seven knots. Our European now gave place to a native pilot. A number of big junks lay anchored at the mouth of the river, deeply loaded with timber, known here as 'poles'. Our progress was much checked by the tide, which runs very swiftly in the river Min. A high ridge of mountainous hills flanked the river on either side; and when an opening occurred, others could be seen as far as the eye could reach. At one time the sides would be highly cultivated with rice, grown in regular bands, the distance between each being marked by a step like a flight of stairs. Next would follow barren and desolate views – rocky mountains, black and purple, according to the light, supporting a few straggling firs. The villages had a peculiarly quaint look, nestled in little nooks, with fantastic roofs to the huts. The military forts, planted at intervals on commanding sites, appeared more ridiculous than formidable. Their positions were indicated by a line of white mounds, something like stout columns cut off at a height of seven or eight feet, and a few feet apart to allow the firing of the cannons, which, nevertheless, were as scarce as they were worthless. The sentinels, too, were no doubt looking after their absent guns, for I never saw a living creature occupying these forts.

We steadily sailed up; and on account of the continuous bends in the river, we had enough to do in squaring and bracing up the yards, setting and hauling down staysails, and even headsails and spanker where the helm could not manage the rounding of an awkward point. Emerging from a narrow reach, we entered a wide expanse of water, almost like a branch of the sea. Here our pilot left us, his navigating knowledge extending no further; and as night was coming on, we let go the anchor after gradually stowing the sails. In the morning we were all engaged buying soft bread and eggs from the 'bumboat' man. For breakfast we had fresh meat; and with half a pound of steak, four eggs, and a small loaf and pint of passable coffee, I set to. I *did* enjoy this meal, and I wanted it badly after my forced abstinence since leaving Hong Kong. Waiting for the tide to turn, and being Sunday morning, we had nothing to do till eleven o'clock, when we took another native pilot, weighed anchor, and proceeded to the anchorage some six miles higher up, where we arrived at 1 pm, furled the sails, and had the rest of the Sunday to ourselves – 13th July.

'Pagoda Anchorage' (named after a very old pagoda built on the top of an island called Pagoda Island) is formed by the river suddenly widening (to an extent of about two miles in some places) into a large sheet of water, having the appearance of an inland lake encompassed with mountains – a few patches cultivated with rice struggling here and there to enliven the otherwise desolate scene. On one side are built some European houses – two ship-chandlers, an English chapel (very small), and several private dwellings belonging to English engineers and officials connected with the Chinese arsenal, of which Foochow boasts the first in the empire; and on the top of a hill stands the doctor's house (resident Englishman – for the shipping principally), a little below that of the British Consul, which latter commands a fine view of the whole anchorage. The only structure on the opposite side is the Chinese Custom-house, of European architecture, and only recently erected. But the Pagoda Island contrasts by its beauty with the melancholy mountains. It rises steeply from the water, and is covered with shrubs and trees, between the openings of which can be seen native houses and huts, with curiously-decorated fronts and roofs: strange little structures some of them, propped

up out of the water by long bamboos, upon whose sometimes doubtful and precarious support the whole concerns depend. Crowning this pretty little oasis stands the old pagoda, built of stone; which, judging by its dilapidated condition and weather-beaten appearance, must be some hundreds of years old.

Another of the principal ports which Symondson visited in the *Inverness* in 1873 was Shanghai, and his description follows:

Saturday afternoon, 14th September, we entered the Yang-tsi-Kiang, the lead being kept constantly going from the main-chains, as shoals are but indifferently marked here. Nothing can be said of the scenery: it is level and unpicturesque; in fact, in many parts it strongly resembles the Thames below London. The water was of a muddy colour, and bore a good sprinkling of European shipping, and the day being thick and cloudy, made the similarity all the more marked. We took in the sails one by one, and evening approaching, we dropped anchor at six o'clock, and having 'chalked' for watches we turned in, mine falling from 12 to 1 am. The following morning, Sunday, before daybreak a steam-tug came alongside flying the Yankee ensign, and made fast to us; and having weighed anchor by five o'clock, we proceeded in tow, and with the tide up, to Shanghai City. Luckily the wind having hauled round ahead we had no sails to loose, so I had more time than usual to look about me. We passed a large American-built river-steamboat painted all white, of which there are several in Shanghai doing the carrying trade between the principal river ports. Towards 1 pm the tide failing us, the tug cast off and we let go the anchor, all hands going to dinner. Between 5 and 6 pm we hove up, the tug towing us as before . . . We anchored for the night below the shipping, waiting for the morning to be berthed higher up. A strange fatality seems to have overruled our Sundays. We entered Portland on a Sunday, we also entered Sydney on a Sunday, and the same day saw us into Hong Kong and Foochow, and now again Shanghai. Sailors do not like going into port of a Sunday, as they believe captains arrange it purposely to get an extra day's work out of them.

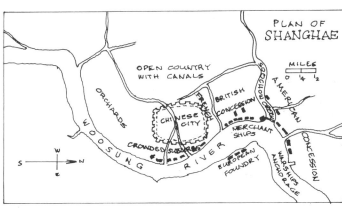

Above: Map of Shanghai with foreign concessions, copied from a plan in *Treaty Ports of China and Japan* by N B Dennys (1867). *(Author)*

Opposite: The river Min and its approaches. *(Author)*

Top: An ink and wash drawing depicting the busy scene at Shanghai with the paddle tug *Fire Cracker* in the foreground. *(Peabody Museum, Salem)*

At eight the next morning we towed slowly up past the shipping lining either side. I was stationed at the gaff-signal-halyards to dip the ensign as customary to the various men-o'-war in harbour. We anchored abreast of the French town. Shanghai is the head-centre of European commerce in China. The city is divided into four distinct parts, each governed by its own laws. The lower end is the American town, the English town comes next, then the French town, and finally and highest up the river stands the native Chinese town. The English is by far the most important, as its wider streets and handsomer buildings denote. Vessels of all nations lay in the stream below us; above, the river swarmed with literally a forest of masts rising from junks and other native craft. In accordance with one of their strange superstitions, they beat gongs and drums every evening at sunset for half an hour or so, causing the most diabolical noise.

Hankow was the most difficult port to get away from, situated as it was almost 900 miles from the sea. A long and expensive tow was requisite which lasted some four to six days when coming down. It was preferable to have the tug lashed alongside for easy manoeuvring, else, if she was towing ahead, a sudden rapid current might make the tow sheer off broadside on to the stream and bring her on to the tug's stern, snapping the tow rope. This happened to Steele's clipper *Guinevere* when towing downstream tea-laden in 1866. She was unable to anchor and striking some rocks sank at once. Of seven ships that went up to Hankow that year, five met with accidents: one, the *Guinevere*, was lost; Green's *Highflyer* (1861) grounded going up as well as coming down and had to repair at Shanghai; the *Coulnakyle* was damaged in collision whilst waiting to load and had to go down empty to Shanghai to repair and then return to Hankow to take on board her tea; the *Min* was damaged by collision, and so was *Sir Lancelot*. It was no wonder that insurance on tea cargoes was up by 2 per cent on other ports. Currents were at places very swift and the river rose and fell rapidly. In the summer months it was some 45 feet above the winter level at Hankow. With the introduction of screw tugs the only tricky piece of navigation left was the crossing at Lang-shan, 50 miles above Woosung. Unless the date is given on which a vessel passed Woosung, about five days should be subtracted from the total number of days spent on the passage in order to compare her work with that made by ships sailing from Shanghai.

The river Whangpoo on which Shanghai was situated, 12 miles above Woosung, could be navigated by a vessel under canvas alone when the wind was favourable or when a tug was not available. The following entries made by Captain Mann in the *Strathmore*'s log were probably typical of many ships:

25 Nov, 1858. At 5.30 began to unmoor ship. At 6 pilot on board. During the day dropped down below the shipping and came to anchor at 10 pm.
26 Nov. At 2 am came to anchor at Half Way point. At 7 am hove up and 3 pm passed Woosung; at 6 came to an anchor outside the marks.
27 Nov. At 6 underweigh and beating down the river. Wind at SE. Anchored 1.30.
28 Nov. Underweigh at 6. Wind SSW. At 10 am pilot left. Off the North Saddle at noon, wind NW fresh. High sea.

The previous year the tug *Meteor* had towed her down to below Woosung. Sometimes a ship would drop down in a day, depending on wind and tide. The date of departure from Shanghai, as given in the shipping reports, was occasionally that on which the vessel passed Woosung. The last land to be sighted was frequently an island known as the North Saddle beyond the mouth of the Yangtze, or even the Two Brothers, two rocks on the edge of the Chusan Archipelago.

At Foochow, navigation of the river Min was rather more hazardous. In several places the river ran through deep narrow gorges with sheer cliffs on either hand where the tide sometimes raced through at 7 knots. Captain Shewan writes that on several occasions he sailed at a speed of 20 knots over the ground with a fair wind through one of these 'passes'. The best known is the 7-mile long Mingan Pass where many ships, including the *Vision*, were wrecked.

If once any part of the ship touched a bank or rock, then the current swept her round out of control and she was soon on her beam ends.

There were not more than three tugs at Foochow of which the paddler *Island Queen* was no good except in still water. Captain Mann describes how the *Strathmore* came down the Min in 1857 with a north-easterly wind:

30 Jan. Took in 100 chests of tea which completes the cargo. Went to Foo Chow Foo and cleared the ship; returned at 8 pm. Blowing and rain: wind NE.
31 Jan. At 6 am unmoored the ship and dropped down to Spiteful Island, and anchored with 25 fathoms cable, the tide being down.
1 Feb. 7 got underweigh and brought down the river, native pilot on board and 23 tow boats to assist, it being very difficult to get ships down the river Min at noon. Anchored at 'Quantoa' in 5½ fathoms.
2 Feb. Proceeded down the river at 7 am and at noon anchored at Sharp Peak; discharged the inside pilot and tow boats. 8 set the anchor watch.
3 Feb. Daylight got underweigh; wind N by E, fine breeze. At 8 am got outside the bar. Outside pilot left. Made sail. Strong breeze. The ship *Wild Flower* in company. At noon abreast of Turnabout Island.

The pilot grounds were situated near the White Dogs, a group of three islands which were frequently the last land to be seen. Sometimes the date on which the bars were crossed was specified as the departure date, in which case it corresponded to that on which the pilot left. With a tug it took less than a day to get down the river.

When the full-rigged ship *Inverness* went down the river Min in 1873, Symondson, who was one of the three apprentices, was writing his log every day and so was able to describe later what happened:

Above: A Canton junk at anchor, with her sails hoisted. The rock-lined shores and backdrop of mountains were typical of many Chinese rivers. (From *Illustrations of China and its People,* 1873)

Opposite: A scene in the vicinity of Chusan. (*MacGregor Collection*)

Early Monday morning, 1st September, the native pilot came aboard, and having weighed anchor, we proceeded slowly down the anchorage, surrounded by swarms of sampans, under charge of the pilot, to guide the ship; but for all the good they do, and all the strength they exert, ships could manage as well without them. The wind blew up the river, and we had the satisfaction of forseeing a beat down to the sea, or rather a drift down, as, with a head-wind in a narrow river, vessels drop down broadside on as far as the ebb tide will carry them, when they let go their anchor and wait for the next ebb. On account of the distance to the sea, we could not possibly do it under two days, and very likely would take more.

Having reached the end of the anchorage where the narrow river opens out, it came on to blow rather strong, which obliged the captain to drop anchor. Being eight o'clock, we went to breakfast after having furled all the sails. During the rest of the day, we were employed at various work upon the rigging, and lashing the harness-casks on the quarter-deck. The weather brightening up in the night, but still with a head-wind, we hove up at 5 am and proceeded on our difficult way, broadside on – and a heavier task it would be difficult to find. Such narrow parts has this river Min, that it is sometimes only three or four ships' lengths in width. Backing and filling, hauling the yards round, hoisting the jibs, and brailing in the spanker, or *vice versa,* we had enough to do; and by the time the tide slackened, and we dropped anchor at 1 pm, we had barely any breath left in us. The wind having died away to a gentle breeze, we left the sails hanging, trimming the yards to the wind, and went to dinner.

We hove up again at seven in the evening and resumed our slow journey, which we could not have done had it not been near full moon and a clear sky. I was stationed on the poop with Reed, giving the lead to a dozen natives (pilot's gang) working the main braces and spanker. We had less hauling about than in the morning, probably because of the moonlight equalising visibly the distances from either shore. I had thus occasionally a little time to look about me, and contemplate the moonlit scenery. What fantastic shapes the rocks on the

mountains had, and what a wild, melancholy aspect the whole view bore! The horse-shoe-shaped white stone graves of native grandees of bygone days shone clearly out from the dark mountain-sides, sadly reflecting the soft rays of the moon; and as we glided noiselessly along the black water, the jib-boom end sometimes almost apparently touching the rocky sides, I thought it a beautifully romantic sight. But my thoughts were suddenly brought back again to their everyday sphere by a stern voice sounding close by, 'Hi there S—! don't you hear? starboard main brace,' which was the captain's, who was walking the poop smoking a cigar. The tide having nearly ceased flowing, we dropped anchor at 11.30 pm, and furled the sails. We gladly rolled into our bunks and got what sleep we could before six the following morning, when we were roused out with 'Man the windlass there, lads'; and tumbling up on the forecastle-head, we took to our old work again of walking round the windlass heaving up the anchor. We worked with a will, as this was to be the last of the 'dropping down', this tide being sufficient to carry us down to the sea, which we reached in the afternoon. We left the anchorage on Monday morning, and this was Wednesday afternoon; we had thus been three days in traversing a distance we might have covered in as many hours had the wind been fair. Unfortunately the breeze died away to a calm at the mouth of the river, and we had to drop anchor again, with the blue expanse of sea stretching out before us. During the latter part of the day we crossed the royal yards, and the native pilot left us – the European sea-pilot taking his place. At eight o'clock we 'chalked' for watches, and my mark being rubbed out amongst the last, I got all night in.

At four o'clock next morning, Thursday, we weighed anchor, loosed the sails from royals downwards, and, wafted by a gentle breeze from land, we stood out to sea under a cloudless sky, with the sun already making his presence felt. We were not favoured long, for a calm succeeded the breeze when near some banks, on which a current was slowly drifting us. The quarter-boat was at once lowered, manned by four men; and with a rope made fast on the forecastle-head, they succeeded, after two hours' hard pulling, in hauling us clear into deep water. The poor fellows were done up when they came aboard again; for pulling under a sun which by this time was little less than scorching, was enough for any man. However, no breeze springing up, we had to drop anchor and wait for it. The heat was very great, and told upon us more than usual. The captain was walking the poop with a wet handkerchief tied round his head. A lot of fishing-boats lay not far from us, their occupiers, in bold defiance of personal appearance, being utterly destitute of clothing. In the afternoon a sea-breeze sprang up, and we once more manned the windlass. We braced the yards sharp up, set every inch of canvas that would draw, and quietly glided through the smooth green water, with the wind just free.

Symondson does not relate when the European pilot left but it was presumably at the White Dogs which were passed at seven o'clock that evening.

Ships leaving Whampoa dropped down over the two bars under easy sail to the Bocca Tigris where they would probably exchange their native pilot for a European who would later be landed at Macao. Departure dates from Whampoa are given when a ship has crossed the second bar. Vessels from Canton of over 11 feet draft had to go by Blenheim Passage and did not pass Whampoa.

Once in the open water a course was shaped for Anjer or the eastern route, depending on winds and other circumstances. A clever master could probably reach Anjer up to a week before his rivals, if he was prepared to take risks. Sandy Nicholson was accustomed to do this in the *Argonaut* and on one occasion sailed through the dangerous and prac-

tically unsurveyed Paracels by night on a long tack which took him right across to the Cochin China coast. After the Java Sea had been entered, possibly by way of Gaspar Strait, the south-east trades would be picked up and the East finally left behind after negotiating Sunda Strait.

The *Strathmore* under Captain Mann took 16 days in 1857 between dropping her pilot off Foochow and reaching the Straits of Sunda. On an earlier page, the log told how the river Min was negotiated at the beginning of this passage and the sixteen-day run to the Straits of Sunda is now described:

4 Feb. Fine breeze from NE; going 9½ knots. *Wild Flower* astern. Hands employed stowing the cables and anchors. Latter part wind failing. Set all std sails, during the light winds and easterly.

5 Feb. Moderate breezes inclining to the SE. Hands employed putting on chafing gear and other necessary work; carpenter variously. Lat 21° 35′ N, long 116° 2′ E. *Wild Flower* out of sight astern. Latter part wind SE. In all std sails. Midnight fresh breeze; in royals and staysails.

8 Feb. Fresh breezes from NE. Carrying all sail. At 7.30 pm hove to and sounded on the 'Macclesfield' Bank in 50 fathoms; coral rock. At 8 bore away and set all std sails.

9 Feb. Fresh breezes all these 24 hours; carrying all possible sail. Lat 13° 46′ N, long 111° 20′ E.

10 Feb. Strong breezes; wind NE. Sees 2 ships going S. Carpenter finishing a new jibboom. People as most requisite. Lat obs 11° 23′ N, long 110° 43′ E.

13 Feb. Light airs. At 8 am passed Saddle Island about 20 miles distant in the lat 4° 7′ N, long 107° 11′ E. At 4 pm seen the 'Low Island' Rocks bearing ESE about 15 miles. Light airs inclining to calms. Weather sultry and warm.

15 Feb. Steady breeze from NE. At noon passed 'Camel Island' about 2 miles distant. Latter part breeze freshens.

16 Feb. Fine breeze. At noon abreast of the 'Catherine' Shoal, but did not see it; shortened sail, and at 8 pm hove to for daylight.

17 Feb. At 4 am bore away under easy sail, and at 6 made 'Gaspar Island' bearing SW by S. At noon in 'Macclesfield'

Strait with a very light air of wind; at 6, well clear of the Straits. The breeze freshens from NW. In all std sails, royals and flying jib; and during the night is squally.

18 Feb. Fresh breezes from NNW. Made sail at daylight. Saw a ship ahead: at 8 is up with her. She is the *Talavera* from Foo Chow, sailed 9 days before me. At 9 passed the 'Brothers'. Noon light airs.

19 Feb. Sharp breeze from NW. Tacked ship off 'Button Island'. At 9 am was boarded by a boat in the 'Straits of Sunda'. Reported my ship, then made sail. At 4 pm fresh breeze from WNW. Took in all the light sails; tacked to the N at 6 pm. At 8 pm a terrific squall took us, laying the ship over very much. Got topgt sails in, mainsail and spanker, and then double reefed the topsails and furled the mainsail and jib. At 10 wore ship to the SW: blowing hard all night and heavy sea. Seen the land all night.

Java Head was passed the following day. ('Std sails' in the log is an abbreviation for studding sails or stunsails.)

A passage to London was frequently made or lost in the run down the China Sea and it will be understood how the season must always be taken into account when comparing lengths of passages, as well as the position of the port of departure. Foochow was some 450 miles from Shanghai and Hong Kong as much again. The distance from Foochow to Anjer was almost 2800 miles, and over 14,000 between Foochow and London.

Of two passages of the same duration, that made against the south-west monsoon was always considered superior by some days. It has already been mentioned how the first starters from Foochow got away before the strength of the south-west monsoon set in and how that August was the worst month in which to leave. Except in the case of the *Fiery Cross* in 1857, the best times made homewards against the south-west monsoon during the 1850s do not bear comparison with the fastest passages made against the monsoon in the next decade; yet the clippers of the 1860s made no better runs during the favourable north-east monsoon than the ships of the previous ten years.

The routes taken by homeward-bound ships sailing either to New York or to London are described in Chapter Five, and also ways of equating the length of passage.

Design of ships had changed sufficiently to meet the exigencies of the China Sea where a successful beat to windward mattered much. Economic conditions had altered too and there was a different outlook on this competition sailed half-way round the world in ships perfectly sparred and built, that could weather a typhoon and yet pile on a cloud of canvas as they held the steady trades on the run to Mauritius across the Indian Ocean. But perhaps it was the men, more than the ships, who had changed.

Opposite: This oil painting of Whampoa does not show any of the prominent pagodas but it does portray the ships clearly. An American ship is on the left and a British ship on the right; in the left foreground a junk is at anchor, and at the extreme left is a small schooner with a Chinese boat alongside. At anchor are a number of 'receiving ships', which are the hulls of sailing vessels whose masts have been removed and superstructures added, and on which cargo is stored and the company servants live. (*Peabody Museum, Salem*)

Below: Map of world showing tracks followed at different seasons of the year by sailing ships. (*Author*)

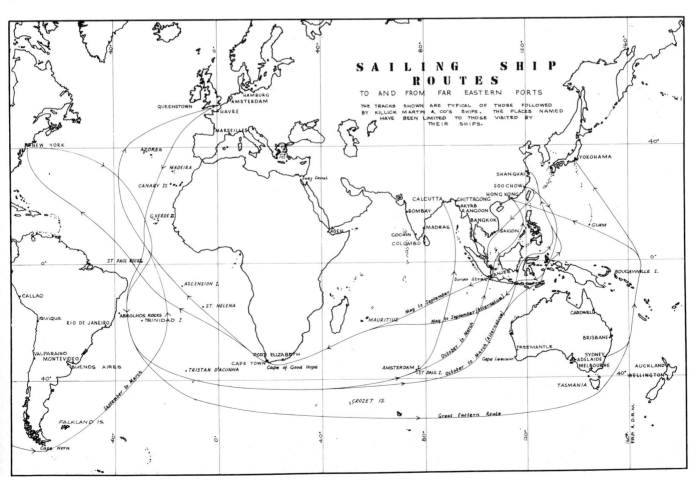

3

FREE TRADE FROM CHINA
AND SHIPS OF 1833-1847

During the first half of the nineteenth century a perceptible change occurred in the outlook of a certain section of the mercantile community of Great Britain. This was occasioned by the opening of the Indian trade in 1813 when the effect of legal competition was experienced there for the first time. This change was chiefly concerned with the sudden shortening of the passage between England and the East. Whereas ships had been taking up to six months and more to make the passage to or from India or China, some had actually returned from China in less than four months. Four years after the monopoly was partially lifted a transport sailed from Ceylon to England in 77 days, whilst the China fleet of thirteen Indiamen was only 109 days on the passage from Canton. The ships, in fact, had not changed but the motive had.

Previously safety and comfort had been all important with these valuable ships and there was neither merit nor profit in arriving at a destination first. By driving these same ships harder and not reducing sail at night the passage was shortened by a month or more. Yet the design of ships remained much the same, while the final abolition in 1834 of the East India Company's monopoly as it affected China, gave a further inducement to short-cut the passage from the East. Thus is was incentive, not fine lines, that gave increased speed, a fact which has always played an important part where speed is concerned. Several of these apple-cheek-bowed Indiamen were reaching London in 110 days or less from Canton (during the favourable monsoon of course) when a further event took place to assist their endeavours.

These ships, like most of their contemporaries, were designed to register as little tonnage as possible and so pay the smallest amount of tonnage dues. Since 1773 tonnage was measured only in terms of length and breadth, depth being assessed as half the breadth. This method of tonnage measurement has been called Old, or (after 1854) Builder's Old, Measurement (bom or om). It was the first tonnage law to apply to all vessels, regardless of their trade or size. The Old Measurement was based on the rule adopted in the Royal Navy in 1677 as well as on the rule applied in 1720 to merchant vessels of over 30 tons that brought cargoes of spirits into the country. The fact that both these rules assessed depth as half the breadth showed that this was the proportion obtaining in contemporary vessels, while the similarity of the 1773 rule to its two predecessors showed that this proportion had remained unchanged. In spite of the fact that the 1720 Act employed internal measurement and the 1773 Act external measurement, George Moorsom

proved by a series of examples in his *Review of the Laws for the Admeasurement of Tonnage* that both rules were actually intended to give the approximate weight of cargoes that could be carried. Prior to 1773, tonnage was often calculated as being the product of the length of the keel, the breadth of beam inside the planking (moulded breadth), and the depth of hold, all divided by 100. Since there was freedom in these years from tonnage laws, design of ships was unhampered and it was not until after the tonnage law was introduced in 1773 that design began to change from its accustomed proportions. There was, of course, no sudden revolution in hull-form. The Napoleonic Wars were largely responsible for accelerating the alterations made in design, since the convoys in which most ships sailed proceeded at such a slow and leisurely pace that good sailing abilities were not necessary. Many owners were quick to take advantage of this opportunity and increased the depth and capacity of their vessels without increasing their register tonnage, to the detriment of their sailing qualities. The average proportions of any vessel then became such that the length was about three-and-a-half times the breadth, and the depth was three-quarters of the breadth. Because the tonnage length was not measured abaft the heel of the sternpost, sterns often had considerable rake, while the entrance and run of the hull were as full as possible. It would have been ruinous for a shipowner to build longer ships in order to get an increase in speed, since the register tonnage figure would have been very high and out of all proportion to the vessel's size, while any degree of sharpness would not have been taken into account at all.

Register tonnage did not therefore give a very accurate representation of a vessel's shape or size and it was to obtain a more correct figure that a new rule became law in 1836. Internal measurement was adopted and the rule was framed with the desire of causing the fewest possible number of measurements to be taken and yet to provide a sufficiently exact result by an easy arithmetical process. The question of better sailing qualities may have been considered, but this was left to improve itself through the medium of measuring the shape of the hull in a new way. It was the paucity of the measurements which led to such a large scale attempt to evade as much of the tax as possible. Appendix VI contains a description of how a ship was measured for tonnage for the 1836 law as well as for the 1773 law.

It will be seen that in the new method, or 'New Measurement' (nm), breadth and depth were measured at three separate points, at the bow, amidships, and at the stern. These measurements were so taken as to give an approxinate cross-sectional area in each case and it will readily be appreciated that to minimize the figure of register tonnage it was an advantage to make the cross-sectional areas as small as possible, and while that amidships obviously had to retain a reasonable fullness, those at bow and stern were cut away considerably. Length for tonnage was measured at half the midship depth and since the length did not now form such an important part in determining the tonnage figure, the whole length of the ship could afford to be increased to make up for the stowage capacity lost by cutting away the shape of the hull at bow and stern, where the cross-sectional areas were measured. The resulting change in hull-form which the new law produced is best illustrated by comparing the sheer plans in which a pre-1836 ship is contrasted with an Aberdeen clipper of 1845. At the three

positions at which breadth and depth were measured, the cross-sectional areas have been drawn. The Merchant Ship has a very full and deep hull and is obviously at a disadvantage compared with the *Acasta* which was a direct result of the New Measurement. The idea for these drawings was taken from a diagram used by John Lyman in *The American Neptune* (Vol V, 1945, p229), in the first of his excellent and readily understandable articles on tonnage measurement. The register dimensions before 1836 consisted of the length, breadth and depth as measured for tonnage pur-

Diagram to show places at which dimensions were taken to calculate tonnage for the 1836 Rule. Double or treble lines indicate that measurements at these points were doubled or trebled in the calculation. (*Author*)

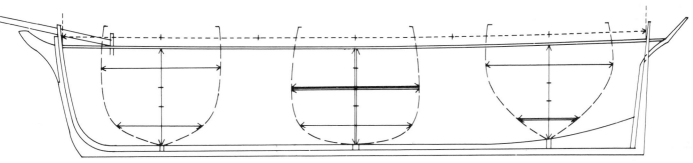

Two ship types to show the change in hull-form caused by the 1836 Tonnage Law. The cross-sections are placed at the three positions at which breadths and depths were measured by this new Rule. The 'Merchant Ship' is typical of many ships; the *Acasta* was a direct result of the 1836 Law. (*Author*)

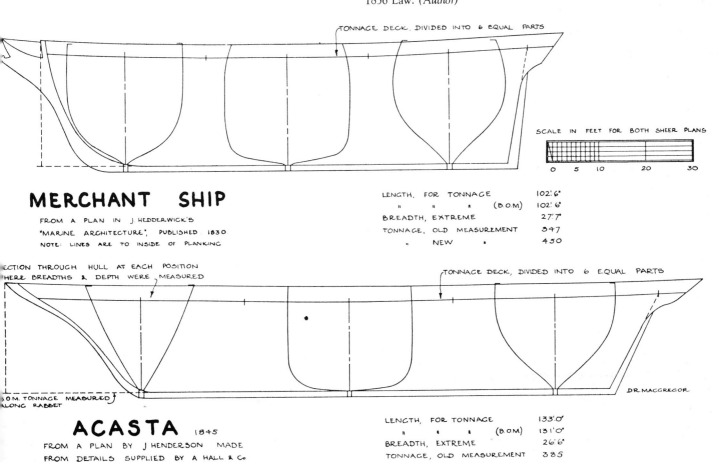

MERCHANT SHIP

FROM A PLAN IN J. HEDDERWICK'S
"MARINE ARCHITECTURE", PUBLISHED 1830
NOTE: LINES ARE TO INSIDE OF PLANKING

LENGTH, FOR TONNAGE	102' 6"
" " " (B.O.M)	102' 6"
BREADTH, EXTREME	27' 7"
TONNAGE, OLD MEASUREMENT	347
" NEW "	450

SECTION THROUGH HULL AT EACH POSITION
WHERE BREADTHS & DEPTH WERE MEASURED

B.O.M. TONNAGE MEASURED
ALONG RABBET

ACASTA 1845

FROM A PLAN BY J HENDERSON MADE
FROM DETAILS SUPPLIED BY A HALL & Co

LENGTH, FOR TONNAGE	133' 0"
" " " (B.O.M)	131' 0"
BREADTH, EXTREME	26' 6"
TONNAGE, OLD MEASUREMENT	385
" NEW "	327

poses, although the depth varied from the actual depth to half the breadth. Under the New Measurement these dimensions were: *length*, from the after part of the main stem to the fore part of the sternpost aloft; *breadth*, the maximum measurement inside at half the length: *depth*, depth of hold.

The *Acasta* illustrates how the proportion of length to breadth began to increase and how the waterlines at bow and stern began to take on the appearance of tapering wedges. When such a vessel was tried at sea, it was found that her sailing powers had been improved, while she had hardly lost any of her former capacity and at the same time registered considerably less tonnage than a vessel built under the old law. Thus a builder now had every inducement to produce a faster and more manageable vessel than anyone had had for some time.

Yet a change was very gradual in coming and an owner was not obliged to have his ship re-measured. John Wilson of Liverpool was certainly quick to profit by the new rule, since his *Athlone* (1836) had a proportion of 6.3 beams to length, and there were probably other forgotten examples.

The assessment of a vessel's fineness by comparing beams to length is, with certain exceptions, a fallacy, since within the register dimensions any shape or size can be had. However, the sudden increase in this proportion in the case of a few ships about 1836 does give an indication of fineness and this relationship can be employed fairly safely up to 1854, after which the method of tonnage measurement changed and the proportion of beams to length can only be considered in conjunction with register tonnage. Another method of judging fineness is by comparing the new measurement tonnage with the old, and the proportionate difference between the two gives a rough idea of how fine a vessel really was, because fine-lined ships usually had a lower tonnage figure by the new measurement than by the old. In the interests of avoiding tediousness when listing a ship's measurements in the text, old measurement and new measurement tonnages have been abbreviated to 'old' and 'new' tons, or 'om' and 'nm'.

Under ideal economic conditions, builders in both Europe and America knew how to design vessels to obtain the highest speed possible under sail. These conditions rarely, if ever, existed, for the governing factor was the purpose or trade for which the ship was built, and the resulting design was usually a compromise. European builders had a long tradition of fast-sailing ships behind them, even though many different theories were entertained. The various trades that required speed amongst other qualities had been developing a certain design, perhaps peculiar to themselves, for as long as that trade had been in operation.

A prime example of a particular trend in design maintained year after year can be had in the ships produced at Whitehaven in T & J Brocklebank's shipyard, where almost all the productions were for their own use. Operating the vessels from offices in Liverpool, they built full-rigged ships, barques, brigs, brigantines, schooners and cutters for trade throughout the world but especially to Newfoundland, the West Indies, South America, India, China and the East Indies. In the period up to 1850, three of their ships, the *Aden*, *Patna* and *Crisis*, traded almost exclusively with China, and others such as the *Bonanza* and *Jumna* made occasional passages to and from it.

One of the principal features found in their ship design after 1815 was that of appreciable deadrise with slack bilges and some tumblehome, and although the entrance was often full and convex the run was often longer and more concave. The head however remained heavy. The three regular China traders maintained a steady average as regards passage times.

Another developing trend in design can be cited in the port of Aberdeen which had built a number of schooners for the Aberdeen and Leith to London packet service. When Alexander Hall was asked in 1839 to build such a vessel, he was commissioned to design a fast schooner, similar to others on the same run. The *Scottish Maid*, as she was called, had thus grown from a very virile branch, and though the design of her bows and entrance was an innovation, due to the inspiration of her builder, she otherwise owed everything to the fast-sailing theory developed locally to meet the exigencies of certain economic and trading conditions. She possessed no similarities with the usual type of Baltimore clipper current at that time, and although Howard I Chapelle has pointed out in his *History of American Sailing Ships* that there are the lines of a Baltimore brig of the 1830s which closely resemble the lines of the *Scottish Maid*, the two vessels had sprung from such different sources that their similarity must be purely coincidental.

The first tea clippers built at Aberdeen were the ships *Bon Accord* (1846) and *North Star* (1847) and they were built with the 'Aberdeen bow'; nevertheless they did not show any remarkable degrees of speed. They are described in Chapter Four.

Shipbuilders in England were called upon from time to time to design and construct a fast vessel for use on the China coast as an opium clipper and so the maiden passage of a small, fast brig or schooner can be compared with that of a bigger ship. The former fruit schooner *Hellas* took 124 days between Gravesend and Canton in 1838 and many of the fast fruiters, opium clippers and yachts could trace the development of their hull-form back to the English cutter. The features of this form were great beam in proportion to length, deadrise with rounded floors, fairly shallow depth, and fine, often convex, lines. The broad hulls gave stability and great power to carry sail. This development did not thus stem from the Baltimore clipper, but when adapted into ocean-going square-riggers, greater length and a deeper hull were required. This hull development was described fully in the author's *Fast Sailing Ships*, Chapters Two and Three.

It was certainly the ending of the East India Company's monopoly with China in 1834 that sparked off the building of several vessels which were undoubtedly of finer lines and possessed greater potential for fast passages than previous merchant ships engaged in long-distance ocean trade. The relative shortness of passages made by the ships built in the 1830s was not equalled until the beginning of the 1850s, according to the random selection of passage times I have made for the years 1834, 1837–38, 1841, 1846 and 1848. Prior to 1834 the fastest outward time to China was probably that claimed by the *Mangles* which was said to have gone from London to Macao in 94 days in 1829. This ship of 545 tons was built at Calcutta in 1802.

The principal ships built as a direct result of the termination of the East India Company's monopoly in 1834 would seem to be the following:

Ship	Built	Builder	Tons (om)	Tons (nm)
Jumna	1833	Brocklebank	364	
Alexander Baring	1834	Green	505	612
Euphrates	1834	Wilson	617	
John o'Gaunt	1835	Wilson	450	
Aden	1839	Brocklebank	312	339

These ships would appear to be more of the 'clipper' category than others built in these years such as the *Robert Small*, which T & W Smith constructed at Newcastle in 1835 and which was probably a reduced version of an East Indiaman and therefore an early Blackwall frigate.

But sentiment was changing as the profit-motive became more evident. In 1834, Baring Brothers had to abandon a speculation in silk for lack of a fast ship and two years later when writing to Russell & Co on 21 April they said:

> We believe too that your shippers will have discovered that it will not answer to employ old worn-out ships that run to your port from New South Wales in search of freight; they are indifferently, and many of them badly, found, sail heavily, frequently damage their cargoes and are not pure enough for fine teas. The *Royal Admiral*, for instance, is so long coming, that the period contracted (1 May) for the delivery of her silk may perhaps expire before she arrives . . . (Baring Bros Archives, Letter Book 5D, 1836).

Their exasperation at losing a fat profit is concealed by the niceties of business politeness.

However, it is unlikely that any ship carrying tea from China to England in the late 1830s was as fine-lined as the *Falcon* which had begun life in 1824 as Lord Yarborough's ship-rigged yacht. According to a model in the Science Museum, London, she had very steep deadrise with fine convex waterlines, which was the usual concept for a fine-lined hull. There are so few plans for the period before 1850 of merchant ships that were intended to sail fast that it is difficult to plot a regular development. The idea of actually racing tea home to England was only being conceived in the later 1840s, and so contests between ships, and the press coverage that resulted from these, were almost non-existent. Hence the selection of ships for inclusion here is difficult. Of course, the Aberdeen bow got reported in newspapers and so did the ships built with it, but speed under sail for commercial square-riggers was quite a novelty in early Victorian times.

The science of making fast passages to and from China and the Far East was a closely-guarded secret by the captains who specialized in this trade, and many potentially fast ships, such as the *Falcon*, made comparatively slow times as a result. As it was, they always took their departure in October or later when the north-east monsoon would be in their favour as they threaded their way down the treacherous China Sea. Only towards the end of the 1840s was tea being brought earlier to the loading ports which obliged the first ships away to beat down in the teeth of the south-west monsoon. In such conditions, the crack ships of the 1830s had to be replaced by longer, larger, and finer-lined clippers of which the Aberdeen clipper *Stornoway*, built in 1850, was the first example.

The somewhat full-bodied tea ships of the 1840s might have been surprised to see a full-rigged ship like the *Sylph* (1831) racing opium up the China Sea. This painting of her at anchor with the sails drying, shows the topsails 'hauled a-bowline', naval fashion. (*C Bull*)

BIOGRAPHIES OF SHIPS BUILT 1833–1847

FALCON, 1824

This full-rigged ship was built in 1824 as a yacht for Lord Yarborough by List, at Wootton Bridge, Isle of Wight, at a cost of £18,000; she was flagship of the Royal Yacht Squadron for twelve years. The naval architect, John Fincham, measured her in the 1820s and gave her dimensions as 107ft 2in (length on deck from rabbet on stem to rabbet on sternpost) and 27ft 4in extreme breadth. Unfortunately his table of offsets has not been discovered. Lines taken off a rigged model in the Science Museum show very steep deadrise and fine convex waterlines. The masts on the model are about the same length as Fincham's dimensions, but the topsail, topgallant and royal yards are much longer, the difference increasing upwards.

Obviously hoping to make money out of the freer China trade, Baring Brothers bought her in 1836 for £5500 and wrote to Russell & Co in Hong Kong: 'The ship seems admirably calculated for an opium ship between your port and Bombay or Calcutta. We believe she will sail faster than any ship in that trade . . .' (Baring Bros Archives, Letter Book 5D, fo 470-3). *Falcon* carried her first cargo of tea to London in 1837–38 but I have not traced the times of this passage; then she sailed out to Batavia in 92 days, again bringing back tea from China. In 1837, *Lloyd's Register*

gave her tonnages as 351 om and 372 nm with a class of 12 A1.

Baring's had vainly tried to sell the ship for £10,500 after buying her; now the asking price was lowered to £6000. She was improved and modernised at Liverpool in 1839 and the following year again sailed to China where Jardine, Matheson bought her and placed her in the opium trade. She sailed from Macao that December to load opium in Calcutta and remained in the trade until her disappearance in the mid-1850s.

Above: The *Falcon* in the China Sea after her purchase by Jardine, Matheson. Lithograph by T G Dutton. (*MacGregor Collection*)

Opposite, top: Falcon sail plan. Drawn from measurements taken off model in Science Museum, London but running rigging omitted. Reconstruction: shape of the royals (royal yards lashed in model's rigging).

Opposite, bottom: Falcon lines plan. Built in 1824 by List at Wootton Bridge, Isle of Wight. Drawn from measurements taken off rigged model in Science Museum, London. Dimensions (scaled off model): 109ft 6in (after part stem to foreside sternpost), 26ft 0in (extreme breadth), 334 tons (calculated). Fincham's measurements vary from these (see text). Reconstruction: load waterline, from Fincham's data.

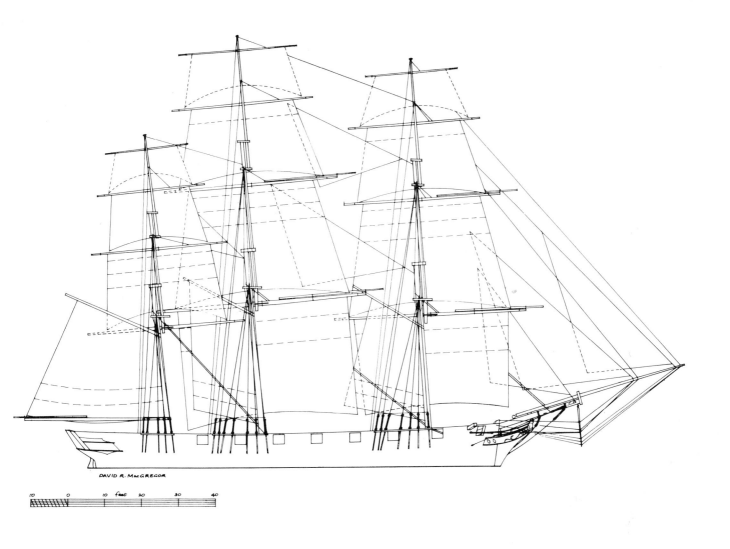

DAVID R. MacGREGOR

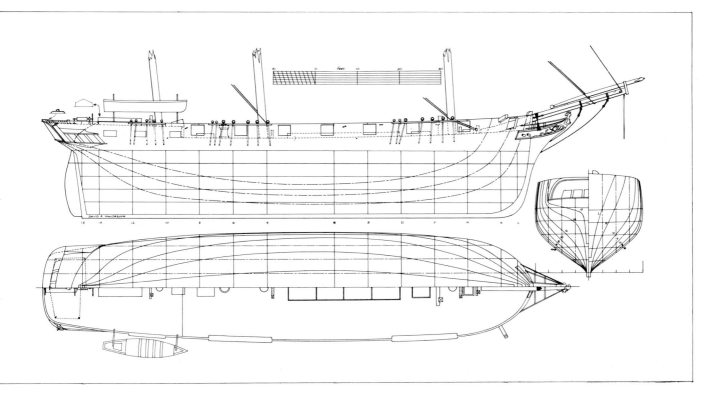

JUMNA, 1833

Many of Brocklebank's vessels possessed a fair turn of speed and she was no exception, her voyage in 1833–34 consisting of a run out to the Ladrone Islands off the Canton river in 110 days from Liverpool and a return trip of 102 days. The latter has been claimed as 97 days – presumably calculated by deducting two days spent at anchor in Gaspar Strait, another day at St Helena and time spent getting down the Canton river. In 1834 she sailed back to Canton in 113 days from Liverpool. These ships, to judge by selected examples of their hull-forms, usually had a fair amount of deadrise with slack bilges and easy waterlines which included a long fine run, and perhaps a smart passage was encouraged by the owners. Certainly the *Bonanza*, at that time rigged as a brig, took the amazingly short time of only 91 days between Shanghai and Liverpool, made at the end of 1844. She had been built in 1830 with a tonnage of 173. It has often been said that vessels built and owned by the same firm as in the case of T & J Brocklebank were not encouraged to sail fast, merely to carry their cargo safely, but it looks as if a reappraisal is required.

The *Jumna* was built at Whitehaven as a full-rigged ship and was designed on the lines of the *Patriot King*, but a foot broader. She was of 364 tons with dimensions of 111.8ft × 27.7ft × 18.9ft and carried a crew of eighteen in 1834. She spent her life trading to India and the East.

Pictured off Whitehaven, ships of the Brocklebank fleet under sail. In the right foreground is the *Jumna* of 1833. The three other identified ships are the *Patriot King* (centre), *Hindoo* (extreme left) and between them is the brig *Globe* (1822). *(Merseyside County Museums)*

In 1856 Brocklebank's sold her to the Tay Whale Fishing Co of Dundee to become an Arctic whaler and in 1863 she had an engine added. On 6 July of the same year she was crushed in the ice in Melville Bay.

ALEXANDER BARING, 1834

Built at Blackwall by R & H Green in 1834 for Baring Bros of London, she was 'built to the specification of the managing partners [and] was a fast sailer' (wrote R W Hidy in *The House of Baring in American Trade*). However, without plan or half-model her actual shape is conjectural, although judging from correspondence the owners obviously expected great things of her. She measured 505 tons om, 612 tons nm, with dimensions of 132.4ft × 28.8ft × 13.8ft. This makes her a ship of unusually shallow draft.

The fastest passage so far found for her was one of 10 days between Deal and Hong Kong in 1838, 26 May to September. After a homeward passage from New Orleans, Barings sold her in September 1845 to Brooke & Co of Liverpool who kept her in the India trade for about twenty years. On one of these India passages she reached Liverpool on 12 March 1851, 107 days out from Bengal. Her name dropped out of the Register in 1866.

JOHN O'GAUNT, 1835

This ship was always being talked about in the 1850s in a manner that suggested she was something out of the ordinary and several fast passages are attached to her name. The particular one for which she is most often credited was a run of 66 days out to Anjer, but the exact year is never specified. Two outward passages I have traced are as follows, all made under the command of John Robertson who remained master until 1844:

1838, Liverpool to Anjer, 12 June to 8 September, 88 days

1839, Liverpool to Batavia, 19 June to 11 September, 84 days.

She remained at Batavia 10 days and then continued to China:

1839, Batavia to Canton, 21 September to 30 September, 9 days. Total elapsed time Liverpool to Canton, 103 days.

Both these must have been considered wonderfully fast at the time they were made. The only homeward passage I have for the ship at this period was of 113 days between Canton and Liverpool, 6 January to 29 April 1838.

She was built by John Wilson at Liverpool for Gladstone & Co, Liverpool, as a full-rigged ship of 449¾ tons with dimensions of 114ft 0in × 29ft 10in (below main wales) × 19ft 3in. This makes her a broad ship with only 3.8 beams to length; perhaps she had steep floors. She is not listed in *Lloyd's Register* until 1848 and I am grateful to Michael Stammers for looking her up in the Custom House Register. The ship continued in the China trade until she was wrecked on 17 January 1854 in Caernarvon Bay near Holyhead when 165 days out from Whampoa bound to Liverpool. Captain McDonald had died at St Helena in November but his widow remained aboard; she was saved and also part of the crew, but all the cargo was lost.

DUMFRIES, 1837

Little is known about this ship as she did not appear in *Lloyd's Register* until 1854 in which year her owner was given as Aiken & Co of Liverpool and that she was barque-rigged, of 468 tons and built in the Isle of Man. They probably also owned *Mencius*, built in the Isle of Man in 1848. The *Dumfries* is inserted here because it is claimed that she once sailed out to Hong Kong in 87 days with the south-west monsoon in her favour. In 1845 she took 111 days between Liverpool and Hong Kong, 7 June to 26 September, but she beat the *John o'Gaunt* under Captain McDonald which left Liverpool 5 days after her but did not reach Hong Kong until 14 October. In 1854 she was wrecked on 11 April on the Pescadores, China Sea, bound from Shanghai to Liverpool with tea which she had loaded at £7 10s per ton.

ADEN, 1839

None of the Brocklebank fleet were listed in *Lloyd's Register* before the 1850s but one can obtain particulars of them from Gibson's history of the firm or from their yard book in the Liverpool Museum. The *Aden*, *Santon* (1839) and *Horsburgh* (1838) were all built by T & J Brocklebank at their Whitehaven yard on the same lines although the number of deadflats varied, the first two having five each and the *Horsburgh* but three. The first two were both barques with similar spar dimensions and carried skysails. The *Aden's* dimensions were 107.2ft × 22.6ft × 17.2ft, with tonnages of 312 om and 339 nm. Although she was in the China trade for over twenty years, I have only traced her passages since 1847. In 1868 she was sold to J Cochran of Liverpool who re-rigged her as a three-masted schooner. In 1877 she was totally wrecked at sea on 20 November.

A typical barque of the 1840s, the *Raymond* carries trysail gaffs on all masts and has skysail masts fidded abaft the royal masts; the spanker is boomless, but is sheeted out to a boom rigged out on each quarter. Built at Sunderland in 1840 of 414 tons om, she was owned in Hull, and this lithograph by John Ward probably celebrates her arrival there in October 1843 as the first ship to come direct from China. (*Parker Gallery*)

MAGELLAN, 1841

This full-rigged ship was built of wood at Cowes in 1841 of 350 tons om and 359 tons nm with dimensions of 103.5ft × 24.5ft × 17.4ft which made her a fairly broad and deep ship for her length. Her first owners were Ravenscroft of Liverpool who sometimes sent her to South America. In 1852, B Sproule of Liverpool became the owner and five years later she was sold foreign on 6 February. Her fate has not been traced.

Her fastest recorded passage in the China trade after 1848 was one of 109 days to Hong Kong from Liverpool in 1849, 28 April to 15 August.

PATNA, 1842

This barque was built by T & J Brocklebank at Whitehaven and operated by them out of Liverpool in trade to the East and China for her entire career under their flag. A small vessel by later standards, she was of probably the same sort of hull-form described for the *Jumna* of nine years earlier. She measured 362 tons with dimensions for register of 113.0ft × 25.1ft × 17.5ft. A breadth also given of 22.8ft is probably the internal tonnage measurement for the 1836 Tonnage Act.

R & H Jefferson of Whitehaven acquired her in 1868 which is also the first date she appears in *Lloyd's Register*. Two years later she passed to W R Kelly of the same port when her tonnage was given as 321 net and 325 under deck. In 1885 she was sold to G H Jones of New Quay and the following year was broken up at Plymouth in June.

VISCOUNT SANDON, 1842

This full-rigged ship was built at Liverpool where a number of China traders were constructed in the 1830s and 1840s. Taylor, Potter & Co who owned a number of early tea clippers were her owners but her builder is unknown. She measured 514 tons om and 540 tons nm with dimensions of 117.5ft × 27.1ft × 18.3ft and was built of wood to class 12 A1. I do not have particulars of any passages made prior to 1848 although she was in the China trade.

In 1861 J Wardley of Liverpool is listed as the owner; he owned shares in a number of Aberdeen clippers in the 1850s. Four years later he sold her to owners in Galle, which was a port in Ceylon, south of Colombo. In 1867 she went to owners in Chittagong but was not listed in the Register in 1870.

EARL OF CHESTER, 1845

Prowse & Co, Liverpool, were her owners and they numbered many interesting vessels in their fleet. She was built at Chester with dimensions of 125.6ft × 28.2ft × 19.5ft and a tonnage of 462, being a full-rigged ship built of wood. In 1852 she left Shanghai on 17 September, the same day as *Countess of Seafield*, and reached London the same day again. She was wrecked in 1867 on the coast of Anglesey on 26 October, the day after sailing from Liverpool for Madras. All hands were lost.

MARY SPARKS, 1845

Built at Workington for J Bushby of that port who owned a number of clippers in the 1850s and 1860s, she was a full-rigged ship of 469 tons om and 544 tons nm with dimensions of 122.0ft × 29.0ft × 20.7ft which made her a fairly

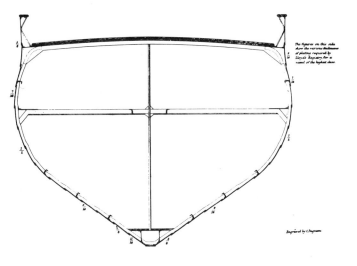

Left: Richard Cobden midship section. Built of iron by James Hodgson at Liverpool in 1844 from a design by Thomas R Guppy of Bristol. Illustrated in *Transactions of Institution of Naval Architects* in 1871. Dimensions: 137ft 7in × 27ft 6in × 19ft 2in, 461 tons nm and 522 tons om.

broad vessel and also on the deep side. Klingender of Liverpool is given as her owner in 1862 and three years later she passed to owners in Dundee who reduced her to a barque and placed her in the Mediterranean trade. D Crighton was the first Dundee owner. She was wrecked on 18 December 1869 on Terschelling Island, bound from Falmouth to Hamburg; only one of her crew of 17 was saved.

ASTARTE, 1846

Built at Cowes by J & R White as an opium clipper, she must have been built on fairly fine lines, probably with big deadrise and convex waterlines. She was a brig of 286 tons om and nm with a square stern, no quarter-galleries and a woman bust figurehead. In 1863 *Astarte*'s measurements were given as 113.4ft × 26.1ft × 15.7ft with tonnages of 283 under deck and 292 gross and net. Her length and breadth were the same as many ships and barques in the trade then, but she was several feet shallower.

Basil Lubbock calls her a 'beautiful brig' and describes how she was laid on the berth at Whampoa to load tea for London in 1850 in competition with the *Oriental* and sailed the following day. However *Astarte* took a month longer on the passage. She returned to China but probably never again carried opium.

Her first owner was J Roberts of London. In 1852 Balcras (or Baleras) of London or Liverpool became owner. In 1860 Tom Crossley of Liverpool was both owner and master; J Forster, London, was the owner for four years from 1868; and then she went to F & A Swanzy, London, who put her into the West African palm-oil trade. In 1885 she was broken up after being run ashore at Grand Bassam on the West African Ivory Coast when it was found that she was leaking.

CRISIS, 1847

Prior to 1850, T & J Brocklebank had several vessels which made occasional voyages from China, but there were only three which remained regularly in the trade. These were the *Aden*, *Patna* and *Crisis*. Like all of their vessels, the last-named was built at Whitehaven in their own yard and registered at Liverpool. She was reputed to have made a fast run home in 1853–54 but there is some doubt as to the correct date of her departure from Shanghai: *Gore's Liverpool Advertiser* has it as 24 October; but *The Times* has 24 September. If the former is correct, it makes a fast passage of only 95 days to Liverpool.

The *Crisis* measured 111.9ft × 25.0ft × 18.8ft; 395 tons om and 426 tons nm. In 1859 she was cut down to barque rig and three years later was wrecked on 23 January on the Arklow Bank, Ireland, bound from Liverpool to Singapore.

MENAM, 1847

Built at Dumbarton with measurements of 110.3ft × 26.5ft × 18.7ft and tonnages of 415 old and 472 new measurement, her first owner was Peter Maxton of Greenock. She was barque-rigged. The son was her first master and he then transferred to the iron clipper *Lord of the Isles* in 1853. It must certainly have been a change! Maxton maintained a good average in *Menam* but she was slow.

Martin & Co, Greenock, are listed as owners in 1857, but probably they and Maxton always retained shares in her; the same was probably the case with *Lord of the Isles*. The *Menam* was abandoned 'north of the Line' on 6 February 1861 bound from Manilla to London with sugar and hemp; the crew were taken off by the French barque *Bahia*. She had begun to leak 11 days earlier.

GANGES, 1847
This wooden full-rigged ship was built at Leith in 1847 for
J Fergus of Kirkaldy and four years later was bought by Muir
& Co of Leith. In 1852 Thomas & Co are given as her
owners, but she is not listed in Lloyd's Register after 1854.
Her dimensions were 133.2ft × 30.0ft × 22.3ft with ton-
nages of 679 om and 770 nm; and she classed 13 A1.

Her only master was Robert Deas, who later had command of *Titania* on her first two voyages and whom Andrew
Shewan described as 'a very cautious man'. He maintained
a good average of homeward passages from China. Her best
time was in 1851 with 111 days to the Downs from Whampoa, and Shewan describes a race with the American clippers *Bald Eagle* and *Flying Cloud* and how she beat them up
the English Channel (*Sea Breezes*, Vol III, 1922). However, as Arthur H Clarke points out in *The Clipper Ship Era*,
Bald Eagle was not built until 1852 and *Flying Cloud* had just
reached San Francisco when the *Ganges* left Whampoa!
The most likely American clipper to have met Deas was the
White Squall, which was off the Isle of Wight on 16
December whereas Shewan claims the *Ganges* to have been
off Portland the following day which somewhat reverses the
claim. But the *Ganges* appears to have docked in London 3
days earlier.

The *John Bright,* built at Dumbarton in 1847, carried trysails on both fore-
and mainmasts and also a crossjack with reef points. She was identified by
the Marryat code hoist 2/5192; formerly this painting was attributed to the
Elizabeth Nicholson (1863). (*National Maritime Museum*)

4

THE ABERDEEN BOW
AND SHIPS OF 1846-1854

Any builder with some knowledge of the best shape for craft designed for speed could have done what William Hall did at Aberdeen in 1839, when he made a suggestion about a schooner, then on the stocks, in order to decrease her register tonnage. He had undoubtedly weighed the matter carefully in his mind, as it was an unusual idea, and it is said that he even made tests with model hulls in a tank, since he obviously thought that he could not only cheat the tonnage laws, but also improve the schooner's sailing abilities. If he merely gave her a very narrow entrance at the place where the first tonnage station occurred, this would only lead to extreme hollows in the waterlines, which was not really good design. He therefore suggested that the stem be extended forward at a very rakish angle, an action that would draw out the waterlines, and thus a sharp entrance with straight or convex waterlines would be preserved. The stem now raked well forward, while the length on deck, along which the tonnage stations were marked, was so increased that the bow station was now almost immediately over the forefoot, at which position the cross-sectional area was reduced to a minimum.

This schooner was the *Scottish Maid* and her design appears to have given something new for the shipping fraternity to talk about. If it is true that she was altered on the stocks from the original design, then her midship section and probably her stern would have been built in the usual local tradition. Her lines and sail plan were reproduced in my book *Fast Sailing Ships* as Figures 97 and 100, but it would probably be as well to run over the salient features of her hull-form.

The profile of her stem was the most unusual thing about her, as it leaned right forward at an angle of some 50° to the vertical. It gave a sense of great purity to the shape of the bows and supported no head knee or false stem, but the rabbet of the planking (the line along which the outside face of the planking met any structural member, in this case the stem) followed the profile of the stem itself, and the bowsprit, pitched as low as possible to give the headsails a large spread, entered the deck on top of the sheer, sometimes between prominent knightheads. The section lines, as shown in the body plan, flared outwards above the rake of the stem, while above the forefoot they were sufficiently full to prevent the craft putting her jibboom under. These features were most successful in the Aberdeen schooners of the 1840s, as predicted by tank experiments, but when enlarged in square-rigged vessels they did not prove so satisfactory, since the bilge was not carried so far forward, with the result that Aberdeen ships were for long noted as being

wet vessels, and their diving qualities, when men were washed off the bowsprit, were long remembered. The waterlines forward were straight or slightly convex, though the lowest one had the merest indication of a hollow which was repeated in the run aft. The midship section had marked deadrise, with evenly rounded bilges and slight tumblehome. The sternpost raked aft under a delicate counter, almost square on plan.

The *Scottish Maid* was herself only important in so far as she was the first vessel to possess the 'Aberdeen bow'. Due to the peculiarities of this feature and her improved sailing and carrying capabilities, she at once set a fashion amongst other Aberdeen-built fast schooners, which was as alive as ever ten years later. From the evidence available it would appear that the Aberdeen schooners, enlarged and rigged as barques or ships, exerted a greater influence on the design and appearance of fast merchantmen than ships launched from any other single port. In several cases, before large ships were effected, design underwent a variety of changes in style through the medium of small craft as in America.

To vessels which adopted this fashion was applied the word 'clipper', and the term was used loosely at the time, especially in shipping advertisements and conversation. Today we differentiate between a 'medium clipper', a 'clipper' and an 'extreme clipper' depending on the degree of sharpness in the hull-form, and the definition should be dependent on an examination of the plans and half-models. In 1861 an advertisement in a shipping paper described the *Stornoway* as 'this far-famed yacht-built clipper and regular trader', and it was not until some two years later that the term 'China clipper' first appeared. Most advertisements styled ships as 'fast-sailing ship' or 'splendid Aberdeen clipper', while the expression 'tea clipper' was probably coined by some writer of more recent times after the vessels he wrote about had all ceased to exist.

After 1836, when Great Britain changed her tonnage laws, there was much less chance of her adopting American forms of design than there was before that year when both countries had much the same rules. While we changed our laws twice in less than twenty years, America retained the same rules until 1864, yet she developed the principle of fine-lined ships to an extreme degree, and that in spite of antiquated and unflattering methods of measurement, which was much to her credit.

The firm of Alexander Hall & Sons commenced at the end of the eighteenth century, and by 1830 when Alexander was 70 the firm were the leading shipbuilders in Aberdeen. He retired about this year and his sons, James, aged

Below: Acasta lines. Built in 1845 by Alexander Hall & Sons at Aberdeen. Redrawn and reconstructed from a diagram issued by her builders to show advantages of their new design methods (figure 105). Dimensions for register: 128.3ft × 23.4ft × 16.7ft, 327⅖ tons nm and 385^{15}/₉₄ tons om. Reconstruction: figurehead, bulwarks, cathead, mast positions; lines developed from three cross-sections in above diagram.

Bottom: Acasta sail plan. Entirely reconstructed and based on a plan drawn by James Henderson. Sources: lines plan; spar dimensions from builder's cost account; spar diameters and mast positions from contemporary practice; paintings of Aberdeen ships. Skysail yards not listed by builder are dotted.

Right: Detail of bows of the early composite ship *Bristow* (1854, of 374 tons) illustrates the raking stem of an Aberdeen bow without the trailboards, hair rails and their supporting brackets. *(MacGregor Collection)*

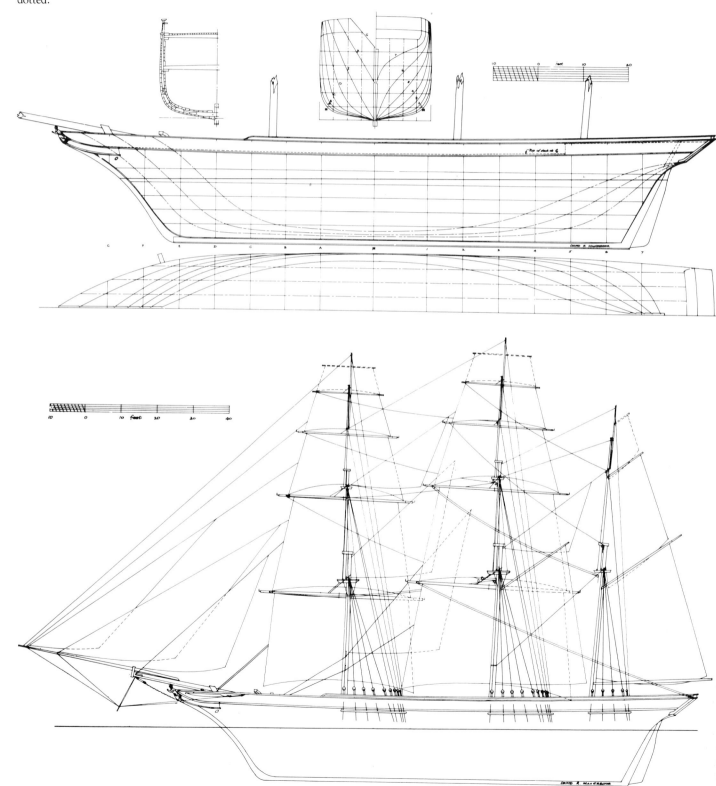

It was a Liberal Parliament which passed the Bill, presented by Lord John Russell, then Prime Minister, for the old Navigation Laws to be repealed. His administration was principally concerned with the policy of *laissez-faire* and of improving conditions by repealing old bills, and the Navigation Laws, previously modified in 1823 by Huskisson, then President of the Board of Trade, did not escape his attention. These laws came to an end as from 1 September 1849, while a new set of rules governing British trade and commerce took effect from the beginning of 1850. Their duty was to shape and encourage trade without a multiplicity of restrictions. At last the government had begun to take a more active part in looking after the welfare of marine commerce, and the great Merchant Shipping Act of 1854, with its 548 clauses covering all aspects of ships, seamen and tonnage measurement, was the foundation on which the British mercantile marine was based. The method of tonnage measurement provided for in this Act is discussed in Chapter Six.

The suspension of the Navigation Laws engendered that spirit of rivalry and competition which was instrumental in rigorously altering the type of ship produced and bringing the shipowner up to date in his business methods. The arrival of the American clipper *Oriental* in London on 3 December 1850, 97 days from Hong Kong with 1600 tons of tea on board at £6 per ton, was an added stimulus to the desire not to be outclassed by foreign ships nor to lose the carrying power in any trade without a stiff fight. The power to fight back came from the shipowners and they turned to British shipyards for help.

The shipbuilders themselves did not benefit directly from the suspension of the Navigation Laws but only in so far as they received orders for ships of new design. British shipwrights held some advantages over American yards, since tools, canvas and copper sheathing were cheaper and cordage was of superior quality.

Whilst the Navigation Laws were being repealed, Aberdeen seems to have built only an odd schooner or two, but as soon as outsiders stepped into the lucrative trades, orders began to pour in. Though the shipyards were not busy in those years, the designers must have been, as a very definite change began to take place, as is evident in the model of the *Stornoway*. Firstly, she was of a larger size than any vessel Hall had built since 1842, and secondly, she was built expressly to carry home Jardine, Matheson's teas in the face of foreign competition. She was built at the close of 1850, and so Hall had had two years in which to examine the performance of his *Reindeer* and also that of the fast *John Bunyan* and *Countess of Seafield*, all Aberdeen ships of 1848, and all head and shoulders above the rest, excluding the *Crisis* (1847) and *Sea Witch* (1848).

The *Stornoway* was a thoroughbred Aberdeen clipper of the same pattern as *Reindeer*, but with slightly less deadrise and a squarer bilge. She was also proportionally deeper, with less projection to her stem, a heavier counter and a more upright sternpost. The reverse curve at the waterline was no doubt designed to give a more balanced hull when heeled, besides giving good spread to the rigging of her lofty masts. This shape of her midship section was well suited to the China trade, but her rather hollow lines, though helping her to windward, made her sluggish in light winds. The *Chrysolite* had hardly any hollows in her lines and was much sharper aft than in her entrance. Though not so good in

4, and William, 25, became the manager and the designer of the firm.

The few drawings extant depicting Aberdeen schooners of the 1840s indicate that they had not changed in general outward appearance from the *Scottish Maid*. The barque *Acasta* was of a deeper model, with flatter floors and a narrower hull. Although the firm launched a few such square-rigged vessels to the new design, the *Bon Accord* and *North Star* of 1846 and 1847 were the first ones put into the China trade, but though individually fast ships, they did nothing very startling in the way of quick passages.

Hall's third square-rigged vessel to be built for the tea trade was the *Reindeer* of 1848 which attained distinction immediately. She was launched the year before the *Benjamin Elkin*, and it is fortunate that their half-models are still in existence, since it is evident that both possessed the peculiarities of the Aberdeen model to a high degree. The *Reindeer*'s stem projected as far forward as *Scottish Maid*'s, while her model was a further development along the line indicated in the drawing of *Acasta*, but with more deadrise. Like other contemporaries of her type, she was virtually an enlarged Aberdeen schooner, just as the *Ann McKim* was an enlarged edition of a Baltimore clipper. William Hall seems to have been experimenting with several designs at this period, since the *Reindeer*'s midship section had a reverse curve at the waterline, like that of *Stornoway* and *Chrysolite*, although each had a different underwater body.

The year of 1848 was certainly a highlight in shipbuilding since *John Bunyan* by Walter Hood and *Countess of Seafield* by Alexander Duthie were both launched in addition to the *Reindeer*. These three vessels were a marked improvement on the general run of ships employed in the China trade and their capabilities were fully recognized when the Navigation Laws were repealed. Although Aberdeen-built ships carried the palm in the China trade for much of the 1850s, the exploits of the first *Fiery Cross* and other individual ships were hard to emulate. The construction of ships with what Hall liked to term the 'Aberdeen bow' gave not only increased speed but a considerable cargo capacity on a comparatively small tonnage, and this factor was of some importance in bringing orders to Aberdeen for ships to contend against American clippers, some of which could barely carry their own register tonnage.

strong headwinds, especially with more deadrise, she was faster in light breezes. Captain Enright of the *Chrysolite* admitted that his ship was slower than *Stornoway* when beating down the China Sea against the monsoon. Yet he showed a better average which must be put down to the fact that he was more energetic and daring than that skilful and renowned master, John Robertson.

Compared with these three Aberdeen clippers, *Cairngorm* was of a much more accepted type of design, having fine enough lines and sufficient rise of floor to make her fast in light and strong favourable winds. Her model was virtually that to which Hall reverted when he built *The Caliph* in 1869 as his last word in clipper ship design.

Walter Hood and Alexander Duthie were the other two most notable Aberdeen builders at this time, but while Hall was producing numerous small and handy clippers of about 500 tons or less, Hood was building several rather larger ones for George Thompson's 'Aberdeen White Star Line', while Duthie, although all his ships were very handsome, does not seem to have built anything spectacular, with the exception of *Ballarat* and *Ben Avon*, and neither of these was very sharp compared with Hall's ships.

COMPARISON OF SHIPS BUILT BY A HALL & SONS 1846–49 WHICH HAD THE 'ABERDEEN BOW' AND WERE PRESUMABLY IN THE CLIPPER CATEGORY

Ships	Date	Dimensions for tonnage (ft)	Dimensions for register (ft in)	Old tons	New tons
Bon Accord	1846	134.2 × 23.7 × 18.4	26 2 max beam	432	380
North Star	1847	135.4 × ? × 18	27 0 max beam	430	385
Reindeer	1848	141.5 × 22.7 × 15.	?	428	329
Bonita	1848	134.7 × 22.5 × 15.2	?	398	299
Pilot Fish	1848	126.0 × 23.7 × 16.0	?	?	303
Benjamin Elkin	1849	136.6 × 23.4 × 16.2	?	425	367

This table indicates somewhat similar dimensions for several of these small clippers, suggesting that there may have been some similarities in profile and shape, although it is likely that their actual hull-forms would have varied as Hall was undoubtedly experimenting with each vessel he constructed.

The true hallmark of the 'Aberdeen bow' is the way in which the rabbet of the stem rakes forward as it follows the curve of the stem, allowing the planking of the hull to stretch right forward without the usual knees, brackets and hair rails. Trailboards bolted to the hull planking itself did sweep downwards from the figurehead and there was also a nameboard on the rail surmounted with carving. As the stem itself raked right forward it meant that the knight-heads also did so, and as the bowsprit entered the hull between them it gave them extra prominence. This was the style from 1839 when the *Scottish Maid* appeared, right through until about 1855; after that the bow was gradually reconverted to the old conventional form of construction although with fewer heavy mouldings. The descriptions by the Lloyd's Register surveyors of the extreme Aberdeen bows provide interesting comments: 'bow termed clipper

with considerably outreach' (*Ben Muick Dhui*); 'is forme with usual so-called clipper bow carried rather to exces (*Bonita*); 'stem raked to form cutwater with little overhan (*Cairngorm*).

Most ships still set up their rigging on channels whic projected outside the ship's side, but it was said that the dragged in the water on the lee side as the vessel heele over under a press of sail and so might reduce the speed. I addition, it was considered they spoiled the looks of a ship Hall's tea clippers *Stornoway*, *Cairngorm* and *Vision* ha channels although they may have only projected some si inches beyond the hull. William Denny's iron clipper o 1850, the *Three Bells*, did not have them and her lowe deadeyes set up on the main rail inside the topgallant bu warks, and the chain plates poked out just below the mai rail and then ran snugly down the outside of the hull t which they were bolted. This was the style adopted in th second half of the 1850s as iron wire became increasingl popular for the rigging, requiring a narrower base in rela tion to the mast height. It was this reduction in the 'sprea which enabled channels to be dispensed with, as they pro vided a wider base for the greater elasticity of hemp riggin Robert S Newall had taken out a patent for iron wire i 1848 and it was soon to be adopted in ships' rigging.

But crews' wages were low – able seamen were paid £ per month – and so there was sufficient manpower to oper ate the handspike windlass, haul the heavy yards round o go aloft and close-reef the deep single topsails with the three rows of reef points. But if the ship's safety could b improved or the replacement of gear could be saved tha was a different matter. So the 'Armstrong patent' windla: with its lever-arm handles geared to the windlass barrel wa generally in use by 1850 and the anchor could now be hov in more quickly than with the handspike variety; at th same time other types of patent capstans began to appea Henry Cunningham first registered his patent for rolle reefing sails in 1850 but by 1853 only a dozen or so ship had fitted them. However in the second half of the 1850 they became more popular and an occasional ship fitte them to the topgallants as well, such as the *Shandon* (1855 and the second *Fiery Cross*, as reported in 1864 in th latter's case. Before the middle of the 1860s, very few Brit ish ships adopted the double topsails advocated in th United States, first by R B Forbes in 1841 and later b Captain Frederick Howes in 1853. Of course, a form c double topsail had already been in use in small square riggers as well as brigs and topsail schooners in countrie bordering the North Sea during the period 1800–1840, so was not unknown over here. In this rig there was only two-piece square-rigged mast – lower mast and topmast.

Flush-decked ships for long deepwater voyages wer never too satisfactory, firstly because the long open dec provided no check for the seas which came aboard, an secondly because all the accommodation was in the 'twee decks and so occupied valuable cargo space. *Ariel* an *Titania* were certainly so built in the 1860s and a few othe as well, but the Aberdeen clippers of the early 1850s appe to have had their accommodation on deck. The crew woul be berthed in a 'topgallant' forecastle or a deckhouse or combination of the two; the master and officers might be i a house on the deck right aft, with a raised quarterdec running around between it and the bulwarks – th arrangement became known as an 'Aberdeen house' – o they might be in a poop, the top of which rounded down on to the upper edge of the bulwarks and was known as a 'half-round'.

Aberdeen clippers are generally reckoned to have been painted with dark green hulls externally down to the copper sheathing or anti-fouling; brown varnish on bulwarks and sides of deckhouses seem to have been popular, but deck-house tops were white and so were the knightheads; iron-work of pumps, winches or windlass was often black or green. On the spars, the doublings on the masts and of the bowsprit were white, as were the tops and mast trucks. Sometimes the lower masts were also white. The topmasts and topgallants between the hounds and the doubling were usually varnished wood or painted dark brown as were the yards. Yardarms were sometimes white. Individual com-manders often had their own tastes; some favoured black yards with masts a lighter varnish. Brasswork on deck fit-tings was much favoured.

Alexander Hall was building a number of vessels for Liverpool owners in these years, of whom Jervis R Wardley owned shares in several: in 1848 he had 48 shares in Rein-deer and bought the remaining 16 shares in 1849; in 1851 he had 40 in Chrysolite and bought the ship in 1860; in 1851 he held 32 shares in John Taylor. McTear & Vining held shares in Bonita, Reindeer when new, and Mimosa. Taylor, Potter & Co owned shares in Chrysolite and John Taylor.

An unusual amount of information is available for some of these clippers built by Alexander Hall & Sons because not only have the firm's yard books survived with the build-ing costs, but they also include spar dimensions.. Then there are the builder's half-models for the Reindeer, Storno-way, Chrysolite, Cairngorm, Vision and Robin Hood. The last is in the Aberdeen Art Gallery and Museum; all the others are in the Glasgow Museum at Kelvingrove. Thus lines plans and spar plans can be drawn for all these ships which is a most unusual form of reconstruction, and it is largely through the efforts and enthusiasm of James Henderson that these reconstructions have been made, many by him-self. One snag is that dimensions scaled off the model do not always agree with the dimensions of the ship as built. This is particularly noticeable in the case of Chrysolite and Robin Hood, and James Henderson, who has reconstructed the former's lines plan, reproduced here, has indicated his method of reconstruction which is given under the plan.

Races between ships were common. For instance Capt Hewitt of the Wild Flower bet Capt Foster 100 dollars at Shanghai in 1853 that he would beat his ship Joseph Fletcher in the passage back to England. Both ships sailed on 8 January 1853, were in company for three days in the Indian Ocean, but Capt Foster in the Joseph Fletcher got back to London in 109 days or 6 days ahead of the the other's arrival at Liverpool. This story of the publicly-made wager was told in the Australian & New Zealand Gazette of 11 February 1854 quoting an Auckland newspaper!

COMPARISON OF DIMENSIONS FOR SURVIVING HALF-MODELS OF TEA CLIPPERS BUILT BY ALEXANDER HALL & SONS 1850–56

Ship	Date	Tonnage New tons	Old tons	Register dimensions of ship (nm rule – ft)
Stornoway	1850	527	595	157.8 × 25.8 (I) 28.8 (X) × 17.8
Chrysolite	1851	440	570	149.3 × 26.1 (I) 29.0 (X) × 17.0
Cairngorm	1853	939	1246	193.3 × 33.6 (I) 36.6 (X) × 20.2
Vision	1854	563	720	170.0 × 27.6 (I) 29.3 (X) × 18.2
Robin Hood	1856	853 (reg)	1185	204.0 × 35.3 (X) × 21.0 (by 1854 rule)

Ship	Dimensions scaled off model (ft)
Stornoway	157.8 × 27.6 (M) × 17.8
Chrysolite	147.0 × 27.5 (M) × 15.5
Cairngorm	190.0 × 35.6 (M) × 20.2
Vision	170.0 × 27.6 (M) × 19.0
Robin Hood	156.5 × 29. 5 (X) × 17.5 (model at Liverpool Museum) 223.0 × 40.0 (M) × 22.0 (model in Aberdeen Art Gallery & Museum)

(I) internal breadth by nm rule; (M) moulded breadth; (X) maximum external breadth.

All the models are at Glasgow Museum, except where stated. Vision was diagonally-built without ceiling and so her internal breadth and moulded breadth are almost identical.

A difference of 2–3ft in the length may signify nothing more than the addition of a frame or two during the course of construction, but 1ft in breadth or depth can make a considerable difference in hull-form. In the above list, some discrepancies occur in each ship and perhaps it is only a table of offsets that produces the most reliable evidence of hull-form, but these seem very rare and none have been discovered for any of the above ships.

BIOGRAPHIES OF BRITISH SHIPS BUILT 1846–1854

BON ACCORD, 1846

She was the first three-masted full-rigged ship which Alexander Hall & Sons built with the raking 'Aberdeen bow' and the second was the *North Star* launched the following year. Their yard numbers were 153 and 159 respectively. The *Bon Accord* had measurements of 134.2ft × 23.7ft (internal) × 18.4ft, 432 tons om and 380 tons nm and was fitted with an iron longboat. When the nm (new measurement) tonnage is less than the om (old measurement) tonnage, it is an indication of a fine-lined hull with a raking stem. *Bon Accord*'s contract price was £18 5s per ton on 388½ tons om but the finished price was £7231. Her principal owners were Hyde, Lennox & Co, London, who owned 16 shares. She was lost in 1856. Hyde, Lennox also owned Hall's schooner *Torrington*.

She was not in Chinese waters in the years 1849-52 nor 1853-54, but the three passages of hers recorded from China are all on the long side, the average being 147 days.

GEELONG, 1847

This wooden barque was built at Glasgow by William Hood Rowan & Co and measured 115.0ft × 24.7ft × 17.2ft and 382 tons; she classed 8 A1. Her owners were Potter, Wilson & Co, Glasgow, who had 32 shares. In October 1850 all shares were transferred into the name of the Clyde & Australian Shipping Co. Two Chinese oil paintings at the National Maritime Museum show her to have had a raking bow with the usual head knees and trailboards, a topgallant forecastle, a full poop, with a shortish hull. There is a jib-headed topsail on the mizen and a large trysail or spencer on the main. No skysails are carried. There does not appear to be a deckhouse abaft the foremast. The full-rigged ship *Melbourne* was constructed the same year by the same builders for the same owners but of 496 tons; she was 4ft longer and 1ft broader but otherwise must have been similar.

The *Geelong* went out to Melbourne in 90 days from Glasgow in 1849–50 and a year later went out in 96 days from London. She made three passages home from China. In 1856 she was sold to owners registered in Singapore for no less than £4000; the next year she was broken up.

LAND O'CAKES, 1847

This wooden full-rigged ship was built at Grangemouth by Adamson for owners of the same name registered at Liverpool, but in 1850 the port of registration changed to London. Her tonnage was 460 om and 496 nm but in 1850 she was lengthened and the new measurements were 146.0ft × 28.0ft × 19.5ft with tonnages of 520 om and 651 nm. She now had 5.21 beams to length and was probably lengthened

by about 20ft to bring her proportions more in line with ships of the 1850s. Her speed would also have been increased. The only passage time I have prior to the lengthening was one of 150 days to Hong Kong from London in 1948–49, 18 August to 15 January, and no other passage she made between the two countries was so long again. In 1852 she made two trans-Pacific voyages across to San Francisco, presumably with gold prospectors or else to bring back lumber.

Wakefield & Co, Liverpool, became owners in 1864 and two years later she passed to P G Carvill & Co, Liverpool, who reduced her to a barque. In 1870, shortly after her purchase by Stewart & Co, she was abandoned on 12 September, leaky, off St Michael's, bound from the Clyde to Boston; but she may have been salvaged later. The master's certificate was suspended for two years.

NORTH STAR, 1847

Constructed by Alexander Hall & Sons, this clipper was of the average size of full-rigged ships being built in Aberdeen at the end of the 1840s. No half-model or lines plan of her is known but she was probably a cross between *Acasta* (1845) and *Reindeer* (1848); she may also have been a sister to *Bon Accord* (1846) as their measurements are so similar. *North Star's* dimensions of 135.4ft × 27.0ft (internal) × 18.2ft gave tonnages of 459 om and 385 nm which suggest a fine-lined hull. She had a round stern with imitation quarter-galleries, a female figurehead, and a raised quarterdeck. She was actually Hall's first barque or ship to be given a round stern. There were trysail gaffs on each mast. The finished cost was £8177 or £17 16s per ton old measurement.

Her first owner was given in *Lloyd's Register* as F Chambers of London who owned 16 of the shares; the remainder were owned by her master, Henry Hale. She first seems to have gone to China in 1851 and the following year her owner was given as Hyde & Co – possibly short for Hyde, Lennox & Co – of London.

The *North Star* was wrecked on the Pratas Shoal on 27 September 1858 (some accounts say 4 October) bound from Hong Kong to Foochow. The master and some of the crew reached Hong Kong by 13 October in the boats; the remainder stayed aboard and HMS *Cormorant* was dispatched to their assistance.

COUNTESS OF SEAFIELD, 1848

One of three clippers built at Aberdeen in this year, she helped materially to give Aberdeen a good name in shipping circles. Alexander Duthie launched her in April for Henry Adamson of Aberdeen who later owned a number of tea clippers. The Lloyd's Register surveyor wrote in his report: 'Has a raised quarterdeck 3ft in height. Clipper bow as termed carried rather to an extreme in outreach and full length figurehead.' She had a 22ft longboat and three other boats, and also a windlass, winch and capstan. Rigged as a ship, she measured 140.2ft × 25.0ft × 18.2ft, 520 old and 451 new tons. Her short life, spent entirely in the China trade, came to an end on 21 March 1855, when she stranded on the Pratas Shoal, China Sea. She was refloated and later sold to Cantonese owners.

JOHN BUNYAN, 1848

She was probably the best-known China trader of her day, though it was a short one with so many new ships on experimental lines continually being launched. Her dimen-

Above: This portrait of the *John Bunyan* must have been executed in the 1860s when the fore and main single topsail yards had been replaced by double ones. *(Alan Stinchcombe)*

Opposite: This painting shows *Geelong* passing Hong Kong under full sail. *(National Maritime Museum)*

sions were 137.3ft × 25.0ft × 18.3ft, with tonnages of 526 old and 466 new. Although her tonnage was slightly greater than *Countess of Seafield's*, with breadth and depth virtually similar, she was some 3ft shorter and may therefore have been of a slightly fuller model. The *Lloyd's Register* surveyor reported: 'This is a highly creditable vessel either as regards workmanship, materials or design. Has the projecting bow carried to a moderate extent with full length figurehead, raised quarterdeck about 3ft in height run over main deck for the space of one beam.' The quarterdeck extended 28ft forward from the sternpost. She had a 22ft longboat and three others.

Walter Hood of Aberdeen was her builder and several of the ships he produced did not compare, on paper, so favourably with their contemporaries, yet in performance they left little to be desired. The *John Bunyan* only once sailed home from China against the monsoon, and on that occasion took three months to reach Anjer. She was owned by George Thompson, Aberdeen, and in appearance maintained the usual Aberdeen characteristics.

On her second voyage she went out to Hong Kong in 104 days, or 78 to Anjer. Then she went up to Shanghai, and after taking on board tea and silk, left on 28 January 1850, reaching Deal on the morning of Saturday 9 May, 101 days later. An earlier fast passage made by Brocklebank's *Jumna* was compared favourably at the time as she had taken 102 days between Canton and Liverpool in 1834–35, or it was claimed to be 97 days land to land. But a much shorter passage, and this between Shanghai and Liverpool, was made by another Brocklebank vessel, the brig *Bonanza* at the close of 1844, and this occupied only 91 days. She had been built in 1830 of 173 tons. This was probably the shortest run yet made from China.

Nevertheless, *John Bunyan's* passage was certainly amongst the quickest that had been recorded up to 1850. Land to land or pilot to pilot she is said to have taken 98 or 99 days. Strangely enough, this fast run was allowed to go unnoticed at the time, and it was not until the American clipper *Oriental* had docked in London, 99 days from Whampoa, 27 August to 4 December 1850, that *John Bunyan*'s claim was put forward. The British press was delighted to find a champion in its midst and devoted much space to bringing to public attention the merits of the Aberdeen model – its speed and carrying capacity.

Many attempts have been made in the past to compare the passages of these two ships, and the answer has been weighted in favour of whichever rival was most favoured, but no true comparison is possible because *John Bunyan* had the monsoon in her favour, but also had to sail from a port 860 miles distant. But *Oriental*'s 91 days to the Lizard shows that the Aberdonian was no match for her.

The *John Bunyan* deserted the China trade in 1856, though she continued to run out to the East. Vanner & Co, London, bought her in 1863, by which year she had been lengthened, her new measurements being 150.3ft × 27.7ft × 18.3ft and 521 tons. C Sayer, Liverpool, had her in 1871, and two years later, bound from Doboy to Barrow, she was posted missing, not having been heard of since 25 September. She had a crew of only thirteen at the time.

PANIC, 1848

Not many iron vessels were ever in use in the China trade and this must have been one of the earliest examples although the *John Garrow* (1840) had been out to India and the *Richard Cobden* (1844) may already have visited China. The latter had very steep deadrise, almost a vee-shaped mid-section, but the shape of her waterlines is unknown. The *Panic* was built by Cato, Miller & Co at Liverpool for Thomas Ripley of that port with register dimensions of 151.0ft × 24.3ft × 16.3ft; this gives a ratio of 6.21 beams to length making her a long, narrow ship, but no plan or

model of her is known. She was built of iron and barque rigged with tonnages of 400om and 450nm.

The prevention of weed-growth on the bottoms and side of iron ships had not then been solved, which presumabl explains her lengthy passages made homewards fron China, three of which average 170 days each. Some iron ships regularly made shortish outward passages after the had been dry-docked in England and their bottoms scrub bed clean, but the homeward runs were almost invariabl long after their stay in tropical salt water where the growth had accumulated.

In 1860 the *Panic* was found to be on fire at Hong Kong and was scuttled in shallow water by firing two shots into her stern; she was later raised. Edward Bates & Co of Liverpool had bought her in 1852 and in 1874 she was acquired by G P Addision & Co of London who renamed her *Aberdour* and re-rigged her as a barquentine. A year later, on 8 May, she was wrecked near Penzance.

REINDEER, 1848

This ship was Hall's contribution to that year of 1848 in which Aberdeen laid down a pattern for China clippers over the next few years. A strange feature about her was the shape of her deck which on plan swelled out to almost its widest point over the sternpost. Perhaps it was intended to give ample bearing aft, though she was not exceptionally fine in the buttocks. Her model has already been mentioned, though not her extreme build when compared with her contemporaries. Her total cost was £3887. She appears to have been ordered by Thomas McTear and Robert Vining of Liverpool, as they paid for her, but the eventual distribution of the shares was that they jointly owned 16 shares and Jervis R Wardley owned 48; in May 1849, Ward-

ley bought them out. He owned the ship until she was lost on 5 February 1856 on the coast of New South Wales.

Her dimensions were 141.5ft × 22.7ft × 15.5ft with tonnages of 427 om and 328 nm. Her entrance was sharp and mostly convex and her run was longer with some hollow in the lower body; she had marked deadrise with rounded floors that curved into the bilge, but above the load line the tumblehome reversed and the bulwarks flared outwards.

Considered with the other two tea clippers built in Aberdeen this year, she was the only one of the three to contend with the south-west monsoon, and her passage of 107 days made against it in 1850 was by far the best of its kind at this period. Her third voyage was not so successful

Opposite: This painting by Arthur Smith depicts the *Bonita* close-hauled under reefed topsails. She was built in 1848, the same year as the *Reindeer*, and although 30 tons smaller, was probably very similar in appearance. (*Parker Gallery*)

Below: Reindeer lines. Built in 1848 by Alexander Hall & Sons at Aberdeen. Drawn from lines taken off builder's half-model in Glasgow Museum and Art Gallery, Kelvingrove. Dimensions: 141.5ft × 22.7ft × 15.5ft, 328 tons nm and 427 tons om. Reconstruction: the figurehead, mast positions, cathead.

Bottom: Reindeer sail plan. Entirely reconstructed and based on a plan drawn by James Henderson. Sources: lines plan; spar dimensions from builder's cost account; spar diameters and mast positions from contemporary practice, painting of *Bonita* and other Aberdeen clippers.

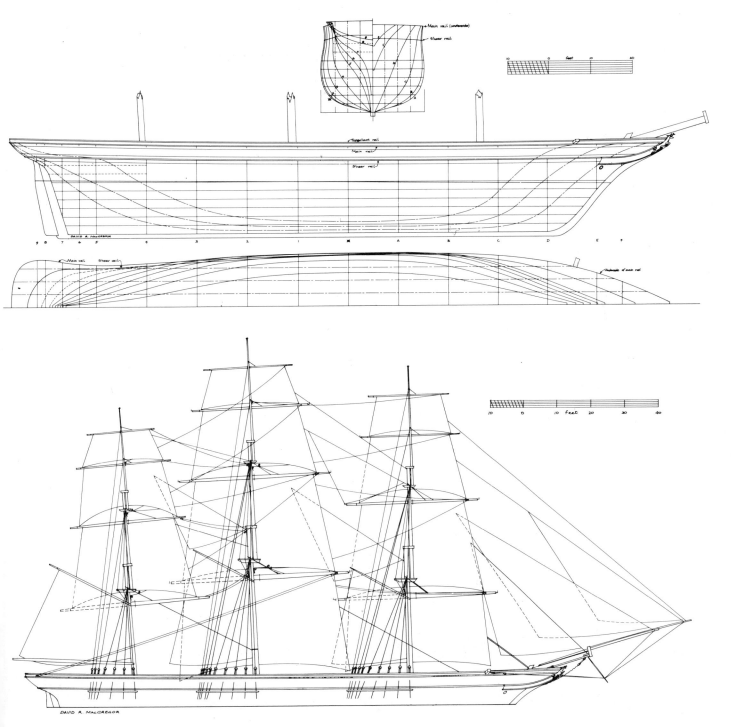

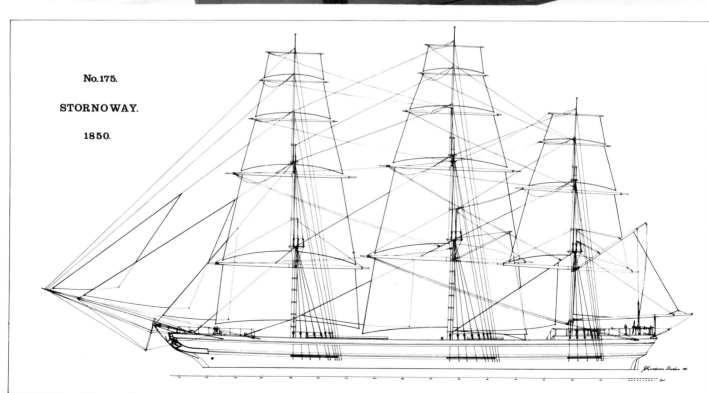

No. 175.

STORNOWAY.

1850.

nder Charles H Hunt as she took 130 days out to Hong
ong from Liverpool in 1850–51 and 140 days to return
om Shanghai. She never visited China again but was in
e trade to South America. For instance, in 1852 she took
days between Liverpool and Rio de Janeiro, 21
ecember 1852 to 12 February 1853.

A WITCH, 1848

ne was the first fine-lined craft launched by Green's
ackwall Yard for the China trade, but no plans exist to
ow her hull-form. Her new tonnage of 337 (401 old) was
ry similar to *Reindeer's*, but her dimensions of 121.5ft ×
.7ft × 16.0ft suggest she was designed on a fuller model.
ne probably had a rather sharp entrance, perhaps even
ightly hollow, but quickly broadening out. She was rigged
a barque. Her owner, G Baine of London, intended her
be an opium clipper, in which lucrative business she was
ever engaged.

On her third outward passage she only took 100 days to
nanghai from Gravesend, 17 March to 25 June 1850, or
5 days land to land. She seems to have been a very handy
nip, her first seven passages from China averaging 116
ays.

Taylor, Potter & Co, Liverpool, bought her in 1855, and
1862 she passed to Sassoon, Hong Kong, and then to
cCully in 1867, who put her into the South American
ade. J M Dean, London, owned her from 1872 until she
as hulked in 1883 in the London Docks by the East &
Vest India Dock Co, for use as a meat store. Her registry
as closed three years later.

A QUEEN, 1849

uilt at Dundee by John Brown for J & R Guild, Dundee,
ne measured 138.1 ft × 23.2ft × 15.1ft, 429 old and 372
ew tons, and was ship-rigged. Sold to Singapore owners in

1858, she passed out of the Mercantile Navy List in 1876. She
appears to be the only vessel built in 1849 for the China trade.

STORNOWAY, 1850.

It seems certain that even as the three Aberdeen ships of
1848 were considerable improvements on the ships then in
the trade, so the *Stornoway* was an advance in design upon
them. She was undoubtedly more fitted for deep sea service
than most of Hall's previous ships had been. She was Alexander Hall's 175th ship, was classed 13 A1, and her measurements were 157.8ft × 28.8ft × 17.8ft, 595 old and 527
new tons, she could carry 632,000lbs of tea.

John Robertson, who had once been master of the *John
o'Gaunt*, had supervised her construction on behalf of her
first owners, Jardine, Matheson & Co. The total cost was
£9948 16s 6½d. As she was launched on 8 August, 20 days
before the American clipper *Oriental* docked in London
with tea from China, she was obviously not ordered with a
special view to beating the Americans but rather to take
advantage of what was going to be a remunerative trade.
Her lines have been redrawn by James Henderson from the
builder's half-model and he has reconstructed her sail plan.
An advertisement in 1861 described her as 'This far-famed
yacht-built clipper and regular trader'.

Her first five outward passages were all made via Bombay
or Calcutta, crossing over to China in about 32 days. Her
early times were amongst her best and though she did not
show better runs than *Chrysolite*, she was probably the faster
of the two. In 1860 she went out to Sydney in 102 days
under Captain Watson and came home via Ceylon. The
next year she was sold to Mackay & Co, London, spending
most of her remaining years in the Australian and New
Zealand trades. Welch & Co, Newcastle, bought her in
1867 and four years later she passed into the hands of
another Newcastle owner, R Chapman. In 1873 she was
wrecked on the Kentish Knock on 7 June.

pposite top: A model of the *Stornoway* made by James Henderson. No
ainting has ever been found of this ship and so the details are entirely
constructed from a half-model, spar dimensions and survey report.
Model in Aberdeen Museum)

elow: Stornoway lines plan. Drawn by James Henderson from lines taken
ff builder's half-model in Glasgow Museum and Art Gallery. Built in
850 by Alexander Hall & Sons, Aberdeen. Register dimensions: 157ft ×
.8ft (internal) × 17.8ft, 527 tons nm, 595 tons om (see table on page
7). Reconstruction: figurehead, midship section.

Opposite, bottom: Stornoway sail plan. Entirely reconstructed by James
Henderson. Sources: lines plan; spar dimensions from builder's cost
account; contemporary paintings of Aberdeen clippers. No painting
known of *Stornoway*. There would have been staysails between the masts.

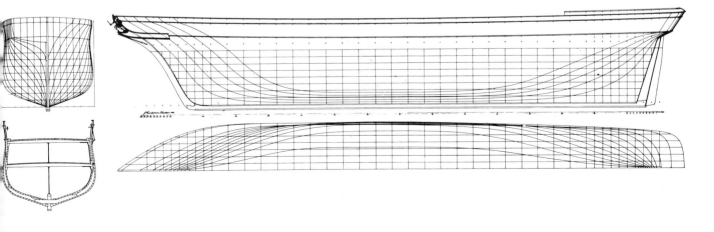

THE " ABERGELDIE," ABERDEEN CLIPPER.

ABERGELDIE, 1851

Built at Aberdeen by Walter Hood with a figurehead of Prince Albert in Highland Dress, she registered 598 old and 600 new tons, with dimensions of 152.3ft × 26.2ft × 19.2ft. She was owned by George Leslie, Aberdeen, and finished her short life in 1854 when she struck a reef on 17 June, 1½ miles off the north end of Pulo Leal, Gaspar Strait. She was abandoned the following day.

On her maiden voyage she took the remarkably short time of 24 days to Mauritius from Woosung and only 80 days to the Western Isles, which were reached on 18 February 1852. Two years later, *Chrysolite* took 11 days from there to Liverpool, so that *Abergeldie* should have reached London in under 100 days. But there must have been a long spell of easterly winds as it took her 44 days to get home.

CELESTIAL, 1851

Built specially for the China trade by Thomas Bilbe & Co, Nelson Dock, Rotherhithe, for James Thomson, London, she was a wood ship of 452 old and 438 new tons, with dimensions of 134.0ft × 26.8ft × 18.2ft. The Lloyd's Register surveyor reported: 'She is a long sharp flush-decked vessel carefully built of the best materials, framed diagonally according to Mr Bilbe's clever plan, the room and space on the keel being 30 inches and at the gunwales 24 inches.' She classed 13 A1. Fore and main lower masts and bowsprit were of teak.

In 1861 she was sold to J Mondel, Liverpool, and after 1864 was managed by Anderson, Thomson & Co. In 1870 she was bought by owners in Valparaiso and vanished into oblivion.

CHRYSOLITE, 1851

Launched in March to the order of Taylor, Potter & Co Liverpool, she was Alexander Hall & Sons' 177th ship. She repeated the reverse curve above the waterline which had been embodied in *Reindeer* and *Stornoway*, but she had another reverse curve between the bilge and keel which gave her great rise of floor, yet a defined bilge. The run of planking immediately above the keel is known as the 'garboard strake', and thus *Chrysolite* could be said to have hollow garboards. Her entrance was sharp and broadened out rapidly just below the waterline, but she had a fine concave run terminating in a very raking sternpost. She was especially suited to light winds, yet had ample bearing forward. A contemporary watercolour and identical engraving picture her clewing up sails when nearing land, and show that she was a tall ship, carrying no crossjack and nothing above royals except lofty poles to her masts, but with trysail gaffs on both fore and main, while her spanker boom projected some considerable distance beyond her taffrail. The builder's spar dimensions confirmed these points with the exception of a skysail yard and mast which he lists.

Thomas Alexander, a Lloyd's Register surveyor at Aberdeen, wrote that she was 'formed with fine ends and great rise of floor, clipper bow with moderate outreach, round stern without transoms, full topgallant forecastle, flush decked otherwise'. The crew drawn on the engraving show

Above: This watercolour drawing of the *Chrysolite* is probably the original from which the *Illustrated London News* engraving was made. Although a stay is drawn from the mizen masthead, suggesting that a skysail could be set, none is listed in the spar dimensions for either the fore or the mizen. (*National Maritime Museum*)

Opposite: E Weedon signed this engraving of the *Abergeldie* in the *Illustrated London News*. He was an accurate artist. (*MacGregor Collection*)

s much above the rail right aft as amidships which indicates the absence of a raised quarterdeck. Of deck fittings, the surveyor referred to a patent windlass, two main pumps, two bilge pumps and a capstan; there was also a 20ft longboat, and two quarter-boats – 24ft and 26ft. All external and main deck fastenings were in copper or Muntz metal. All internal iron fastenings in ceiling including iron work on deck & connected with the spars electro tinned.' She cost £9179 17s 9d.

She was well built to class 14 A1 and measured 570 old and 440 new tons, 156ft overall, 149.3ft long on the upper deck, 130ft length of keel, 29ft extreme breadth, and 17.2ft depth of hold. In good sailing trim she drew 15.5ft forward and 17ft aft and could carry almost 900 tons of tea. The best 24-hour runs on her first voyage were 320, 290 and 289 miles. Sailing by the wind she made $10\frac{1}{2}$ knots and $13\frac{1}{2}$ when running free under all sail, 14 knots being attained for short periods. She was said to be very buoyant and to handle easily.

The *Chrysolite* got good 'press notices' because there was an engraving in the *Illustrated London News* with an enthusiastic account of her maiden voyage, and she had the rare 'distinction' for a British clipper of being mentioned by the American naval architect John W Griffiths, in the *Monthly Nautical Magazine* of which he was editor. He referred to her critically in a special article; but he said that Aberdeen was on the river Clyde; remarked that 'so far as the sailing qualities of British ships are concerned, we suppose many of their finest performers are built in Canada and New Brunswick'; and supplied a totally inaccurate lines

plan for her, from which he worked out a long string of calculations. The Dutch author H W Schokker probably used Griffiths' material in 1861 in his *Handboek voor de kennis van den Scheepsbouw*, as he perpetuated the fallacy that the *Chrysolite* was built on the Clyde; if so, then his table of offsets is worthless.

In considering the records of all ships in those days when navigation was undertaken with greater risk and less knowledge than today, the performance of a ship depended more on her captain's ability and skill than on almost any other factor. Some men would go from ship to ship and always be in the forefront. Others – and unfortunately there were many of this kind in the trade – never got the best out of their vessels. *Chrysolite* had the misfortune to have one of the latter sort, after four splendid voyages under Anthony Enright, who had come from the *Reindeer*, and under whom she averaged $105\frac{1}{4}$ days from China; but the next four under Alexander McLelland averaged 135 days. What a difference! Yet this took place in the same ship.

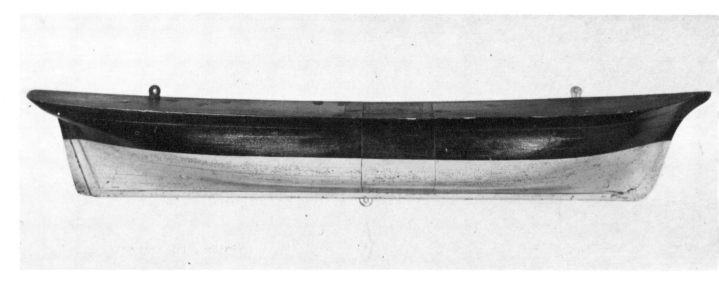

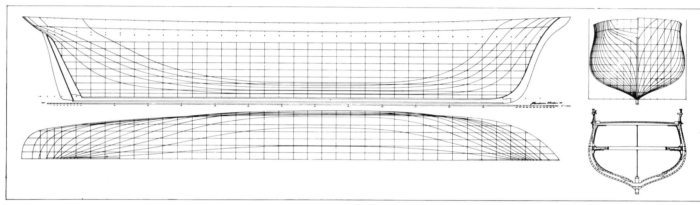

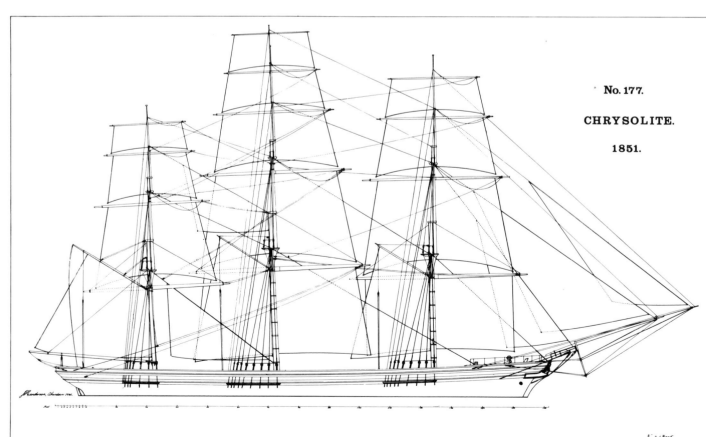

No. 177.

CHRYSOLITE.

1851.

Opposite, top: The builder's half-model of *Chrysolite* was one of several loaned to the Glasgow Museum by her builder, Alexander Hall & Sons, in 1881, but never returned. The model is about 1ft 6in less in depth than the ship as built. The two saw-cuts in the hull have never been explained; usually it means that a new length was inserted in the model after it was first made. (*Glasgow Museums & Art Galleries*)

Opposite, centre: Chrysolite lines plan. Drawn by James Henderson from lines taken off builder's half-model in Glasgow Museum and Art Gallery. Built in 1851 by Alexander Hall & Sons, Aberdeen. Register dimensions: 149.3ft × 26.1ft (internal) × 17.0ft, 440 tons nm, 570 tons om (see table on page 47). Reconstruction: depth of hold increased about 18in to agree with register dimensions by proportionately increasing spaces between waterlines; midship section; sheer lessened. Stations now spaced equal to 'room and space' in *Lloyd's Register* survey report.

Opposite, bottom: Chrysolite sail plan. Entirely reconstructed by James Henderson. Sources: lines plan; spar dimensions from builder's cost account; watercolour painting of ship. She would have carried staysails between the masts and stunsails.

Chrysolite's fastest outward time was made in 1853 when she ran from Liverpool to Hong Kong in 87 days, 16 April to 12 July, 6 days of which were spent in beating out of the Channel. On the return passage, her times were as follows:

Left Whampoa	30 July
Left Hong Kong	1 August
Passed Anjer	31 August
Off Cape of Good Hope	28 September
Passed Ascension	11 October
Passed the Western Isles (Azores)	2 November
Heavy NNW gales, in which paint house was washed away	2–5 November
Off Mizen Head	12 November
Arrived Liverpool, 108 days out	15 November

Being of a handy size, she was nearly always able to load the first teas and get a good freight, such as £7 to £8 per ton for 565,200lbs of tea in 1855. The previous year she had had a crew of twenty-four.

A curious interlude occurred in 1852–53 after the end of her second voyage from China and before the beginning of her third. Under Enright she sailed for Bahia on 28 November 1852 and returned to Liverpool on 25 March 1853 on passage from Paraiba. Presumably there was a good freight to be earned. In the same manner, Killick, Martin & Co were sending some of their clippers such as *Kaisow* and *Miako* across the Atlantic to load grain at good rates in late 1879 and early 1880.

Jervis R Wardley of Liverpool had always held 40 shares in the ship and in 1860 he appears as owner, perhaps because he bought out Thomas Taylor and William Potter. In this year she had a new keelson fitted but continued to trade almost exclusively with China until 1866 when McPherson, Liverpool, bought her, had her remetalled and recaulked and sent her out to Japan. Four years later she was sold to J Brodie, London, and was trading to Colombo when she was wrecked on 28 March 1873 in a hurricane off Mauritius with a cargo of bullocks from Madagascar. She had been a barque since 1870.

FOAM, 1851

Several well-known masters commanded this ship, such as R Findlay, G Innes (who later had the *Serica*), and J Watt (who had the *Hallowe'en*). James Findlay of Greenock owned her – he was later to own *Serica, Spindrift* and others – and she was built in Greenock by William Simons. She measured 131.4ft × 28.0ft × 20.6ft with tonnages of 604 old and 628 new, and she was a full-rigged ship built of wood.

Clink & Co bought her in 1868 and then in consecutive years she went to three Glasgow owners: Cree, Renison & Co in 1871; Barton in 1872; J Blair in 1873; and was finally sold foreign at Valparaiso in 1874.

JOHN TAYLOR, 1851

'She is a beautiful Aberdeen-built ship . . . and sails remarkably fast' commented the *Sydney Morning Herald* on 9 December 1853, on her arrival from Lyttleton. She was a full-rigged ship built in Aberdeen by Alexander Hall & Sons and the Lloyd's Register surveyor stated that she had 'a clipper bow with moderate rake'; she was assigned a class of 15 A1. She measured 164.4ft × 24.8ft × 19.6ft with tonnages of 784 old and 788 new measurement, and was fitted with a topgallant forecastle and a full-height poop with a 'half-round'. The finished cost was £14,670. She carried skysails on each mast and the main yard was 69ft long. She was built for Taylor, Potter & Co, Liverpool, who owned the *Chrysolite*, also built by Hall in the same year. J R Wardley was the principal shareholder in both ships.

On her maiden passage to Bombay in 1851 she was dismasted off the Cape Verde Islands during a severe gale in August, only the main and mizen lower masts being left standing. One man was killed and three others injured. She was supplied with sails and other equipment by the *Eleanor Thompson* as she was preparing to rig jury masts. On her second voyage she sailed out to Melbourne in 90 days from London, 12 June to 10 September 1852, and returned in 120 days of which 11 days were spent at Bahia. She sailed out to Lyttleton in 1853 and is said to have made the passage in 88 days.

She first went to China in 1855 and loaded tea at Whampoa at £6 10s per ton. The following year she reached Hong Kong on 28 May 1856, 103 days from London. In 1857 she sailed from Shanghai for Liverpool on 16 October, passed Anjer on 15 November and was never heard of again, being officially posted 'missing'.

BALLARAT, 1852

She was a medium clipper which, although built at Aberdeen, did not have an Aberdeen bow but what the Lloyd's Register surveyor termed a 'common bow'. She had a powerful hull with a full-ish entrance but a finer run; there was deadrise and undoubtedly good cargo capacity. Andrew Shewan considered her to be of the same calibre as the *Robin Hood*. She was owned for the first eleven years of her life by Duncan Dunbar and during this time her first two voyages were made to Australia during the gold rush but thereafter she was in the China trade. On her maiden passage in 1852 she is credited with 78 days to Melbourne from the Lizard. On her second voyage she took 79 days to Melbourne from the Lizard, 11 July to 28 September 1853, and returned in 69 days to London, or so it is claimed. She never made a passage out or home in the China trade in less than 105 days.

Her builder was Alexander Duthie & Co at Aberdeen and her dimensions were 131.9ft × 27.4ft × 20.0ft (tonnage dimensions); with tonnages of 637 om and 713 nm.

After Dunbar's death she was acquired by Vanner & Co of London and in 1871 she was bought by Shaw, Savill & Co, who probably reduced her to barque rig; all this time she was in the New Zealand trade. In 1874 she was sold to Norwegian owners at Kragerö and renamed *Freia*. Still under this flag, she was abandoned at sea in December 1891.

CAMBALU, 1852

Charles Lamport built this ship at Workington for John Atkin & Co, Liverpool, with dimensions of 140.0ft × 28.4ft × 19.0ft and tonnages of 528 om and 536 nm. When her tonnage was calculated again in the 1880s it produced 495 net, 508 gross and 493 under deck. The latter figure gives a coefficient of under deck tonnage of 0.65. Lamport built the *Aerolite* for the same owners the following year, and *Cambalu*'s first master, Edward Alleyne, later transferred to her.

The *Cambalu* was in the China and Far East trades for eighteen years until sold to Samuel & Co, Llanelly, in 1870 when she was reduced to a barque. J Thomas of the same port acquired her six years later and in 1883 she passed to owners in Swansea, Thomas Watkins & Jenkins, who further cut down her rig, this time to a barquentine. W Grove & Co, also of Swansea, purchased her in 1892 and four years later she was dismantled.

HANNIBAL, 1852

Built at Aberdeen by Alexander Hall & Sons for Cook & Co of the same port, she had a short life of only two years, being wrecked on 3 August 1854 on rocks near New Caledonia, bound from Syndey to China. At the start of the voyage she had gone ashore near Folkestone but had been towed off and had returned to London for repairs. She measured 158.0ft × 25.6ft × 18.3ft, with tonnages of 618 old and 577 new. She was a full-rigged ship built of wood, having a 'clipper bow with moderate outreach' and trysail gaffs on each mast, but carried a skysail on the mainmast only. The final cost was £9338.

JOHN KNOX, 1852

This square-sterned, wooden barque was built at Aberdeen by Walter Hood for J Munro & Co of the same port, with dimensions of 128.2ft × 21.7ft × 14.0ft and tonnages of 358 old and 296 new. This is quite a difference for a small vessel and suggests a sharp hull-form, although the only two passages I have recorded for her from China were slow ones of 128 and 120 days, both made with the favourable monsoon. But to confirm the suggestion of fine lines comes this report by the Lloyd's Register surveyor at Aberdeen: 'This is a vessel of long, low, sharp construction; little outreach forward.' She was equipped with a longboat, a quarter-boat and a jolly-boat, and there was a raised quarterdeck level with the main rail. She obviously had a drag aft as the height of the yellow metal sheathing was 12ft forward and 13ft 3in aft.

In 1865 she was made a full-rigged ship and was managed by George Thompson in London. In 1876 she passed to owners in Sydney: first to J Merriman; then four years later to Jenkins; and four years after this to J Henderson, when she is again listed as a barque of 291 tons net. She was condemned in 1886.

JULIA, 1852

This full-rigged ship was built at Aberdeen by Alexander Hall & Sons for Melhuish & Co, Liverpool, and measured 624 old and 510 new tons, and was capable of carrying 574,300lbs of tea. The figure of 476 new tons was crossed through in the Lloyd's Register survey report and replaced with 510 tons. The surveyor commented:

> This is a sharp low vessel with considerable rise in floor, formed with the clipper bow and round stern. Main deck runs fore and aft with house built for cabin abaft having raised quarterdeck across the stern and on each side of house. Stern formed without transom timbers, being filled in and centred round . . . Frame is diagonally trussed from upper deck shelf down over long floor ends with 12 pairs 24ft × 4½in × 5/8in flat rod iron scored into the timbers and bolted to each.

Register dimensions under the 1836 Act were 158.2ft × 26.2ft × 16.8ft. The breadth here is internal and the length between closer parts of stem and sternpost than by the 1854 Rule. Register dimensions by the 1854 Act were 162.8ft × 28.3ft × 16.6ft; and tonnages were 434.81 under deck and 477.04 net register. The coefficient of under deck tons works out at 0.57.

Described as a 'frigate-built yacht', she was intended to take passengers out to Australia and cross over to China to bring home a tea cargo. On her maiden voyage she sailed out from London to Melbourne in what was called a 'fast passage of 79 days', although the dates of 17 July to 10 October 1852 give 85 days. Then she crossed over to Shanghai in 46 days from Sydney, in ballast, to load tea at Woosung. Shipping reports give the master as G W Britton outwards and as Butler homewards. In 1853–54 she made a round trip out to Adelaide and back home without visiting China.

In 1859, *Julia* had a fast run out to Hong Kong in 89 days from London, 29 January to 28 April, and on her return made the quickest passage of any ship leaving China for London prior to 6 August.

Joseph Bland, Liverpool, bought her in 1857, and four years later she went to John Brodie & Co, London. In 1862 she was bought by B D Freeman of London who sold her foreign in 1866. A year later, she was owned by David Forman (or Foreman) in Hong Kong, sold foreign again, only to turn up under British ownership in 1870 as the *Nadesda* of Bristol, belonging to S Adey. He disposed of her at Barcelona in the following July, and then she disappeared.

WILD FLOWER, 1852

Described as 'clipper ship (Aberdeen model) *Wild Flower*' on the occasion of her race from Shanghai with *Joseph Fletcher* as described in the introduction to this Chapter, she was built at Liverpool and measured 133.0ft × 27.0ft × 18.4ft with tonnages of 452 om and 478 nm. She was a full-rigged ship built of wood and her first owner was Anderson of Liverpool. In 1860 the owner is listed as Thompson Jnr, Aberdeen, but three years later she reverted to R Anderson, Liverpool. In 1866 she was owned by W Dunn, Aberdeen, and the following year was bought by Nattrass & Co, Sunderland, and reduced to a barque. Spain and the Mediterranean became the destination of her voyages. She was wrecked in 1872.

CAIRNGORM, 1853

As the largest ship Alexander Hall & Sons of Aberdeen had ever built up to this time, measuring 1246 old and 939

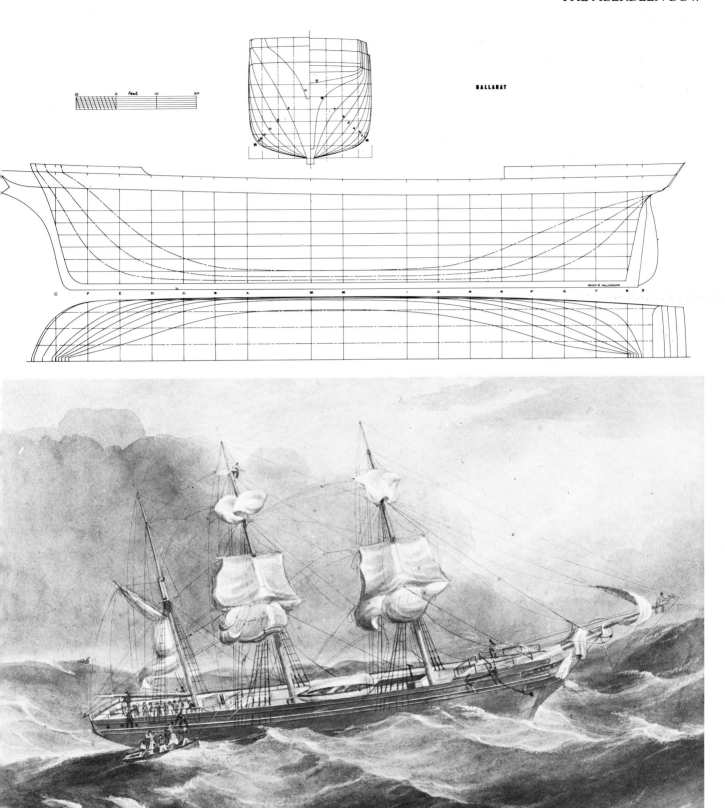

new tons, she was also probably their most perfectly-designed one at the time of her launch in January 1853. From an analysis of her design published in the *Illustrated London News* on 5 March 1853, it appears that the owners' wishes had always restricted Hall's ambition to build the perfect clipper and he accordingly decided to build one on speculation which would embody his concept of the ideal

Top: Ballarat lines. Built in 1852 by Alexander Duthie & Co at Aberdeen. Lines taken off builder's half-model by James Henderson and drawn from his draft. Dimensions: 141.9ft × 27.4ft × 20.0ft, 637 tons om and 713 tons nm. No reconstruction.

Above: The *John Knox* hove-to, as the crew of a wrecked ship are taken aboard. Watercolour by an unknown artist. (*National Maritime Museum*)

tea clipper. The writer in this weekly periodical explains how this came about:

> But while the passage to China has thus been greatly shortened, and teas are now brought from Shanghae in 98 days instead of four or five months, which used to be the ordinary length of the voyage, it was still felt that the Americans had a great advantage in the large size of their clippers, some of them being double the registered tonnage of the largest of the British ships. To meet this objection, the Messrs Hall resolved to lay down a clipper of larger size and finer lines than had been previously built in Scotland; and to construct her so that any

purchaser might challenge in good faith the fastest of the American fleet.

Captain John Robertson of the *Stornoway* brought this to the notice of his owners, Jardine, Matheson & Co, and as a result they purchased her while still on the stocks. She was launched with the name of *Cairngorm*, and dimensions of 193.3ft × 33.6ft (inside) × 20.2ft; length overall was 215.0ft and maximum breadth outside 36.6ft; due to the softwood in her timbers she only classed 7 A1. The Lloyd's Register surveyor commented on her: 'This is a vessel of sharp construction, having great rise in floor and finely

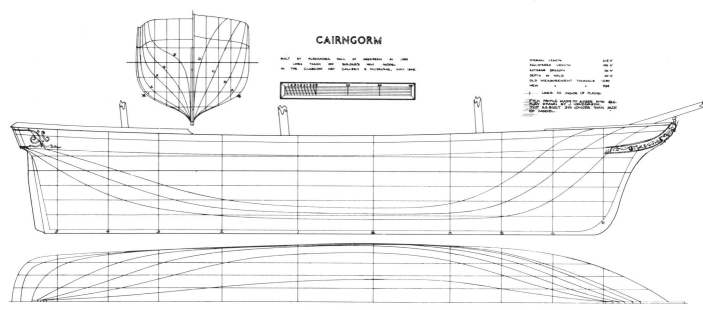

Cairngorm sail plan. Entirely reconstructed by James Henderson. Sources: lines plan; spar dimensions from builder's cost account; engraving of ship in *Illustrated London News*. Although both the latter and the painting of *Mimosa* show no stay from main topmast to head of fore lower mast, I have added one to Henderson's plan. Stunsails would have been set up to the royals.

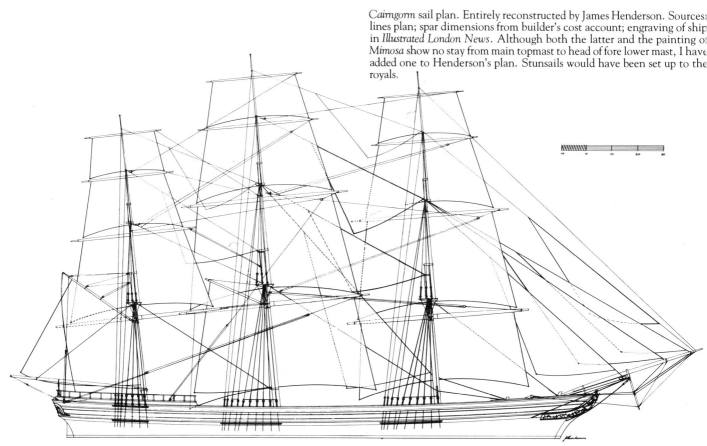

Opposite, top: Cairngorm lines plan. Built in 1853 by Alexander Hall & Sons, Aberdeen. Lines taken off builder's half-model in Glasgow Museum and Art Gallery. Register dimensions: 193.3ft × 33.6ft (internal) × 20.2ft, 939 tons nm, 1246 tons om. Reconstruction: figurehead of Highland chieftain; profile of stem made to agree with sail plan drawn by James Henderson. Ship as built was 3ft longer than size scaled from model.

THE ABERDEEN CLIPPER "CAIRNGORM."

Above: This engraving of the *Cairngorm* is the only illustration ever found of this famous ship, but fortunately there are spar dimensions and a half-model. It is surprising that Hall continued to give his ships channels right through into the 1860s. (*MacGregor Collection*)

tapered ends; stem raked to form cutwater with little overhang.' She had a full-height poop, the sides of which were rounded down on to the topgallant rail.

From lines I took off her half-model in the Glasgow Museum can be seen her remarkably fine-lined hull with the long sharp entrance and run, but one of the most remarkable things about this clipper is the enormous deadrise above the concave garboards. Of the American clippers, *Samuel Russell* (1847), *Staghound* (1850) and *Nightingale* (1851) all had large deadrise but none had hollow garboards as well. Like many of Hall's clippers in the 1850s, *Cairngorm* was not unduly lofty but the yards were long, those on the mizen being not much shorter than those on the fore, the mizen royal yard being only 3ft 4in shorter than her counterpart on the fore. The total cost was £15,434 10s 1d of which the principal items, to the nearest pound, were:

Timber and plank	£4545
Carpenters' wages	£2882
Ironwork (hull and rigging)	£1574
Chains, anchors, etc	£633
Making and sewing sails	£1095
Cordage	£800
Knees and beam plates	£499

The sails were made by Hall & Co of Limehouse, London, and a description of her in the *Shipping Gazette & Sydney General Trade List* (13 June 1853) said that she could 'set no fewer than fifty sails of all descriptions', which would require some imaginative flying kites, especially as

she did not cross any skysail yards. This paper said that the 'lower masts are solid sticks and not built . . . having been felled expressly for her last year in the forests of America.' Her figurehead was of a highland chieftain in full dress with targe on arm. There were two items for carving in the accounts: Robert Hall £21 15s; and James Wishart £12 18s. Perhaps the former carved the figurehead. To give greater strength and stowage capacity, all her main deck beams and half of her hold beams were of iron.

Her first commander was John Robertson, who also owned 16 shares in her, and she was undoubtedly a fast sailer, a speed of 14 knots being credited to her on her maiden voyage. On a load line length of 188ft, this yields a speed-length ratio of 1.02 which is not exceptionally fast when a ratio of 1.25 is considered to indicate a fast vessel. With a load line length such as 188ft, *Cairngorm* had a speed potential of 17.14 knots which would give a speed-length ratio of 1.25. (This ratio is obtained by dividing the highest speed, in knots, by the square root of the load line length, in feet.)

The time taken on her first outward passage is unique, since she was only 77 days at sea between London and Hong Kong, 24 March to 12 July, or 110 days port to port. Unfortunately she had to put into Lisbon when five days out with the loss of her mainmast. She took a month to refit and left Lisbon on 1 May, arriving in Hong Kong 72 days later. Two years afterwards she went out to Hong Kong in 93 days, 29 March to 30 June. On her second, fourth and sixth voyages she sailed to China via Bombay, taking cotton on to Hong Kong. On her fourth voyage she reached Bombay on 21 April 1856 and leaving there on 19 May reached Hong Kong 29 days later on 17 June. A month later she was away from Whampoa with a tea cargo. Her low class of 7 A1 made no difference to the freights she earned as Jardine, Matheson were her owners; for instance, in 1855 she loaded at Whampoa in July at £7 per ton.

Nearly all her homeward passages were made from Whampoa or ports in the vicinity. Her fastest tea-laden passage, irrespective of the season, was one of 91 days between Macao and Deal, 6 November 1858 to 5 February 1859, when the *Lammermuir* is said to have beaten her by a few hours on elapsed time. This race is related in more detail in the biography on *Lammermuir* (1856) in Chapter Six.

Her class terminated in 1860, and the next year Baines & Co, London, bought her and put her in the Australian trade under Captain Cairncross. In 1863 when bound from Sydney, she was wrecked on 29 September whilst attempting to enter the river Min, and so never again loaded a cargo of sweet-scented teas.

A list of *Cairngorm's* outward passages when under Jardine, Matheson's ownership is as follows:

CAPT ROBERTSON
1853, London to Lisbon, 24 March to 29 March, 5 days (put in partially dismasted).

1853, Lisbon to Hong Kong, 1 May to 12 July, 72 days (7 days at sea and 110 since leaving London).
1854, London to Bombay, dep 24 June.

CAPT IRVINE
1855, London to Hong Kong, 29 March to 30 June, 9 days.
1856, London to Bombay, arr 21 April.
1856, Bombay to Hong Kong, 19 May to 17 June, 29 Day (cargo of cotton).

CAPT RYRIE
1857, London to Hong Kong, 29 January to 26 May, 11 days (in Straits of Sunda 28 to 30 April).
1857–58, London to Bombay, dep 3 December.
1858, Bombay to Hong Kong, 14 May to 17 June, 34 days.
1859, London to Hong Kong, 17 March to 19 July, 12 days (off Anjer 25 June).

LEICHARDT, 1853
Alexander Hall & Sons were launching numerous clippers in these years which were suitable for the triangular trade rout – out to Australia with gold prospectors, across to Chin with coal, and then home to London with tea. Some voyage were extremely profitable. Dr Leichardt, who was a explorer in Australia, may have provided the name of th clipper which was first owned by Barnes Bros in Liverpool. She measured 152.8ft × 26.9ft × 18.0ft, 634 tons om an 589½ nm. She had two decks, a round stern without quarter galleries and a male bust figurehead. The above dimension were for the 1836 Tonnage Rule and were internal becaus when measured again in 1865 the dimensions were 160.5 × 29.6ft × 18.0ft with tonnages of 558 under deck and 62 net register. The coefficient of under deck tonnage is 0.65.

The Lloyd's Register surveyor wrote: 'This vessel is formed [wi]th flared out stem and bow; round stern with full poop and [to]pgallant forecastle; poop beams rounded down in a circular [fo]rm at ends . . .'. This was later termed a poop with a [h]alf-round'. The equipment included two capstans, two [m]ain pumps, two bilge pumps and a fire engine. She did not [c]arry any skysails but a main trysail gaff was fitted. The [c]ontract price was £15 per ton on 611¾ tons which totals [£]9176¼; this was also the finished price.

She did not get to China until 1855 although she had been [a]t Akyab and Singapore. Easily her fastest passage was a run [o]f 92 days between Shanghai and New York in 1861–62. J [C]rowse, London, became owner in March 1865. When [o]utward bound for New Zealand in 1868, she was run down [a]nd sunk off Gravesend on 23 October by SS *North Star* of [2]19 tons, which was found entirely to blame. All on board [w]ere saved.

MIMOSA, 1853

[O]wned by the Liverpool shipowner Robert Vining, she was a [w]ooden ship built by Alexander Hall & Sons, Aberdeen, [w]ith dimensions of 139.9ft × 25.5ft × 15.6ft and tonnages [o]f 540 om and 447 nm. She cost £5916. Her sail plan was not [lo]fty and no skysail yards were crossed. Vining still owned [h]er in 1865 but Stuart & Douglas, Liverpool, were the [o]wners in 1873, which is the first year she appeared in *Lloyd's Register*. She dropped out of the Register in 1880. I [h]ave not traced many of her passages.

VISION, 1854

[S]he must have been one of Hall's last ships to be built with [t]he Aberdeen bow while there was still a logical reason for its

use and the principles governing its introduction still operated, because the Tonnage Law which was responsible for this feature was about to be repealed. She was actually launched on 31 December 1853, but of course was not delivered until the following year. She was smaller than *Cairngorm*, but equally sharp, with great deadrise, long sharp entrance and long tapering run.

Her counter was much more delicate and she continued the practice of lessening the rake to stem and sternpost, though there was no mistaking her Aberdeen bow. Compared with *Cairngorm*, her hull gave the appearance of a more finished and better conceived design, and her builders expected her to be very fast. J H Beazley described her in *Sea Breezes* (Vol V, 1923, p63) as 'an expensive and peculiarly-built ship, of 563 tons, on the diagonal principle with two thicknesses of 2-inch larch worked diagonally and one thickness vertically; also one outside of an average thickness

Opposite: Built in 1853, the *Mimosa's* portrait throws corroborative details onto what is known about *Cairngorm*. In particular, these two form the only examples I have been able to find in which no stay goes from the mainmast to the head of the fore lower mast at the doubling, which is most unusual. The main topmast stay on *Cairngorm* could not cross the foremast so high up, or the foresail would not set properly. (*Parker Gallery*)

Below: The Aberdeen clipper *Vision* from a painting by Samuel Walters after restoration. Gracie, Beazley allowed me to have the picture photographed some years ago. The spike bowsprit listed among the builder's spar dimensions is not drawn here, but the half-round forecastle is shown. (*Gracie, Beazley & Co*)

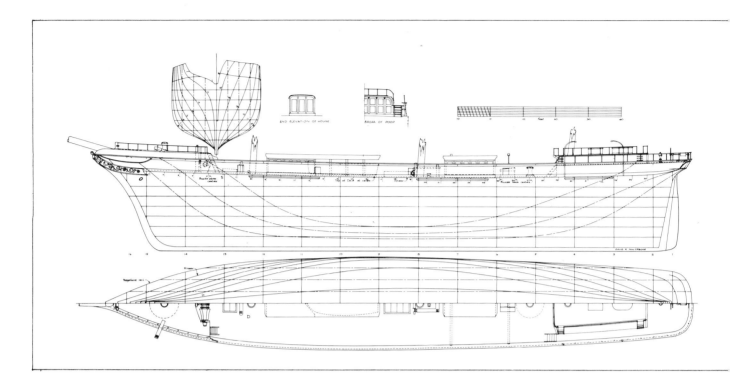

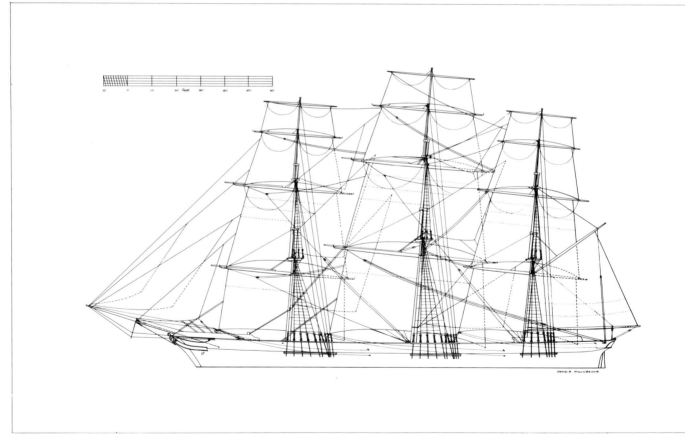

Top, Vision lines plan. Built of wood on diagonal system in 1854 by Alexander Hall & Sons at Aberdeen. Lines taken off half-model in Glasgow Museum and drawn to inside of plank. Dimensions by 1836 Act: 170.0ft × 27.6ft (inside) × 18.2ft, tonnages 563 nm and 720 om. Reconstruction: All deck fittings, based on painting of ship by S Walters owned by Gracie, Beazley & Co, Liverpool, and half-model of ship in Liverpool Museum; Lloyd's Register survey report; and contemporary paintings of other ships built by Hall.

Above: Vision sail plan. Reconstructed from builder's spar dimensions, painting of ship by S Walters, and contemporary illustrations of ships built by Hall; also from research by James Henderson. The spike bowsprit accords with the spar dimensions but is not shown in Walters' painting. No stunsails are listed in the spar dimensions, but a full suit would have been carried.

f 4½ inches worked longitudinally – the sheer strake was eak, and the top-sides Dantzic red pine, etc, and there were wo complete layers of hair-felt between the planking, all oated with vegetable tar.' This construction made her trong, although she was only classed at 7 A1, but caused loss f speed through being too rigid. Her measurements were 70.0ft × 27.6ft × 18.2ft, 720 om and 563 nm tons. These re dimensions by the 1836 Act and the breadth is internal.

Lines taken off the half-model in Glasgow were used to econstruct the lines plan and the steep deadrise is confirmed y a midship section amongst the Lloyd's Register survey eports. Another half-model in the Liverpool Museum has much less deadrise and is also 13ft 6in shorter than the Register dimensions. But this model has useful deck fittings mong which is shown how the longboat is stowed under a ontinuation of the deckhouse roof. The American clipper *Witch of the Wave* (1851) used a similar method but the boat vas laid on rollers for easier handling. The Lloyd's Register urveyor wrote a very detailed account of the diagonal con-truction, which is analysed in more detail in my book *Fast ailing Ships 1775–1875*. Of her hull-form the surveyor wrote hat she was a 'very sharp vessel in ends and bottom . . . lared stem and bow; round stern, no transoms'.

Her sail plan has been reconstructed from the builder's par dimensions and a painting by Samuel Walters. One pecial point of interest is the spike bowsprit; another is the omewhat similar lengths of the yards on the mizen to those n the fore, and the much greater length of the yards on the nainmast. The builder does not list stunsail booms but they vould of course have been carried, probably up to the royals n fore- and mainmasts.

James Beazley, Liverpool, was the principal owner with 32 shares, and the shipbuilder George R Clover held 16; Joseph Hubback held the remaining 16. The ship cost £9400.

On her maiden voyage she went out to Hong Kong in 95 days from Liverpool, 18 March to 21 June 1854. Loading at Whampoa, she was the first ship to arrive home with the new teas that year, taking 103 days to Liverpool, but she had to be content with a freight of £2 per ton less than the American clipper *Architect* which in the previous year had made the best passage. In the following year, 1855, she sailed from Singapore to Hong Kong in 9 days with the help of the monsoon, arriving on 23 May.

In 1857 she had loaded some 5000 chests of old teas at Hong Kong and whilst proceeding to Foochow to complete her cargo, she took the ground (through the fault of her pilot) on the north bank of the river Min near the Mingan Pass, on about 10 to 15 June, and the strong tide capsized her. She later became a total wreck.

An unidentified barque with Aberdeen bow painted in China and flying the houseflag of Doublas Lapraik. The presence of roller-reefing gear on the topsail yards makes the date between about 1855–1865, but Lapraik is not given as owner or shareholder to any vessel built by Alexander Hall in this period nor earlier. Perhaps she came from some other Aberdeen yard. A trysail gaff on the fore but not on the main is worthy of attention. (*N R Omell Gallery*)

5

AMERICAN TRADE TO LONDON
AND SHIPS OF 1847-1856

The rivalry and competition between British and American masters and agents for ascendancy in the China tea trade may fairly be said to have commenced when the American clipper *Oriental* reached Hong Kong on 8 August 1850, just under 81 days after leaving New York, a record which has never been beaten. Such an outstanding feat gained her immediate prestige and the ability to command a high rate of freight. Owing to the fact that the British Navigation Laws had been repealed in September 1849, ships of any nationality were now free, for the very first time, to carry tea to England from China. There was great excitement in Hong Kong when it was learned that *Oriental* was to load tea for London and she had no difficulty in procuring a freight of £6 per ton which was £2 higher than British ships were being offered.

Actually it was the barque *Jeanette* which was the first American to depart from Whampoa with tea for London, leaving on 25 August 1850, two days before the *Oriental* under Captain Palmer, but she was 148 days on the passage whereas the *Oriental* was only 91 days to the Lizard and 99 days to London, and as her run down the China Sea was made against the south-west monsoon, this was a very fast passage.

Her arrival in London caused a great stir because no one had seen such a large clipper ship before – she registered 1003 tons – and her short passage was the subject of general discussion. Another American ship, the *Argonaut*, had sailed the same day as *Oriental* but neither she nor the small *Jeanette* had yet reached port and so the new arrival received all the glory as crowds visited her in the West India Docks, and surveyors Waymouth and Cornish took off her lines in dry-dock for the Admiralty's benefit.

The majority of the clipper ships built in the United States were destined for the California trade, which meant rounding Cape Horn on the outward passage at least, so vessels of over 1000 tons were favoured as being better able to withstand the heavy seas of the southern latitudes and carry a larger cargo. Many of these ships crossed the Pacific Ocean, once their passengers and goods had been off-loaded at San Francisco, in order to get a cargo on the homeward passage, and now the tea trade to London was open as well as the already proven one to Boston and New York. Many of the Far Eastern ports were unaccustomed to ships larger than 500 tons, which necessitated either a long wait to collect cargo or else a series of coasting trips to different ports to pick it up. But as the 1850s progressed, so did the cargo-handling facilities.

The American clippers were all built of wood and so were the lodging and hanging knees, the hold pillars, and all the massive sister keelsons which these long ships required. These wooden ships had a big sheer, a large freeboard, lofty masts with long yards from which the white cotton canvas hung, and they were quite a new feature in British ports. The double channels from which their rigging was set up and their generally plainer bows with less decorative hair rail and trailboards evoked much interest in shipping circles. American clipper ship masters must have carried press cuttings with them, because the local papers always managed to print fulsome reports extolling any American ship that happened to be lying in the harbour. The public interest in all things nautical was kept alive by such cases and the awareness that international news could only be disseminated by the safe arrival of some ship, often a clipper, made everyone keen to scan the 'Ship Arrivals' in the columns of the daily newspapers.

According to Appendix III in Carl Cutler's *Greyhounds of the Sea*, there were altogether 139 passages made by American ships between ports in China and England in the period 1850–60. (The name of *Invincible*, Captain Graham, sailing in January 1856 from Hong Kong should be omitted because she was the British vessel of this name.) The maximum number of times any of these ships loaded for England was three times and only three of them did so, namely the *Oriental*, *Celestial* and *Nightingale*. A number made two passages to England but the majority made but one. Irrespective of the season, only nine ships made runs of less than 100 days to the English coast, as listed here:

Oriental, Whampoa to London, 27 August to 4 December 1850, 99 days

Wisconsin, Whampoa to London, 14 December 1850 to 13 March 1851, 99 days.

White Squall, Whampoa to Isle of Wight, 8 September to 16 December 1851, 99 days; arrived London 22 December.

Witch of the Wave, Canton to London, 3 January to 6 April 1852, 92 days.

Celestial, Foochow to London, 27 October (?) 1853 to 31 January 1854, 96 days.

Golden Gate, Shanghai to Beachy Head, 25 November 1854 to 23 February 1855, 90 days; 4 days spent at Batavia repairing damage = 86 days at sea.

Nightingale, Shanghai to Beachy Head, 8 February to 18 May 1855, 99 days; arrived London 21 May.

Kingfisher, Macao to Deal, 20 October 1855 to 24 January 1856, 96 days; arrived London 28 January.

Florence, Woosung to Deal, 26 December 1858 to 2 April 1859, 97 days; arrived London 4 April.

Of all the above passages, only two were made against the south-west monsoon, namely those by *White Squall* and *Oriental*. All the others had the monsoon behind them which could shorten the passage considerably down the China Sea. The record passages are listed here in Appendix III from which it will be seen that the fastest passage from Shanghai to Dover was made in 89 days by *Lord of the Isles* in 1858–59 with the fair monsoon, a month before the *Florence*. Between Macao and Deal, the fastest passage in the fair monsoon was made by *Lothair* in 88 days in 1873–74.

Some of the American ships listed by Cutler made excessively long passages such as the 207 days of *North Star* which left Canton on 12 August 1855 for London. There were a number of extreme clippers carrying tea to London such as *Challenge*, *Flying Cloud*, *Nightingale*, *Romance of the Seas*, *Staghound*, *Sovereign of the Seas* and *Witch of the Wave*, but some of them made long passages. Most American ships sailing at any time in 1855 made long passages to England.

In *Greyhounds of the Sea*, Carl Cutler makes the following statement on page 350 when referring to American ships

A clipper built in 1851 but not in the China to London trade was the *Syren* of 876 tons new measurement. Her photograph is included to illustrate an American medium clipper better than any painting could do. She still had a lofty sail plan when photographed at New Bedford although the skysails with which she was first equipped had been removed. She once made a passage from Batavia to London of 96 days. (*Peabody Museum, Salem*)

participating in the China to England trade for the year 1858: 'It was the first time since the days of the *Oriental* that a Yankee ship had failed to hang up the record passage of the year from China to a port in England.' Perhaps at the time he wrote he had only the passage times which Basil Lubbock had extracted for British clippers, but due to the research conducted since his day it can be shown that British clippers of those days were by no means slow-coaches, and so his forthright comment must be treated with reserve. In Appendix II I have now set down side-by-side many passages made by ships of both nationalities so that they may be compared easily for the first time.

From these tables it can be seen that *Oriental*'s passage time of 99 days between Whampoa and London against the monsoon was never beaten by an American ship sailing at

this time of the year, and that the first British ship to equal it was *Fiery Cross* with 99 days from Foochow in 1857. Prior to this, no British ship had made a decisively shorter passage home than an American ship, differences in departure ports making comparison impossible.

During the favourable monsoon, American ships had conclusively beaten British ships every year until 1855–56 when the British *Kate Carnie* took 92 days from Shanghai against the American *Kingfisher* with 96 days to Deal from Canton.

But American ships on the loading berth for London at the principal ports in China early established a reputation for speed and so could command higher freight rates than British ships in the period 1850–53. Agents and consignees had only to look at the dramatically short passages being made in the China-to-Boston or -New York run to realize the potential in the ships they were loading and offer freight rates accordingly. With record times set by the *Sea Witch* of 74, 77 and 81 days from Canton to New York, 79 days by the *Sea Serpent*, 82 days by the *Surprise* to Boston, they can be forgiven for expecting extra fast passages to London.

Matthew F Maury analysed passages of ships bound from China to America or England in his *Sailing Directions*, published in various editions. Ships bound to either destination took the same route until just south of the equator in the Atlantic, but then there was 'a fork in the track of homeward-bound Indiamen', he wrote in the eighth edition, published 1859. And he continued: 'The shortest sailing distance from the Line, where it is crossed by the American [ships], to New York is about 3350 miles. The practical sailing distance from the European crossing to the Lizard is 500 miles greater, and yet the average distance of time in making the run is 12 days!'

Ships bound to the Lizard and English Channel were usually braced sharp up against the north-east trades as they steered north to pick up the westerlies, while the ships bound for America had the wind abeam. This time difference of 12 days is important. It explains why the record passages of ship bound to America were so much less than those bound to England and it shows, if 12 days are subtracted from the fastest times to England, that the records to either country are about the same.

There seems to have been greater confrontation between British and American clippers in their first few years of competition than in later years, possibly due to press coverage and the endeavour to try and find an excuse for English shipping, if indeed it needed one. After *Oriental* reached London 99 days out from Whampoa in December 1850, editors were looking for some scapegoat, but to their relief found that a small Scots-built clipper, the *John Bunyan*, had taken 101 days between Shanghai and Deal early the same year and efforts were made to equate the times. The following year, 1851, things were allowed to rest, but *Oriental* loaded at £7 per ton as a result of her previous year's exploit and *Surprise* got £6 per ton. The former took 128 days from Woosung and the latter 107 from Whampoa, although the *Stornoway*'s 104 days from Whampoa was noted.

But in 1852 there was a great hullabaloo. The extreme American clipper *Witch of the Wave* made a 92-day passage to London from Canton, arriving in April. Then there were suggestions that the new clipper launched by R & H Green was named *Challenger* to really challenge American ships in the tea trade. Next, there was the challenge issued in September by the American Navigation Club of Boston for a race between British and American clippers to China and back for stakes of £10,000 each. Lastly there were the arrivals of the clippers themselves in the last three months of the year, which made the editors get their pens out again. The times are listed here in Appendix II, but a simple comparison is given now.

From Whampoa (or Canton) in 1852:
SAILING IN JULY
Chrysolite, British, 105 days to Liverpool
Stornoway, British, 108 days to London

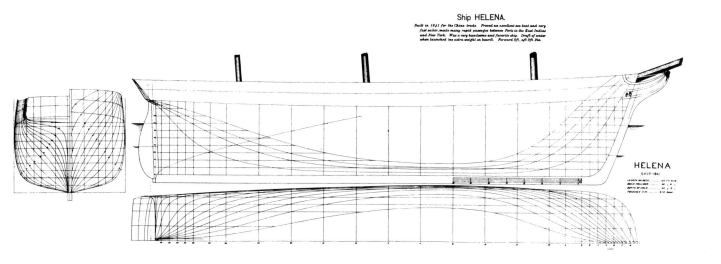

Ship HELENA.

Built in 1841 for the China trade. Proved an excellent sea boat and very fast sailor, made many rapid passages between Ports in the East Indies and New York. Was a very handsome and favorite ship. Draft of water when launched (no extra weight on board). Forward 8ft., aft 9ft 9in.

HELENA
SHIP-1841

Sea Queen, British, 116 days to London
Racehorse, American, 125 days to Liverpool
Surprise, American, 107 days to London
SAILING IN AUGUST
Challenge, American, 106 days to London
From Shanghai in 1852:
SAILING IN JULY
Challenger, British, 112 days to London
Nightingale, American, 133 days to London

It was the contest of *Challenge* versus *Challenger* that excited great interest, but they took their departure from ports 860 miles apart and, in the adverse south-west monsoon when they left, this had the effect of making Shanghai dead to leeward and adding at least a week to comparable passage times; so it looks as if honours were about even all round. Captain Fiske of *Nightingale* was so disappointed in the performance of his ship that he resigned the command in London and her owners had to send out a new skipper. Nevertheless, so convinced were they of their ship's potential that they wagered £10,000 on her next voyage to China and back, but they received no bids.

In 1853 a definite race took place between *Challenger* and *Nightingale* because they both left Shanghai on 8 August; the former reached Deal on 26 November, 110 days out, and the *Nightingale* two days later. Just as the latter made a long passage of it the previous year, so intrinsically fast ships could not regularly be relied upon to make a quick passage on every occasion without fail. Some captains could not get the best out of a ship, while others seemed to have a close rapport with their ship. The extreme clipper *Sovereign of the Seas* – built by Donald McKay in 1852, which made such an astounding passage of only 82 days between the Sandwich Islands and New York in 1853, and which could sail at 19 knots and cover 421 nautical miles in 24 hours – loaded tea at Shanghai for London in 1855. Now owned by a German firm, she made a protracted voyage with eleven of the crew dying of cholera and, with others ill, she took no less than 170 days on the passage to London. Another of McKay's clippers, the *Staghound*, had taken 141 days to London from Shanghai earlier the same year.

In 1855, of five American ships sailing in July from Foochow to London, four made long passages averaging 145½ days but the *Don Quixote* took 106 days. In 1857 the number

Above: Helena lines plan. Built in 1841 by William Webb at New York. Reproduced from plan in his book *Plans of Wooden Vessels*. Dimensions on plan: 135ft 0in (length on deck) × 30ft 6in (moulded breadth) × 20ft 0in (depth of hold), 856 tons. Built for the China trade where she made some fast passages home to America.

Opposite: The American clipper *Sea Witch* never carried tea to London but her unrivalled passages to New York set a standard for speed. (*Peabody Museum, Salem*)

of American ships carrying tea decreased and a year later only two loaded for London, but in 1859, in spite of being able to load at only £2 to £3 per ton, twelve ships cleared for England. In this year the *Bald Eagle* and the British *Challenger* both sailed from Shanghai on 6 August; the former took 120 days to Portsmouth and then went to Liverpool; the latter took 107 days to London. Other times of ships were roughly comparable. The conflict of the Civil War was to bring this contest to a speedy end and although American ships continued to load tea for London in various years throughout the 1860s those early days of keen competition were not to be repeated.

BIOGRAPHIES OF AMERICAN SHIPS BUILT 1847-1856

It should be noted that prior to 1865, American ships were measured for tonnage by the equivalent of the British 'Old Measurement' Rule, except that the divisor was 95. In 1865 America adopted the Moorsom system which was the rule used since 1854 by Great Britain. In this system the tonnage falls noticeably so that American clippers registered less tonnage by the new system. Howe & Matthews often differentiate between old and new American in their *American Clipper Ships*.

MEMNON, 1847
Her hull-form was a combination between a good cargo carrier and a medium clipper and her lines plan in Howard Chapelle's *Search for Speed under Sail* (Plate 99) shows a full midship section with a short, sharp entrance and a slightly longer run. Since she was built by Smith & Dimon of New York, who the previous year had produced the fine-lined *Sea Witch* from a design by John Griffiths, Chapelle suggests that

the *Memnon*'s design was a retreat, but she made some fast passages such as a record run of 14 days 7 hours between New York and Liverpool in 1848, and 36 days between San Francisco and Hong Kong two years later. She sailed out to San Francisco in 122 days from New York in both 1849 and 1850. In 1851 she loaded tea at Whampoa in August for London but was wrecked in the Gaspar Strait on 14 September.

She was owned in New York by F A Delano and had a tonnage of 1068 and dimensions of 170.0ft × 36.0ft × 21.0ft.

WISCONSIN, 1847
Carl Cutler calls her a 'fast sailing vessel' not a clipper and says she owed her fast passages to the ability of her master, Oliver R Mumford. She made a passage out to California in 1850 of 121 days, and then went across to China; and sailing from Hong Kong on 4 December 1850 got to the Downs 96 days later, but took a further 3 days to reach London. She again took tea to London in 1852. She had been built at New York with measurements of 925 tons and 157.0ft × 39.0ft × 21.0ft, being owned by B A Mumford and others in New York. In 1869 she was owned in South America.

ARCHITECT, 1848
This shallow-draft Baltimore clipper was really an enlarged schooner-hull rigged as a ship, according to Howard I Chapelle in *The Baltimore Clipper*, and he surmised that she was not as sharp as the *Ann McKim*. Perhaps like the latter she had a big drag aft. She was built at Baltimore by L B Culley and owned by her master, Adams Gray, of the same port. She measured 140.0ft × 30.0ft × 13.6ft and 520 tons.

She made several passages out to California in early gold rush days. She carried tea to London in 1853 and 1854, both passages being made against the monsoon; the first of these occupied 107 days from Whampoa. She was sold at Hong Kong in 1854. According to *American Clipper Ships* she continued in trade between China and England for a few years but did 'not appear in the register of 1857/58'. She certainly never appeared in *Lloyd's Register*.

ARGONAUT, 1849
Another ship of the China packet class and considered a good sailer, she was amongst the first of the American ships to load tea for London in August 1850, but she took 143 days on the passage, 27 August 1850 to 17 January 1851. These are the dates given in Cutler's *Greyhounds of the Sea* (p467) but Howe & Matthews, while agreeing with the departure date, give the days for the passage as 107 which would make the arrival date 12 December.

The *Argonaut* was built at Medford, Massachusetts, by S Lapham, was of 575 tons and measured 147ft 5in × 29ft 0in × 21ft 0in. She was owned in Boston by J E Lodge, who kept her in the Far Eastern trades until 1864 when he sold her to Norwegian owners. Her name dropped from the registers after a few years.

ORIENTAL, 1849
To Captain Nathaniel Palmer is credited the design of *Houqua* (1844), *Samuel Russell* (1847), *Oriental* (1849) and *N B Palmer* (1851) but his claim is not fully substantiated by fact. A A Low & Bros of New York owned all four of them: the first two were built by Brown & Bell, the third by Jacob Bell and the last named by Westervelt & Mackay. The design of

Opposite: Although never in the trade to London, the *N B Palmer* was often in Hong Kong or Shanghai, and this broadside photograph illustrates the proportions of an American extreme clipper. She was built in 1851, of 1124 tons new measurement. *(A J Nesdall)*

Bottom: This engraving in the *Illustrated London News* was signed by E Weedon and portrays the *Oriental* with a light breeze from the starboard quarter. Two headsails are set from the fore topgallant. *(MacGregor Collection)*

Below: Oriental lines plan. Built in 1849 by Jacob Bell at New York. Plan redrawn by E N Wilson from plan in National Maritime Museum, Greenwich. Dimensions: 185ft × 16ft × 21ft and 1003 tons. Reconstruction: scroll head; cathead and moulding; bowsprit and masts; rudder.

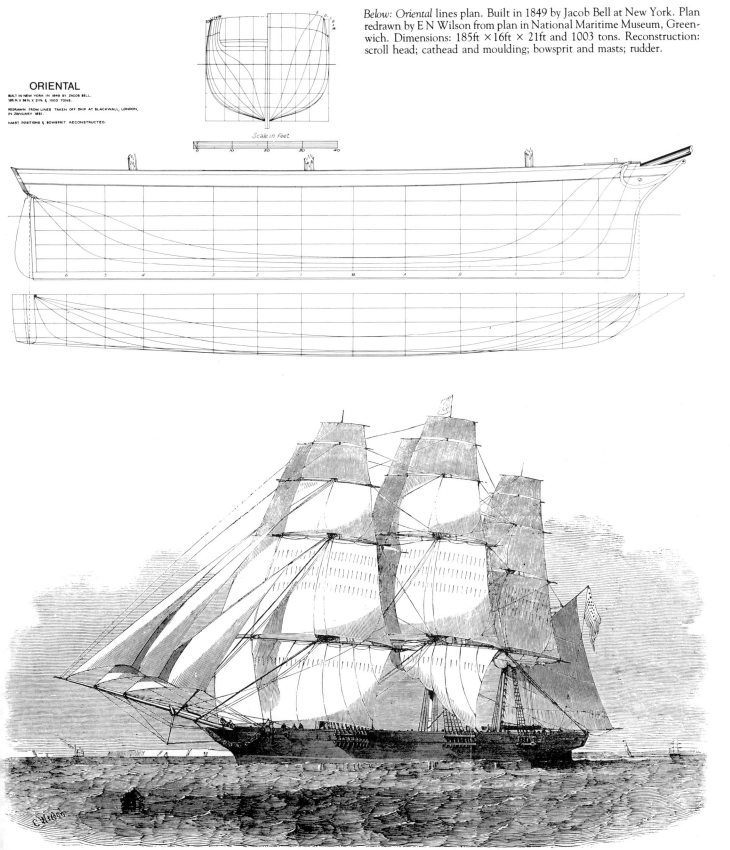

ORIENTAL

BUILT IN NEW YORK IN 1849 BY JACOB BELL.
185 Ft X 36 Ft X 21Ft & 1003 TONS.

REDRAWN FROM LINES TAKEN OFF SHIP AT BLACKWALL, LONDON, IN JANUARY 1851.

MAST POSITIONS & BOWSPRIT RECONSTRUCTED.

Scale in Feet

THE SHIP "ORIENTAL," OF NEW YORK.

fast ships for the China trade had produced such clippers as *Sea Witch* designed by Griffiths and the fine-lined China packets such as *Oriental.* In the latter's case, there was a hull which could carry a good paying cargo but with a sharp enough entrance and run, and also steep enough deadrise to produce some short passages. If gold had not been discovered in either California or Australia, it is doubtful if the China tea trade alone would have called for the production of any large out-and-out clippers. The *Oriental* was thus the culmination of a decade of experience in building fast ships for the China trade. These ships were deeper and broader than the Aberdeen clippers and usually much larger as well.

Oriental was built by Jacob Bell, New York, the successor to Brown & Bell, with register measurements of 185.0ft × 36.0ft × 21.0ft, and 1003 tons. *Sea Witch* had been given a raking stem rather like an Aberdeen bow although the bowsprit grew out of the stem. In *Samuel Russell* and *Oriental* the cutwater became the stem and the planking was carried right forward, the bowsprit coming down on top of the main rail and butting against the forward end of the topgallant rail. Both were fast powerful ships capable of sailing at 15 or 16 knots.

The *Oriental*'s maiden voyage was from New York to Hong Kong and back. Her second voyage began on 18 May 1850 when she left New York and reached Hong Kong in the record time of 81 days, her best day's run being 302 miles. Russell & Co were her agents and they offered her £6 per ton of 40 cubic feet if she would load for London; British ships usually loaded at 50 cubic feet per ton. As she loaded 1618 tons of tea, she got a most remunerative freight. Leaving Whampoa on 27 August 1850 she got down to Anjer against the monsoon by 18 September, passed the Lizard only 91 days out and locked into the West India Dock on 4 December, 99 days later. The time was also given as 97 days from Hong Kong, perhaps to Deal. This was a passage and a performance that could not be ignored and being made against the monsoon was so much quicker than previous fast passages.

Unfortunately in comparing this fast passage with others made by British ships on previous occasions, no less an authority than W S Lindsay, MP and shipowner, stated in a letter to the *Manchester Guardian*, which was reprinted in the *Shipping Gazette* on 20 December 1850, that the *John Bunyan* had already made a passage from Shanghai to London of 98 days 'against the monsoons'. Of course she had sailed *with* the monsoon, having sailed in January. The China merchants Phillips, Shaw & Lowther wrote to *The Times* on 27 December correcting the errors which they described as 'so glaring a mis-statement', but the damage was done, and people believed for many years that a British ship had never really been beaten.

It is instructive that no British shipowner ordered a ship of comparable size which could emulate the speed of *Oriental* and so obtain equally high profits, and it was not until *Cairngorm* was built three years later that a comparable challenger appeared.

However, *Oriental* obtained a charter for a round voyage to Hong Kong and back, sailing out in 116 days and returning against the monsoon in 128 days, all in 1851. She returned once more to China but this time loaded at Shanghai for New York, where she arrived on 16 December 1852, 106 days out. Her next outward passage was to San Francisco from where she crossed over to China and once more loaded tea for London, first at Canton and then completing her

cargo at Foochow. Unfortunately whilst being towed down the river Min by local boats she struck a rock and sank on 25 February 1854.

CELESTIAL, 1850
She was William Webb's first clipper ship design and was intended for the China trade, having register measurements of 158.0ft × 34.0ft × 19.0ft and 860 tons, her owners being Bucklin & Crane of New York. Like all Webb's designs, she had a short, sharp entrance with the maximum beam between the fore- and mainmasts after which there was a long run. She was a broad vessel with 4.64 beams to length and she had appreciable deadrise and marked tumblehome.

Many of her outward passages were from New York to San Francisco after which she crossed over to China, but she carried tea to England on three occasions. On the first she left in May 1852 which meant she must have carried old 1851 teas; on the second she left in October 1853 and took only 96 days to London; on the third she sailed in August 1857. On both the first and third of these passages she took 137 days, which was on the long side.

Early in 1858 she was sold to Spanish owners but in 1861 she was once more owned in New York, this time by B Blanco.

STAGHOUND, 1850
This extreme clipper was the first built by Donald McKay but she only once loaded tea for London and that was in 1855 when she left on 8 April from Woosung and made a long passage of 141 days to Deal. Most of her voyages were out to San Francisco, across to China and then home to New York with tea. Her best day's run is said to have been 358 miles.

She had very fine lines with a long entrance and run without much hollow anywhere; there was considerable deadrise with slack bilges and little tumblehome; she was of course a full-rigged ship carrying skysails on each mast. She was owned by G B Upton and Sampson & Tappan, Boston, with register measurements of 215.0ft × 39.8ft × 21.0ft and 1534 tons which was about 1100 tons by the 1854 British rule. On a passage from Sunderland to San Francisco with coal, she was found to be on fire off Pernambuco on 12 October 1861 and was abandoned the same day with the ship burned to the water's edge. The crew reached Pernambuco next day in the four boats.

SURPRISE, 1850
Another product of this first year that witnessed the launch of large clippers was the *Surprise* which was built at East Boston by Samuel Hall for A A Low & Bros of New York. From the evidence assembled by Howard I Chapelle it seems that she was designed by Samuel H Pook as a clipper combining speed with good carrying capacity, and she earned her owners some handsome profits. Many ships launched this year were good money-spinners when freights to California were at their peak. Her measurements were 183.3ft × 38.8ft × 22.0ft and 1261 tons. She had not so much deadrise as *Staghound* but was more like *Celestial.*

She made two passages with tea to London: both were made from Whampoa in July in the years 1851 and 1852, and both occupied 107 days, which was within a few days of the shortest time each year. On her first round voyage to San Francisco, Whampoa and London she earned sufficient to pay the cost of building and the voyage expenses, and still have a clear profit of $50,000. Apart from two passages out to California in 1853 and 1854, her life was spent in trade with the Far East. Even in 1870–71 she went from Shanghai to New York in 83 days, arriving in February. She struck Plymouth Rocks on 4 February 1876 off the Japanese coast bound for Yokohama and was abandoned when on her beam ends, the crew getting safely to land. The 'pilot' who had been in charge was later found to have been a drunken beachcomber who then disappeared.

WHITE SQUALL, 1850

Built by Jacob Bell as a larger and sharper version of the Oriental, she measured 190.0ft × 35.6ft × 21.0ft and 1119 tons, being a full-rigged ship. Her first cost was $90,000, including stores and provisions for one year, but owing to the high freights to California she obtained $74,000 for the trip and then from Canton to London a further $58,000; in addition, passengers at $600 each for the passage to San Francisco augmented the profits. There were only a few ships which happened to be available that could earn these enormous profits, but that is just what stimulated the building of the clippers, although many came on the scene too late to participate. Her owners, W Platt & Sons, Philadelphia, were delighted with this maiden voyage.

There are enough paintings of ships carrying every rag of canvas, and by way of contrast the American clipper *Surprise* is here pictured close-hauled on the port tack under reefed topsails and whole courses. (*Peabody Museum, Salem*)

This voyage was the only one in which she loaded tea for London and she took 99 days to the Isle of Wight from Whampoa, 8 September to 16 December 1851, which was a very fast run at this date, being the shortest of any American ship sailing against the monsoon that year.

Her outward passages were made to California. On 26 December 1853 she caught fire from sparks blown on to the ship from a conflagration ashore and burned to the water's edge, but she was rebuilt as a barque of 896 tons. In 1856 she was sold to French owners and was renamed *Splendide* of Marseilles. In 1877 a vessel of this name was beached at Gibraltar in a sinking condition.

CHALLENGE, 1851

This extreme clipper ship reached England on the last leg of a voyage around the world which had excited the deepest emotions, from admiration at the splendour of the ship to stupefaction at the brutality meted out to the crew on the passage to San Francisco. She was built by William Webb of New York for N L & G Griswold of the same port and was intended to be the finest and fastest clipper afloat. Her dimensions of 230ft 6in × 43ft 2in × 26ft 0in and 2006½ tons register show her to have been much larger than previous clippers, although these measurements were soon to be exceeded. She was Webb's finest-lined clipper and was given great deadrise with rounded bilges which flowed into the tumblehome; the entrance was very sharp and concave; the maximum beam was midway between the fore- and mainmasts and then the extremely long run flowed aft with much hollowness in the lower body. She had a long, open deck with only a small deckhouse abaft the foremast, a very short poop, and only a monkey forecastle. The owners secured Robert Waterman from the *Sea Witch* as master and, in superintending her construction and outfit, he obliged

Webb to increase the lengths of the masts and spars considerably beyond what had been designed for her. The distance across from the outer leech of one of her square lower stunsails to the outer leech of the other was 160ft. She was undoubtedly 'overhatted' and this probably contributed to her poor performance on the maiden voyage.

She was launched on 24 May 1851 and her maiden passage to San Francisco took 108 days, but Waterman had to relinquish his command after a near-mutiny aboard and other problems. She crossed over to Hong Kong and on the return trip was only 18 days from opposite Japan to San Francisco, which remains the record. Recrossing the Pacific she loaded tea at Whampoa for London and leaving in August 1852 took 105 days to the Downs. Attempts were made to compare her passage with that of the British clipper *Challenger*, presumably because of a similarity of names, but

the latter had taken her departure a week earlier from Shanghai which was 850 miles dead to leeward in the south-west monsoon and the equivalent of one or two weeks sailing. So any comparison was really impossible.

The Admiralty got permission to take off *Challenge*'s lines in London. She sailed back to China direct from London and again loaded tea for England, but on the homeward run she was obliged to put into Fayal in the Azores, leaky, with crew and passengers manning the pumps, and the entire passage to Deal occupied 160 days. She never loaded tea again for London.

In 1861 she was sold in Hong Kong and renamed *Golden City*, and continued to work out of that port. Five years later she was bought by Wilson & Co, South Shields, who put her in the trade to India and the Far East without altering her name. She was wrecked off the French coast in 1876.

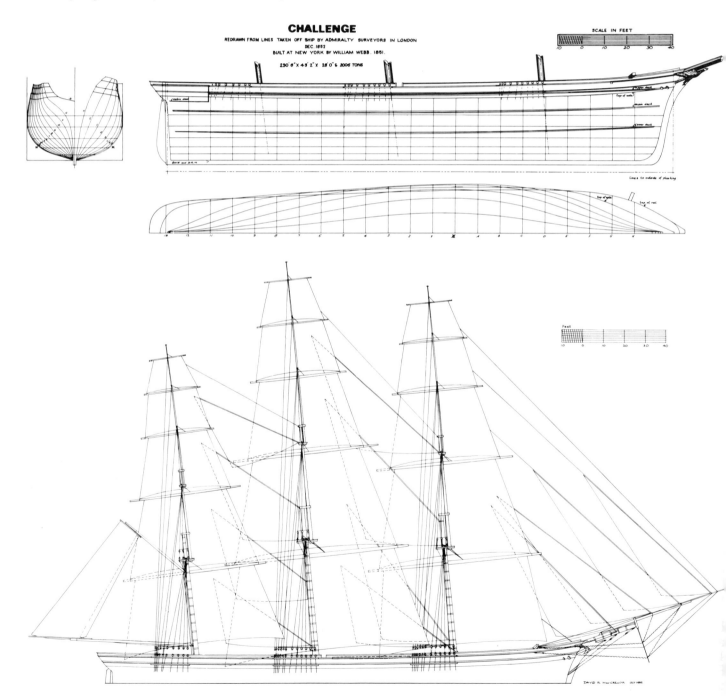

CHALLENGE

REDRAWN FROM LINES TAKEN OFF SHIP BY ADMIRALTY SURVEYORS IN LONDON
DEC. 1852
BUILT AT NEW YORK BY WILLIAM WEBB. 1851.

230' 6" X 43' 2" X 26' 0" 6 2006 TONS

SCALE IN FEET

DAVID R. MacGREGOR. OCT 1983

Above: This lithograph of *Challenge* measures 10½in × 7in image size and is signed by L Lebreton; it was published in Paris with a heading at the top *Marine Americaine*, and is numbered '42' under the title beneath. It has been used extensively in reconstructing the sail plan. (*MacGregor Collection*)

Opposite, top: Challenge lines plan. Built in 1851 by William Webb at New York. Redrawn and reconstructed by E N Wilson from take-off (dated 1852) in National Maritime Museum, Greenwich. Dimensions: 230ft 6in × 43ft 2in × 26ft 0in and 2006 tons.

Opposite, bottom: Challenger sail plan. Entirely reconstructed to show ship as first built. Souces: lines plan; spar dimensions listed on plan of lines taken off in London December 1852 by Admiralty Surveyors and from spars in Howe & Matthews *American Clipper Ships* (1926); headsails based on Lebreton's lithograph.

FLYING CLOUD, 1851

It was not until she was nine years old and had had her spars twice reduced in length that this famous ship carried tea to London, making the passage in 123 days from Foochow which she left in August 1860. Her days as an out-and-out clipper in the California trade around Cape Horn were over by this time, as well as her chance to achieve any more of those record runs of under 90 days – she had twice made the passage from New York to San Francisco in 89 days – and she had had the mortification of being idle at New York for two year and eight months.

Now having been sold by Grinnell, Minturn & Co she had left New York in December 1859, and in London loaded a cargo for Hong Kong which had been reached on 21 May 1860, 97 days from Deal. After the passage with tea from Foochow, she had sailed from London to Melbourne in 85 days and then gone to Hong Kong where she was chartered

to carry troops to London for £6000. This passage began on 29 December 1861 and occupied 112 days of which 11 were spent at St Helena. During 1862 she was sold to British owners: between 1865 and 1870 she was owned by T M Mackay of London, who may have had her for a longer period, but she was not listed in *Lloyd's Register* until 1874 when H S Edwards, South Shields, became her owner. In 1874 she went ashore on Beacon Island bar after leaving St Johns. After being got off, she broke her back, was condemned, and finally was burned for her metal work in June 1875.

The *Flying Cloud* had been built by Donald McKay as an extreme clipper with dimensions of 225ft 0in (on deck) × 40ft 8in × 21ft 6in and 1782 tons. By British registration the measurements were 221.1ft × 40.2ft × 21.8ft, 988 tons under deck and 1098 tons net. The coefficient of under deck tonnage works out at 0.51, which is sharper than any British tea clipper.

GOLDEN GATE, 1851

Jacob A Westervelt, New York, built her for Chambers & Heiser of the same port with dimensions of 186ft 8in × 40ft 4in × 21ft 6in and 1349 tons. The *Golden State* built by him the following year for the same owners had very similar dimensions and was said to be a sister ship.

During her short life, the *Golden Gate* was in the California and China trades and in 1854 loaded tea at Shanghai for London. Leaving on 25 November she was run into by the barque *Homer* when 9 days out and had to put into Batavia to replace her jibboom where she remained 4 days. She reached Beachy Head on 23 February 1855, 89 days after leaving Shanghai and 86 days at sea, which was a record passage,

Opposite, top: This painting by Charles Robert Patterson of the *Flying Cloud* evokes the spirit of the clipper ship era with a fore topmast stunsail set although men are on the fore royal yard furling the sail. (*National Maritime Museum, San Francisco*)

Opposite, bottom: The *Nightingale* at anchor; the doublings are very long. (*Parker Gallery*)

Right: *Nightingale* sail plan. Entirely reconstructed from hull profile, mast positions and rake of masts on lines plan. Sources of reconstruction: spar dimensions from *American Clipper Ships* by O T Howe and F C Matthews 1927, vol II, p427, with exception of bowsprit, jibboom, flying jibboom, spanker boom and gaff; rigging from oil painting of ship in *American Sail* by Alexander Laing, 1961, p264.

Below: *Nightingale* lines plan. Built in 1851 by Samuel Hanscom Jnr, at Portsmouth, New Hampshire. Redrawn from plan drawn by G Hillmann (probably in Liverpool *c*1860) in the Mariner's Museum, Newport News, Virginia. Dimensions (customs measurement): 185.0ft × 36.0ft × 20.0ft, 1060 tons. Dimensions on plan: 171ft 3in (length on load waterline) × 35ft 0in (moulded breadth) × 20ft 0in (depth of hold), 1100 tons burthen. Reconstruction: figurehead and trailboards.

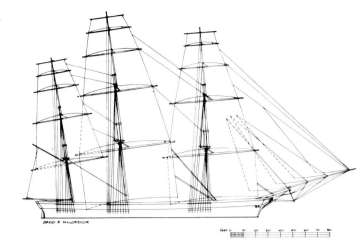

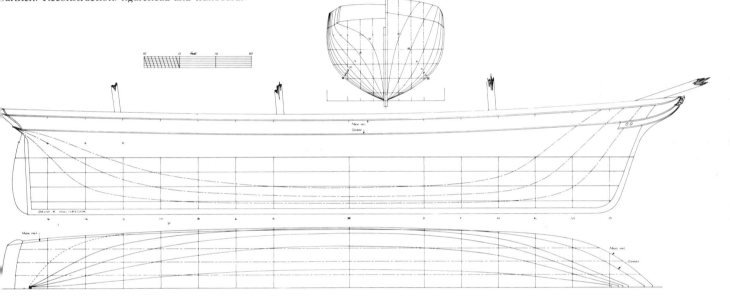

even though made in the favourable monsoon. This ranks with the 91 days of *Nightingale* made the following year between the same points and also the 89 days of *Lord of the Isles* in 1858–59. It is difficult to evaluate the time of so many days 'at sea' in assessing a record run.

The *Golden Gate* was destroyed by fire at Pernambuco on 26 May 1856, into which port she had gone after being partially dismasted at sea. The scarred hull and cargo were sold for $700.

NIGHTINGALE, 1851

This ship possessed extremely steep deadrise bordering on a vee-section, but the floors were slightly convex and curved all the way up; the entrance and run were long and sharp but with very little hollow anywhere except near the stem. She was built by Samuel Hanscom Jnr at Portsmouth, New Hampshire, with dimensions of 185.0ft × 36.0ft × 20.0ft and a tonnage of 1060. She was a lofty ship crossing skysails on each mast and the mainmast was stepped a long way aft, which placed the mizen rather in the stern.

Ordered by Captain E A Miller to carry passengers for a trip across the Atlantic to visit the Great Exhibition in London, she was named after the singer Jenny Lind, who was known as the 'Swedish Nightingale'. Miller, however, refused to accept delivery and so the builder was obliged to

put the clipper up for auction to pay his debts. Sampson & Tappan acquired her and sent her out to Sydney where she arrived in January 1852 after a slow passage of 90 days. Then she crossed over to China and loaded tea at Shanghai for London. The British *Challenger* was also on the berth and left first on 28 July, taking 38 days to Anjer and 112 to London. *Nightingale* left three days later but took 61 days to Anjer and 133 to London. A year later she and *Challenger* both sailed on the same day from Woosung but again she was beaten to Deal, although this time by only two days. But she did make a record passage between Shanghai and Beachy Head of 91 days in 1855, 16 February to 18 May, reaching London three days later.

After further trade to and from China, she was sold in 1860 and fitted out to carry slaves, but after capture became an armed supply ship for the Federal Navy. At the end of the Civil War she became a merchant ship again and traded to California. In 1876 she was sold to Norwegian owners who retained her name and employed her in the North Atlantic timber trade, where she was abandoned on 17 April 1893.

TYPHOON, 1851

She was launched fully rigged with skysail yards crossed on 18 February from the yard of Fernald & Pettigrew in Portsmouth, New Hampshire, and it must have been a splendid

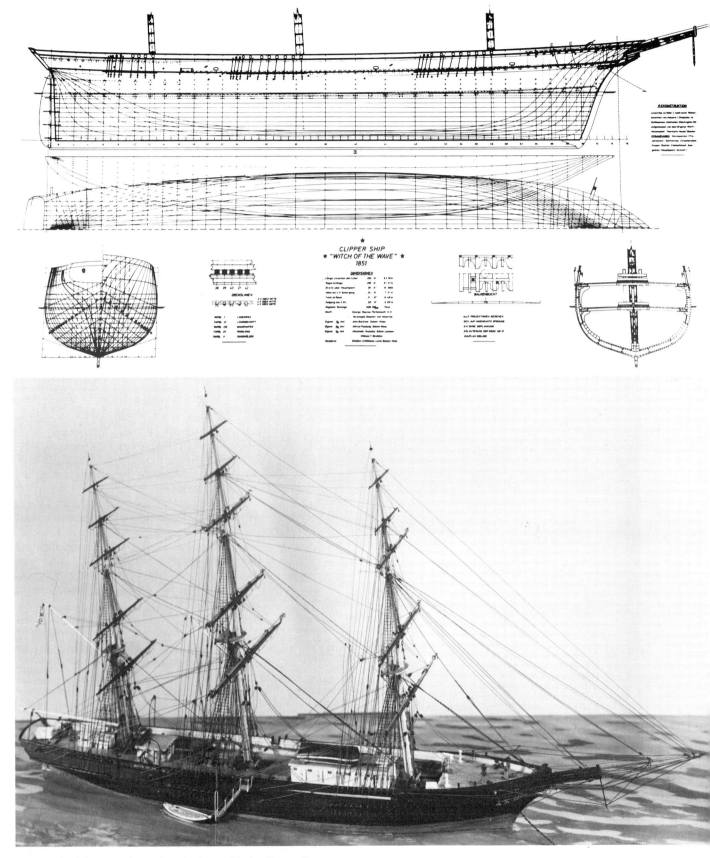

Top: Witch of the Wave lines plan. Built in 1851 by George Raynes at Portsmouth, New Hampshire. Plan reconstructed and drawn by Peter Rückert. Dimensions 220.0ft × 40.0ft × 21.0ft and 1498 tons.

Above: Model of *Witch of the Wave* by Donald McNarry. *(Parker Gallery)*

The *Archer* in dry dock at Foochow, probably after going ashore in the Min river in 1865. An unusual sight in a photograph is the lower stunsail boom which is hinged back beside the hull across the fore upper channel. *(A J Nesdall)*

ight to see her enter the water or, as the papers of the time would have said, her 'native element'. She measured 1611 ons and 207ft × 41ft × 23ft; tonnage by the new American measurement was 1215. Her first owners were D & A Kingsland & Co, New York, for whom she traded to California, India and China. In November 1853 she loaded t Shanghai for London and made the run in 106 days to Deal. In 1862 she was at Whampoa, loading for Cork, and ater completed her cargo in Manila, but put into Fayal, Azores, on 24 December, leaky and damaged with several of he crew dead through over-exertion. She did not get to Liverpool until 19 February 1863.

She returned to Hong Kong with coal from Newport and owards the end of 1863 was sold in Singapore for $39,000. By 1869 she was owned in Dublin by J Martin & Sons with he name of *Indomitable* and was still under their ownership hree years later. I have not traced her subsequent fate. Lloyd's Register was not listing her at this date.

WITCH OF THE WAVE, 1851

This large and beautiful clipper ship,' stated the *Illustrated London News*, 'commanded by Captain Millett, arrived in he East India Docks, Blackwall, from Canton, having made one of the most extraordinary and rapid voyages on record . .' She took her pilot off Dungeness on 4 April 1852, 90 days out from Whampoa and docked two days later, '. . . a rip surpassing the celebrated runs of the *Oriental* and *Sunrise* clippers.'

Although this very fast run was made in the favourable monsoon and from the closest loading port in China, rather than from Shanghai, yet at the time it was the fastest properly authenticated passage between China and London. At the end of 1844 the brig *Bonanza* had taken only 91 days between Shanghai and Liverpool; but, as usual, the basis for accurate comparison is not constant.

Howard I Chapelle published the lines of *Witch of the Wave* in *Search for Speed under Sail*, and showed that she had considerable deadrise with rounded bilges, sharp entrance and long, sharp run; and he commented favourably on the large number of fast passages she had made, indicating the ability to sail fast under a variety of wind and weather conditions. She was built by George Raynes of Portsmouth, New Hampshire, for Glidden & Williams, Boston, and measured 220.0ft × 40.0ft × 21.0ft and 1498 tons, or 997 tons by foreign measurement. After various passages to and from Far Eastern ports, she was sold to Dutch owners in Amsterdam in 1856–57 and renamed *Electra*. She was still afloat under Dutch colours in 1871.

ARCHER, 1852

This full-rigged ship was launched on 29 December 1852 and so could not have been completed until the next year, but 1852 is the year usually given as her date of build. She was not large by American standards, with a tonnage of 1095 tons old measurement and 905 tons new American. Dimensions worked out at 176.0ft × 37.0ft × 21.5ft. She was built at Somerset, Massachusetts, by James M Hood for Crocker & Warren, New York. In 1862 she was bought by William Perkins, Boston, who partially rebuilt her at a cost of $25,000. In 1876 she was sold by her then owner, S G Reed, Boston, to Captain Crossman. On 12 February 1880 she was abandoned in the North Atlantic and her crew, exhausted from pumping the leaking hull, were taken off by ss *Naworth Castle*; she foundered and sank shortly afterwards.

She had various accidents and it was as a result of grounding in the river Min in 1865 that she was dry-docked at Foochow and the famous photograph of her was taken then. Josiah P Cressey, famous as captain of the *Flying Cloud* on her record runs, was her master in the early 1860s.

FLYING DUTCHMAN, 1852

Several clippers built by William Webb carried tea to London or made passages from there to China. *Flying Dutchman* embodied all Webb's ideas – short, sharp entrance, extremely long run with the whole body tapering aft, large deadrise and slack bilges. Her builder wrote on the lines plan he published that she 'proved a very fast sailer and excellent sea boat, successful and popular ship'. She was owned by George Daniels of New York, and had measurements of 191ft 0in × 37ft 8in × 21ft 6in and 1257 tons.

She twice carried tea to London, leaving on both occasions during the favourable monsoon. On the second, O T Howe in *American Clipper Ships* gives the date of her arrival at London as 9 January 1856, which would give her a passage of 93 days from Shanghai, but Carl Cutler in *Greyhounds of the Sea* gives her arrival as 24 January at Deal, making 108 days.

Two years later, bound from San Francisco to New York, she ran ashore on Brigantine Beach, New Jersey, on 13 February 1858 and was a total loss.

COMPETITOR, 1853

This ship was built by J O Curtis at Medford, Massachusetts, for W F Weld & Co, Boston, with measurements of 175ft 0in (overall) × 33ft 5in × 20ft 2in and 871 tons. She had an eagle figurehead and a round stern. She had a long life for a hard-sailed clipper and made some quick passages as well as some protracted ones.

Many wooden clippers suffered from constructional defects, and on her maiden passage around Cape Horn she was hove-to for five days strapping her bow together with chain in an attempt to remedy the effects of a split stem which was causing a serious leak. She visited China on many occasions but only once carried tea to London in a passage of 163 days in 1857.

Weld & Co sold her in 1863 to owners in Hanover who renamed her *Loreley*, but in 1874 she reverted to her original name of *Competitor* under the ownership of A F Freeman of London, who owned her in the 1870s. At this time her dimensions in *Lloyd's Register* were 164.0ft × 32.8ft × 20.7ft, 713 tons under deck and 734 tons net and gross. She was sold to German interests at Pillau about 1878; in 1897 she was sold to Norway, with ownership changes annually. In 1899 she was acquired by owners in Kalmar, Sweden, who overhauled her and renamed her *Edward*, but as a result of litigation following a collision in 1901, she was sold to Finland and disappeared from the Register in 1908.

KINGFISHER, 1853

Another ship to be built at Medford, Mass, but this time i the yard of Hayden & Cudworth, she measured 1286 tor and 217.0ft × 37.0ft × 21.0ft, being owned in Boston b Wm Lincoln & Co. She traded to and from China in man years but of the two passages made to London with tea that 1855–56 was the quickest, as it occupied only 96 days be ween Macao and Deal, 20 October to 24 January. Sh returned to Foochow in 109 days from the Lizard and her te passage in 1856–57 lasted 109 days.

She was damaged by running aground on three occasion In 1871 she put into Montevideo in distress, leaking, an was condemned and sold. The purchasers renamed her *Jaim Cibils* after a member of their family and kept her in trad until 1890 when she was sold for breaking up in Montevide Bay.

NONPAREIL, 1853

Several American clippers were sold to British owners in th early 1860s as a result of the depression caused by the Civ War. Amongst these was the *Nonpareil* which was built b Dunham & Co at Frankfort, Maine, in 1853 with a tonnag of 1431, or 1097 British measurement, with dimensions c 200.0ft × 41.6ft × 22.5ft. During the 1850s she was tradin from Philadelphia, but in February 1860 arrived in New Yor 128 days out from Shanghai. Then followed some voyages t San Francisco, returning to Liverpool. She was sold to th Globe Navigation Co, Liverpool, in 1864, after her fa passage of 87 days from Shanghai made in 1863–64; therea ter she was trading to the East until she foundered on 1 October 1871 in a Force 12 gale, 600 miles from New Yor when bound there from Bombay.

Many of the ships sailing from Shanghai in 1863 about th same time as *Nonpareil* made good passages, and the times ar listed here:

Note: the arrival port is Liverpool unless otherwise stated

Heroes of Alma (Lass), 15 December to 19 March (c Plymouth for London) 95 days.

Chryseis (Hedley), 16 December to 16 April, 122 days.

Young England, ex-*Oracle* (Smith), 18 December to March (off Anjer 2 January), 90 days (cargo = 3966 bal cotton and about 10 chests tea etc).

Nonpareil (E W Smith), 19 December to 15 March (c Anjer 1 January), 87 days (cargo = 4500 bales cotton ar 21 cases tea).

Offor (Bertram), from Hong Kong, 20 December to 14 Apr (Anjer 2 January), 116 days.

Amazone (Nielson), from Hong Kong, 21 December to April (Anjer 28 December), 105 days.

Esmerelda (Pollock), from 'China', 22 December to 1 Apri 101 days.

Zingra (W Gould), 26 December to 20 March (Anjer 3 December; spoken on 16 January in 26°S, 60°E), 85 da (cargo = 2100 bales cotton).

Agra (Bell), from Macao, 26 December to London 18 Apri 114 days.

It is curious that two ships owned by J Clay of Sunderlan the *Chryseis* and the *Zingra*, were both taking part. In th latter's record run, the dates allow her but 5 days to get dow to Anjer or 6 if the days of departure and arrival are bot counted. Of the others listed above, *Amazone* was built a

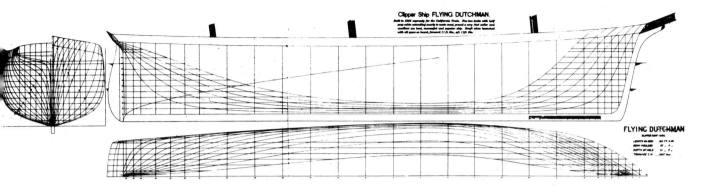

Sunderland in 1852 of 411 tons and owned in Amsterdam; *Esmerelda* was built at Hamburg in 1860; *Offor* was a brig built in Jersey in 1861 and of 172 tons.

ORACLE, 1853

Built in 1853 at Thomaston, Maine, by Chapman & Flint, of 1196 tons or 1017 British measurement, she was owned in New York and in 1854–55 took 122 days Shanghai to London. One account says she was sold to British owners in November 1862 and renamed *Young England* (Howe & Matthews *American Clipper Ships*, Vol II). Another account says she was sold to England in 1861 and renamed *Young England* (VDFQ of Liverpool) but was abandoned at sea in March 1863 (D R Bolt 'Later History of American Sailing Ships "Sold Foreign" ', *American Neptune*, Vol IV, p244). This abandonment would be *before* her run of 90 days from Shanghai to Liverpool in 1863–64. The *Mercantile Navy List* of 1864 and 1865 has the *Young England* as VDFQ of Liverpool, 1017 tons and owned by T N Mackey of London, so Daniel Bolt's account would appear to be incorrect, unless she was salvaged. Her subsequent career has not been traced. It seems possible that T N Mackey was the same person as T M Mackay of 1 Leadenhall Street, London, who owned *Flying Cloud* in the same years.

Above: The *Competitor* in the English Channel, from the painting by R B Spencer. (*MacGregor Collection*)

Top: Flying Dutchman lines plan. Built in 1852 by William Webb at New York. Reproduced from Webb's book *Plans of Wooden Vessels*. Dimensions 191ft 0in × 37ft 8in × 21ft 6in and 1257 tons.

ROMANCE OF THE SEAS, 1853

She was an extreme clipper built at East Boston by Donald McKay with very long, sharp ends, possessing hollowness in the lower portion, and considerable deadrise, and her proportions were much longer, narrower and shallower than in most large American clippers. Her register dimensions were 240.75ft × 39.6ft × 20.0ft and 1782 tons. Her ratio of breadth to length was 6.09. Howe & Matthews in *American Clipper Ships* (Vol II) write that 'she was designed by her owner, George B Upton of Boston', but Howard I Chapelle who reproduces her lines plan in his *Search for Speed under Sail* makes no mention of this, calling her 'one of McKay's experiments in hull proportions'. Previously he had commented, 'McKay seems to have been uncertain as to what hull form to use for a given trade' and these inconsistencies are most noticeable when the plans are examined.

Her outward passages were usually to San Francisco and on her maiden one she got there in just under 97 days from

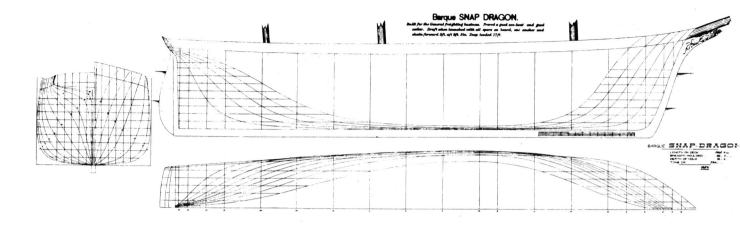

New York. Then she went across to China and loaded tea for London at Whampoa, leaving on 9 June and taking 104 days. Then followed a round trip to China and back to London, after which her China voyages did not take her to England. In 1863 she was posted 'missing' on a passage to San Francisco, not having been heard of since leaving Hong Kong on 31 December 1862.

SNAP DRAGON, 1853
This clipper barque was built at New York by William Webb and her lines plan shows flat floors but a sharp entrance and run, although due to her shorter length the long tapering run found in some of his clippers is here absent. It states on her plan that she was built for 'the general freighting business'. Her owners were Wakeman, Dimon & Co of New York and her dimensions were 142ft 2in × 30ft 10in × 18ft 2in and 618¾ tons. In 1858 she left Whampoa on 1 May with old teas, but got down to Anjer in 19 days against the monsoon, taking 104 days on the entire passage. *Romance of the Seas* had taken the same time from Whampoa in 1854 and these appear to be two of the four fastest runs made to London by American ships against the south-west monsoon. The *Snap Dragon*'s size was more akin to British clippers. Her fate is unknown to me.

SPITFIRE, 1853
Reputed to be a fine-lined clipper as well as an attractive-looking ship, she was constructed in Frankfort, Maine, by J Arey & Sons for T Gray and Manning & Stanwood of Boston and had dimensions of 224.0ft × 40.0ft × 23.0ft and a tonnage of 1549. She made the usual outward trips to California whilst freight rates were high, but when depression set in on that trade, she made a round voyage from London to Hong Kong and back in 1856–57, and at the end of the 1850s was trading on the China coast. In 1863 she was sold in London for £9000 to W N de Mattos of that port and he retained ownership during the 1860s. Howe & Matthews say she dropped out of 'Lloyd's' (presumably *Lloyd's Register*) in 1874, but I could not find her listed at all. The *Mercantile Navy List* of 1865 records her with a tonnage of 1241.

SWALLOW, 1854
Built at East Boston by R E Jackson for Dugan & Leland of New York, she measured 210ft 0in × 38ft 6in × 23ft 6in and 1435 tons. She traded to and from ports in England for much of her life and her maiden voyage took her there and thence

to Melbourne in 73 days from Deal, rather than out to California. The freight on the Australian run netted £5500 and bound back from Shanghai she loaded at £6 per ton of 40 cubic feet. However, although sailing in November with the favourable monsoon, she made a slow passage to London of 135 days. Two years later she took 101 days to Land's End from Shanghai.

Thatcher Magoun of Boston bought her in 1862 and put her into the California trade; eleven years later she was sold to Howes & Crowell, New York. In 1883 she was put up for auction at New York and sold for $19,000, and two years later the leaky old clipper was abandoned at sea when bound for Sydney, soon after leaving Liverpool, as the pumps had become choked.

MAURY, 1855
This clipper barque had a close race home in 1856 with the British iron clipper *Lord of the Isles*. The latter left Foochow on 10 June, a day after the American, and they were in company on several occasions. The *Maury* averaged 272½ miles per day for twelve days whilst crossing the Indian Ocean, her best being 370 miles on one day. Eventually both vessels reached the Downs on the same morning and towed past Gravesend within ten minutes of each other on 15 October; but with a better tug, *Lord of the Isles* passed the *Maury* and docked first, so gaining the premium of £1 per ton which was awarded to the first ship in dock with the new teas. *Maury*'s passage time of 128 days was not particularly short.

She carried tea to London again the following year when she raced home against the *Fairy* which she beat by one day.

The *Maury* was built at New York by Roosevelt, Joyce & Co for A A Low & Bros of the same port, with measurements of 141ft 0in × 30ft 1in × 16ft 3in and 594 tons; she had a draft of 17ft. Carl Cutler omits her name from his list of clipper ships in Appendix I to *Greyhounds of the Sea* but the *American Lloyd's Register* for 1861 gives her model as 'sharp'. Her end has not been discovered, but she is not listed in the *American Lloyd's Register* of 1863 and the Peabody Museum of Salem had no copy for 1862. (My thanks are due to Andrew Nesdall for obtaining particulars for me from these Registers.)

FAIRY, 1856
She was rigged as a barquentine at a time when there were only a few afloat of this rig and when they were at first called schooners. One was the *Jenny Ford* which reached San Francisco in June 1855 after a passage of 141 days from

Boston and thereafter traded in the Pacific. She was of 397 tons and was built in 1854 at East Machias, Maine. Other early ones were the *Mary Stockton* (1853) and *Lamplighter* (1854). (See notes by John Lyman in *American Neptune* Vol VII, pp315–6.)

An early use of the word 'barkentine' occurs in the log-book of the American ship *Cremorne* for the years 1861–63, now in the library of Mystic Seaport, where the *Fairy* is so described when seen at Shanghai. Carl Cutler calls her a 'clipper barkentine' in *Greyhounds of the Sea* and gives her measurements as 141ft 3in × 31ft 6in × 18ft 2in and 629 tons. She was built at New York by Roosevelt, Joyce & Co for Gordon, Talbot & Co of the same port. This yard also produced the barques *Maury*, *Benefactor* and *Penguin* which were in the China trade.

Sailing from Foochow on 4 July 1857, a day after the *Maury*, the *Fairy* got to London in 107 days which was a fast passage and a day longer than *Maury*. *Cairngorm* which left Foochow on 3 July took 120 days to London and all the passages by British ships this year were of about this average length, with the exception of *Fiery Cross* which took only 99 days or 94 to off Dartmouth. The *Fairy* again carried tea to London in 1860. I have no particulars of her later career.

FLORENCE, 1856

There have always been ships built with moderately fine lines and good stowage capacity which, due to the skill of their master, the placing of their masts in relation to the hull, the finding of suitable favourable winds, or perhaps a combination of all three, have been able to perform faster passages than ships of extreme-clipper build. Certainly a good master who was able to drive his ship along was all-important and one such man was Philip Dumaresq, who superintended the construction of the *Florence* and then had her until 1859. Her log-books carry numerous references to

ships being passed, an extract when crossing the Indian Ocean in 1857 reading in part: '. . . passed two barks under reefed courses standing the same way, we having topgallant studding-sails and royals set.' Her design allowed *Florence* to stow a large cargo.

In 1858, after two voyages to China from America and back, she loaded vegetable wax in Nagasaki and completed at Shanghai, from where she was 97 days to Deal, sailing with the favourable monsoon. The following year she again reached London from China.

In 1862 she crossed the Atlantic to Liverpool where she was sold to Jones, Palmer & Co who renamed her *Hypatia*. Her tonnage was then given as 869. In 1872 she was sold to Norwegian owners at Skien, her dimensions in Norwegian feet being given as 168 x 34 x 21. She was now barque-rigged. L W Flood was her master and later he became her owner, running her in the North Atlantic timber trade. In 1888 when bound from Nova Scotia to Liverpool with deals she was wrecked on Clippera Rocks, Anglesey, on 16 November, but the crew of fifteen were saved.

Her first owners were J M & R B Forbes, Boston, and her builder was Samuel Hall of East Boston. Her first dimensions by American registry were 171ft 7in × 36ft 6in × 22ft 6in and 1045 tons.

Opposite: *Snap Dragon* lines plan. Built in 1853 by William Webb at New York. Reproduced from Webb's book *Plans of Wooden Vessels*. Dimensions: 142ft 2in × 30ft 10in × 18ft 2in and 618¾ tons.

The *Golden State* in Russell's Floating Dock at Quebec in 1884 when she bore the name of *Annie C Maguire*. By this date her rig had been reduced to that of barque. There are still stunsail boom irons on some of the yards. (*Peabody Museum, Salem*)

6

WOOD, IRON OR COMPOSITE
AND SHIPS OF 1852-1857

It was not until 1852 that ships produced from building yards in the rest of Britain could be favourably compared with those emanating from Aberdeen. This building-centre led the way throughout the first half of the 1850s, after which ships from other ports were of equal merit until the Clyde took the lead in the 1860s. Most yards were still experimenting with various types of designs, so that one ship might differ totally from another, even though she followed her closely off the stocks. And experiments were not limited only to design and fitting out, for new combinations of materials were tried out in the construction of hulls.

Timber had been master of shipbuilding for as far back as men could remember and with it had been constructed an immense variety of craft for every purpose. For ease of working, adaptability, cheapness where readily available, it was unsurpassed. Yet so great were the demands made on it in Great Britain that hardwood was becoming scarce, whilst the import duty on foreign-grown woods was exorbitant. The clipper schooner *Mayville*, for example, registering 73 tons and built at Leith in 1847 of foreign oak to class 7 A1, cost £20 per ton, but had she been built abroad, say at Dantzic, the cost would have been some £8 less for the same materials. The mark awarded by such classification societies as Lloyd's Register, fixed the type of timber to be used and therefore the relative cost. In the middle of the century, ships classed at 10 A1 or less had varying amounts of softwood in their construction. Some of Hall's ships, such as the *Friar Tuck*, rated only 8 A1 being built chiefly of larch and cost £13 12s per ton om. Larch was itself light and buoyant but limited the life of a ship. Shortly after this Hall's regretted having stained their reputation by building so many low-classed softwood ships. Their *Robin Hood*, however, classed 13 A1, cost £18 5s per ton om, which was an appreciable increase on the softwood *Friar Tuck*. Expenses in London were higher and Blackwall frigates built of teak on oak frames and fitted for Far Eastern trades came out at from £22 10s to £25 per ton, at 12 A1, such prices including a complete outfit.

Lloyd's Register of British and Foreign Shipping, established in 1834, awarded varying classification marks to the vessels registered on its books. At the beginning of the 1850s, the letter designated the class to which the vessel was assigned. Thus the highest was A which indicated a ship of the 'First Description of the First Class'; Æ indicated a First Class ship of the Second Description; E a Second Class ship; and I a Third Class. Then followed the figures 1 or 2 which described whether the ship was well-found or lacking in that respect. Hence we get the term A1 which all British ships

mentioned in this book possessed when new. The figure preceding the letter indicated the number of years at which the vessel might be classed A1. Naturally the higher the standard of materials used the longer a ship could remain in first class condition, and hence this number gives some indication of the type of timber used in the construction. At first the period of classification ranged from 4 to 12 years but was later extended. To retain her classification mark a vessel had to be surveyed at least once every four years and could be reclassed for a few years when the original period had elapsed. An additional year of classification could also be obtained by building the vessel under a roof.

A saving of timber was tried with diagonally planked ships, in which the frames were placed much further apart and probably were not so massive as in traditional work. The planking was then laid on diagonally in two layers with a longitudinal layer outside. Ships so built did not consume so much timber of large scantling in their construction, while the method of working produced a very strong build, capable of long life, and softwood could be used with greater success, since the seams did not open when hard pressed and allow the tea cargo to become saturated. In extreme cases this might mean digging the choice tea out of the hold with a spade. Alexander Hall's *Vision* was so built, and J & R White later built several such vessels at Cowes, notably the *Solent*.

Economies had been successfully practised over a number of years in ships built for the Navy and the East India Company, by the introduction of iron knees, straps and various small structural members. As the number of iron foundries and rolling mills increased, so did the use of iron in shipbuilding. A rapidly increasing number of iron vessels had been built during the first half of the century and by the beginning of the sixth decade iron ships were no longer looked upon as novelties. Lloyd's had admitted iron ships to A1 classification in 1838, dependent on an annual survey, but without a term of years. In 1854 various periods of years were granted for A1 classification, still subject to annual and special surveys. These rules were altered in 1863 and modified seven years later. There were some 156 iron ships on the Society's books in 1852, of which 98 were steamers and the rest sailing vessels. There were also many iron ships not classed or listed by Lloyd's Register. But they were iron ships by designation of material only. By methods of construction they differed little from their wooden contemporaries.

Due to the fact that only short lengths of iron could be rolled and that the craftsman who worked it had been brought up to handle timber, the structure of an iron ship was built up on the same principle as a wooden one. The keel was a solid iron bar two or more inches thick, while the keelson was often a plate and angle girder secured to the top of the floors which consisted of vertical plates running from bilge to bilge at each frame, with reverse angles at each end. The frames, which were normally spaced at eighteen inches centre to centre, consisted of an angle bar running across the top of the keel and up to the deck. The reverse angles from the top of each floor were carried up the side of these frames, being riveted to them to form a Z-section. At first the plating was of relatively great thickness, but by the 1850s was about ⅞in thick at the garboard strake, that is to say, beside the keel. The decks were usually wood-planked and there were deck beams at every second or third frame. Such a vessel was said to be 'transverse framed' as opposed to some of Brunel's and Scott Russell's 'longitudinal framed' steamers, which were novelties until iron came into more general use in the 1880s. Iron construction, of course, enabled a much larger cargo to be stowed with greater ease while it was especially popular in steamers. It did ensure a very long life with the added advantage of not becoming strained or water-soaked by constant driving. The best-built iron ships cost £18 to £20 per ton with a class of 13 A1 and a full East India outfit. This was at the start of the 1850s, but later in that decade prices of iron ships fell by £4 per ton.

The first iron ship in the tea trade was probably the Liverpool barque *Panic*, launched in 1848 by Cato, Miller & Co, followed in 1852 by the *Vanguard*, which John Reid built at Port Glasgow as a fine-lined carrier. About a dozen such ships visited Chinese waters in the 1850s, but only the *Gauntlet*, *Lord of the Isles* and *Vanguard* were regular traders.

There were a number of reasons why iron ships took such a long time to gain favour, not the least of them being the additional cost for a well-built ship of the highest class, while the question of conservatism cannot be overlooked as it tended to enlarge the disadvantages of this new material. Higher insurance premiums and all-round working costs were certainly a deterrent, as well as the fact that ventilation of ships proceeding through tropical climates was not yet sufficiently perfected to prevent condensation and the deleterious effect it would have on the cargo. In the case of tea, it was said that iron ships 'sweated' their cargoes, but probably only in the early days. Yet it took some years to live down such a reputation.

But perhaps the most important reason why iron took so long to be universally adopted was the fact that there was no really satisfactory anti-fouling preparation available to protect the underwater parts of a ship. This was especially troublesome in Eastern waters, and the immense growth on a hull would seriously affect the length of the homeward passage – a factor of great importance in the tea trade. Constant dry-docking to have the bottom scraped was essential and this became a heavy financial burden. Such preparations as McInnes' patent green copper soap as used in the 1850s and the superior Peacock & Buchan's pink composition used in the next decade and afterwards were by no means as effective as the use of copper sheathing which would remain clean for about ten years, or as long as it was exfoliating. Copper was being replaced in the 1840s by Muntz' metal, or 'yellow metal,' a mixture of copper and zinc, and both cheaper and more effective. There was no difficulty in attaching copper plates to the hull of a wooden ship, but it was an impossibility to so protect an iron hull. One alternative, occasionally adopted in naval vessels, was to completely encase an iron ship with wood planking and then lay on copper plates. But this was a waste of an iron shell. Instead, wood planking took the place of iron plating, and a ship having 'iron frames, wood planked' emerged. This combination of materials has been called 'composite construction'.

An equally important reason for its introduction was the great saving of weight compared with wooden ships. The timbers for wooden vessels of over 150 feet or so in length needed to be very massive and closely spaced, and their replacement with iron frames saved weight and enabled longer and larger ships to be built with greater ease. The increasing difficulties of obtaining timber of sufficient size and strength were also avoided.

The first patent granted for such a construction was to William Watson, Dublin, in 1839, who proposed using iron T-bars as frames, wood planking being secured by rivets or bolts. In that year a composite-built steamer, the 450-ton *Assam* was made in India by Captain Andrew Henderson, but details are lacking regarding her exact construction. A number of patents were applied for on these lines during the 1840s, and builders at Newcastle, Peterhead and probably other centres, launched a few such ships.

The first really scientific approach to the problem was made in 1849 by John Jordan of the Liverpool firm of Jordan & Getty. He proposed laying an iron plate on top of the wood keel and carrying it up both stem and sternpost. Iron frames were bolted to this plate and iron plate stringers were riveted on at the outside to tie them together, while iron plates or 'doublings' were also used to strengthen the wooden deck beams. The planking was butt-jointed over iron plates. Jordan & Getty's first craft on this principle was the schooner *Excelsior* (1850), followed by the barque *Marion MacIntyre* (1851). The latter was probably the first composite ship to trade with China as she carried tea cargoes in 1853 and 1857. Three other ships followed her off the ways – *Tubal Cain* (1851), *George Jordan* (1853) and *Bristow* (1854) – and although French yards at Nantes and Bordeaux built such ships, the system did not immediately gain in popularity. Deck beams, however, and the pillars and knees supporting them were made of iron in numerous vessels during these years, a system which persisted till the end of the 1860s. They gave added strength and capacity and were considered an advantage.

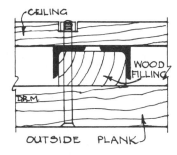

Thomas Bilbe's compound frame for his composite construction. The bolt was driven through without passing through any metal. (*Author*)

85

In 1856, Thomas Bilbe of Rotherhithe devised a system of compound frames. Two iron angles were placed apart, but facing one another, and the area so formed, similar to a broad channel, was filled solid with wood which was bolted to the flanges. Planking was then laid on each side of this compound frame, and bolts passed through the wooden section without having to touch any metal. Had the planking been secured by treenails, the corrosion arising from bilge water coming into contact with iron frames and copper bolting would have been eliminated. This method was advocated in 1863 by James C Richardson, who used either double angles or a T-bar, the inner skin being bolted to the flanges, while the outer was secured to the inner with treenails. The other method was to use galvanised metal screw bolts and to surround the wood through which they passed with waterproof glue or some bituminous substance.

Thomas Bilbe's first composite ship was the *Red Riding Hood* for the China trade. In the same year, 1857, he built the *Gondola*, and in the next the *Lauderdale* for John Willis. Further composite vessels were launched by the yard in the 1850s and 1860s.

The important role played by Alexander Stephen in furthering the progress of composite shipbuilding is told in Chapter Seven.

In trades where speed was not the essential factor, iron ships developed rapidly, but the tea trade still relied on wooden hulls whilst owners and builders were presumably watching the performance of the few composite ships afloat. Then in 1862 and 1863 there was a rush to build such ships.

Composite ships held advantages over both wood and iron craft. Compared with wood-built ships they could stow a relatively larger cargo, due to smaller scantlings, while over the course of years they did not become strained or water-soaked, but possessed the strength of iron hulls which enabled constant hard-driving, without suffering from too much stiffness which prevented speed in strong winds. In light breezes they were as fast as wooden ships and delivered their cargo in excellent condition. They eventually received a high class mark from Lloyd's and could have their class renewed when it elapsed, if they were still sound, which was a great saving to the owner in insurance. Their ability to be yellow-metalled has already been discussed.

But developments in design were no less important than experience with new materials. Hall's *Cairngorm* proved a very fast ship in fresh and strong winds and perhaps, after the *Lord of the Isles*, one of the fastest clippers of the 1850s in reeling off the knots. In the *Robin Hood* Hall had so improved his fast-sailing theory as to produce his fastest and most successful all-round clipper until the advent of *Flying Spur* in 1860. Another advocate of fine midship sections was Charles Scott of Greenock, whose first iron sailing ship, the *Lord of the Isles*, was launched in 1853. The most significant remark made at the time of her launch was that she bore a greater resemblance to a fast screw steamer than to a sailing ship, and on her arrival in Australia at the end of her maiden passage, the *Sydney Morning Herald* said that her model 'surpasses that of the sharpest steamers that have yet been in these seas'. Up till this time all emphasis for the development of fast sailing had been laid on small craft such as the Aberdeen schooners, but here is a reminder that vessels propelled by screws or paddles, regardless of their size, were accustomed to be built on finer lines than large sailing ships. The lines of *Lord of the Isles* are reproduced in this chapter.

She had marked rise of floor with rounded bilges and a long, sharp entrance and run; she was especially fast in a fresh breeze.

The lines of the *Cairnsmore*, which appear in Basil Lubbock's *Last of the Windjammers*, Vol II, show that other builders on the Clyde believed in sharp floors. John Reid & Co were her builders, as they were of *Vanguard*, launched two years earlier, and *Cairnsmore* was a refinement of the latter.

A valuable comparison is afforded by the sharp-floored Aberdeen model as opposed to the more generously moulded Sunderland hull, as recorded in *The Stowage of Ships and their Cargoes* by R W Stevens (on p582 of the 1869 edition). The *Friar Tuck*, 193 feet long and 31 feet broad, registered 662 tons, and the *Kelso* (1855), 145 feet overall and 32 feet broad, 529 tons. The former was almost 50 feet longer yet registered only some 130 tons more, being of a more cut-away design. However, the *Friar Tuck* not only carried less tea than the *Kelso* but required 200 tons more ballast, a disadvantage which the owner could only tolerate so long as high freights were obtainable. On the only passage when they both left at the same time, in 1858, *Kelso* beat the other by four days to London, though she took four days longer down the China Sea. From this it would appear that Hall's ship was better suited to the conditions prevailing in the China Sea than the *Kelso*, though the reverse seems to have been the case after leaving Anjer. Alternatively, there may have been some unrecorded incident in which *Friar Tuck* was damaged in a gale and so lost several precious days. It was in this year that *Cairngorm* and *Lammermuir* had their famous duel, and as they both left Whampoa at the same time as the two mentioned above, they must have experienced the same weather. *Lammermuir* and *Kelso* were both built by William Pile and excelled in the same conditions, while *Cairngorm* and *Friar Tuck* both came from Hall's yard. Yet *Cairngorm*'s master must have been far more energetic than *Friar Tuck*'s and got the last ounce of speed from his ship, since he took one day less than *Lammermuir* on the passage from Macao.

The brothers John and William Pile were responsible together with their father, for introducing the clipper bow to Sunderland. When John, the elder brother, moved to West Hartlepool in 1853, William remained at North Sands. Both produced a number of ships for the tea trade, and J R Kelso over a period of 25 years ordered nearly all his ships from William. The latter was in partnership with Richard Ha between 1861 and 1867 but died in 1873 at the age of fifty His ships were perhaps more celebrated than his brothe John's, though the latter produced flyers like *Mirage* an *Spirit of the Age*. Above the waterline they looked much lik an Aberdeen clipper with forecastle and poop level with th bulwarks, the bowsprit entering the hull on top of the shee or frequently emerging, as it were, from the apex of the ster and the sheer. Underwater, however, it was considered tha a good beam and a clean run could beat the sharp-floore Aberdeen ships, and in certain conditions this proved to b the case.

There is a saying that 'any fool can design the entrance but it takes a genius to design the run'. On the half-breadt plan, the 'run' consists of the underwater body abaft amic ships. A fine run gave an ability to keep moving in a weathers. Many of the British ships had inherited the narro deep hulls produced by the pre-1836 tonnage laws, an although they could go to windward well, could not run s st as some of the Aberdeen ships, produced from 1853 wards, which were not quite so deep.

The cheap cost of materials made Sunderland one of the rgest shipbuilding centres in the country, but no owner of pute would purchase a ship built there unless he had pervised her construction. The fifty-odd builders there in e middle of the century had to make a quick profit or else ake way for someone else, and most of their ships were assed under 10 A1.

Other builders who preferred moderately full midship sec ons without excessive rise of floor were Rennie, Johnson & ankin who built the first *Fiery Cross* with hollow water nes, making her one of the fastest of the early ships though ther deep, and the Greenock firm of Robert Steele whose rst tea clipper was the *Kate Carnie*. This vessel was appar ntly much fuller than some of Steele's later ships although e was by no means slow. William Steele, who was respons le for the designs, had had much experience in producing st-sailing ships and yachts prior to the *Kate Carnie* and he as perhaps more successful with his second tea ship, the *len Rodger*, which was good all round. The firm's third ip, the *Falcon*, was a much finer-lined vessel and was a rerunner of their incomparable masterpieces of the 1860s, hich were the pattern for every ship calling itself a China ipper.

The firm had been in existence at Saltcoates prior to 1786 nder the name of Steele and Carswell. In 1796 they moved Greenock, and in 1816 the firm became Robert Steele & o, under which name it remained until the yard became art of Scott's shipbuilding establishment in 1883. The andsons of the first Robert Steele, Robert and William, ailt the clippers. Their success depended as much on the perb workmanship and excellence of materials over which obert was in charge, as on the design.

All these advances in shipbuilding had been greatly accel ated by the introduction of yet another set of rules for nnage measurement. The 1836 Act had been a step for ard in an attempt to assess more correctly the volume f a ship's hull, and the system of measurement had directly helped to improve sailing qualities. Yet the portunities for partial evasion of the Act had become too eat to be ignored, even though they had led to a revolution design, whilst it was also considered that steamers had an nfair advantage over sail, in that the whole of their engine oom, often a third of the volume of the ship, was deducted om the gross tonnage. So a commission, of which George loorsom was secretary, had been appointed in 1849 to make irther investigations concerning tonnage measurement, nd though its report was not adopted, the system advocated y Moorsom in 1852 which he published in book form, was acorporated into the Merchant Shipping Act two years ter. A description of how to measure a sailing vessel to etermine her tonnage, according to Moorsom's method, ill be found in Appendix VI.

The new system was concerned with internal measure ment, found by computing the areas of a number of trans verse sections below the tonnage deck from which the inter nal volume could be determined. Whereas the 1836 law had given an answer at once in tons, Moorsom's rule gave it in cubic feet and for the sake of convenience there were said to be 100 cubic feet in a ton. The internal volume of all enclosed spaces above deck was also computed and added to the above figure and the total was then described as the gross tonnage. Net or register tonnage was found by the deduction from the gross of certain enclosed spaces. The 1854 rule at first only allowed the space occupied by the propelling power in steamships to be deducted, and thus the gross and net tonnages in sailing vessels remained the same for some years. Any above-deck space occupied by the crew up to one twentieth of the remaining tonnage, as well as any shelter for passengers, was exempted from being included in the gross tonnage total. In 1867 all crew spaces, wherever they were placed, were deducted from the gross tonnage. From time to time other deductions have been added to reduce the net or register tonnage figure, such as master's accommodation, chart house, sail locker, water ballast, etc. There is a third tonnage figure, namely, under deck tonnage, which is the amount of gross tonnage included under the tonnage deck. Most sailing vessels had only two decks of which the topmost was the tonnage deck, so that the under deck tonnage was similar to the internal volume of the hull, calculated as previously described. It will be seen that the under deck tonnage figure more accurately describes the shape of the hull than either the gross or the net. Moorsom's rule is still in use today and has been adopted by all maritime nations, America being the first to do so in 1864.

Naval architects have always made use of the under deck tonnage figure for the calculation of fineness, but they have always had detailed measurements concerning displacement etc to give them an accurate figure. Unfortunately data about most ships of the past is limited merely to under deck tonnage and register dimensions, but nevertheless a relation between these two can be worked out which will give useful information when none else is available. W L A Derby pointed this out in *The Tall Ships Pass* – which contains such a wealth of detail – referring to it as an approximate form of architect's Block Coefficient. The measurements involved, usually taken from the books of the various classification societies, consist of under deck tonnage and register dimen sions. The register dimensions lie between the following points: *length*, from the fore side of the stem to the after side of the sternpost measured along the tonnage deck; *breadth*, extreme outside; *depth*, from the underside of the tonnage deck to the top of the floors or ceiling at half the registered

Diagrams to show differences between 'tonnage length' and 'register length', according to the 1854 Tonnage Law. (*Author*)

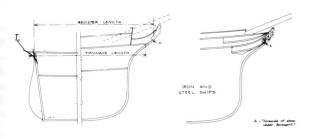

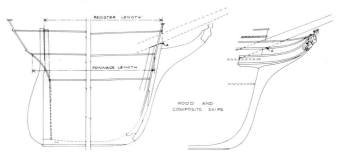

length. There is no objection to using these dimensions, since although the under deck tonnage was not calculated on them, they are so very similar to the tonnage dimensions that any differences are negligible in so approximate a ratio. The tonnage dimensions are: *length*, measured along the tonnage deck but from the inside of the stem to the stern planking; *breadth*, measured internally; *depth*, from a point one-third of the round of the beam (or deck camber) below the tonnage deck to the top of the ceiling at the limber strake. To avoid confusion with the true Block Coefficient of Fineness based on displacement at a given draft, this tonnage ratio has been called the 'Coefficient of Under Deck Tonnage'.

Suppose a model hull is to be carved from a solid piece of wood, the block of wood would be cut down to the smallest size as given by the overall dimensions. Proceeding from this stage, the block is cut away until the correct hull shape appears, a greater amount of wood having to be removed for an extreme clipper or a racing yacht than for a wall-sided carrier. The proportion of wood remaining, when the correct hull shape is obtained, to the complete block before any cutting began, gives a ratio by which any vessel's degree of sharpness can be ascertained. This is the principle behind the naval architect's Block Coefficient of Fineness which is found by dividing the volume of displacement in cubic feet by the product of the moulded length and breadth and the draft. The measurements available in the case of almost all the tea clippers are limited for the most part to register dimensions and tonnages. Yet these can be employed to obtain the rough and very approximate figure already referred to, found by dividing the under deck tonnage in cubic feet (when one ton equals 100 cubic feet) by the product of the register dimensions. The ratio so obtained does not bear comparison in any way with the accepted coefficient of fineness, which always works out at a much lower figure than that given by the 'coefficient of under deck tonnage'. Throughout this book, when ratios of fineness are referred to, they should be taken as being coefficients of under deck tonnage.

The comparison of ratios amongst ships of a similar category is most valuable, as it affords some degree of description where no other information is available. A considerable amount of research has been devoted to this particular subject by Basil Greenhill who has found that a comparison of, say, clipper schooners of under 300 tons with larger sailing vessels, gives very misleading results and that the same objection applies if square-rigged ships are compared with tramp steamers or ocean liners. He has found that a comparison can only be had amongst categories formed by vessels which possess the same relative number of frames amidships off the bevel. This objection only occurs when coefficients of under deck tonnage, not coefficients of fineness, are being compared. A list of ratios possessed by some of the tea clippers is given in Appendix V.

The internal measurement of tonnage now gave designers the chance to develop their ideas freely according to the most approved patterns. No longer were they influenced by the desire to evade the full burden of the law and so force themselves into designing something unnatural. There was no longer any reason for using the Aberdeen bow which had been developed solely to cheat the tonnage laws. But because it had become the trademark of Aberdeen ships and expressed the use of constructional timbers in a very attrac-

tive manner, it was unthinkingly put into ship after ship an persisted in most vessels for some ten years, and in a modifie form until the early 1870s.

Prior to 1854 the influences on British shipbuildin had been mostly native to this Island, due to the peculia tonnage laws in force. American fast-sailing clippers stimu lated rivalry and enthusiasm, but they had little direct effe on the design of British ships. Ships required for speed we ordered chiefly from builders at Aberdeen or possibly fron White of Cowes, who had built several sharp-floored bri and schooners. Firms in these two places had therefore bee able to build up some form of tradition which they could ca upon when commissioned to build a fast-sailing ship. Th influence of Aberdeen gradually extended to all shipbuildin centres, which modified the extreme views held by that po to suit their own requirements.

It will be noticed that the biographies of ships considere in this chapter overlap those in Chapter Four by two year the latter ending in 1854. This was done deliberately so tha all the Aberdeen clippers which fell under the influence o the 1836 Tonnage Law could be considered together, and u to the end of 1851 the few tea clippers built elsewhere whic bore evidence of Aberdeen. But in 1852 comes the earlies known lines plan of a ship designed for the tea trade whic did not carry Aberdeen characteristics, namely the *Cha lenger*, and so this year is a convenient one for commencin further biographies.

BIOGRAPHIES OF SHIPS BUILT 1852–1857

CHALLENGER, 1852

Richard Green of the Blackwall Yard, London, who bui this ship, probably intended her to challenge Americ competition in the China trade which in 1851–52 appeare in the ascendancy. A year later Alexander Hall built th *Cairngorm* on speculation in order to have a completely fre hand at designing his ideal of a tea clipper, but wheth Green did the same thing a year before is not now known. H was strongly patriotic and the ship he built nobly upheld h aspirations and under the command of James Killic achieved an enviable reputation in the tea trade.

Perhaps it was because the *Challenger* was built in Londo where the *Oriental*'s lines were taken off or due to her choic of name that her design is mistakenly imagined to have falle under American influence. Basil Lubbock was unfortunate guilty of stating in *The Blackwall Frigates* that *Challenger* design was based on that of the *Oriental*, but a study of the plans makes it quite obvious that they were quite differen both in dimensions and in hull-form. The entrance and ru of *Challenger* are somewhat concave, but in *Oriental* they ar convex; the bilges are firm and there is little tumblehome i *Challenger*, but in *Oriental* they are slack, there are no wa sides and they tumble home in a continual curve. It may b that the *Challenger*'s hull-form is that of a fast Blackwa frigate or at least that it is a development of one. In appea ance she was probably like the *Anglesey* built in the Black wall Yard the same year which a Lloyd's Register survey wrote was 'of a smart clipper style', or like the *Northfle* which was also built in the same year on the Thames for th China trade.

Captain Andrew Shewan, writing in *Sea Breezes*, refers *Challenger* as 'of a different type from the Aberdeen clipper

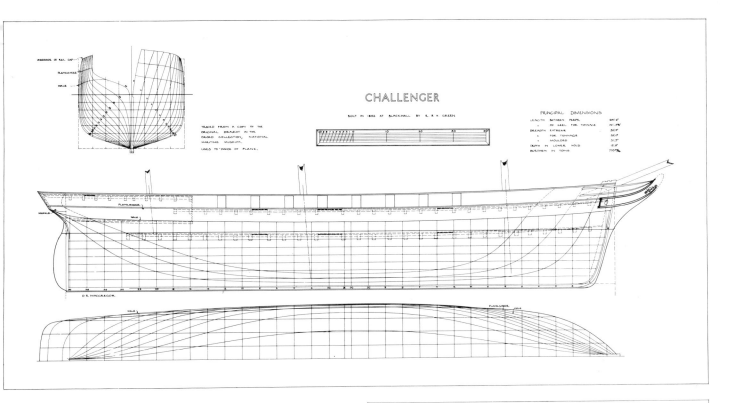

Top: Challenger lines plan. Built in 1852 by Richard Green at the Black-wall Yard, London. Redrawn from a copy of the original plan found in the Croad Collection, National Maritime Museum, Greenwich. Dimensions: 174ft 0in × 32ft 0in × 20ft 0in and 699 tons nm.

Above: Challenger sail plan. Entirely reconstructed. Sources: lines plan for hull and mast positions; *A Treatise on Masting Ships* by John Fincham (3rd edition, 1854) for spar dimensions calculated by his rules; contemporary ship plans and paintings. Spars represented by a single line along their centres.

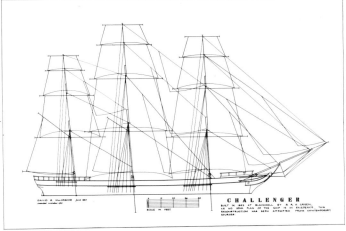

not so sharp forward, more of the "cod's head and mackerel tail" type, and consequently faster in light winds.' She was certainly not of the Aberdeen type, nor yet was she an extreme form of the cod's head and mackerel tail, which consisted of a fairly full entrance contrasted with a very fine run. Her performance was very steady, and when the general average of her passages is examined, it will be seen that she retained a higher level of good runs than almost any other ship in the trade. She also traded exclusively between London and Shanghai for about fifteen years, a most unusual record.

The *Challenger* was launched on 23 December 1851 but as she was completed in 1852, this is given as her year of build. She was of 699 tons nm with dimensions of 174.0ft × 32.0ft × 20.0ft. She had a round stern, no galleries, and a woman bust figurehead. By the 1854 Act, the tonnage was 614 under deck and 650 net and gross. Her first owner was Hugh H Lindsay of London.

The facts concerning her first passage home from China have been exaggerated on a number of occasions. It is true that she took six days longer on the passage to Gravesend than the big American clipper *Challenge*, but as the latter had sailed from Whampoa on 5 August, while the *Challenger* had sailed from Shanghai, there was no suggestion of a race from ports 860 miles apart. The passages must, however, be deemed equal considering the extra distance sailed by the

British ship. In the following year there was no doubt as to the result of the contest, as the *Challenger* beat the American *Nightingale* by two days to Deal, both ships having left Woosung on the same day.

Her best outward time was 101 days in 1856, when she arrived in May. Leaving Woosung on 31 July that same year with a cargo of tea and silk worth £500,000, she went ashore on the South Spit, at the entrance to the Woosung river, and lay on her side for a day and night before she was refloated. Repairs at Shanghai took about one month.

In November 1865, H H Lindsay sold her and Killick, Martin & Co of London acquired 27 shares, her old commander, James Killick, held another 16 shares on his own behalf, and the remaining 21 shares were owned by others. They retained ownership for just over three years until William Stewart of London became her sole owner in December 1868 – but only for four days – and then Grice & Co of London acquired her. In January 1871 her registry was transferred to Melbourne and the same year she was abandoned at sea on 14 May in 48°N 13°W.

Above: Photographed under the Danish flag, the *Carl* was built as the *Vanguard* in 1852 with an iron hull; the bow seems very plain here. (*Jens Malling*)

Top: In ballast on her epic voyage to Norway in 1917; the *Tinto* was then 65 years old. Photograph by her master on that passage, Captain Karl Richarz. (*Harold D Huycke*)

CRYSTAL PALACE, 1852

Probably of clipper build as the new measurement tonnage was so close to the old measurement figure, namely 480 old as against 494 new, she was built at Teignmouth by J B Mansfield for John Lidgett & Co, London. How an order for a tea clipper was secured by this Devon shipyard is not known unless they built her on speculation. She measured 131.0ft × 25.3ft × 17.7ft, being a full-rigged ship classed 11 A1. She was taken to London to be yellow-metalled but her master was a Devon man. Her maiden passage was a fast run of 83 days to Hobart and she distinguished herself in 1858–59 by taking only 92 days between Foochow and New York under the command of Shewan. (It could not have been Andrew Shewan, who left the *Merse* in 1856 for the *Lammermuir*.)

Crystal Palace put into Swatow in September 1857 partially dismasted in a typhoon. She was wrecked in 1862.

JOSEPH FLETCHER, 1852

This was very much a family affair as she was built for Fletcher & Co, London, by Fletcher of Limehouse, London. She measured 132.0ft × 26.3ft (internal) × 18.6ft with tonnages of 621 old and 672 new. She was a full-rigged ship built of wood. She always sailed out to New Zealand and then crossed over to China to load tea; she maintained a good average throughout her life. In 1859, bound from Auckland to Shanghai, she ran ashore on the island of Wukido in the Loochoo Group, China Sea, during the night of 2 November in thick squally weather and was a total loss. Five out of her crew of 29 were lost in escaping to the reef where they were kindly treated by the locals; they were later picked up by the *Kate Cleather* on passage from Hong Kong to Shanghai.

TINTO, 1852

The qualifications for this ship as regards clipper status are unknown, but she is included because of her final curious voyage.

She was a full-rigged ship carrying skysails on each mast and was built at Liverpool by J Steel Jnr for himself. She measured 137.8ft × 26.8ft × 18.0ft, 466 old tons and 480 new tons and several passages from China have been found for her. In 1870 McCubbin of Liverpool acquired her and she was reduced to a barque the following year. In 1882 J Martin of Liverpool became owner. From 1884 she was owned abroad, first in China and after 1886 in Valparaiso with various changes of ownership. In 1917 the owner is listed as C Oelckers of Calbuco, Chile.

In that year 28 German sailors from various ships interned in Chilean waters because of the War bought her and, under the Chilean flag, sailed her safely around the Horn to Trondheim, Norway. This was quite a feat for an old water-soaked wooden ship that had been neglected for years. Enquiries were made concerning her fate, and a letter sent to me from the Port Office at Trondheim, dated February 1949, states in part:

> After the German seamen arrived in Trondheim . . . she was sold to a Salt Company and was rigged down to a barge. The barge was later towed to Fosen in the Norwegian skerries where she was used for years as a mooring-ship for fishing boats . . . After the Salt Company ceased to exist, what happened to the barge afterwards is not known.

VANGUARD, 1852

Judging by a half-model in the Glasgow Museum and Art Gallery, this iron full-rigged ship was no finer than a medium clipper and it was obviously hoped to find a good compromise in her hull-form between carrying capacity and a reasonable turn of speed, which is what many builders and owners wanted to achieve. She was built at Port Glasgow by John Reid & Co and constructed of iron for Nicholson & McGill of Liverpool, although the latter's name appears as either Nicholson or McGill in the Registers before 1878. The *Vanguard* measured 171.0ft × 26.8ft × 19.4ft, 643 old tons and 687 new tons; she had two decks and four bulkheads.

In 1874 she was given much new iron plating and received a new foremast, new bowsprit and a general overhaul at a cost of £4500. Most of her voyages were to India and the East, but after 1881 when she was sold to J Boumphrey & Co, Liverpool, she started trading with South America as did many ex-China traders. She was then reduced to barque rig. Three years later she was sold to J Wallis & Sons, Barth, Germany and renamed *Carl*, and in 1897 sailed from Wilmington, North Carolina, to Stettin in 49 days. In 1904 P Poulsen of Veile, Denmark, became owner and she was renamed *Anna*, and the tonnage was given as 605 gross. Four years later she stranded on 18 July on the Parapato bar, in Mozambique Bay, and sank. At the time she was bound for Punta Delgade in the Azores with 750 tons of mangrove bark; the ship was valued at Kr25,000.

AEROLITE, 1853

Many China traders were built at Workington and this ship was one of the fastest, and though no plans or model are known of her, the large reduction of new measurement tonnage compared with the old – 911 as against 1160 – suggests a fairly fine hull-form. Her builder, Charles Lamport, also constructed the *Scawfell* which made a record run of 85 days from Macao to Liverpool. The *Aerolite* measured 183.6ft × 36.5ft × 20.0ft which made her a fairly beamy full-rigged ship. To increase her longitudinal strength there were two sister keelsons, and 10in × 4in diagonal wood trussing in the 'tween decks instead of the ceiling. The fore and main lower masts were formed of iron plates, and she had a poop and topgallant forecastle.

She was employed in the Australian trade at first but in the 1860s was in the China and India trades. John Atkin & Co, Liverpool, owned her throughout her life; her end is not known, but she was dropped from *Lloyd's Register* in 1872. Edward Alleyne who became her master in 1860 has previously commanded the *Cambalu* from 1852 to 1856; she was also owned by Atkin and built by Lamport a year before the *Aerolite*.

CREST OF THE WAVE, 1853

An extreme clipper, built by William Pile, Sunderland, of white oak, for Brice, Friend & Co, Liverpool, she measured at the time of her launch 180.0ft × 32.1ft × 20.8ft, 924 old and 856 new tons. She was a very sharp vessel and her coefficient of under deck tonnage was as low as 0.56; *Spray of the Ocean*, built the following year, was probably equally sharp. *Crest of the Wave* set three skysails, had a long projecting bow and a half-round poop. She could carry 920,000lbs of tea. In 1854 on her maiden voyage, she ran out to Melbourne in 73 days.

In 1867 she was sold to Wright Bros, London, and to Bullard, King & Co ten years later. E T Stromberg, Gothenburg, bought her in 1881 and renamed her *Gurli*. Several owners at this port had her during the next ten years, after which she went to T G Tarabochia, Trieste, Austria, who changed her name to *Tomaso T*. She never sailed for him since she was condemned in September 1892.

GAUNTLET, 1853

In spite of the fact that iron ships were still something of a novelty in the tea trade, the year 1853 saw two such ships of the first rank built for it. *Gauntlet* was one and *Lord of the Isles* was the other.

Below: J R Isaac's lithograph of *Crest of the Wave* produces a rather 'wooden' effect. The topsails only carry two rows of reef points each. *(Parker Gallery)*

Opposite: Built seven years after *Lord of the Isles* and by the same yard, the *Horsa* must have had similarities with the clipper. In this picture she is ashore in the Scilly Isles but was towed off. *(James Gibson)*

Bottom: The iron-hulled *Gauntlet* seems devoid of sheer. She appears to have a long Aberdeen house aft and another big deckhouse through which the foremast passes. Another of Weedon's engravings. *(MacGregor Collection)*

"THE GAUNTLET" CLIPPER SHIP.

Denny & Rankin, Dumbarton, were responsible for the *Gauntlet*, which was designed by William Rennie, and they fitted her out for the Australian passenger trade in a very sumptuous manner. Great care was taken with her building, and her frames and plating were of extra thickness. The hull was divided by five watertight iron bulkheads and a fire engine was also provided. Her stern was elliptical yet had quarter-galleries, and her rakish bow terminated in only a scroll fiddlehead. She had a raised quarterdeck through which the roof of the main saloon projected. The saloon was 15ft wide with a coved ceiling, and gilded pilasters divided the walls into panels which were filled with medallion views, while the seats were of crimson velvet. Shower and 'plunging' baths and an ice house were also carried. Her measurements were 189.5ft × 29.8ft × 19.1ft, 784 old and 693 new tons.

James Smith, Liverpool, was her first owner, and under Captain W Inglis, later master of the *Hero* and the *Black Prince*, she traded out to the East. But her maiden passage took her out to Melbourne at the height of the gold rush with a passage of 90 days from Liverpool, which was rather long for such a clipper. She left for Bombay in January 1854 and loaded her first cargo of tea at Whampoa the same year. In 1856, homeward-bound from Whampoa, she ran down to Anjer in only six days, 23 to 29 October. Four years later she took coolies to Demerara. Although a sharp ship, with a rise of floor of 3ft 9in and a coefficient of under deck tonnage of 0.58, Inglis did not really let her show her paces.

In 1874, Taylor, Bethel & Roberts, London, bought her, and then J W Harper in 1880. Five years later he sold her to C Poulsen & Co, Elsfleth, Germany, who renamed her *Argo*. She was wrecked two years afterwards.

LORD OF THE ISLES, 1853

The fineness of her lines were not only favourably compared with those of a fast screw steamer, but it was also said in 1855 that she was 'the finest [vessel] ever seen at Shanghai – unmatched for symmetry of form and beauty of model.' Built by Charles Scott & Co of Greenock as their first iron ship, she was luxuriously fitted up to carry passengers in two large deckhouses and in the 'tween decks if necessary, since these were fitted with portholes throughout their length, and she was equipped with such things as shower baths and expensive furnishings. The crew lived in the forecastle and the after-guard under the poop. She had practically no sheer, a heavy counter, but a graceful stem surmounted by a figure-head of a Scots lord. She had several new labour-saving devices such as friction rollers in the sheaves of her large blocks, small winches worked by a hand-spike lever to hoist topsails and work the main braces, and the helm worked by a double screw which took up the sudden pull of the rudder. She carried a main skysail. Her dimensions were 185ft length of keel, 210ft overall, 27.8ft beam, 18.5ft depth of hold. She registered 770 old and 691 new tons. Maxton & Co, Greenock, were her owners until she was lost by spontaneous combustion on 24 July 1862, in 115°E 12°N, bound for Hong Kong. Captain Davies reached Macao in the boats with his crew and passengers numbering 30 all told.

On her maiden passage out to Sydney in 1853–54, the times were as follows:

Left Greenock	12 November
Passed Tuskar Light	19 November
Off Madeira	26 November
Crossed the Line in 28°30'W	11 December
Crossed Cape of Good Hope Meridian	2 January
Passed Cape Otway Light	26 January
Passed Kent Group Lighthouse	30 January
Arrived Sydney Harbour (7 pm)	1 February

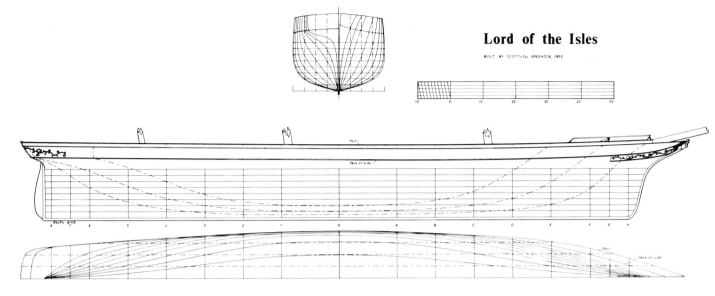

Lord of the Isles

BUILT BY SCOTT+Co, GREENOCK, 1853

Left: Close-hauled on the starboard tack, the large size of the staysails s
on *Lord of the Isles* can be seen. (*Alexander Turnbull Library*)

Right: The *Northfleet* in the Thames off Gravesend in 1872. Doub
topsails had replaced single ones by this time. (*Nautical Photo Agency*

Above: Lord of the Isles lines plan. Drawn by Ralph Bird from pla
published as Plate IV in *Theory and Practice of Ship-Building* by Andre
Murray (1861). Built in 1853 by Charles Scott & Co, Greenock, with
dimensions: 185ft keel, 210ft overall, 27.8ft beam, 18.5ft depth of hold
691 tons nm, 770 tons om. Reconstruction: re-plotting waterlines t
ensure they conformed to sections in body plan; omitting some stations fo
greater clarity in reproduction.

The time works out as 74 days from the Tuskar Light near
Liverpool to Sydney, and 68 days from the same point to
Cape Otway Light near Melbourne. Numerous erroneous
times of much shorter duration were cited at the time. As
regards speed through the water, a passenger wrote to the
Sydney Morning Herald of 2 February 1854: 'In a strong breeze
the rate attained has been as high as 18 knots per hour.
Several days' runs reached from 360 to 400 miles, and in one
day the distance sailed, with only a few hours of maximum
speed, was 428 miles.' She carried 17 passengers and 1240
tons of cargo.

The return passage from Sydney to London occupied 98
days, 21 March to 27 June 1854. Her second voyage was
again made to Australia with a passage to Adelaide from
Southampton of 94 days, 30 August to 2 December 1854
with 308 Government emigrants. Then she crossed over to
Shanghai in 50 days and returned direct to London with tea
in 96 days, 24 March to 28 June 1855, one of the fastest
passages made up to that date by a British ship.

In that autumn she sailed from Land's End to Hong Kong
in 98 days against the monsoon, 19 October to 25 January
1856, or 97 days land to land and 103 from Portsmouth.
Three years later she was 97 days between the Downs and her
Yangtze pilot, 22 April to 28 July 1858. But her best China
passage was made in 1858–59 when, loaded with 1030 tons
of tea, she sailed from Shanghai on 29 November, lost sight
of the coast the next day, passed the Lizard 25 February and

reached London two days later, 90 days out or 87 days land t
land. She was said to have averaged 320 miles for fiv
consecutive days whilst crossing the Indian Ocean. In 187
the *Hallowe'en* took 91 days between Shanghai and Londo
or 89 days to Start Point, and these two passages, irrespectiv
of season, appear to be the fastest made by British ship
between these two points.

Of American ships sailing from Shanghai, the *Golde*
Gate took 89 days to Beachy Head in 1854–55, 25 Novembe
to 23 February, and presumably reached London in 90 day:
This time includes three or four days' detention at Batavia t
repair minor collision damage. The *Nightingale* took 91 day
to Beachy Head in the spring of 1855.

Between Shanghai and Liverpool the record is probabl
held by the Sunderland-built ship *Zingra* which in 1863–6
took only 85 days, 26 December to 20 March, while th
American *Nonpareil* took 87 days, 19 December to 1
March, sailing at the same time.

The fast passages of the clippers of the 1850s have ofte
been dismissed as merely due to the influence of favourabl
monsoons. This is partly correct; yet passages like the abov
were still a rare experience in the life of the later clippers.

NORTHFLEET, 1853

The Blackwall frigates have become almost legendary an
their course of development is apt to be forgotten. Though

utward appearance they seemed antique yet their hull-form ollowed the fashion of fine lines from the 1850s onwards. ike the ill-fated *Dunbar* they probably had a slight rise of oor with a shortish entrance embodying some hollow near he stem but a longer, finer run. A few were diverted to ustralia during the gold rush fever in the earlier 1850s and ome occasionally visited China, but *Northfleet* was the only gular trader there.

Built on the Thames by William Pitcher at the place to hich she owed her name, *Northfleet* bore all the resemb- nces of a true Blackwall frigate with her heavy appearance oove the waterline and her quarter-galleries, which con- ined windows for her stern cabins, two of which were 11ft quare. A large crowd watched her launch on Saturday 25 ne 1853 although it was marred by a man being killed at it. he was described as having an entrance 'as sharp as a knife', nd perhaps her hull-form generally matched this as she ade many fast passages. That she was especially built for e China trade is evidenced by the fact that her first owners ere Dent & Co, London, the well-known China mer- hants, who sold her to Duncan Dunbar at the end of her rst China voyage. She had spacious 'tween deck accommo- ation and was normally employed to take out troops and ring home invalids and tea. She measured 896 old and 951 ew tons on dimensions of 180.0ft × 32.3ft × 20.9ft, with a 0ft poop, being classed 14 A1.

On her maiden voyage in 1853 she went out to Welling- n in 87 days, crossed over to Hong Kong, and from there

went to San Francisco in 41 days, returning to Shanghai in 48. She finally reached home 97 days out from Shanghai in the spring of 1855. After spending from 19 March to 1 January 1856 as a Crimean transport engaged at 18s per ton per month, she returned to the China trade for the next twelve years or so. She frequently brought home, say, 120 naval invalids and 650 tons of tea.

She has been credited in the past with a remarkable run of 82 days, Hong Kong to London, in 1857. A careful examina- tion of all shipping reports shows that she actually left Hong Kong on 6 August in tow of the SS *Tribune*, which was to take her to the coast of Luconia to shorten her passage down the China Sea. She made sail two days later and from there took 117 days to Plymouth which was reached on 3 December. But she did make three fine outward passages: 1856, London to Hong Kong, 18 March to 20 June, 94 days. 1857, London to Hong Kong, 26 February to 31 May, 96 days. 88 days from Start Point. 1858, London to Hong Kong, 15 February to 27 May, 101 days. 89 days from Start Point.

In the last two years she probably called at Portsmouth.

Benjamin Freeman, her commander, bought her in 1863 on the death of Dunbar and sold her five years later to A Pearson. The next year she went to J Patton Jnr, London, and in 1873 was run down and sunk on 22 January off Dungeness, by the SS *Murillo*. She had a large number of emigrants on board, and the total loss of life amounted to 293.

POLMAISE, 1853

A full-rigged ship built at Dundee by Alexander Stephen & Sons for Campbell & Murray, Glasgow, she measured 178.9ft × 32.2ft × 21.2ft, 878 old and 887 new tons, and classed 14 A1, being designed to carry troops. Up to 1859 she had only twice gone to China, trading out to Australia and India and had once run from Port Phillip Heads to Point de Galle in 37 days. An advertisement in *The Times* in February 1862 claimed a day's run of 304 miles on the previous voyage.

John Brodie, London, bought her in 1872 and the following year she was wrecked on 4 February near Rockhampton, Queensland.

PRIDE OF THE OCEAN, 1853

Although built in the United States of America this clipper was sold to British owners the year after she was built and so it seems more logical to consider her amongst other British ships.

Launched under the name of *Pride of America* from the yard of Patten & Sturdevant in Richmond, Maine, for themselves, she had measurements of 213.0ft × 38.0ft × 22.0ft and 1826 tons, or 1282 tons by British measurement, and she was a full-rigged ship. C Gumm of London acquired her in March 1854 and renamed her *Pride of the Ocean*.

It was in 1857 under the command of John Kyle that she sailed from London to Hong Kong in 89 days, 11 May to 8 August. An advertisement in *The Times* on 1 November 1859 included this statement about her: 'Just returned from Bombay in 64 days, and made her last passage to Hong Kong in 79 days.' The latter time presumably refers to the passage made out in 1857. A correspondent to *The Times* claimed

outward time as 69 days from Land's End, but there seems
way of verifying either of the two claims.

I have no particulars of any passage she made homewards
om China, although she often visited Hong Kong. In 1858
e sailed from Manila to Deal in 126 days, 2 April to 6
ugust.

In 1871 she was sold to French owners and renamed *Leone*
Bordeaux but was re-sold to London owners the same year,
verting to her previous name. In 1879 she was condemned,
it was repaired and acquired by owners in Gibraltar; and
ur years later she foundered by stranding on 11 January on
e Shipwash Sand in the North Sea, bound from Hamburg
New York with empty casks.

PIRIT OF THE NORTH, 1853

Sunderland clipper barque, built by John Pile for T A
ibb, London, who the following year ordered *Spirit of the
ge*, she measured 169.0ft × 30.0ft × 18.5ft, and 671 tons.
he was described as having only one deck, with a half-poop
d topgallant forecastle. Her bow was decorated with a
roll figurehead and her stern was elliptical. She usually had
crew of twenty-seven. Classed 10 A1, she was quite a fast
ssel, although all her homeward passages were made dur-
g the favourable monsoon. She had her share of accidents
r she was dismasted in a typhoon in 1856, while in 1861

pposite, top: A model of *Polmaise*, presumably contemporary, but the
curacy of the hull lines is not known. *(Merseyside County Museums)*

pposite, bottom: *Polmaise* in the river Thames in 1872 when cut down to a
rque. *(Nautical Photo Agency)*

low: The large wooden Canadian clipper *Star of the East* hove-to, from a
inting by Samuel Walters. *(Gracie, Beazley & Co)*

she stranded on a reef homeward-bound and had to put into
Singapore to discharge and repair.

Baines & Co, Liverpool, bought her in 1863 and sold her
five years later to G Maule. In 1873, H P Samuelson,
Norway, purchased her and renamed her *Panama*. She went
out of the Register in 1883.

STAR OF THE EAST, 1853

She was another large softwood clipper which immediately
came under British ownership, having been constructed by
W & R Wright at St John, New Brunswick, with measurements of 206ft 0in keel, 237ft 0in overall, 40ft 10in breadth
and 22ft 0in depth of hold; tonnage was 1219. She had an
elliptical stern. A comment on her design is to be found in
the C W Kellock papers in the Liverpool Museum, where a
contract with James Smith & Son of St John regarding the
ship *Queen of the Seas* states: '. . . it is also guaranteed by the
seller that this ship will have a longer floor and not such
sharp ends as the *Star of the East* or the *Guiding Star*.' (Vol III,
369, 9 Jan 1853).

Being built at the height of the Australian gold rush, she
was obviously built on speculation and sent over to Liverpool
to find a buyer, which was a common practice by Canadian
yards. On this occasion, James Beazley bought her at once
for £16,000, and lavishly fitted her out for carrying passengers at a cost of a further £6681.

On her first voyage she sailed out to Melbourne in 78 days
from Liverpool, 7 July to 23 September 1853, and was off
Port Phillip Heads when 75½ days but had to anchor as she
could not get a pilot. During the passage she made 1000
miles in three days on more than one occasion, according to
the *Sydney Morning Herald*, and often made 15 knots. After
only a week's detention she went on to Sydney and crossed
over to Shanghai where she loaded for Liverpool, returning

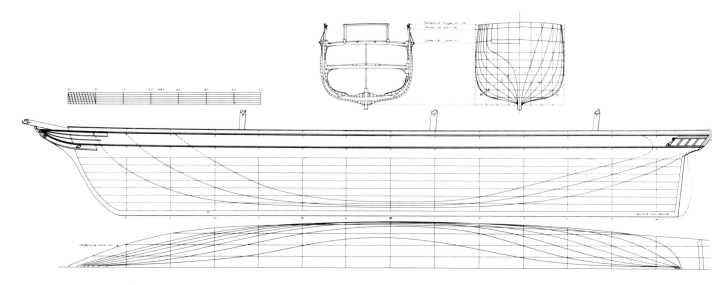

in 107 days during the favourable monsoon or 104 days from Woosung. She cleared a profit of £8018.

On her second voyage, the pattern was repeated, the outward passage to Melbourne occupying 77 days from Liverpool in 1854, 6 July to 21 September, during which she ran at 17½ knots on one occasion. She was 34 days between Melbourne and Hong Kong late in the year, and then going up to Shanghai she was 105 days to London. Profits on this voyage were given as £8920, according to Basil Lubbock in *The Colonial Clippers*. Other passages to Australia, India and China followed. In 1861 she left Bombay on 11 January for Liverpool, but stranded on a rock 30 miles west of Cape Infanta on the South African coast. However she was floated off only to be wrecked on 12 April the same year in Storring Bay, South Africa, close to where another of Beazley's ships, the *Miles Barton*, had been wrecked only a matter of two months earlier.

ANNANDALE, 1854
This ship was remarkable for her great length in relation to breadth with dimensions of 226.9ft × 28.5ft (inside) × 18.5ft by the 1836 Tonnage Act. The maximum external breadth was 31.8ft which yields a ratio of 7.13 beams to length. Tonnage was 1131 om and 759 nm, a clear indication of extremely fine lines. Although she did not have much deadrise or tumblehome, the entrance and run were very long with considerable hollow, all of which produced one of the most extreme hull-forms to be found in a British clipper. The firm of John Nicholson & Co, Annan, Dumfriesshire, both built and owned her, the design being made by Benjamin Nicholson, one of the partners, then aged twenty. Thus he was able to produce a design unhindered by an owner's strictures. A list of other long narrow ships is given in the biography of the *Queensberry* (1856).

At the start of the *Annandale's* maiden voyage from Liverpool in 1854, she had to put back twice with the loss of her topmasts, the reason for which was not stated in the shipping reports. Then she went out to Bombay in 83 days, her biggest day's run being 381 miles and her maximum speed 18 knots. She returned home to Liverpool in 98 days. In January 1856 she began a long voyage which took her first out to Melbourne in 80 days, and thence to various Eastern ports and home via Bombay. It was on this voyage that she sailed from Singapore to Hong Kong in only 7 days, 6 to 13 September

1856. She brought her only cargo of tea home for Nicholso in 1859–60, taking 117 days to Plymouth, where she put disabled. The master had died 14 days earlier.

Nicholson's sold the ship in September 1860 to Stuart Douglas of Liverpool for £5287. Two years later Isaac Wilso of Liverpool bought her; in 1863 M G Klingender purchas her and then she went to Wigg & Haig in 1865. The san year she went ashore on 5 December at Key West, USA, a was condemned the following March.

ASSYRIAN, 1854
Launched in November by Walter Hood of Aberdeen fo Alexander Nicol of the same port, she proved to be a spee vessel, spending her first fifteen years trading solely wit China. She measured 156.1ft × 28.5ft × 18.5ft, 605 old ar 555 new tons, being ship-rigged.

Her passages out and home were very consistent, but sh usually sailed both ways with the fair monsoon averagir something like 114 days in each direction. In 1863 she wei to Shanghai in 93 days from the Downs, 4 February to 8 Ma and three years later arrived off Falmouth on 3 April, 96 da out from Foochow.

J T Rennie, Aberdeen, purchased her in 1871 and place her in the Algoa Bay trade. Six years later she was con demned in October on arrival home with guano from th Lacepede Islands, after springing a leak.

INVINCIBLE, 1854
She was built under special survey at Workington in the ya of Peile, Scott & Co for whom Jonathan T Fell was th manager, and was owned by Bushby & Co of the same po She measured 174.0ft × 30.6ft × 20.0ft with tonnages 764 old and 718 new and classed 13 A1. The Lloyd's Regist surveyor reported that 'the vessel is flush, having merely raised quarterdeck'. Her coefficient of under deck tonna was 0.60, similar to *Sir Lancelot*.

Her first voyage was out to Calcutta and back to Liverpo in 7 months 3 days in 1854. On her second voyage she we out to Calcutta in 87 days with 1000 tons of cargo; then sh loaded rice and opium for Hong Kong which she reached c 19 May 1855, but two days earlier she was almost on h beam ends for four hours in a typhoon. Four-and-a-ha months later, she left Shanghai on 8 October with a cargo tea and silk worth £193,750 but when 90 miles south-east

above: The *Invincible* must be experimenting with Cunningham's roller-reefing topsail gear, because it is only fitted to the main topsail, the fore and mizen having conventional reef points.

opposite: *Annandale* lines plan. Built of wood in 1854 by Benjamin Nicholson at Annan. Lines taken off builder's half-model in possession of B E Nicholson. Lines drawn to inside of plank. Dimensions by 1836 Act: 126.9ft × 28.5ft (inside) × 18.5ft; maximum outside breadth 31.8ft; tonnages 759 nm and 1131 om. Reconstruction: Head, trailboards, cutwater, mast positions and quarter galleries from paintings of the *Queensferry*; midship section from drawing in *Lloyd's Register* survey report.

Hong Kong – another account says 10 miles – she collided on 5 October with the *A Cheeseborough**, and although not much damaged got back to Hong Kong with 11ft of water in the hold. Most of the tea was ruined although the silk was almost undamaged. After repairs were made, she finally got away on 21 January 1856 and reached London 99 days later. Her first master was George Graham who had come from the *Mary Sparks*, also owned by Bushby.

In 1875, John Gibson, of London, became her owner at which date her tonnage was given as 626 net and 646 under deck. Two years later, still rigged as a ship, she was acquired by J C & R Porrett, Sunderland. In 1884 she was wrecked on 2 October on Caicos Bank, Turks Island, in the West Indies, when bound from Haiti to Rotterdam with a crew of fifteen. By this time her rig had been altered to that of a barque.

* not listed in *Lloyd's Register*.

SPIRIT OF THE AGE, 1854

When many full-rigged ships registered little more than 300 tons it was unusual to find a vessel of over 700 tons rigged as a barque from the time of her launch. Yet this was the case with John Pile's beautifully-named clipper *Spirit of the Age*. T G Dutton's lithograph shows a finely-proportioned hull with a bowsprit growing from the head of the stem which was curved much like an Aberdeen bow. T A Gibb, London, owned her, and she was probably built on more extreme lines than his other 'Spirit', *Spirit of the North*. Classed 10 A1 of

wood, dimensions of 173.0ft × 32.0ft × 18.5ft gave tonnages of 878 old and 737 new. She could carry 880,800lbs of tea.

There is a story that she once went to Sydney in 73 days, but the only occasion on which she deviated from the China trade was on her maiden passage when she took 91 days between London and Sydney, 11 April to 11 July. In 1857 her anchor fouled the Calais to Ostend submarine cable, but her master was exonerated from all blame.

In 1859, bound for Shanghai, she passed through Sunda Strait leaking badly, and was towed into Batavia making 10 inches of water per hour. She was condemned there on 24 September.

Perhaps this leak had developed as a result of the damage she suffered in April of that year when HM steam tug *African* collided with her in the Thames. She had been dry-docked at Fletcher, Son & Fearnall's yard and was inspected there by Mr J Brown, foreman of the Deptford Dockyard. He reported to the master shipwright at the Dockyard that the following repairs were needed:

> replace sprung bowsprit with new; repair broken figurehead; repair broken jibboom; repair broken rails on bows; caulk wood ends; remove deck; fit new canvas coatings to bowsprit; leather on bowsprit cap; new paintwork. Cost of timber £89 13s 6d; cost of ironwork £10 2s 6d; cost of labour £16 15s.

The work was completed by 19 April and the old bowsprit was valued at £5 13s. She sailed from London for Shanghai on 12 May 1859.

SPIRIT OF THE DEEP, 1854

This evocatively-named ship was constructed at Sunderland by J T Alcock for D MacDonald of Liverpool with tonnages of 785 old and 733 new measurement. Her dimensions were 173.5ft × 31.0ft × 20.0ft and she classed 13 A1. In 1861 she left Shanghai on 23 October on the same day as the *Solent*, *Wellington* and *Mallard*, and beat them all on the passage home to London. In 1867 she was wrecked in June on a reef off Achen Head on the north-west corner of Sumatra, having sailed from Penang on 25 May for London.

Top: In this lithograph, Thomas G Dutton has achieved a great sense of activity, and the barque *Spirit of the Age* is really alive. (*MacGregor Collection*)

Above: The *Wynaud* when rigged as a barque, but still carrying singl topsails. There are long spars resting on top of the forward deckhouse there is a second abaft the mainmast. (*National Maritime Museum*)

SPRAY OF THE OCEAN, 1854

A wood ship built by William Pile at Sunderland for Brice, Friend & Co, Liverpool, owners of *Crest of the Wave*, she measured 181.0ft × 33.6ft × 20.5ft, 996 old and 908 new tons. She carried a battery of six guns, and was built of white oak to class 13 A1. She may have had a flush deck.

On her maiden passage she ran out to Melbourne from Liverpool in 86 days, 26 September to 21 December 1854. In 1859 she went out to Auckland in 86 days, and it was claimed that on one occasion she ran at 17 knots under close-reefed topsails.

Thomas and John Gourlay, Glasgow, bought her in 1868, only to sell her three years later to be broken up at Rio de Janeiro.

WYNAUD, 1854

This vessel was originally intended for the opium trade and was fitted out more like a yacht than a merchantman, being built to the order of Dent & Co, the well-known Eastern merchants, by Bilbe and Perry, Rotherhithe, who launched her as a wood full-rigged ship, very lofty and with an unusually long, hollow bow. She was found to be slightly tender and needed careful handling, but was withal a speedy ship. Most China ships carried a small armament including signal guns with which to frighten off piratical craft: the *Wynaud* mounted six 9-pounder carronades and also carried a trained gunner. Alexander Remington of London is registered as her owner until 1855, when she became the property of Dent & Co, Hong Kong. A G Robinson, London, bought her three years later. Dimensions of 150.0ft × 29.0ft × 17.9ft gave her tonnages of 596 old and 546 new.

Her maiden passage was one of 93 days out to Adelaide from London, 29 August to 30 November 1854. In January she cleared for Shanghai but I have not traced her passage home to England. Her second voyage again started outwards to Adelaide and again she crossed over to China, loading at Foochow for Cowes, an unlikely destination for any commercial sailing ship. Her arrival date has not been traced, and only the month of her departure from Foochow on her third homeward run could be found.

She never made a passage with a cargo of opium but carried tea from China until the beginning of 1863, when she passed into the hands of W H Tindall who placed her in the Ceylon trade in which she averaged about 110 days on the passage home. Details of her first two tea-laden passages were only partially reported at the time, but both were made between Foochow and Cowes in 1855 and 1856. C P Jones bought her in 1870, and James Alexander was registered as her owner at the end of the following year. She was wrecked on the east coast of Tasmania on 16 February 1874.

BEEMAH, 1855

This full-rigged ship was built of wood under a roof by Alexander Stephen & Son at Dundee for Willis, Marwood & Co of Liverpool. She measured 189.0ft × 33.6ft × 21.1ft, 1021 old and 887 new tons, and this big difference between the two tonnages suggests a fine-lined hull; also the coefficient of under deck tons was 0.58, the same as *Thermopylae*. Stephen's had another shipyard at Glasgow which was managed by Alexander, the second eldest son, but William, the eldest son, and his father, Alexander, ran the Dundee yard. Alexander Jnr got the Glasgow yard transferred to him in 1858.

Beemah had a fairly consistent record as to passages, and her fastest homeward run was one of 98 days from Shanghai to Deal in 1864–65. An advertisement in *The Times* of November 1861 claimed the following fast passages for her: England to Java Head [*ie* Anjer] in 69 days; England to Hong Kong in 89 days; Foochow to St Helena in 56 days. No dates, needless to say, were given although the last one was probably made in 1858–59, as she sailed from St Helena on 26 February 1859, 58 days after leaving Foochow.

In 1880 she was bought by the British India Steam Navigation Co of Glasgow and was surveyed at Hong Kong. Perhaps she was used as a hulk there. She dropped out of the Register in 1886.

FIERY CROSS, 1855

Two ships which successively bore the name *Fiery Cross* and were designed by the same man, rank amongst some of the fastest ships seen in the trade between 1856 and 1865.

The first ship to carry this name was one of the last vessels to be built by the Liverpool firm of Rennie, Johnson & Rankin, to the design of William Rennie, with measurements of 174.0ft (keel and rake of stem) × 31.0ft × 19.1ft and tonnages of 788 old measurement and 686 new. Unfortunately Rennie's went bankrupt in January 1855 and his yard at Brunswick Dock was taken over by Thomas Vernon. As the *Fiery Cross* was not launched until 31 July, she was completed by either Vernon or some other builder, perhaps Chaloner, who is the builder named by Basil Lubbock. The *Liverpool Chronicle* of 4 August 1855 says that John Campbell of Glasgow purchased her, which implies that she was either built on speculation or that her contract was cancelled following the firm's failure.

The *Liverpool Albion* of 8 April 1856 wrote that her

> frame is of British oak, and she is planked with teak and greenheart, and copper-bolted throughout. In both decks there are horizontal iron knees, and a hanging knee to every beam in upper and lower hold, the latter of which have two bolts in short floor heads. She has staple knees abreast of the rigging, which is of galvanised wire throughout, which gives her a very light appearance. The lines of this magnificent vessel are by Mr Rennie, of Liverpool, celebrated as the finest marine draughtsman in England.

Her lines, which appear in *The China Clippers* by Basil Lubbock, show a vessel with much less deadrise than the Aberdeen ships and with hollows in her lowest three waterlines, both fore and aft. It should be noted that a vertical stem tended to give a hollow entrance in fine-lined ships. The stern is rather undeveloped, square and heavy with a 'half-round' poop, and there is practically no tumblehome. The bows flare outwards considerably to support a very broad forecastle head.

On her maiden passage under Captain John Dallas she went from Liverpool to Melbourne in 81 days, 9 October to 29 December 1855, with 1200 tons of cargo, and because she was so deeply laden and was detained within 100 miles of her destination for 10 days, it was said at the time that she had made one of the best runs out of the season. The Melbourne *Argus* called her 'a smart and race-horsey looking ship'. Her best day's work on this passage was one of 316 miles and on six consecutive days she averaged 255 miles.

From Melbourne she took only 33 days to off Point de Galle, Ceylon, 27 January to 29 February 1856, which knocked 4 days off the record previously held by the *Polmaise* which was under the same ownership. She continued her passage to Bombay where she loaded cotton for Whampoa and then came home with tea in 104 days against the monsoon.

In 1857 she made the remarkable passage of only 94 days from Foochow to Dartmouth, 9 August to 11 November, London being reached five days later. Made as it was against the monsoon in the bad month of August, it was the fastest time to London under these conditions until 1866 when *Ariel*, *Taeping* and *Serica* went from pilot to pilot, Foochow to the Downs, in a few hours under 99 days. The next year *Fiery Cross* went out to Hong Kong in 96 days, 12 January to 18 April 1858, and was able to load tea at £6 6s per ton.

In 1859, John Dallas relinquished his command in order to stay ashore and superintend the construction of a new clipper which was in due course christened with the same name. This event occurred because the *Fiery Cross*, when bound from London to Hong Kong under Captain Duncan, stranded on 4 March 1860 on an uncharted reef in the China Sea, which lay near the NW Investigator Shoals and stretched from 9°32′N 112°53′E, to 9°41′N 113°04′E. The crew reached Labuan safely in the boats.

FRIAR TUCK, 1855

A comparison has already been drawn earlier in this Chapter between this example of an Aberdeen clipper and the Sunderland ship *Kelso*. Alexander Hall built *Friar Tuck* of wood at a cost of £11,739 to class 8 A1. She was his 204th ship, the *Robin Hood* being launched immediately afterwards and therefore probably very similar in design to *Friar Tuck*, especially as they were both built for the same owner. *Friar Tuck* measured 193.2ft × 31.0ft × 17.0ft, 585 tons under deck and 662 tons gross, being owned by James Beazley, Liverpool. Beazley already had the large St John clipper *Star of the East* in the China trade as well as Hall's *Vision*. In six voyages *Friar Tuck* made £15,215 in profits. Other items of expenditure in the builder's cost account were: steering gear £24 9s 9d; cannons £37; Hughes – carver £24; capstans £25 17s; muskets £12 3s; upholsterers £37 10s. She carried nothing above royals, had a main spencer gaff and the main yard measured 63ft. The coefficient of under deck tonnage was 0.57.

Outward-bound to Hong Kong in 1858, she lost a man overboard off the Cape of Good Hope when going 14 knots

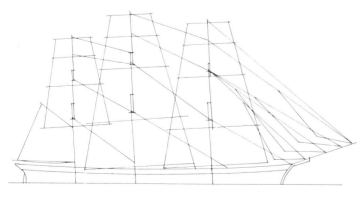

Friar Tuck sail plan. Traced from photocopy supplied by Bergen Maritime Museum, possibly from a note book. No scale specified; diagram titled: '*Friar Tuck* built by Hall brothers Aberdeen'.

with all starboard stunsails set but although the ship was hove-to, he could not be saved. This passage occupied 102 days from London.

In 1858–59 when she raced home against *Kelso*, *Cairngorm*, etc, her captain and crew were promised a bonus of £150 if they were the first to arrive, but unfortunately they were unable to pass the four ships ahead of them.

When homeward-bound from Shanghai in 1863, she put into St Mary's Bay, Isles of Scilly, on 27 November, but her anchor cables parted and she drove ashore on Newford Island becoming a total loss. Her figurehead is preserved at Tresco.

KATE CARNIE, 1855

Robet Steele's first tea clipper was the first British ship really to short-cut the distance between China and England, when at the end of her first voyage she ran from Shanghai to London in only 92 days, 4 January to 5 April 1856, loaded with tea and silk at £4 10s per ton.

Built of wood to class 13 A1, she measured 148.4ft × 26.0ft × 19.0ft and 576 register tons. Alexander Rodger was part owner with C Carnie of Glasgow. She had a forecastle 14ft in length and a poop of 46½ft, and she probably possessed a full midship section. When fully-laden with tea she carried 704,000lbs.

In 1873 J B Foley, London, bought her but sold her in 1882 to T P Dobbin, Norway. A J Arnesen, Frederickstad had her three years later and in 1887 she went to A L Löversen of Arendal. She sprang a leak the following year bound for Montevideo, and in January 1889 was abandoned.

KELSO, 1855

Mention of this vessel has previously been made in connection with *Friar Tuck*, when it was pointed out that her builder, William Pile, gave her a good beam and a clean run as opposed to great rise of floor. In light and moderate wind she was as good as any other ship and was able to maintain a very consistent average under the command of Captain Coulson, later in the second *Kelso* and the crack *Maitland*.

Pile's yard was at North Sands, Sunderland, and there he built the *Kelso* of 529 tons, 145.0ft (overall) × 32.0ft × 18.0ft, and rigged as a ship. John R Kelso was her owner until she was lost on 9 February 1861, when she ran ashore at Hartlepool. Outward-bound, it was the beginning of her first voyage under Captain Vowell. There was a pilot aboard and in the gale she had been struck by a schooner and made 8 inches of water in ten minutes. The lifeboat rescued nineteen of the crew from the rigging but one was lost.

In 1857 when leaving the river Min on 24 November, she struck the bank and put into Hong Kong on her way home to repair. She probably did not leave Hong Kong until about 10 December, or even later if she had to dry-dock. In 1862 she reached Deal on 1 January, only 63 days from Anjer – a remarkably quick run – having passed the Cape of Good Hope on 21 November and St Helena six days later, and was altogether 102 days between her pilots. This passage of 63 days still stands as the record. In 1980 the 'Spice Race' was organized by Nedlloyd in an attempt to beat it and a number of yachts completed the course from Jakarta (Batavia) through the Straits of Sunda to the Straits of Dover and then Rotterdam. The quickest elapsed time to Dover, made by the *Flying Wilma*, was almost a day longer than *Kelso*'s.

An oil painting by Thomas G Dutton of the *Mirage* with stunsails set 'alow and aloft'. The stunsail yards are all set abaft their adjacent sails. (*Parker Gallery*)

MIRAGE, 1855

An excellent product from the yard of John Pile, West Hartlepool, builder of *Spirit of the Age*, she measured 180.0ft × 32.5ft × 19.0ft, 965 old and 833 new tons, being owned by A Orr Ewing, Liverpool. Like some of Pile's other ships she had heavy railings round poop and monkey forecastle.

On her second voyage she went out to Bombay in 81 days and came home to Liverpool from Tuticorin in 77. After trading out to the East all her life, she was sold at Hong Kong in March 1868 for $7500. She finally came to grief after leaving Bangkok on 20 May 1871 for Hong Kong. One account says she was wrecked on Sailing Island, also called Tyho or Tyoa Island, on 7 June. Another account in the *Overland China Mail* says that the rice cargo choked the pumps in a heavy gale and that she was abandoned in a sinking condition on 17 June 1871 near Tyho Island, which is on the 'West Coast'.

VALDIVIA, 1855

This small barque of only 356 tons net, with dimensions of 148.4ft × 26.4ft × 16.7ft, had a coefficient of under deck tonnage of 0.60. She had only one deck, a square stern with an imitation quarter-gallery, and the hull was painted green. Her builder was Lumley, Kennedy & Co of Whitehaven and her first owners were Nicholson & Co, Liverpool.

Her first voyage to China was made in 1859 and on the outward passage between Liverpool and Hong Kong she lost a man overboard, five days after her departure, when going 13 knots. The passage occupied 102 days and she arrived on 4 September. In 1861 at Manilla she loaded moist sugar at £3 10s per ton and hemp at £4 5s per ton for Liverpool. In 1864 she had a minor race home from Shanghai with *Assyrian* and *Chaa-sze*.

R & W King of Bristol became her owners in 1874 and in 1883 she was posted missing, having been last heard of on 26 November bound from Old Calabar on the west coast of Africa to Bristol, with 492 tons of palm kernels and a crew of thirteen.

BANIAN, 1856

Described by Andrew Shewan as 'a favourite ship especially at Canton' and the equal of *Assyrian* or *Vision*, she was one of the many fine China traders built at Workington, most of which made a series of regular passages out and home, but never did anything spectacular. The *Banian* was built by Peile, Scott & Co (for whom J T Fell was manager), for Bushby & Co of Liverpool, who also owned *Corea* and *Dunmail*, and she had dimensions of 186.0ft × 30.5ft × 20.8ft and tonnages of 760 nm and 812 om. She had a raised quarterdeck 47ft long. H Williams of Bangor became owner in 1880 and three years later she was wrecked on 23 April on Parangua Bar, Brazil, bound to Valparaiso.

HERCULEAN, 1856

She was built at Whitehaven in the shipyard of T & J Brocklebank for their own use and was registered at Liverpool. She measured 164.8ft × 28.7ft × 18.9ft and 531 tons, being a full-rigged ship constructed of wood. The *Liverpool Mercury* of 9 June 1856 commented on the shape of her hull when describing the launch in these words: 'The fashion of late has been to build models exceedingly sharp and fine and in this respect the *Herculean* is far ahead of anything ever turned out at Whitehaven.'

She never made a passage home with the new teas. In 1860 she was wrecked on 30 November in Gaspar Strait on Pulo Pongo Island, the master and crew of twenty-six being saved by the Dutch barque *Antonia Gertruida* and landed at Batavia on 4 December.

LAMMERMUIR, 1856

This ship was probably the first vessel John Willis owned that had any pretensions to being a clipper. He had previously had the *St Abbs* and the *Merse* in the China trade, but both were built primarily as carriers. His *Lammermuir* came from William Pile's yard at Sunderland and was a fast vessel, having his usual proportion of length to breadth, which was somewhat lower than many another builder's. She set nothing above royals, but her sails had great spread, her topsails being Cunningham's patent. Classed 13 A1, she measured 178.0ft × 34.0ft × 22.0ft and 952 tons. Her life came to an end on 31 December 1863, when she was wrecked on the Amherst Reef, in the Macclesfield Channel, Gaspar Strait, homeward-bound under Captain Jones.

After going out to Melbourne in 77 days on her maiden passage, she crossed over to Shanghai and spent the next year voyaging between there and Singapore. In 1860 she was chartered to carry home invalids at £20 per man, but this was dropped and instead she was engaged at £3800 for the voyage with permission to take cargo in the lower hold.

Probably her most noteworthy performance was her contest with *Cairngorm* in 1858–59. It happened that, on the Canton river being re-opened to shipping at the close of 1858 after the Chinese War came to an end, there were a number of ships ready to load tea at Whampoa. There was a great rush to load and *Cairngorm*, chartered by Jardine & Matheson, was the favourite. Owing to their smaller size, *Chieftain* and *Morning Star* were the first to finish loading and left on 5 November. *Cairngorm* had begun unmooring on 30 October and, like *Lammermuir*, dropped down the river on the afternoon of the 5th, and was fortunate enough to be towed to Lantow Island, which lies at the mouth of the Canton river on the opposite side to Macao, by the steamer *Hong Kong*, taking her departure from Macao the next day. She was off Banka Strait on 18 November. *Lammermuir* did not leave Macao until the 7th. On 22 November, Anjer was passed by *Chieftain*, *Cairngorm* and *Lammermuir*. The last two named both passed St Helena on 2 January 1859, and then *Cairngorm* went ahead, reaching Deal on 5 February, 91 days from Macao. She reached London the day after and received a premium of 10s per ton. *Lammermuir* got to Deal on 7 February, which would give her a passage of 92 days from Macao or 96 from Whampoa to London. The late Captain Andrew Shewan wrote that *Lammermuir* actually beat *Cairngorm* by six hours on time, but the dates given here were taken from contemporary shipping reports.

The passages of all those ships leaving Whampoa at about the same time in the 1858–59 season are set out below. All made the passage to London except where indicated:

Morning Star (D Forman), 5 November to 11 February, 98 days.

Chieftain (Tocque), 5 November to 19 February, 106 days. Off Anjer 22 November.

Cairngorm (J Ryrie), 5 November to 6 February, 93 days. Dep Macao 6 November; arr Deal 5 February. Off Anjer 22 November; off St Helena 2 January.

Lammermuir (A Shewan), 5 November to 9 February, 96 days. Dep Macao 7 November; arr Deal 7 February. Off Anjer 22 November; off St Helena 2 January.

Warrior Queen (Cresswell), 12 November to 18 March, 126 days.

Friar Tuck (Richardson), 13 November to 24 February, 103 days. Off Anjer 30 November.

West Derby (Sargent), 13 November to 1 March, 108 days. Off Anjer 28 November.

Veloz (Jones), 15 November to 24 February, 101 days. Off Anjer 29 November. Went to Belfast.

The *Morning Star* was on her maiden voyage, having been launched at Dundee in 1858, and had gone out to Hong

Kong in 111 days with coal from Newcastle. *Chieftain* was built in Jersey the year before and was wrecked on the Pratas Shoal in 1859, tea-laden. Particulars of ships not having individual biographies are listed briefly in Appendix I.

QUEENSBERRY, 1856

A most unusual feature in this vessel was that her dimensions of 206.9ft × 28.6ft × 19.2ft gave her a proportion of 7.2 beams to length. Together with the *Annandale* and the *Fairlight* they formed the narrowest tea clippers afloat. A list of sailing ships with a ratio of 7 beams to length and over contains these names for the 1850s:

Built	Name	Ratio	Material	Tons
1853	*Hurricane*	7.0:1	iron	979 nm
1854	*Annandale*	7.1:1	wood	759 nm
1854	*John Bell*	7.3:1	iron	1207 nm
1854	*Glen Roy*	7.0:1	iron	1219 nm
1855	*Tempest*	7.5:1	iron	845
1856	*Queensberry*	7.2:1	wood	635 nm
1858	*Fairlight*	7.1:1	wood	588 net

Both *Annandale* and *Queensberry* were designed by Benjamin E Nicholson and built by the family firm of John Nicholson & Co at Annan, Dumfriesshire. The builders were also the owners but they were managed by cousins in Liverpool, Nicholson & McGill, who also owned tea clippers.

The *Queensberry* registered 635 tons nm and 767 tons om and was built of wood to class 9 A1. On her maiden passage she arrived at Hong Kong on 20 July 1857, 97 days out from Liverpool.

Arnold de Beer Baruchson, Liverpool, bought her in 1863, and then Hargrove, Ferguson & Co of the same port acquired her in 1869, followed by J Dawson, Queenstown, five years later. In 1877 she was wrecked by stranding on the island of Palawan, China Sea, on 13 October.

ROBIN HOOD, 1856

She was 'perhaps Hall's most successful tea ship, up to the advent of *Flying Spur*', wrote Captain Shewan in *Sea Breezes*. She certainly was a profitable ship but her passages were not exceptional in spite of her undoubtedly fine lines. Unfortunately her half-model represents a larger ship than the one built, dimensions scaled off it producing 223.0ft × 40.0ft (moulded) × 22.0ft, whereas the dimensions of the ship as built were 204.0ft × 35.3ft (maximum) × 21.0ft; also 853 tons net and gross, 776 tons under deck, and 1185 om. This lovely mahogany half-model shows an extreme clipper which is broadly similar to the lines of the American extreme clipper *Sweepstakes* with a long sharp entrance and run, steep deadrise and straight floors, but without any tumblehome. This model in the Aberdeen Regional Museum, after years of neglect and damage, will at last be repaired by James Henderson for the new Maritime Museum in the city. It is

impossible to say whether the *Robin Hood* as built was a scaled-down version of this model or not.

The *China Mail* of 5 March 1857, quoting from the *Liverpool Daily Post* of 31 December 1856, wrote of the *Robin Hood*:

She was built for Mr James Beazley by Messrs Alexander Hall & Co, who, we hear, received a *carte blanche* to build a ship that either for speed, strength, or finish should not be excelled by any vessel afloat . . . we cannot conceive any vessel to possess finer lines, or be more handsomely finished; indeed, the common remark is, 'She is more like a nobleman's yacht'.

She was built under a shed, but because it was very cold when she left Aberdeen with snow lying thick on the ground, she did not receive her final coat of paint; but otherwise she was considered one of the finest ships ever to have been built in Aberdeen.

The quotation in the *China Mail* continued:

We noticed her very handsome spars and wire rigging, and all her adjuncts are of the newest and most approved description; all her anchors are Trotman's patent. She has patent blocks, and throughout the ship no expense seems to have been spared. She has a spirited half-length [figurehead] of Robin Hood, with his bow in hand; a very long forecastle, and a poop cabin most chastely fitted up.

The finished cost to the builder was £21,655, and in eight voyages she made some £26,000 in profits. Her first master was George Cobb who had been in the *Swordfish* out of Liverpool, had made one voyage in the *Vision* and was later to be master of *Wild Deer*. She set nothing above royals and the yards on the fore and main were of similar lengths, the lower yards being 79ft overall. Her bowsprit was said to have a higher steeve than was then common in Aberdeen ships.

Although *Robin Hood*'s passages seem only to be a good average when looked at on their own, it can be seen that when compared with other clippers sailing at the same time her's are almost invariably shorter. Her fastest homeward passage was made from Foochow in 1858 at the end of the south-west monsoon in 99 days with 1,032,660lbs of tea on board – the second fastest run that had yet been made at this time of the year.

She could stow 1,124,500lbs of tea at Whampoa. As an example of her work, when outward-bound, London to Hong Kong in 1860–61, she ran from the Line to 14°00'S 102°30'E, in 46 days, an average of over 200 miles per day. It is also said that once, homeward-bound from China, she did 1200 miles in four consecutive days, her greatest run being 364 miles in 24 hours. There is no record to substantiate her claim of 90 days to Hong Kong; indeed her fastest outward time was 102 days from the Scillies in 1859. In 1862, homeward-bound from Foochow, she damaged her rudder near the Line and had to rig a tiller which was steered below deck. Captain Mann received a bonus of £100 from James Beazley for bringing his ship safely home, as told in Chapter One.

After eight voyages she was sunk off Dungeness on 22 November 1864, bound for Hong Kong, after colliding with the ship *Spirit of the Ocean*, inward-bound from Quebec. All her sails were unbent or cut away later. She was insured for £12,577.

SIR W F WILLIAMS, 1856

This full-rigged ship was one of the few built in Canada for the tea trade and her low class of 7 A1 indicates why Canadian ships were not employed more frequently amongst the front-runners in this trade. She was built at St John, New Brunswick, and owned by Shaw & Co, Liverpool, but whether she was built to their order or on speculation is not known. She measured 181.1ft × 34.5ft × 20.8ft and 870 tons. The height in the 'tween decks was 8ft.

Her maiden passage was made out to Hobart and crossing over to China, she loaded tea and silk at Shanghai; from there she made the run home in 99 days to London, arriving on 31 March 1858, her fastest passage in the tea trade. She was at Zebu in the Philippines in April 1865 and loaded sugar, shells, coffee, hemp and hides, and took 120 days on the run home, reaching London on 8 August.

The owner's name is not given in *Lloyd's Register* in 1867–73. In 1874 she was condemned, but was bought by P Olivari of Genoa who renamed her *Marietta D*. After twenty years under the Italian flag she was condemned in 1894.

SPARTAN, 1856

To be owned by John R Kelso of North Shields and built by William Pile at Sunderland was a combination that inevitably produced a fast ship and *Spartan* was one of these. She was a full-rigged ship constructed of wood with a tonnage of 665 and dimensions of 156.5ft × 31.5ft × 19.0ft. In 1861 she went ashore at the mouth of the Min river, having left Foochow on 30 January, but was pulled off and towed back to Foochow where her cargo of tea was discharged and most of it was then loaded into the *Panic*. Her dismantled hull was sold for a mere $1300 and the masts etc for a further $1200. She was then condemned because her back was broken and the dry-dock at Foochow was not yet ready. Had she been at Whampoa she could have been repaired.

STRATHMORE, 1856

This clipper barque, registering 450 tons net and gross, w built by the Dundee Shipbuilding Co, Dundee, and was I far their most successful China clipper. It has been said th she was designed by William Rennie. Classed 9 A1, s measured 146.3ft × 27.0ft × 17.2ft, and had an und deck tonnage of 421.28 which gives a coefficient of 0.6 Her first owners were William Young and Alexand Fotheringham, Glasgow. Much of the information abo her is available to me through the kindness of J Kenned Mann, grandson of her first master, who loaned me th log-book in 1950.

The *Strathmore* was launched on 21 May with topmas and lower rigging set up. The fore and main rigging, bac stays, fore and main lower and topmast stays were of 7 cordage, the rigger making a charge of £40 for his service Cunningham's patent topsails were carried and also flyin kites up to royal stunsails. At sea a main skysail yard w sent up, and occasionally one on the fore. Carpenters ca ried by these clippers spent much of their time making ne stunsail booms. The livestock when she carried passenge consisted of two cows, twelve sheep, two goats, some pi and numerous fowls.

The photograph of her model admirably illustrates th sort of deck layout in these ships. The little platform in th bows was barely large enough to accommodate those wor ing the anchors. There were cargo hatches abaft the wind lass and the mainmast, and on the raised quarterdeck aba the mizen mast were companion, skylight, binnacle ar wheel. On the model the main fiferail appears to hav become dislodged from its correct place. The position the longboat lying on chocks on the deck or sometimes o the main hatch was frequently to be met with in vessels under 1000 tons. There is a particularly good drawing this by Roger Finch in Basil Greenhill's *The Mercha Schooners* (Vol 1, 1951 edition) showing how it was don on the 52-ton ketch *Clara May*. The stern was almo square and had some gilded carving which was sent fro Glasgow with the trailboards. For protection in the Chin Sea she carried four swivel guns on the poop and four bra 9-pounders on the main deck, together with 24 muske and the same number of cutlasses. The felt and copperin cost some £630.

Captain John Mann was 37 years old when he took h from the stocks and he received £200 per annum an weekly board wages of 25s. The first mate received £6 p month. Mann was later in command of the *Robin Hood* an was accustomed to take his wife and small son to sea wit him, which was unusual in the hard-driven tea clippers. lithograph of the barque was published by William Fost but I have never seen a copy.

After going out to Port Chalmers with 158 steerage an second cabin passengers on her maiden voyage in 90 day land to land, she crossed over to Foochow in 51 days to loa tea. Almost a year later she was loading her second te cargo of 566,700lbs at £2 10s per ton and 249 bales of silk £5 to £6 at Shanghai. On this passage in 1857–58 she wa 95 days 1 hour between the East Saddle and the Lizard. A epitome of her log-book reads as follows:

Left Shanghai at 5.0 pm	21 December
Passed Woosung at 3.0 pm	22 December
Dropped pilot at 1.30 pm	23 December

This model of the *Strathmore* is contemporary, and like the *Wynaud* has two deckhouses and a raised quarterdeck. (*J K Mann*)

East Saddle bore W at 10.0 pm	23 December
In Macclesfield Channel, Gaspar Strait	6 January
Passed Anjer	9 January
Crossed meridian of Cape of Good Hope	10 February
Passed St Helena	19 February
Ascension Island bore E 100 miles	24 February
Passed the Lizard at 11.0 pm	28 March
Passed Start Point at 9.0 am	29 March
Picked up pilot off Dungeness at 9.0 pm	30 March
In London Dock at 4.0 pm	31 March

Between 20 and 24 January 1858, she went from 17°07'S 9°27'E, to 23°24'S 64°47'E, and the log entry for the 24th records that 'for the last four days we have had almost constant rain, with thick weather, and since our last observation [on the 20th] we have made 925 miles.' On no occasion did she ever log more than 14 knots.

Her next outward passage to China took her to Woosung in 117 days in 1858, laden with coal, which was her usual outward cargo. Following this, she went from the North Saddle to Start Point in 97 days 3 hours, 28 November 1858 to 5 March. Though she left Shanghai on 26 November, she had to anchor each day and was not fully underway until the 28th.

By June 1857, William Young had sold his original 32 shares and Alexander Fotheringham had reduced his 32 by half. Edward Harwood now had 36 shares, and there were some other shareholders, including the master. Harwood had a clipper named after him in 1857 and in the same year Young & Fotheringham had the *Strathallan* built by the Dundee Shipbuilding Co.

Wilson & Co, London, bought her in 1861, and apart from 1863 when she beat Hood's clipper *Garrawalt* by one day from Whampoa, she did not load tea again but traded out to Swan River, Singapore, etc. In 1872, towing up the Mersey on the night of 2 April, she came into collision with the anchored barque *Glengaber*, and sank in a few minutes. A week or so later the hull was brought into shallow water, but the fore part remained in mid-channel.

HARWOOD, 1857

This full-rigged ship traded with New Zealand and China for many years and was built for Edward Harwood, according to the inscription on the well-known lithograph of her hove-to. However, *Lloyd's Register* gives the first owner as E Young & Co of London, probably because they were the managing owners. As Fotheringham is listed as the owner from 1862, all three of them were probably the same men who held shares in the *Strathmore*.

The *Harwood* was built at Montrose of 462 tons with dimensions 145.0ft × 27.1ft × 16.3ft. Although her maiden passage between Shields and Shanghai, laden with coal, occupied 151 days from 3 July to 1 December, she returned to London in only 99 days with a cargo of tea and silk. Her name drops out of the Register in 1870.

JUBILEE, 1857

This ship had the longest life afloat of any of the tea clippers since she was not broken up until 1944, giving her a life of 87 years. *Cutty Sark*, now preserved in dry-dock, was built in 1869 and entered the dry-dock in 1954, giving her 85 years afloat. On the other hand, neither ship was working under sail all this time – *Jubilee* had only 35 years of this as against *Cutty Sark*'s 53 years – but the tea clipper with the longest working life under sail was surely the *Cleta*, built in 1866 and under sail until condemned in 1937, which gives a working life of 71 years.

The *Harwood* hove-to for picking up the pilot, whose cutter lies head to wind on the starboard bow. (*MacGregor Collection*)

The *Jubilee* must have had a fine-lined hull since her coefficient of under deck tonnage was 0.58 which is the same as *Thermopylae*. Her dimensions of 192.4ft × 31.0ft × 21.3ft gave her a ratio of almost six beams to length. Mr R F Monteath, who saw her as a hulk in Auckland, wrote to Rhoderick Glassford in 1857 that 'when in light trim she appeared a long vessel of moderate beam' and that she 'had a nice hull – rather wall-sided'. She had a raised quarter-deck 45ft long and a tonnage of 764, when built.

Her builders were the Workington & Harrington Ship-building Co of Workington for whom Jonathan T Fell was the manager, and she was their first ship. Fell had moved from Peile, Scott & Co's yard to take up this new post, but how much he was responsible for the design of the ships is unknown. The owners were Bushby & Co of Workington.

In February 1859, when 104 days out from Shanghai and going at 8 knots, she drove ashore on the French coast near Étaples, the master having mistaken the lights there for those of Portland. The ship was then valued at £18,000 and carried a crew of twenty-six which included the master, two mates, and two boys. Only 44,000lbs of tea out of the 763,900lbs loaded were recovered. The ship was salved the same year and sold to J Brodie, London, but John Douglas was no longer her skipper.

She remained in the China trade throughout the 1860s and in the 1870s was trading to New Zealand. In 1875 she put into Milford Haven, leaking, on 27 January, 137 days out from San Francisco. In 1880, W Heselton of London bought her and two years later she passed into the hands of T Cowlishaw of Sydney. In 1884 the Gear Meat Preserving

& Freezing Co, Wellington, acquired her to carry mea from their works to the loading berths. She was eventuall hulked in 1893, and was out of *Lloyd's Register* in 1894.

The Westport Coal Co bought her in the early 1900s and used her as a coal hulk at Wellington until about 191' when she was towed to Auckland to continue in the same work. She had been cut down to her fore and main lowe masts and the coal was worked by ship's gear and baskets while the more modern hulks used cranes and grabs. Even tually the wood of her hull was found to be worth more than her use as a coal hulk and so she was broken up towards the end of 1944.

RED RIDING HOOD, 1857

This ships seems to have been the first craft Thomas Bilb and William Perry, his partner built on the composite plan She was launched in August from the Nelson Dock Rotherhithe, London, for their own use, and measured 183.2ft × 29.6ft × 19.7ft, 720 net and 709 under deck tons. Her deck layout became a standard pattern in many ships of the 1860s. She had a woman's bust figurehead, wa metal bolted, but with galvanized bolts only in her topsides Her stern was rounded and quite attractive. On her maiden passage she carried a master, two mates, and twenty-fou men and boys.

Red Riding Hood's coefficient of under deck tonnage 0.66, was simlar to *Lauderdale*'s, indicating that they pos sessed the same degree of sharpness even though the *Lauderdale* was slightly larger in dimensions and tonnage Thus they had equal chances to make good passages, and i is worth noting their performances under different captains

That intrepid navigator and reckless sail carrier, Alexander Nicholson, had *Red Riding Hood* for some four or five years, and in 1864 brought her from Foochow to Falmouth in 115 days against the monsoon, an easy victory over others sailing at the same time, excluding *Childers*. The following year she went to Trinidad, presumably with Chinese coolies.

Anderson, Anderson & Co acquired *Red Riding Hood* in 1876, but sold her in two years' time for something over £2100 to Arabs, who rechristened her *Iscandria*. In 1886 she was in the hands of Sandberg, Zoon & de Jong, Batavia, under the name of *Barend-Christiaan*. She was broken up in 1890.

ROBERT HENDERSON, 1857

She was typical of the very best type of vessel turned out by Aberdeen yards at the end of the 1850s – faultless in finish, equipment and sailing powers. This particular vessel was built by the younger Duthie for the Glasgow shipowner Robert Henderson and his New Zealand trade, and was specially designed to meet these requirements, having a very spacious saloon some 50ft long and 7ft high, to accommodate twenty passengers. The poop was raised above the bulwark level and reached forward of the mizen. She had a topgallant forecastle, was fitted with Cunningham's patent topsails, and her steering gear was on the principle of the reverse screw, then a novelty, but very efficient. She was taken round to Greenock to be coppered and on the way ran from Stromness to Scalpa Light at 14 knots, reaching the Clyde 48 hours from Stromness. The wind was very strong on this trip, yet she displayed great stiffness under canvas. At Greenock she was much admired, where it was seen that like other Aberdonians she had fine lines, being of the same relative sharpness as the second *Fiery Cross*. She measured 163.0ft × 28.3ft × 17.3ft and 552 tons.

Her maiden voyage took her out to Dunedin in only 79 days, land to land; across to Hong Kong in 47 days; then to New York with tea from Amoy, and home to Liverpool in 23 days. She usually went out via Dunedin, except in 1859, when she went out to Hong Kong from Liverpool in 98 days against the monsoon, 15 July to 21 October. Altogether she made twelve outward passages to New Zealand.

In November 1864, the Albion Shipping Co, Glasgow, acquired 48 shares and in the following August they became the sole owners. In 1877 she was sold to Rogerson of London, and three years later she passed into the hands of J Hay & Co, another London owner. She was condemned in 1881–82.

SHAKSPERE, 1857

Built by Benjamin Nicholson at Annan for the use of his Liverpool firm, John Nicholson & Co, she did not go out to China until 1860, having previously been trading to South America around Cape Horn. In this trade she made such passages as Caldora to Swansea in 71 days in 1857, and Swansea to Valparaiso in 78 days in 1858. With dimensions of 164.8ft × 27.2ft × 18.0ft she had six beams to her length; tonnage was 565 old and 496 new. Her half-model has survived to show that she was one of the finer-lined hulls designed by Nicholson, but fuller than *Annandale* or *Mansfield*. In the autumn of 1870 she was wrecked on the French coast, homeward-bound for London from Shanghai.

Top: The *Solent* under easy sail with none of her royal yards crossed. Shepherd's houseflag had white and blue squares. Lithograph by Thomas G Dutton. *(MacGregor Collection)*

Above: The London-built *Caduceus* under full sail off Hong Kong. Par ticulars can be found in Appendix I. *(Parker Gallery)*

SOLENT, 1857

Most vessels built on moderately sharp lines had by this year dispensed with such features as quarter-galleries and the omission of a sail bent on the crossjack yard; but not so the *Solent*, a diagonally-constructed ship by J & R White, Cowes. These builders had had a long association with fast ships designed to suit the requirements of the China trade, and the *Solent* was accordingly able to make a series of fine runs during the favourable monsoon, the average for her first four homeward passages being 101¾ days. Her bow was graceful, supporting a lengthy bowsprit and jibboom, and behind prominent knightheads she had a forecastle 25ft long. Her poop, 52ft in length, stretched to midway between her main and mizen masts.

The London firm of J Shepherd owned her all her life until she stranded in 1876 in the Macclesfield Channel, Gaspar Strait, on 31 July, bound for Yokohama with a crew of 19.

On her maiden voyage she took 80 passengers out to Auckland and brought home 895,500lbs of tea and 589 bales of silk from Shanghai. She measured 163.7ft × 33.2ft × 20.4ft, and 732 tons. Due to the soundness of her diagonal construction she survived hard driving as well as a composite ship, and at the end of the 1860s made two fine homeward runs of 92 and 93 days.

STAR OF THE NORTH, 1857

This wooden ship was built at Sunderland in 1857 and her tonnage of 935 made her fairly large for a ship in the China trade. She had dimensions of 190.0ft × 34.0ft × 21.0ft and her first and only owner was George Leslie, Aberdeen. Her fastest passage was one of 99 days from Foochow to London in 1858, her departure being taken in February. In 1860 she sailed from Foochow on 5 May but in fact loaded the last teas of the previous season. In 1868 she was engaged as a transport for the Abyssinian War. She was condemned in 1871–72.

VANGUARD, 1857

Built by William Pile of Sunderland for John R Kelso of North Shields, she was a wooden full-rigged ship of 626 tons with dimensions of 154.0ft × 32.0ft × 19.0ft and she had a poop 48ft in length. She always seems to have taken her departure from China in february, March or April but no passage either out or home has been found of less than 100 days.

On 25 June 1859 in the North Atlantic, homeward-bound from Foochow, she was making 9½ knots in a gale when she was caught aback and lost the lower, topsail and topgallant yards on the mainmast. However she was off the Scillies five days later, 107 days out, but easterly winds in the Channel delayed her arrival for a full week.

J Baker of London acquired her in 1870, by which time the rig had been changed to that of barque, and in 1878 her name dropped out of *Lloyd's Register*.

This painting of *Corriemulzie* shows her at Hong Kong in 1864. She was built at Dundee in 1856. Particulars of the ship are given in Appendix I. *(Paul Mason Gallery)*

7

REQUIREMENTS OF DESIGN
AND SHIPS OF 1858-1862

The ranks of the extreme China clippers had been very much thinned out by the end of the 1850s and there had not been many satisfactory replacements. There were few ships left that could make a passage home against the monsoon in 110 days or less. Earlier in the decade a host of swift ships had been launched but the majority were by now worn out and strained with hard driving. Furthermore, the pick of the fleet, the *Fiery Cross*, had been lost in 1860.

It will have been noticed how varied in design and appearance were the ships built in these years, whilst the impetus which had launched and sailed these early clippers with such success appeared, temporarily, to have almost died out. There had been a slump in world-wide freight markets after the end of the Crimean War when so much tonnage was again free for charter. This was also bad for the shipbuilding industry as orders were cut back while the cheaper softwood American and Canadian ships were available for purchase. In the China tea trade the emphasis was still on quality – weatherliness, speed, dry holds, high-classed ships – and this protected builders of such vessels from the worst effects of the recession.

With the change in the rules for tonnage measurement which occurred in 1854, no reduction in the register tonnage figure could any longer be given by the 'Aberdeen bow' style of hull, however extreme it might be, and so Alexander Hall & Sons began gradually to alter their designs by giving less rake to the sternpost and the stem rabbet. The bow now became more conventional although the knightheads were often prominent. There was now no reason to thicken up the ceiling at places where the internal breadths were measured for tonnage nor to have that curious cross-section as seen in *Reindeer* where the sides curve in and then flare out to the bulwarks.

But deadrise, in addition to fine waterlines, was still favoured by tea clippers as can be seen in the hull-form of the *Scawfell*, which Charles Lamport built at Workington in 1858. She was designed with a raking mid-section and very steep deadrise, and there are no hollows in the waterlines. Occasional experimental designs continued to appear: *Fairlight* (1858) was unusually long with 7.1 beams to length; *Mansfield* (1861) had an exceptionally long concave run; *Chaa-sze* (1860) was converted from an auxiliary whaler and so had flattish floors and wall sides.

A fine midship section with very steep deadrise made a vessel fast when running before favourable winds, whatever form the rest of her hull may have taken. She would also be a good all-rounder in light breezes since her section offered the least resistance to the water. But she was not always so good beating to windward in strong winds, as, when heeled, she possessed little depth.

A fuller midship section, on the other hand, was as it best in good whole-sail breezes and on a beat to windward. When heeled the whole body of the hull would continue to give the necessary depth and power. The first *Fiery Cross* was so designed and her hollow entrance helped her sailing powers when beating against the monsoon. Hollow bow lines were not so satisfactory in other circumstances, and the fuller the sections the stronger was the wind required to send the ship along. But *Fiery Cross* had a fine run which helped for speed in light winds. Some of Robert Steele's ships had this sort of midship section with a long clean run which was carried to excess in the *Ariel* and her contemporaries. Before this time, most ships favoured rather fuller quarters.

The ability to make a quick run to Anjer against the monsoon made all the difference on a homeward passage and a ship that could do this was preferred above all others. Sailing down the China Sea with the new teas meant contending with head winds all the way and for the reason already given excessive deadrise was not satisfactory. Furthermore, a clipper with great rise of floor stowed much less tea, whilst requiring more ballast, a point which has already been mentioned in the last chapter when comparing *Kelso* with *Friar Tuck*.

The second *Fiery Cross* was a good all-rounder and excelled in the China Sea, proving superior to all her contemporaries. Before she entered the lists, Captain Shewan listed the following ships in order of speed: first, the *Falcon*; second, the *Ellen Rodger*; third, the *Challenger*; and, tying for fourth place, the Aberdeen clippers *Robin Hood*, *Ocean Mail* and *Friar Tuck*.

Aberdeen had been launching many ships for the trade throughout the 1850s and in 1863 sent five lovely new clippers out to China to load tea. But clipper freights were falling and more economical vessels were gaining preference. Aberdeen ships, many with great rise of floor, carried less tea than other equally fast ships of the same dimensions, yet required the same expensive upkeep. The next year found only one Aberdeen ship to join the tea fleet, and she usually sailed with passengers to Australia on the outward passage. In the next few years Hall concentrated on Australian passenger ships where cargo capacity was not so important.

A number of iron ships were constructed for the China trade about 1860, perhaps because owners were tempted by lower shipbuilding costs compared with wooden vessels. In

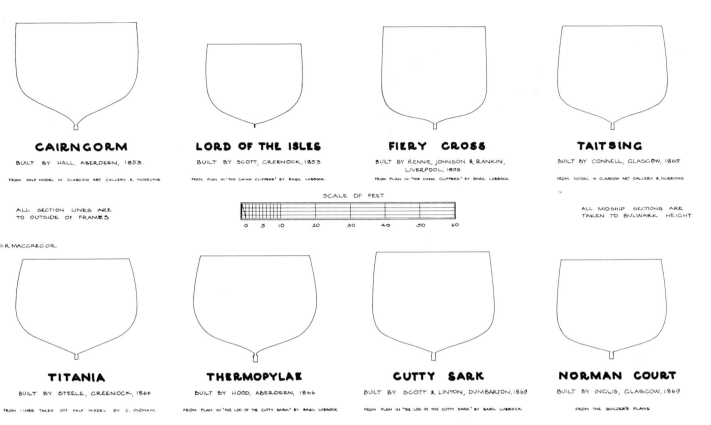

CAIRNGORM
BUILT BY HALL, ABERDEEN, 1853.
FROM HALF MODEL IN GLASGOW ART GALLERY & MUSEUMS

ALL SECTION LINES ARE
TO OUTSIDE OF FRAMES

LORD OF THE ISLES
BUILT BY SCOTT, GREENOCK, 1853
FROM PLAN IN "THE CHINA CLIPPERS" BY BASIL LUBBOCK

SCALE OF FEET

0 5 10 20 30 40 50 60

FIERY CROSS
BUILT BY RENNIE, JOHNSON & RANKIN,
LIVERPOOL, 1855
FROM PLAN IN "THE CHINA CLIPPERS" BY BASIL LUBBOCK

TAITSING
BUILT BY CONNELL, GLASGOW, 1865
FROM MODEL IN GLASGOW ART GALLERY & MUSEUMS

ALL MIDSHIP SECTIONS ARE
TAKEN TO BULWARK HEIGHT

TITANIA
BUILT BY STEELE, GREENOCK, 1866
FROM LINES TAKEN OFF HALF MODEL BY C. OLDHAM

THERMOPYLAE
BUILT BY HOOD, ABERDEEN, 1866
FROM PLAN IN "THE LOG OF THE CUTTY SARK" BY BASIL LUBBOCK

CUTTY SARK
BUILT BY SCOTT & LINTON, DUMBARTON, 1869
FROM PLAN IN "THE LOG OF THE CUTTY SARK" BY BASIL LUBBOCK

NORMAN COURT
BUILT BY INGLIS, GLASGOW, 1869
FROM THE BUILDER'S PLANS

Outline midship sections of some of the best known ships compared at the same scale. (*Author*)

1862, the *King Arthur* by Steele, the *Helen Nicholson* by Reid and the *Vigil* by Vernon, all made their appearance. But after this year the successful construction of composite vessels proved a better alternative to wood than did iron and for a while no more iron tea clippers were to join the front ranks.

The name of a new builder who was to have a profound effect on tea clipper design now appears on the scene. This was Robert Steele & Co of Greenock who had begun there in 1816 after the partnership with Carswell was terminated. The firm had achieved fame with the huge wooden steamers built for Samuel Cunard but there is no evidence that they had any experience of building a clipper. In 1854 they built two 700-ton ships of identical dimensions, one for George Smith's 'City Line' to India, the other for J & A Allan's Atlantic service. Then in 1855 they launched the *Kate Carnie* for the China tea trade. She was yard No 131. In 1858 came the *Ellen Rodger*, yard No 140, followed a year later by the *Falcon*, yard No 144. Plans of the latter have survived and possibly the two previous tea clippers bore some resemblance to her even though much shorter in length.

Presumably Steele got the order for *Kate Carnie* by quoting a lower price than his competitors – it was the usual way to get an order. Tea clippers were not built irrespective of cost, because the future owner wanted a reasonable return on his investment. We can get some idea of prices quoted by Steele on reading Alexander Stephen's diary for 1861. When in the London office of Phillips, Shaw & Lowther he quoted a price of £17 9s per ton for an iron ship of 12 A1, and £18 10s per ton for a composite ship at 14 A1. This was

on 14 November. Next day he went aboard the new *Fiery Cross* and commented: 'Our price higher than Steele's.' Robert Steele was also in London visiting the shipowners' offices.

Like Steele, Alexander Stephen was to build many tea clippers in the 1860s although none was as extreme as the splendid iron clippers he constructed a decade earlier.

BIOGRAPHIES OF SHIPS BUILT 1858–1862

ELLEN RODGER, 1858

Robert Steele's second ship for the tea trade was built to the order of Alexander Rodger and C Carnie of Glasgow, owners of *Kate Carnie*. She was a wood ship of 585 tons, 155.8ft × 29.4ft × 19.5ft and classed 13 A1.

In 1860, before the second *Fiery Cross* entered the field, Captain Andrew Shewan placed the *Ellen Rodger* as the fastest clipper in the China trade after the *Falcon*.

Ellen Rodger ran out to Singapore on her maiden passage and then on to Macao. In 1862–63 she went out to Shanghai in 98 days from London, 28 December to 5 April. It was in 1862 that, in company with *Falcon*, *Robin Hood* and *Queensberry*, she met the Blackwaller *Kent* near the Line when homeward-bound. *Ellen Rodger*, with a recently increased sail plan, was able to leave the others behind, and when the wind freshened and backed to the north-east, the *Falcon* and the smooth sided *Robin Hood* also drew ahead of the *Kent*. Yet the *Kent* just managed to beat the tea ships into dock by a few hours, the *Queensberry* arriving at Liverpool the next day, 134 days out from Kanagawa, Japan.

In 1866, the homeward-bound *Ellen Rodger* went ashore on Belvidere Reef, Gaspar Strait, on 20 September. The hull was sold for $700. Later the same year she was passed by another ship, still hard and fast aground, her hull and bowsprit intact but her masts gone.

FAIRLIGHT, 1858

It was in this ship that Captain Kemball first made his name before obtaining command of the *Yang-tsze* in 1864 and later of the famous *Thermopylae*. The *Fairlight* was built at St Helier, Jersey, by F C Clarke who constructed a number of ships for the China trade, such as *Wagoola* (1856) and *Chieftain* (1857). The *Fairlight* had a tonnage of 588 and measured 191.2ft × 27.0ft × 17.6ft which gives her a ratio of 7.1 beams to length. The *Annandale* and *Queensberry* were the only other ships in the China trade to have such long narrow hulls, and I was unaware that the *Fairlight* had such extreme proportions until I began this biography on her. Since then the Channel Islands Shipping Research Project at University College, London, of which Robin Craig is the editor, has drawn my attention to other points about her construction.

Redfern & Alexander, London, who were her owners, wrote to Lloyd's Register on 30 September 1857 informing the Society that they were having a ship built in Jersey of wood on the same principle as the *Florence Nightingale* which Bilbe & Perry had built on the Thames two years earlier (probably with radiating frames). The *Fairlight* received a class of 11 years A1, of which 9 years were for materials, 1 year was for yellow metal fastenings and 1 year for being built under a roof. The Lloyd's Register surveyor in Jersey commented in his report on her 'great length and experimental construction' and how the builder and owners adopted his suggestions to make her stronger.

The *Fairlight* spent all her life in the China trade until wrecked in the China Sea in June 1866, but Kemball had left her three years before. A painting of the ship depicts her with Cunningham's roller-reefing topsails on which three rows of reef points are drawn, thus ensuring that if one reefing system refused to function then the other would work instead.

LAUDERDALE, 1858

A composite ship built by Bilbe & Perry, Rotherhithe, for John Willis & Son, London. John Willis Jnr had had a hand in her design, but neither his father nor Captain Andrew Shewan Snr, of the *Lammermuir*, approved of her lines. She was obviously not an extreme clipper, though she was no fuller than *Wild Deer*. Dimensions of 187.0ft × 32.0ft × 20.0ft gave her tonnages of 851 net and 794 under deck. The latter gave a coefficient of 0.66. She could carry 1428¼ tons of cargo based on 50 cubic feet per ton with 280 tons of ballast. (Entry in Alexander Stephen's diary for 3 Oct 1861.)

Right: Scawfell *at anchor off Hong Kong, flying Rathbone's houseflag. (Merseyside County Museums)*

Opposite, top: This painting of the Ellen Rodger *by G R Barr makes an attractive ship's portrait.* Falcon, *built by Steele the following year, was probably very similar. (National Maritime Museum)*

Opposite, centre: The long narrow hull of Fairlight *is not brought out in this painting by P J Ouless; but the interesting feature of her rig is that the topsails have two modes of reefing gear: Cunningham's roller and reef points. (Parker Gallery)*

Opposite, bottom: The Lauderdale *in Eastern waters. The open ports may have been painted ignorantly at the wrong deck level as they are not so much gunports as ventilation ports for the 'tween decks; in any case, some are painted right across chainplates. (Alexander Turnbull Library)*

Lauderdale had Bowers at first and made an average performance. She was less successful under Hutchings, but Moodie, who took over in 1867, made her show her paces by bringing her back in 99 days in the favourable monsoon.

In 1860, she met *Friar Tuck* and *Lord of the Isles* in Sunda Strait, all bound for Hong Kong. She arrived the same day as *Friar Tuck*, 22 days later, and one day before *Lord of the Isles*, having had the south-west monsoon behind her up the China Sea. The following year she went out to Hong Kong in 95 days from Land's End, 29 May to 31 August. In 1877 she was posted missing in July, bound from Nagasaki to Shanghai with a crew of twenty-two and 1195 tons of coal.

SCAWFELL, 1858

The comparison of unusually fast passages made from different starting points in different seasons and years always proves a controversial subject. It has already been stated how *Lord of the Isles* in 1858 and *Hallowe'en* in 1874 ran from Shanghai to London in 90 and 91 days respectively, and how *Zingra* took 85 days from there to Liverpool. The best times from Foochow were both made in 1869 by *Sir Lancelot* and *Thermopylae* in 89 and 91 days, and both against the monsoon. From Amoy the *Taeping* took 88 days to Deal in 1864. From Whampoa in the spring of 1861, *Scawfell* went to Liverpool in 88 days.

The times of *Scawfell*'s passage are 13 January to 11 April (noon), but she did not leave the Canton river until 14 January and picked up her pilot off Point Lynas at daybreak on 11 April, or 86½ days later. These dates seem quite certain; but, quoting from *Sea Breezes*, the overlooker to Lamport & Holt sent a note to the wife of *Scawfell*'s captain as follows: 'Mr William Ellis' compliments to Mrs Thomson, and begs to inform her that the *Scawfell* is off Point Lynas in 85 days from China. Liverpool, 11th April, 1861.'

The only solution to this is that Captain Robert Thomson sent letters ashore at Macao, dated 16 January. It appears that Thomson himself always maintained he took only 84½ days, but between what points is not specified. This passage seems worthy of ranking with the other six mentioned, even though made over a shorter distance.

The *Scawfell* was built of wood at Workington by Charles Lamport to class 13 A1. Of 826 tons she measured 198.0ft × 32.6ft × 21.8ft, with a 40ft raised quarterdeck. Her coeffi-

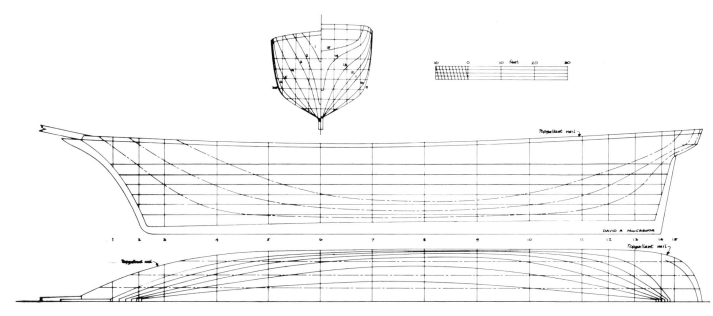

Above: Scawfell lines plan. Built of wood in 1858 by Charles Lamport at Workington. Lines taken from half-model in Liverpool Museum. Dimensions of *Scawfell*: 198.0ft × 32.6ft × 21.8ft, 826 tons. Dimensions scaled off this model: 184.0ft × 31.5ft × 18.0ft (approx). No reconstruction.

Opposite: Ziba sail plan. Entirely reconstructed, and based on a plan drawn by James Henderson. Sources: spar dimensions from builder's cost account; portrait of barque as frontispiece to *The Great Days of Sail* by Andrew Shewan (1927 edition). Hull profile typical of Hall's ships.

cient of under deck tonnage was 0.57 which made her as sharp as *Serica*.

There is a half-model in Liverpool Museum made to a scale of ⅛in to 1ft which is said to represent the *Scawfell*, but the drawback is that the dimensions are different from the vessel as built. The model scales 184.0ft × 31.5ft × 18.0ft (approx). Perhaps it was a preliminary model and the design was altered because it was considered too experimental. I took off the lines and drew them out. They show a ship with very steep deadrise and flaring topsides but with convex waterlines which are finer in the entrance than in the run. The keel is also much deeper aft than forward, the depth changing from 4ft to 2ft 3in. An interesting point about the design is that she had a raking mid-section, the broadest point of each waterline being further aft than the one below. On the lowest waterline, the maximum beam comes at the centre of the load line, but the maximum beam on the load line is about 25ft abaft the centre. This sort of hull-form increases stability, decreases pitching and assists fast sailing.

Two pointers indicating that *Scawfell* did have a sharp hull are that when she was lost she was still carrying 50 tons of permanent iron ballast, whereas most ships had removed theirs in the 1870s to improve stowage capacity. Secondly, the 1059 tons of coal and coke she was carrying represents only 29 per cent more than her register tonnage which is most unusual, as ships would expect to carry 50 per cent more than their net register tonnage and many twice as much. Of other ships built at Workington about the same time as *Scawfell*, the dimensions of the *Dunmail* come nearest to those of this half-model.

Her fastest outward passage was made in 1866 between London and Hong Kong, in 104 days, 8 March to 20 June.

Thomson, who joined the ship in 1858 from the *Cathaya* left her in 1871 and for the next ten years commanded the Blue Funnel steamer *Agamemnon*.

Rathbone Bros, Liverpool, were her first owners. Wilson & Blain, South Shields, purchased her in 1872 and then W Hutchinson, Newcastle, in 1880. Three years later she was abandoned on 9 January in 47°30′N 11°10′W, with 7ft of water in the hold and her pumps choked with small coal. There was a heavy sea running and the ship was straining and labouring in the gale. The crew numbered seventeen, but I do not know how they were rescued. At the time the ship was in one of the main shipping channels, bound from South Shields to the telegraph station on Cabo Garajo – the report spells it 'Garrucha' – which lies on the east side of Funchal Bay, Madeira; this was a principal coaling station.

WEYMOUTH, 1858

This iron full-rigged ship was built at Port Glasgow by J Reid & Co for Temperley, Carter & Darke of London and measured 187.0ft × 32.2ft × 21.0ft, and 830 tons. She had a poop 43ft long. None of her homeward passages which I have so far traced was less than 100 days, and her fastest outward passage was one of 99 days between London and Shanghai in 1864, 28 March to 5 July. In 1862 she stranded off Newchang but floated off safely on 14 May.

The Hamburg owner Ferdinand Laeisz bought her in 1881, renamed her *Poncho* and placed her in the South American trade. Ten years later she was sold to another Hamburg owner, H D J Wagener, and was finally lost in February 1898 after collision with the SS *Karnak* near Borkum.

ZIBA, 1858

Described in the early 1860s as the 'favourite Aberdeen-built China Clipper', this vessel was a jackass barque, with Cunningham's patent topsail on the fore and double topsails on the main. There was no main course, but a large gaff-sail instead. Her staysails were numerous and very large. The hull was typically Aberdeen and very beautiful.

Alexander Hall & Sons, Aberdeen, built her for John Wade and Captain Charles Tomlinson but Wade & Co,

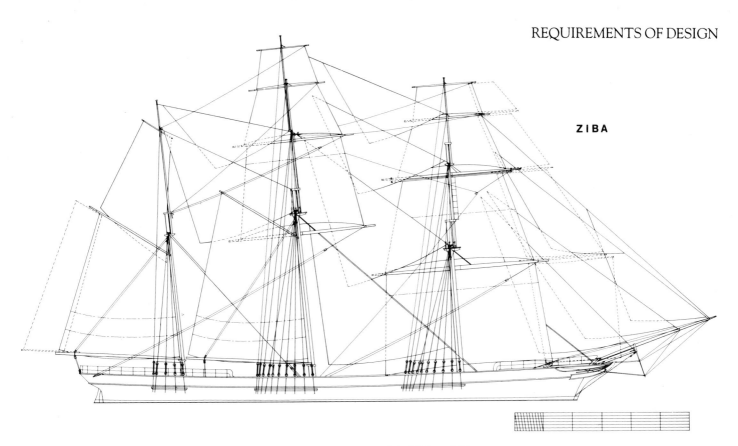

ZIBA

London, are listed as the managing owners. Her sail plan was probably designed by these two from their own practical experience but there seems no contemporary comment on it. The builder's certificate describes her as having 'three masts, schooner-rigged, round stern'. With the exception of 1861, she loaded in May or June with the first flight of clippers in every year until 1869 when she loaded in July, so she was obviously liked by the agents. On her maiden passage home she loaded at £5 per ton and was promised an extra £1 per ton if first ship home but was beaten into third place by *Ellen Rodger* and *Fiery Cross*.

The *Ziba* was possibly the only jackass barque in the tea trade but her rig was not unique, although comparatively rare. Darcy Lever illustrated one in his book on rigging in 1808 – *The Young Sea Officer's Sheet Anchor* – and there were various vessels so rigged in the 1860s and 1870s. The reconstructed sail plan has been drawn from the builder's spar dimensions and a painting of the clipper.

The *Ziba* measured 169.4ft × 28.4ft × 17.3ft, according to the builder's certificate, with tonnages of 497½ gross and net, and 465 under deck. She was built of wood with a raised quarterdeck 43ft long, and cost £8909. She was named after Wade's eldest daughter, Ziba. On her maiden passage she carried a cargo of 820 tons deadweight out to Shanghai, as well as measurement goods; on her third passage home she brought back 777 tons of tea and silk as well as 110 tons of ballast. This is a large proportion of ballast and suggests she had steep deadrise. Charles Tomlinson, her first master and part owner, died in China in 1862 and the ship was brought home by Captain Fine who was a stranger to the China Sea, according to Captain Andrew Shewan. Perhaps that accounts for her long passage of 150 days, of which 59 days were spent in sailing down to Anjer from Shanghai.

In 1881, J S Whitehead & Co, London, bought her only to have her wrecked three years later on 28 January in Samana Bay, Bahamas, bound from Haiti with dyewood.

COREA, 1859

Although the builder's name was at first written down on the Lloyd's Register survey report as Workington & Harrington Shipbuilding Co, Workington, it has been crossed through and an accompanying letter from the surveyor states that Jonathan Fell wished his own name to be inserted as the builder. Perhaps this was the first time he had achieved sole control of a shipyard, although he had been signing documents and reports on behalf of Peile, Scott & Co as far back as the *Clymene*, built in 1851.

The *Corea* measured 167.1ft × 29.0ft × 19.3ft with a tonnage of 581 and a raised quarterdeck 41ft long. An under deck tonnage of 566 gives a coefficient of 0.60. She was built of wood as a full-rigged ship but she had been reduced to barque rig in 1874. John Bushby, Workington, was her first owner; the firm's name became Shaw, Bushby & Co in 1880. In 1883 she was sold to J E Sassoon of Bombay and the registry was transferred to Shanghai, but she may have been used as a hulk, as the *Mercantile Navy List* leaves the rig blank in the appropriate column.

DUNMAIL, 1859

This was another ship from the yard of the Workington & Harrington Shipbuilding Co, Workington, of which Jonathan Fell was manager. They had built the *Jubilee* in 1857 and late in 1859 delivered the *Corea* for the same owner as the *Dunmail*. This was John Bushby of Workington who owned a number of ships in the China trade. The *Dunmail* measured 184.6ft × 31.5ft × 21.3ft with a tonnage of 768; the raised quarterdeck was 1ft 8in high.

She was not in China every year but also traded to India and Burma. In 1866 she got ashore in Gaspar Strait in May but managed to get off. But four years later when inward-bound from London she struck a sunken rock off Kowloon Point, Hong Kong, and was wrecked on 8 May. This loss was attributed to the neglect of using the lead; her general cargo was valued at just under £100,000.

FALCON, 1859

The firm of Robert Steele & Co, Greenock, had already launched two ships for the tea trade: the *Kate Carnie*, reputed to have a full midship section; and the *Ellen Rodger* on finer lines. But both these two were easily outclassed, as were most of the other clippers, by Steele's *Falcon*. From her were directly developed the splendid Clyde-built clippers of the 1860s. The *Taeping* was similar to her, though possessing a slightly finer run. *Falcon*'s coefficient of under deck tonnage works out at 0.59, and although this is 0.01 less than either *Ariel* or *Sir Lancelot* it is only an approximate indication of form. In fact, both these later clippers had more deadrise than *Falcon* and were somewhat finer in the ends. The *Falcon* had appreciable rise of floor, the sides tumbled home, and the entrance and run were long and sharp with some concavity near to the stem and sternpost. She was altogether a pleasing ship and obviously capable of a good turn of speed as well as having a reasonably good cargo capacity.

She had an Aberdeen house aft which stood on the main deck and was surrounded on each side and across the stern by a low deck, similar to *Vision* or *Thermopylae*. She had a row of four buckets standing in a rack on the top of the forward end of this house and abaft the skylight. The house, which had coved sides like *Cleta*'s, could be entered by a door on the main deck, but there was also a sliding hatch giving access to the cabins, at the after end of the house. *Falcon* carried channels for the rigging at a time when some of the more developed clippers had given them up and she was also fitted with roller reefing topsails. Her spar dimensions are given in Appendix IV. She also carried a main skysail.

John Keay was her second master, and in 1863–64 took her out to Hong Kong in 97 days, 7 November to 12 February, and then up to Hankow where she loaded tea at £8 per ton.

She had been built of wood for Phillips, Shaw & Lowther, London. Dimensions of 191.4ft × 32.2ft × 20.0ft gave a

DUNMAIL

Above: A splendid painting of the *Dunmail* under sail with no stunsails set, but sporting a main moonsail, a ringtail and a Jamie Green. This painting was formerly in James Burr's collection. *(Parker Gallery)*

Right: The *Falcon* at sea under a press of sail. A reconstructed drawing based on an oil painting by John Catnach, first mate, and given to the master, J L Dunn, in 1873. *(Author)*

Below: *Falcon* lines and deck plan. Redrawn from tracing made by Michael Costagliola of a plan in the Massachusetts Institute of Technology. Built 1859 by Robert Steele & Co, Greenock. Dimensions: 191.4ft × 32.2ft × 20.0ft and 794 tons. Reconstruction: deck fittings, cathead etc from portrait of ship painted in 1873 by John Catnach (mate).

Opposite, top: *Falcon* outline sail plan. Entirely reconstructed. Sources: lines plan for hull and mast positions; spar dimensions from *Committee of Lloyd's Register's Report* on the *Dismasting of Large Iron Sailing Ships* (1886); painting of ship done by John Catnach, mate, in 1873.

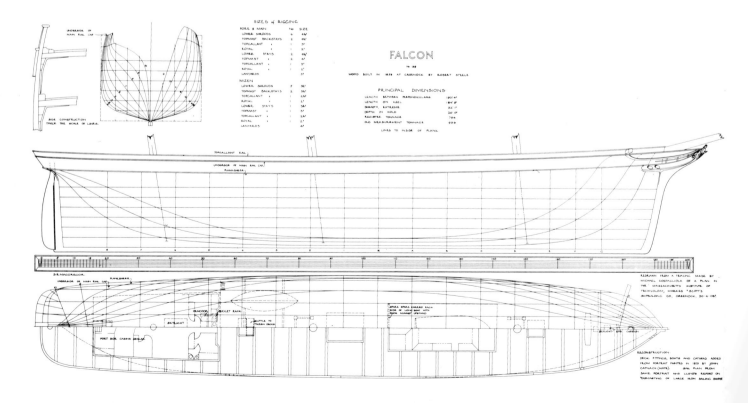

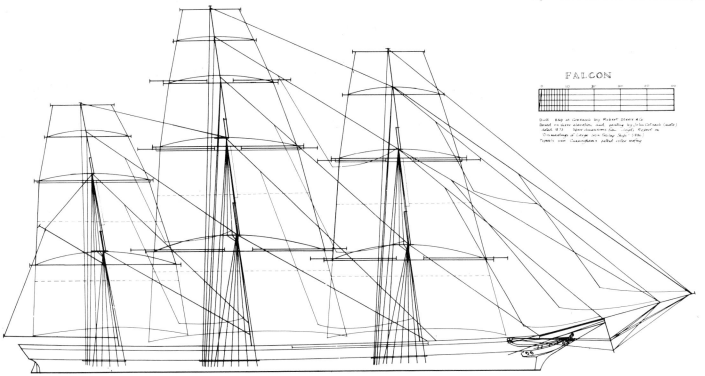

FALCON

Built 1859 at Greenock by Robert Steele & Co
Based on sheer elevation and painting by John Cutnach (mate)
dated 1873. Spar dimensions from Lloyd's Report on
Dismastings of Large Iron Sailing Ships (1886)
Topsails were Cunningham's patent roller reefing

register tonnage of 794. In 1865 Maxton joined the firm which became known as Shaw, Lowther & Maxton. They sold her in 1879 to J Brailli of Orebich, Austria, who renamed her *Sofia Brailli*. She was broken up in 1900.

JUANPORE, 1859

The builder's draft shows a fair amount of deadrise and moderately slack bilges drawn on the body plan, but with virtually no tumblehome; the entrance is fairly short and convex, but the run is longer and convex in the upper part and concave lower down. It had been expected that she would be a fast sailer, although her lines suggest the opposite, and so her outward passage of 136 days to Hong Kong disappointed everyone; it was 29 days longer than the *Herculean*'s. However, the return passage was made in 109 days.

She was built by T & J Brocklebank at Whitehaven for their own use as a wooden full-rigged ship of 459 tons with dimensions of 144.4ft × 26.7ft × 18.6ft. She crossed skysail yards on each mast according to her sail plan which lists the main yard as 54ft 'cleated' or with the length of the yardarms extra.

T Davies & Co, London, bought her in 1874 at which time she was barque-rigged; and in 1890 she passed into the hands of R Ferguson, Dundee. A year later she was posted missing on a passage from Sunderland to Santos with coal, not having been heard of since passing Orkney on 24 October.

CHAA-SZE, 1860

This ship was ordered by a Peterhead firm as a whaler with an auxiliary steam engine and was designed by the noted architect William Rennie. For some reason the owner did not take delivery, but Captain Andrew Shewan Snr, who had been commissioned to find a ship for the China tea trade, saw her on the stocks at the Aberdeen yard of Alexander Hall & Sons and thought she looked suitable. As a steam whaler she would have had a fine run into the propeller and was probably fairly fine forward, but a midship section shows her to have had flattish floors with firm bilges and wall sides. Her coefficient of under deck tonnage is 0.55 which is equal to *Cutty Sark*, indicating a fine-lined hull. Of course, having Andrew Shewan as master from 1860 to 1868 was a big advantage. In the latter year he left to take command of the new clipper *Norman Court*; previously he had been master of the *Niagara* (1850–53), *Merse* (1853–56) and *Lammermuir* (1856–60).

The *Chaa-sze* – which is the Chinese word for 'tea taster' – measured 170.0ft × 29.2ft × 18.2ft, 556 tons gross and net, and 495½ under deck. Her total cost was £10,285. The framework was of oak and she was diagonally planked with three skins of oak and teak, each 1½in thick; the average distance between the frames was 3ft 3in. She carried a skysail on the mainmast only; the main lower yard measured 63¼ft long overall, and Shewan thought her over-sparred. His son wrote that the yards were shortened in Hong Kong at the end of her maiden outward passage.

John W Dudgeon of London was her first owner, having all her 64 shares. Her passages from China were usually made against the monsoon and several occupied 120 to 125 days. On her maiden outward passage from Sunderland to Hong Kong, 15 June to 4 October 1860, she was caught in a squall

Left, top: Brocklebank's shipyard at Whitehaven in 1862, with tw
wooden vessels under construction: furthest is *Burdwan* of 803 tons, whic
traded to China; nearest is the brig *Ariel* of 130 tons. (*Merseyside Count
Museums*)

Left, centre: *Chaa-sze* midship section: reproduced from shipyard plan
Built 1860 by Alexander Hall & Sons, Aberdeen. She was diagonall
planked.

Left, bottom: Emerson & Walker's patent windlass. One of these was fitte
to the *Chaa-sze* at a cost of £100 in 1860. (*Author*)

Opposite, top: *Fiery Cross* lines plan. Built of wood in 1860 by Chaloner
Liverpool, from a design by William Rennie. Drawn from lines taken o
whole-hull model in Science Museum, London. Dimensions: 185.0ft ×
31.7ft × 19.2ft and 695 tons net and gross. No reconstruction.

Opposite, bottom: *Fiery Cross* sail plan, during years 1866-68. This wa
reconstructed from the oil painting reproduced here, using the other sai
plan as a basis. The skysail masts and yards have gone and double topsail
are fitted on the main only as an experiment.

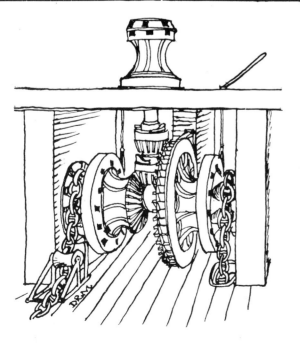

off the Natuna Islands in the China Sea which carried awa
her fore topmast, fore topgallant mast, main topgallant mas
and main royal mast. On the homeward passage she carriec
730 tons of tea of which 500 tons carried a freight of £4 pe
ton for Turner & Co, tea merchants. Hall's account bool
records that she carried no less than 300 tons of ballast. Or
her second voyage she loaded 815 tons of tea at Whampo
but also carried 240 tons of ballast. In 1863 she loaded tea a
Shanghai at £6 10s per ton.

In 1867, Baring Bros of London are listed as her owners
and the following year the owner was Devitt & Moore wh
placed her in the Australian trade. In 1874 she was sold t
J Delaney of London and two years later was lost when sh
stranded on 28 June, five miles north of the Grand Conne
table Islands, French Guiana, with a crew of twelve.

FIERY CROSS, 1860

The story of the first half of the 1860s could easily be tol
through the medium of the *Fiery Cross* – the fastest and mos
successful ship in these years. She was designed by Willian
Rennie who had previously produced the first *Fiery Cross*
and she was an improvement on that ship. She did not have
so much tumblehome as some of Steele's ships, but hac
moderate deadrise and hollow garboards. The waterline
were slightly hollow both fore and aft which enabled her t
go to windward well. Her stern was round, heavy and per
forated with seven windows surrounded by much ginger
bread work. A raised quarterdeck extended to midway bet
ween the mizen and main masts. There was a short ancho
deck level with the rail and although there was a small house
abaft the foremast, the crew must have berthed below deck.

She was built at Liverpool by Chaloner for John Campbel
of Glasgow, and William Walker of London may have hac
an interest in her or perhaps was the London manager. She
measured 185.0ft × 31.7ft × 19.2ft with a tonnage of 695
net, gross and under deck. She had steel masts, channels fo
spreading the rigging, and Cunningham's roller-reefing top
sails; in 1864 it was reported that this roller-reefing gear hac
been fitted to her three topgallant sails. An oil painting done
when George Kirkup was master in the years 1866–68 show
that the single main topsail had been replaced with double
topsails, and this is confirmed by the photograph of five
clippers lying at Foochow. Kirkup was poisoned by his Chin
ese cook and died at Hong Kong in 1868, and Beckett
brought the ship home.

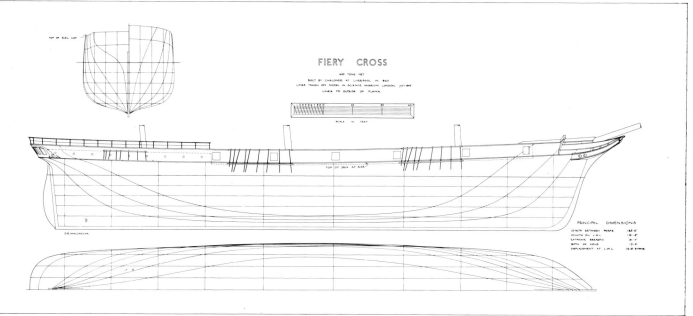

FIERY CROSS

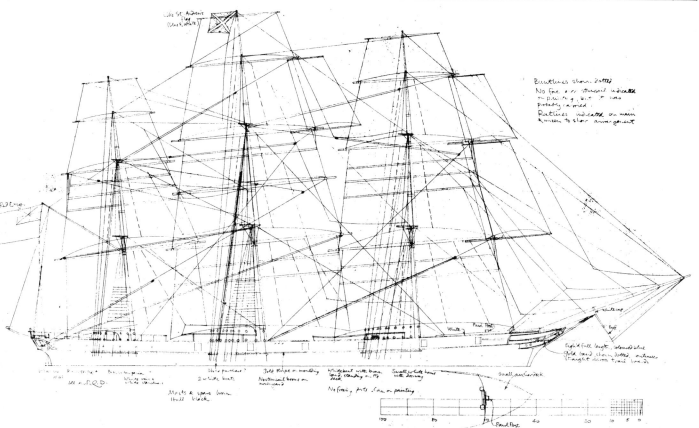

Alexander Stephen Jnr went aboard the *Fiery Cross* in November 1861 when visiting London and noted in his diary the lengths of the lower yards: fore yard 68ft, main yard 74ft, crossjack 58ft. Another note stated that she carried 1050 tons of tea at 40 cubic feet to the ton (entry for 15 Nov 1861). Stephen was often quoting Campbell with prices for shipbuilding. For instance, on 9 September 1862 he received a letter from him asking a price to build a composite ship of 750 tons register on the model of the *Fiery Cross*. The two men met in Liverpool two days later and had a long talk about ships in the China trade and their construction. Some

particulars of the *Fiery Cross* were obviously passed to Stephen as he recorded the following, some of which do not agree with the register details:

Length between perps (ft)	185
Length load line (ft)	181.6
Breadth (ft)	31.3
Hold depth (ft)	19.6
Depth amidships from top of keel (ft)	21
OM tons	$863^{54}/_{94}$

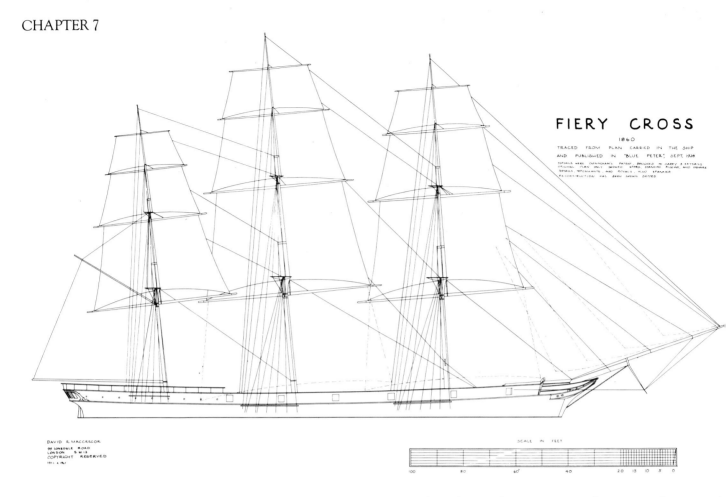

FIERY CROSS
1860
TRACED FROM PLAN CARRIED IN THE SHIP
AND PUBLISHED IN 'BLUE PETER' SEPT. 1928
TOPSAILS WERE CUNNINGHAM'S PATENT DESIGNED TO CARRY 3 SKYSAILS
ORIGINAL PLAN ONLY SHOWED SPARS, STANDING RIGGING AND SQUARE
SAILS, TOPGALLANTS, AND ROYALS, ALSO SPANKER
RECONSTRUCTION HAS BEEN SHOWN DOTTED

DAVID R MACGREGOR
99 LONSDALE ROAD
LONDON SW13
COPYRIGHT RESERVED

SCALE IN FEET

100   80   60   40   20 15 10 5 0

Reg tons	702.31
Area of midsection to LWL (sq ft)	424.12
Area of load WL (sq ft)	4394.90
Displacement at ditto (tons)	1615.84
Displacement per inch at ditto (tons)	10.46
Raised quarterdeck	52 feet from sternpost

At first Stephen quoted Campbell £22 for a composite ship at 14 A1 with East India outfit, but later reduced this to £20 15s. Campbell thought both prices too high. Alexander Stephen's conclusion was: 'Fiery Cross is the fastest ship in the China trade at present' (diary entry 9 Sept 1862).

On her first passage home she loaded 870,000lbs of tea at 5 guineas per ton, with a promise of 10s extra if first home, which she won easily. Her departure date has in the past been given as 14 June, but The Times said she left the Min in company with the Ellen Rodger and Falcon and that was on 11 June. This would make her passage 103 days to the Downs. Her steel masts proved very satisfactory on this voyage. The next year she just beat the Flying Spur by taking the tug for which Captain Ryrie had refused to pay £100. Fiery Cross got the coveted premium for the first ship in dock in 1861, 1862, 1863 and 1865. In the last year the premium was £1 per ton.

Yet her outward passages in these years were even more remarkable and were all made under Captain Richard Robinson who had just made two voyages to China in Brocklebank's Veronica:

1862–63, London to Hong Kong, 1 November to 30 January, 90 days.

1863–64, London to Shanghai, 8 November to 8 February, 92 days.

1864–65, London to Hong Kong, 29 October to 29 January, 92 days; 88 days pilot to pilot.

Three such consecutive outward passages made against the

strength of the north-east monsoon have never been equalled, whilst her 92 days to Shanghai in such circumstance stands as a record. Fiery Cross was indeed the fastest ship yet built for the trade.

In 1866, after passing Serica in the north-east trades outward-bound, and making a coasting voyage to Rangoon and back, she loaded in haste at Foochow with Ariel, Serica and Taeping. Ariel was the first to finish loading and left in tow of the weak paddle tug Island Queen. But so keen was Robinson to get away that he bolted without his papers and without signing bills of lading, gaining a 12-hour start on the rest and, it is said, driving Captain Innes of the Serica into a state bordering on insanity. Fiery Cross procured a good tug and passed Ariel at anchor inside the bar, which she crossed on the evening of 29 May, 14 hours ahead of Ariel. Anjer was passed on 18 June, only 20 days out, after making a better run down the China Sea than any of the others. It was a neck and neck race all the way home and she passed Flores in the Western Isles (Azores) on the same day as Ariel, Serica and Taeping, but somehow she was left behind after this in spite of a fair south-west wind, since she did not reach the Downs until somewhat over 24 hours after the Serica, or 101 days from Foochow. Robinson left her after this for Sir Lancelot, being replaced by Kirkup.

In 1874, the Fiery Cross passed to J Morrison & Co, London, and continued trading to the East throughout the 1870s and early 1880s. G P Addison, London, bought her in 1877, and sold her to William Wright, London, in 1883, who in turn sold her to J Gilbody, London, four years later. In the same year (1887) she was sold to owners in Fredrikstad, Norway, being rechristened Ellen Lines. Two years later she was towed into Sheerness with her coal cargo on fire and sank in Stangate Creek on the Medway.

Another account sent me by Captain Daniel states that she remained in the North and South Atlantic trade until 1893, when on 21 November she stranded on Red Sand near Whitstable, bound from Skelleftea to Britain with firewood. She was refloated and towed waterlogged into Sheerness by a tug on 24 November, and anchored in Saltpan Reach. Ship and cargo were then disposed of. The Norwegian master from 1891–93 was Christopherson.

FLYING SPUR, 1860

Jardine, Matheson's softwood clipper *Cairngorm* was too strained for further tea-carrying by the end of 1859, and so it was decided to replace her with a new ship which was ordered from Alexander Hall. Jardine's crest was a winged spur, and so the new vessel was given the name of *Flying Spur*. This was also the name of one of Sir Robert Jardine's racehorses and the figurehead was a likeness of this horse's head with his crest on a shield below. John Robertson of London was her managing owner in England for many years.

She was the 219th ship to be launched from Hall's yard, and was built of teak and greenheart to class 15 A1 at a cost of £13,787. She was a fairly sharp ship being of the same comparative fineness as either *Sir Lancelot* or the second *Kelso*. She had a raised quarterdeck which was 48ft long. Her forecastle measured 43ft, and her hull 184.0ft × 31.4ft × 19.4ft and 732 tons. In 1862 she loaded 1100 tons of tea. In 1881 she stranded on 13 February on Martin Vas, North Rock, in the South Atlantic, having on board a cargo of coal and a crew of 18. She later drifted ashore.

In a long letter to Basil Lubbock in 1910, which was loaned to me, Frederick Paton, who served aboard *Flying Spur* from November 1865 to early in 1870, first as apprentice and latterly as third mate, listed the crew and the sails:

bove: This painting of *Fiery Cross* was done during the years 1866–68 hen Captain Kirkup was master, and shows how the main topsail was vided into upper and lower sails while single ones were retained on fore d mizen. This was presumably a measure of economy. I photographed e painting in 1957 in the house of Mr Floyd, who was Kirkup's great-ephew. (*Author*)

pposite: Fiery Cross sail plan. Redrawn from copy of plan said to have een carried aboard the clipper. Reconstruction shown by dotted lines, ut skysails on each mast, staysails between the masts, and stunsails would ave been carried; also, probably, a crossjack.

elow: Photographed by John Lamb at Aberdeen in 1861, *The Murray* is tting out. Her flying jibboom is not yet rigged out nor is her main skysail rd crossed. Although built by Alexander Hall & Sons as an Australian ipper, she must have been very similar to *Flying Spur* or *Ocean Mail*. MacGregor Collection)

We had 20 able seamen, 2 ordinaries, 2 midshipmen, Captain, 3 officers, carpenter, joiner, boatswain, sailmaker, cook, 2 stewards and a butcher; 36 in all, which was a big crew for a vessel of 735 tons reg. But then, of course, she was very heavily rigged [with] two reefs in foresail and mainsail and also a reef in the crossjack; the topsails were Cunningham's patent and very large, as were also the topgallant sails and royals. When she went out of the China trade, they cut 15 feet off her lower masts and shifted the yards down.

Commenting on the number of stunsails carried in the clippers, he wrote that 'in the *Flying Spur*, the first three years I was in her, we set as many as fourteen, and these were hoisted and taken in sometimes twice in one watch.' This total makes four per side on the foremast and three per side on the mainmast, assuming no lower stunsails were set on the main. The ship carried no skysails.

As to her speed and that of other clippers, Paton commented: 'I do not think any of the tea clippers were capable of more than 14 knots, except in squalls when the water was smooth. As soon as the sea began to rise they began to wallow and lose speed; but in the China Sea in squalls I have often seen the *Flying Spur* do about 15 knots for a time.' And he continued:

The best day's run of the *Flying Spur* that I know of was 328 miles, but she repeatedly made over 300; and once, when on the way to Sydney, did 2100 miles in one week. That time we made the passage to Sydney in about 73 days, discharged the cargo (general), loaded a full cargo of coal and some racehorses, and then reached Shanghai on the 120th day from London. This I fancy is a record.

This would have been in 1866–67. Basil Lubbock noted on this letter that on a similar voyage *Thermopylae* took 128 days in 1868–69.

Comparing her with other noted clippers, Frederick Paton thought her the equal of the fastest:

The *Flying Spur* was certainly a very fast vessel, as good as the fastest, I should say, with the exception perhaps of the *Ariel* and *Spindrift*, but we were never in company with either. We were 7 days in company with the *Taeping* once, and 10 days with the *Sir Lancelot*, and proved quite a match for them in any wind. Their Captains were a good deal more enterprising, however, and drove their ship harder in strong winds. I do not think they owned any shares in them whereas Capt Ryrie was quite a large owner in the *Flying Spur* and nursed her . . . We passed the old Blackballer *Lightning* once, very fast indeed; also the tea clippers *Black Prince, Falcon, Ada, Ziba, Chinaman, Maitland* [and] several more also that I do not remember. One of the best tussles we ever had was with an iron ship named *Hippolyta* of Liverpool; she certainly sailed very well indeed in light winds and it took us a good while to leave her out of sight. The *Macduff* also . . . proved to be fast . . .

The *Macduff* was built by Alexander Hall in 1859 and was a wooden ship of 1135 tons gross. The *Hippolyta* was built of iron at Port Glasgow by John Reid in 1856 and was of 853 tons.

Elsewhere in the letter, Paton dramatically tells of the *Flying Spur* making 13 knots when close-hauled on the starboard tack in the north-east trades with her lee rail under water, and of how they passed the 'Glasgow clipper ship' *Lochleven Castle* whose main topgallant sail split to ribbons as they did so. Of Captain John Ryrie he writes that he 'believed in plenty of good food' and that when he left the

ship in 1867 he retired from the sea and lived in Liverpool which is where his mother and sisters lived.

At this date, her fastest passage from China had been 11 days made that year.

HORSA, 1860

This iron full-rigged ship is of interest because she was built by Scott & Co, Greenock, seven years after they built the *Lord of the Isles* and it may be that from the excellent photographs taken by James Gibson in 1893 when she went ashore in the Scilly Isles some useful details can be had to reconstruct the famous clipper. *Horsa* was somewhat bigger measuring 220.0ft × 34.2ft × 21.7ft which made 6.4 beams to length; 1094 tons under deck and 1128 net. The coefficient of under deck tonnage was 0.67.

Her first owners were Rathbone Bros, Liverpool; the Star Navigation Co of the same port became owners in 1876. I have only traced two of her passages from China. She survived her grounding at the Scillies and was towed off. However, her name is not listed in *Lloyd's Register* or the *Mercantile Navy List* for 1894. In 1890 she had been acquired by Ship Horsa Co Ltd, Liverpool (G McAllester & Sons).

OCEAN MAIL, 1860

Early in February this full-rigged ship was launched from Alexander Hall & Sons' yard at Aberdeen. Built of wood especially for the China trade at a cost of £13,252 or £21 per register ton and classed 14 A1, she measured 179.0ft × 31.0ft × 19.6ft and 630 tons net and gross. Her cut keel was 164ft long and she had 12ft rake of stem. She had a flush deck, a shield figurehead and wire rigging; her Emerson & Walker's patent windlass cost £105; the patent roller-reefing gear to her topsails cost £93. The yards on the mizen were of the same lengths as those on the foremast which was a feature found in some of Hall's ships and which tended to make for a powerful appearance. There was a main skysail yard, 30ft long, but the skysail mast was a gunter pole fidded abaft the main royal mast and secured by a cranse iron. The main yard measured 68ft and the main lower mast was much longer than the foremast. When in 1860 she was laden with 990 tons of tea and 2810 bales of cotton at Shanghai, in addition to 200 tons of ballast, she drew 16ft aft making her 10in down by the stern. She was considered a handsome craft and had the reputation of being very fast. Henry Adamson of Aberdeen owned her; he had once been the owner of *Countess of Seafield*, and in 1862 took delivery of *Star of China* from Hall.

On her maiden passage, bound for Shanghai, she passed thirty northbound ships including the American *Swordfish* after leaving Anjer. She brought home 364,600lbs of tea and 2841 bales of raw silk in 100 days between her pilots. Outward-bound the following year, Captain Adams was washed overboard in May, whilst *Assyrian* and *Wynaud* were caught up off Anjer on 26 June, all bound for Shanghai. *Ocean Mail* and *Wynaud* took 24 days to port and *Assyrian* 23. In 1863, Linklater took her out to Shanghai from London in only 88 days, 9 February to 8 May. This is almost as good as *Fiery Cross*'s superb run of 92 days against the monsoon in 1864.

Linklater must have been a smart captain but not smart enough to avoid wrecking her when leaving Shanghai late that year. With a cargo valued at £150,000 she had anchored outside the marks on the night of 1 August. Next morning

when leaving the estuary of the Yangtze her heel struck a wreck, whereupon she swung round on to the North Bank and the strong tide immediately capsized her. She was a total wreck within fifteen minutes. Many ships had come to grief on this bank though the *Cairngorm*, which had gone ashore there eight years before, had got off undamaged.

PEGASUS, 1860

Built in the same year as *Flying Spur*, the *Pegasus* also came from Alexander Hall's shipyard at Aberdeen but she was about 200 tons smaller, her actual tonnage being 525 gross with dimensions of 166.0ft × 28.0ft × 17.7ft, and she was rigged as a ship. The fore and main lower masts as well as the bowsprit were of iron, and were the first iron spars put into one of Hall's ships. She cost £9328. Her first owners were Potter Bros, Liverpool, who had her until she was sold to J J Bordes of Bordeaux in 1872 who renamed her *Esperance*. V Oriot, Havre, bought her in 1881 and five years later her name dropped from the Register.

VERONICA, 1860

Built a year after *Juanpore* but about 100 tons smaller, this wooden barque was constructed and owned by Brocklebank's, with dimensions of 127.5ft × 25.3ft × 17.2ft and a tonnage of 343. She was almost too small by 1860 for the

Left: Sporting a main skysail yard, the iron-hulled *Horsa* lies beside a wharf at Geelong in the late 1880s. A photograph of her ashore in the Scilly Isles appears in the last chapter. (*MacGregor Collection*)

Below: The *Maiden Queen* was owned by Brocklebank's but not built by them, which was unusual. Williamson of Harrington was the builder in 1860. All Brocklebank ships carried the broad white stripe on their hulls. Further particulars are in Appendix I. Her first five passages home with tea averaged 131.4 days. (*Merseyside County Museums*)

China trade, yet she was in it throughout the 1860s. Her first commander was Richard Robinson who arrived back in the river Mersey on 5 November 1861 at the end of her second voyage, and on 2 December he left London in command of *Fiery Cross*.

On her maiden voyage, *Veronica* took 106 days to Hong Kong from the Mersey, 30 March to 14 July in 1860, which was her fastest outward run. On her second outward passage she met so few strong winds that her royals were never furled nor any reefs taken in her topsails for the entire passage. She passed the *Invincible* in Gaspar Strait which had left Liverpool 26 days before her. This was in 1861. A year later, on the day she took her pilot some 48 miles from Hong Kong, bound from London, she beat off a pirate junk which tried to board her.

She was managed from 1864 to 1874 by Anderson, Thompson & Co, London, and in the latter year they acquired her. Ten years later she passed to Robertson of Swansea, and in 1886 she sank on 8 February after colliding with the barque *Marquis of Worcester* at Port Nolloth, when bound from Cape Town to Swansea with copper ore.

GLENAROS, 1861

A wood ship built at Sunderland by William Pile for Adamson, London, she measured 182.0ft × 32.5ft × 19.0ft and 679 tons, being later reduced to barque rig, like so many of her contemporaries. It will be noted that on her first passage home in 1862, under the command of W P Buckham who had come from *Star of the North*, her passage time of 108 days was easily the quickest of any made against the monsoon, and at the same time her run from Anjer only took 66 days, just three days outside the record set by the first *Kelso*.

J Morrison of London bought her in 1869, and then three Aberystwyth owners had her: first Hopkins in 1877, then Owens the next year and Doughton in 1880. The following year she was abandoned on 21 March in the North Atlantic in a fierce north-east gale, her grain cargo having choked the pumps.

HIGHFLYER, 1861

R & H Green built this ship in their Blackwall Yard, London, as a sloop-of-war for a South American republic; but

when ready to receive her engines no more money was forthcoming and so Green's took possession of her, plugged the propeller shaft, filled in the screw aperture and completed her as a pure sailing ship. This is the story submitted to *Sea Breezes* in August 1924, Vol VI, by E Branston Heath who served in her from 1872 to 1875. He said the old shaft always leaked. A lines plan in the Croad Collection, National Maritime Museum, shows the screw aperture. She has a sharp entrance and run and there is appreciable dead rise with slightly concave floors, hard bilges, wall sides and tumblehome above the wale. Another lines plan of the lower body only gives the amended lines where the screw aperture was filled in which has the effect of lengthening the run and making it finer. A lines plan has been reconstructed by Frederick Claydon combining the two drawings.

She measured 192.6ft × 35.5ft × 22.0ft, 907 tons under deck and 1011¾ tons net and gross. Although built of wood she had iron deck beams; she had an eagle figurehead and was a full-rigged ship. Anthony Enright, who had commanded the *Chrysolite* and the *Lightning* took her from the stocks and made two fine runs out to Sydney on her first two voyages, on each of which she crossed over to Shanghai and then brought home tea. On the first of these two, she took 84 days to Sydney in 1861 and then 32 days to Shanghai, but homeward-bound, she sailed from St Helena a day after *Glenaros* yet took an extra 29 days to get back. On her second voyage, the run to Sydney was accomplished in only 74 days. After a voyage-and-a-half in *Childers* Enright retired from the sea in 1868 to become overlooker for Gracie, Beazley & Co. In 1897 he finally retired at the age of 82 and died shortly before the First World War.

In 1866, *Highflyer* was towed up the Yangtze to Hankow to load tea and took the ground on the way up. Coming down she grounded again, this time at Langshan, 80 miles above Woosung. As she heeled over, the crew rapidly deserted her fearing she would capsize, but the tug *Fusi-yama* managed to get her off as the tide rose and she eventually reached Shanghai, where she had to go into dry-dock. The master Captain Shutter, died at Shanghai; a large number of masters died in China from various causes but anxiety must have been a major factor.

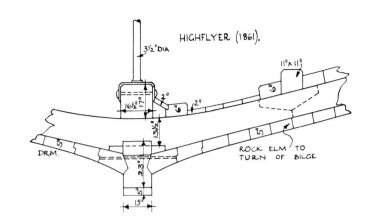

HIGHFLYER (1861).

Left: Although cut down to a barque, *Glenaros* was still a handsome vessel. *(James Burr)*

Right: Constructional details around the keel of a wooden vessel having pillars and deck beams of iron; as illustrated by R & H Green's *Highflyer.* *(Author)*

Bottom: The black-hulled *Highflyer* on a buoy off Gravesend on 7 August 1873. No sail is bent to the crossjack yard, a feature which Dutton's lithograph also repeated. *(Nautical Photo Agency)*

Below: Highflyer lines plan. Drawn by Frederick A Claydon, combining two plans at the National Maritime Museum, Greenwich; that in the Croad Collection has the lines and deck fittings, but also a screw aperture; the other shows the amended after body with the aperture blocked-in. Built in 1861 by R & H Green at the Blackwall Yard, London. Dimensions: 192.6ft × 35.5ft × 22.0ft, 1011¾ tons.

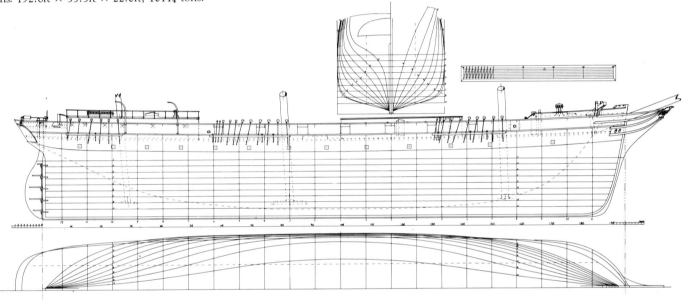

In 1870, probably on the death of Richard Green, Henry Green became the sole or principal owner. She sailed as a passenger ship in the Melbourne trade for some years. Ten years later she was sold to H Ramien of Elsfleth and was reduced to a barque. In 1889 she was owned in Christiania, Norway, and in November 1900 she caught fire at sea and was abandoned. The year before she had sailed from Montevideo to Halifax in 64 days, 7 February to 12 April.

KELSO, 1861

As the first vessel to bear this name had been lost, J R Kelso of North Shields ordered another ship from William Pile to replace her. The new ship was wood-built and measured 150.0ft × 31.3ft × 18.5ft and 557 tons. Captain Coulson, who had left the first *Kelso* before she was wrecked, took her from the stocks. He was one of the most experienced masters in the trade, and later did great things in the *Maitland*.

The *Kelso* was sold to Ross & Co, Liverpool, in 1880, and six years later went to owners in Mandal, Norway, being renamed *Bayard*. She was posted missing in September 1892.

MANSFIELD, 1861

This barque of 357 tons was the next finest-lined vessel t have been built at Annan by Benjamin Nicholson aft *Annandale* and *Queensberry*. She was not nearly so long i proportion to breadth as these two, having dimensions 133.1ft × 25.6ft × 16.9ft which gives 5.2 beams to lengt instead of over 7.0. The builder's half-model was made at ½ scale and is about 6ft long, but it must be a prelimina design as it scales 116.5ft × 24.0ft (moulded) × 15.5ft. Th length must have been increased by 16½ft on the mould lof The model has not much deadrise with hard bilges, and th maximum beam kept low; there is a sharp entrance, conve above and concave below; the run is especially long and ve hollow, and the quarter-beam buttock is almost straigh where it crosses the assumed load line.

The *Mansfield* was owned in Liverpool and operated t John Nicholson & Co, but she had a very short life. Sh went out to Shanghai in 115 days, departed from Amoy an reached New York 117 days later, and on the return tr across the Atlantic to Llanelly was posted missing, no

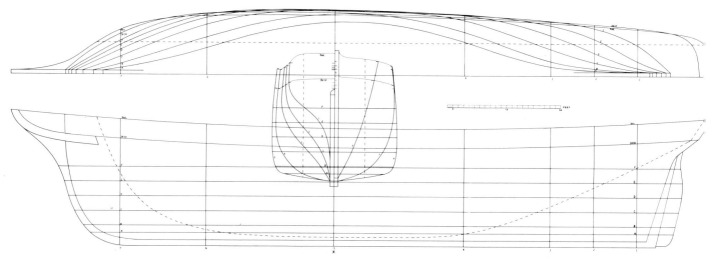

Above, left: Captain Thomas Mitchell (1832–70) All his commands were with the Aberdeen White Star Line: first was the *Phoenician* in 1857, followed by *Transatlantic;* then came *Queen of Nations,* 1861–68; and the wooden *Centurion* of 1869 was his last command. *(Dr and Mrs Donald)*

Above, right: A discoloured painting of the *Queen of Nations* when commanded by Thomas Mitchell in the 1860s. *(Dr and Mrs Donald)*

Opposite, top: Mansfield lines plan. Built in 1861 by Benjamin Nicholson at Annan with dimensions as given in the accompanying biography. This plan portrays a preliminary design and how it varied from the actual vessel is difficult to say. I took the lines off the model, but owing to pressure of work did not have time to ink in my own drawing; this was done by F A Claydon. Reconstruction: head, trailboard, rudder.

Opposite, bottom: The *John Nicholson,* built in 1859 at Annan, was of fuller hull-form than *Shakspere.* Particulars of her in Appendix I. *(Collection of the late Dr R C Anderson)*

having been heard of since leaving New York on 4 April 1862 with a cargo of grain.

MIN, 1861

Robert Steele built three ships for the tea trade in 1861–62 but none was as successful as the *Falcon.* One was the *Guinevere,* lost after three-and-a-half voyages; another was the *King Arthur,* built of iron and lost on her maiden voyage; and the third was the *Min,* built of wood, but with iron beams, for Captain Alexander Rodger, measuring 174.5ft × 29.8ft × 19.3ft and 629 tons. The *Min* was relatively as sharp as the *Falcon* but was said to be rather full in the buttocks which detracted from her speed in light winds. In the 1870s *Norman Court* easily outsailed her.

The *Min* was sold to Ewing & Co, Glasgow, in 1877 and bought from them by Picken of the same port in 1884. Four years later she passed to owners in Honolulu, being renamed *W B Godfrey.* On 9 March 1891, she was wrecked near Lorne, Australia, bound from San Francisco to Melbourne.

QUEEN OF NATIONS, 1861

A painting of this full-rigged ship depicted her as carrying skysails on each mast and being fitted with Cunningham's roller-reefing topsails. She was built of wood at Aberdeen by

Walter Hood for George Thompson & Co of the same port and measured 190.9ft × 32.5ft × 20.1ft, 738 tons under deck and 827 tons net. The cargo she loaded at Shanghai in 1864 was listed in *The Stowage of Ships and their Cargoes* by R W Stevens (p589) as follows: 3452 chests of tea; 3615 half-chests; 6832 tea packages; 507 boxes of tea; 58 bales silk; 32 bales waste silk; 34 other packages and 2 passengers. There was 35 tons of kentledge ballast, presumably iron, and 230 tons of shingle ballast; the dunnage, consisting of staves and bamboos, was 18in thick in the bottom and 19in thick in the bilges. Tonnage dues cost £126.

Her second master, Archie Donald, who had been mate of *Chaa-sze* in 1860, was washed off her poop in 1870. He had succeeded Thomas Mitchell. George Thompson still owned *Queen of Nations* in 1881 when she stranded on 31 May when 3 miles north of Wollongong, which lies about 20 miles south of Sydney Heads. She was bound from London to Sydney at the time with general cargo and a crew of 26, one of whom was lost. The wind was southerly Force 9 and she had presumably stood too close inshore.

Writing of his time in *Queen of Nations* on the maiden voyage of the *Centurion* in 1869, Captain Thomas Mitchell recalled in a letter to his wife: 'I never saw but one ship go past the *Queen* [*of Nations*] the whole eight voyages I was in her but I have already seen several go past the *Centurion.*' The latter was built by Hood in 1869 for Thompson's.

In 1865, Mitchell purchased four shares in *Queen of Nations* for £750 which valued the ship at £12,000 in all. The joint owners in the Bill of Sale were given as 'George Thompson Junior' and William Henderson, both of Aberdeen, and also Stephen Thompson and 'George Thompson Youngest', both of London. These men operated the 'Aberdeen White Star Line' and their ships usually made the outward passage to Australia and a number of them crossed over to China to load tea for London.

SILVER EAGLE, 1861

This was the only tea clipper built at Troon, by the Portland Shipbuilding Co, and her owner was Joseph Somes of London who later owned the extreme clipper *Leander.* The *Silver Eagle* was a full-rigged ship built of wood with dimensions of

185.2ft × 34.5ft × 20.8ft, 903 tons net and 805 tons under deck. The latter figure produces an under deck tonnage coefficient of 0.61. She had an eagle figurehead, an elliptical stern, a forecastle 33ft long and a poop 52ft long; the chart room and roundhouse were added to the poop in 1877, in which year her rig was reduced to that of barque. Somes' interests were transferred into the Merchant Shipping Co, London, as from 1 January 1869. In 1884 she was bought by P A Christensen of Langesund, Norway, and renamed *Aquila*; she was abandoned in April 1895.

WHINFELL, 1861
Built three years after the *Scawfell* by the same builder at Workington, Charles Lamport, the *Whinfell* was 8ft shorter but almost similar in breadth and depth of hold, having dimensions of 190.2ft × 32.6ft × 22.2ft, and her net and gross tonnage was 834. She was a full-rigged ship constructed of wood. She must have been a fast ship because on her passage home from Foochow in 1862, she sailed two days after the *Falcon* under the command of John Keay, but reached London on the same day. A year later she reached London on the same day as *Friar Tuck* having sailed three days later.

C Lamport of Liverpool, possibly the builder, was the first owner until 1874 when she passed to David Jones & Co, Liverpool. She foundered in a severe gale on 6 June 1881, 270 miles from Juan Fernandez Island, when bound from Antofagasta, Bolivia, to Great Britain with 1280 tons of nitrates. Out of her crew of eighteen, two were lost.

ZINGRA, 1861
Her claim to fame is the exceedingly short run she made between Shanghai and Liverpool of 85 days, when she left on 26 December 1863, passed Anjer five days later, and reached Liverpool on 20 March. Her cargo included 2100 bales of cotton. Two American clippers of over 1000 tons each took part in this remarkable race. They were the *Non-pareil* and *Young England* ex-*Oracle* which likewise sailed between Shanghai and Liverpool, the former taking 87 days and the latter 90 days. The dates and times of all the participants are set out in Chapter Five, in the biography of the *Nonpareil*. Of these other ships, one was the *Chryseis*, built at Sunderland in 1856 of 477 tons, which was under the same ownership as the *Zingra*.

The Sunderland firm of Taylour & Scouler at South Dock built the *Zingra*. This partnership built only in wood and lasted from 1857 to 1868 and in 1869 the yard was taken over by Bartram & Haswell. The *Zingra* measured 486 tons net and gross, 460 under deck, and had dimensions of 138.6ft × 28.6ft × 18.8ft for register. *Lloyd's Register* gives the depth incorrectly as 21.0ft until 1869 and the dimensions it gives are probably for tonnage. She was constructed of wood and rigged as a barque. Her first owner was John Clay of Sunderland, the sole owner, and on his death in 1865 John James Clay and Alfred Clay mortgaged the barque to James Burness of London as from November 1867. The registry was transferred to Liverpool in July 1870 in the name of Percival Tonge, and later the same year J R Ellis of Bangor, North Wales, became the owner. He placed her in general trade. Ten years later she was sold to owners in Japan and disappeared from the Register.

COULNAKYLE, 1862
An Aberdeen clipper as sharp as *Scawfell* and said to be as fast as *Serica* or *Fiery Cross*, she was built of wood by Alexander Hall for J Jamieson of Aberdeen, and measured 168.1ft × 30.6ft × 18.1ft and 579 tons. She cost £11,808 or £20 7s 10d per net register ton. On her first voyage she loaded 902 tons of tea at Shanghai at £6 10s per ton; she also carried 180 tons of ballast.

In 1864 she left Shanghai on 1 July in company with the brand-new clipper *Taeping* and both ships were partially dismasted in a typhoon ten days later; *Coulnakyle* put into Hong Kong and *Taeping* into Amoy, and so both sailed later

n the season, the latter taking only 88 days to Deal. It has already been told in Chapter Two how *Coulnakyle* was badly damaged at Hankow in 1866.

In 1883 she was sold to C M Boden of Umea, Sweden, for £1100. In either 1886 or 1888 she got ashore in the river Tamar, near Launceston, Tasmania, but it was found that repairs would cost £4000 and so she was sold by auction in Sydney for £300 to Ostermeyer Dewez & Co, Sydney. In 1890, Schiaffino of Genoa bought her and renamed her *Splendidezza*. She was condemned seven years later in July.

GUINEVERE, 1862

John MacCunn of Greenock had two near sister ships completed for him this year by Robert Steele & Co and they were appropriately named *Guinevere* and *King Arthur*. All his ships bore names from the Arthurian legends and he later owned *Sir Lancelot* and *Geraint*. *Guinevere* was launched on 1 July and was built of wood; *King Arthur*, launched on 5 November, was built of iron. *Guinevere* measured 647 tons net and 603 under deck, and had dimensions for registry of 174.5ft × 30.1ft × 19.8ft.

She was wrecked on 4 June 1866, off Hwangchow in the Yangtze, 50 miles below Hankow, as described in Chapter Two. The wreck was plundered but some tea was saved. The pilot was held to blame.

HELEN NICHOLSON, 1862

Iron ships were never popular in the tea trade because the lack of ventilation caused them to damage the cargo through condensation; in addition the attachment of barnacles and weed to the bottom slowed down their speed and the cost of putting them in a dry-dock, if one existed at all, was expensive in China. Altogether there were only about ten or so that were regular traders.

The *Helen Nicholson* was one of these, built by John Reid at Port Glasgow for Nicholson & McGill, Liverpool, who already owned the iron China trader *Vanguard*. The latter was, however, hardly a clipper, although she made several short passages. The *Helen Nicholson* measured 180.0ft × 30.0ft × 19.7ft and 717 tons. From her half-model in the Glasgow Museum, it can be seen that she had an almost square stern, a fair amount of deadrise with slack bilges, and that her run was rather finer than her entrance, so that she conformed to the best standards of tea clipper design without being an extreme model.

In 1865–66 under Halliday who had come from *Spirit of the North*, she went from Shanghai to Deal in 95 days, 1 November to 4 February. The following year she was 102 days from Hankow to the Downs, and by deducting the time spent in towing down the Yangtze, she was probably about 98 days from Woosung. She stranded fatally on Princes Island in the Straits of Sunda on 7 April 1870, outward-bound to Shanghai.

JOHN LIDGETT, 1862

In appearance she set a standard for Alexander Stephen's ships during the 1860s with a topgallant rail that enclosed a topgallant forecastle and a full height poop, the cutwater having a big overhang with numerous brackets and long trailboards. In hull-form there was only a small amount of deadrise, with hard bilges, wall sides and not much tumblehome; the entrance and run were only moderately fine so that she could only be classed as a medium clipper.

Opposite: This painting of the *Thomas Blythe* probably shows the ship at Singapore. Built of iron at Preston, Lancashire, in 1859 of 387 tons, she forms an example of the small forgotten ships that thronged Far Eastern ports. (*Hullform International*)

Below: John Lidgett sail plan. Built in 1862 by Alexander Stephen & Sons and reproduced from the builder's plan. This was photographed in 1961 when still in their possession.

A sail plan dated 26 July 1862 shows double topsails on fore- and mainmasts and a single one on the mizen. This is a very early date for double ones in Great Britain, but a painting of the ship portrays her with Cunningham's single roller-reefing variety, so the innovation may not have been approved by the owner.

The *John Lidgett*'s real claim to fame is that she was the first ship to be constructed on the composite principle as developed by Stephen and for which Lloyd's Register were willing to assign a class of 15 years A1. This was the type of composite construction – iron frame and wood planking – that was used by various builders throughout the 1860s with such success.

The contract price for building *John Lidgett* was £18 18s per ton for 750 tons builder's measurement, including an East India outfit, but the actual finished cost to Stephen was £15 17s 1d so he made a good profit. Composite ships were nearly always more expensive than wooden ones. Stephen's fear that Alexander Hall would complete a composite ship before

he did, resulted in the *John Lidgett* being launched only months and 24 days after laying the keel. In fact, Hall's ship the *Reindeer*, was not launched until February 1863.

The *John Lidgett*, named after her London owner, measured 178.7ft × 30.1ft × 20.4ft and 770 tons. Her passages in the China trade were nowhere out of the ordinary. In 187 she was posted missing since 20 October, bound from New York to London with a crew of nineteen.

WHITEADDER, 1862
Built at Rotherhithe by Bilbe & Co for John Willis, London she was constructed of wood with iron beams and a partly iron frame, measuring 180ft along the keel with register dimensions of 191.4ft × 34.0ft × 20.7ft and a tonnage of 915. When laden with some 1,375,000lbs of tea she drew just over 19ft.

She remained with Willis till sold for breaking up in 1884 In 1866 she probably did not carry tea as she took troops to Port Elizabeth on the way home.

Pictured off St Helena is the *Whiteadder* in a moderate gale. An early form of double topsail is in use here with a yard across the middle of the sail at the height of the lower mast cap, rather like the French *baleston* topsail. The yardarms are short but are fitted with braces. This watercolour is in the style of Thomas Dutton and the manner in which the bow profile follows the land is reminiscent of the portrait of *Mirage* in the last chapter. (*Parker Gallery*)

8

THE GREENOCK MODEL
AND SHIPS OF 1863-1866

The term 'tea clipper' has become legendary amongst those who discuss the merits and capabilities of the square-rigged ship and is employed to epitomize a perfect fusion between speed and beauty, and when used it is often considered only applicable to the composite clippers of the 1860s. Yet many of the ships sailing to China before 1863 were equally fast, successful and attractive in appearance, although each was finished off in an individual manner, according to the practice of each separate yard. Thus a ship was labelled as an 'Aberdeen clipper', 'River-built ship' (launched on the Thames) and so forth; never as a 'tea clipper'. In the early 1850s when the Aberdeen bow was so popular, there were indeed a few ships that merited the distinction 'tea clipper', but this small band was early swamped by other varieties. Ten years later when builders had had a chance to learn something of the peculiarities best suited to the design of a China clipper, one firm emerged with such a satisfactory hull and rig that it immediately became the fashion.

Situated at Greenock this yard produced some of the finest models ever to be seen in the trade and before long other yards on the Clyde were producing very similar vessels. Though hull-form was variable, the appearance above the waterline was at a glance so similar in numerous examples, that these vessels could only be termed 'tea clippers'. Although it has been remarked that when one had been seen, they all had been seen, they nevertheless continued to attract admirers wherever they went. A specialized trade always tends to produce a class of vessels similar in performance and design and the China clippers of the 1860s were no exception.

It is said that the Greenock firm of Robert Steele & Co modelled their earliest tea clippers on the lines of brigs that they had previously built for the West Indies trade. The *Falcon* was the most successful of their early ships – indeed she was hardly inferior to the second *Fiery Cross* – and though neither *Min* nor *Guinevere* were so satisfactory, Steele's had been able to build into their ships some of the features of design most necessary in a China clipper. These were discussed in the last chapter. Compared with other vessels in the trade, Steele's ships possessed an average amount of deadrise and a long, clean run, skilfully designed, which was contrasted in some of their ships with a rather shorter entrance. Many of the composite tea clippers possessed these characteristics to a lesser or more marked degree.

Robert Steele had already launched the *Young Lochinvar* in 1863 (lost on her third voyage) and the *Serica*, both wood-built ships, before he sent the *Taeping* afloat late in December as his first composite ship for the China trade. Launched for rival firms, *Serica* and *Taeping* seem to have been evenly matched and both were hard-sailed. Perhaps *Taeping* just had the best of it. Her half-model has survived showing a typical Steele vessel, very similar to *Falcon*, with slightly less deadrise, yet finer aft. The stem had become much more upright than formerly, with an inclination of only some 12° to the vertical, but a lot of false wood had to be bolted to the stem head to provide an aesthetic support to the bowsprit and figurehead. The stern was rounded, with a very shallow delicate counter, and the deadwood was carried high up the sternpost so that the hull had to flare suddenly outwards to take the shape of the stern. This was very marked in the case of *Ariel* and her contemporaries whose quarters were so fine that they did not give sufficient buoyancy, and it was only the underside of the counter, bearing on the water, which prevented the stern sinking under a following sea. On several occasions when running

Robert Steele (1821–1890) as a young man. The painting was photographed when in the possession of the late Mrs James Steele. *(MacGregor Collection)*

heavily, *Ariel* herself had her decks swept in seas that gave ships with fuller quarters or greater beam no cause for anxiety.

According to the builder's lines plan, *Ariel* and *Sir Lancelot* had similar hull lines although as they were built for rival owners this seems extraordinary, and the probability is that they were altered somewhat in the mould loft. Nevertheless the register dimensions and under deck tonnage remained surprisingly similar, varying only by a few inches in one case and six tons in the other. *Ariel* had more deadrise than *Taeping* but not quite such a fine entrance. *Titania* had the most extreme hull-form of any, with big deadrise and an exceedingly long entrance and run. Steele's later ships had more beam and so the fear of being pooped was less real. *Titania*'s coefficient of under deck tonnage, 0.58, is the smallest of all Steele's ships except *Serica* and gives sufficient reason for describing her as one of the more extreme tea clippers.

Charles Connell at the Scotstoun Shipyard, Glasgow, also built numbers of fast China traders. He built most of Thomas Skinner's 'Castles', which made a voyage or two to China as part of their trading to the East, but he also launched flyers like *Taitsing, Spindrift* and *Windhover*. Most of the other well-known ships came from individual yards of good repute. Rennie designed the *Black Prince* built by Hall, and the *Norman Court* built by Inglis. Another consulting naval architect was Bernard Waymouth, a Lloyd's surveyor, who designed *Leander* and *Thermopylae*. *Leander*, with a coefficient of 0.54, was the finest-lined ship in the trade, having a marked tumblehome and considerable rise of floor. Her two lowest waterlines were slightly hollow both fore and aft. *Thermopylae*'s ratio was 0.58, and she found this extra power very useful without it detracting from her speed. Built the year after *Thermopylae*, Alexander Hall's three-skysail-yarder, *The Caliph*, was one of the last tea clippers to be both built and designed at Aberdeen. This ship, whose great rise of floor and marked hollows in her garboard strakes emphasized the depth of her keel, was of the relatively shallow form of hull which Hall fancied. There is no doubt but that she

was incredibly fast, yet was an untried ship when lost on her second voyage. *Norman Court*, built in the same year, was of quite a different mould, with long deep sides, less deadrise and a very powerful midship section having, like Steele's ships, an angular forefoot, and she was fast and handy in the China Sea especially in a head sea. *Cutty Sark* was another individualistic ship built by an unknown firm, but though differing in appearance from the other clippers, she was fast and soon made a name for herself.

Most of the clippers had slight hollows in their lowest waterlines to aid them in working to windward, but in no case as marked as some of the ships of the previous decade. The midship sections continued to vary from one builder to another and Aberdeen yards maintained distinct differences in design and finish. A less extreme form of Aberdeen bow was still built by Hall and Hood and also a heavier form of stern. A full poop was frequently fitted and sometimes a topgallant forecastle.

In sail plans the general practice was becoming one more of spread than hoist. *Cutty Sark* had the greatest spread of any ship in the trade, having especially square topgallants and royals. *Spindrift* was also noted for her sail area with a main yard 84ft long. Double topsails had made their appearance by the middle of 1860s, *Ariel, Maitland* and others coming out with them in 1865. Many ships still carried a single mizen topsail which was frequently Cunningham's patent. Indeed, ships with single topsails were usually fitted with the roller reefing variety and it was estimated that some 4000 ships had been so equipped. In light winds single topsails were undoubtedly best, but double ones more satisfactory when the wind freshened. Steele's ships set the fashion for a main skysail only, but the number of flying kites was limited only by the master's fancy or the owner's purse. Many carried royal stunsails and most a Jamie Green. The lithograph of *Ambassador* gives a good idea of what an over-masted tea clipper looked like when under all plain sail. Thomas G Dutton's lithographs practically never show stunsails set although the booms are always drawn.

Above: Clippers lying at Foochow in 1866 waiting to load tea. According to names written at the bottom of the photograph, they are, from left to right: *Black Prince, Fiery Cross, Taeping, Ariel* and *Flying Spur*. The names attributed to *Taeping* and *Ariel* are surely incorrect, but the others are right. The late David M Little suggested the names should be: *Black Prince, Fiery Cross, Taitsing, Taeping* and *Flying Spur*, which seems quite possible. (*Peabody Museum, Salem*)

Opposite: Clippers at Pagoda Anchorage, Foochow, with awnings rigged. In the foreground is *Serica* with staysails hoisted; stern-on, to her right, is *Lahloo*. The names of the other three vessels are unknown. (*Peabody Museum, Salem*)

Ariel and *Titania* were flush-decked ships, but otherwise most clippers carried a raised quarterdeck, often commencing a few feet forward of the mizen. This was more sightly than a full-height poop which would have stuck up above the top of the low main rail but it meant that some cargo capacity was lost as the after accommodation occupied half the height of the 'tween decks, as shown in the longitudinal section of *Sir Lancelot*. On the raised quarterdeck were placed the usual saloon skylight, companionway, binnacle and wheel. To avoid taking up valuable cargo space and yet preserve the low profile afforded by a raised quarterdeck, a compromise was reached in which a deckhouse was erected on the after deck and a low deck surrounded it on three sides. This was the 'Aberdeen house' with the binnacle and wheel abaft it and entrance-ways built into the fore and after ends. Quite a number of clippers preferred this arrangement.

Forward of the mizen came the after hatch and boat skids, and between the fore- and mainmasts there was a large panelled deckhouse containing the crew, petty officers, galley, sail locker, etc. But a number of vessels only carried a small deckhouse in this position, the crew berthing forward in the 'tween decks. The longboat was either lashed on top of the deckhouse or aft on the main hatch. A forecastle raised level with the main rail was only fitted for easier working of the anchors and was only just long enough to enable the capstan bars to be manned. The crews were sometimes hand-picked and numbered about thirty-five all told before economies were adopted. At the beginning of the 1850s many British ships were manned on the principle of five men for every 100 tons. Thus *Northfleet* carried a crew of forty-eight a late as 1866.

During the 1860s the design of clippers that might be considered 'full-bloods' was generally less extreme than in the previous decade because the experiments in hull-form had been largely tried out by then and builders knew which forms would sail fast and which would not. This meant that shipbuilding costs followed a more standard and predictable pattern throughout the country and certainly benefited the owner as clippers were not costing much more than cargo ships. Lloyd's Register did not draw any distinction in its rules between clippers and carriers, but for vessels of any hull-form that were long and narrow in proportion to breadth and depth there were rules concerning the tie-members required. Wooden ships in which the proportion of breadth to length exceeded five, or in which depth to length exceeded eight, were to be given diagonal iron plates fitted inside or outside the frames. The tonnage of the ship governed the size of the plates, and as the proportions of depth and breadth to length increased, then extra precautions were required to ensure stiffness of the structure such as the incorporation of additional keelsons and minimum distances between shifts of planking. Iron ship-building was also subject to similar rules concerning strength of materials in relation to size.

However, ships built primarily to carry cargo were becoming longer and were beginning to enter the shipbuilding categories formerly applicable to clippers. An additional cost for a clipper was the so-called 'East India outfit' which was a more lavish supply of equipment than the 'Baltic outfit'. Ships were usually priced for hull, spars and rigging, and in some cases the owners supplied the rest. But a builder usually liked to fit out a ship complete. In these two outfits were included all the sails, warps and cables, boats, anchors, and the entire equipment required on board as well as all the spares for these; blocks were supplied with the rigging in the basic price, but spare blocks were scheduled in the outfit. In Vol I of his *Modern System of Naval Architecture*, John Scott Russell lists East India outfits for a sailing ship of 1400 tons builder's measurement and another for a ship of 560 tons bm; each occupy an entire page. He then lists a Baltic outfit for a sailing ship of 400 tons bm which occupies only half a page. All ocean-going ships would be fitted with an East India outfit which Alexander Stephen assessed as costing £2 to £3 per ton when working out his estimates.

Shipbuilders based their costs on the quality of materials put into a ship in order to obtain a particular class at Lloyd's Register and the exact form of the ship did not come into the calculation. Therefore tea clippers were not built without relation to cost and no shipowner would have been crazy enough to allow a builder to complete his ship without adherence to a strict budget and specification. No doubt extra carving on the outside, a more elaborate figurehead, panelling inside the bulwarks and some special joinery work would cost a little more but would not vastly alter the building costs.

But one thing which did alter building costs was the introduction of composite construction which became generally popular amongst tea-clipper owners from 1864 onwards. It had developed, to briefly restate the case, because of a desire to build longer ships without increasing their weight unduly, which was unavoidable with wood ships, whilst the rapid expansion of iron foundries had greatly lowered the cost of this new material. Composite ships were also tighter, could be coppered, delivered their cargoes in good order and did not become strained. And because of the prejudice against iron ships, the ranks of the crack tea clippers were almost entirely composed of composite-built ships by the end of the 1860s. In other trades iron ships had gradually been adopted and antifouling devices somewhat improved. Steamers required more strength and rigidity than even composite hulls could give, so that the China and Far Eastern trades when worked by sailing ships were chiefly responsible for propagating composite shipbuilding. When the Suez Canal was opened and steamers could reach India and the East so quickly that they could make three voyages to the sailing ships' one, thereby taking over the cream of the trade, there were no more orders for tea clippers and therefore no composite ships to build. Indeed, *Lothair* (1870) and *Torrens* (1875) were, with a few others, the only exceptions.

Though not the first to make use of this principle, Bilbe & Co of Rotherhithe were, as already mentioned in Chapter Six, the first to build composite ships specially for the China trade. But the comparatively new idea did not catch on at once. Possibly it needed a more widely known builder to adopt it. Bilbe's method of compound frames must have been very difficult to construct, yet something had to be done to overcome the disadvantages of securing the planks to iron frames with copper bolts. But it was the younger Alexander Stephen who made this method of construction a thoroughly practical and acceptable proposition.

While his father, Alexander (1795–1875), and his brother, William, remained at Dundee building only in wood, a second yard was opened on the Clyde at Kelvinhaugh in 1850 to build in iron. Alexander Stephen Jnr (born 1832) was placed in charge under his father who must

have been busy travelling between the two yards. The son gradually gained control of operations with the success of the yard until, in 1858, it was transferred to him and his brother James, although the latter was soon to quit.

As early as 1856, Alexander Stephen Jnr had shown an interest in composite construction but five years later things started to move more rapidly. He got to know John Jordan who was the successor to the Liverpool firm of Jordan & Getty which had built some composite ships in the early 1850s, and he discussed the whole question not only with shipowners but also with Lloyd's Register itself. The two problems were to prove to shipowners that such a system of iron frames and wood planking was practical and so win orders, and also to convince Lloyd's Register of the soundness of the idea. He made numerous visits to shipowners in Glasgow, Liverpool and London to discuss the problem, made models, experimented with various methods of fixing bolts, drew out his ideas on paper, and finally submitted a written report to Lloyd's Register on 25 September 1861. To his delight they agreed in writing on 11 October to his scheme which permitted him to build vessels up to 15 years A1 which was the highest class then allotted, and the first time Lloyd's Register had actually assigned a number of years to such a form of construction.

On the following day he contracted with John Lidgett & Co to build a composite ship for them of 750 tons bm to class 15 A1 with an East India outfit at a cost of £18 18s per ton bm. According to his calculation he anticipated making a profit of £3 0s 11d per ton bm. The keel was not laid until 4 March 1862 because the iron ship *City of Bombay* had to be launched first, and this delay drove Alexander Stephen nearly to despair as he was afraid that Alexander Hall & Sons in Aberdeen might get their first composite ship into the water before he did; so the Glasgow yard really worked hard and the new ship, christened *John Lidgett*, was launched only five months and twenty-four days after laying the keel. This must have required some organization and sleepless nights to get everything so well planned in advance that an entirely new form of construction could be brought so swiftly to fruition. Hall must have had problems, as his ship, the *Reindeer*, was only finished in 1863. In February 1862 Alexander Stephen had patented his ideas for protecting copper bolts to avoid them from coming into contact with the iron frames, and he also covered the iron frames and bolt heads with cement.

Of course, other shipbuilders were not slow to utilize the permission given by Lloyd's Register and by April 1862 five other builders had submitted their proposals to them. Robert Steele first visited Stephen's yard in December 1862 to inspect his composite construction and the following March was there again discussing the matter, as he had contracted to build a composite ship for Alexander Rodger. This was to be the *Taeping*. On 15 April 1863, Alexander

Opposite, top: A typical midship section with explanatory key for a composite vessel. The drawing is based on a plan found in the files of Alexander Stephen & Sons and is dated 1861. (*Author*)

Opposite bottom: This was the second of Hall's ships to bear the name *Reindeer* but was only a medium clipper. Painted ports were unusual for a ship from this yard; the builder's spar dimensions allow a moonsail on the main above the skysail. Particulars are in Appendix I. (*Aberdeen Museum and Art Gallery*)

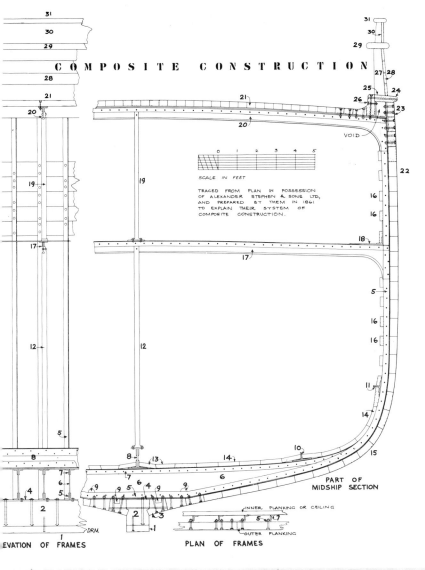

COMPOSITE CONSTRUCTION

SCALE IN FEET

TRACED FROM PLAN IN POSSESSION
OF ALEXANDER STEPHEN & SONS LTD,
AND PREPARED BY THEM IN 1861
TO EXPLAIN THEIR SYSTEM OF
COMPOSITE CONSTRUCTION.

VOID

PART OF
MIDSHIP SECTION

INNER PLANKING OR CEILING

OUTER PLANKING

ELEVATION OF FRAMES   PLAN OF FRAMES

KEY

1. False keel (timber)
2. Keel (timber)
3. Garboard strake (timber)
4. Keel plate (iron)
5. Frame (iron)
6. Floor (iron)
7. Reversed frame (iron)
8. Single plate keelson (iron)
9. Limbers
10. Side keelson (iron)
11. Bilge keelson (iron)
12. Hold pillar (iron)
13. Limber boards (timber)
14. Ceiling (timber)
15. Bilge planking (timber)
16. Cargo battens (timber)
17. Lower deck beam (iron)
18. Lower deck stringer (iron)
19. Upper deck pillar (iron)
20. Upper deck beam (iron)
21. Upper deck (timber)
22. Topsides (timber)
23. Sheerstrake (timber)
24. Planksheer (timber)
25. Covering board (timber)
26. Waterway (timber)
27. Bulwark stanchion (timber)
28. Bulwark planking (timber)
29. Main rail (timber)
30. Topgallant bulwark (timber)
31. Topgallant rail (timber)

Stephen entered in his diary: 'Killick, Rodger and I went to Steele's yard to see ships building for China trade. Steele's first composite ship commencing for Rodger . . . Copper bolts same as ours. They intend protecting them similar to my patent . . . Killick and Rodger afterwards dined with me.'

Unfortunately Lloyd's Register required that all these new composite ships be classed as 'Experimental' and subject to biennial survey which deterred some prospective shipowners. In 1867 Lloyd's published their own rules for composite construction and the term 'experimental' was deleted. In fact, these ships generally enjoyed very long lives and it was not long before orders for them were flooding in to shipyards all over the country.

Elsewhere I have covered in some detail the royalties demanded by John Jordan on every composite ship built in the 1860s, as he claimed it infringed the patent taken out in 1849 and renewed in 1863 for a further seven years. Alexander Stephen got a large reduction because he claimed that but for him composite building would not have been so widely acclaimed. Jordan's royalty demands varied all the time at anything from 1s to 6s per ton and he must have made good profits on all the trouble he caused the builders. Stephen's usually only paid 3d to 6d per ton. There were variations on Jordan's system, such as that patented in 1864 by Charles Lungley of London who built the *Dilpussund* and others for the China trade.

It was mostly in the North of England and in Scotland that composite ships were built. In August 1863, Hall launched the *Black Prince* as his second composite tea clipper and later the same year came the *Yang-tsze*. On the Clyde, Charles Connell's first composite ship was the *Wild Deer* launched in December of that year and Robert Steele's was the *Taeping*, launched in the same month. By 1864 composite construction was in full swing.

In essence this system was remarkably simple in dealing with a particular task, rather than side-stepping the issue as iron ships did, built as they were on a traditional pattern of wooden shipbuilding with no appreciation for the immense strength and flexibility of shape that iron gave. In composite construction, frames and floors were built up in the same manner as in an iron ship. The keelson usually consisted of a plate and angle girder situated on or between the floors and with special stiffening incorporated in way of the masts. The keel, stem and sternpost were of wood, with an iron plate bolted to the inside edge to which the frames were secured. The first ten feet of planking above the keel consisted of elm, and teak above that in twelve inch widths where possible, the thickness varying from about six inches at the garboard strake to just under five at the sheer strake. Beams supporting the wood decks occurred at every other frame. Three or more stringers ran round inside the frames tying the whole together, whilst diagonal iron plates between the planking and the frames gave additional strength. Bulwarks and bulwark stanchions were of either wood or iron. Most of the composite ships had iron or steel lower masts with the lower and topsail yards and bowsprit of the same material.

During the 1860s the approximate cost of building a first class iron sailing ship varied from £15 to £17 per gross ton; for a composite ship from £17 to £21 per gross ton to class 15 A1; and for a wooden ship from £18 to £22 per ton of the same class. Shipbuilders often continued to use the old

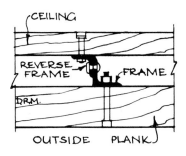

The iron Z-frame, composed of two angle irons, used in nearly all composite ships after 1862. (*Author*)

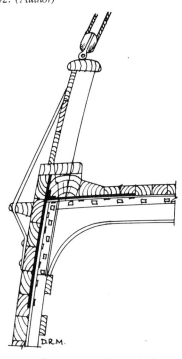

Typical bulwark construction of a composite ship with channels. (*Author*)

measurement tonnage when quoting prices which had the effect of reducing the price per ton, so it then becomes necessary to divide the total cost by the gross or net tonnage to obtain a comparable figure. For instance, Alexander Hall's clipper *Fychow* built of wood in 1863 measured $853^{22}/_{94}$ tons om – 853.26 in decimals – and if multiplied by the price per ton, £18 10s, it gives a total of £15,785 6s 3d as the contract price. When this is divided by the gross tonnage of 710, the cost becomes £22 4s 7d per gross ton. So it is important to compare like with like.

Builders taking up composite construction were early encouraged in their task by the reduction of tea duties in 1863 from 1s 5d per lb to 1s. Two years later they fell to only 6d which brought a spate of orders for first class ships. Both 1863 and 1865 produced a host of fast handy clippers, an event which was repeated as late as 1869. When the entire period can be reviewed as a whole it is surprising to note the large number of clippers built just before the eclipse; but then no owner thought that steam would immediately prove so successful in areas affected by the opening of the Suez Canal.

Although freight rates began to decline slowly towards the end of the 1860s, the fastest clippers of the front rank could still expect to receive £4 per ton at Foochow at the

An example of a vessel built on the Scilly Isles by Edwards for Banfield & Co of the same place, with a tonnage of 390 and dimensions of 122.3ft × 26.7ft × 17.0ft and classed 13 A1. Several vessels from the Scillies traded to the East. *(F E Gibson)*

tart of the season, declining to £3 per ton by July, and £2 0s from Shanghai or Whampoa. In 1865, *Serica* and *Fiery Cross* got £4 10s per ton at Foochow plus £1 per ton premium for the first ship home; all other ships there got £3 0s plus 10s premium. Therefore, by being dismasted in a yphoon during the 1864 season, *Taeping* had no chance to demonstrate to the shippers how fast she could sail *against* he monsoon – 89 days home late in the season from Amoy ould not be judged aright – and so probably lost £1 per ton reight. Going back to the beginning of the 1860s, we find hat in 1861 at Foochow in July *Falcon, Fiery Cross, Ellen Rodger, Flying Spur* and *Robin Hood* all loaded at £5 5s per on plus 10s per ton for first cargo in dock. Rates from Hankow were usually £2 per ton higher in order to defray he cost of being towed all the way up the Yangtze Kiang nd down again, as well as the high insurance premiums. Nevertheless up to the end of the 1860s, freights were still ust high enough for owners to maintain their clippers in op class condition.

One owner who figures prominently through the two lecades of the tea clippers' progress was John Robert Kelso of North Shields. He was born in 1816, but I have found out nothing about his early years as the obituary notice in 899 was more interested in his long illness. It did mention hat he had built up a large fortune out of shipowning, had xtensive interests in Harrogate and was well-known as a good horseman. He was survived by only one son and his our daughters. The best known of his clippers were the *Maitland* and *Undine*, and Coulson was his most capable captain who went from ship to ship in the fleet.

The younger Andrew Shewan (1849-1927) who took command of the *Norman Court* in 1873, and who has recorded such valuable first-hand information on the subject in early issues of *Sea Breezes* and in his book *The Great Days of Sail*, discussed at some length the relative merits of he best-known clippers in Chapter 23 of the latter, and finally came to the conclusion that the first place should be warded to *Ariel*. Next he placed *Cutty Sark, Leander, Spindrift, Thermopylae* and *Titania* in the same group, with little o choose between them. After them came *Kaisow, Lahloo,*

Lothair, Norman Court, Sir Lancelot, Taeping, Undine and *Windhover;* followed by *Black Prince, Coulnakyle, Falcon, Fiery Cross* (1860), *John R Worcester, Maitland, Serica* and *Taitsing.* The groupings, but not the ships, are arranged in descending order of merit and apply, of course, only when the ships were in the China trade.

It has already been mentioned more than once that the attitude of the master determined to a great extent the duration of the passage. This naturally applied to any trade, but the master of a tea clipper had more inducement to carry sail than many another man. Yet first class captains were always in short supply in the China trade. The best masters endeavoured to carry on as long as possible without losing a sail or a spar and then make sail again at the first opportunity. No instance of seamanship gives a better idea of how a clipper should be handled than the method of luffing her through a squall. It was essential, especially in the China Sea, to keep to windward as much as possible. The captain who squared away his yards and ran before the squall lost a number of miles made good against the wind. But the man who kept his ship as near to the wind as possible, with the canvas frequently shaking violently, and who avoided being taken aback or thrown over on to his beam ends when the wind shifted, would come through little the worse for it, but with the satisfaction of being far to windward of those that had run off before the squall. The master who lacked nerve was useless in such a crisis and in attempting to get his ship off the wind would find himself on his beam ends and possibly lose a spar or some sails. When the wind was fair, all flying kites that would draw were set and constantly changed or taken in to suit the wind. The carpenter was always busily employed making and repairing stunsail booms.

As an example of the work of constantly shifting sails on a small clipper, Captain John Mann's log aboard the barque *Strathmore* records:

A magnificent photograph of tea clippers in their prime at Pagoda Anchorage, Foochow. The photograph is dated 1868 and the ships named as *Sir Lancelot* (nearest) and *Spindrift* on the right. But the ships did not look like this. The most likely candidates are *Ariel* (left) – as the ship is flush-decked – and *Thermopylae* (right), and the year 1869. The flags are at half mast. I have reconstructed the rigging above the top of the hills where it had been printed out. (*Peabody Museum, Salem*)

> *22 Aug 1856.* Blowing fresh. Took in the royal and topgt std sails. At 2 pm foretopmast std sail carried away. At 5 pm in topgt sails. Through the night squally: wind W – a high sea on.
> *23 Aug.* Do weather. Shortening and making sail accordingly.

And again, three months later:

> *27 Nov.* Commences with light breezes from the ENE to E. Carrying all sail to the best advantage. Set all the starboard std sails. Latter part gloomy. At 7 took in all the std sails, royals and light sails. At 10.30 heavy rains, thunder and lightning. Clewed up topgt sails. 4 am set topgt sails. Lat at noon 18°30'S 172°59'E.

Yet in spite of this driving, experienced masters rarely lost a spar. Many of them, prompted not by the premium but by a sporting instinct, drove their ships hard all the way from Foochow to the Downs, and if they could beat by only one or two days some noteworthy rival, they might be so favoured the following year by the shippers in China that they could load tea at a higher rate of freight than formerly.

A very fine picture is painted by Captain Shewan of an outward-bound clipper, when he writes in *The Great Days of Sail* (reprinted in 1973 by Conway Maritime Press):

> I myself met the *Ariel* twice at sea. Once, in 1868, when homeward-bound in the *Black Prince*, while we were running into the chops of the Channel, the *Ariel* passed close to us, outward bound, and standing south on the starboard tack. I was but a youngster at the time, and was up aloft loosing the topgallant sail. I had a good view of her slashing through the water, her men aloft, reefing the fore topsail. She certainly looked every inch a clipper – very low in the water, travelling very fast, and apparently shipping much water.

BIOGRAPHIES OF SHIPS BUILT 1863–1866

BELTED WILL, 1863

Besides this ship, John H Bushby of Liverpool owned number of ships in the China trade mostly built at Working ton, such as *Banian*, *Corea* and *Dunmail*, to mention but few; but *Belted Will* was the only one with any pretensions t speed, being as sharp as the *Falcon*.

J T Fell built her at Workington of wood, with iron beams on dimensions of 186.4ft × 32.4ft × 20.8ft and 812 tons She nearly always loaded tea at Canton and was fortunate i having such a capable master as Locke. On her maide voyage she was said to have gone out to Hong Kong from Liverpool in 93 days, but port to port the time is 103, 2 September to 5 January, 1863–64.

The firm's name changed to Shaw, Bushby & Co in 1880 and in 1884 she was sold to J O Hulthen of Helsingborg Sweden. Nine years later she stranded on 2 July at Söderarn soon after leaving Sundsvall with a cargo of lumber for Por Elizabeth. Later she was refloated and condemned; then sh was towed to Helsingborg and broken up in 1894.

BLACK PRINCE, 1863

William Rennie who had designed the two *Fiery Crosses* wa called upon to design this clipper and John Robertson, lat master of the *Cairngorm*, who had an interest in her, saw t her equipment. No expense was spared and when ready fo sea she was considered capable of beating any clipper in th trade. Yet she lacked one thing which undid all the rest, an that was the insufficient daring of her master, Willian Inglis. His inconsistency of purpose time and again spoile what might have been a good passage; or it may have been his natural caution because he owned 16 shares in her and this always curbed a master's inclination to race. Duncan Kay, London, registered as the owner, held the same numbe of shares; John Scarth held 8, and William Walkinshaw, partner in Baring Brothers, held 24 shares. The account were rendered to the latter by the builder.

Three years before *Black Prince* was built, the celebrated *Fiery Cross* had been launched and the fact that she was so successful probably encouraged William Rennie to repeat her hull-form in this new tea clipper. The great similarity in the register dimensions would certainly confirm such a theory and for ease of comparison they are set out here: *Black Prince*, 185.0ft × 32.0ft × 19.0ft, 707 tons under deck, 750 tons net, 0.62 coefficient of under deck tons. *Fiery Cross*, 185.0ft × 31.7ft × 19.2ft, 695 tons under deck, 695 tons net, 0.61 coefficient of under deck tons.

In addition, the dimensions of the masts and yards are very similar; the lines and sail plan of *Fiery Cross* are reproduced here. It would be interesting to know whether Alexander Hall & Sons, who constructed the *Black Prince*, had the same misgivings about employing someone else's design that Alexander Stephen had in building the auxiliary steamer *Sea King* in 1863. She was also to Rennie's design.

In Hall's cost account, *Black Prince*'s spar dimensions are listed, amongst which are skysail masts and yards on each mast. In addition the stunsail boom dimensions are given, which is unusual. She had topmast, topgallant and royal stunsails on fore- and mainmasts and also topmast stunsails on the mizen. The mizen booms were 31ft long which was the same as the fore topgallant booms.

Designers liked to provide low bulwarks for the sake of elegance but this was at variance with accommodation in the forecastle, and in *Black Prince* a compromise of a sort was reached by making a low break in the rail to give a height of 5ft at the after end. But this meant that the men had to bend double to get in and out from the main deck and some serious accidents took place as they forgot the low headroom. The forecastle measured 39ft long and the raised quarterdeck 56ft. The total finished cost was £17,540 16s 1d or £23 7s 10d per ton for 17 years A1 in composite construction.

Finlay, Hodgson & Co, London, were the managing owners in 1866 in which year they were bought up by Baring Brothers who thus became the new owners. Ten years later, the ship is listed in the name of C L Norman, one of Baring's partners, and in the next year William Inglis of London is given as the owner. The clipper was wrecked on 5 August 1882 on Arendo Reef in the Java Sea bound from Manilla to London with a crew of twenty-two. On one of her earlier passages in 1868 she was struck by a swordfish when homeward-bound from Foochow and the first eight inches of its sword remained sticking in her side.

In spite of Captain Andrew Shewan's misgivings about William Inglis' ability to get the best out of the *Black Prince*, she made a number of fast passages such as 93 days between Hong Kong and London in 1864, 23 March to 24 June, loaded with 1150 tons of cotton at £4 10s per ton. Then in 1866, having gone out to Hong Kong in 102 days from London, she made the passage back from Foochow in 109 days, 3 June to 20 September, with 1148 tons of tea loaded at £5 per ton, a good rate. On this last passage she beat *Ziba*, *Chinaman*, *Flying Spur*, *Ada*, *Falcon* and *Min* which sailed at about the same time. Her net earnings on her first four voyages amounted to £10,060 19s 4d.

These particulars from the archives in Baring Brothers show that Captain Inglis could well afford to smile when chaffed at being called the 'whipper-in' after one of the tea races, and the other shareholders must have been well pleased.

Alexander Hall's composite ship *Black Prince* in Aberdeen harbour when newly completed. No sail is bent on the crossjack yard, but the spanker is hooped to the mast, and so she probably has a hoisting gaff. (*MacGregor Collection*)

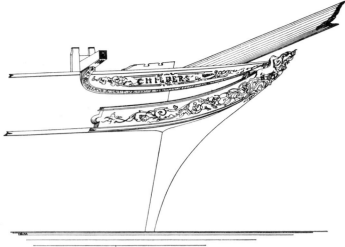

Left: Bow decoration of *Childers*. Redrawn from one of four designs in the Croad Collection, National Maritime Museum. (*Author*)

Below: An oil painting by Samuel Walters dated 1864 of the *Eliza Shaw* which was built the previous year. The arrangement of the half-round poop can be made out, with the chainplates of the rigging secured to it and the short space at the stern for the helmsman. (*Parker Gallery*)

Bottom: *Eliza Shaw* sail plan. Reproduced from a modern shipyard copy of the original builder's plan in which only the spars, sails and standing rigging was shown. The royal backstays are rather feint.

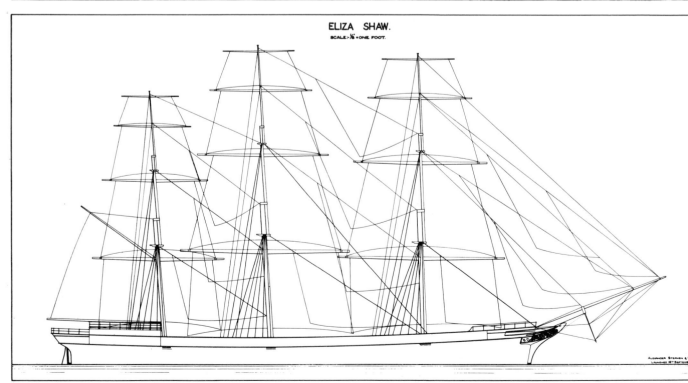

ELIZA SHAW.
SCALE:-⅛ = ONE FOOT.

CHILDERS, 1863

Described as 'a very fine ship', she was built of wood by R & H Green at Blackwall for their own use. Of 1016 tons she measured 194.3ft × 35.4ft × 21.9ft. Captain Anthony Enright who had just made two voyages to China in their own *Highflyer*, upon which the *Childers* was an improvement, was transferred to the new vessel.

Leaving London on 22 December 1863, she reached Hong Kong on 30 March, 99 days later. Her return passage was equally good. The following year, loaded with 1,388,000lbs of new teas insured at $800,000, she was towed down the river Min on 30 May by the SS *Vulcan*, but when two miles outside Sharp Peak she struck the North Sand Bank and became a total loss. Green's never built another ship for the tea trade.

ELIZA SHAW, 1863

A composite ship launched in September by Alexander Stephen & Sons, Glasgow, for C Shaw & Co, London, of 596 tons, measuring 184.5ft × 30.7ft × 18.4ft. Killick, Martin & Co may have acted as agents for Charles Shaw in negotiating a price, placing an order and providing supervision during construction. Alternatively Killick's may have ordered the ship for themselves and then transferred her to Charles Shaw. In October 1862, Alexander Stephen named a price of £19 19s builder's measurement to Killick, Martin for a 14 A1 ship copper-bolted, but they thought a price of £18 10s to £19 more realistic. Stephen prepared a model and specification for Killick's and his quotation was accepted on 14 November 1862 for a total price of £15,400, which on 596 tons net and gross works out at £22 2s 7d per ton. On 800¹⁰⁄₉₄ tons bm the price per ton is £19 5s. Stephen made a clear profit of £3300 on the contract. Captain Killick visited the ship whilst she was under construction in June 1863, but Charles Shaw paid the second instalment of £4002.

The first of the iron frames was erected on 16 March 1863 and the framework was completed on 7 April; on 20 April the first timber plank was fixed on – the fore hood – and she was planked to the gunwale by 27 May. In July Killick was again in the yard looking at her and on 8 July Charles Shaw paid his first visit to the yard to see the ship, which was No 44. She was built under a roof and classed 15 A1.

The *Eliza Shaw* was launched by Mrs Shaw and Alexander Stephen entertained twenty-two guests to dinner at his home. The ship was launched without any masts in her. Captain Killick's opinion of the ship was that she 'is a beautiful piece of naval architecture and highly finished'. The Builder's Certificate was sent to Killick's before the ship left Glasgow on 27 October 1863 under tow for Liverpool, where she was to load for Shanghai.

Alexander Stephen was in London early the following month and noted in his diary for 4 November 1863 that he went with Killick aboard Hall's new ship *Yang-Tsze* [sic]. 'She is much inferior to the *Eliza Shaw*. She is iron frame & wood planked – no sheer strake.'

Most of Stephen's ships for the China trade which were launched in the 1860s were only medium clippers, and *Eliza Shaw* is the finest-lined of them all with moderate deadrise and firm bilges; the entrance and run are fairly sharp. There was a small monkey forecastle and the crew were housed in a large deckhouse abaft the foremast. Close abaft the mizen stood another big deckhouse for the officers and any passengers, but instead of having low decks on each side of it, the top curved down on to the bulwarks. The gap of 15ft between the after end of this house and the taffrail had a low deck on which were placed the binnacle, wheel and wheel box. The only ways to the wheel from the main deck were either through the deckhouse or up over it and down the after side. Two other tea clippers had this arrangement – the *Highflyer* and the *Ethiopian*. The sides of the house above the main rail were painted white. Perhaps it made the counter less heavy-looking than taking the poop right to the stern with a 'half-round' completely encasing it, but it was an awkward arrangement and possibly dangerous for the helmsman. The bulwarks were faced inboard with decorative panels.

Like many of Stephen's ships she looked under-canvassed, both in the sail plan and in an oil painting of her done by Samuel Walters. She did not set skysails, but the sail plan has large staysails drawn and perhaps big studding sails were provided to augment the square sails. The main yard was 66ft long and the mainmast 113ft from deck to truck.

The *Eliza Shaw* loaded at either Hankow or Shanghai throughout the 1860s and once carried 400 tons of weight and 688 tons of measurement goods. She always sailed in June or July, her fastest passage being 114 days from Shanghai to off Plymouth in 1865. In 1868 she loaded at £7 7s per ton at Hankow but the rate was usually £6 or so; sometimes she got this rate at Shanghai as in 1864. In 1871 Captain Gerrard Gaye recorded in his meteorological log-book that he had made the passage to Japan six times in the ship by the 'Great Eastern Route round Tasmania' in 112 to 122 days for the entire passage and getting to Tasmania in February. But in 1871 he was so delayed by easterly winds that he headed for Anjer where he found sixteen ships that had spent three weeks trying to beat through the Straits of Sunda. The wind was NE.

Outward-bound to Shanghai with coal in 1875, she was involved in a collision with an unknown barque, believed French, and put into Rio de Janeiro to repair. The cargo was sold and once the repairs were completed she abandoned a voyage to China and instead sailed to Bahia where she loaded a cargo for London.

In 1877, Charles Shaw sold the ship for £4750 to John Willis & Son, who renamed her *Fantasie* and reduced her to a barque. Willis kept her in the China trade and in 1878 she loaded tea at Foochow and sailed on 6 November, reaching London 144 days later on 30 March. She went missing in 1884 bound from India to Dundee, not having been heard of since 11 July; it was supposed that she foundered off the Cape of Good Hope. She had a crew of nineteen.

ELIZABETH NICHOLSON, 1863

Built of wood by John Nicholson & Co, Annan, and designed by Mr Brown for their own use, she measured 192.5ft × 32.5ft × 22.2ft and 904 tons. An oil painting of her in the National Maritime Museum shows a vessel with painted ports (rare in the tea trade), square stern, old fashioned bow, full poop with diagonally crossed wire mesh panels secured to the rail, and no deckhouse. She carries trysails on both fore and main and nothing above royals. Unfortunately this painting carries Marryat's code flags '2/5192' which is the ship *John Bright* that was built at Dumbarton in 1847 of 591 tons. The presence of the fore trysail certainly suggests an earlier ship than one of 1863.

Top: *Elizabeth Nicholson* with her sail cloths painted very prominently. The Chinese artist has drawn the tell-tale track of the Cunningham roller-reefing gear not only on the topsails but also on the main topgallant; however, he has omitted the second yard, which did not revolve. (*Merseyside County Museums*)

Above: The *Fychow* shortening sail. The topsails were Cunningham patent. (*Gellatley, Hankey & Co*)

Right: The Sunderland clipper *Pak Wan* at Port Adelaide when rigged as barque. The framing on the coved sides of her Aberdeen house has bee picked out in black or some dark colour. (*A D Edwardes*)

There is another painting ascribed to this ship which the Liverpool Museum owns, and on this there are no signal flags nor any name discernible. However the distinguishing track in the centre of the topsails identifies Cunningham's roller-reefing sails – there is even one on the main topgallant – and makes the ship post-1855. This painting depicts a vessel which differs in almost every way from the other one.

Elizabeth Nicholson had about 2500 sheets of Muntz metal on her bottom as sheathing. She was registered at Dumfries. In 1867–68 she made a very fast run of 92 days to London from Foochow in the favourable monsoon.

Montgomerie & Workman, London, bought her in 1888 and four years later sold her to Chilean owners in Antofagasta who renamed her *Elisa*. In 1899 she returned to the British flag when owned in Shanghai. She was given back her original name and by 1913 had become a hulk at Shanghai. She was still afloat there ten years later under the ownership of S C Farnham & Co, Shanghai.

EVEREST, 1863

Brocklebank's ships were noted for sound construction and an ability not only to complete their voyages safely but also to deliver their cargoes in good condition. Several of their ships – the *Burdwan, Crisis, Herculean, Juanpore, Maiden Queen* and *Veronica* – were in the China trade during this period, but perhaps *Everest* was the fastest member of the fleet. She often loaded new teas, whilst most of the others sailed with the fair monsoon.

A lines plan in the Brocklebank archives at Liverpool Museum shows that she had marked deadrise with slack bilges and almost no tumblehome; the ends were long and sharp with a little hollow in the lower body. She had a square

stern. No sail plan or spar dimensions exist, nor have I come across a painting of her.

Everest was built by T & J Brocklebank at their Whitehaven yard for their own use. Constructed of wood as a full-rigged ship, she measured 171.8ft × 30.0ft × 19.2ft and 571 tons. She was lost on Danger Reef in the China Sea on 5 September 1873.

FYCHOW, 1863

This wooden full-rigged ship was built by Alexander Hall & Sons to the order of Duncan Dunbar, London, but as he died in the year before she was launched, Gellatly, Hankey & Sewell, London, became the owners. She measured 180.0ft × 31.5ft × 19.2ft with a tonnage of 710 and cost £15,785 or £22 5s per ton. The builder's cost account lists an 'engine' supplied by Chaplin & Co at a cost of £200 1s 7d; presumably this was situated in the after end of the deckhouse with a donkey boiler to drive the pumps, cargo winch and windlass. There were two lower swinging booms, each 42ft long, for setting the lower stunsails on the foremast, and stunsails on fore- and mainmasts up to the royals were fitted; the topsails were roller-reefing and there was a mizen trysail mast for the spanker, which shows on a painting of the ship.

In 1867 she went missing in the North Atlantic on passage from New York to London with a crew of twenty, loaded with barley.

PAK WAN, 1863

Originally built as a full-rigged ship, this composite clipper was launched in May by George Peverall, Sunderland, for J S Patton, London. Dimensions of 186.2ft × 32.6ft × 19.0ft gave a tonnage of 818. The photograph taken of her when she was a barque shows a typical clipper with a short fore-

castle head for working the anchors, deckhouse with boats on top, raised quarterdeck with a low house containing companion and skylights to saloon, and aft of that the wheel. On her second voyage she went out to Hong Kong in 93 days from London, 30 June to 1 October 1864.

A Lawrence, London, bought her in 1875, and W Smith, Newcastle, NSW, in 1885. After three years he sold her to J Gillan, also of Newcastle, during which time she was in the inter-island trade in the Pacific. In 1889 she sustained hull damage in a hurricane at Tahiti and reached Honolulu on 20 May in distress. Soon afterwards she was sold by auction and bought by her master who renamed her *Mauna Ala*. In 1892 the owner was G Walker of Honolulu. In 1903 she was wrecked on 27 July on the bar of Topolobambo on the west coast of Mexico.

SERICA, 1863
Robert Steele's designs were still in the experimental stage, for the *Serica*, launched at the beginning of August, had an under deck tonnage coefficient of only 0.57 as against *Taeping*'s 0.63. In spite of her hard-driving master and sharper hull, *Serica* was never so good a passage-maker as *Taeping*, which with a somewhat fuller section was more weatherly in the China Sea. In 1866, *Taeping* gained two days on her in the homeward run to Anjer but lost it after passing the Cape.

Serica was built for James Findlay of Greenock, being Steele's last but one wooden tea clipper. Dimensions of 185.9ft × 31.1ft × 19.6ft gave a net tonnage of 708. She was fitted with a half-poop and four boats, the lower masts and their yards being of iron.

In 1864, loaded with the new Kaisows, she won the premium for the first ship home and then went out to Shanghai in 99 days from Torbay, 25 October 1864 to 1 February, or 106 from London. Another fast outward

run was 98 days between London and Shanghai in 1868–69, 11 October to 17 January. In 1865 she loaded 1,021,800lb of tea at £4 10s per ton, and leaving on the same day as *Fiery Cross*, they both reached the Isle of Wight together. *Serica* was the leading ship off Beachy Head, but failed to get a tug and so docked 12 hours after her rival.

In 1872 she left Hong Kong on 2 November for Montevideo, but was wrecked on the Paracels the next day, there being only one survivor out of twenty-eight.

TAEPING, 1863
Described two years after her launch as a 'magnificent vessel', she was Robert Steele's first composite tea clipper. Her planking was of greenheart and teak secured to the iron frames by Elliot's phosphorated metal screw bolts. Her bowsprit was of iron and her lower masts and topmasts with their yards were probably of the same material, as this was fast becoming the fashion. She had a short anchor deck, a raised quarterdeck, and small deckhouses abaft both the fore- and mainmasts. Her longboat lay on chocks on the deck forward of the mainmast. All her deck fittings were beautifully finished.

She was launched for Alexander Rodger of Glasgow in December, measuring 183.7ft × 31.1ft × 19.9ft and 767 tons, classed at 14 A1. She excelled in light winds. On her maiden voyage she left Shanghai tea-laden on 1 July 1864, but was towed into Amoy 22 days later by HM gunboat *Flamer*, having lost her bowsprit, figurehead, foremast, and main and mizen topmasts overboard in a typhoon off Formosa. She left again on 8 October and was only 88 days to Deal. Then, leaving London on 8 February, 1865, she went out to Hong Kong in 94 days, or 92 days between her pilots, 9 February to 13 May. She made the best homeward run of her career in 1866 during the 'Great Tea Race', taking only

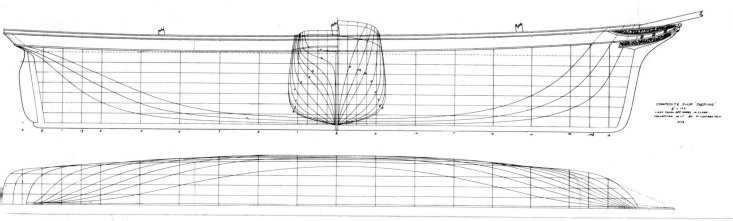

Above: Taeping lines plan. Drawn by Michael Costagliola from lines he had taken off a half-model in the Clark Collection at the Massachusetts Institute of Technology. Ship built 1863 by Robert Steele & Co with dimensions of 183.7ft × 31.1ft × 19.9ft and 767 tons.

Right: Iron bulwark construction in a composite ship such as *Wild Deer.* (*Author*)

Opposite: One of Dutton's most impressive lithographs of a clipper under full sail pictures *Taeping* racing up-Channel in 1866. The *Illustrated London News* pictured her with these same sails and in addition a Jamie Green, watersail, and jib topsail. (*MacGregor Collection*)

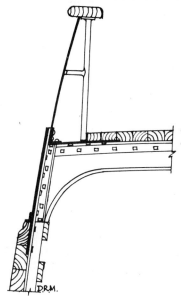

99 days to the Downs, and although ten minutes behind *Ariel* there, managed to dock almost half an hour before her. This is described in the biography of *Ariel*.

MacKinnon, her master, was landed at Algoa Bay on 3 December 1866, very ill, when bound for Shanghai, and died at Table Bay whilst returning home, aged 41. The first mate, Dowdy, took command with a crew of 26. At Foochow *Taeping* loaded 1,099,900lbs of tea, unmoored on 3 June and crossed the bar at 11.45 am next day. Five days later she was up with *Serica* off Hong Kong, having started two days after Findlay's crack clipper. Anjer was passed at 8.0 am on 27 June and the Cape rounded on 1 August. On 13 August Ascension was passed and the Line was crossed at 10.0 am three days later. On 12 September Portland Light bore 20 miles at 8.0 pm and with a west wind she was abreast of the Isle of Wight at 3.0 am next day. She took two tugs off the Owers Light and reached Gravesend at 10.30 am on 14 September. She was in London Dock just after 2.0 pm, 102 days 2½ hours after leaving the river Min, being the first ship home with the new teas. But the premium had been discontinued following the dead heat the year before. Nevertheless, in spite of this fine run which terminated a week ahead of any other ship, *Ariel* was estimated to have beaten her by four hours on time, between leaving the Min and entering the docks in London, 13 June (8.30 am) to 23 September (7.0 am in dock) or 101 days 22½ hours, while *Sir Lancelot* took only 99 days from Woosung. The race home in 1868 is described in the account of *Spindrift*. In 1869 *Taeping* went from Plymouth Sound, where she had sheltered from a south-west gale, to Shanghai in 97 days, 27 November to 4 March.

On 22 September 1871, she was wrecked on Ladd's Reef, China Sea, under Captain Gissing, bound from Amoy to New York.

WILD DEER, 1863

Launched as Charles Connell's first composite ship, she had an elm bottom fastened with treenails and yellow metal; teak planking above the turn of the bilge, fastened with yellow metal screw bolts; and iron bulwarks above the sheer strake. She came out with a 75ft main yard and roller-reefing topsails, but was dismasted on her maiden passage and put into Lisbon. Captain George Cobb who had been in *Robin Hood* took her from the stocks, but died at Anjer on his fourth outward passage. A Dutchman named Ganzwyk brought the ship home.

She was built for Walker, London, and in 1866 became the property of the Albion Shipping Co, which merged with Shaw, Savill in 1882. In 1883 she was wrecked on 12 January on the North Rock, Cloughey, Co Down, with 200 emigrants for New Zealand, in which trade she had been since the early 1870s. Of 1016 tons net she measured 211.0ft × 33.2ft × 20.7ft; under deck tonnage was 955.

YANG-TSZE, 1863

A composite ship built by Alexander Hall & Sons at Aberdeen for Lewin & Co, London, who held half the shares, she measured 636 tons under deck, 688 tons gross and net, with dimensions of 179.5ft × 31.0ft × 18.3ft. Captain James Killick held 8 shares in a personal capacity but Killick, Martin & Co were never shareholders although they were often the loading brokers.

Above: Stern view of *Wild Deer* in dry dock at Port Chalmers; after 1871 she was in the New Zealand trade. *(Alexander Turnbull Library)*

Right: Bows of *Wild Deer* when in dry dock. *(Alexander Turnbull Library)*

Opposite: Gossamer sail plan. Built in 1864 and reproduced from the builder's plan. This was photographed in 1961 when still in their possession.

She was built under a shed and the Lloyd's Register surveyor, William Wallis, inspected her thirty times between April and October 1863 for which his fee was £39 8s. She had a dragon figurehead and was built with a poop. She was launched without masts or bowsprit fitted but was to be equipped with roller-reefing topsails and a main skysail. She cost £14,724 or £21 8s per gross ton; the contract price was £19 per ton om on 772 tons om.

Alexander Stephen had met David Lewin, who was to be *Yang-tsze*'s future owner, at Killick, Martin's London office on 21 October 1862 and had named a price of £19 19s for a composite ship to class 14 A1 which had been thought too high; those present had said that £19 or £18 10s was what they had in mind, so it is interesting to note that the *Yang-tsze* was contracted for at £19. (All these prices are for om tons.) David Lewin visited Stephen's yard in June the following year; Stephen's remarks on the *Yang-tsze* are given in the biography of *Eliza Shaw*. In *The China Bird*, I gave a description of *Yang-tsze*'s construction from her survey report, a copy of the Builder's Certificate, a statement of accounts in building and lists of her spar dimensions.

Captain Kemball's fine performance in her in 1867 when he beat five ships all acknowledged to be faster than his, gained him the command of *Thermopylae*. In 1871 *Yang-tsze* was wrecked on 2 October on the Paracels, bound for New York from Foochow under Captain Smith, who was amongst those lost.

YOUNG LOCHINVAR, 1863

Built by Robert Steele & Co at Greenock in the same year as his *Serica* and *Taeping*, she had an identical breadth measurement and the same depth of hold to within 0.2ft as these two, but she was 2ft shorter than *Taeping* and 4.2ft shorter than *Serica*. Her actual measurements were 181.7ft × 31.1ft × 19.8ft, with tonnages of 680 under deck, and 724 net. Her coefficient of under deck tonnage was 0.61.

Launched only 25 days after the *Serica* on 29 August, she was built of wood as a full-rigged ship fitted with Cunningham's roller-reefing topsails, the lower masts and topmasts with their respective yards all being made of steel plates. Her owners were McDiarmid & Greenshields, Liverpool. She had but a short life, being wrecked on 9 May 1866 when off the China coast bound from Hong Kong, presumably towards Foochow to load tea. The reason was put down to thick weather, uncertain currents and poor charts.

BOREALIS, 1864

Her builders were Bilbe & Perry of Rotherhithe who had constructed several vessels on the composite principle before

Stephen's method appeared in 1862, as well as several other composite tea clippers in the 1860s. The *Borealis* had 6.4 beams to length with dimensions of 205.0ft × 32.0ft × 21.0ft, and there were not many tea clippers with a register length of over 200ft before this date. She was a full-rigged ship of 920 tons, built on the composite principle, and owned by her builders, although William Perry is listed as owner when she was sold in 1876 to Anderson, Anderson & Co who ran the Orient Line. In 1884, G Brailli & Co, Trieste, became the owner; he registered the ship at Orebich and renamed her *Marietta Brailli*. Later he moved to Cardiff but the registration port did not alter. She was broken up in 1897.

She made a very fast passage of 89 days between Amoy and New York in 1875–76, 29 December to 27 March, with the north-east monsoon, under the command of Richard Bear (or Beard); but her passages in the 1860s under Alexander Henderson have not been obtained. After 1876 she was in the Adelaide trade.

CORAL NYMPH, 1864

The more exotic names of ships were confined largely to the euphoric 1850s and especially to the gold rush era, but fancy names still appeared from time to time. The above name seems to be tempting providence and indeed this fine ship was wrecked on 20 May 1869 on a coral reef in the Macclesfield Channel, South China Sea, when bound from Sunderland to Shanghai with a cargo of coal. She had already been ashore at the start of this passage, going aground off Dungeness on 6 December 1868, but was towed off and back to the East India Docks three days later.

John Hay of London, who two years later owned the *Cleta*, ordered the *Coral Nymph* from the Sunderland builder William Pile. She measured 176.6ft × 33.2ft × 18.7ft and 725 tons, being built of composite construction and rigged as a ship.

DILPUSSUND, 1864

Five full-rigged ships were built on the River Thames in the middle of the 1860s, all to the order of Smith, Fleming & Co, London, for the India and Far East trades, and the first syllable of each comprised the letters 'Dil'. They were as follows:

1864 *Dilkoosh*, 816 tons, 167.2ft × 32.4ft × 21.2ft, by Major.
1864 *Dilpussund*, 624 tons, 180.0ft × 29.0ft × 18.0ft, by Lungley.
1865 *Dilawur*, 1306 tons, 226.0ft × 34.0ft × 22.8ft, by Lungley.
1865 *Dilbhur*, 1308 tons, 226.0ft × 34.0ft × 22.7ft, by Lungley.
1865 *Dilharee*, 1293 tons, 227.7ft × 34.0ft × 22.7ft, by Fletcher.

All were composite-built. Lungley's yard was at Deptford; Fletcher, Sons & Fearnall had theirs at Limehouse, and they built the *Dilharee* on Lungley's principle. In the case of *Dilpussund* this was described as having the usual iron frames, stringers and tie plates. 'The inner skin is of teak planking fastened to the frames with galvanized nut and screw bolts.' Diagonal iron straps were then let in to this skin and fastened through the planking to the iron frames. 'The outer skin is then brought on longitudinally, as before, and fastened to the inner skin with copper clinch bolts.' She was then sheathed with yellow metal.

I have only obtained passages from China for the first two of the above five ships, of which *Dilpussund* made the shorter passages. She was sold in 1880 to S D Grant & Co, London, and three years later they transferred her to C Brandt of Hamburg who changed her name to *Europa*. In 1894 she came back to London ownership and reverted to her original name of *Dilpussund* to be used for 'cruising purposes', but to what extent the new owner, Hanks, employed her thus is not known. In 1896 she arrived at Lyttleton on 27 September, 217 days out from New York via Dunedin. In 1901, Nelson

Below: The *Douglas Castle* when under Danish ownership. *(Jens Malling)*

Bottom: A typical Dutton lithograph portrays the *Ethiopian* under easy sail without any of her royal yards crossed. The after house, with its coved sides, and surrounded by a raised quarterdeck, was placed much further forward than usual. *(Paul Mason Gallery)*

& Robertson of Sydney became her owners and six years later she was turned into a hulk at Sydney, but she survived until 1933 when she was broken up at Wellington.

DOUGLAS CASTLE, 1864

Thomas Skinner's ships, none of which were extreme clippers, were all named after castles and were built by various Clydeside yards, this one coming from Charles Connell who had a shipyard at Overnewton, Glasgow. Of 678 tons net and gross, she had dimensions of 176.6ft × 30.6ft × 18.7ft

and was composite-built and rigged as a ship. She had quite a good average in the China trade.

She passed to J Casey, Glasgow, in 1883 and a year later to T Rhys, London. In 1888 she was sold to G Brandi of Thisted, Denmark, who placed her in the Calcutta and Mauritius trade. Three years later she was posted missing being last heard of on 23 June, bound to Valparaiso from Swansea with coal.

ETHIOPIAN, 1864

Built of wood for George Thompson's 'White Star Line' by Walter Hood, Aberdeen, she measured 195.8ft × 34.0ft × 20.2ft with a raised quarterdeck of 51ft, forecastle of 42ft, and registered 839 tons. She went out to Melbourne in 68 days on her maiden passage.

In 1867 she had gone out to Melbourne and then loaded a cargo of coal and cleared Port Phillip Heads on 23 February. On 1 March almost due east of Sydney in 164°34'E, the ship was under reefed topsails and foresail with a strong easterly gale blowing until 6 March. On 7 March in 16°50'S 170°10'E, and so not far from the New Hebrides, the ship was struck by great gusts of wind and tremendous seas which threw her over on to her beam ends, until the water came as high as the bell on the poop. The ship seemed to be settling in the water with 'all hands standing outside the weather rail expecting that they had only a few minutes to live', as Captain Faulkner later wrote in his log. The main and mizen masts were cut away; after only a few lanyards were cut, the masts went over the side, but the ship would not come up until the foremast was cut away too. The master summed it up a few days later in his log-book:

During the hurricane the sea was one sheet of foam, and at 6 o'clock it was so dark that you could not see anyone standing beside you except when the lightning flashed, which was awful, and with the wind, sea and rain, you could not keep your eyes open a second, for it cut like a knife; the heaviest of the hurricane lasted for about an hour-and-a-half and there is not one on board ever expected to see morning; and I think, if the masts had not been cut away, that the ship would not have come up again, and if the ship had not been strong she could not have stood what she did.

The crew were sent into the hold to trim the cargo of coal as there was seven feet of water in the well. The masts had broken off just above the deck but the hull was intact and apparently undamaged. Jury masts were rigged from a few spare spars left on deck, the pumps were repaired and the ship got back on to an even keel on 8 and 9 March when the wind died away. They were 1800 miles away from Sydney with no masts. There was a flat calm in the heat until 22 March, followed by squally south-east winds, and on the 27th they just avoided drifting ashore on New Caledonia. By 7 April the ship had got to within 14 miles of Sydney Heads when a strong south-east gale sprang up and drove the helpless clipper a hundred miles to the north-east with the sea making a clean breach over the ship. On 13 April the French warship *Marceau* appeared and towed the *Ethiopian* back to Sydney. Repairs were put in hand quickly and the ship sailed for China, where she loaded a cargo at Shanghai and sailed from there for London on 27 October.

She was sold to owners at Frederikstad, Norway, in 1886, and in 1894 was abandoned in September in the North Atlantic. She was passed derelict on 3 October, towed into St Michael's, and condemned.

GOLDEN SPUR, 1864

This full-rigged ship was built of wood at St Sampson's, Guernsey, by P Ogier for G T Carrington of Guernsey with dimensions of 177.4ft × 31.4ft × 19.9ft and a tonnage of 657. The presence of a long house on deck abaft the foremast and another one aft through which the mizen mast passed, as shown in a photograph, suggests that she had a flush deck. She had an oak frame and was planked with teak and greenheart. She was wrecked on 28 February 1879 on Haiphong Bar, Hong Kong, with rice from Cochin China.

ADA, 1865

Apart from *Lufra* and *The Caliph*, this was Alexander Hall's last ship built for the tea trade. Her finished cost was £13,120. Composite-built for John Wade & Co, London, she measured 182.0ft × 30.0ft × 18.0ft and 686 tons. Her first master, Jones, had come from *Ziba*.

In 1878 she stranded on 11 December near Chefoo, bound from Swatow in ballast with a crew of sixteen.

The *Golden Spur* dried out in Town Harbour, Guernsey. She was flush-decked with two large deckhouses and had Cunningham's roller-reefing topsails. The stern carving looks elaborate. She had double topsails by 1871. *(J D Attwood)*

Above: The Aberdeen Clipper *Ada*. (James Burr)

ARIEL, 1865

Most designers sought primarily to produce a ship capable of speed in light or head winds with the frequent result that a ship moderately fast on all points of sailing made better passages. Rennie was one of the most successful men at designing a fast, weatherly clipper and Robert Steele was also concentrating on this factor. The *Taeping* excelled in light airs and the *Ariel* was even better in this respect.

A half-model of *Ariel* in the M'Lean Museum, Watt Institution, Greenock, the lines of which I took off in 1949 as well as those of *Taeping* and *Lahloo*, unexpectedly turned out to be of smaller dimensions in breadth and depth than the vessel as finally built, as proved by the register dimensions and the discovery of the plans from which the vessel was built. All the extreme clippers had lines on the same principle as *Ariel* and *Sir Lancelot*, the greatest difference being the shape of the midship section. The only record of *Ariel* being passed at sea was when the *Lahloo* weathered on her, but the latter was then on her maiden voyage. In a strong gale she had to be quickly relieved of her canvas or even hove-to, for the lack of bearing aft increased the likelihood of being pooped. If carefully nursed she would run at 16 knots and could make 12 when on a wind. Captain Keay found her a knot faster all round than the *Falcon*.

The builder's plan states that the *Ariel* and *Sir Lancelot* were both built from the same lines, but as I commented in the preamble to this chapter it seems unlikely that rival owners who were in competition for the 'Blue Ribband' of the China tea trade should have acquiesced in having identical hulls for their clippers. The fact that *Ariel* was tender aft but that there are no special reports to this effect concerning *Sir Lancelot* suggests that *Ariel*'s run was altered on the mould loft. *Ariel* has more deadrise than *Falcon* although the waterlines are fairly similar, but she was 6ft longer. Her sail area was considerably larger than *Falcon* which could give additional speed as well.

The *Ariel* was No 162 at Robert Steele & Co's yard, Greenock, and was launched on 29 June, having been ordered by Shaw, Lowther & Maxton of London. Her regis-

Opposite, bottom: Ariel general arrangement plan. It is considered that this general arrangement plan for *Ariel* is equally suitable for *Titania*, but allowance should be made for the slightly different dimensions of the two ships. Built of composite construction in 1865 by Robert Steele & Co at Greenock. Entirely reconstructed. Dimensions for register: 197.4ft × 33.9ft × 21.0ft, 852.87 tons net. Sources for reconstruction: lines plan; longitudinal section and deckplan of *Sir Lancelot* for position of most fittings with exception of wheel, monkey poop, davits, windlass, fore scuttle and catheads; *Lloyd's Register* survey report; log of ship printed in Basil Lubbock's *The China Clippers*; paintings of ship; contemporary illustrations and plans.

ter dimensions were 197.4ft × 33.9ft × 21.0ft with a tonnage of 852.87 under deck and net; she classed 14 A1 and was of composite construction. The coefficient of under deck tonnage works out as 0.60.

The Lloyd's Register survey report gives scantling sizes of which the following are a sample:

Timber and space	18in
Floors (iron)	22⅛in × ⁹⁄₁₆in
Keel (wood)	15in × 15in
Keel plate	27in × ¹²⁄₁₆in
Keelson (plate)	16in × ¹²⁄₁₆in
Futtocks (angle iron)	4½in × 3½in × ⁹⁄₁₆in
Garboard plank	9in
Planking up to topsides	5½in
Topsides planking	5in to 4½in
Decks in yellow pine	4in
Bottom planking 'to height in Table A'	American rock elm
Remainder of outside planking	East India teak
Deck beams (bulb iron)	8in × 5in × ¹¹⁄₁₆in
Hold beams (bulb iron)	9in × 6in × ¹¹⁄₁₆in
Average spacing between deck and hold beams	4ft

The surveyor's own comments follow and describe the way the hull structure was held together. The longitudinal section and deck plan of *Sir Lancelot* illustrate the various tie plates specified below:

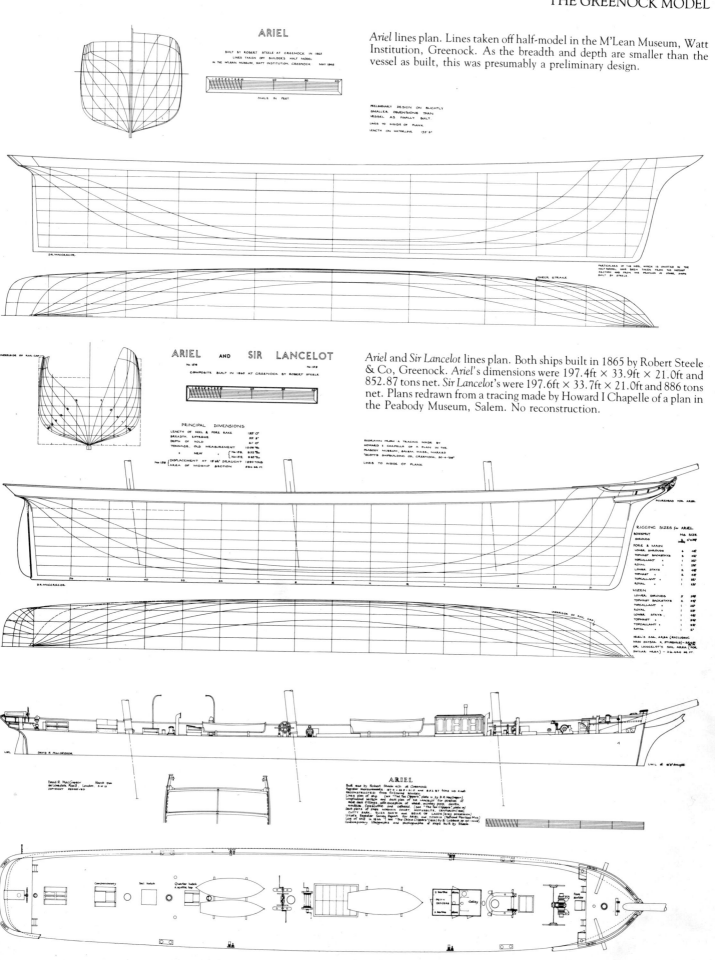

Ariel lines plan. Lines taken off half-model in the M'Lean Museum, Watt Institution, Greenock. As the breadth and depth are smaller than the vessel as built, this was presumably a preliminary design.

Ariel and *Sir Lancelot* lines plan. Both ships built in 1865 by Robert Steele & Co, Greenock. *Ariel*'s dimensions were 197.4ft × 33.9ft × 21.0ft and 852.87 tons net. *Sir Lancelot*'s were 197.6ft × 33.7ft × 21.0ft and 886 tons net. Plans redrawn from a tracing made by Howard I Chapelle of a plan in the Peabody Museum, Salem. No reconstruction.

This ship has been built under special survey as per order No 346. Is ship-rigged and has a flush deck, with a small house on deck for galley &c forward. Is a composite ship, iron frame and wood planking; and fastened entirely with yellow metal screw bolts and nuts throughout; with the exceptions allowed as per Rule section 46; viz – fastened with galvanized iron for one-fifth the depth of hold below the upper deck. The keel is fastened with 1½in galvanized iron wood screw bolts, as shown in sketch herewith [missing], 18in apart. The frames are doubled in the bottom for one half the length of the ship amidships from the keel upwards to the upper part of the bilges. Has a sheer belting plate at the gunwale 30in broad by ½in thick and another at the turn of the bilges all fore and aft 20in broad, the same being connected by double diagonals laid across each other 10in broad by ½in thick and spaced 8ft apart on a square all fore and aft; has thick garboard strakes, the same being yellow metal bolted athwartship through the keel as shown in sketch [missing]; is fitted with sister keelsons and a bulb iron to ditto 8in × $^9/_{16}$in with double angle irons to ditto 5in × 4in × $^8/_{16}$in. Has longitudinal tie plates fitted on each side of hatchways to each deck, and diagonals very efficiently fitted all fore and aft on upper deck beams, with a substantial iron pillar fitted to every beam to each tier of beams.

There had always been some confusion about *Ariel*'s deck layout but the surveyor's opening remarks settle the matter completely. It is further confirmed by an oil painting by W B Spencer, a watercolour of the *Titania* and a sheer elevation of the latter in her own survey report in which a freeing port is drawn 23ft abaft the mizen, which automatically rules out a raised quarterdeck. *Ariel*'s survey report specifies a few other deck fittings: one longboat and two others; Brown's [ie Brown & Harfield's] patent windlass; patent steering gear; wire standing rigging and hemp running rigging; two lead pumps; three bower anchors (with stock), one stream anchor, two kedges.

The deck plan is accordingly based on this evidence: there is a monkey forecastle with a small capstan, mooring bitts and ventilator to forecastle; the heads each side of it on the main deck, and in the centre a scuttle leading to forecastle in 'tween decks; Brown & Harfield's patent windlass abaft it; fore hatch; cargo winch; fife rail around foremast; deckhouse; longboat on chocks; main hatch and cargo winch; mainmast and pumps with fife rail each side; two boats – a lifeboat and a gig – on chocks with standard compass in between; quarter hatch; capstan with a ventilator on each side; sail hatch; mizen mast; companionway to after accommodation; skylight to saloon; binnacle and close abaft it a monkey poop on which is placed wheel and wheel box. The deck plan of *Sir Lancelot* provided details of some of the fittings.

The *Ariel* had her lower masts made up of three iron plates ½in thick without internal angle stiffeners; the fore and main were 30in diameter and the mizen was 28½in diameter. The bowsprit was 30in diameter made up with three plates but stiffened inside with 4in × 3in × $^7/_{16}$in angles. Presumably a boy or man crawled inside as a 'holder-upper' as the plates were being riveted together.

The sail plan is reconstructed from an undated plan traced in the Science Museum, London, and as it had only masts, yards and standing rigging drawn just like the sail plan of *Wylo*, it must have been a copy of Robert Steele's original, as this was the technique used by him for mast and rigging plans. So, sails and running rigging have been added but the stunsails have been drawn dotted.

Later in her life, *Titania* had two deckhouses erected on her main deck to increase cargo capacity by taking the accommodation out of the 'tween decks; this is authenticated by an oil painting and by photographs. Perhaps the same thing was done to *Ariel* before she was lost in 1872. There is a large painting in the National Maritime Museum supposedly of her with two big deckhouses, but also with a

Opposite: This spirited engraving in the *Illustrated London News* was signed 'E W' which was Edward Weedon. Here the *Ariel* has many fancy racing sails set but no main skysail yard. (*MacGregor Collection*)

Above: Painted in oils by W B Spencer, the *Ariel* is seen in the chops of the Channel with a quartering wind. She is flush-decked with only a smallish deckhouse abaft the foremast. Although royal stunsails are set, the artist has not crossed the main skysail yard. (*Parker Gallery*)

ong poop, a topgallant forecastle, double channels, topgallant rail, and headsails cut in the fashion of twenty years later. The figures painted about the decks are also too small for a tea clipper and suggest a vessel of 1500 tons with an American or Canadian pedigree. The *Ariel*'s original sail area of 25,451 sq ft, excluding skysail and stunsails, was reduced later in her life to 23,471 sq ft.

Her only outward passage under 100 days was in 1866–67 on her second voyage, but this was the fastest ever made out against the monsoon:

Left Gravesend	14 October
Left Start Point	15 October
Dropped pilot (noon)	17 October
Crossed the Line in 25°30′W	3 November
Passed meridian of the Cape in 44°S	14 November
Passed Island of Savoby	13 December
Passed through Gillolo Passage	23 December
Passed Pelew Islands and Bashees	3 January
Picked up pilot (9.0 am)	5 January
Anchored at Hong Kong (11.0 pm)	5 January

The time was 83 days, or 79 days 21 hours, pilot to pilot. Commenting on the public reaction to this passage, Captain John Keay wrote in his journal: 'Our 80 days (79 days 21 hours) from pilot to pilot & 83 from Gravesend to Hong Kong made quite a sensation in Hong Kong & at home when telegram reached, 'twas scarce believed. So *Ariel* up to present date has exceeded every other sailing ship, specially is extraordinary in NE monsoon.'

Cairngorm's fast run of 77 days at sea out to Hong Kong has already been mentioned, but *Ariel*'s was the fastest allowing for an unfavourable monsoon and for making the passage at one attempt. Two other fast times were made by American ships in the 1850s. *Eagle Wing* took 83 days 12 hours in 1855,

pilot to pilot, between leaving the Downs on 17 April and arriving at Hong Kong on 10 July. The previous year the *Comet* had taken 83 days 21 hours between her pilots from Liverpool to Hong Kong, 17 June to 7 September or 86 days 16 hours anchor to anchor. Both were made with the help of the monsoon. There has always been a mystery about a fast run made by a ship called *Pride of the Ocean*. This vessel was built at Maine in 1853 as *Pride of America*, but was renamed when sold soon after her launch as described in Chapter Six. Owned in London, she sailed from there on 11 May 1857, and reached Hong Kong on 8 August, 89 days later – not 69 from Land's End as was asserted in a letter to *The Times*. In their turn, shipping advertisements called it 79 days. Another unverified time is the 72 days claimed by HMS *Vindictive* in the early 1840s on the passage out to Hong Kong.

Ariel early gained fame by being the first ship in 1866 to reach the Downs. She had loaded 1,230,900lbs of tea at Foochow at £5 per ton on 340 tons of iron kentledge and shingle ballast. Her bills of lading, like those of the other early starters, were endorsed for '10s per ton extra if first sailing vessel in dock with new teas from Foochow'. But she was unlucky with her tugs. She finished loading first and left at 5.0 pm on 28 May behind the paddler *Island Queen*. The tug was too weak to take her across the bar next day and she had to wait 24 hours during which *Fiery Cross* passed her, so

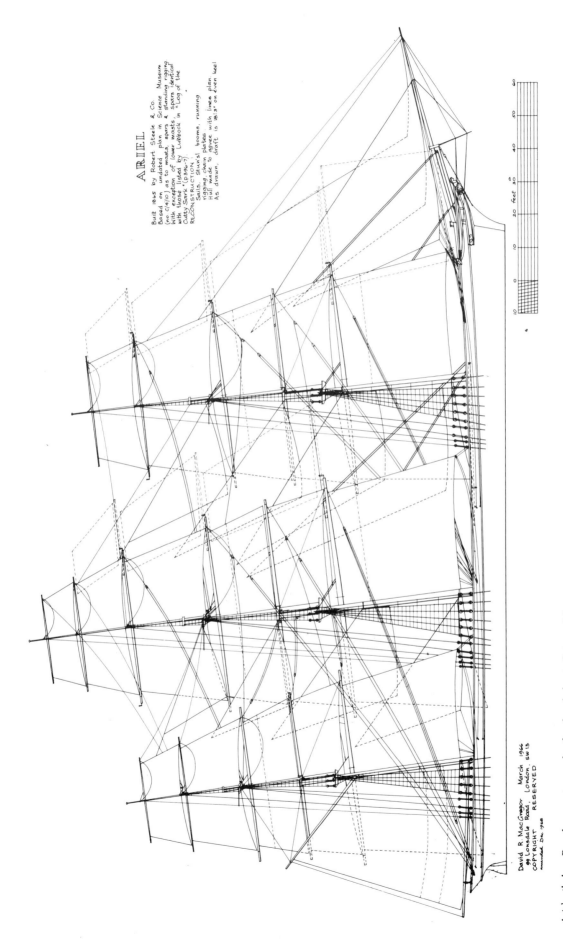

ARIEL

Built 1865 by Robert Steele & Co.
Based on undated plan in Science Museum
(no C/4/10) as to masts, spars & standing rigging
with exception of lower masts, spars identical
with those listed by Lubbock in "Log of the
Cutty Sark" (p396-7).
RECONSTRUCTION:
Sails, Stunsail booms, running
rigging, chain plates.
Hull made to agree with lines plan.
As drawn, draft is 18.3' on even keel

David R. MacGregor   March 1966
99 Lonsdale Road, London, SW13
COPYRIGHT   RESERVED

Ariel sail plan. Based on tracing made of undated plan in Science Museum,
London, which gave only spars and standing rigging. Reconstruction: hull
made to agree with lines plan; sails; stunsails (dotted); running rigging;
chain plates.

hat she eventually got across closely followed by *Serica* and *Taeping*, all three making sail at about 10.30 am. *Taitsing* left next day.

Fiery Cross made the best time to Anjer by one day and all five ships made big runs across the Indian Ocean, *Ariel* on one occasion logging 330 miles and *Fiery Cross* 328. The positions of the ships altered slightly, with *Taitsing* gradually catching up. She passed Flores on 1 September, the other four having passed it on 29 August. *Ariel* and *Taeping* ran up Channel logging 14 knots for most of 5 September. *Ariel* signalled her number off Deal at 8.0 am on 6 September, 98 days 22½ hours from dropping her pilot. *Taeping* was off Deal 10 minutes later, and *Serica* not until noon. *Fiery Cross* arrived about 36 hours later. With her better tug *Taeping* docked the same day at 9.47 am, *Ariel* at 10.15 pm, and *Serica* at 11.30 pm, just before the dock gates closed. The consignees must have been very loth to award the premium to either ship because with so much tea arriving at the same time on the market prices would be sure to fall and a loss would be sustained. The premium was in future abandoned, after being divided on this occasion between *Ariel* and *Taeping*.

The following year *Ariel* obtained 10s per ton more freight than any other ship, and though not sailing with the first flight passed every ship ahead of her except *Taeping* and *Fiery Cross*. Her third passage was her fastest since she was only 95 days to 'off Falmouth'.

A résumé of her first four outward passages is as follows:
1865, Liverpool to Hong Kong, 4 September to 15 December, 102 days.
1866–67, Gravesend to Hong Kong, 14 October to 5 January, 83 days (79 days 21 hours pilot to pilot).
1867–68, London to Shanghai, 19 October to 5 February, 109 days.
1868–69, London to Shanghai, 22 September to 8 January, 106 days.
The first three were made under Keay, the fourth under Courtenay.

Basil Lubbock copied Captain Keay's private journal and these hand-written copies are now in the National Maritime Museum. They provide some informative background data on the ship's fittings and are summarized here:

There was so much brasswork that it took three to four men twelve hours to clean and oil it all round outside and inside rails, gun mountings, bucket straps, &c; there were eight side winches [I have only drawn four on my deck plan]; eight capstan bars of teak were fitted in rack on after side of deckhouse; pig house was stowed under longboat; hen coops kept under monkey poop but could be moved out for cleaning; there was a sheep pen, but position not stated; steering gear stated to have screw and guide rods which implies the standard wheel box of the period; bower anchors kept abaft windlass on main deck and brought on to forecastle when approaching land and painted red [this may have been done to distribute weights further aft]; sidelight screens placed in mizen rigging on three foremost shrouds; prior to entering port, all fancy gratings, buckets and racks, brass ventilator, standard of compass, headboards, boom boards, guns &c got on deck, and were put away when ship got to sea; spare spars stowed along waterways, three each side, and one each side of quarter hatch; 'lower ends of carved ornaments on house too fragile, shortened them a little' [perhaps this refers to acanthus leaves on pilasters]; manger situated at fore part of main hatch [presumably for animals]; temporary breakwater built across deck from side to side to protect wheel, binnacle, skylight and companionway when running the Easting down, as there was a lot of water on deck.

The only reference to colours of paint is that on the second passage the fore- and mainmasts were painted a stone colour as 'owners had put on board different paint from first voyage'; also that waterways were painted cream.

As regards the setting of flying kites, all those pictured by the *Illustrated London News* were regularly set at different times and in addition there were: a main skysail, main sky staysail, jib topsail, save-all to spanker, main middle staysail [partly shown in *Illustrated London News* engraving], water-sail below ringtail, and a mizen staysail laced to the outside of a lower stunsail; the Jamie Green was cut from No 4 canvas similar to a main topgallant stunsail but with 3ft more hoist; the clews of the upper topsails were sometimes 'hove out . . . and laced to head of lower topsails'; two spare topmast stunsail booms were lashed across fore hatch making a total length of 65ft as a passaree boom to haul out the sheet of the lower stunsails.

I am also grateful to F A Claydon for allowing me to use some of the extracts he had made from Captain Keay's journal. Captain Keay left the ship in the autumn of 1868 to take command of the company's new clipper *Oberon* and his first mate, Courtenay, took command. In 1870 *Ariel* was dismasted south of Yokohama on an intermediate passage. After refitting, Captain Courtenay left Yokohama for New York on 1 September, and going across the Pacific and by way of Cape Horn, he passed Diego Ramirez on 22 November and reached New York on 15 January 1871, 136 days out. In 1872 she left London for Sydney on 31 January and was never heard of again. It is usually assumed that she was fatally pooped when running her Easting down.

CHINAMAN, 1865

A composite ship built by Robert Steele, Greenock, for Park Brothers, London, measuring 171.0ft × 31.1ft × 19.1ft and 668 tons. She was relatively as sharp as *Black Prince* though that ship outsailed her on occasions. She was run down and sunk on 21 January 1881 by a steamer at the mouth of the Yangtze. She was at the time barque-rigged, having been cut down in the middle of the 1870s, a fate which happened to many of the clippers.

FUSI YAMA, 1865

This composite barque was typical of Alexander Stephen's productions in the 1860s: the lines were slightly fuller than *Eliza Shaw* with some concavity in the run but less in the entrance; there was medium deadrise and some tumblehome; the stem did not rake forward much; she had a monkey forecastle, a house to accommodate eighteen crew between the foremast and main hatch, and a raised quarterdeck. Stephen contracted with Killick, Martin & Co, London, who held 20 of the shares, to build a barque at £18 10s per ton of about 618 tons builder's measurement, and he made a profit of £632. All three lower masts, the lower and topsail yards, and also the bowsprit were of iron; the remaining spars were of wood. The iron spars cost £218 13s. She had measurements of 165.6ft × 28.1ft × 17.0ft, 556 net and gross tons.

She never made any passages either out or home in less than 119 days although she did go from Singapore to Boston in 91 days in the spring of 1870. Mogens Christian Borup,

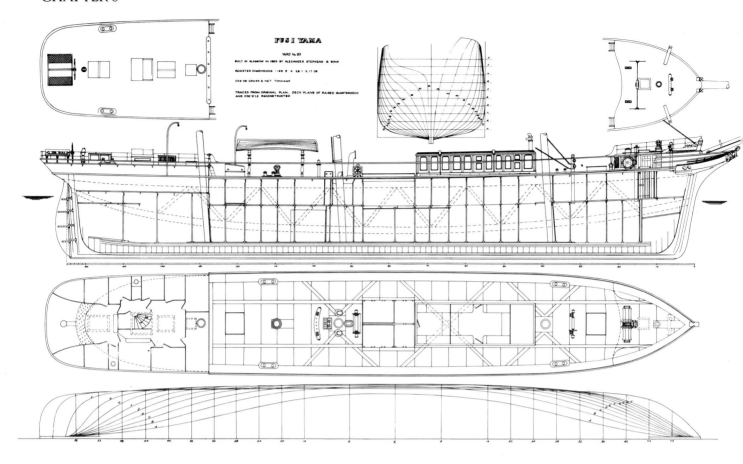

FUSI YAMA

YARD No 83

BUILT IN GLASGOW IN 1865 BY ALEXANDER STEPHENS & SONS

REGISTER DIMENSIONS 165 5 X 28 1 X 17 0S

556 38 GROSS & NET TONNAGE

TRACED FROM ORIGINAL PLAN . DECK PLANS OF RAISED QUARTERDECK
AND FOC'S'LE RECONSTRUCTED

Above: Fusi Yama lines, longitudinal section and deck layouts. Redrawn by E N Wilson from tracing made of builder's plan. Built in 1865 by Alexander Stephen & Sons, Glasgow, with dimensions 165.5ft × 28.1ft × 17.0ft and 556 tons net and gross. Reconstruction: deck layouts for fo'c'sle and raised quarterdeck; some stations omitted amidships for sake of clarity. Diagonal iron trussing outside iron frames shown dotted on section.

Below: Fusi Yama sail plan. Redrawn by E N Wilson from tracing made of builder's plan. Reconstruction: chain plates and channels (from midship section). Running rigging and studding sails would be as on other vessels; the builder did not draw these.

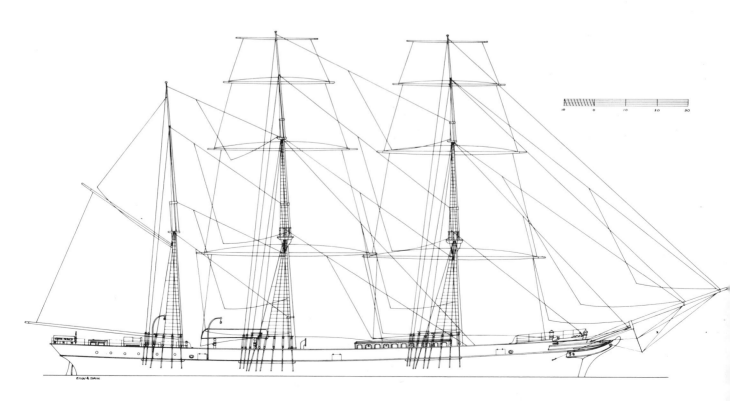

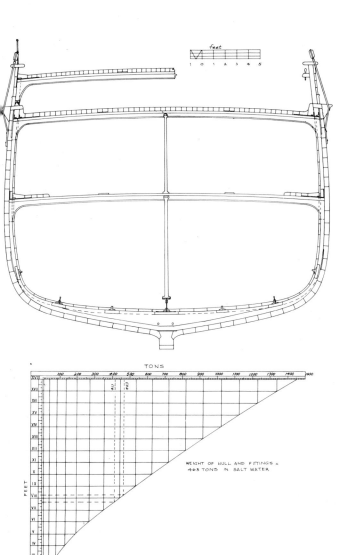

WEIGHT OF HULL AND FITTINGS = 463 TONS IN SALT WATER

previously first mate, who became master in 1868, had his name spelled in a variety of ways: Barup, Birup, Borup, Burup and Bomp. The crew shipped in London in January 1869 for a passage to Shanghai received the following monthly wages:

Captain Borup	[not stated]	
1st mate Wright	£7	age 26
2nd mate Gunn	£5	age 24
carpenter	£6	age 32
sailmaker	£4 10s	
steward	£4 10s	
cook	£3 5s	
9 able seamen	£2 10s each	
2 boys	10s each	
1 boy	1s	
3rd mate	1s	

These rates are from the official log.

In 1870 she was run into and sunk by the American ship *Liverpool* on 26 July off the Lizard when outward bound to Hong Kong. The American was first seen about ten minutes before the accident but after the collision the *Fusi Yama* sank in only a few minutes, and those who were saved jumped overboard and were picked up by the *Liverpool*. However the master, two ABs and two boys were drowned.

JOHN R WORCESTER, 1865

Her model was described as an improvement on the lines of the *Fiery Cross*, and she herself was composite-built at Port Glasgow by the Marine Investment Co Ltd, for John R Worcester of London, on measurements of 191.5ft × 32.4ft

I have attributed the name *John R Worcester* to this previously unidentified painting, firstly because she is wearing the flag of John Patton Jnr who became owner after her first voyage, and secondly because her two large deckhouses so closely resemble those of the ship in the following illustration. Patton did own other ships but the sky stunsails indicate a clipper of the front rank, which is just what the *John R Worcester* was. (*Parker Gallery*)

Top: The *John R Worcester* seen in a typhoon off the east coast of Formosa, in which the deck layout is clearly depicted. *(C J Cawse)*

Above: *Lennox Castle* under all plain sail. *(National Maritime Museum)*

× 19.9ft and 844 tons. In 1866, ballasted with 100 tons o pig iron and 250 tons of shingle, she took 18 days at Shang hai to load 12,500 chests of tea, 221 bales of raw silk and 12 casks of wine, which gave a draft of 18ft forward and 19ft aft.

When Worcester became bankrupt a year after the shi was built, J Patton Jnr of London bought her in 1867. At tha time Wawn, who had previously commanded *Pak Wan*, wa the master. Thomas Cawse took command in 1868 and hel the position until 1875, when he gave it up to his brothe James, who had been first mate with him. While Thoma Cawse was master, the clipper made three round voyage between Shanghai and New York in the years 1872–7 without ever returning home to London. The fastest passag claimed by Cawse was one of 84 days from Shanghai to Ne

York, although the shipping reports make it 89 days. A statement by Cawse detailing his tenure of command was pasted on the back of a painting depicting the ship in a typhoon off Formosa which his descendant, C J Cawse, showed me. A close-up photograph I took of this clearly illustrates her deck layout, from which it appears that she might have been flush-decked.

J Patton sold the clipper to J Stewart, London, in 1884. Five years later she passed to Italian owners in Castellammare who renamed her *L'Immacolata*. When owned in Naples she grounded in 1896 and was dismantled.

LENNOX CASTLE, 1865

Thomas Skinner & Co, Glasgow, owned a number of fine ships trading to the East in the 1860s, all of which were named after castles. Many traded to China, Manilla or Singapore but if they sailed against the south-west monsoon their passages were usually longer than 120 days home, which suggests they were only of the medium clipper category unless their masters were of an easy-going temperament. *Lennox Castle* is included here because of her rapid passage between Anjer and London in 1867 which occupied only 63 days, 30 September to 2 December, according to contemporary shipping reports. This is equal to the time taken by *Kelso* in 1860–61. The *Lennox Castle* on this occasion took 82 days to get to Anjer from Shanghai, and the *Wild Deer*, sailing a month later, took 70 days to Anjer via the Eastern Route and the Java Sea. In her first four voyages, *Lennox Castle* had a new master each time which implies that the owners were dissatisfied with each.

She was built in Sunderland by G S Moore & Co as a full-rigged ship with a tonnage of 693 and dimensions of 178.6ft × 30.1ft × 18.9ft; there was a raised quarterdeck 41ft long and a forecastle of 17ft. She was of composite construction and carried a main skysail. *Elmstone*, built by Moore in 1866, was of almost the same tonnage but was 12½ft shorter and 1.4ft broader and had rather flat floors, according to her midship section. *Lennox Castle* was damaged in a hurricane at Astoria in 1875; in 1887 she was broken up. She had been reduced to a barque in 1870.

MAITLAND, 1865

Two important discoveries have been made since the first edition of this book was researched and written thirty years ago and they are the builder's half-model of *Maitland* and Waymouth's sail plan of *Thermopylae*, which have enabled a complete set of plans of each ship to be drawn.

In the case of *Maitland*, her half-model was found in the offices of Joseph L Thompson & Sons, who were the successors in Sunderland to William Pile who built the ship, and through their courtesy I was able to take off the lines and draw them out with the help of the builder's longitudinal section and deck plan from the Science Museum, London. The *Maitland* measured 183.0ft × 35.0ft × 19.65ft for registry with tonnages of 754.58 under deck and 798.72 net and gross. She classed 12 A1 and was a full-rigged ship of composite construction built to the order of John R Kelso, North Shields, and was launched on 2 December 1865.

This lines plan is the only known one for a tea clipper built by William Pile, although the midship section is of the same shape as Pile's iron clipper *Ganges* built in 1861. The *Maitland* has a sharp entrance with the maximum beam well forward of the centre of the load line, and abaft this is a long and very concave run. There is not much deadrise but the bilges are slack and the sides tumble home. This is a different hull-form from Robert Steele's clippers where the ends are more balanced with greater deadrise. *Maitland* is 15ft shorter on the load line than *Ariel* but 1ft 6in broader. *Maitland* was credited with a speed of 15 knots in 1869, and on a load line length of 179ft this gives a speed-length ratio of 1.12; for the 17 knots claimed by Captain Coulson on his maiden passage, the ratio becomes 1.27 which indicates an extremely fast hull-form.

The hull is very attractive and the topgallant rail does not spoil her looks while it provides sufficient headroom to fit a forecastle on the main deck forward of the foremast, inside of which is an Emerson & Walker's windlass and the capstan above. Aft, there is a raised quarterdeck and on it and the remainder of the deck are to be found the usual deck fittings. Cunningham's brace winches were fitted to both fore and main lower yards, although not shown on the deck plan.

Her great beam provided good stability for her large and lofty sail plan, which is based on the builder's sail plan in the Science Museum on which the spar dimensions are written. The respective yards on fore and main masts are of equal length. The lower masts are of iron and the lower and two topsail yards of steel. What makes the sail plan of particular interest is its 'squareness' aloft which is disguised by the loftiness of the masts. For instance, *Spindrift* had a load line 37ft 6in longer than the *Maitland* and yet her mainmast is only 2ft taller from deck to truck; at the same time, *Spindrift*'s main yard is 11ft longer than *Maitland*'s and yet her royal yard is 3ft shorter. The following table compares lengths of lower and royal yards on six tea clippers:

LENGTHS OF YARDS COMPARED ON SIX TEA CLIPPERS (in feet)

Ship	Length on load line	Fore lower yard	Fore royal yard	Main lower yard	Main royal yard
Maitland	179	73	37	73	37
Titania	197	71	33½	76½	36
Thermopylae	207	81	35	81	37
The Caliph	208	80	35	85	38
Cutty Sark	211	78	38	78	38
Spindrift	216½	76	33	84	34

Thomas Dutton's lithograph of *Maitland* provides rigging details and the number of staysails, although storm staysails on the lower stays would have been made for her. No dimensions of stunsail booms and yards are known for her, and so these have been dotted, although the ones drawn are of standard size. Contemporary descriptions are the source for the flying kites drawn – moonsails, sky stunsails, ringtail, watersail and jib topsail – which are just the sails to be set and taken in that Captain Keay is contantly describing in his private journal aboard *Ariel*. As regards the moonsails, it is unknown if they had yards or were triangular but several people mentioned them. On 31 May 1867, Captain Keay wrote in his journal that *Maitland* left Foochow with a fine north-east wind 'with moonsails set'. Alexander Hall's medium clipper *Reindeer* of 1863 is allotted a moonsail yard in the builder's cost account.

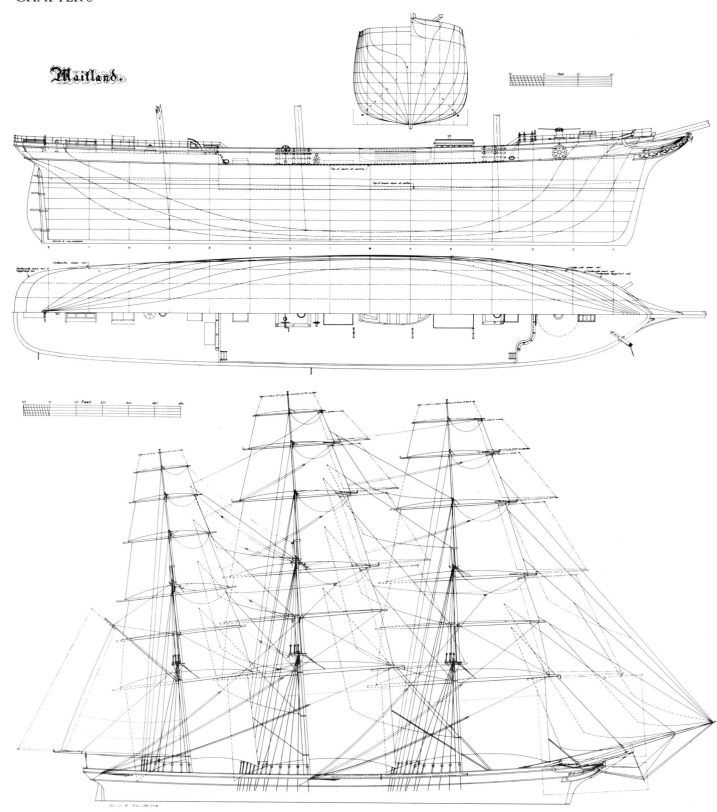

Above: Maitland sail plan. Redrawn from sail plan in Science Museum, London. Reconstruction: running rigging; stunsail booms, yards and their sails; moonsails; ringtail; watersail; jib topsail; crossjack. Ship was equipped with Cunningham's braces on fore and main lower yards, but this was not discovered until sail plan had been drawn with conventional braces. Principal source was T G Dutton's lithograph of ship; flying kites from eye-witness accounts.

Unfortunately, position of masts on sail plan in Science Museum do not agree with position on longitudinal section, also in Museum. This error has been repeated in drawings here. Neither plan in Science Museum is dated and so it is impossible to tell which is correct.

Top: Maitland lines. Built of composite construction in 1865 by William Pile at Sunderland. Lines taken off builder's half-model in possession of Joseph L Thompson & Sons Ltd, Sunderland; deck details from plan in Science Museum, London. Dimensions for register: 183.0ft × 35.0ft × 19.6ft, 798.72 tons gross and net. Reconstruction: plan view of deck fittings on raised quarterdeck; binnacle; wheel and wheel box; whisker booms on catheads.

Right: The lofty *Maitland* as portrayed by Thomas G Dutton. (*MacGregor Collection*)

Maitland was favoured by the shippers when she loaded at Foochow in 1867, and not without reason, for on her maiden voyage Coulson drove her out to Hong Kong in 87 days from Sunderland, 24 February to 22 May 1866, the medium Aberdeen clipper *Fychow* being beaten by 14 days to Anjer and the *Everest* by 6 days up the China Sea. She is said to have crossed the Line 16 days out and reached port in 84 days, counted perhaps after passing Deal. She passed Anjer on 25 April. It will be seen that during the south-west monsoon her homeward passage was the next best after the first five starters. She was passed by *Sir Lancelot* in 1867, homeward-bound, and there is a story that later the *Flying Spur* sailed through her lee, but Captain Shewan declared that this could only have happened if the *Maitland* had been at anchor.

In 1867–68 she made the best outward time except *Sir Lancelot*, taking 103 days between London and Shanghai, 5 November to 16 February. She sailed late in 1868 because she struck the Ariadne Rock when leaving Woosung and had to be beached with five feet of water in the hold, but was later taken back to Shanghai. In 1869 she is credited with sailing from Sunderland to the Downs in only 22½ hours outward-bound, her fastest speed on the homeward run being 15 knots. In 1871 she ran out to Hong Kong from Cardiff in 96 days, 12 February to 19 May.

In 1874 she was wrecked on a coral reef in the Huon Islands (just north of New Caledonia) on 25 May, bound from Brisbane to Foochow.

PETER DENNY, 1865
Built at Aberdeen by John Duthie, Sons & Co, successors to Alexander Duthie, his brother, who died in 1863, she was a wooden full-rigged ship of 997 tons and measuring 197.0ft × 34.2ft × 20.0ft, having been built to the order of Patrick Henderson's Albion Shipping Co, Glasgow, and she embodied some of James Galbraith's ideas for the carrying of emigrants. In the mid-1860s, Duthie's yard turned out several ships of this size, the *John Duthie* (1864, of 1031 tons), *Australian* (1866, of 1016 tons), *Agnes Rose* (1867, of 991 tons) and *Ann Duthie* (1868, of 993 tons). Probably they were all fairly similar to the latter whose lines and sail plan I published in *Fast Sailing Ships* (Figure 237), in which there was a sharp entrance and run, convex in the upper body but concave below, some deadrise with slack bilges, but little tumblehome. Skysails were carried on each mast.

The *Peter Denny* took emigrants out to Dunedin from Glasgow on her maiden passage in 92 days, 2 June to 2 September 1865 and in the next three voyages was in the China trade. In *Colonial Clippers*, Basil Lubbock recounts a close race from Gaspar Strait to Gravesend between her, *Wild Deer* and *Douglas Castle* in 1868 with the ships frequently in sight of each other, and all three arriving close together. *Peter Denny* had started from Foochow and the other two from Shanghai.

She was sold in 1883–84 to L G S Larsen of Sandefjord, Norway, and was renamed *Inga*; she was wrecked in 1888.

SIR LANCELOT, 1865
Although reservations have already been expressed as to whether *Ariel* and *Sir Lancelot* were exact sisters, it is worth quoting a letter from James MacCunn to Basil Lubbock, written in November 1911, in which these two clippers were mentioned: 'I've no doubt both ships were the same almost throughout as they were practically the same model.'

After a voyage to China, Japan and back in 1864 aboard *Guinevere*, 'my father and I,' wrote James MacCunn to Basil Lubbock in June 1911, 'contracted with Robert Steele & Co

The *Peter Denny* at Port Chalmers, New Zealand, in the 1880s. The channels run across her line of painted ports. *(Cyril L Hume)*

for *Sir Lancelot*. My first idea was 10ft longer than the dimensions ultimately decided upon. But the latter had much to commend them. So I saw this noble clipper built from keel to truck to my entire satisfaction.' These letters are in the National Maritime Museum.

Sir Lancelot's dimensions were 197.6ft × 33.7ft × 21.0ft, 886 tons net and 847 tons under deck. The crew's quarters were below deck and were entered through a scuttle abaft the windlass, as shown on the deck plan. The hatch at the forward end of the raised quarterdeck communicated direct with the sail locker. She carried double topsails on fore and main and a single roller-reefing topsail with Cunningham's patent on the mizen, the total sail area being 32,811 sq ft, including a set of stunsails for each mast. She had an iron frame planked with elm below the bilge and teak above. The size of the iron lower masts and the bowsprit were similar to *Ariel*.

Her first master, McDougall, was a failure and was dismissed on the ship's return from her maiden voyage, and MacCunn was fortunate enough in persuading Captain Richard Robinson to leave the *Fiery Cross* to take charge of his new clipper. She had hardly started, however, before she was completed dismasted on 13 December 1866, only her mizen iron lower mast remaining intact. The wind shifted in time to prevent her drifting on to Ushant, and Falmouth was reached later. She was hastily re-rigged in six weeks with a set of Oregon pine masts which proved very satisfactory.

After a successful passage out, she sailed from Woosung on 16 June 1867, with 1,255,041lbs of tea, and in spite of going by the long Eastern passage through the islands, she managed to overhaul every ship sailing ahead of her except *Taeping* which arrived 9 days before, and *Ariel* and *Fiery Cross* which arrived the same day. *Chinaman* and *Yang-tsze* were spoken off Madagascar on 3 August and *Flying Spur* on

11 August off Algoa Bay. Later *Maitland* was passed under sky stunsails and moonsails. *Sir Lancelot* took her pilot off Dungeness at 1.0 pm on 22 September and was said to have been only 96 days, land to land. She was at Blackwall at 7.0 am next day.

On the occasion that *Flying Spur* and *Sir Lancelot* met on this voyage, Frederick Paton was an apprentice on the former, and he recalled the dramatic meeting in a letter he wrote to Basil Lubbock in 1910. (I have a copy of this letter):

In the year 1867 when off the coast of Cape Colony, racing home with the 1st Season's tea, it was a stormy day and we were carrying what was thought by us to be a heavy press of sail, viz whole topsails and courses with outer jib, whilst other ships in company were close-reefed, when we sighted a clipper ship on the other tack carrying three topgallant sails and flying jib. This was an enormous amount of sail considering the wind and she could not have possibly done so but the swell was running abaft her beam whilst it was right ahead with us. Well we were, of course, anxious to know the name of that ship and as soon as she got near enough, we began signalling; she proved to be the *Sir Lancelot* from Hankow, Capt Robinson, who had previously commanded the *Fiery Cross*. She crossed our bows and just then when the signalling was going on, her helmsman, paying too much attention to us, allowed her to come up in the wind and get aback. We thought that she would have been dismasted, she heeling right over and getting sternway. However, they managed to get some sail off her and she righted, but it was a close thing. As the ships were fairly close we could see all that took place on board of her: we saw Capt Robinson knock down the man at the wheel and jump on him! After that we were in company some days, the ships being of the same speed.

What an exciting moment to have witnessed and how well Paton tells the story of such an event. He must often have re-lived that day and recounted the meeting of the two clippers to an admiring audience.

James MacCunn thought highly of Robinson, as in a letter to Basil Lubbock dated 7 July 1911 he wrote: '[Capt Robin-

Dutton's lithograph of *Sir Lancelot* is a good action picture of the hard-driven clipper under Richard Robinson's command. It was published in October 1867. (*Parker Gallery*)

on] was really a fine fellow in every way with dash, daring and energy quite exceptional. He died about fifteen years ago.' MacCunn said that he lured Robinson away from his previous employer, Campbell, who owned *Fiery Cross*, by paying him much more. 'As a matter of fact,' wrote Mac-Cunn in another letter, 'Robinson was the best man I ever had in any ship, and I knew he had got the best racing results out of *Sir Lancelot* . . .' These last quotations are from letters in the National Maritime Museum.

Sir Lancelot left London again for China on 26 October 1867 but put into Cowes to shelter from a strong gale. She then made the following good passage:

Left Cowes and dropped pilot	2 November
Crossed the Line in 27°36′W	27 November
Passed the meridian of the Cape in 41°15′S	19 December
Passed through Clayer Straits	20 January
Crossed the Line in 130°50′E	25 January
Caught monsoon and passed to E of Bashees	27 January
Picked up pilot	4 February
Anchored at Hong Kong	5 February

The time was 94 days, pilot to pilot. She came home in 98 days, but *Spindrift* beat her by 23 hours on time. In 1869 *Sir Lancelot* reached Hong Kong on 10 January, 99 days from London, which she left on 3 October 1868.

Then followed the usual number of so-called 'intermediate passages' between various ports, usually going to Saigon or Bangkok for rice and so earning a little money. On this occasion in 1860, *Sir Lancelot* made the following short hauls:

Hong Kong to Bangkok, 27 January to 5 February, 9 days.
Bangkok to Hong Kong, 3 March to 24 March, 21 days.
Hong Kong to Saigon, 10 April to 20 April, 10 days.
Saigon to Yokohama, 5 May to 26 May, 21 days
Yokohama to Foochow, 14 June to 20 June, 6 days.

Now that she was at Foochow she waited for a tea cargo, but she had missed the first flight of clippers. She unmoored at the Pagoda Anchorage, Foochow, on 17 July, 1869, and her times for the famous record passage were as follows:

Unmoored from Foochow (7.0 am)	17 July
White Dogs bore NNE 15 miles	18 July
Passed Anjer ESE 10 miles	7 August
Off Buffalo River	28 August
Off Cape Agulhas NE 12 miles	1 September
Passed St Helena 12 miles off	11 September
Passed the Lizard	10 October
Passed Dungeness	12 October
At Gravesend (2.0 pm)	13 October
Docked	14 October

Her best run was 336 miles in the Indian Ocean, and off the Cape she caught up *Spindrift*. The Lizard was passed on the 85th day after leaving Pagoda Anchorage and Dungeness on the 87th. After making due allowance for the season, this was undoubtedly the best passage ever made between China and England. *Thermopylae* and *Titania* made passages of 91 days from Foochow and 98 days from Shanghai respectively in the same year.

A writer to the *Nautical Magazine* on 2 April 1908 claimed that *Sir Lancelot* had made a run of 359 miles in 24 hours in the 1869 passage. James MacCunn concluded that the claim was probably made by Captain Owen, who knew Robinson well, and on 17 July 1911 he wrote to Lubbock: 'I have no doubt from [Capt Owen's] complete knowledge of *Sir Lancelot*'s work and acquaintance with Robinson, that the 359 knots day's run (between Anjer and landfall at Buffalo River 21 days) is correct . . . *Sir Lancelot* could and did sail at the rate of 15 and even 16 knots across the SE trades. A beam wind (slightly abaft the beam) was her best point.'

Maintaining her remarkable performance, now under Edmonds – Robinson having left due to the sudden death of

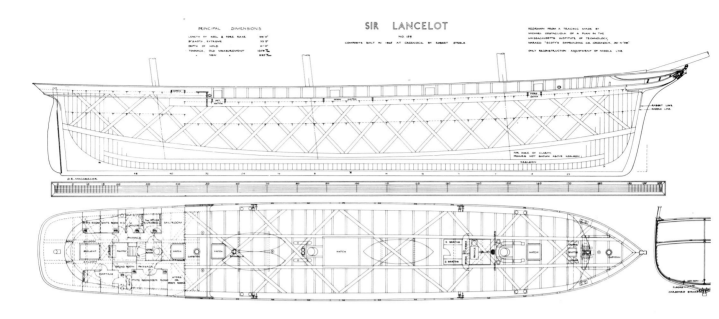

Above: Sir Lancelot longitudinal section and deck layout. Redrawn from a tracing made by Michael Costagliola of a plan in the Massachusetts Institute of Technology. Reconstruction; adjustment of middle line.

Below: Because the main royal mast is not lofty enough to carry a skysail, this photograph cannot be *Sir Lancelot* as attributed; suitable candidates could be *Taitsing* or *Leander*. (*Peabody Museum, Salem*)

his wife – the *Sir Lancelot* went out to Hong Kong in 97 days from London, sailing on 20 November 1869 and arriving on 25 February 1870. She came home from Foochow in 104 days. But now that the Suez Canal was open, the racing between the clippers had lost its real significance and several pasages were made to New York. The best of these was made in 1877–78 in 95 days under Captain Hepburn, who had been first mate under Felgate.

Her 100 tons of permanent iron ballast was removed at New York in 1871 to improve her cargo capacity, and three years later 8ft was cut off her mainmast and the other spars shortened in proportion; at the same time all stunsails were abolished. It is not clear from MacCunn's letters if she was reduced to a barque in 1874 or in January 1877, but she was still a fast sailer. In the 1874 Tea Season she had the distinction of making two passages with tea from China.

In the early 1880s she was trading between Europe and India, and then was chartered by the Parsee merchant Vis ram Ibrahim, who bought her outright in 1886, placing the experienced Eurasian master C W Brebner in command. He kept her like a yacht while in the India to Mauritius trade and it was in 1892 that a correspondent to *The Times* late recalled having been in Mauritius harbour when she 'cam stealing in like a ghost from the past' (*The Times* 16 Nov 1931). Captain Brebner survived four cyclones in her.

In 1895 she was sold to Persian owners and in the sam year was supposed to have foundered on 1 October in a cyclone off the Sand Heads, Calcutta, deeply laden with sal from the Red Sea.

TAITSING, 1865
Launched on 8 July by Charles Connell & Co at Glasgow she was a fine-lined ship with a long sharp entrance and run in which there was the minimum of concavity; the buttock lines were easy and the quarter-beam buttock was straigh where it crossed the load line in the run, indicating a fas hull-form; in the body plan, there was marked deadrise hollow garboards and slack bilges but without much tumblehome. These points can be assessed from the line taken off the builder's rigged model in the Glasgow Museum and Art Gallery by Frederick Claydon who ha drawn an impressive set of plans.

Taitsing was composite-built to class 14 A1 with registe dimensions of 192.0ft × 31.5ft × 20.15ft and a tonnage o 815. The first owners were Findlay & Longmuir, Greenock Translated from the Chinese, her name meant 'Grea Arrow'. Although she had a topgallant rail, the counte raked aft to include it and so reduced a possibly heav appearance. The bulwarks were just under 5ft high permitting a topgallant forecastle for the crew and a raised quarterdeck aft.

It is interesting to note her two small deckhouses, o which the forward one probably contained the galley and paint locker, and the after one berths for the apprentices, a one end, and the bosun, carpenter, sailmaker and cook a the other. The lever handles for the windlass are on the forecastle head but as was normal practice the windlas

Below: Taitsing lines and General Arrangement. Drawn by F A Claydon from lines and measurements taken off rigged builder's model in Glasgow Museum and Art Gallery (Transport Museum). Ship built in 1865 by Charles Connell & Co, Glasgow with dimensions of 192.0ft × 31.5ft × 20.1ft and 815 tons.

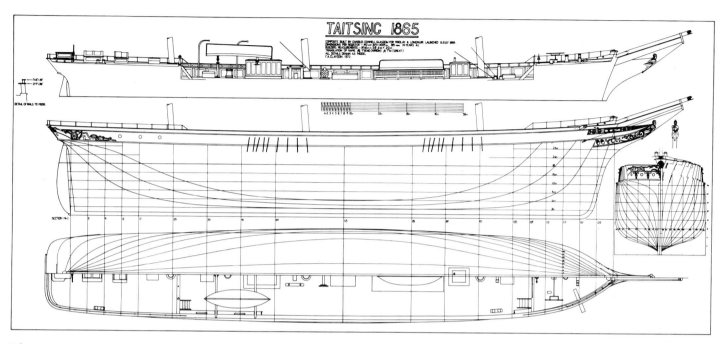

Below: Taitsing sail plan. Drawn by F A Claydon from measurements taken off builder's rigged model in Glasgow Transport Museum. Reconstruction: sails, including stunsails, as there are none on model; stunsail booms where dotted; royal mast poles.

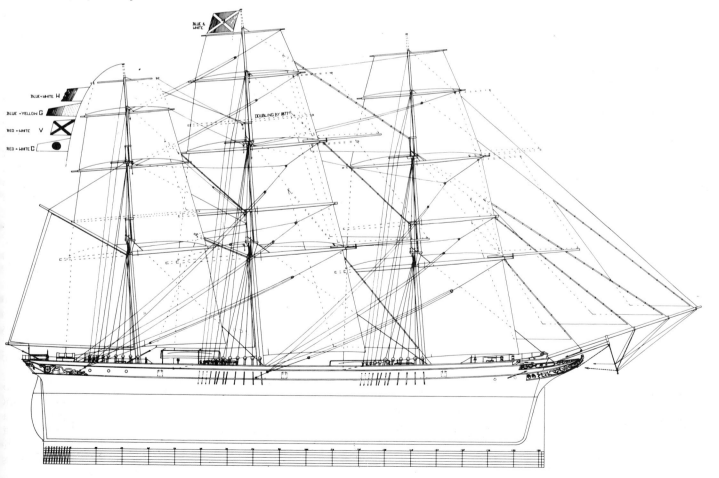

barrel is inside the forecastle. There is a substantial range of poultry and pig pens abaft the galley with the lifeboat or longboat placed on top, keel uppermost. There is only one cargo winch and the pumps are in the space abaft the mainmast between the fife rails. The small hatch abaft the mizen was probably the sail locker; there are two capstans for use on various jobs; and the fittings on the raised quarterdeck are standard. Two omissions are mooring pipes through the bulwarks for mooring ropes – one by the break of the forecastle and another by the break of the raised quarterdeck as a minimum; also there are no gypsy winches on the bulwarks for running rigging – two per side would have been normal.

The model of *Taitsing* had masts and spars, standing rigging and braces, but no sails, and so Frederick Claydon has reconstructed these according to contemporary practice and with the help of a painting by a Chinese artist done in 1877. The deep fore and main upper topsails would have had at least one row of reef points in each; it is not known if the single mizen topsail had point reefing or roller-reefing gear, but there is nothing on the model to indicate the latter. The stunsails have been drawn dotted.

On her maiden passage she left London on 23 October 1865, took her departure from the Downs on 28 October and reached Hong Kong on 1 February, 96 days from the Downs. She was always hard-driven under Daniel Nutsford and was at her best when running free. She had her decks swept clear and lost her topgallant masts in a heavy gale on 4 September 1867.

James Findlay of Greenock acquired her in 1876, and Robert D Willis, London, in 1880. Still trading to the East, she was lost on 20 September 1883 on Nyuni Island off the Zanzibar coast, bound from Swansea with patent fuel.

ARGONAUT, 1866

She was one of the larger ships in the trade and though 5ft shorter than *Wild Deer* she was some 30 tons larger under deck. Though sharp in the ends she had a long floor which gave her a high coefficient of 0.69. With a quartering wind, Shewan described her as a 'galloper'. What she lost in ability to contend with head winds was made up by the daring of her first master, 'Sandy' Nicholson. In 1873, anxious to carry the somewhat westerly monsoon for as long as possible, Nicholson kept on too long and stranded on the Pescadores, being forced to jettison 300 tons of tea before

getting off. The previous year he had sailed through the dangerous Paracels on a moonlit night and did not have to tack till off the Cochin China coast. Episodes like these were frequent amongst the hard-driven ships.

Thomas Bilbe & Co had built her on the composite principle at Rotherhithe for their own use to dimensions of 206.4ft × 33.2ft × 20.6ft and a net tonnage of 1073. Anderson, Anderson & Co, London, bought her in 1877 but sold her to Jacob Brothers, London, in 1883. In 1888 she was condemned at Port Natal after putting in, leaking, when bound for Hamburg from Western Australia.

CLETA, 1866

As she was actively engaged in trade from 1866 to 1937, a space of 71 years, it seems safe to award her the prize as the tea clipper with the longest working life. Although *Cutty Sark* was afloat for 85 years, only 53 of these were spent carrying cargoes under sail and the rest were spent at anchor as a training ship. The *Cleta* began life as a barque, and she was composite-built by Gardner at Sunderland with tonnages of 546 gross, 505 net and 481 under deck. Her coefficient of under deck tons was 0.63, the same as *Taeping*. Dimensions worked out at 151.2ft × 29.3ft × 17.3ft.

John Hay of London was her first owner but in 1873 she passed to Balfour, Williamson & Co, Liverpool, who put her into the Australian trade. Davis of Liverpool became owner in 1885 and two years later she was sold to E T Norrman of Malmö, Sweden, who changed her name to *Nelly & Mathilda*. Her period of Swedish ownership lasted until 1926 during which time she had four collisions but usually came off best; she also went ashore twice but was refloated. In 1917 she was partially dismasted in a squall and was then re-rigged as a three-masted barquentine.

Top: The *Nelly & Mathilda*, formerly the *Cleta*, photographed under the Swedish flag sometime before 1917, when she was re-rigged as a barquentine. *(A Ericsson)*

Above: The Aberdeen White Star Line clipper *Harlaw* at Circular Quay, Sydney, in the seventies. *(Cyril L Hume)*

Right: The white-hulled *Kagosima* in Aberdeen harbour when new. *(J Henderson)*

In 1926 she went under Finnish colours, being acquired by Engblom & Henriksson, Kumlinge, Åland Islands, and was renamed *Frideborg*. From 1934 she was engaged in the lumber trade between Denmark and England, and many people saw and photographed her in the river Thames or in the Docks. She went ashore at Kalix in September 1937 and although she was not even leaking when they dragged her off, her owner declined to have her repaired: so she was condemned and broken up. She had had a proud life which had been lengthened by her splendid construction.

HARLAW, 1866

An Aberdeen clipper as sharp as *Titania*, she was built of wood for George Thompson, Aberdeen, by Walter Hood and was very similar to *Ethiopian* in appearance. With a tonnage of 894 she measured 194.0ft × 34.0ft × 21.2ft with a 40ft forecastle and 52ft poop.

Although sailing usually with the fair monsoon her passages were well above the average, her best being in 1870 when she was 87 days between her pilots, Shanghai to New York. Sailing against the monsoon under Phillips in 1872, she went from Foochow to London in 112 days, 1 August to 21 November. She was wrecked on 31 July 1878 on Tung Sha Banks, at the south entrance to the Yangtze, bound from Sydney with 1100 tons of coal.

KAGOSIMA, 1866

A small white-hulled clipper of 394 tons, she was built for trade between China and Japan, and her portrait, which was taken in the harbour at Aberdeen when she was completed, is a splendid and detailed record of a clipper ship of the mid-1860s. She was constructed by John Humphrey at the Inches, Aberdeen, as a wooden full-rigged ship with dimensions of 143.0ft × 26.3ft × 15.6ft. Her owner was J Glover of Aberdeen and her first master was W Glover. She had Colling and Pinkney's roller-reefing topsails and her main lower mast was long. Unfortunately I have not traced any of her passages.

John Humphrey had been chief draughtsman to 'Yankee' Smith, who was of German extraction, and had taken over the business on the latter's death.

TITANIA, 1866

When describing this extreme clipper in the original edition, I was very concerned with her deck layout and how and why it was altered, but now it is firmly established that she began life as a flush-decked ship, and that the deck plan and fittings for *Ariel* are equally applicable to her. The only difference is that *Titania* was some 2ft broader and so this must be allowed for in the deck layout. The Lloyd's Register survey report states unequivocally that 'she has a flush deck with a small house on deck for Galley &c forward' and a sheer elevation accompanying the report to indicate the planking at the bilge has a freeing port right aft in the bulwarks; but whereas there is no direct pictorial evidence to prove that *Ariel*'s deck arrangement was altered in her lifetime, the reverse is the case with *Titania*, because it is well authenticated in actual photographs that her accommodation was taken out of the 'tween decks during the 1870s and placed in two substantial deckhouses, thereby

171

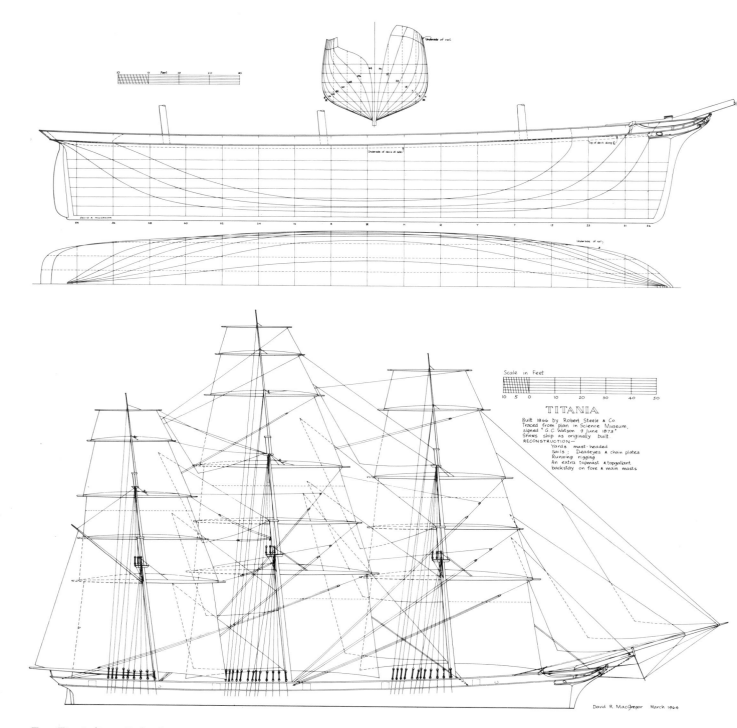

Top: Titania lines. Built of composite construction in 1866 by Robert Steele & Co at Greenock. Drawn from lines taken off builder's half-model in Science Museum, London. Dimensions for register: 200.0ft × 36.0ft × 21.0ft, 879 tons. Reconstruction: mast positions; bowsprit; figurehead and trailboards.

Above: Titania sail plan. Redrawn from outline plan in Science Museum, London, signed and dated 'G C Watson 9th June 1873'. Reconstruction: yards mast-headed; sail outlines; running rigging; one extra topmast and topgallant backstay on fore- and mainmasts; deadeyes, lanyards and chain plates.

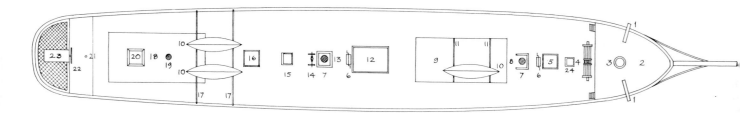

Opposite, bottom: Diagrammatic deck plan of *Titania* after the two large deckhouses were erected in the 1870s. *(Author)*

KEY
1. Catheads
2. Anchor deck, with bosun's lockers under
3. Capstan
4. Windlass, with ship's bell fixed on top
5. Fore hatch
6. Cargo winch
7. Fife rail
8. Foremast
9. Deckhouse containing galley and accommodation for petty officers and crew
10. Lifeboats, keel uppermost
11. Wooden skids
12. Main hatch
13. Mainmast
14. Pumps
15. Scuttle leading to sail locker
16. After hatch
17. Skids, curving down each side on to main rail
18. Deckhouse containing accommodation for master and officers
19. Mizen mast
20. Skylight
21. Binnacle
22. Wheel
23. Wheel box, surrounded at about half its height by a grating not more than two feet above the deck
24. Scuttle, leading to bosun's stores, etc

increasing her cargo capacity. As she had her spars shortened in 1872, this may have been the time when the deckhouses were erected.

Above: Although the main skysail mast and yard are gone and the masts have been shortened, this picture of *Titania* shows what she and *Ariel* would have looked like in their clipper days. Of course, the big deckhouses now spoil the long sleek hull, but she still rides the water like a queen. The photograph was taken at Esquimalt, BC, while under the ownership of the Hudson Bay Company. Robert Weinstein identified *Titania* in this old photograph, and this portion of the old glass plate measured 3in × 1¾in. *(Provincial Archives, Victoria, BC)*

As regards hull-form, the *Titania* was the finest-lined clipper Steele ever built, with very steep deadrise, and an extremely long sharp entrance and run; there was also marked tumblehome. Dimensions of 200.0ft × 36.0ft × 21.0ft gave her great power to carry sail. She was 16ft longer than *Taeping* and 5ft broader, for example. Tonnage was 879.45 net and under deck, which gives a coefficient of under deck tonnage of 0.58.

Robert Steele & Co, Greenock, were the builders of *Titania* and Shaw, Lowther, Maxton & Co, London, the owners. The fore, main and mizen lower masts were of steel plates 10ft long and 5/16in thick, but the thickness was less than that normally allowed for masts without angle iron stiffening inside. These steel plates were manufactured in Prussia and as the builders had no test certificates from the makers, the plates were tested in Greenock to 20 tons per square inch. A year after she was launched, the owners wrote to Lloyd's Register asking them to examine her specification again and re-class her at 16 A1 instead of 14 A1, as was being done to other composite-built ships.

The lines plan is derived from a builder's half-model in the Science Museum, London, which I measured, and the sail plan has been reconstructed from a copy of the builder's

Top: A watercolour drawing of *Titania* as a fairly new ship, before the two large deckhouses were erected. The freeing port right aft indicates the flush deck. (*MacGregor Collection*)

Above: Moored off Gravesend, the *Dilbhur* has masts of almost equal height and their comparative shortness gives the impression of a long hull. The deckhouses are very large: the forward one extends a long way aft; the after one extends right up to the boats on skids abreast of the main rigging and there are men standing on it by the boats. (*National Maritime Museum*)

lan which is signed 'G C Watson 9th June 1873', also in he Museum; presumably the future celebrated yacht esigner traced this spar plan when an apprentice on the Clyde. Robert Steele's spar plans never had sail outlines rawn, only masts, yards and standing rigging. A list of her par dimensions in Lubbock's *Log of the Cutty Sark* agrees airly well with this plan.

Titania's first two voyages were not marked with the success expected because Robert Deas, her master, had neither he nerve nor temperament to drive her and he was getting n in years. He had done great things with the old *Ganges* n the early 1850s, but *Titania* was a type of thoroughbred e had never met before. On her maiden passage she was lismasted on 29 January 1867 in a squall near the Cape Verde Islands, through her bobstay carrying away. She put nto Rio to repair, with the loss of her foremast.

But under Burgoyne and Dowdy it was a different story. n 1869 she came home in 96 days, Woosung to Deal, aving loaded at £4 per ton. She had her spars cut down on er return in 1872, whilst in 1874 she was again dismasted vhen out in the East, only the bowsprit remaining intact.

The late Vernon C Boyle collected information on the *itania* because her fifth master, England, was an Appleore man and his bosun, Boon, came from the same North Devon port. The latter's son collaborated with Boyle who ound some paintings of the ship owned locally as well as a model. The descriptions which follow are collected from his period when there were two deckhouses.

Titania's hull was beautifully finished, like all Clyde-built lippers. Her two deckhouses had white tops and panels, nd the panels had green borders; the pilasters separating he panels, and a narrow band above them, under the pro-

jecting white moulding of the roof, were light brown. The deck stanchions had green faces and the approximately square space between each was filled with a panel with gilded decoration on it. These panels were deached on the commencement of a voyage and stowed below a big iron box, leaving the green bulwarks uncovered. The trailboards with their gilt scrollwork were likewise stowed away. The deck structure aft was probably identical with *Ariel*'s. The wheel box was surrounded behind and on each side by a grating filling the whole stern space. This grating was less than two feet above the deck and the forward side was probably left open.

From the position of the aftermost deckhouse, the latter probably abutted on the platform on which the wheel box stood, but whether there was a low raised deck each side between the house and bulwark is not known.

Captain W England had her from 1874 until the end of the 1870s but the owners given by *Lloyd's Register* changed frequently, although the name 'Shaw' was always the first: in 1873 it was Shaw & Co; in 1874 and 1876 it was Shaw, Savill & Co; in 1878 it was Shaw & Son; in 1881 Shaw, Bushby & Co.

She continued trading to Australia and the East until she was bought by the Hudson's Bay Company at the end of 1885, for whom she made six voyages out round the Horn and back, averaging 115 days on each passage. In 1892 she went from Pisagua to Falmouth in 76 days; in 1907–08 she took 71 days between Marseilles and Rio.

Maresca of Castellammare, Italy, bought her in 1894 and placed her in the Mauritius and South American trade until she was broken up at Marseilles in March 1910.

Below: Woosung break of poop. Reproduced from builder's plan and photographed in 1961 when still in their possession. Built in 1863 by Alexander Stephen & Sons, Glasgow, of iron with dimensions of 176.5ft × 31.3ft × 19.0ft and 729 tons. The original was coloured in purple and blue, if I recall it correctly.

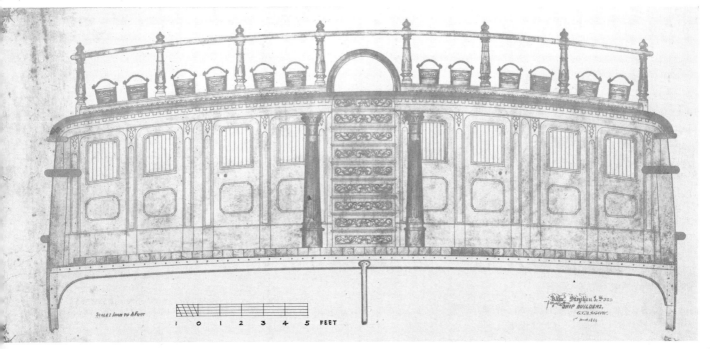

9

THE FINAL CLIPPER SHIP BOOM
AND SHIPS OF 1867-1869

Today it is hard to understand what prompted the building of so many extreme clippers in the last three years of the 1860s, when freights were slowly falling and the returns on the capital invested were being reduced annually. Perhaps a certain temperament induced shipowners to have one final fling to build a really out-and-out full-blooded clipper and no doubt the spirit of rivalry and competition caught on. Some of them may have made good profits and had money to invest and it was probably being found that first class ships of composite construction were keeping their values in the secondhand market. Or it may have been due to the shareholders, who had had their appetites whetted by the excitement of the 1866 Tea Race or the distribution of dividends, and so wanted an extreme clipper built.

Of the ships described in this chapter, no fewer than six of them were of extreme clipper build, according to the survival of plans or models, and perhaps the number could be increased if further plans had survived. The extreme clippers were the *Leander* and *Spindrift* built in 1867, *Thermopylae* built in 1868, and *Cutty Sark, Norman Court* and *The Caliph* built in 1869. Of the others, plans show *Derwent* to have been a clipper; *Omba* was only a medium clipper with little deadrise and a fullish entrance; *Norham Castle* and *Forward Ho!* were finer versions but not full clippers. A half-model of *Lahloo* shows her to have been of similar sharpness to *Ariel*, and although no plans or models are known of *Kaisow* or *Wylo*, they were probably not much fuller than *Ariel*. *Undine* was probably a repeat of *Maitland* and so would have been a clipper with a broad beam. With the exception of *Titania*, the six extreme clippers listed above are the finest-lined clippers to have been built in the 1860s, according to the evidence of surviving plans or models.

Frederick Claydon has reconstructed the plans of two of these ships, the *Spindrift* and *The Caliph*, and drawn out splendid sets of lines, deck and sail plans. My thanks are due to him for allowing me to reproduce them here. In the case of the former, he had to measure the rigged model in the Glasgow Museum, which required considerable skill and patience. He performed the same task for the *Taitsing*.

An interesting account of how *The Caliph* was constructed was published by Charles Chapman in *All About Ships* and it is reproduced here as it describes work in a shipyard engaged on composite construction. Some punctuation has been altered where the printer misinterpreted the original and some spelling has been corrected. Chapman's puerile phraseology has also been amended or omitted. By his use of 'we' and 'our' it sounds as if he was in the employ of Alexander Hall & Sons, Aberdeen, the builder of *The Caliph*.

Building of 'The Caliph'

Her dimensions are as follows: length between perpendicular 213ft 3in, extreme breadth 36ft, depth in hold 20ft 4in. The first order was the iron for frames, beams, stringer plates, &c the dimensions of whch are to be found in *Lloyd's* [*Register*] and the lengths, &c, measured from the model and plans. The line of the vessel having been laid down on the loft floor an made all correct, the body plan, as it is called, is scratched on a wooden platform near the furnace for bending frames, &c.

The 27th of March [1869] we launched the Japanese corvette *Jho-Sho-Maru*, 1500 tons register, 280hpn; and that da the keel, stem and sternpost of our new ship, No 263 (after wards to be known as *The Caliph*), was lying alongside th corvette, ready to be laid down, which was done on the 29th the intervening day being Sunday. The keel is of a peculia construction, being a sort of double keel, composed of tw American elm logs, 17in by 18in, one above the other, a shown in the midship section which accompanies this. Th sternpost, composed entirely of teak, with rabbet cut on it t receive hood ends. The stem, in two parts: the lower of goo British oak, the upper of teak, with knightheads bolted on, next hoisted up, planked, raked, and shored. The deadwoods of teak, are next fitted on, and dressed from the bearding lin to the rabbet. The keel-plate, one inch in thickness, and of breadth to suit the shape of the bottom, is laid along the top c the keel, and kept up about four inches to allow of rivetting the holes for securing the frames to it, and for bolting th plate to the keel being all punched in it. While the carpenter have been getting the keel ready, gangs of ironworkers have been preparing the iron frames, beams, keelsons, &c.

A wooden platform is now laid across the top of the keel whereon to build the frames, which consist of frame bars, floc plates, and reverse bars, with sundry cleats for securing kee sons and stringers. When so many of the frames, say 20, ar built and hoisted into their places, they are then rivetted t the keel-plate, which is then lowered down on top of the kee and bolted to it by 1¼in yellow-metal bolts through an clenched – one between each two frames; that is to say, one every 18in, as that is the distance the frames are apart. Th keelsons and stringers are now commenced, and consist c main keelson, bilge keelsons, intercostal keelson, and ho stringers, which meet at the stem and sternpost, and so forr breasthooks. As the frames are hoisted up they are set fair an ribands put on them. The beams are hoisted along with th frames, and are composed of bulb iron with double angle iro on top, and connected to the frame by knees or bracket-plate The ship being all framed, fore and aft, we now put on th sheer strake, a plate 3ft broad, and extending along the top c

the frames from stem to stern. Then follow stringer plates, bilge plate, and diagonal straps, &c., all of which you will see in [the] midship section.

The planking consists of American rock elm, and mountain teak, the elm extending up to the 7ft waterline; the planking on the bottom is 6in thick, tapering to $4\frac{3}{4}$in at gunwale. It is secured to iron frames by $^{15}/_{16}$in and $^{13}/_{16}$in yellow-metal bolts, and nuts screwed up inside, the head of the bolt being covered over with teak dowel dipped in marine glue. The two paint strakes or uppermost planks being put on, the stanchions, waterways and covering board are fitted; then the deck is laid, yellow pine 5 by 4 fastened with $^{5}/_{8}$in galvanised iron bolts. The outside skin is now caulked, the oakum being driven back within $\frac{3}{4}$in of inside. While one or two gangs are caulking [the] outside others, having caulked the deck, go on fitting deck work, including [the] windlass, which in this ship is Brown and Harfield's, according to the wish of the owner. For our own part we always prefer a good common windlass with patent purchase; there is no fear of anything going wrong with the old ones but what can be easily repaired, whereas these patent ones, if they are not carefully looked after, soon rust up, and they are not so simply handled in a dark night, and, if they do break, it is beyond your power to mend them; in *The Caliph's* windlass the purchase is very slow. I prefer Emerson & Walker's. As the hatch combings are of iron, they are generally fitted when the beams are in; the mast combings, fife rails, and stanchions, chain plates, catheads, capstans, pumps, mooring pipes, mooring bitts, likewise acting as ventilators; the deckhouse is built of teak with iron frames, with accommodation for galley and engine room, with rooms for petty officers and midshipmen; attached to the cooking apparatus is a condensor capable of distilling 50 gallons in 12 hours; besides this the ship has two tanks holding 2000 gallons each. In the after end of the house stands the steam engine, of 8 horsepower, which works cargo, lifts the anchor, pumps the ship, and hoists sails, yards, or warps ship. This engine is made in such a way that it can be attached to a shaft for driving two small screws, one on each side of the vessel, worked by a

bevelled wheel on end of shaft across the deck, and a similar wheel on the end of the shaft which is along the ship's side, at an angle, and can be lifted out of the water at pleasure; this machinery is expected to drive the ship about $2\frac{1}{2}$ knots per hour in a calm. The pumps are two 7in pumps with brass chambers and boxes. The companion and skylights having been made by the joiner, they are now fitted on the raised quarterdeck. The upsides being caulked, are next planed, dressed and sand-papered, the seams filled with a composition for the purpose and puttied. The chain-plates, being all made and galvanised, are bolted on with three $1\frac{1}{4}$in iron bolts, the plates for fore and main sheets, bobstay, bowsprit shroud, jibboom guys, likewise the bumpkins, fore and main braces. The scuppers, three on each side, 6in by 3in, are made of thick lead, with brass grating inside to prevent their getting stopped up with dirt, and to keep Jack from poking holes in them with a broom handle. The bulwarks are fitted with yellow pine, with four large ports of a side to clear the water off the decks; sheaves are fitted in the bulwarks for fore and main sheets and studdingsail sheets; belaying pins put in the rails with small metal heads for tacks and sheets. The vessel's bottom is cemented [inside] with Portland cement over all bolt heads and iron plates, to prevent the action of the water on the bolts and rivets. The ceiling is close up to the upper turn of the bilge, with every third strake left loose, so as to reach the frames for painting, &c; from the bilge up to the main deck she is sparred with upright hardwood battens, put on as permanent dunnage. The forecastle is fitted below for thirty men, with scuttles inside for light and ventilation, and a small stove for cold weather.

The chain-locker is by the foremast, and is all below the lower deck; the coal-hole is down in the fore peak; the sail cabin and store rooms alongside the main hatch. I can't recommend the arrangements, and they are no plan of ours. I should have had all the stores and sails aft, and taken a piece off from that useless fore cabin, with a companion from the deck so as to reach your stores when the rest of the place was filled with tea. The cutwater and figurehead are fitted, which may be called the ornamental part, along with stem knees, wing rail, sword rail, head board, trail boards, cross knees, &c; the hawse-pipes, two on each side, 10in diameter, come through between [the] stem knees. The rudder-stock is English oak, 16½in diameter, and is what is known as a gooseneck or gunstock; [the] rudder [is fitted] with four pairs of rudder-braces of brass. The ship's bottom receives two coats of Archangel tar, and is ready for the copper sheathing which is 26 and 28oz, fastened with 1⅛ nails, and extends up to 22ft waterline.

The ship is launched upon two side-ways and a centre-way below the keel, on which most of the weight rests, the side-ways merely serving to steady the ship. Owing to the extreme sharpness of the bottom, the side-ways, were the whole weight to rest on them, would fly out beneath her. As it is, we are obliged to put chains under the keel to hold in the side-ways. The ship, until ready for launching, is steadied by shores, and kept from running down before she is wanted by dogs driven into the running and laying ways, and a strong lashing, which is the last link which connects her with *terra firma*. When the time is up, these shores are taken away, the dogs driven out, and the word being given the lashing is cut, when the vessel is expected to move off, which in most cases they do, but sometimes they require a lot of screwing and hammering.

However, *The Caliph* moved away just when she ought to, and made a most capital launch. This was Monday, Sept 6th, 1869.

The ship is next taken under the sheer legs to receive her masts, tanks, &c, and the work of rigging commenced. . . . The ship's keel was laid on 29 April; launched 6th September; left Aberdeen, 19th; arrived at London on the 21st September; was coppered, loaded, and sailed (I understand) on the 12th of October.

I should have mentioned before that she was built under a watertight shed; classed 17 years A1 at Lloyd's; register tonnage under tonnage deck, 888; gross register, 961; deduction for crew space, 47; net register, 914 tons. Builders' measure, 1330.

Alexander Hector who owned *The Caliph* was not one of the regular group of shipowners who had been connected with China clippers all their lives. These men were all well known to each other and James MacCunn, in a letter to Basil Lubbock dated 7 July 1911, remarked on some of them. Some of the comments are his own, as indicated in single quotes, but some I have summarized in his own language:

I knew Maxton well, a native of Greenock like myself. His father was a shipmaster. He was very go-ahead 'and, I think, the pioneer of the real clipper'. He became a partner in Shaw, Maxton. He's dead long ago.

So is Rodger, shipmaster and later owner of *Min*, *Taeping*, &c.

Findlay, owner of *Spindrift*, was never the same man after her uninsured loss.

John Willis, owner of *Cutty Sark* is long dead. 'He was a fine affable sportsman [?] and built his hopes in that ship – in vain.'

'Killick Martin & Co were my agents and I saw a great deal of Killick, who formerly commanded *Challenger*, built 1852. He was in the very thick of the fight re China races. Old Mr Ritchie was the last survivor of that firm.'

'Skinner too is dead. He was a great moving spirit in building clippers on spec and selling them as well as owning. I regarded him as a very clear, level-headed, practical man.'

His letters are with the Lubbock papers at the National Maritime Museum.

The sort of enthusiasm produced by the races amongst the first starters with the new season's tea spilled over into newspaper reports, of which the following is typical. The cutting was pasted in a scrapbook of maritime items which I was loaned but the collector had failed to record the source and date of the cutting; but the race described took place in the year 1868.

The Great Ship Race from China
The 16,000-mile race among the large fleet of the finest clipper ships in the world with the new spring teas from China has this year been watched with more than ordinary interest. In all about forty sailing ships were engaged in the contest. Their departure from Foo-chow-Foo and its neighbouring ports in China ranged over a space of twenty-five days. Of these ships were those which accomplished such extraordinary quick passages in last year's race and the race the year before – viz the *Ariel* and the *Taeping* as well as others which have obtained considerable notoriety for their swift-sailing qualities, such as the *Serica* and *Fiery Cross*. This year's contest has at least displayed most splendid seamanship on the part of the officers and crews commanding the different clippers; and, though there was no prize held out as in former years (a handsome premium), there was no lack of the determined courage and perseverance which characterized their seamanship in former contests. The leading ships in the race, with the days of sailing, tonnage, and cargo, will be found detailed in the following list:

May 27 [1868]	*Belted Will*	934,496lbs tea
May 27	*Undine*	1,088,398lbs tea
May 28	*Ariel*	1,230,900lbs tea
May 28	*Sir Lancelot*	1,250,057lbs tea
May 28	*Taeping*	1,165,459lbs tea
May 29	*Spindrift*	1,306,836lbs tea
May 30	*Lahloo*	1,231,397lbs tea
(her first voyage and considered the favourite)		
May 31	*Black Prince*	1,051,300lbs tea
June 1	*Serica*	967,500lbs tea
June 2	*Fiery Cross*	867,600lbs tea

[I have omitted date of build, tonnage, owners and class at Lloyd's from the list.]

It will be seen that three of the ships, the *Ariel*, *Sir Lancelot* and *Taeping*, left on the same day, the 28th of May, and that the *Spindrift* sailed on the 29th of May, and the *Lahloo* on the 30th of May. The next heard of them was from Anjer, showing that these vessels passed the Straits about the 22nd and 23rd of June, and from subsequent accounts most of the other vessels passed down the China Seas all together.

The *Ariel* was the first ship to reach the Channel. She passed through the Downs at two o'clock on Wednesday morning [ie 2 September], and was hauled into the East India Dock at noon that day.

The *Spindrift* was the next ship. She passed through the Downs at thirty minutes past twelve o'clock on Wednesday forenoon, and got into the East India Dock at twelve o'clock that night.

The *Ariel* was undoubtedly the first ship in dock; but the *Spindrift* was the winning ship, according to nautical time, by 15½ hours, the *Spindrift* having, it is said, accomplished the run in little more than 94 days; while the *Ariel*, which left China the day before the *Spindrift*, took about 95 days 12 hours.

[The reports by the two respective captains are here omitted].

Since the arrivals mentioned, the *Sir Lancelot* passed up the River on Thursday [*ie* 3 September]. She left China the same day as the *Ariel*. The *Lahloo* which sailed two days afterwards, arrived in the Downs on Friday [4 September], and it is doubtful whether she will not be third in the race. Two other ships are reported in the Channel, the *Taeping* and the *Belted Will*. As yet the laurels fall on the *Spindrift*; unless some of the ships which left China later beat her by time.

But none did.

Thus did one newspaper after another report on the China tea race and perhaps the owners and shareholders enjoyed the publicity earned by their ships.

BIOGRAPHIES OF SHIPS BUILT 1867–1869

DERWENT, 1867

This iron barque built by Barclay, Curle & Co, Glasgow, forms a good example of a fine-lined iron clipper of the 1860s. The ends are long and sharp, and although there is not much deadrise the bilges are slack with some tumble-

home above. Although there is a topgallant rail, the after accommodation is in a raised quarterdeck, not a poop, thus retaining the elegant sheer of the long hull. The frames are at 21in centres and the beams 3ft 6in apart on average. There are 6.46 beams to length. The two skysails on the fore- and mainmasts of a barque make a noble rig. The running rigging, stunsail booms and some of the staysails have been reconstructed from a painting owned by the Little Ship Club, London.

The *Derwent* had dimensions of 186.0ft × 28.8ft × 17.1ft and tonnages of 599.37 net and under deck. She was owned by William H Tindall of London and her name drops out of *Lloyd's Register* in 1876, although the *Mercantile Navy List* still includes her name that year. She traded to China under

Below: Derwent lines plan. Redrawn from tracing made of builder's plan. Built of iron in 1867 by Barclay, Curle & Co, Glasgow, with dimensions of 186.0ft × 28.8ft × 17.1ft and 599.37 net. Reconstruction (from painting in Little Ship Club, London): wheel and wheel box; boat in davits; deckhouse panels.

Bottom: Derwent sail plan. Redrawn from tracing made of builder's plan. Reconstruction: running rigging; houseflags; some of the main and mizen staysails; stunsail booms. Source: painting in Little Ship Club, London.

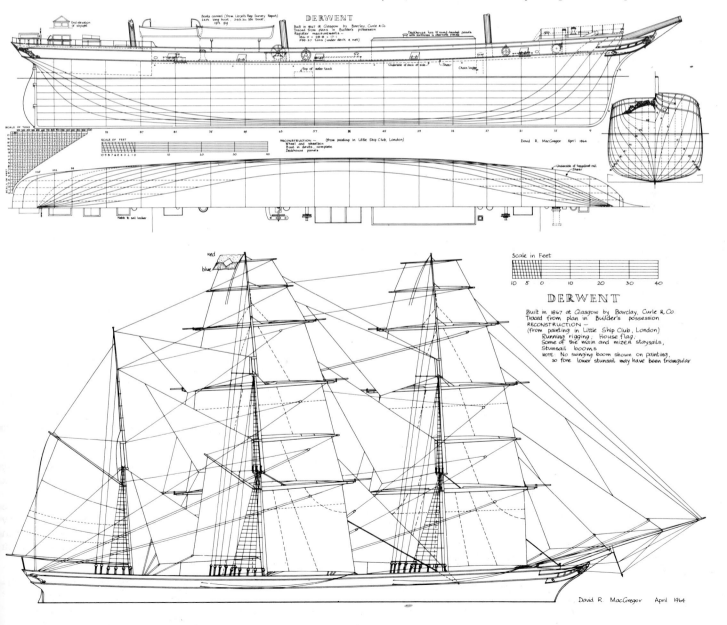

Captain Gadd at various times in her life but I have not traced any of her passages. In 1874 she sailed from Manilla on 18 July, passed Anjer 1 September and St Helena 16 October, and reached New York on 3 December, 138 days later, which was 21 days quicker than the *Elmstone*.

FORWARD HO!, 1867

A composite ship built by Alexander Stephen & Sons, Glasgow, for J Catto, Aberdeen, measuring 193.7ft × 33.6ft × 20.6ft and 943 tons, classed 17 A1. She was a powerful ship, equally suited for the Australian or China trades and made runs of 332 and 312 miles in the Roaring Forties in 1873.

In 1880 Hossack, Liverpool, bought her, but she was wrecked the next year on 28 October at Sendoe, Japan.

This ship was No 110 in Stephen's yard. The contract price was agreed on 16 April 1867 and the terms were for a ship of 1014 tons bm at £17 15s per ton bm to class 15 A1. In fact she was classed 17 A1 by Lloyd's Register – the first composite ship built on the Clyde to be awarded 17 years. The profit on the contract was £2865, and Alexander Stephen noted in his diary that it was 'very good to get it off Aberdonians'.

GERAINT, 1867

This was another of James MacCunn's short-lived ships, which went 'missing' in 1871 at the same time as *The Caliph*, not having been heard of since 1 March that year, bound Cardiff to Shanghai with coal, and a crew of twenty-six. She had been built on the Clyde by McMillan as a composite full-rigged ship of 1075 tons with dimensions of 207.0ft × 33.5ft × 21.2ft.

LAHLOO, 1867

Of the few good photographs that exist of tea clippers, perhaps that of *Lahloo* resembles more than most the picture conjured up by the imagination of a heavily-sparred clipper with little freeboard. *Lahloo* was of the same class as *Titania* and *Ariel*, and of the same sharpness as the latter, yet with more deadrise and tumblehome and a slightly fuller run. Robert Steele & Co, Greenock, built her for Alexander Rodger, Glasgow, owner of *Taeping*, and she came out with Cunningham's roller-reefing single topsails. Like the *Ariel* her courses were tremendously deep. Composite built to class 14 A1 she measured 191.6ft × 32.9ft × 19.9ft and 799 tons.

John Smith, from the *Min*, took her from the stocks and drove her hard all the time. On her second voyage, having gone out to Shanghai against the monsoon in 100 days, pilot to pilot, she came home by the Eastern route as did many others that year such as *Spindrift* and *Ariel*. In 1869, leaving London on 28 October she reached Shanghai on 3 February, 98 days later, or 95 pilot to pilot, beating *Ariel* by 10 days.

She was wrecked on 31 July 1872, on Sandalwood Island, one of the Sunda Islands, bound from Shanghai for London with tea.

LEANDER, 1867

This extreme clipper ship was designed by Bernard Waymouth, who also designed *Thermopylae* which was built the following year. *Leander*'s lines plan was reproduced in *L'Art Naval . . . Jusqu'en 1869* by Admiral Paris and he devotes a page-and-a-half to her description in the separate volume of text. Her lines are amongst the sharpest of any tea clipper, with a long entrance and run in which there is considerable hollow in the lower body; there is great deadrise with hollow garboards and floors that round up into slack bilges and this curve continues as the topsides tumble home. The head and counter are light and there is no topgallant rail.

This extreme hull-form produced a clipper that was at her best in light winds and performed well going to windward or in a head sea, but when pressed in heavy weather she was inclined to be tender and very wet. There are no known examples of ships designed by Bernard Waymouth prior to *Leander* and yet he must have been practising to have conceived such a sophisticated design. The mid-section is styled on the traditional English cutter which was the basis from which many clipper designs developed. Waymouth had been a surveyor with Lloyd's Register since 1854 and so would have been able to examine all the finest clippers built. He became Principal Surveyor in 1871 and Secretary two years later, a position which he held until his death in 1890.

Thermopylae, Waymouth's next clipper design, although very slightly fuller, was hardly less fast in light winds and far superior in strong ones. Due to her fine lines, *Leander*

Opposite: The magnificent Lahloo *moored off Gravesend in the early 1870s. She was actually fitted with single topsails when built in 1867. (MacGregor Collection)*

Below: Leander *lines, sail plan and midship section. Reproduced from* L'Art Naval a L'Exposition. . .de Paris en 1867 . . . jusqu'en 1869 *(plate XXVII) by Vice Admiral Paris. Built of composite construction in 1867 by J G Lawrie, Glasgow, with dimensions of 215.5ft × 35.2ft × 20.7ft and 848 tons net.*

required so much ballast that she was down to her marks before fully laden and only carried about 1,151,000lbs of tea. This was the cause of her being outsailed by *Thermopylae* in 1869, which gained 32 hours on her in the run to Anjer and, when in the south-east trades, dropped her astern in three days; but then *Leander* was immersed a foot deeper.

Leander was composite-built by J G Lawrie, Glasgow, and measured 215.5ft × 35.2ft × 20.7ft, 848 tons net and under deck, and 886 gross. This made the coefficient of under deck tonnage 0.54 which was very low indeed. She was built for Joseph Somes, London, and was known as 'Somes yacht'. Later he transferred his interests into the Merchant Shipping Co.

Although the lines plan reproduced by Basil Lubbock in *The China Clippers* shows an Aberdeen house aft with its side decks, a painting by William Clark depicts a raised quarter-deck with railing across the front, a smallish deckhouse abaft the foremast, all the boats stowed on deck, and a monkey forecastle. The crew's quarters must have been below deck forward.

Some fine-lined ships had small sail areas but this was certainly not the case with *Leander*, and although she set nothing above royals, the topgallant sails were especially deep. The main topgallant was a roller-reefing sail with Colling and Pinkney's gear and there was a row of reef points on each of the upper topsails. The single mizen topsail had three rows of reef points. There would have been a full suit of stunsails up to the royals.

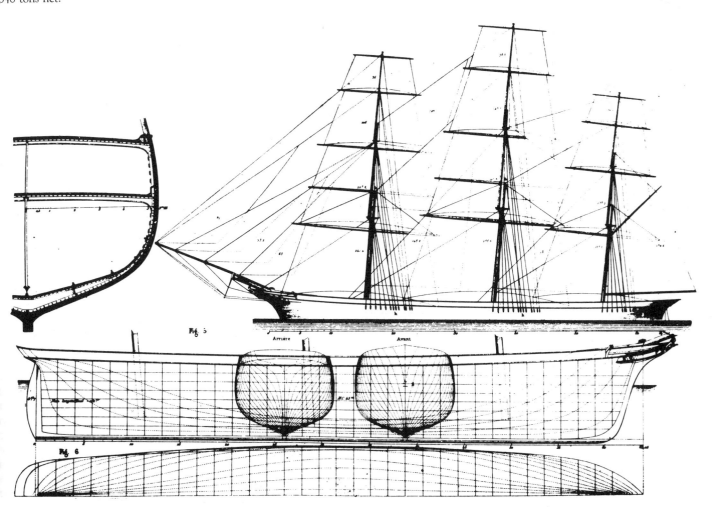

She made some fast passages in the tea trade, although during the 1870s she usually carried tea direct to New York with the exception of the year 1879–80. She made two fast outward passages to China:

1868, Plymouth to Shanghai, 27 October to 30 January 1869, 95 days.

1871, London to Hong Kong, 15 March to 18 June, 95 days.

Some of the passages between Amoy and New York were said to have been made in under 90 days.

She had many contests with the *Hallowe'en* which was always the better ship in strong winds. In 1874 *Leander* went out to Sydney from the Isle of Wight in 74 days. In 1886 she and *Hallowe'en* were still managing to load tea.

R Anderson bought her in 1887 and Ross & Co the following year. In 1895 she was bought by Arab owners in Oman and rechristened *Nusrool Mujeed*. She was broken up in 1901.

SPINDRIFT, 1867

Many of the clippers had short lives, but of the extremely sharp ships *Spindrift* had one of the shortest, being wrecked at the commencement of her third voyage. She had been built and designed by Charles Connell, Glasgow, for James Findlay of Greenock, and she was undoubtedly her builder's finest tea clipper. She was somewhat longer than other ships in the trade and together with a large sail area was extremely fast on a reach, at which she was almost equal to *Ariel* and perhaps a little better than the latter in strong winds. *Spindrift*'s sail plan included a mainyard 84ft long, double topsails on fore and main and a roller-reefing mizen topsail. The table in *Maitland*'s biography comparing lengths of yards shows how much *Spindrift*'s square sails tapered up to the royals and in fact the sails overlap very little.

Perhaps the winning of the China tea race was an ambition held by many owners and although to some it was a lovely dream impossible to realize, to others the trophy seemed almost within their grasp. However, James Findlay was one of the winners. His *Serica* won the race in 1864 but just failed to grasp the prize in 1865 and 1866; unfortunately his *Taitsing* was not fast enough. Perhaps he determined to

Above: This oil painting by William Clark of *Leander* shows that she had a large spread of canvas and that her main topgallant was fitted with Colling & Pinkney's roller-reefing mechanism, like *Thermopylae*'s. There are also four buntlines to this sail. (*Parker Gallery*)

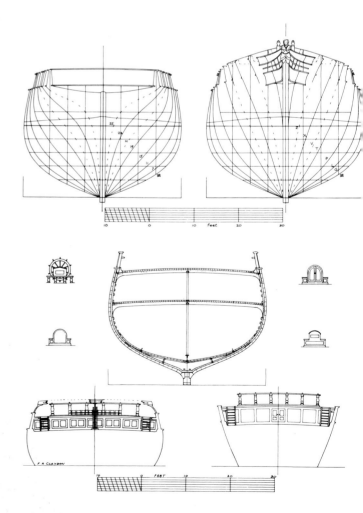

Opposite, centre: Spindrift body plans. Instead of the conventional way, the afterbody sections on both sides of the hull appear on the left-hand diagram and all the forebody ones on the right-hand diagram. Drawn by F A Claydon. No reconstruction.

Opposite, bottom: Spindrift midship section (centre), break of raised quarterdeck (left), break of forecastle (right), and end views of other fittings.

Below: Spindrift lines and deck layout. Drawn by F A Claydon from lines and measurements taken off rigged builder's model in Glasgow Museum and Art Gallery (Transport Museum). Ship built in 1867 by Charles Connell & Co, Glasgow, with dimensions of 219.4ft × 35.6ft × 20.25ft and 899.43 tons net.

Bottom: Spindrift sail plan. Drawn by F A Claydon from measurements taken off builder's rigged model in Glasgow Transport Museum. Reconstruction: sails, as there are none on model; stunsail booms, yards and sails.

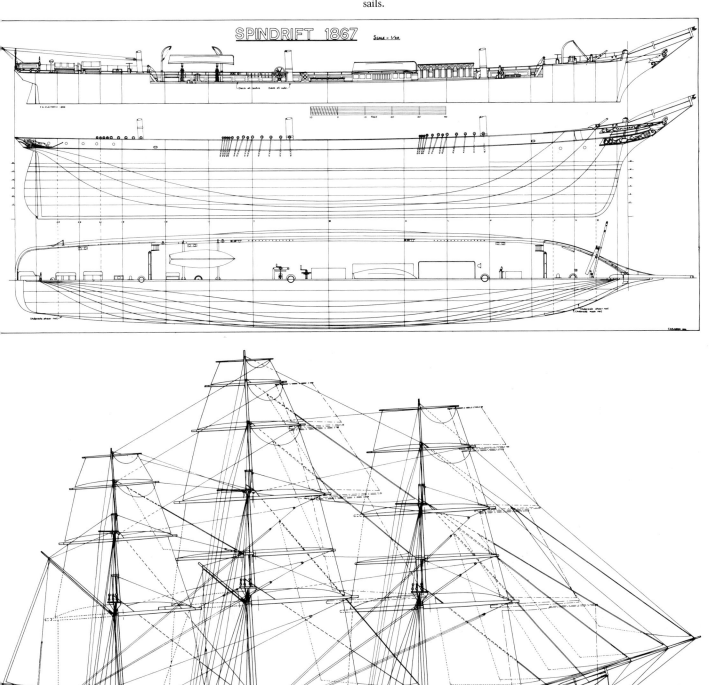

have a final attempt, because with his third clipper, the *Spindrift*, he owned an extremely sharp-bodied ship with exceedingly fine waterlines and great deadrise, whose cargo capacity was small and which could not be made to pay without high freight rates. His gamble, if that is not an inappropriate word to call it, paid off because *Spindrift* was judged to have beaten *Ariel* by 14 hours on time on her maiden passage with tea.

Spindrift was launched on 18 July with a tonnage of 899 net and under deck, according to the Lloyd's Register survey report, and dimensions of 219.4ft × 35.6ft × 20.25ft, which gives a coefficient of 0.57 under deck tons. A rigged model of the ship at ¼in scale in the Glasgow Museum and Art Gallery was measured by F A Claydon, who produced the fine set of plans reproduced here.

The deck layout was typical for a composite-built ship with a raised quarterdeck and only a monkey forecastle, but one point of interest was that the panels of the deckhouse were of pointed Gothic style, which was rare for a sailing ship although it was all the rage ashore and also in some passenger steamers.

Middleton took her out on her maiden passage to Shanghai in 108 days from London, 13 September 1867 to 1 January 1868, and he and Innes, who had gone out on *Serica*, changed ships when in China. There was some keen racing on the run home in 1868 with *Ariel*, *Sir Lancelot* and *Taeping* all leaving one day before *Spindrift*. *Ariel* was the first through Sunda Strait and led for most of the way home. The four ships, together with *Lahloo*, were in close contact all the time. On 30 August they were all clustered round the Scillies with hardly any wind. *Ariel*, however, found just enough to take her up Channel, 6 hours ahead of *Spindrift* and *Sir Lancelot*. Although *Ariel* docked first – at 1.0 pm on 2

September – the race was awarded to *Spindrift* which, having left on 29 May, 25 hours behind *Ariel*, docked at midnight on 2 September and so won by some 14 hours on time, 9[?] days 7 hours from Foochow, *Ariel* having taken 96 days 2[?] hours. The next year *Spindrift* took 105 days to Gravesend via the longer Eastern route.

In 1869, under Nutsford, she left London for Shanghai on 20 November with cargo worth £200,000 and a crew numbering 35, but was wrecked the next day near Dungeness. She was not insured.

THYATIRA, 1867

This was George Thompson & Co's first ship built of composite construction with an iron frame and wood planking: she was constructed by Walter Hood at Aberdeen with dimensions of 201.0ft × 33.0ft × 21.7ft and a tonnage o[f] 962. Her raised quarterdeck was 48ft long and the forecastle was 36ft long. But Thompson was obviously not truly convinced that his 'Aberdeen White Star Line' could dispense with ships of all-wood construction, because he had three more built: in 1867 the *Jerusalem* of 901 tons, followed by *Ascalon* in 1868 and *Centurion* in 1869. His first iron ship wa[s] the *Patriarch* of 1869. Photographs of *Thyatira* show outside channels. Although trading principally to and from Australia she carried home cargoes occasionally from China.

Thompson sold her to Woodside of Belfast in 1894 and two years later she was abandoned on fire on 16 July, bound from London to Rio de Janeiro with a crew of eighteen. The presence of 800 cases of dynamite in the cargo probably hastened the decision to leave the ship.

UNDINE, 1867

This was another of William Pile's attempts to build an out-and-out clipper for the tea trade, but though several other fast ships came from his yard he was not to improve upon *Maitland*. J R Kelso of North Shields was her owner, as

Spindrift was another heavily-canvased extreme clipper of 1867, as portrayed in this fine lithograph by Thomas G Dutton. *(Paul Mason Gallery)*

might be expected, and his new composite ship registered 796 tons on dimensions of 182.6ft × 35.1ft × 19.5ft.

In 1868–69 she went out to Shanghai against the monsoon in 100 days, pilot to pilot. Three years later a correspondent to the *London and China Telegraph* wrote that she reached Shanghai on 22 April 1871, 89 days from the Downs; but he was misinformed, as she actually reached Shanghai exactly one month later, or 119 days out.

She was still in the trade in 1884, but in that year was sold to Austrian owners in Trappano and after passing through various hands, capsized and sank in February 1893.

GUINEVERE, 1868

When his first clipper of this name was wrecked in 1866, James MacCunn of Greenock ordered a replacement to which he gave the same name, and the new ship had a long life. She was composite-built at Glasgow by Randolph, Elder & Co with dimensions of 197.0ft × 34.0ft × 19.7ft, 879 tons net and 904 gross, and a raised quarterdeck of 42ft. of 42ft.

Left: Photographed at Melbourne in the 1880s, *Thyatira* was a beautiful product from Walter Hood's yard. A painting showing her when new depicts Cunningham's roller-reefing gear fitted to all her topgallants. (*The late David M Little*)

Below: Built to replace the first *Guinevere*, the second one of the same name is here seen cut down to a barque and bearing the name *Luna*. (*Nautical Photo Agency*)

The year before MacCunn disposed of her, she put into Mauritius on 5 August, leaking, being four months out on a passage from London to Wellington. In 1887 Carl Rathkens of Rostock became the new owner; four years later he sold her to Norwegian owners in Arendal who renamed her *Luna*. In 1900 she was dismasted in October and five years later a passage is recorded for her across the Atlantic from Preston to Bay Varte, New Brunswick, in 47 days, 7 July to 23 August. Her end came in 1907 when she was broken up at Dunkirk in September.

KAISOW, 1868

This was the last tea clipper, apart from *Wylo* launched the following year, to be built by Robert Steele of Greenock, and though slightly fuller than *Lahloo* she was equally fast and could go to windward in a remarkable fashion. She came out as a full-rigged ship with a single mizen topsail, skysail, and the usual host of stunsails, being composite-built of teak and elm planking on iron frames. The fore and main lower masts and the bowsprit were of iron plates, but the mizen was a solid stick of Oregon pine. She was launched on 19 November at Greenock with tonnages of 767 under deck, 820 gross and 795 net register, with dimensions of 193.2ft × 32.0ft × 20.3ft.

Alexander Rodger Snr of Glasgow began by owning 48 shares with his son Alexander having 16 shares, but within a year the father had disposed of all his shares to female members of his family living at the same address and his son became the managing owner. At the end of 1875, the ship was bought by Killick, Martin & Co, London, and re-registered there in January 1876. This firm was appointed the managing owners, and there were four other shareholders. holders.

A description of *Kaisow* is best given by Captain Harry Davis who served all his time in her and then rose to become first mate until she was sold in 1885. In a letter to me, he wrote:

She was a joy to sail and handle and very fast. I was in her for nearly six years and never saw her passed by anything under canvas. With a beam wind or close-hauled she was, in my opinion, the equal of any of the clippers and faster than most of them, and certainly so in light winds and catspaws.

With the wind dead astern she was not at her best, and consequently whenever practicable the wind was always brought on to one quarter or the other; this meant jibing over every 8 or 12 hours when running before the SE trades between the Cape and St Helena.

When running before a heavy gale and high sea she never pooped, which was most remarkable considering her fine quarters; but the sea sometimes tumbled over the rails at the end of the poop on to the quarterdeck. The foresail was seldom or never taken off her when she was running before a gale, and the weather had to be very bad before it was reefed or furled. She had good shoulders and overhang, and never dived badly, nor did she ship heavy water over the bows except when being driven into a head sea, such as one encounters off the Agulhas Bank and Cape or in the Formosa Channel, wind against tide: but she flung the spray wide and high.

She could log 12 and 13 knots easily for hours, and at times, in favourable circumstances, could reach 14, but things were straining then. Daily runs of from 280 to 310 knots were considered satisfactory and she required careful watching and handling, but steered beautifully.

Coming home under Captain John Gadd from San Francisco, to which port we had been with tea from Yokohama, we came up with the *Wild Deer* to the eastward of the Falkland Islands. The wind held very light from SW, dead astern, and we were in close company with her for two days. On the third day the wind came out of a northerly quarter; *Kaisow* was braced up on an easy bowline and in a few hours *Wild Deer* was hull down astern.

According to Davis, Flores was passed on the 80th day and Falmouth reached on 24 July 1881, 88 days out, a very fast passage.

Unfortunately, Davis' memory played him false as the dates of this passage were 6 November 1880 to 19 February 1881 at Falmouth which equals 105 days. No evidence could be found to substantiate the time of 88 days. On 24 July 1881, the ship was in harbour at Manilla.

Davis continued:

Kaisow was perfectly masted. I say this because we used to set a ringtail when she was reduced to barque rig, but she did not like it and griped a good deal, and it was therefore discontinued. She would do almost anything for one who understood and could handle her. One had to be very quick with her when going about, and get the fore yards round promptly or she would gather her sternway and kick.

He described the setting of the ringtail as follows:

A boom was lashed or fastened on to the extreme end of the spanker boom. The sail was triangular, the apex hoisted to the end of the gaff, the clew hauled out to the end of the temporary boom and the tack to a cleat on the spanker boom. Everything was made fast to the spanker boom so that the whole thing moved with it.

The diagrammatic deck plan was constructed from Captain Davis' description. The whisker booms were of greenheart, fitted with a wire jumper stay down to a bolt in the ship's side, the booms being hinged on a gooseneck and clamped down in a groove on the forecastle rail. They could be unshipped or topped up in port. The iron-framed teak deckhouse with brass-framed ports housed the crew, carpenter's shop, paint locker, lamp room, and on the port side aft, the galley, containing a small condenser for emergency use as the ship only carried a 90-day water supply. The passaree booms hinged on the foremast and were laid fore and aft with their ends on the forecastle head deck when not in use. The miniature winches, fitted with brass whelps and fixed to the 4ft high bulwarks, were used for heaving taut the fore and main sheets and were in the ship from the first. On the raised quarterdeck the skylight to the after cabin carried brass mesh frames which protected exquisite glass panes engraved with the tea plant and flowers in all stages. Teak was used throughout.

In the early 1870s she made these fast outward passages:
1869–70, Anderson, London to Shanghai, 1 December to 10 March, 99 days.
1871, Anderson, Cardiff to Hong Kong, 19 March to 19 June, 92 days. Passed Lundy 21 March.
1875, Tropp, Deal to Hong Kong, 5 March to 10 June, 97 days (92 days from the Lizard). Passed Anjer 23 May.

Although *Kaisow* loaded tea at £3 10s per ton on her maiden passage home in 1869, things were difficult thereafter as steamers began to take the cream of the trade, and a year later freights from Foochow were only £1 5s or £1 10s per ton in August and £2 in September. In 1871 she secured a private charter from Batavia to London in which she

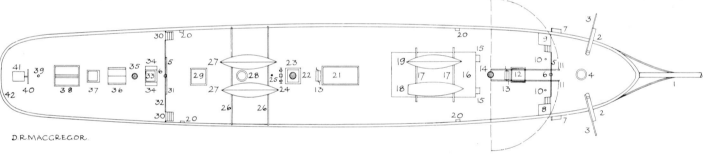

D.R.MACGREGOR.

Above: Diagrammatic deck plan of *Kaisow.* The dotted line represents the position of the passaree booms as they are swung out. *(Author)*

KEY

1. Figurehead of a mandarin in a pleated blue robe, with a red hat and yellow tassel, and holding a small scroll in his right hand
2. Oak catheads
3. Whisker booms
4. Capstan geared to Emerson & Walker's patent windlass (with compressor)
5. Capstan bar rack (of teak)
6. Ship's bell
7. Side light screens
8. Lavatory for crew
9. Bosun's locker
10. Chain locker
11. Passaree booms, hinged on foremast
12. Fore hatch
13. Cargo winch
14. Foremast
15. Poultry pens
16. Teak deckhouse
17. Wooden skids on top of deckhouse, fastened to ring bolts on deck
18. Longboat
19. Lifeboat
20. Miniature winches
21. Main hatch
22. Mainmast
23. Fife rail
24. Pumps
25. Fresh water pump
26. Skids supported on iron stanchions and curved down each side on to main rail
27. Lifeboats, keel uppermost
28. Capstan
29. After hatch with seat each side
30. Teak ladders
31. Bucket rack with 12 buckets
32. Teak rail
33. Booby hatch leading to quarters for apprentices and petty officers (to starboard)
34. Teak hen coops
35. Mizen mast
36. Fire cabin skylight
37. Companion hatch
38. Elaborate after cabin skylight
39. Binnacle
40. Wheel
41. Wheel box
42. 12 lifebuoys lashed to inside of rail

Top: The *Kaisow* bound down-Channel on her maiden passage in 1868, as seen by T G Dutton, but her main skysail yard has not been drawn by the artist. There is a photograph of her as a barque but it is too poor to be worth reproducing. *(MacGregor Collection)*

probably carried sugar. In 1872 she took tea to New York, loading at £4 and £3 10s at Shanghai. One shipping paper gives the passage times as 17 August to 8 December; another gives it as 21 August to 8 December. Perhaps the latter dates were pilot to pilot. In 1874 she sailed out to Melbourne and then to China; the next year she took a cargo to London from Bangkok.

After Killick, Martin & Co became owners, John Gadd replaced Anderson as master. In 1877, Gadd took the ship out to Hong Kong in 96 days from London, 18 April to 23 July. *Sir Lancelot* had left a month earlier on 10 March and took 119 days to Shanghai. Between September 1877 and January 1879, the *Kaisow* sailed to and fro across the Pacific making three round voyages in all, and carrying timber from Vancouver Island to Shanghai, often loading at Burrard's Inlet. Her fastest run from west to east was in 1878 when she sailed from Shanghai for Guam in ballast on 26 March and reached Victoria on 29 April, 34 days later. Ships not wishing to carry mail used to clear out 'for Guam', which at that time was uninhabited! Later the same year she took 38 days between the same ports. Trans-Pacific passages loaded with timber took 68 days 1877–78, 61 days in 1878, and 58 days (25 November to 22 January) in 1879–80. Her last cargo of tea was loaded at Yokohama in 1884, and she sailed on 23 July for San Francisco which she reached 35 days later on 27 August.

In April and May 1885, Killick, Martin & Co sold *Kaisow* to William Bowen Jnr of Llanelly in South Wales, and he placed her in the South American trade, although in 1888 she did get to Amoy and Hong Kong again. William Davies became her master the following year and in a letter he wrote to *Fairplay*, dated 3 April 1896, he claimed

to have made a passage of but 60 days between Coquimbo and the Old Head of Kinsale, in southern Ireland, or 62 days to Liverpool. He was trying to refute the claim made by the editor that a recent fast passage of 71 days performed by the *Preussen* between Valparaiso and Germany had broken the record. Davies gives no dates in his letter but it could have been in 1890 when *Kaisow* left Coquimbo on 15 May and reached Liverpool on 21 July, 67 days later, with a cargo of 1196 tons of manganese ore and a crew of twenty-one. (I am grateful to Robin Craig for details of her passages when owned by Bowen.)

In 1891, when bound from Valparaiso to Queenstown she foundered in a southerly gale, Force 10, after having been thrown on to her beam ends when the cargo of manganese ore shifted. At the time she was 60 miles WSW of Valparaiso and had a crew of sixteen.

OMBA, 1868

This composite-built full-rigged ship had a similar hull-form to the *Fusi Yama* which Stephen's had built three years before for the same owners, namely Killick, Martin & Co, London. But *Omba* was a larger vessel, being some 20ft longer and 3ft broader, her actual dimensions being 186.6ft × 31.8ft × 19.5ft with tonnages of 789 under deck, 861 gross and 836¼ net register. Like *Fusi Yama*, she had a monkey forecastle and a large deckhouse abaft the foremast to house the crew, but unlike her there was also a full-height poop with a 'half-round'. The external planking was of American rock elm and teak, and the decks were yellow

Omba sail plan. Built in 1868 by Alexander Stephen & Sons, Glasgow, and reproduced from builder's plan. This was photographed in 1961 when still in their possession. This is more detailed than *Gossamer's* plan and suggests a new employee in the draughting room.

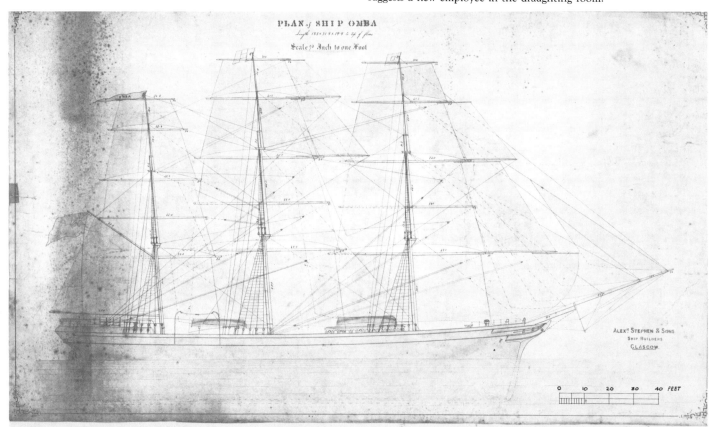

In this photograph, taken in Sydney harbour in 1882, *Thermopylae* has just had her topgallant masts shortened by 7ft. At this date she carried double topgallant yards on fore- and mainmasts but a single on the mizen. (*MacGregor Collection*)

ine. Like *Fusi Yama* she was only a medium clipper and cargo capacity was an important factor, especially when freight rates were low. Here are examples of cargoes she carried: 1266 tons of tea and general goods (1875); 1,229,000lbs tea (1871); 1136 tons of coal and coke (1874); about 1200 tons of sugar (1881); 19,500 piculs of rice (1868). *Omba*'s cost or contract price is not recorded by Alexander Stephen & Sons, Glasgow, but they made a profit of £2257.

She managed to load a cargo in China or the Philippines for London in most years, although she went to New York on two or three occasions. None of her passages was particularly fast and because she usually left China with the favourable north-east monsoon she had to sail out again against it, which made her outward passages long. Her fastest out was in 1879 between London and Shanghai, 26 April to 12 August, which equals 108 days. On this voyage she sailed across to San Francisco in 44 days from Shanghai, and then loaded grain, reaching Queenstown, for orders, 119 days later. From there she was ordered to Newcastle, and it took her 18 days to get there up the English Channel. However, it was probably a good loading port for coal; at any rate she made a quick passage out to Batavia in 87 days, 3 May to 29 July 1880, or 85 days from Folkestone. Her second voyage was recorded by W C Crutchley in *My Life at Sea* (1912).

At the end of a long outward passage to Shanghai in 1872, the *Overland China Mail* commented: 'The British ship *Omba*, which has been expected at Shanghai for some time, made her appearance there on the 28th ulto, [*ie* December] after a passage of 164 days, a tenth portion of which was passed within sight of the small island after which the vessel is named.'

The ship was posted missing since passing Anjer on 14 September 1881, bound from Samarang to Sydney with sugar. It was supposed that she had foundered in a gale off Newcastle, NSW, as wreckage was washed ashore near there, but no bodies were found and there was no trace of the crew.

THERMOPYLAE, 1868

This extreme clipper ship was designed by Bernard Waymouth and bore a strong similarity to *Leander*, launched the previous year for Joseph Somes. The dimensions of the two ships were:

Leander, 215.5ft × 35.2ft × 20.7ft, 848 tons under deck, 883 tons net.
Thermopylae, 212.0ft × 36.0ft × 20.9ft, 927 tons under deck, 947 tons net.

The lines plan of *Thermopylae* was drawn by James Henderson from a copy of the builder's offsets which had been made by James R Melville (1885–1957) when he was an apprentice in the yard of Hall, Russell & Co. Allowing Henderson to transcribe the offsets and trace his profile of the ship, Melville added, 'Now you can draw up the plan of a *real* ship.' The result is a thoroughly accurate hull plan of this famous clipper, which was constructed in Aberdeen by Walter Hood & Co to the order of George Thompson & Co, London. In fact, all their ships were built by Hood.

The entrance and run of *Thermopylae* were exceptionally long and fine without any deadflats amidships; there was great deadrise and the floors curved right up through the bilges into the topsides and then tumbled home. The drawing is to the inside of the planking; externally the garboard strake was concave. *Leander*'s slightly narrower hull increased the deadrise fractionally and made the entrance and run a little finer. *Thermopylae* had more sheer from amidships to the knightheads than *Leander*.

Thermopylae was built with wood planking over an iron frame; American rock elm was used from the garboard to the light water mark, and teak above that. She had a monkey forecastle, an Armstrong patent windlass, a deckhouse abaft the foremast, a raised quarterdeck with an Aberdeen house, and the usual arrangement of other fittings. She had four boats but no longboat; the steering gear was enclosed in a vertical pillar of a type then popular in some ships; the fore yard was braced round with Cunningham's patent gear and the winch for this was placed under the foremost of the after boat skids. All this can be seen on the deck plan which was reconstructed from Cyril Hume's model in the Museum of Applied Science at Melbourne and from photographs of the ship.

The sail plan is based on Bernard Waymouth's original which was found in Lloyd's Register archives and was drawn to a scale of ³⁄₁₆in to 1ft. A single mizen topsail fitted with Colling & Pinkney's roller-reefing gear was drawn but this was amended in red ink to double mizen topsails. A note stated that the main topgallant was to have Colling & Pinkney's rolling gear. Reconstruction consists of the running rigging and stunsails.

She was undoubtedly a fast ship and in 1874–75 on her first passage under the command of Charles Matheson to Melbourne, her best day's run was 348 miles and during the previous 22 days she averaged 262 miles per day. This run of 348 miles means an average speed of 14½ knots, and Basil Lubbock wrote that this was her fastest day's run. She was fast under all points of sailing and was especially quick at going to windward.

On the occasion of her Lloyd's Register survey report dated Aberdeen 17 September 1868, the master's name is given as William Edward, but the survey report dated London 6 October 1868 gives the master as Robert Kemball.

Kemball, who had commanded the China ships *Fairlight* and *Yang-tsze*, took out to Melbourne on her maiden passage in 60 days from leaving the Lizard on 8 November 1868 to sighting Cape Otway on 7 January, or 63 days Gravesend to Hobson's Bay, Melbourne. Before this year the record run stood at 63 days from Rock Light or 65 from Liverpool as made by the *James Baines* in 1854–55. On the passage to China she was only 31 days between Newcastle and Shanghai, 10 February to 13 March, or 28 days taking her pilot off Video Island in the Chusan Archipelago.

Her brilliant run from China completed a momentous maiden voyage. Towed down the river Min on 3 July 1869 she took her departure the same day and was 25 days to Anjer and 49 to Cape Agulhas. She was off the Lizard on 30 September, 89 days out, and docked two days later.

Thermopylae usually sailed out via Australia and her first ten passages between the Lizard and Melbourne averaged 69 days, whilst her eleven tea passages averaged 106½ days.

This green-hulled clipper with her white yards and long white lower masts was surveyed in London at the end of each voyage from China or Australia. The yellow-metal sheathing was either repaired or else it was stripped off and she was re-sheathed. The fore and main lower masts and their yards were of iron; in November 1872 the mizen lower mast was replaced with a new Oregon pine spar; two years later the two fore topsail yards were renewed with pitch pine spars. She was fitted with double topgallants on fore and main early in the 1870s like other ships in Thompson's 'Aberdeen White Star Line' fleet. A photograph taken of her at Sydney in 1882 states that 7ft had been cut off her topgallant masts. In April 1887 the Lloyd's Register survey report said that her fore- and mainmasts had been reduced 5ft in height – presumably the lower masts – and a number of other spars were renewed, but no others were shortened.

She failed to load tea for London in 1879 and 1880, but in 1881 managed to load her last tea at Foochow and sailing on 30 October in the fair monsoon, took 108 days to London. During the 1880s she raced home with wool from Sydney around Cape Horn, but here her record was not so good as *Cutty Sark*, which revelled in the strong winds of the southern latitudes, whereas *Thermopylae* excelled in light winds. *Thermopylae*'s fastest passage from Sydney was 76 days to Start Point in 1882, but *Cutty Sark*'s average for seven passages from Sydney up to 1890 was only 73¼ days.

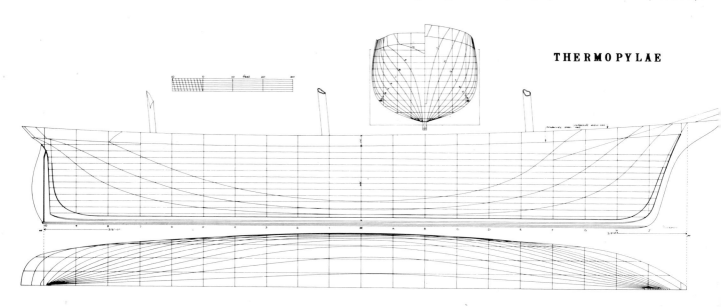

THERMOPYLAE

In 1890 *Thermopylae* was sold for £5000, the first owner being William Ross, according to a survey report at Rotterdam in May 1890. Perhaps Ross acted as an agent; he had bought the *Wylo* in 1886 but sold her within three months. *Thermopylae*'s new owner was soon to be Mr Reford, President of the Mount Royal Milling and Manufacturing Co, Montreal.

In May 1892 she was examined by W R Clarke, the Lloyd's Register surveyor at Victoria, British Columbia, who reported that her topsides were in bad condition, that

Opposite, bottom: Thermopylae lines. Built of composite construction in 1868 by Walter Hood & Co at Aberdeen from a design by Bernard Waymouth of London. Drawn by James Henderson from builder's offsets given him by James R Melville. Dimensions for register: 212.0ft × 36.0ft × 20.9ft, 947 tons net. Reconstruction: mast positions from sail plan. *Below: Thermopylae* general arrangement plan. Entirely reconstructed, with assistance of James Henderson. Sources: midship section from survey report in archives of *Lloyd's Register*; deck fittings based mostly on Cyril Hume's model of ship in Museum of Applied Science at Melbourne and from photographs of ship; spacing of deck beams from Bernard Waymouth's drawing at National Maritime Museum used to position principal fittings, forecastle, raised quarterdeck, etc.

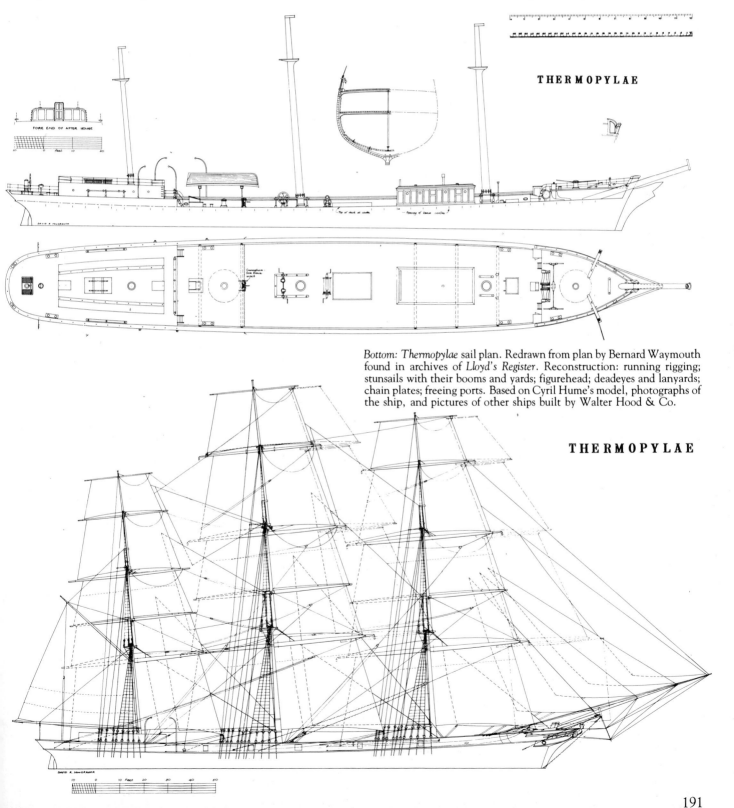

THERMOPYLAE

FORE END OF AFTER HOUSE

Bottom: Thermopylae sail plan. Redrawn from plan by Bernard Waymouth found in archives of *Lloyd's Register*. Reconstruction: running rigging; stunsails with their booms and yards; figurehead; deadeyes and lanyards; chain plates; freeing ports. Based on Cyril Hume's model, photographs of the ship, and pictures of other ships built by Walter Hood & Co.

THERMOPYLAE

Above: Thermopylae under sail while in Canadian ownership, after being reduced to a barque in 1892 and being painted white. Loaned by Ralph Bird. *(Provincial Archives, Victoria, BC)*

Left: Thermopylae's lean after body shown to perfection when photographed about 1895 at Bullin's Way, Esquimalt, BC. *(Provincial Archives, Victoria, BC)*

her woodwork around the stern was rotten and that 'the vessel's seams were thoroughly empty, there scarcely being one thread of oakum in them'. But the iron frames were in excellent condition. A bow port was cut on the starboard side and a beam was cut out in the lower deck for stowing timber; and the necessary repairs were effected. Simultaneously she was reduced to barque rig: the fore and main topmasts were each shortened by 2ft; new fore and main topgallant masts were fitted, and the lower topgallant yards were removed altogether, single topgallants now being sufficient; she was also given a new mizen topmast. Hall, Ross & Co, of Victoria, were listed as the owners.

Between 1892 and 1895 she was in the trans-Pacific trade, her fastest passage being one of 23 days between Victoria and Hong Kong in ballast, 15 February to 10 March 1893. In 1896 she was sold to the Portuguese Government for use as a training ship and was renamed *Pedro Nunes*. After eleven years, she was towed out of the Tagus on 13 October 1907 and sunk by gunfire.

WINDHOVER, 1868

Like the *Spindrift*, she was built in Glasgow by Charles Connell for James Findlay of Greenock and exactly resembled this clipper in appearance, both in hull shape above the waterline and in deck and sail plans, being essentially a light-weather flyer. In 1879, she was passed by *Cutty Sark*, homeward-bound off the Cape. Composite built, she measured 201.1ft × 34.0ft × 19.8ft and 847 tons net. Her rig was reduced to barque by 1880.

Top: Built a year after *Spindrift* by the same shipyard and for the same owner, *Windhover* is said to have resembled her greatly. (*National Maritime Museum*)

Above: The *Ambassador* under all plain sail. Like many of the clippers, she was rather 'over-hatted'. (*MacGregor Collection*)

On her second voyage under Captain Orr she loaded 1,064,645lbs of tea at Foochow, left Pagoda Anchorage on 31 August 1870, when the south-west monsoon was not quite so strong, dropped her pilot off the White Dogs on 1 September at 4.0 pm, passed Anjer on 26 September at midnight and was in the Downs early in the morning of 7 December, 96½ days later, docking at 1.0 pm on 8 December, 99 days out, which was the best time of the year before the monsoon changed. After this passage she did not load tea until 1876.

J Halden, Glasgow, bought her in 1875 and Kerr & Co, Greenock, in 1881. In 1889 a northerly current set her on to Bramble Cay in Torres Strait on 20 August, where she was abandoned. She was bound from Newcastle, NSW, to Batavia with coal and had a crew of eighteen.

AMBASSADOR, 1869

One of the last composite ships to be launched on the Thames, *Ambassador* was built by William Walker at the Lavender Dry Dock, Rotherhithe, for W Lund, London, and was the fourth composite ship he had built there in the last four years. She measured 176.0ft × 31.3ft × 19.1ft and 692 tons, with a coefficient of under deck tonnage of 0.63. Walker had built the *Shun Lee* four years earlier, and a short description of her build, taken from the *London and China Telegraph*, may well apply to *Ambassador*:

> The frame is of double-angle iron, diagonally trussed, with extra angle and bulb iron stringers worked longitudinally on frames right fore and aft. The vessel is entirely planked with teak. The bottom is double to the underside of the wales, the inner bottom being fastened to the frames with galvanized iron

Inside the hold of *Ambassador's* decaying hull at Punta Arenas in 1970. The timber planking of the composite hull has been stripped off to reveal the iron framework. The step of the mainmast is at the bottom left on the keelson – we look forward – with the hold pillars rivetted to the lower deck beams stretching away towards the foremast. The opening for the main hatchway is visible with twin pillars providing a ladder into the hold. (*Norman Brouwer*)

bolts, and the outer bottom being worked diagonally and fastened to the inner bottom with pure copper bolts.

After 1871 her best passage against the monsoon was one of 108 days between Foochow and London, 23 July 1872 to 8 November. Her rig was reduced to barque in 1874 and she was still trading to the East eleven years later. She had had an unfortunate experience in 1877 on a passage from New York to Melbourne under the command of Captain C Prehn and a crew of twenty: running before a westerly gale, Force 10, in the South Atlantic, the decks were swept by enormous seas, carrying overboard the master, four of the crew, the wheel and the boats.

George Milne, Aberdeen, bought her in 1888. In 1889 she passed to G Shaddick, Swansea, and two years later to Burgess & Co, London. She was sold to Christiansand three years later and in December 1895 was condemned at Stanley, Falkland Islands, after putting in with damage, on passage from Jacksonville to Honolulu. The ship was eventually towed round to the Straits of Magellan where she served as a hulk at Punta Arenas, and was photographed there in 1970, with her iron frame still intact but most of the timber gone.

CUTTY SARK, 1869

The composite clipper *Cutty Sark* was one of the finest vessels to be launched at the close of the sailing ship's monopoly of the tea trade, yet she was built by an unknown yard at Dumbarton owned by Scott & Linton, who went bankrupt through building her, Denny Bros finishing her off. She was designed by Hercules Linton who is said to have modelled her entrance lines on those of *The Tweed*, which had been built in 1852 as the paddle steamer *Punjaub*; John Willis had bought her in 1862–63, removed the engines and paddle wheels and converted her into a sailing ship. Like a typical paddle teamer *The Tweed* had very little deadrise, a hard bilge and vertical sides, and she would have had a long sharp entrance and run that was fairly straight at the load line and so unlike most clippers. The *Cutty Sark* certainly possesses some of these characteristics in her lines, but she also had marked deadrise, a firm bilge and tumblehome. Her entrance was unusually long and straight at the load line, but in the run the load line swelled out more. Above this the buttock lines were concave. In Robert Steele's clippers such as *Ariel* and *Titania*, the knuckle of the counter was close up to the rudder trunk; in *Thermopylae* it was further away; but in *Cutty Sark* there was a generous overhang to the stern. This was achieved by making the rudder trunking closer to the load line thus thickening the hull at this point. The sharpness of the run was not minimized, but there was a little more bearing given to the clipper, which proved advantageous when she was running before big following seas in the Roaring Forties.

The *Ariel* was fuller at the load line aft than *Cutty Sark* and yet was found to be tender in big following seas; *Titania* had more beam than *Ariel* and safely made the passage around Cape Horn on several occasions. *Cutty Sark*'s midsection bears a similarity with *Titania* although she has less deadrise, because both have a firm bilge. With dimensions of 212.5ft × 36.0ft × 21.0ft, *Cutty Sark* had identical breadth and depth measurements to *Titania* but was 12½ft longer; this naturally gave her a larger tonnage with 963 gross, 921 net and 892 under deck. Her coefficient of under deck tonnage was 0.55 as against *Thermopylae*'s 0.58.

The *Cutty Sark* at sea under full sail, photographed by Captain Woodget from one of the ship's boats. The skysail and stunsails had been removed by the time she entered the wool trade. (*C L Hume*)

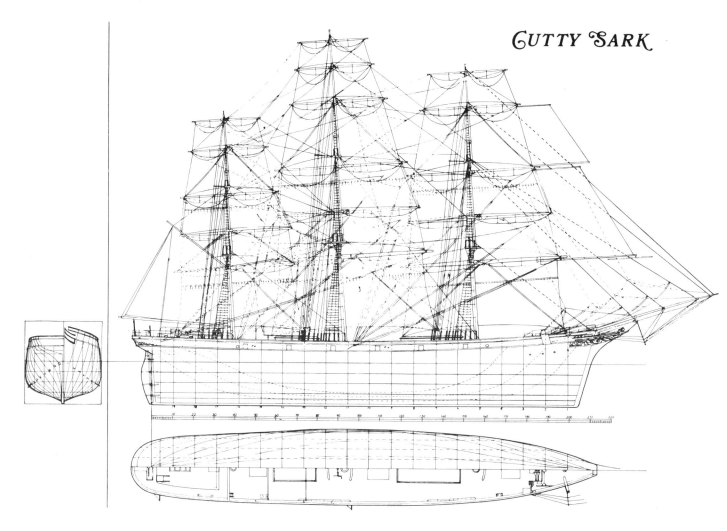

Cutty Sark

John Willis of London, whose father had founded the firm of J Willis & Son, already owned several ships in the China tea trade – the *Merse*, *Lammermuir* and *Whiteadder* – but none of them was a full-blooded clipper. In 1868 he contracted with the newly-formed partnership of Scott & Linton to build a composite ship not exceeding 950 tons at a price of £16,150 and to class 16 A1. This works out at £17 per ton for 950 tons or £16 15s 5d per ton on 963 tons gross, which is a very keen price for such a clipper. Of course, prices of composite ships had been falling towards the end of the 1860s and Alexander Stephen & Sons got £16 15s per ton on 700 tons for building the composite ship *Norham Castle*, contracted for in October 1868. On this contract they made only £65 clear profit.

So it might just have been possible for Scott & Linton to break even on building the *Cutty Sark* had not Captain Moodie, on behalf of Willis, rejected any materials he thought were not the best obtainable. Work was suspended in the yard in early September 1869 as the builders could not meet their debts, but the creditors decided to complete the clipper. The yard was taken over by Denny Bros and the ship was launched on Monday 23 November, and then towed over to Greenock to have her masts fitted and be rigged.

The deck layout as originally drawn by John Rennie, who was Scott & Linton's chief draughtsman, shows the conventional arrangement: monkey forecastle, with quarters for the crew below; deckhouse abaft foremast; house on

main deck aft with the raised quarterdeck surrounding it; but Tudgay's painting dated 1872 depicts an additional deckhouse between the main and mizen masts which the ship still has, and which was probably added after the end of the first voyage.

In the biography of *Maitland* (1865) I give a table comparing the lengths of yards on six tea clippers which shows how little the yards tapered aloft on either her or *Cutty Sark*. The latter's yards on the fore- and mainmasts were of equivalent lengths, and at 78ft, the main lower yard was shorter than on *Spindrift*, *Thermopylae* or *The Caliph*. John Rennie's drawing of her sail plan shows the fore lower stunsail to be triangular which was an economy being forced on owners, although enterprising masters possibly got the sailmaker to cut larger stunsails at sea.

Cutty Sark was at her best in strong beam and quartering winds when none of the other clippers could equal her. Her career is a long story of ships being passed at sea, although in light winds the *Wylo* hung on to her for eight days in the China Sea on her maiden passage. She was capable of higher bursts of speed than most of the other ships, often going at 15 and 16 knots, and once at $17\frac{1}{2}$ when under the command of Captain Moodie, who also made a day's run of 363 miles. Coulson claimed to have driven the *Maitland* at 17 knots and she was undoubtedly fast with a large spread of sail.

In the China trade, the *Cutty Sark* was not the first vessel to bear this name since there was already a Siamese barque

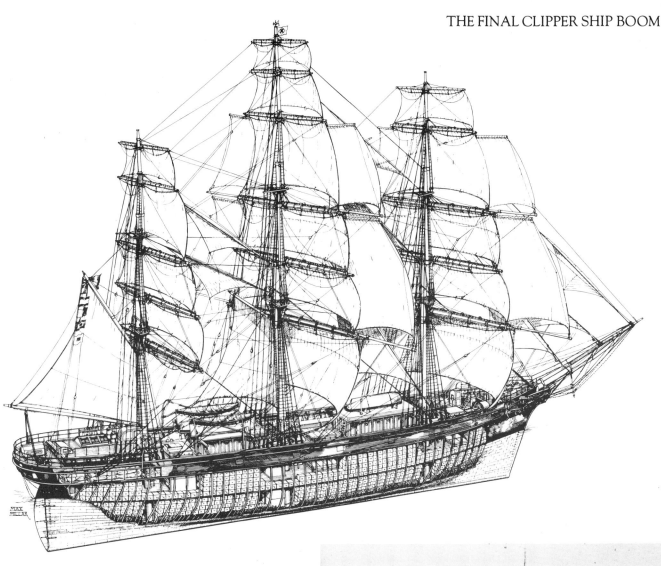

Opposite, top: Cutty Sark lines, deck and sail plan. Drawn by Cyril L Hume from authentic sources. Ship built in 1869 by Scott, Linton & Co, Dumbarton, with dimensions 212.5ft × 36.0ft × 21.0ft and 921 tons net.

Above: Cutty Sark. A perspective view of the clipper under full sail, but with most of the starboard planking removed to show the stowage of the tea chests and the iron frames. The diagonal iron trussing outside the frames has also been removed (Cutty Sark Society).

Right: The legend on the back of this photograph, which I bought with others, reads: 'The famous *Cuttysark* [*sic*]. Last Photograph taken of her as a fullrigged ship before her being dismasted off the Cape. She is now a painted port barquentine. Taken at Mossamedes, Portugese East Africa. [signed] F G Layton.' The date would be between July and October 1915. At the time she was named *Ferreira*, and wore the Portuguese flag. (*MacGregor Collection*)

of 474 tons called *Cutty Sark* trading at the end of the 1860s, between Hong Kong and Bangkok. Willis' clipper never made a homeward passage under 100 days, yet she compared favourably with the clippers still carrying tea. On her third passage there was some keen racing with *Thermopylae* in the China Sea in which the latter managed to pass Anjer first. However *Cutty Sark* was some 400 miles ahead off the Cape when her rudder gave way, and though forced to carry easy sail from then on for fear of injuring her jury rudder, she reached London only a week behind *Thermopylae*. She only made one passage from China in under

Above: Three of the crew aboard *Cutty Sark*; on the right is Tony Robson, the Chinese cook. In the bottom right is the main hatchway, and then comes the cargo winch, mainmast, pumps and after house. The break of the raised quarterdeck is on the left, level with the man's shoulder. (*National Maritime Museum*)

Below, left: The fife rail on the fore side of the *Cutty Sark*'s mainmast, showing the grooves in the timber worn by ropes through long usage. The two lugs in the deck were for the mizen stay. Drawn from life by T W Ward. (*MacGregor Collection*)

Below and right: Two hand winches aboard *Cutty Sark,* on the starboard side, drawn by T W Ward. On the left, mounted on the bulwarks abaft the fore rigging; on the right, abaft the main rigging. (*MacGregor Collection*)

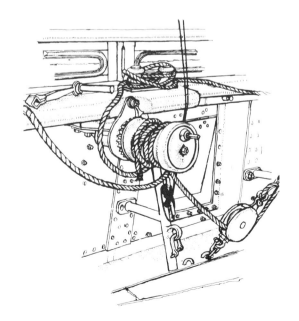

110 days after 1871, and that was in 1876 when under Captain Tiptaft she went from Woosung to London in 109 days, 9 June to 26 September. Her best outward passage was in 1870–71 when she went from the Downs to the North Saddle in 98 days, 10 November to 16 February, or 101 days London to Shanghai.

From 1883 until she was sold, *Cutty Sark* made twelve passages home with Australian wool, a trade in which she was at the top of her form, making some fast runs. The last ten of these passages were made under the command of Richard Woodget who drove the clipper as never before. Under him, the fastest passage home with wool was one of 70 days from Newcastle to the Lizard, 28 December 1887 to 7 March 1888, and she was off Dungeness next day. In December 1885 she had been off Ushant only 67 days out from Sydney. It was probably during this period that her rivalry with *Thermopylae* began to be established, or else it may be due to twentieth century writers.

In 1895, Willis sold *Cutty Sark* to the Lisbon firm of Ferreira & Co for £2100. They renamed her *Ferreira* and placed her in the trade to South America or Florida. During the First World War she was dismasted in 1916 off Cape Agulhas when loaded with 1142 tons of coal and was towed into Cape Town. Here she was re-rigged as a barquentine and continued trading under sail. In 1922 she changed hands and her name was altered to *Mario Do Amparo* of Lisbon.

Fortunately it was in this year that Captain Dowman succeeded in purchasing the old ship for £3750 and restored her to her original rig at Falmouth. In 1938 she was towed round to Greenhithe in June and moored alongside HMS *Worcester* to form part of the Thames Nautical Training College's establishment. After spending the War years with her topgallant masts housed, she was drydocked at Millwall in March 1951 and passed survey satisfactorily.

At the time of writing the first edition of this book, the clipper lay in the Thames off Rotherhithe and I expressed the hope that she would be preserved. This has happened. She was floated into a permanent dry-dock at Greenwich

on 10 December 1954 where she has been fully restored to her clipper ship appearance. She is now under the ownership of the Maritime Trust.

DEERHOUND, 1869
A composite barque built by William Pile for John R Kelso, North Shields, she measured 157.1ft × 31.0ft × 18.5ft and 573 tons. In the same year Pile built *Miako* and the white-hulled *Osaka* for the China trade. In 1875 she was abandoned after stranding on the Palawan Shoal, China Sea, tea-laden, on 30 August. She once loaded 661,762lbs of tea.

In 1869 she had raced out to Hong Kong against the *Maitland*, leaving Sunderland on 23 February, 4 days ahead. She crossed the Line 8 days ahead and passed the Cape of Good Hope meridian 5 days ahead, but both ships passed Anjer on 18 May, and although *Maitland* spent 2 days at Singapore, she reached Hong Kong the same day as *Deerhound*, 10 June. The latter took 107 days.

DUKE OF ABERCORN, 1869
A composite ship built by Charles Connell, Glasgow, for Montgomerie & Workman, London, on lines said at the time to be something between those of *Spindrift* and *Windhover*. She registered 1050 tons net on dimensions of 212.0ft × 35.1ft × 20.5ft. She could carry 1730 tons of tea. In 1892 she went missing after being spoken on 21 May bound to Callao from Cardiff laden with coal.

EME, 1869
J Wade & Co, London, were the owners of this full-rigged composite-built ship which Charles Connell & Co constructed on the Clyde at Glasgow with dimensions of 199.7ft × 32.6ft × 19.0ft and a net tonnage of 774. She was named after one of Wade's daughters and was pronounced 'Eemie'. Basil Lubbock in *The China Clippers* describes her as a 'very pretty vessel' and a 'light-wind flyer', and he recounts how she took 135 days to return home on her maiden voyage via the longer Eastern Route, and how the unfortunate master was sacked on his arrival by Captain Wade with a rich 'flow of language'. The fact that she had gone ashore at Dungeness *en route* for London no doubt contributed to her owner's annoyance. Robertson & Co, London, acquired her in 1876 and retained ownership until she was hulked in December 1895.

MIAKO, 1869
The year in which the Suez Canal opened, Killick, Martin & Co had two medium-sized clipper barques, the *Miako* and *Osaka*, delivered by the yard of William Pile, Sunderland, but they were destined for a trade which was immediately to be depressed by the influx of steamers through the Canal. Freight rates began falling year by year, although it may be that these small barques could occasionally be chartered to lift 700 or 800 tons at a freight 10s per ton above the berth rate. Both were intended for the Japan trade and they occasionally got there.

The *Miako* had dimensions of 160.1ft × 30.1ft × 17.1ft with a raised quarterdeck of 40ft; tonnages were 496¾ under deck, 535⅔ gross and 515⅓ net; the coefficient of under deck tonnage was 0.60.

She never actually brought a cargo home from China although she sailed out there several times, her fastest passage being in 1876 between London and Hong Kong, in

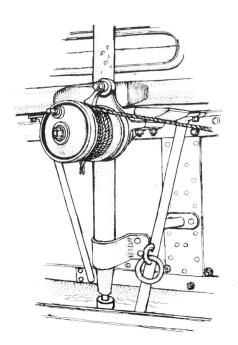

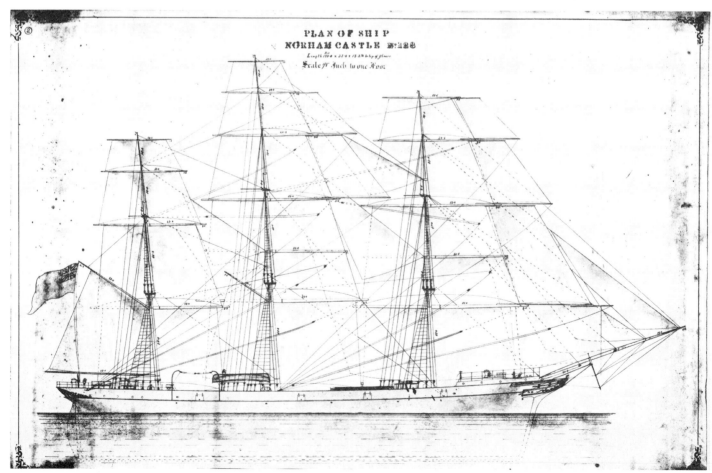

PLAN OF SHIP
NORHAM CASTLE №123

which she took 99 days from Deal, arriving on 8 September, having probably loaded at the berth rate at a mere £1 5s per ton deadweight. Four years earlier, on passage between New York and Yokohama, she was dismasted in a gale off Cape St Francis, South Africa, and went over on her beam ends when the coal cargo shifted; eventually she managed to put into Port Elizabeth on 29 June 1872 with only the fore and main lower masts still standing. Repairs took 3½ months. She finally got to Yokohama where she loaded 304,783lbs of tea at £3 per ton and about the same quantity at Kobe, and taking her departure on 5 March 1873, was 114 days on the passage to New York.

Killick, Martin & Co sold her in 1885 to Thomas Roberts, Llanelly; and in 1891 we find her making a fast run from Mauritius to Melbourne of only 26 days and then sailing from Sydney to Boston in 84 days. In 1894 he sold her to Borbones & Borotau of Barcelona who changed her name to *Asuncion*. After some changes of ownership she was registered at Santa Cruz de la Palma in 1908 under the ownership of Perez, Castro & Co, who renamed her *Isla de la Palma*. In 1911 she was registered at Teneriffe and the following year she became a barge at Cuba, and thereafter her name is dropped from the Register.

Opposite, top: The *Duke of Abercorn* in the 1880s, waiting to load wool. (*C L Hume*)

Opposite, bottom: *Norham Castle* sail plan. Built in 1869 by Alexander Stephens & Sons, Glasgow, and reproduced from builder's plan. This was photographed prior to 1961 when still in their possession.

Below: Waiting to pick up her pilot, *Norman Court* lies hove-to under topsails. Thomas G Dutton has created a great atmosphere in this lithograph. (*Parker Gallery*)

NORHAM CASTLE, 1869

Another of the many clipper ships built the year the Suez Canal opened was delivered to Thomas Skinner & Co, Glasgow, by Alexander Stephen & Sons of the same port. She was of a slightly finer hull-form than *Omba* with more deadrise and slacker bilges; she was also shorter, broader and shallower, the actual dimensions being 177.4ft × 32.1ft × 18.0ft. Tonnages were 735 gross, 698 net, 672 under deck, giving a coefficient of under deck tonnage of 0.65. The contract price was £16 15s per ton for 700 tons, but the builder made a profit of only £65. She was a full-rigged ship of composite construction, but had been reduced to a barque by 1880. In 1886 she was acquired by the 'Norham Castle' Sailing Ship Co, Glasgow, managed by P H Cowley & Co. She dropped from the Register in 1888.

NORMAN COURT, 1869

This extreme clipper was certainly William Rennie's masterpiece and compared most favourably with the other clippers. She was of sharper form than the second *Fiery Cross* built in 1860; her entrance and run were longer and finer; there was about the same amount of deadrise but hardly any concavity in the floors; and there was more tumblehome. The lines plan in the archives of Baring Bros was entitled 'Drawing of a Composite Clipper Ship'.

A letter from the builders, A & J Inglis of Glasgow, to one of Baring Bros partners concluded the verbal negotiations which must have been conducted during a visit of the builders to London. The letter which was written in London reads as follows:

Wm Walkinshaw Esq   London 27 Nov/68

Dear Sir
With reference to what has passed between our senior and yourself on the subject of a new ship, we beg to say that we are

prepared to undertake the contract for building said ship from the lines to be furnished by Mr Rennie, at the price of seventeen pounds seventeen shillings and sixpence per ton register. The ship to be built and furnished in accordance with the Specification agreed and to be delivered to Messrs Baring Brothers & Co or their Agent ready for loading not later than the 15th (fifteenth) June 1869.

Payments to be made as follows: one fourth of the total cost on laying of the keel; one fourth when the ship is planked; one fourth after launching and the remaining fourth on delivery.

We quite understand that Mr Rennie is to inspect the lines when laid down and that his plan of masting is to be strictly adhered to.

We are Dear Sir,
Your obedt. serts.,
A & J Inglis

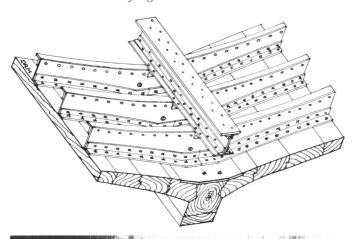

The ship was launched on 29 July 1869 with dimensions of 197.4ft × 33.0ft × 20.0ft and with tonnages of 795.84 under deck, 855.02 gross and 833.87 net register. She was composite-built. Loaded with 150 tons of pig iron and 50 tons of iron kentledge she was brought round from Glasgow to London with a crew of sixteen 'runners'.

The total cost of the ship was £16,005, made up of the following items:

A & J Inglis account	£14,894	0	2
Wm Rennie for model and a/c	123	10	0
Runners wages	76	5	10
Capt Shewan superintending ship –			
8 months @ £25 per month	200	0	0
Capt Shewan's travelling expenses	14	9	3
R Young, brokerage sundries	132	12	9
ditto, for Clyde Shipping Co towage	51	17	0
– for drawing heraldic arms	1	15	0
pig iron 50 tons for kentledge	128	15	0
supplies in Glasgow per Capt's a/c	77	13	0
	15,700	18	6
less 1/- difference too much	15,700	17	6
chronometer £20			
interest 20 Oct £284 2 6			
Total cost of Ship 20 Oct 1869	£16,005	0	0

This calculation gives some idea of the extras to be added on top of the builder's account when computing the final cost of a ship, which is often called the 'First Cost' of the ship. In this case the extras amounted to £1110 19s 10d which works out to be £1 6s 7d per register ton.

Not added to the First Cost was the pilotage from Glasgow to London (£14 17s 6d) and the cost of towage from the Downs to the dock (£30). These were added to the disbursements for the first voyage.

The 64 shares of *Norman Court* were allotted to the following: C L Norman (of Baring's) 16, Andrew Shewan 16, Wm Walkinshaw (of Baring's) 8, Wm Hutchinson 8, Patrick Dudgeon 8, D J Kay 4, John M Ryrie 4. The last was presumably the man who had been the master of *Flying Spur* and *Cairngorm*.

Norman Court's deck layout was typical for a tea clipper with a monkey forecastle, deckhouse for crew, low bulwarks, raised quarterdeck, all beautifully finished. The windlass was Harfield's patent, the pumps were Kirkland's patent, and the steering gear was Skinner's patent vertical gear. In December 1874 repairs to the latter cost £12 10s.

The sail and rigging plan indicates very little overlap of the plain square sails, but the stunsails seem large. Even though the fore lower stunsail is basically triangular, with only a short foot, it has a long head. The mainmast is very lofty which the main skysail accentuates, so that the mizen

Above, left: Isometric projection of keel, floors and keelson of a typical composite ship. (*Author*)

Left: Model of *Norman Court* by John Alderson. The deck layout from the mainmast to the stern is typical of a tea clipper. (*Baring Brothers*)

looks somewhat diminutive. There are two main topmast stays, but a staysail is only set from the upper one that sets up to the foremast hounds. There is only one other staysail on the mainmast and that is the main royal staysail. On the mizen the only staysail is the mizen topgallant. The head-sails are large sails and the foot of each is cut higher than was formerly the case.

In the matter of performance at sea, the *Norman Court* was very fast in light airs, being at her best in a head sea, under which conditions *Kaisow* was once run out of sight in a single day, only to reappear again later. *Norman Court* was equal to *Serica* and slightly superior to *Fiery Cross* and once, going a knot faster, passed the *Harlaw* when homeward-bound in the north-east trades.

Captain Andrew Shewan, the younger, who was master of her from 1873 to 1879, writing in an old volume of *Sea Breezes* said: 'Though so staunch and tight, yet at times the whole fabric [of the *Norman Court*] would tremble like a piece of whalebone. When we were driving her into a head sea, I have noted, as I lay on the after lockers, that after a heavy plunge as she recovered herself the after end would vibrate like a diving board when the pressure is released.'

In 1870–71 she went to Shanghai by passing to the east of Australia. Leaving the Lizard on 27 December 1870, she was within 500 miles of Sydney 65 days later but kept on going northwards to the east of the New Hebrides, crossing the Line on 22 March and skirting the Ladrone and Loochoo Islands. Sulphur Island near the Saddles was reached 102 days from the Lizard. *Serica* had followed this route the previous year, taking 106 days, London to Shanghai, over a course of 20,463 miles. She had left London on 24 December 1869, being only 19 days to the Line, and had once run at 14 knots in the Roaring Forties.

The *Norman Court* managed to load tea at fairly good rates in the early 1870s. She loaded 1180 tons of tea at Foochow in August 1873 at £3 per ton. At Shanghai in July 1875 she discharged 1094 tons of coal and 326 tons of shingle ballast.

In June and July 1877 she was converted to a barque at the Nelson Dock, Rotherhithe. Making and mounting a new mizen topmast of Vancouver pine cost £15 10s; at the same time, a new shorter fore topgallant mast of red pine was fitted at a cost of £10 10s. Total cost of new spars was £35 8s. Charges by John Phillips, rigger, at Poplar were £39 10s. New sails by Coubro & Potter connected with this conversion cost £155 16s 1d.

By 1878 Shewan was writing to his owners complaining of the low freights and that he was trying in vain to load tea at £1 15s for New York. Eventually he got a charter to Port Elizabeth from Hong Kong. She loaded her last tea cargo in 1879 and made the passage from Foochow to Dover in 117 days with the favourable monsoon. Low freights did not suit Baring Bros. They declined to sell the ship for £5000 in 1880 but in the following year sold her to Jamieson, Grieve & Co, Greenock, for £7500. He placed her in the Java sugar trade.

In 1882 she had gone out to Batavia in 84 days from Cardiff and returned in 103 days to Queenstown, arriving on 29 March 1883. She had left the same day for Greenock and that night ran ashore at 8.30 pm in Cymmeran Bay, Anglesey, in a violent south-westerly gale. She became a total wreck. Her crew of twenty-two were eventually rescued after spending 25 hours lashed in the rigging although two of them succumbed during that bitter experience.

OSAKA, 1869
Launched on 12 July, about two months after *Miako*, she was of very similar measurements and doubtless in appearance. She was a composite-built barque of 507 tons under deck, 546½ tons gross and 527 tons net, having dimensions of 165.0ft × 30.1ft × 17.2ft, with a raised quarterdeck of 38ft. She was built at Sunderland by William Pile for Killick, Martin & Co, London, and when they sold her the advertisement stated that 'she will stand without ballast in dock' which was a most useful feature.

A Chinese artist's impression of a clipper ship being dismasted in a typhoon. She has not been identified. (*Parker Gallery*)

The *Osaka* at Port Adelaide, probably after Killick, Martin & Co had sold her. (*The late A D Edwardes*)

Perhaps her large beam saw to that. Her lower yards, each 60ft long, were of 15in diameter at their centres and were made of steel plates manufactured by Palmer & Co at Jarrow. She could carry 730 tons of coal.

Unlike *Miako*, she made two passages from China to England, and had to beat down the China Sea against the south-west monsoon in each case: on the second she actually carried tea. She also made several passages out to China as well as innumerable short hauls between Far Eastern ports. For instance, on her maiden voyage which lasted almost two years, she left London on 15 October 1869 and called at the following ports in this order: Yokohama (arrived 25 February, 133 days); Yokohama to Hong Kong, 18 days; Hong Kong to Saigon, 20 days; Saigon to Kobe; Kobe to Hong Kong, 13 days; Hong Kong to Saigon, 22 days; Saigon to Hong Kong, 24 days; Hong Kong to Bangkok, 10 days; Bangkok to Hong Kong, 34 days; Hong Kong to New York, 108 days; New York to London, 25 days (arrived 4 September 1871).

In 1878 she left London on 14 May for Shanghai on what was to be an even longer voyage because she never returned to a port in Great Britain until 21 June 1883, when she arrived in London. During this interminable voyage away from home, the nearest she got back was to Marseilles, which she visited twice. Her master for this long voyage was Robert Lowe who had previously been master of *Kate Carnie*.

Like *Miako*, she was sold to Thomas Roberts, Llanelly, in 1885 but he kept *Osaka* for one year longer. In 1889 she made a passage of 80 days between London and Fremantle, arriving out on 14 June. Roberts sold her in 1895 to N E

Möller & Son, Shanghai, for not less than £2250, and she was kept trading in the China Sea. In 1904 she was wrecked on 14 September on the Kurile Islands, Japan, in a Force 8 gale, whilst carrying a general cargo from Tsingtao to Nicolaieosk with a crew of sixteen men.

THE CALIPH, 1869

Alexander Hall had not built a first class tea clipper since *Black Prince*, and by launching *The Caliph* he hoped to produce a rival to *Thermopylae*. *The Caliph*'s design was a natural development from such a vessel as *Cairngorm* in which the distinctive mid-section was repeated. In this the hollow floors turn down into the garboards, thus forming the equivalent of a deep keel, presumably to assist the clipper in sailing to windward. In *The Caliph* the bilges are firmer than in *Cairngorm* but again there is great deadrise and some tumblehome. The composite construction must have helped to strengthen the shape of the hull and reduced the amount of solid timber that would have been used in *Cairngorm*'s bottom. *The Caliph*'s entrance and run are very long and sharp, and as the deck line narrows in more at bow and stern than in *Cairngorm* there is less flare in the sections above the load line. *The Caliph* was designed to be fast in light winds and the Duthies of Aberdeen thought her to be faster than, and of a superior model to, either *Cutty Sark* or *Thermopylae*.

Below: The Caliph lines and general arrangement. Redrawn by F A Claydon from a lines plan at the National Maritime Museum and from the plans in Chapman's *All About Ships* (1869). Ship built in 1869 by Alexander Hall & Sons, Aberdeen, with dimensions of 215.1ft × 36.1ft × 20.4ft and 914 tons net.

Bottom: The Caliph sail plan. Redrawn by F A Claydon from the following sources: sail plan in Chapman's *All About Ships* together with a list of sails, and sizes of standing and running rigging; spar dimensions from Hall's cost account, supplied by James Henderson.

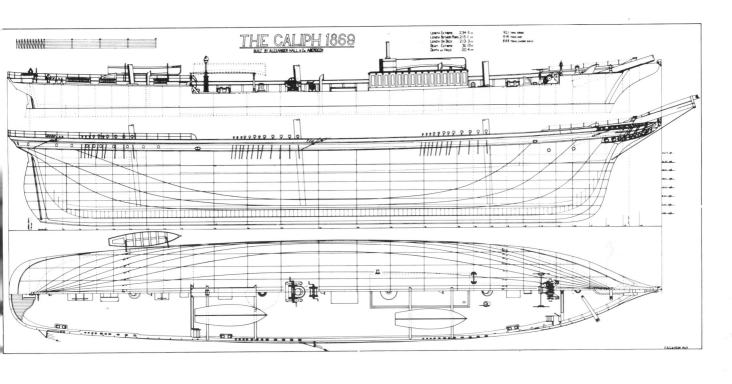

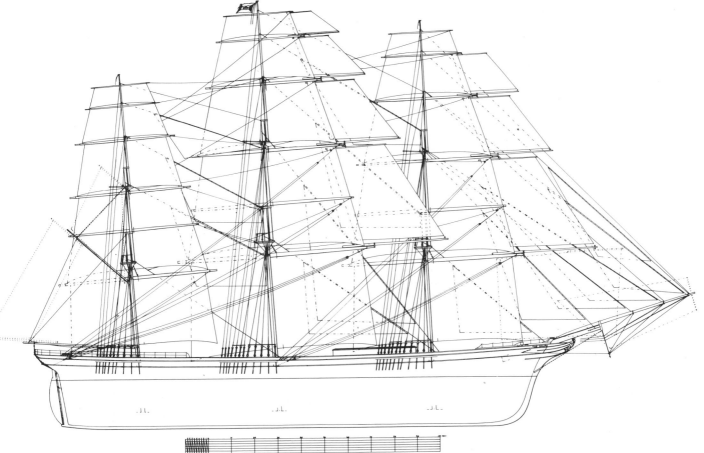

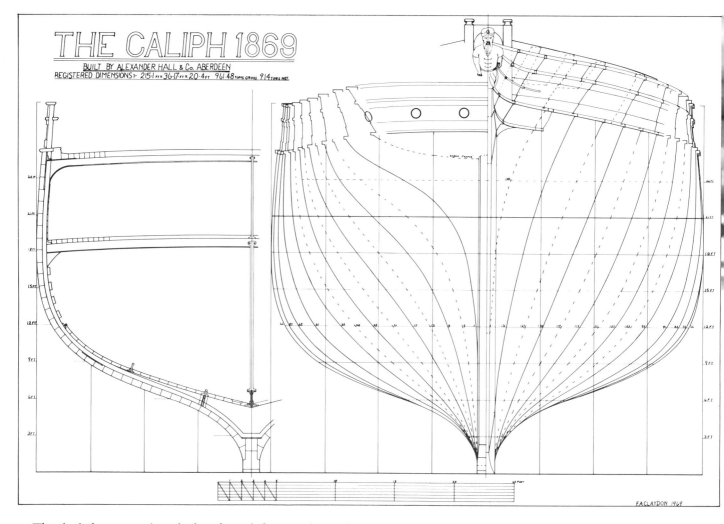

THE CALIPH 1869
BUILT BY ALEXANDER HALL & Co. ABERDEEN
REGISTERED DIMENSIONS:- 215.1 FT × 36.17 FT × 20.4 FT 961.48 TONS GROSS 914 TONS NET.

FA CLAYDON 1969

The deck fittings and outfit for *The Caliph* were obviously of the best to judge by a report in *All About Ships* by Captain Charles Chapman in which the ship's construction is described and her sails and inventory listed. The method of construction is quoted at the start of this chapter. In her after deckhouse she sported an 8hp engine which, apart from providing driving power to the pumps, cargo winch and windlass, also could be fitted to drive auxiliary screw propellers. The latter could be mounted on each side of the ship, the driving shafts being connected by bevelled gear wheels. No drawing of this machinery was given by Chapman. Barclay, Curle & Co's ship *Ben Nevis* had a similar arrangement. However, raising steam in mid-ocean on a clipper ship in a calm may not have appealed to the master and mates, and one wonders how often this machinery was put to practical use.

The Caliph had a very lofty sail plan with skysails on each mast and a host of stunsails up to main skysail ones. According to the builder's list of spars, these had yards 10ft long and were set on 22ft booms.

Alexander Hall & Sons, Aberdeen, built *The Caliph* for Alexander Hector, a London merchant and a cousin of John Willis. The contract price was £17 per ton on 900 tons which totals £15,300, but as the final cost was £16,655 16s 4d, Hall's lost £1355 16s 4d on the contract. The final cost was about £500 more than *Cutty Sark*'s contract price. Dimensions of the ship were 215.1ft × 36.1ft × 20.4ft, with tonnages of 888 under deck and 914 net. The

Above: The Caliph body plan and half mid-section; separated from the rest of the lines makes it difficult to relate the two drawings. The sources are the same as for the main drawing.

Below: The Caliph midship section. Reproduced from plate in Charles Chapman's *All About Ships*.

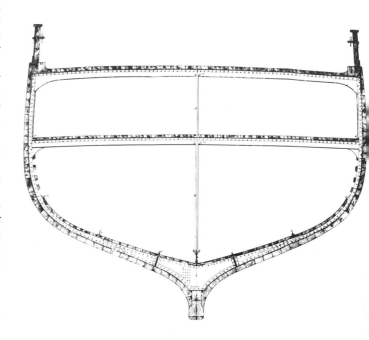

coefficient of under deck tonnage works out at 0.56. She was of composite construction and built under a watertight shed to class 17 A1.

The Caliph took 36 hours to the Thames on her maiden passage and then went out to Shanghai in 101 days from the Isle of Wight, 23 October 1869 to 1 February, the same number of days as taken by Titania. She left Foochow on 6 December 1870 for New York, dropped her pilot off Sharp Peak the next day, passed Anjer 17 December, took a pilot on 2 March, and docked the following day, 87 days out or 85 pilot to pilot.

On her outward passage in 1871 she went missing after passing Anjer on 15 August. Strangely enough, MacCunn's Geraint also went 'missing' in the China Sea at the same time, likewise bound for Shanghai.

WYLO, 1869

The London shipowners Killick, Martin & Co had had the new ships Fusi Yama, Omba, Miako and Osaka built to their order; they had purchased the clipper Challenger, which Killick himself had once commanded; they had purchased the Heversham in 1864, and The Sir Jamsetjee Family in 1867, but neither of the latter were anything more than medium clippers, if that. Later they were to purchase the clippers Lothair in 1873 and Kaisow in 1875, both of which were very fast, as well as other ships, but Wylo was the only real clipper ship which they ordered brand-new.

She was built by the celebrated Greenock firm of Robert Steele & Co with dimensions of 192.9ft × 32.1ft × 20.2ft and had a raised quarterdeck of 52ft. Her tonnage was 766⅔ under deck, 829 gross and 799½ net. She was a full-rigged ship, reduced to a barque in 1878, and composite-built with wood planking on iron frames. Steele's yard list gives identical dimensions for Kaisow (yard No 173) and Wylo (yard

No 174) and the latter's under deck tonnage is only 0.53 less than Kaisow's. The size of the raised quarterdeck is identical in the two, but whereas Kaisow's deckhouse measures 15.20 tons, Wylo's is much bigger and measures 24.44 tons.

Andrew Shewan described Wylo as a 'pretty vessel and speedy' but said that some speed was sacrificed to carry more cargo. However, she is credited with having outsailed Cutty Sark in the light winds of the Java Sea. Her coefficient of under deck tonnage is 0.61, which is the same as Norman Court, so she was just a bit fuller-bodied than Ariel. She had the same master, Henry W Browne, for her entire career with Killick, Martin & Co, and it is the master who really brings out the last bit of intrinsic speed in a clipper.

As might have been expected, she traded extensively between England, China and the East for many years. Her fastest outward passage was one of 99 days between London and Shanghai, 14 April to 22 July 1876. On this occasion, Lothair sailed on the same day and the two passed Anjer on the same day, 29 June, but Lothair sailed on to Yokohama.

In 1870 Wylo only managed to load 1,132,251lbs tea at £2 per ton. The result of such low freights was that for her next three homeward passages she did not load in China. They were as follows:

1871, Rangoon to Falmouth, 23 May to 31 August, 99 days.

1872, Indramayoe (Java) to Falmouth for orders, 21 September to 15 December, 80 days (discharged at Hamburg).

1873–74, Manilla to New York, 24 September to 15 February, 144 days.

The Wylo painted by a Chinese artist. She was the last tea clipper built by Steele. (Parker Gallery)

In 1883 and 1884, *Wylo* loaded wheat at San Francisco. On the first occasion, she took 111 days to Queenstown for orders and discharged at Galway. On the second occasion she was 104 days to Barrow. Leaving Barrow on 8 January 1885 for Victoria, BC, she had to put into the Falkland Islands on 1 April 1885, 93 days out, with loss of bulwarks and her mizen mast, presumably due to storm damage. Repairs took a month and she reached Victoria 94 days later. At Burrard Inlet she loaded lumber for Shanghai and on arrival was put on the berth for London at the rate of £1 10s per ton of 50 cubic feet. The cargo was a general one, and the passage occupied 111 days, 2 March to 12 June 1886, with a crew of sixteen.

The owners could no longer afford to run the clipper at such rates and they accordingly sold her in July that year to William Ross, a London merchant and shipowner. In turn he sold her on to James Gibb Ross that autumn for £2375 and the registration was transferred to Quebec. What connection these two persons named Ross had is unknown. William Ross purchased *Thermopylae* four years later; perhaps he acted as an agent for Canadian shipowners. In the case of *Wylo*, J G Ross of Quebec owned her until she was sunk by collision in 1888, but I have no particulars of the accident.

Below: Wylo spar plan. Traced from a plan in the Whitby Museum, it is of the style drawn by her builder, Robert Steele & Co. By mast-heading the yards and drawing in sails, the plan could be converted into the more conventional sail plan.

Right: Crew agreement for *Wylo* on a voyage beginning at London in October 1871. (*From the records of the Registrar General of Shipping and Seamen*)

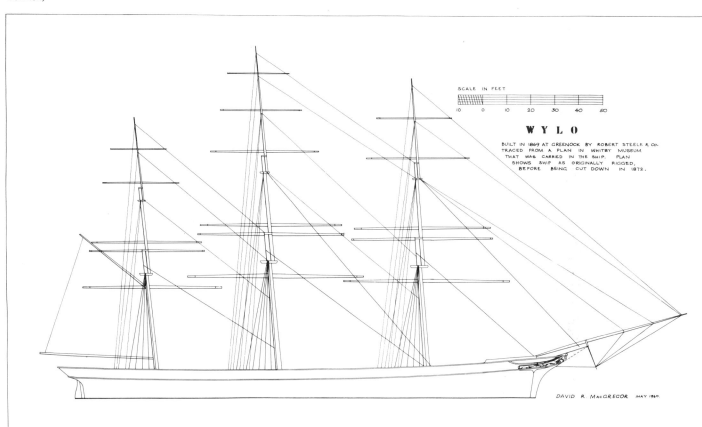

WYLO

BUILT IN 1869 AT GREENOCK BY ROBERT STEELE & CO.
TRACED FROM A PLAN IN WHITBY MUSEUM
THAT WAS CARRIED IN THE SHIP. PLAN
SHOWS SHIP AS ORIGINALLY RIGGED,
BEFORE BEING CUT DOWN IN 1872.

DAVID R. MACGREGOR MAY 1960.

10
CHANGING TRADE
AND SHIPS OF 1870-1876

The last year of the 1860s had seen some hard racing amongst the tea-laden ships: new records had been made and everyone was looking forward to next year's contest in which the new cracks would try their mettle against some of the renowned clippers. Indeed, not since 1865 had so many fine ships been built expressly to carry tea. Those ships that had returned from China in the autumn of 1869 were refitted, some with new suits of sails, others with new copper sheathing in place of ragged and missing plates – for in those palmy days a racing ship had her copper renewed after two voyages – and all were dispatched to the Far East once more, as had been the practice for some years past.

But these same ships did not find the trade quite as they had left it. It is true there had been some talk when they first arrived with last season's teas about the opening of a canal which would link the Mediterranean with the Red Sea, yet their owners had refused to realize the effect such a canal would have on their own lucrative trade in China. Nevertheless the effect was noticeable as soon as the clippers reached the loading ports.

Throughout the 1860s the number of steamers trading to the East had been gradually increasing, but due to their immense fuel consumption the majority of hold space was given up to coal bunkers and their cargoes consisted chiefly of passengers, mail, specie and valuable goods in small quantities. Some of them loaded a little tea, but it was worth their while, since their ability to put their cargoes on the market, only 80 days or so from China, meant that the shippers were willing to pay a high rate of freight, frequently as much as £8 8s at Hankow. Some steamers, especially the auxiliaries, made very lengthy passages, and freight was usually graded according to the length of passage they were likely to make. In 1869 sailing ships started to load at from £4 to £4 10s and £6 at Hankow, with the steamers' freights graded from £3 to £4 10s. Sailing over the same course as the clippers the SS *Achilles* made the quickest time of 62 days, but 76 or 80 was the average.

When the clippers reached the loading ports in 1870 they found that the steamers had increased in number and that their services were much in demand. Practically all had gone out by way of the Suez Canal in almost half the time taken by the Cape route. Coaling stations were being established at Gibraltar, Port Said, Aden and at other ports of call on the way to the East. This route was almost half the distance taken by sailing ships so that many steamers, like the *Hipparchus*, went out to Shanghai in 53 days, including all stops. With coaling stations so frequent, bunkers could take up less room and more cargo could be car-

ried. As supplies of tea were abundant, steamers were quickly taken up at £7 from Hankow and £4 10s from Shanghai, with a premium of 10s per ton for the first ship home, the rates formerly given to sail. Clippers asked £4 per ton of tea but only got £2 10s. The rates to New York were nearly always in advance of those to London but in every case steamers could load at £2 per ton more than sailing ships in the months of June and July, and later in the season at 10s to £1 more. The clippers needed high freights and readily accepted cargoes to New York, whilst the steamers returned to London in 60 days, much to the astonishment of the sailing ship owners.

So successful was the China trade becoming for steam that in 1871 no fewer than 45 steamers were built on the Clyde alone for Far Eastern trades. In that year Foochow was thronged with racing steamers and the clippers began to disperse to where they could load without competition from steam. A number went to Yokohama, many took cargoes to New York, and others like *Assyrian* and *Kaisow* sailed from the Philippines or Batavia to Europe. Yet in 1871 sailing ship freights were slightly higher from China than in the previous year, commencing at from £2 10s to £3 and not dropping throughout the season. Occasionally some ships would load at £4, but freights were beginning to fall for all classes of vessels.

Sailing ships trading to the East were not only at a disadvantage with regard to lower freights but also found that insurance companies were reducing premiums on goods carried by steamers using the Suez Canal. In the China trade, tea carried by sailing ships had to be insured at £5 per ton from Hankow and £3 10s from Shanghai and Foochow, while the rate for steamers was £3 and £2 10s respectively. Yet many thought this rate too high for steamers carrying tea, especially since outward cargoes to Shanghai were written at only £1 15s. A consignee would prefer to incur a smaller insurance premium, while the risk by steamer was only two months as against four or five by sail. Here, then, on the face of it were two strong reasons in favour of steam propulsion. But add to this that the steamer could carry teas twice a year, even though she might have to wait much longer to fill up and leave not fully loaded, and it will be seen why no real tea clippers were built after 1870 and why those afloat began to look for cargoes elsewhere.

Steamers did not bring the only mechanisation to the trade, for with the steady improvement in telegraphic services, the head office shifted to London and instructions about what teas to buy and when began to be sent out to the chaa-szes, whilst with a booming trade the number of

LLOYD'S LIST, NOVEMBER 18, 1869.

LONDON.—Vessels Entered Outwards for Foreign Ports.

Destination	Ship's name	Master	Nat.	Tonnage	Dock	Broker	Sailing date	Class
	City of Dublin	Waugh	B	813	LD	Anderson	Nov.10	A 1
Swan River	Witch of the Tees	Bartley	B	300	LD	Devitt	Sept.27	A 1
Yokohama	Ziba	Bowes	B	513	WID	Robertson	Nov. 8	A 1
" & Kanagawa	Black Watch	Kerruish	B	491	EID	Norris	Oct. 8	A 1
" "	Eleanor	Maxwell	B	433	WID	Killick	Nov. 2	A 1
Kanagawa & Yokohama	Eliza Shaw	Gaye	B	696	EID	Killick	Oct. 14	A 1
Tientsin & Newchwang	Walton	Mercer	B	576	WID	Robertson	Oct. 29	—
Shanghai	Spindrift	Innes	B	899	EID	Robertson	Oct. 18	A 1
"	Taeping	Dowdy	B	767	EID	Killick	Oct. 25	—
"	Huntley Castle	Stewart	B	623	EID	Shaw	Nov. 6	A 1
"	Kaisow	Anderson	B	795	EID	Killick	Nov. 8	A 1
"	Windhover	Nutaford	B	846	EID	Robertson	Nov. 8	A 1
"	Helen Nicholson	Halliday	B	716	LD	Killick	Nov. 8	A 1
"	Whiteadder	Moore	B	915	EID	Gellatly	Nov. 9	A 1
"	Whinfell	Jones	B	834	EID	McDiarmid	Nov.15	A 1
"	Falcon	Dunn	B	793	EID	Shaw	Nov.15	A 1
Hong Kong	Sir Lancelot	Edmonds	B	885	EID	Killick	Oct. 14	A 1
"	Taitsing	Bloomfield	B	815	EID	Robertson	Oct. 14	A 1
"	Belted Will	Looke	B	812	EID	Shaw	Oct. 21	A 1
"	Burdwan	Douglas	B	803	WID	Robertson	Nov.11	A 1
"	Guinevere	Spowart	B	879	EID	Killick	Nov.15	A 1
" & Whampoa	Manuelita	Findlay	B	271	MilwDk.	DBrwn	Nov. 9	—
Bangkok	Wild Curlew	Parnell	B	353	WID	RCSmith	Oct. 26	—
Batavia & Sourabaya	New Brunswick	Lurvey	B	839	VID	Harward	Oct. 9	A 1

A list of ships loading in London for Eastern ports. The columns contain the following information: destination, ship's name, master, ship's nationality, tonnage, at which dock loading, broker's name, sailing date, classification symbol. (*MacGregor Collection*)

shippers increased out of all proportion. As more and more steamers were sent out to China so the clippers were squeezed out, whilst freights also fell away with so many ships on the berth. When the trade became stabilized again in the 1880s, the sailing ship was employed in more economical occupations.

It must have been very hard for men brought up in the old China trade to see it radically alter before their eyes, whilst the masters and crews of the clippers waiting to load a few hundred tons of tea thought that they might never lie in the Pagoda Anchorage again. Captain Harry Davis, lying there in the *Kaisow* at the end of the 1870s, admirably describes the scene:

There were eight or ten of our clippers anchored there, waiting for tea – glossy black sides, brasswork gleaming in the early sunlight, yards squared by lifts and braces, house flags fluttering at the main, and the glorious red ensign at peak or staff. Some of the ships had been there many days, ours only a few.

Enter the SS *Aberdeen* of Aberdeen under her own steam. She anchored below all of us and was admired by all, I think, for she looked very smart in her green dress. But although we all admired her, I think we resented her intrusion into what had been our freehold and domain for long, long years. She was optical proof to most of us that the day of the tea clipper proper was swiftly drawing to its close. And when, at dawn on the fourth day, she hove up by steam, the rattle of her cables and windlass sounded the knell of our lovely vessels as tea carriers, for she had gobbled up all there was in the godowns, except ours (for we were loading for the Cape), and left the fleet waiting for their cargoes which she had swallowed whole!

After the middle of the 1870s, the racing was almost wholly confined to the tea steamers, which were at great pains to make as short a passage as possible. In 1882 the SS *Stirling Castle*, loading at £6 per ton instead of the usual £4, went from Hankow to London in 32 days at an average speed of 19 knots, stopping only at Singapore and Port Said for bunkers which were ready waiting for her. Many of the

clippers had had their spars reduced in length or been cut down to barques or refitted with shorter spars after being dismasted. Flying kites had been reduced, and lower, topsail and topgallant stunsails were only carried on the foremast. All had lost their large crews and had their racing iron kentledge taken out of the floors. None of them was driven as formerly but some of the more energetic masters still made good passages, especially during the fair monsoon. Yet a few ships still managed to load tea, the *Hallowe'en* and *Leander* keeping together longer than any others.

By the beginning of the 1880s freights at Manilla, Penang etc, were higher than at the tea ports. Many of the clippers had by then drifted into the Indian, East Indies or Australian wool trades. They were maintained as economically as circumstances would permit since their build did not allow them to carry large cargoes, yet their turn of speed allowed the making of more voyages than a mere carrier could hope for. Several of them must often have been run almost at a loss, but owners were loth to part with them and maintained them in their employ for as long as possible. Killick, Martin & Co, for instance, never turned to steam, and in the middle of the 1880s were forced to sell their fleet of small lovely clippers.

Just as there had been a slump in shipbuilding whilst the Navigation Laws were being repealed, so there was almost a cessation of the building of large sailing ships for a year or two after the Canal was opened. In 1869, 132 large iron sailing ships, as well as many composite ones, were built. Practically no more composite vessels were constructed, whilst in the following four years only 51, 10, 14 and 37 iron ships were built. In 1874, there was a boom and 109 were launched, followed by 198 the next year. Sailing ship tonnage, at first astounded by the rapid success attained by steamers using the Canal and their consequent increase in numbers, seemed about to be overwhelmed, but the high maintenance costs and increasing price of coal, together with the realization that many trades could still be worked as yet unchallenged by steam, brought about a sudden revival and there sprang into being fine loftily-rigged iron clippers, many designed on medium clipper lines and produced by renowned clipper ship builders. They rank amongst some of the stateliest and most beautiful ships ever built and fittingly continued the story of sail which the composite clippers had brought so far.

The desire for speed was rapidly being sacrificed to the carrying of bulk cargoes where fine lines were at a disadvantage. Nevertheless, the strength given by iron and later by steel in the construction of hulls, masts and rigging, enabled ships, with the aid of their powerful hull-forms, to be driven for longer periods in strong winds. Thus many remarkably fast runs were still made in the wool, nitrate and grain trades. Even in the changed China trade some astounding passages were made by ships carrying oil in bulk from New York or deeply laden with Welsh coal. The fast four-masted barque *Muskoka* ran from Cardiff to Hong Kong in only 86 days in 1898, 25 March to 19 June, while the *Metropolis* took only five days longer. In 1894–95, the *Alcides* had gone to New York in 83 days from Hong Kong, 18 December to 11 March. Admittedly they were made in the fair monsoon in each case when head winds were at a minimum and they were considered exceptional at the time; yet that they were made at all shows how slim is the

The unlucky *Blackadder* under sail. (*Nautical Photo Agency*)

difference between the clippers and carriers where fast passages are concerned.

In their heyday, the clippers were fine money-makers by reason of their speed. The energies used to build and design them and drive them round the world roused the maritime community out of its lethargy. The clippers were especially remarkable when compared with their ancestors or with their own contemporaries, rather than with the ships which were developed from them, even though these had to live and work in more straitened circumstances.

In the battle between sail and steam the sailing ship had to progress and develop to survive at all. Each stage seemed slight and hardly noticeable at the time, but reviewed a century later the changing scenes all fit into a continuous story of development towards a single end. Looked at from the historian's point of view, it seems incredible that the square-rigged sailing ship survived so long in competition with steam. Even after square-rigged tonnage had practically ceased to be built anywhere in the world it was not the end of deepwater sail, for sail training has caused an unexpected revival today.

The last hundred years have seen considerable changes in sailing ship design, but always made against increasing economic difficulties, so that the result was bound to be a compromise. How unhurried and yet how remarkable was the progress in the years preceding 1869 when sail was still supreme! It was the last chance for square-rigged ships to be built along untrammelled lines. Of the main trades served, the China trade was the least touched by steam and the last one to be worked by vessels that could be described as 'all ship'. The fine-lined clippers that ran out to China with picked cargoes and then raced each other home with holds full of fragrant teas were the last of their kind ever to serve the trade they were built for. All who saw them were impressed by their beauty and perfection of design, for they were the queens in the days when steam competition held no terrors and when sailing ships were an accepted part of daily life.

BIOGRAPHIES OF SHIPS BUILT 1870–1876

BLACKADDER, 1870

An iron clipper launched on 1 February at Greenwich by Maudslay, Sons & Field, for John Willis, London, her lines were said to be based on those of *The Tweed* and when skilfully handled she proved a fast ship. Her builders were good engineers but had had hardly any shipbuilding experience and made serious errors in fitting her masts, which caused her to be dismasted on her maiden passage. She was extremely sharp, registering 908½ tons net and 872⅓ tons under deck on dimensions of 216.6ft × 35.2ft × 20.5ft, with a 30ft poop and a 34ft forecastle. *Hallowe'en* was her sister ship.

Her maiden voyage was one of collisions and dismastings. On her second she sailed from Deal on 3 January, 1872, was off Dartmouth two days later, passed Anjer 23 March and reached Shanghai 7 April, 95 days later. She came home in 121 days from Foochow, 28 June to 27 October. She was

again dismasted in 1873, this time in a typhoon. Her passages with wool from Brisbane in the 1890s were good and she could still log 16 knots. The photograph showing her under sail has previously been reproduced as the *Dharwar*, but there is little doubt that it is in fact *Blackadder*.

J Aalborg, Kragerö, Norway, bought her in 1900 on Willis' death. She was wrecked on 5 November 1905 bound from Barry to Bahia with coal. She had sailed on 11 September.

HALLOWE'EN, 1870

Although launched on 4 June, she was not handed over until late in 1871 when the numerous lawsuits had ended between her owner, John Willis, the underwriters, and Maudslay, Sons & Field of Greenwich, her builders, concerning the dismasting of *Blackadder* which was her sister ship. Built of iron, *Hallowe'en* measured 216.6ft × 35.2ft × 20.5ft, with tonnages of 872.38 under deck, 970.99 gross and 920 net; she had a 78ft main yard and an under deck tonnage coefficient of only 0.55. She was very fast in light airs but was not so powerful as *Cutty Sark*, although she made runs of 360, 341 and 338 miles in the Roaring Forties. On her maiden passage she went out to Sydney in 69 days and brought home wool, being too late to load tea. She was in the tea trade all

Opposite top: Blackadder's sister Hallowe'en at Circular Quay, Sydney, on her maiden passage in 1872. The mainmast was 141ft high from deck to truck. (C L Hume)

Opposite bottom: A sad scene on the South Devon coast at Sewer Mill Cove where the Hallowe'en lies wrecked in January 1887. (MacGregor Collection)

Below: Lothair flying Killick, Martin & Co's houseflag. The chart house close abaft the mizen does appear in the photograph also. (Parker Gallery)

her life and was finally wrecked on 17 January 1887, after going ashore at Sewer Mill Sands, Salcombe, with tea from Foochow. The wind was SSE Force 9.

Her early China passages are truly remarkable, even though made in the fair monsoon. These consisted of:
1873–74, J Watt, Shanghai to London, 17 November to 17 February, 92 days.
1874–75, J Watt, Shanghai to London, 21 October to 20 January, 91 days.
1875–76, J Watt, Woosung to London, 23 November to 24 February, 92 days.
1876, Fowler, London to Shanghai, 11 March to 24 June, 105 days (96 days from the Lizard).
1876–77, Fowler, Woosung to London, 13 November to 23 February, 102 days.
1878, Fowler, Woosung to London, 7 January to 16 April, 97 days.

LOTHAIR, 1870

This lovely clipper was probably the last composite ship to be built on the Thames and was launched from William Walker's yard at Lavender Dock, Rotherhithe, on 2 July. Unfortunately no plans or half-model of her appear to have survived, but all accounts state her to have been fast, especially in light winds, and there is only one record of her having been passed at sea, which was done by *Thermopylae* when both ships were driving into a head sea. She probably looked like the *Ambassador* which Walker had built the previous year and which Dutton's lithograph shows to have been very lofty.

Lothair was named after one of Disraeli's novels which had just been published. She measured 191.8ft × 33.5ft × 19.0ft with tonnages of 765.90 under deck, 823.95 gross and 793.58 net register. She had a monkey forecastle and a raised

Heeling to the wind, *Lothair* in ballast trim in her old age. (*MacGregor Collection*)

quarterdeck; she had a female figurehead; the windlass was Harfield's patent and the pumps were Redpath's. The planking at the garboard was 12in and from there to the topsides it was 5½in, and 4½in above that in rock elm and teak. The fore and main lower masts, 78ft and 79ft long respectively, were formed of two ½in iron plates 'in the round' and were both 26in diameter. All other spars were of wood. She carried two lifeboats and two other boats. Her deckhouse was calculated at 24.55 tons. Her coefficient of under deck tonnage works out as 0.63, the same as *Taeping*.

William Walker, her builder, held 56 shares for six months, and Emlyn Peacock, her first master, held the remaining 8. Although Walker owned shares in a number of clippers including *Wild Deer*, this is the only instance in which I have checked the actual shareholdings of a ship he built, and so I cannot say with certainty whether it was his practice to own some of the shares himself. But there was a slump in building sailing ships in 1870 which leads one to wonder if he built the clipper on speculation or whether the person who had contracted for the ship failed to pay one of the instalments so that the ship reverted to the builder. In any case, William Walker mortgaged his 56 shares in March 1871 to Arthur, William and Thomas Forwood, three London merchants, and the shares remained in their hands until the mortgage was redeemed in July 1873 when the ship was sold to Killick, Martin & Co. Peacock's shares were also sold. Killick, Martin acted as managing owners, retaining 16 shares and farming out the others to various individuals as was their customary habit. They remained owners for twelve years.

By 1870 the tea races were really over and the dispersal of the tea clippers into other trades was beginning. The *Lothair* traded frequently to Japanese ports and often made the homeward passage to New York so that she did not often sail in company with other tea clippers. The following are her outward and homeward passages until the end of Orchard's command:

CAPTAIN EMLYN PEACOCK

1870–71, London to Yokohama, 10 September to 23 January, 135 days. (*Crest of the Wave* was 9 September to 8 February, Newcastle to Yokohama). Was partially dismasted about this time, losing her topgallant masts.

1871, Yokohama to New York, 23 March to 1 July, 96 days. Passed Anjer 14 April; loaded tea at £2 15s per ton. *London & China Telegraph*, 19 June 1871, stated: 'The *Lothair*, despatched by Hudson, Malcolm & Co, Yokohama to New York, has arrived in 82 days.'

1871–72, London to Yokohama, 21 October to 13 February, 115 days.

1872, trading between Japan and China carrying rice; whilst in Hong Kong harbour in July, a son was born to the master's wife aboard ship; arrived Yokohama 20 August dismasted.

1872–73, Kobe to New York, 15 December to 9 April, 115 days. Berth rate £3 per ton; loaded some tea at Yokohama.

CAPTAIN BENJAMIN ORCHARD

1873, London to Hong Kong, 12 July to 26 October, 106 days. Sailed from Portland 17 July; off Anjer 3 October. Lost a man overboard running Easting down.

1873, at Macao loaded 26,250lbs Congou, 472,168lbs Scented Caper, 239,829lbs Orange Pekoe, 167 bales Punjum, 609 bales Waste, 2210 rolls matting & sundries at £3 per ton.

1873–74, Hong Kong to London, 11 December to 10 March, 89 days. Anjer 16 December; arrived off Scillies 4 March, 83 days out; passed Prawle Point 6 March; Deal 9 March. (Twenty-five crew.)

1874, London to Shanghai, 15 April to 4 August, 107 days. Anjer 2 July, 78 days out. Loaded 1,132,056lbs tea at Shanghai; berth rate £3 per ton increasing to £3 10s.

1874, Shanghai to London, 22 August to 28 December, 128 days. Anjer 4 October; passed Prawle Point 24 December.

1875, London to Sydney, 23 January to 28 April, 95 days. Passed Lizard 27 January; rounded Tasmania 21 April. (*Lammermuir*, Lizard to Sydney, 28 January to 28 April.)

1875, Sydney to Shanghai, 22 May to 1 July, 40 days (coal).

1875, Shanghai to Hiogo, 29 July to 15 August, 17 days (in ballast).

1875–76, Yokohama to New York, 29 September to 26 January, 119 days. Anjer 2 November; Cape of Good Hope 12 December. On 10 November in southerly gale, 1st mate and two seamen thrown overboard when link of tye to fore upper topsail yard carried away; they were on yard repairing it, where sprung, with topmast stunsail yard. Capt Orchard had previously climbed up to yard himself to inspect it. Ship put about and boat lowered but men could not be found.

1876, New York to London, 12 February to 2 March, 19 days.

1876, London to Yokohama, 14 April to 3 August, 111 days. Anjer 29 June; 76 days to Anjer (dep London and arr Anjer same days as *Wylo* which went on to Shanghai).

1876–77, Yokohama to New York, 12 November to 2 March, 110 days. Anjer 8 December in company with *Ambassador*; met again 11 January near Cape of Good Hope (general cargo). (*Ambassador*, Yokohama to New York, 4 November to 26 February, 114 days.)

1877, New York to London, 18 March to 7 April, 18 days.

1877, London to Yokohama, 19 May to 14 September, 118 days. Anjer 13 August, 86 days out. (Loading tea and general at Yokohama and Hiogo for New York.)

1877, Kobe to Amoy, 21 November to 26 November, 5 days (completed loading at Amoy).

1878, Amoy to New York, 8 January to 2 April, 84 days. Sunda Strait 19 January; spoken 12 February in 30°6'S, 37°5'E; Cape of Good Hope 18 February; crossed Line 11 March in 36°W. *New York Herald* stated: '. . . had fine weather to Hatteras, thence variable weather – making the passage in 83½ days.'

1878, New York to London, 14 April to 9 May, 25 days. At the end of this voyage, Orchard was succeeded by Thomas Boulton as master, who was another hard-driving captain.

The writer to *Sea Breezes* in 1923 who stated that *Lothair* had sailed from Yokohama to New York in 81½ days sometime between the years 1876 and 1882 was presumably thinking of the passage made in 1878 when tea was loaded at Yokohama, although the departure was actually taken from Amoy. The time of 82 days between Yokohama and New York claimed by the *London & China Telegraph* for 1871 is another possible candidate, but this time is at variance with the departure and arrival times given by the *New York Herald* on 2 July 1871, unless a later departure from, say, Kobe was overlooked. On her arrival at Sydney in April 1875, the *Sydney Morning Herald* wrote on 29 April: 'The *Lothair*, one of the celebrated composite-built tea clippers, arrived yesterday from London, having on this voyage come out to the Colonies previous to proceeding to Shanghai. She has the reputation and appearance of being a remarkably fast vessel . . .'

On her arrival at Melbourne in July 1884 she was described as having 'all the clean and trim appearance of the tea clippers of those days' (*Argus* 8 July 1884).

An interesting coinciding of dates occurred with *Wylo* in the mid-1870s, as the *London & China Telegraph* of 16 April 1877 explains: 'The *Lothair* which left London on April 14, 1876, for Japan, took from there a cargo to New York, and arrived at Gravesend on the 7th inst. The *Wylo* also left London on April 14 for Shanghai, proceeded to Manilla, and loaded for Boston, arriving at Gravesend on the 7th inst. Both vessels are in the employ of Messrs Killick, Martin & Co.'

Two fast passages were made in the 1880s: the first, under Boulton, took 95 days from London to Hong Kong in 1882, 12 June to 15 September, with 1020 tons of coal – 92 days were claimed for this run; and the second was 98 days from Hong Kong to New York in 1884–85, 31 October to 6 February, under Captain F W Dester.

In 1885 the clipper was sold to William Bowen of Llanelly who put her into the South American trade, although she also got to China again. In 1891, he authorized the master to sell her at Callao for not less than £6000 and it was there she was acquired by Genoese owners and the British registry was closed in January 1892. G Buccelli and D Loero were the new owners, but they disposed of her about 1905 to Peruvians. F G Piaggio of Callao owned her when she was lost about 1910. Her name was not removed from *Lloyd's*

Register until 1922, partly because the owner was lax in notifying the authorities and partly because no returns from owners of unclassed ships in South America were received in London during the First World War.

LUFRA, 1870

She was the last composite-built sailing ship to be constructed at Aberdeen by Alexander Hall & Sons, bearing their yard number 265. She was built for Anderson & Co, Banff, for a sum of £10,000 based on a contract tonnage of 704. She measured 178.7ft × 31.1ft × 17.9ft and 672 tons register. She began life as a full-rigged ship with a single topsail on the mizen. She made two voyages to China and then three out to Adelaide.

In 1874 she was bought by Alexander McGregor & Co, Hobart, and was reduced to a barque. She was placed in the Hobart to London trade for the next twenty-three years and proved a fast vessel. Her average time on the passage to London was 89 days and for the passage to Hobart the average was 90 days. In 1876 she had a close race out to Tasmania with the *Wagoola*: both vessels, sailing from London, left England on the same tide – 20 July – and reached Hobart on the same tide on 25 October, 97 days out.

Right: Built seven years after *Thermopylae,* the *Salamis* was said to be a copy in iron with an extra 10ft added amidships. This photograph was taken at the Alfred Graving Dock, Williamstown, near Melbourne. (*The late D M Little*)

Below: The *Lufra* at anchor at Hobart, soon after being bought by local owners, who reduced her to barque rig. When new, she had crossed skysail yards. (*The late A D Edwardes*)

The *Lufra* was sold to L Castellano of Naples in 1897 for £1250 and was renamed *Letizia*. She was broken up in 1905.

So the real tea clippers pass from the scene and the few still to be built for the China tea trade, although splendid ships in themselves, were not true inheritors of the tea clipper traditions.

SALAMIS, 1875

She is said by Basil Lubbock to have been virtually an iron copy of the composite *Thermopylae* and that Bernard Waymouth, designer of the latter, adapted the plans; but she was 10ft longer and 1ft deeper, her actual dimensions being 221.6ft × 36.0ft × 21.75ft for register, with tonnages of 1020¾ under deck, 1130 gross and 1078¾ net register. Walter Hood & Co, Aberdeen, built her in 1875 for George Thompson & Co, London.   She was intended to trade out to Australia and then bring home tea, but in fact she never did precisely this. On her maiden voyage she took 68 days out to Melbourne in 1875 from Start Point, but came home with wool. On her second voyage, she took 76 days out to Melbourne, crossed over to Shanghai in in only 32 days from Sydney but then, even after going to Hong Kong, was unable to get a tea cargo because of the low freights and so brought home 18,000 bags of sugar to London in 119 days in 1876–77. On her third voyage, Captain Phillips twice crossed over to Shanghai in an attempt to load tea for London, but with freights only £1 15s per ton or less, he twice returned to Australia, and finally came back to London with wool. No further attempts were made to load tea.

She proved a fast and successful ship in the wool trade, thirteen consecutive outward passages to Melbourne averaging 75 days, pilot to pilot. So she continued until 1899 when sold to L Gundersund of Porsgrund, Norway; she was wrecked on Malden Island, South Pacific, on 20 May 1905.

SERAPIS, 1876

Presumably William Lund, London, had some special reason for ordering a sailing ship especially for the China tea trade at this late date. He was already the owner of *Mikado* (1868) and *Ambassador* (1869), both composite-built by Walker at Rotherhithe, so he had sufficient experience of Far Eastern trade in the 1870s.

Serapis was built of iron by J E Scott of Greenock – not to be confused with Charles Scott & Co – with dimensions of 224.0ft × 35.5ft × 20.1ft, which gave her 6.31 beams to length. Tonnages were 933 under deck, 1027 gross and 995 net, and she was a full-rigged ship. A contemporary report on her launching stated that she was 'designed for speed, also elegance'. The latter may be correct, but her two passages in the China trade of 139 and 142 days from Shanghai show that the former was not achieved. Perhaps she was unlucky in the matter of captains, as a broadside photograph suggests, by the shadow running forward from her stern, that she was fine aft.

In 1889 she was bought in London on 4 July by P N Winther of Nordby, Fanø, for £7070 and four years later was converted to a barque at Flensburg. In 1901 she made a passage of 94 days between Sydney and Liverpool, arriving on 2 June; five years later she was sold in Antwerp on 28 August for £1920 to Italian owners and registered at Genoa. Her end came in January 1912 when she was scrapped and broken up.

Seen at Balmain, Sydney, the *Serapis* has been converted to barque rig by removing the yards from the mizen but the masts have yet to be altered. She looks fine aft. *(The late A D Edwardes)*

11

CONCLUSIONS

The ships described in these pages were the pick of the British or American merchant service and were almost invariably constructed of good materials to high standards, but they were not built regardless of cost. They were designed on fine lines and in some cases this was carried to excess with hulls being given great deadrise and exceedingly long sharp waterlines. Such hulls had high speed potential but their stowage capacity was greatly curtailed. Some compromise nearly always had to be reached, and *Cairngorm* and *Annandale* are the only two British tea clippers which were designed and constructed as the builder's ideal of what a clipper should be.

In addition to sharp hulls, the ships were heavily-sparred to set the maximum amount of canvas, and the plain canvas was augmented with stunsails and other flying kites as the captain's fancy dictated. So the ships themselves were perfect examples of the shipbuilder's art and they probably well deserved the description of looking like a nobleman's yacht. Large crews were provided to handle the sails and gear, but wages were low and seamen possessed of great skill were in plentiful supply.

However, captains capable of handling these large racing machines were in short supply, and although many aspired to the command of a clipper, comparatively few achieved the highest honours. To know what course to take to find favourable winds, to overcome the hazards of the reef-strewn China Sea, and to survive the strain of sail-carrying in an ocean race, called for masters of the highest calibre. There are too many examples of a clipper's chances being spoiled by the captain's ineptitude or over-caution, but when a skilled man was appointed, then the ship's speed potential was utilized to the full. Many masters succumbed to all these trials and not a few died on the China coast from various causes.

Were the inducements sufficient to recompense the owners for having these ships built and to send them out to the East, year after year? At the time of the gold rush to California or Australia, in the early 1850s, some clippers made a passage out to the goldfields and returned home with tea at freight rates which were high enough on that one voyage to repay the cost of building the ship and yet leave something over for a dividend. Of course this was exceptional, but it may have spurred others to order ships in the hopes of achieving similar profits. For ordinary ships in general trade, an annual return of 10 to 15 per cent on the capital invested was the maximum that could be achieved, which meant that the original or first cost of building might only be cleared when the vessel was sold. But with freights from China at £4 per ton and over, the first cost was cleared more quickly in the case of the tea clippers. Undoubtedly the profit element must have been strongly in existence or extreme clippers could never have been built at all.

It is strange how rarely the wind and weather combined to provide the ideal conditions under which a record passage could be made, but a ship that had made a record could be sure of getting a high rate of freight. Hence a fast run out to China could influence the agents favourably.

The tea clippers were small in number – less than one per cent – compared to the total British merchant service, yet as so much thought was put into their construction and design, could it be said that they influenced the development of the sailing ship? The desire for speed does tend to hasten the development of any moving object as the inefficient parts get eliminated, and it cannot be denied that fast-sailing ships got sleeker hulls, were more strongly rigged with iron wire standing rigging, or had to be strongly built to withstand hard driving and yet deliver their cargoes in first class condition. The fairly expensive composite construction developed entirely because of the tea clippers and the belief that the condensation in ill-ventilated iron ships damaged tea cargoes. Perhaps one view would be that composite shipbuilding delayed the earlier adoption of all-iron construction in clippers, and that the cheaper building costs of iron would have resulted in higher profits for the owner.

There were two shipbuilding booms for clippers in Great Britain – in the early 1850s and in the later 1860s – whereas in America there was only the one of the early 1850s. Shiplovers do tend to concentrate their worship and interest in a few of the best-known ships and an attempt has been made here to widen the field a little. Without a doubt the forgotten names of other clippers will come to light and it will be interesting to discover whether any other record passages are unearthed.

APPENDIX I
ADDITIONAL BRITISH AND AMERICAN CHINA TRADERS 1834-1875

This list records names of vessels for which I have found a minimum of three passages homewards from China or the East, or for which I have evidence that they were regular traders. Also included are vessels which would have been regularly in trade had they not been wrecked early in their careers.

There are many sources which have been consulted, but the principal ones are:

Lloyd's Register of Shipping
Mercantile Navy List
Custom House Registers
Lloyd's Register Survey Reports
D R Bolt's records at Tower Hamlets Central Library
Contemporary newspapers

Key to List and Abbreviations

Column 3 Rig: S=ship; bk=barque; bkn=barquentine.

Column 4 Tons: om = old measurement; nm = new measurement; nt = net; where no qualification is stated, it will almost certainly be 'om' before 1854 and 'net register' afterwards.

Column 5 Hull: Constructional material – W = wood; 1 = iron; C = composite.

Column 6 Builder: In a number of cases, the builder's name is not known to me.

Column 7 Owner: This is usually the 'managing owner' and not the principal shareholder.

Column 8 Change of Name given with first year it occurred; 'out of Register' signifies year when ship's name dropped from Lloyd's Register or MNL (= Mercantile Navy List) indicating her probable loss or disappearance.

City of Hankow with her sails hanging in the buntlines. Particulars of the ship will be found in Appendix I. *Nautical Photo Agency)*

Name	Built	Rig	Tons	Hull	Builder	First owner	Name change, fate, etc
Acasta	1845	bk	385om 327nm	W	Hall, Aberdeen	Moir, Aberdeen	still afloat 1858
Agnes Muir	1869	S	851nt	I	Duncan, Pt Glasgow	Henderson, Glasgow	Adele 1885, hulk Melbourne 1909
Anglo Saxon	1854	S	890	W	Sunderland	Frost, London	abandoned 1878
Aracan	1854	S	911om 864nm	W	Brocklebank, Whitehaven	Brocklebank, Liverpool	sunk 1874
Ashmore	1851	bk	430om 512nm	W	Sunderland	Alcock, Sunderland	not in MNL 1868
Ascalon	1868	S	938	W	Hood, Aberdeen	Thompson, London	wrecked 1907
Bacchante	1856	S	717	W	Sunderland	Beazley, Liverpool	wrecked 1870
Balmoral	1848	S	345om 357nm	W	Peterhead	Leslie, Aberdeen	out of Register 1857
Ben Avon	1854	S	664om 684nm	W	Duthie, Aberdeen	Leslie, Aberdeen	wrecked 1856
Beautiful Star	1861	S	547nt	W	Duthie, Aberdeen	Cook, Aberdeen	out of Register 1888
Bonanza	1830	bkn	174om	W	Brocklebank, Whitehaven	Brocklebank, Liverpool	lost 1856
Burdwan	1862	S	803nt	W	Brocklebank, Whitehaven	Brocklebank, Liverpool	wrecked 1885
Caduceus	1854	S	1106	W	Fletcher, London	Fletcher, London	wrecked 1873
Cathaya	1850	S	407	W	Lamport, Workington	Lamport, Workington	wrecked 1857
Centurion	1850	S	656om 639nm	W	Hood, Aberdeen	Thompson, London	stranded 1867
Chieftain	1857	S	579nt 715om	W	Clarke, St Helier	Fruing, Jersey	wrecked 1859
Cinderella	1855	S	877nt	I	Bachelor, Newport	Bachelor, Newport	Shakespeare 1867, Felix Quebracho 1895, out of Register 1912
Cissy	1859	S	649	W	Duthie, Aberdeen	Temperley, London,	Genevieve 1874
City of Aberdeen	1862	bk	569nt	W	Duthie, Aberdeen	Tulloch, Aberdeen	Louis 1888, abandoned 1893
City of Hankow	1869	S	1195nt	C	Stephen, Glasgow	Smith & Sons, Glasgow	hulked 1904 as Hankow
Colinsburgh	1854	bk	436om 474nm	W	Newcastle	Cowan, Newcastle	Manila 1862, out of Register 1870
Confucius	1846	S	432om 380nm	W	Isle of Man	Atkin, Liverpool	lost 1857 (typhoon)
Corriemulzie	1856	S	672	W	Dundee	Cruikshank, Macduff	still afloat 1863
Countess of Seafield	1852	bk	436om 492nm	W	Turnbull, Stockton	Brown, Stockton	disappeared 1865
Dartmouth	1859	S	915nt	W	Stephen, Dundee	Somes, London	Flecha 1895, still afloat 1901
Deerfoot	1865	bk	499nt	W	Gardner, Sunderland	Kelso, N Shields	sunk 1878
Dennis Hill	1856	bk	370om 349nt	W	Adamson, Shields	Hill & Sons, S Shields	stranded 1865
Dilkhoosh	1864	S	810nt	C	Major, R Thames	Fleming & Co, London	Inveravon 1873, Gotha 1882, hulked 1898
Dunkeld	1863	S	699 .	W	Duthie, Aberdeen	Foley & Co, London	stranded 1876
Elmstone	1866	bk	698nt	C	Moore, Sunderland	Buckle, Bristol	out of Register 1903–06
Epsom	1853	S	556om 619nm	W	Hall, Sunderland	Temperley, London	still afloat 1868
Ethereal	1856	S	796nt	W	J Pile, Hartlepool	Mills, Stockton	Diane 1875, still afloat 1878
Euphrates	1834	S	617om	W	J Wilson, Liverpool	Jamieson, Liverpool	wrecked 1867
Euphrates	1845	bk	368om 428nm	W	Sunderland	R C Wilson, Liverpool	out of Register 1865
Ferozopore	1846	bk	497om 558nm	W	Newcastle	Henderson, London	abandoned 1872
Fire Queen	1864	S	766nt	W	Portland SB, Troon	Somes Bros, London	stranded 1878
Florence Nightingale	1855	S	537	W	Bilbe, Rotherhithe	Bilbe, London	dismasted & condemned 1881, wrecked 1882
Forfarshire	1840	S	614	W	Moulmein	Ingram, London (1845)	stranded Bombay 1854, registered Bombay 1864
Garrawalt	1862	S	627	W	Hood, Aberdeen	A Nicol, Aberdeen	wrecked 1865
Glen Clune	1857	S	471	W	Dumbarton	Turnbull, Glasgow	foundered 1869
Glenavon	1868	S	830	I	Hood, Aberdeen	A Nicol, Aberdeen	arrived Deal 31 Jan 1870, 100 days from Foochow on maiden voyage, out of Register 1872

Name	Built	Rig	Tons	Hull	Builder	First owner	Name change, fate, etc
Glendover	1858	S	485	W	Sunderland	Blackwell, Dartmouth	ashore but got off 1858, stranded 1871
Gossamer	1864	S	734	C	Stephen, Glasgow	Potter Bros, Liverpool	wrecked 1868
Hamilla Mitchell	1850	S	561om 540nm	W	Lunnan & Robertson, Peterhead	J Mitchell, Glasgow	wrecked 1865
Harkaway	1852	S	899nm	W	Stephen, Dundee	Somes Bros, London	stranded 1885
Hero of the Nile	1852	S	356	W	?White, West Cowes	Remington, London	first British ship home with new teas 1853, stranded 1876
Heroes of Alma	1855	S	537	W	White, Cowes	Shepherd, London	Shanghai to Plymouth in 95 days 1863–64, missing 1867
Heversham	1856	bk	464nt	W	Greenwell Bros, S Shields	Middle Dock Co, Newcastle	stranded 1876
Hoang Ho	1864	S	566nt	C	Stephen, Glasgow	Smith, Preston Co, Liverpool	out of Register 1888–89
Hope	1867	bk	454nt	I	Readhead, Softley Co, S Shields	J Robinson, S Shields	*Rewa* 1882, out of Register 1899
Inverness	1869	S	744	C	Hall, Russell, Aberdeen	Grant & Co, London	out of Register 1893–97
Isles of the South	1859	S	821nt	W	Laing, Sunderland	Cox & Co, London	*Löining* 1880, broken up 1908
Jerusalem	1867	S	900	W	Hood, Aberdeen	Thompson, London	missing 1893
Jessie Beazley	1859	S	447	W	Clover, Liverpool	Beazley, Liverpool	*Jessie* 1866, out of Register 1874
John Bright	1847	S	515om 591nm	W	Dumbarton	Hamlin, Greenock	still afloat 1863
John C Munro	1862	S	613nt	I	Laing, Sunderland	G L Munro, London	*Noman* 1892, wrecked 1896
John Dugdale	1834	S	371om 407nm	W	R Hardie, Whitehaven	Little & Co, Liverpool	lengthened 1842, not in MNL 1861
John Temperley	1856	S	976	W	Hall, Sunderland	Temperley, London	missing 1872
John Nicholson	1859	S	685nt	W	Nicholson, Annan	Nicholson, Liverpool	*Eloy Palacio* 1891, later *Ninie*, hulk in Brazil in 1923
Jungfrau	1867	S	585nt	C	Doxford, Sunderland	Glover Bros, London	*Glycas* 1886, *Leonidas* 1892, *Leonidas Glycas* 1899, broken up 1901
King Arthur	1862	S	699	I	Steele, Greenock	MacCunn, Greenock	wrecked 1863
Lady Hodgkinson	1853	S	946om 925nm	W	Sunderland	Hodgkinson, London	out of Register 1862
Lammermuir	1864	S	1054nt	W	J Pile, Hartlepool	J Willis, London	missing 1876
Lancastrian	1849	S	503om 591nm	W	Liverpool	Langley, Liverpool	lost 1854 (grounded)
Leucadia	1871	S	896	I	Hood, Aberdeen	A Nicol, Aberdeen	*Edwardina* 1902
Loo Choo	1863	bk	445om 321nm	W	Barr, Ardrossan	MacCunn, Greenock	lost 1864
Lord Hardinge	1846	S	378om 424nm	W	Whitehaven	Treacy Co, Whitehaven	wrecked 1871
Lord Macaulay	1860	S	846nt	W	Hall, Sunderland	Munro & Co, London	*Flora* c1884, foundered 1898
Lucia ex-*Maria Fidela*	1868	bk	640nt	C	Blumer, Sunderland	Killick, Martin & Co, London	under Spanish registration 1868–74, *Lucia* 1875, lost 1904
Maiden Queen	1860	S	814	S	R Williamson, Harrington	Brocklebank, Liverpool	*Betty* 1886, hulk at Santos, Brazil, by 1892
Marion Macintyre	1851	bk	283	C	Jordan & Getty, Liverpool	Macintyre, Liverpool	stranded and condemned 1859
Marquis of Argyle	1860	S	550	W	Hood, Aberdeen	Munro, London	foundered c1880
Melbourn	1847	S	496	W	W H Rowan, Glasgow	Potter & Co, Glasgow	driven ashore 1859
Mencius	1848	S	463om 510nm	W	Isle of Man	Atkin & Co, Liverpool	wrecked 1863
Menzies	1845	S	448	W	Lumley, Kennedy Co, Whitehaven	Jones & Younghusband, Liverpool	condemned 1881, broken up 1883
Merse	1853	S	699	W	W Pile, Sunderland	J Willis, London	wrecked 1877
Monarch	1840	S	464om 551nm	W	Leith	Duncan & Co, Leith	out of Register 1870
Monarch	1844	bk	338	W	Scilly Isles	Percival, Scilly Isles	lost 1857
Morning Star	1858	S	562	W	Tay SB Co, Dundee	Soot, Dundee	*Van Artevelde* 1875, condemned 1881, ?*Morning Star* of Sourabaya 1886

Name	Built	Rig	Tons	Hull	Builder	First owner	Name change, fate, etc
Neville	1856	S	715nt	W	Arbroath	Shallcross, Liverpool	out of Register 1876
Niagara	1845	bk	327om 326nm	W	Sunderland	Henderson, Glasgow	out of Register by 1865
Norna	1851	S	460om 392nm	W	Pile, Sunderland	Pryde & Co, Liverpool	out of Register 1862
Prince Alfred	1859	bk	663	W	Kelly, Dartmouth	Pile & Co, London	out of Register 1876
Pudsey Dawson	1853	S	693om 762nm	W	Lumley, Kennedy Co, Whitehaven	Hutchinson, Liverpool	hulked at Plymouth 1887
Red Deer	1863	S	775	W	Barr, Ardrossan	Walker, London	condemned 1884
Reindeer	1863	S	964nt	C	Hall, Aberdeen	J R Wardley, Liverpool	wrecked 1868–69
Richard Cobden	1844	bk	522om 461nm	I	J Hodgson, Liverpool	Darby & Sim, Liverpool	broken up 1870
St Abbs	1848	S	505om 592nm	W	Pile, Sunderland	J Willis, London	wrecked 1855
Sarah Nicholson	1865	S	934nt	W	Nicholson, Annan	Nicholson, Liverpool	dismasted 1878, hulked in Singapore, still a hulk 1920
Sea Star	1855	S	590nt	W	Hall, Aberdeen	D & J Louttit, Wick	stranded 1877
Shun Lee	1866	S	650nt	C	Walker & Co, Rotherhithe	W Walker, London	burnt 1891
Sir Robert Sale	1843	S	741	W	T & W Smith, Moulmein	T & W Smith, Newcastle	wrecked 1889
Star of China	1862	S	794	W	Hall, Aberdeen	Adamson, Aberdeen	Holmenkollen 1890, broken up 1906–07
Swithamley	1844	S	620om 727nm	W	Liverpool	Moore & Co, Liverpool	afloat 1858
Tartar	1851	S	641om 670nm	W	Greenock	Adams & Co, Greenock	wrecked 1865
The Sir Jamsetjee Family	1863	S	1049nt	W	Stephen, Dundee	Cursetjee Ferdunjee, Bombay	in China trade from 1867 under Killick, Martin; wrecked 1886
Tung Yu	1857	S	1137	W	New Brunswick	Shaw & Co, Liverpool	out of Register 1863
Tyburnia	1857	S	1027om 962nm	W	Stephen, Glasgow	Somes Bros, London	hulked at Townsville, Queensland c1890
Veloz	1854	S	571	W	J Salter, Moncton, NB	Jones & Co, Liverpool	sold to Sweden 1868
Venelia	1854	S	674	W	Hardy, Sunderland	Shields & Son, Newcastle	missing 1869
Vigil	1862	S	529nt	I	Vernon, Liverpool	Potters Bros, Liverpool	Aldgate 1899, hulked at Beira, East Africa 1902, beached c1922 and survived
Wagoola	1856	S	549	W	Clarke, Jersey	Redfern & Alexander, London	stranded 1860 but got off, wrecked 1887
Wellington	1853	S	444om 428nm	W	Harrington	Kendall Bros, Liverpool	lost 1885
West Derby	1855	S	853om 914nm	W	Chaloner, Liverpool	J Browne, Liverpool	Ocean c1876
William Connal	1852	S	607om 596nm	W	W Simons, Greenock	Campbell, Glasgow	wrecked 1854
Yaratilda	1857	S	720	W	Workington	Alexander, Workington	still afloat 1866

The *Houqua*, built in 1844 of 583 tons, was called a 'China packet' because she was built to carry cargo with a fair turn of speed. Although not in the China to London trade, this picture is included as it vividly portrays a ship labouring in a hurricane. *(Peabody Museum, Salem)*

APPENDIX II
CHINA PASSAGES 1840-1876

The following tables only list ships for which biographies appear in the text, and an attempt has been made to chronicle every passage between China or Japan and Great Britain performed by these ships in the years 1848 to 1879. Also, the passages which British ships made to America are included. After the early 1870s, the racing abilities of the clippers were impaired by the economies introduced and so the passages after the 1875–76 Tea Season are largely academic, even though some of the masters remained as keen as ever to race. During this last period, times of departure from ports in Java and the Philippines are included in order to keep track of well-known clippers.

The number of ships listed in any one Tea Season gives no true indication of the actual number of sailing ships carrying tea, as many non-clippers also loaded it. Details of passages have largely been taken from reports in contemporary newspapers and occasionally from log-books, backed by modern published works when necessary. Inaccuracies and conflicting dates were not uncommon in papers published in China and elsewhere, and so the information considered most nearly correct is given in doubtful cases.

The absence of a ship's name in any one Tea Season can be put down to a variety of reasons: obtaining lucrative coasting charters; damage from a typhoon or from stranding; low freight rates; or even loading two cargoes – at the beginning and end of a single season. The names of masters sometimes drop out, perhaps because they were superintending the construction of a new vessel to whose command they had been appointed.

The passages have been divided into separate tables for each Tea Season, since the interest lies in following the departures of the first clippers to load the new season's teas during the unfavourable south-west monsoon, through the change in direction of the monsoons in the early autumn, to the final departures at the end of the season in the following spring. The number of days has been calculated to facilitate the method of comparison and the total is correct to the nearest whole day between the first and last dates given.

Durations of passages can be shortened if taken between pilots or landfalls, and dates of the latter are given when known, but the majority of passages are calculated from port to port, so that the number of days is worked out between the first and last dates given.

Distances between ports are worth noting, but the distances covered by sailing ships depended on wind and weather and were always longer than a steamer's course. Hong Kong and Shanghai were some 900 miles apart, with Foochow roughly in the middle. In 1869, *Thermopylae* covered 2650 miles from Foochow to Anjer against the monsoon and the entire passage from Adam's Point – perhaps the last point seen on the China coast – to the

Lizard, was 13,910 miles that year. From Hong Kong to New York the sailing distance was 14,500 to 16,000 miles, but 1000 miles more in the opposite direction. A passage by the Eastern Route might add 1000 to 1500 miles to the course. In 1854, the American clipper *Comet* sailed 17,500 miles between Liverpool and Hong Kong. The sailing distance from Anjer to the Cape of Good Hope was approximately 5500 miles.

Some abbreviations should be noted: 'CGH' stands for Cape of Good Hope; 'St H' is St Helena; '(A)' denotes an American-built ship. When a ship spent several days at St Helena, the date given is the day of departure.

Ship/Master	Sailed	Passed	Arrived	Days
TEA SEASON 1848–49				
Aden Michael	Whampoa 19 Jun	?with last season's teas	Liverpool 20 Nov	154
Mary Sparks J Bushby	Whampoa 26 Jul		London 11 Dec	138
Bon Accord Buckle	Whampoa 26 Jul		London 29 Dec	156
Patna Mann	Whampoa 26 Aug		Liverpool 15 Jan	142
Sea Witch Reynell	Woosung 20 Sep		London 13 Jan	115
Magellan Sproule	Woosung 23 Oct		Liverpool 12 Mar	140
John o'Gaunt McDonald	Hong Kong 18 Nov		Liverpool 18 Mar	120
Earl of Chester Blackstone	Whampoa 24 Nov		London 20 Mar	116
Viscount Sandon Perry	Whampoa 21 Dec		Liverpool 9 Apr	109
Menam P Maxton	Hong Kong 20 Jan		London 24 Jun	155
John Bunyan J Thomson	Woosung 26 Jan		London 16 May	110
Panic R Howard	Woosung 17 Apr		Liverpool 12 Sep	148
TEA SEASON 1849-50				
Mary Sparks G Graham	Whampoa 8 Jul		London 15 Nov	130
Aden Smith	Hong Kong 8 Jul		Liverpool 18 Nov	133
Land o'Cakes J B Grant	Hong Kong 29 Jul	Anjer 7 Sep	London 6 Dec	130
Ganges R Deas	Canton 2 Sep		London 24 Dec	113
Patna Rorison	Whampoa 10 Sep		Liverpool 22 Jan	134
Magellan Sproule	Hong Kong 19 Sep	Anjer 22 Oct	Queenstown 22 Jan Clyde 25 Jan	128

225

Ship/Master	Sailed	Passed	Arrived	Days
Reindeer / A Enright	Whampoa 5 Oct		Liverpool 19 Jan	106
Sea Witch / Reynell	Shanghai 6 Oct		London 21 Jan	107
Crisis / W Gibson	Shanghai 23 Oct		Liverpool 3 Mar	131
Countess of Seafield / W Leask	Shanghai 9 Nov		London 28 Feb	111
Viscount Sandon / Perry	Woosung 28 Nov		London 28 Mar	120
John Bunyan / J Thomson	Shanghai 28 Jan	St H 25 Mar	Deal 9 May / London 10 May	102
Menam / P Maxton	Hong Kong 13 Mar		London 25 Jul	134
Earl of Chester / Blackstone	Whampoa 5 Apr	St H 31 Jul	London 23 Sep	171
Panic / R Howard	Woosung 12 May	Anjer 27 Jul	London 10 Nov	182

TEA SEASON 1850–51

Ship/Master	Sailed	Passed	Arrived	Days
Sea Witch / Reynell	Shanghai 26 Jul	St H 15 Oct	London 2 Dec	129
Patna / Rorison	Shanghai 3 Aug	St H 6 Nov	Liverpool 13 Dec	132
Reindeer / Hawkins	Hong Kong 20 Aug	Anjer 15 Sep	Liverpool 5 Dec	107
Magellan / Sproule	Whampoo 26 Aug	St H 19 Nov	London 3 Jan	130
Oriental (A) / T Palmer	Whampoa 27 Aug	Anjer 18 Sep	Lizard 27 Nov / London 4 Dec	99
Astarte / J Roberts	Whampoa 28 Aug	Anjer 9 Oct / St H 19 Nov	London 3 Jan	128
Aden / Smith	Hong Kong 29 Aug	CGH 8 Nov	Liverpool 4 Jan	128
Ganges / R Deas	Whampoa 23 Sep	St H 12 Dec	Deal 19 Jan / London 20 Jan	119
Countess of Seafield / W Leask	Shanghai 8 Oct	St H 17 Dec	London 20 Jan	104
Mary Sparks / G Graham	Whampoa 25 Sep		Liverpool 15 Feb	143
Wisconsin (A) / Mumford	Whampoa 4 Dec		Downs 10 Mar / London 13 Mar	99
Crisis / W Gibson	Whampoa 6 Dec		Liverpool 21 Mar	105
John o'Gaunt / McDonald	Whampoa 4 Jan		Liverpool 7 May	123
Land o'Cakes / J B Grant	Shanghai 15 Jan		London 18 May	123
John Bunyan / J Thomson	Shanghai 25 Jan		Deal 16 May / London 17 May	112
Viscount Sandon / March	Shanghai 1 Feb		London 7 Jun	127
Menam / P Maxton	Whampoa 8 May		London 6 Oct	151

TEA SEASON 1851–52

Ship/Master	Sailed	Passed	Arrived	Days
Stornoway / J Robertson	Whampoa 5 Jul		London 17 Oct	104
Reindeer / C H Hunt	Shanghai 9 Jul		Liverpool 26 Nov	140
Oriental (A) / T Palmer	Woosung 15 Jul		London 20 Nov	128
Surprise (A) / Dumaresq	Whampoa 28 Jul		Brighton 10 Nov / London 12 Nov	107
Magellan / J N Gittens	Woosung 6 Aug		London 24 Jan	171
Patna / Rorison	Whampoa 15 Aug	Anjer 17 Sep	Liverpool 6 Dec	113
Memnon (A) / Gordon	Whampoa 16 Aug		wrecked Gaspar Strait 14 Sep	–
Chrysolite / A Enright	Whampoa 19 Aug		Liverpool 1 Dec	104

Ship/Master	Sailed	Passed	Arrived	Days
Ganges / R Deas	Whampoa 30 Aug	Anjer 27 Sep	Downs 19 Dec	111
Aden / Smith	Whampoa 30 Aug		Liverpool 25 Dec	117
White Squall (A) / Goodwin	Whampoa 8 Sep		Isle of Wight 16 Dec / London 22 Dec	105
Mary Sparks / G Graham	Hong Kong 17 Sep		London 16 Jan	121
Sea Witch / C Gribble	Hong Kong 18 Sep		London 10 Jan	114
Panic / R Howard	Shanghai 1 Oct	Anjer 4 Nov	Queenstown 27 Jan (to repair damage) / Liverpool 5 Feb	127
Countess of Seafield / W Leask	Shanghai 4 Oct	Anjer 1 Nov / St H 23 Dec	London 29 Jan	117
Astarte / Oppenheim	Hong Kong 8 Oct		Queenstown 7 Feb / Dublin –	122
Crisis / W Gibson	Shanghai 10 Oct		Liverpool 28 Jan	110
Sea Queen / G Shearer	Shanghai 15 Oct		London 3 Feb	111
North Star / T Smith	Whampoa 31 Oct		Clyde 6 Mar	127
John Bunyan / J Thomson	Shanghai 6 Nov	Anjer 28 Nov	Dover 19 Feb / London 22 Feb	108
Abergeldie / L Wilson	Woosung 30 Nov	Mauritius 24 Dec	London 2 Apr	104
Witch of the Wave (A) / Millett	Canton 5 Jan	Anjer 12 Jan	Dungeness 4 Apr / London 6 Apr	92
John o'Gaunt / McDonald	Whampoa 15 Feb		London –	–
Geelong / R Barr	Woosung 15 Apr	St H 11 Jul	London 31 Aug	138
Celestial (A) / Palmer	Shanghai 8 May	Anjer 17 May	Liverpool 22 Sep	137
Celestial / J O Raymur	Woosung 31 May		Halifax –	–

TEA SEASON 1852–53

Ship/Master	Sailed	Passed	Arrived	Days
Chrysolite / A Enright	Whampoa 9 Jul	Anjer 8 Aug / St H 16 Sep	Liverpool 22 Oct	105
Stornoway / J Robertson	Whampoa 10 Jul	Anjer 10 Aug / St H 16 Sep	London 26 Oct	108
Surprise (A) / Ranlett	Canton 19 Jul	Anjer 18 Aug	Downs 2 Nov / London 3 Nov	107
Patna / Smith	Whampoa 26 Jul		Liverpool 21 Nov	118
Challenger / J Killick	Shanghai 28 Jul	Anjer 4 Sep	London 17 Nov	112
Sea Queen / R Robertson	Whampoa 28 Jul		London 21 Nov	116
Hannibal / A Walker	Shanghai 29 Jul	St H 13 Nov	London 21 Dec	145
Nightingale (A) / Fiske	Shanghai 31 Jul	Anjer 30 Sep	Deal 10 Dec / London 11 Dec	133
Magellan / J N Gittens	Whampoa 1 Aug	Anjer 25 Oct	Clyde –	–
Challenge (A) / Pitts	Canton 5 Aug	Anjer 12 Sep	Deal 18 Nov / London 19 Nov	106
Cambalu / Alleyne	Shanghai 14 Aug		Liverpool 15 Jan	154
Foam / R Findlay	Whampoa 6 Sep		Liverpool 15 Jan	131
Aden / H P Fletcher	Whampoa 6 Sep	Anjer 10 Oct	Liverpool 21 Jan	137
Mary Sparks / G Graham	Hong Kong 8 Sep	Anjer 6 Oct / St H 4 Dec	Liverpool 14 Jan	128
Menam / P Maxton	Shanghai 10 Sep	Anjer 24 Oct / CGH 29 Nov	London 4 Feb	147
Ganges / R Deas	Whampoa 12 Sep	Anjer 7 Oct	Deal 13 Jan / London 16 Jan	126
John Bunyan / J Thomson	Woosung 13 Sep	Anjer 19 Oct	Deal 14 Jan / London 15 Jan	124

Ship/Master	Sailed	Passed	Arrived	Days
Countess of Seafield / Gibson	Shanghai 17 Sep		London 16 Jan	121
Earl of Chester / F P Johns	Shanghai 17 Sep	Anjer 18 Oct CGH 4 Dec	London 16 Jan	121
Crisis / W Gibson	Shanghai 17 Sep		Liverpool 21 Jan	126
Viscount Sandon / March	Shanghai 22 Sep	Anjer 30 Oct St H 22 Dec	Liverpool 3 Feb	134
Wisconsin (A) / Scott	Shanghai 3 Oct		London 3 Feb	125
Panic / R Howard	Shanghai 15 Oct	St H 22 Dec	off Liverpool 1 Feb Liverpool 3 Feb	111
John Knox / Elmslie	Shanghai 22 Oct	Anjer 1 Nov St H 27 Dec	London 27 Feb	128
Aberdeldie / G Brook	Shanghai 31 Oct	Anjer 28 Nov	Deal 27 Feb London 1 Mar	121
Sea Witch / G H Heaton	Shanghai 5 Nov	St H 16 Jan	Plymouth 4 Mar London 8 Mar	123
Land o'Cakes / J B Grant	Hong Kong 4 Dec	Anjer 17 Dec	London 2 Apr	119
Wild Flower / Hewitt	Shanghai 8 Jan	Anjer 27 Jan	Liverpool 3 May	115
Joseph Fletcher / J Foster	Shanghai 10 Jan		London 28 Apr	108
North Star / T Smith	Whampoa 19 Jan		London 21 May	122
Julia / Butler	Woosung 19 Feb		London 4 Jul	135
Crystal Palace / N K Narracott	Shanghai 27 Feb		London 20 Jul	143
Bon Accord / Buckle	Shanghai 5 Mar		London 21 Jul	138
Geelong / A Bowers	Woosung 1 Apr		London 26 Aug	147

TEA SEASON 1853–54

Ship/Master	Sailed	Passed	Arrived	Days
Architect (A) / Potter	Whampoa 25 Jun		London 10 Oct	107
Sea Queen / R Robertson	Whampoa 4 Jul		London 1 Nov	120
Challenge (A) / Pitts	Canton 13 Jul	Anjer 10 Aug Fayal 20 Oct (leaky)	Deal 20 Dec	160
Stornoway / H L Hart	Whampoa 15 Jul		Liverpool 31 Oct	108
Patna / Smith	Whampoa 16 Jul	Anjer 17 Aug Ascension 2 Oct	Liverpool 19 Nov	126
John Bunyan / J Thomson	Woosung 17 Jul	Anjer 15 Oct St H 27 Nov	London 11 Jan	178
Chrysolite / A Enright	Whampoa 30 Jul Hong Kong 1 Aug	Anjer 31 Aug	Liverpool 15 Nov	108
Celestial / J O Raymur	Canton 30 Jul Hong Kong 1 Aug		Deal 9 Dec London 11 Dec	134
Cairngorm / J Robertson	Whampoa 2 Aug off Lintin 3 days	Anjer 1 Sep	Deal 17 Nov London 19 Nov	109
Hannibal / A Walker	Whampoa 2 Aug		London 1 Dec	121
John o'Gaunt / McDonald	Whampoa 5 Aug	St H 23 Nov (master died)	Holyhead 17 Jan (wrecked there)	165
Challenger / J Killick	Woosung 8 Aug		Deal 26 Nov London 28 Nov	112
Nightingale (A) / Mather	Woosung 8 Aug	Anjer 11 Sep	Deal 28 Nov London 29 Nov	113
Aden / H P Fletcher	Whampoa 17 Aug	Anjer 26 Sep St H 8 Nov	Liverpool 31 Dec	136
Crisis / J Bell	Shanghai 24 Sep	Anjer 30 Oct	Liverpool 27 Jan	125
Sea Witch / G H Heaton	Woosung 27 Sep	Anjer 29 Oct St H 14 Dec	Deal 22 Jan London 24 Jan	119
Cambalu / Alleyne	Woosung 28 Sep	Anjer 30 Oct	London 28 Jan	122

Ship/Master	Sailed	Passed	Arrived	Days
John Knox / J Munro	Shanghai 29 Sep	Anjer 31 Oct	London 27 Jan	120
Abergeldie / G Brook	Whampoa 30 Sep	Anjer 2 Nov	London 31 Jan	123
Celestial (A) / Palmer	Foochow ?27 Oct		London 31 Jan	96
Panic / Ingleton	Woosung 30 Oct	Anjer 11 Dec	London 29 Apr	181
Ganges / R Deas	Whampoa 3 Nov	Anjer 22 Nov	London 6 Mar	123
Typhoon (A) / Salter	Shanghai 4 Nov	Anjer 24 Nov	Deal 16 Feb London 21 Feb	109
Menam / N Andrews	Woosung 24 Nov	Anjer 1 Jan	London 1 May	159
Vanguard / J Crosbie	Whampoa 27 Nov		Deal 15 Mar London 16 Mar	109
Foam / R Findlay	Foochow 13 Dec		London 11 Apr	109
Countess of Seafield / G Innes	Whampoa 26 Dec		London 29 Apr	124
North Star / T Smith	Whampoa 2 Jan	Anjer 18 Jan	London 5 May	123
Joseph Fletcher / J Foster	Woosung 11 Jan	Anjer 30 Jan	London 9 May	118
Star of the East / J B Robertson	Woosung 18 Jan		Liverpool 5 May	107
Flying Dutchman (A) / Hubbard	Canton 12 Feb	Anjer 3 Mar	London 25 May	102
Oriental (A) / Fletcher	Foochow 25 Feb		wrecked river Min 25 Feb	–
Geelong / A Bowers	Shanghai 9 May		London 24 Oct	168

TEA SEASON 1854–55

Ship/Master	Sailed	Passed	Arrived	Days
Romance of the Seas (A) / Dumaresq	Whampoa 9 Jun	Anjer 2 Jul	London 21 Sep	104
Architect (A) / Potter	Canton 9 Jul	Anjer 13 Aug	London 30 Oct	113
Patna / Smith	Whampoa 11 Jul		Liverpool 16 Nov	128
Celestial / J O Raymur	Whampoa 14 Jul	Anjer 19 Aug	Liverpool 31 Oct	109
Vision / A Douglas	Canton 15 Jul Hong Kong 16 Jul	Anjer 14 Aug	Liverpool 27 Oct	104
Polmaise / J Allen	Whampoa 16 Jul	Anjer 17 Aug	London 29 Oct	105
Chrysolite / A Enright	Foochow 18 Jul		London 30 Oct	104
Bon Accord / Buckle	Foochow 26 Jul	St H 31 Oct	London 21 Dec	148
Gauntlet / W Inglis	Whampoa 29 Jul	Anjer 18 Sep	London 5 Jan	160
Stornoway / H L Hart	Whampoa 5 Aug	Anjer 7 Sep	London 7 Dec	124
Challenger / J Killick	Shanghai 9 Aug	Anjer 15 Sep	London 4 Dec	117
Aden / H P Fletcher	Whampoa 26 Aug	Anjer 3 Oct	Liverpool 29 Dec	125
Archer (A) / Thomas	Shanghai 4 Sep		London 9 Jan	127
Cairngorm / J Robertson	Shanghai 6 Oct Yangtze R 9 Oct		London 26 Jan	112
Crest of the Wave / J Steele	Shanghai 20 Oct		Liverpool 17 Feb	120
John Bunyan / B Grant	Hong Kong 24 Oct	St H 19 Dec	Liverpool 22 Feb	121
Spirit of the Age / G H Heaton	Shanghai 8 Nov		London 25 Feb	109
Golden Gate (A) / Dewing	Shanghai 25 Nov	at Batavia 4 days; Anjer 10 Dec	Beachy Head 23 Feb (for London)	89

Ship/Master	Sailed	Passed	Arrived	Days
Northfleet / N Pentreath	Shanghai 26 Nov		London 3 Mar	97
Crisis / J Bell	Foochow 15 Dec	Anjer 3 Jan	London 24 Apr	130
Mimosa / Kemp	Shanghai 21 Dec	Anjer 7 Jan	Halifax ?	–
Spirit of the North / C Tomlinson	Shanghai 23 Dec	Anjer 9 Jan	London 15 Apr	113
Oracle (A) / Ranlett	Shanghai 7 Jan	Anjer 26 Jan	London 9 May	122
Tinto / D Jones	Shanghai 16 Jan		Liverpool 11 May	115
Sea Witch / Lewes	Hong Kong 24 Jan		London 9 May	105
Joseph Fletcher / J Foster	Shanghai 31 Jan		London 28 May	117
Star of the East / J B Robertson	Shanghai 8 Feb		London 24 May	105
Wild Flower / Barclay	Shanghai 14 Feb	Anjer 11 Mar	Liverpool 13 Jun	119
Nightingale (A) / Mather	Shanghai 16 Feb	Anjer 5 Mar	Beachy Head 18 May / London 21 May	94
Countess of Seafield / G Innes	Shanghai 17 Mar		stranded 21 Mar (for London)	–
Lord of the Isles / P Maxton	Shanghai 24 Mar		London 28 Jun	96
Land o'Cakes / Miller	Whampoa 27 Mar	Anjer 24 Apr	London 2 Aug	128
Julia / S Balfour	Shanghai 4 Apr		Liverpool 22 Aug	140
Staghound (A) / Behm	Woosung 8 Apr		Deal 27 Aug	141

Ship/Master	Sailed	Passed	Arrived	Days
Romance of the Seas (A) / Henry	Shanghai 1 Nov	Anjer 29 Nov	Deal 7 Mar	127
Cambalu / Alleyne	Shanghai 3 Nov	Anjer 2 Dec	Liverpool 2 Mar	120
Swallow (A) / Tucker	Shanghai 9 Nov		Scilly 14 Mar / London 24 Mar	135
John Bunyan / T Henry	Hong Kong 20 Nov	Anjer 3 Dec	London 21 Mar	122
Leichardt / H Oakley	Shanghai 22 Nov	Anjer 10 Dec	Liverpool –	–
Crisis / J Bell	Whampoa 4 Dec		Liverpool 21 Mar	108
Foam / R Findlay	Hong Kong 5 Dec		London 4 Apr	121
Spirit of the North / C Tomlinson	Foochow 7 Dec		London 4 Apr	119
Kelso / Coulson	Hong Kong 21 Dec		London 4 Apr	105
Kate Carnie / A Rodger	Shanghai 4 Jan	Anjer 31 Jan	London 5 Apr	92
Invincible / G Graham	Hong Kong 21 Jan		London 29 Apr	99
Tinto / D Jones	Foochow 1 Feb		London 14 May	113
Joseph Fletcher / J Foster	Shanghai 4 Feb		London 7 Jun	124
Viscount Sandon / E Hughes	Whampoa 13 Mar	Anjer 15 Apr	Liverpool 30 Jul	139
Star of the East / W Christian	Shanghai 8 Apr		London 26 Aug	140

TEA SEASON 1855–56

Ship/Master	Sailed	Passed	Arrived	Days
Chrysolite / A McLelland	Foochow 13 Jun		London 1 Nov	141
Patna / Rodgers	Hong Kong 28 Jun		Liverpool 2 Nov	127
Vision / A Douglas	Foochow 13 Jul		Liverpool 29 Nov	139
Cairngorm / Irvine	Whampoa 24 Jul	Anjer 27 Aug	London 19 Nov	118
John Taylor / J Cawkitt	Whampoa 11 Aug	Anjer 13 Sep	London 26 Dec	137
North Star / T Smith	Whampoa 12 Aug	Anjer 16 Oct	London 26 Jan	167
Challenger / J Killick	Shanghai 13 Aug	Anjer 14 Sep	London 8 Dec	117
Spirit of the Age / G H Heaton	Shanghai 13 Aug		London 24 Dec	133
Aden / H P Fletcher	Shanghai 14 Aug	via Singapore Anjer 12 Oct	Liverpool 24 Jan	163
Celestial / J O Raymur	Whampoa 22 Aug	Anjer 24 Sep	London 24 Dec	124
Stornoway / H L Hart	Whampoa 29 Aug	Anjer 2 Oct	Liverpool 27 Dec	120
Wynaud / R A Hunt	Foochow 1 Sep		Cowes ?	–
Spray of the Ocean / Slaughter	Shanghai 8 Sep		Liverpool 16 Jan	130
Mirage / Carter	Shanghai 14 Sep	Anjer 25 Oct	London 22 Jan	130
Assyrian / G Wood	Shanghai 3 Oct	Anjer 4 Nov	London 25 Jan	114
Flying Dutchman (A) / Hubbard	Shanghai 8 Oct		Deal 24 Jan / London 26 Jan	110
Kingfisher (A) / Z Crosby	Macao 20 Oct	Anjer 7 Nov	Deal 24 Jan / London 28 Jan	100
Spirit of the Deep / J Hewitt	Whampoa 27 Oct		London 8 Feb	104

TEA SEASON 1856–57

Ship/Master	Sailed	Passed	Arrived	Days
Maury (A) / Fletcher	Foochow 9 Jun		London 15 Oct	128
Chrysolite / A McLelland	Foochow 10 Jun		Downs 31 Oct / London 1 Nov	144
Lord of the Isles / P Maxton	Foochow 10 Jun		London 15 Oct	127
Sea Witch / Pentreath	Foochow 2 Jul	Anjer 24 Aug	London 25 Nov	146
Vision / G Cobb	Foochow 13 Jul	Anjer 19 Aug	Liverpool 19 Nov	129
John Taylor / Charleson	Foochow 17 Jul	Anjer 25 Aug	London 27 Nov	133
Cairngorm / Irvine	Whampoa 19 Jul	Anjer 20 Aug	Downs 20 Nov / London 22 Nov	126
Patna / Rodgers	Whampoa 19 Jul	Anjer 19 Aug	Liverpool 25 Nov	129
Spitfire (A) / Jackson	Canton 23 Jul	Anjer 30 Aug	Deal 21 Nov	121
Julia / S Balfour	Shanghai 6 Aug		London 8 Dec	124
Fiery Cross / J Dallas	Foochow 12 Aug	St H 17 Oct	London 24 Nov	104
Celestial / J O Raymur	Whampoa 18 Aug	Gaspar Strait 17 Sep	London 8 Dec	112
Spirit of the Age / W Billing	Whampoa 21 Aug	Anjer 13 Sep	Deal 28 Nov / London 30 Nov	101
Northfleet / B Freeman	Whampoa 5 Sep	Anjer 8 Oct	London 9 Jan	126
Challenger / J Killick	Shanghai 8 Sep	St H 18 Dec	London 14 Jan	128
Aden / H P Fletcher	Whampoa 9 Sep	Anjer 21 Oct	Liverpool 7 Feb	151
Stornoway / H L Hart	Shanghai 10 Sep	Anjer 24 Oct / St H 18 Dec	Downs 16 Jan / London 20 Jan	132
Mimosa / Kemp	Shanghai 22 Sep	Anjer 25 Oct	London 18 Jan	118
Wynaud / R A Hunt	Foochow – Sep		Cowes 30 Dec	–

Ship/Master	Sailed	Passed	Arrived	Days
Kingfisher (A) Z Crosby	Foochow 4 Oct	Anjer 1 Nov	London 21 Jan	109
Foam R Findlay	Shanghai 27 Nov		Deal 23 Mar	116
Polmaise J Smith	Foochow 8 Dec	Anjer 25 Dec	London 2 Apr	115
Leichardt R Barrett	Shanghai 13 Dec	Anjer 30 Dec	London 1 Apr	109
Cambalu Fawcett	Shanghai 22 Dec		Liverpool 5 Apr	104
Spray of the Ocean Slaughter	Shanghai 9 Jan		London 17 May	128
Competitor (A) White	Shanghai 9 Jan	Anjer 5 Feb	London 21 Jun	163
Swallow (A) Tucker	Shanghai 19 Jan	Anjer 7 Feb	Land's End 29 Apr London 4 May	106
Crisis J Black	Shanghai 19 Jan	Anjer 14 Feb	Liverpool 10 Jun	142
Wild Flower H Brown	Foochow 26 Jan	Anjer 19 Feb	Cowes for orders 11 Jun	136
Strathmore J Mann	Foochow 31 Jan over bar 3 Feb	Anjer 19 Feb St H 11 Apr	off Tuskar Lt 28 May Liverpool 31 May	120
Ballarat H Jones	Foochow 10 Feb		London 30 Jun	140
Spirit of the North C Tomlinson	Hong Kong 12 Feb	Anjer 23 Feb	London 27 May	104
Herculean J Bell	Shanghai 15 Mar		London 14 Jul	121
Joseph Fletcher Pook	Foochow 4 Apr		London 14 Sep	163
Crest of the Wave J Steele	Foochow 25 May		London 28 Sep	126

TEA SEASON 1857–58

Ship/Master	Sailed	Passed	Arrived	Days
Maury (A) Fletcher	Foochow 3 Jul		off Dartmouth 14 Oct London 17 Oct	106
Fairy (A) Blish	Foochow 4 Jul	Anjer 29 Jul	London 19 Oct	107
Cairngorm J Ryrie	Hong Kong 10 Jul		Deal 30 Oct London 31 Oct	113
Chrysolite A McLelland	Shanghai 19 Jul		London 16 Nov	120
Stornoway H L Hart	Foochow 20 Jul		New York 19 Nov	122
Julia W Miller	Shanghai 29 Jul		London 27 Nov	121
Viscount Sandon E Hughes	Macao 3 Aug	Anjer 10 Oct St H 5 Dec	Liverpool 3 Feb	184
Challenger J Killick	Shanghai 5 Aug		London 1 Dec	118
Northfleet B Freeman	Hong Kong 6 Aug	Anjer 7 Sep	Plymouth 3 Dec London 7 Dec	123
Robin Hood G Cobb	Shanghai 6 Aug	Anjer 15 Sep	London 30 Nov	116
Spirit of the Age W Billing	Foochow 8 Aug	Anjer 14 Sep	Liverpool 1 Dec	115
Fiery Cross J Dallas	Foochow 9 Aug	Anjer 29 Aug	off Dartmouth 11 Nov London 16 Nov	99
Patna Rodgers	Foochow 9 Aug	Anjer 19 Sep	Liverpool 17 Dec	130
Mirage J Roberts	Shanghai 13 Aug	Anjer 23 Sep	London 18 Dec	127
Lord of the Isles P Maxton	Shanghai 25 Aug	Anjer 9 Oct	London 13 Jan	141
Sea Witch T Roy	Shanghai 2 Sep	Anjer 1 Nov	Dublin 31 Jan	151
Assyrian S Shepherd	Shanghai 18 Sep	Anjer 14 Oct	London 9 Jan	113
Aden Howson	Macao 19 Sep	Anjer 12 Oct	Liverpool 18 Jan	121
Lammermuir A Shewan	Shanghai 4 Oct	Anjer 2 Nov	London 31 Jan	119

Ship/Master	Sailed	Passed	Arrived	Days
Spitfire (A) Arey	Foochow 25 Oct	Anjer 22 Nov	Plymouth 15 Feb (for London)	113
Wynaud R A Hunt	Foochow 9 Nov		London 29 Mar	140
Kelso Coulson	Foochow 24 Nov	via Hong Kong	London 29 Mar	125
Friar Tuck Fordyce	Shanghai 30 Nov	Anjer 19 Dec	London 26 Mar	116
Menam N Andrews	Shanghai 20 Dec		London 2 May	133
Strathmore J Mann	Shanghai 21 Dec Woosung 22 Dec	Anjer 9 Jan St H 19 Feb	off Lizard 28 Mar London 31 Mar	100
Sir W F Williams D Rees	Shanghai 22 Dec	Anjer 3 Jan	London 31 Mar	99
Solent M Brooks	Shanghai 31 Dec	Anjer 20 Jan	London 16 Apr	106
Harwood Forsyth	Shanghai 16 Jan	Anjer 2 Feb	London 25 Apr	99
Spirit of the North E Martin	Foochow 19 Jan	Anjer 26 Jan	London 27 Apr	98
Cambalu Fawcett	Shanghai 30 Jan		Montreal –	–
Spirit of the Deep J Hewitt	Foochow 5 Feb		Belfast 24 May	108
Vanguard (1857) A Scott	Shanghai 12 Feb	Anjer 25 Feb	London 24 May	101
Star of the North W P Buckham	Foochow 16 Feb	Anjer 3 Mar	London 26 May	99
Crisis J Black	Foochow 19 Feb	Anjer 28 Feb	Liverpool 9 Jun	110
Herculean J Bell	Shanghai 23 Mar	off South Latunas 18 Apr	London 21 Jul	120
Invincible Wilson	Shanghai 23 Mar	Anjer 4 May	London 15 Aug	145
Pride of the Ocean (A) J Kyle	Manilla 22 Apr		Deal 6 Aug	126
Banian G Graham	Hong Kong 9 Apr	Anjer 1 May	London 4 Aug	117
Star of the East Gaggs	Shanghai 16 Apr	Anjer 21 May	London 13 Aug	119
Crest of the Wave J Steele	Whampoa 17 Apr	Anjer 15 May	London 13 Aug	118
Snap Dragon (A) Davis	Whampoa 1 May	Anjer 20 May	London 13 Aug	104
Wild Flower Barn (?Brown)	Foochow 10 May	St H 4 Sep	London 9 Nov	183
Red Riding Hood J Rossiter	Shanghai 14 May		New York 1 Oct	140

TEA SEASON 1858–59

Ship/Master	Sailed	Passed	Arrived	Days
Fiery Cross J Dallas	Foochow 27 Jun		London 19 Oct	114
Julia W Miller	Shanghai 30 Jun	Anjer 8 Aug	London 31 Oct	123
Chrysolite A McLelland	Foochow 13 Jul		London 25 Nov	135
Northfleet B Freeman	Hong Kong 22 Jul	Anjer 24 Aug St H 29 Oct	Plymouth 25 Nov London 30 Nov	131
Mirage J Roberts	Shanghai 7 Aug	Anjer 22 Sep	London 17 Dec	132
Kate Carnie Lewis	Foochow 19 Aug		Deal 1 Dec London 2 Dec	105
Stornoway H L Hart	Shanghai 6 Sep		London 21 Jan	137
Robin Hood G Cobb	Foochow 9 Sep	Anjer 7 Oct	London 17 Dec	99
Ballarat H Jones	Foochow 9 Sep	Anjer 11 Oct	London 27 Dec	109
Challenger J Killick	Shanghai 18 Sep	Anjer 22 Oct	London 11 Jan	115
Crystal Palace Shewan	Foochow 15 Oct		New York 15 Jan	92

Ship/Master	Sailed	Passed	Arrived	Days
John Taylor Charleson	Shanghai 16 Oct	Anjer 15 Nov	posted missing (for Liverpool)	–
Spartan W Storey	Macao 19 Oct	Anjer 8 Nov	London 4 Feb	108
Jubilee J Douglas	Shanghai 22 Oct		Start Pt 2 Feb ran ashore near Étaples 3 Feb	104
Aden Howson	Macao 22 Oct		Liverpool 9 Feb	110
Cairngorm J Ryrie	Whampoa 5 Nov Macao 6 Nov	Anjer 22 Nov St H 2 Jan	Deal 5 Feb London 6 Feb	93
Lammermuir A Shewan	Whampoa 5 Nov Macao 7 Nov	Anjer 22 Nov St H 2 Jan	Deal 7 Feb London 9 Feb	96
Joseph Fletcher Pook	Shanghai 7 Nov	Anjer 26 Nov	London 28 Feb	113
Friar Tuck Richardson	Whampoa 13 Nov	Anjer 30 Nov	London 24 Feb	103
Assyrian S Shepherd	Shanghai 14 Nov	Anjer 3 Dec	London 25 Feb	103
Patna Rodgers	Foochow 16 Nov	at Singapore to repair damage 3 Dec to 10 Jan	Liverpool 19 May	184
Kelso Coulson	Whampoa 18 Nov	Anjer 9 Dec	London 25 Feb	99
Spray of the Ocean Slaughter	Foochow 21 Nov	Anjer 9 Dec	London 18 Mar	117
Strathmore J Mann	Shanghai 26 Nov N Saddle 28 Nov	Anjer 13 Dec St H 23 Jan	Start Pt 5 Mar London 7 Mar	101
Lord of the Isles W Jamieson	Shanghai 29 Nov	St H 23 Jan	off Lizard 25 Feb London 27 Feb	90
Robert Henderson W J Cubitt	Amoy 2 Dec		New York 17 Mar	105
Celestial J Legoe	Whampoa 7 Dec	Anjer 20 Dec	Deal 25 Mar	108
Spirit of the Age W Billing	Foochow 8 Dec	Anjer 23 Dec	London 29 Mar	111
Wynaud D Reid	Macao 16 Dec	Anjer 30 Dec	London 1 Apr	106
Beemah J Pickernell	Foochow 30 Dec	Anjer 12 Jan St H 26 Feb	London 11 Apr	102
Scawfell R Thomson	Foochow 5 Jan	Anjer 21 Jan	Deal 29 Apr	114
Spirit of the North E Martin	Shanghai 12 Jan	Anjer 31 Jan	London 19 May	127
Gauntlet W Inglis	Shanghai 14 Jan	Anjer 3 Feb	Montreal –	–
Solent M Brooks	Whampoa 3 Feb	Anjer 11 Feb	Deal 13 May	99
Herculean J Bell	Foochow 15 Feb	Anjer 5 Mar	London 31 May	105
Crisis J Black	Whampoa 19 Feb	Anjer 12 Mar St H 28 Apr	Liverpool 23 Jun	124
Menam N Andrews	Whampoa 28 Feb	Anjer 20 Mar St H 17 May	London 15 Jul	137
Star of the North W P Buckham	Foochow 2 Mar	Anjer 18 Mar	London 12 Jun	102
Vanguard (1857) A Scott	Foochow 15 Mar	Anjer 30 Mar	London 7 Jul	114
Sir W F Williams D Rees	Shanghai 24 Mar	St H 25 May	London 14 Jul	112
Banian G Graham	Whampoa 31 Mar	Anjer 17 Apr	London 1 Aug	123

TEA SEASON 1859–60

Ship/Master	Sailed	Passed	Arrived	Days
Star of the East Gaggs	Manilla 7 Jun	St H 26 Sep	Liverpool 3 Nov	149
Ellen Rodger J Keay	Foochow 10 Jun		London 24 Oct	136
Fiery Cross Duncan	Foochow 11 Jun		London 26 Oct	137
Crest of the Wave J Steele	Foochow 16 Jun		London 10 Nov	147
Ziba Tomlinson	Foochow 19 Jun	Anjer 30 Jul	London 31 Oct	134
Julia W Miller	Foochow 7 Jul	St H 24 Sep	London 4 Nov	120
Chrysolite A McLelland	Foochow 23 Jul		New York 9 Nov	109
Polmaise Guthrie	Foochow 2 Aug		London 9 Dec	129
Challenger J Killick	Shanghai 6 Aug	Anjer 11 Sep	London 21 Nov	107
Cairngorm J Ryrie	Whampoa 18 Aug	Anjer 20 Sep	London 7 Dec	111
Falcon P Maxton	Shanghai 23 Aug	Anjer 25 Sep	London 7 Dec	106
Stornoway H L Hart	Shanghai 4 Sep	Anjer 13 Oct	London 30 Dec	117
Spirit of the Deep J Hewitt	Foochow 6 Sep	Anjer 17 Oct	London 18 Jan	134
Ballarat H Jones	Shanghai 9 Sep	Anjer 13 Oct	London 31 Dec	113
Cambalu Fraser	Shanghai 13 Sep	Anjer 22 Oct	London 21 Jan	130
Northfleet B Freeman	Macao 29 Sep	Anjer 27 Oct St H 18 Dec	London 21 Jan	114
Annandale Aitchison	Whampoa 29 Sep	Anjer 24 Oct	Plymouth 24 Jan London 31 Jan	124
Robin Hood G Cobb	Whampoa 1 Oct Hong Kong 3 Oct	Anjer 22 Oct	Start Pt 11 Jan London 16 Jan	107
Assyrian S Shepherd	Shanghai 8 Oct		London 1 Feb	116
Wynaud D Reid	Shanghai 9 Oct	Anjer 7 Nov CGH 14 Dec	off Penzance 14 Feb London 19 Feb	133
Mirage J Roberts	Whampoa 21 Oct		London 1 Feb	103
Lammermuir A Shewan	Whampoa 22 Oct	Anjer 10 Nov	Downs 31 Jan London 1 Feb	102
Valdivia A Halliday	Whampoa 25 Oct	Anjer 11 Nov	Dublin 13 Feb	111
Kelso Coulson	Foochow 26 Oct		off Scilly 13 Feb London 20 Feb	117
Kate Carnie D McLean	Whampoa 27 Oct		Downs 5 Feb London 8 Feb	104
Beemah Pickernell	Shanghai 3 Nov	Anjer 28 Nov St H 23 Jan	off Plymouth 6 Mar London 12 Mar	130
Friar Tuck J Darlington	Shanghai 9 Nov	Anjer 1 Dec St H 23 Jan	London 14 Mar	126
Strathmore J Mann	Shanghai 9 Nov Woosung 10 Nov	Anjer 4 Dec St H 26 Jan	London 14 Mar	126
Lord of the Isles W Jamieson	Whampoa 13 Nov	Anjer 29 Nov	London 14 Mar	122
Aden Bell	Whampoa 25 Nov		Liverpool 17 Mar	113
Lauderdale F Bowers	Foochow 29 Nov	Anjer 15 Dec	London 15 Mar	107
Florence (A) Wadsworth	Whampoa 12 Dec	Anjer 24 Dec	London 23 Mar	102
Spray of the Ocean Slaughter	Shanghai 23 Dec	Anjer 5 Jan	London 13 Apr	112
Florence (A) P Dumaresq	Woosung 26 Dec	Anjer 8 Jan	Deal 2 Apr London 4 Apr	99
Herculean J Bell	Whampoa 31 Dec	Anjer 15 Jan	London 11 Apr	102
Solent M Brooks	Shanghai 1 Jan	Anjer 18 Jan	London 10 Apr	100
Scawfell R Thomson	Foochow 14 Jan	Anjer 30 Jan	London 4 May	111
Robert Henderson A Walker	Whampoa 15 Jan	Anjer 28 Jan	London 4 May	110
Patna Smith	Shanghai 16 Jan	Anjer 3 Feb	London 11 May	116
Juanpore M King	Macao 19 Jan	Anjer 31 Jan	Portland 1 May London 7 May	109
Spirit of the North E Martin	Foochow 2 Feb	Anjer 20 Feb	London 25 May	113

Ship/Master	Sailed	Passed	Arrived	Days
Spartan / W Storey	Foochow 2 Feb	Anjer 20 Feb	London 30 May	118
Vanguard (1857) / A Scott	Shanghai 22 Feb		London 27 Jun	126
Banian / G Graham	Hong Kong 9 Mar	Anjer 3 Apr	London 28 Jun	111
Sir W F Williams / D Rees	Shanghai 24 Mar	Anjer 9 Apr	London 19 Jul	117
Corea / J Garry	Canton 28 Mar	Anjer 15 Apr	Liverpool 29 Jul	123
Star of the North / W P Buckham	Foochow 5 May	Anjer 7 Jun	London 11 Sep	129
Invincible / C Rollason	Shanghai 16 May		London 3 Oct	140

TEA SEASON 1860–61

Ship/Master	Sailed	Passed	Arrived	Days
Ellen Rodger / J Keay	Foochow 7 Jun		Deal 4 Oct / London 6 Oct	121
Ziba / Tomlinson	Foochow 7 Jun	Anjer 14 Jul	London 11 Oct	126
Falcon / P Maxton	Foochow 10 Jun	Anjer 10 Jul	London 28 Sep	110
Julia / J H Carter	Foochow 21 Jun		London 27 Oct	128
Chrysolite / A McLelland	Foochow 29 Jun	Anjer 5 Aug	London 30 Oct	123
Leichardt / R Barrett	Foochow 3 Jul		London 21 Nov	141
Jubilee / M A Jones	Shanghai 18 Jul	Anjer 27 Aug	London 20 Nov	125
Robin Hood / G Cobb	Foochow 19 July	Anjer 11 Aug	London 20 Nov	124
Polmaise / Guthrie	Foochow 24 Jul		London 3 Dec	132
Northfleet / B Freeman	Whampoa 27 July	Anjer 22 Aug	Deal 16 Nov / London 17 Nov	113
Veronica / R Robinson	Whampoa 2 Aug	Anjer 31 Aug	London 21 Nov	111
Flying Cloud (A) / Winsor	Foochow 6 Aug		London 7 Dec	123
Fairy (A) / Blish	Hong Kong 10 Aug	Anjer 30 Aug	London 3 Dec	115
Crest of the Wave / J Steele	Foochow 20 Aug	Anjer 10 Oct	London 8 Jan	141
Challenger / J Killick	Shanghai 24 Aug	Anjer 29 Sep	London 10 Dec	108
Celestial / J Legoe	Foochow 3 Sep		Belfast 7 Jan	126
Spirit of the Deep / J Hewitt	Whampoa 7 Sep	Anjer 31 Oct	London 26 Jan	141
Ballarat / H Jones	Shanghai 9 Sep	Anjer 10 Oct	London 24 Dec	106
Kelso / Coulson	Macao 19 Sep	Anjer 30 Oct / St H 27 Nov	Deal 1 Jan / London 3 Jan	106
Crystal Palace / Davey	Hong Kong 24 Sep	Anjer 29 Oct	London 31 Jan	129
Assyrian / S Shepherd	Shanghai 5 Oct	Anjer 27 Oct	London 24 Jan	111
Lord of the Isles / W Jamieson	Whampoa 23 Oct	Anjer 18 Nov / St H 3 Jan	London 18 Feb	118
Kate Carnie / D MacLean	Shanghai 26 Oct	Anjer 19 Nov	London 16 Feb	113
Wynaud / D Reid	Shanghai 26 Oct	Anjer 16 Nov / St H 3 Jan	Deal 16 Feb / London 18 Feb	115
Foam / G Innes	Foochow 28 Oct	Anjer 17 Nov	Deal 26 Feb / London 27 Feb	122
Chaa-sze / A Shewan	Whampoa 4 Nov		London 18 Feb	106
Friar Tuck / J Darlington	Hong Kong 5 Nov	St H 5 Jan	London 22 Feb	109
Ocean Mail / Adams	Shanghai 7 Nov / Woosung 8 Nov		Deal 16 Feb / London 18 Feb	103
Herculean / J Bell	Whampoa 13 Nov		wrecked 30 Nov (for Liverpool)	–
Mirage / J Roberts	Foochow 13 Nov		London 28 Feb	107
Solent / Passmore	Shanghai 27 Nov	Anjer 11 Dec	Deal 8 Mar / London 9 Mar	102
Lauderdale / F Bowers	Foochow 28 Nov	Anjer 13 Dec	Deal 19 Mar / London 20 Mar	112
Valdivia / A Halliday	Macao 3 Dec	Anjer 16 Dec	Liverpool 20 Mar	107
Patna / Smith (?)	Canton 12 Dec	Anjer 28 Dec	off Lizard 6 Apr / London 16 Apr	125
Aerolite / E Alleyne	Shanghai 22 Dec	Anjer 8 Jan	London 1 Apr	100
Queensberry / G Hefferman	Canton 29 Dec	Anjer 14 Jan	off Scilly 7 Apr / London 16 Apr	108
Cambalu / Fraser	Shanghai 3 Jan	Anjer 31 Jan	London 10 May	127
Scawfell / R Thomson	Whampoa 13 Jan / Canton R 14 Jan	Anjer 25 Jan	Liverpool 11 Apr	88
Spray of the Ocean / Slaughter	Foochow 31 Jan		London 27 May	116
Vanguard (1857) / A Scott	Macao 16 Feb	Anjer 26 Feb	London 19 Jun	123
Corea / J Garry	Canton 12 Mar	Anjer 1 Apr	London 9 Jul	119
Panic / Robinson	Hong Kong 2 Apr	Anjer 29 May / St H 23 Aug	London 25 Oct	206
Weymouth / Thomas	Whampoa 6 Apr	Anjer 10 May	London 21 Aug	137
Strathmore / J Mann	Whampoa 9 Apr	St H 20 Jul	London 5 Sep	149
Ziba / Tomlinson	Shanghai 14 May	Anjer 30 Jun	London 30 Sep	139

TEA SEASON 1861–62

Ship/Master	Sailed	Passed	Arrived	Days
Ellen Rodger / J Keay	Foochow 11 Jun		London 10 Oct	121
Falcon / P Maxton	Foochow 11 Jun	Anjer 21 Jul	London 9 Oct	120
Fiery Cross / J Dallas	Foochow 11 Jun		Downs 22 Sep / London 23 Sep	104
Flying Spur / J Ryrie	Foochow 14 Jun		off Falmouth 16 Oct / London 21 Oct	129
Robin Hood / G Cobb	Foochow 14 Jun		Liverpool 14 Oct	122
Veronica / R Robinson	Foochow 20 Jun		Liverpool 5 Nov	138
Highflyer / A Enright	Shanghai 27 Jun	St H 21 Sep	London 3 Nov	129
Banian / G Graham	Foochow 5 Jul	St H 27 Sep	London 8 Nov	126
Shakspere / Crosbie	Foochow 10 Jul		London 15 Nov	128
Chrysolite / T Roy	Shanghai 12 Jul		London 28 Nov	139
Northfleet / B Freeman	Canton 16 Jul / Macao 19 Jul	Anjer 27 Aug / St H 11 Oct	London 23 Nov	130
Invincible / Rollason	Foochow 17 Jul		London 6 Jan	169
Challenger / T Macey	Shanghai 18 Jul		London 21 Nov	126
Chaa-sze / A Shewan	Whampoa 23 Jul	Anjer 2 Sep	London 25 Nov	125
Sir W F Williams / D Rees	Foochow 25 Jul		London 2 Dec	130
Jubilee / M A Jones	Shanghai 2 Aug		London 3 Dec	123
Spirit of the North / C E Wise	Macao 5 Aug / Singapore 22 Oct	ashore Carimata Strait 21 Sep	London 10 Mar	217
Polmaise / Carter	Shanghai 20 Aug		off Plymouth 2 Jan / London 6 Jan	139
Kelso / Coulson	Canton 29 Aug	Anjer 27 Sep	London 17 Dec	110

Ship/Master	Sailed	Passed	Arrived	Days
Star of the North McQueen	Foochow – August		London –	–
Assyrian S Shepherd	Shanghai 13 Sep		London 14 Jan	123
Pegasus J Penrice	Shanghai 16 Sep	Anjer 25 Oct	London 14 Jan	120
Wynaud D Reid	Amoy 16 Sep		London 23 Jan	129
Gauntlet Welch	Foochow 17 Sep	CGH 26 Nov	London 16 Jan	121
Ballarat H Jones	Shanghai 28 Sep	Anjer 25 Oct	London 20 Jan	114
Lord of the Isles Barnett	Whampoa 2 Oct	Anjer 6 Nov	Deal 31 Jan London 3 Feb	124
Ocean Mail J Thomson	Shanghai 15 Oct		Deal 16 Feb	124
Spirit of the Deep J Hewitt	Shanghai 23 Oct	Anjer 23 Nov	London 22 Feb	122
Solent Passmore	Shanghai 23 Oct	Anjer 22 Nov	London 10 Mar	138
Foam G Innes	Foochow 24 Oct	Anjer 20 Nov St H 15 Jan	London 11 Mar	138
Leichardt T Clark	Shanghai 28 Oct		New York 28 Jan	92
Kate Carnie D McLean	Shanghai 30 Oct	Anjer 21 Nov	London 20 Feb	113
Mansfield Netherway	Amoy 12 Nov		New York 9 Mar	117
Patna Paul	Whampoa 14 Nov		Liverpool 9 Mar	115
Mirage J Roberts	Foochow 27 Nov	Anjer 7 Dec	C Hatteras 20 Feb New York 27 Feb	92
Celestial T Jones	Shanghai 16 Dec	Anjer 11 Jan	London 24 Apr	129
Flying Cloud (A) Winsor	Hong Kong 29 Dec	Anjer 7 Jan at St H 26 Feb to 9 Mar	London 20 Apr	112
Robert Henderson P Logan	Foochow 13 Jan		London 28 Apr	105
Juanpore M King	Shanghai 31 Jan		London 26 May	115
Fairlight Kemball	Shanghai 8 Feb		London 23 May	104
Vanguard (1857) A Scott	Hong Kong 13 Mar	Anjer 27 Mar St H 29 May	London 17 Jul	126
Corea J Garry	Canton 14 Mar	Anjer 1 Apr	London 5–12 Jul	–
Spray of the Ocean Slaughter	Shanghai 1 Apr	Anjer 10 May St H 3 Jul	London 7 Sep	159

TEA SEASON 1862–63

Ship/Master	Sailed	Passed	Arrived	Days
Fiery Cross R Robinson	Foochow 28 May		Wight 26 Sept London 29 Sept	122
Robin Hood J Mann	Foochow 29 May		London 13 Oct	137
Min John Smith	Foochow 31 May		London 9 Oct	131
Flying Spur J Ryrie	Foochow 2 Jun	Anjer 5 Jul	Wight 26 Sept London 29 Sept London 29 Sep	119 119
Falcon J Keay	Shanghai 13 Jun		London 13 Oct	122
Scawfell R Thomson	Hong Kong 14 Jun		London 15 Oct	123
Whinfell Yeo	Foochow 15 Jun		London 13 Oct	120
Ziba Fine	Shanghai 15 Jun	Anjer 13 Aug	London 12 Nov	150
Ellen Rodger Mackinnon	Foochow 19 Jun		London 13 Oct	116
Glenaros W P Buckham	Shanghai 19 Jun	Anjer 31 Jul	London 5 Oct	108

Ship/Master	Sailed	Passed	Arrived	Days
Banian Mumble	Hong Kong 30 Jun	St H 19 Sep	London 5 Nov	128
Challenger T Macey	Shanghai 9 Jul		London 14 Nov	128
Veronica Douglas	Foochow 12 Jul	St H 25 Oct	Liverpool 10 Dec	151
Kelso Coulson	Whampoa 17 Jul	Anjer 18 Aug	London 28 Nov	134
Shakspere Crosbie	Foochow 26 Jul	St H 25 Oct	London 10 Dec	137
Invincible Locke	Foochow 3 Aug	Anjer 4 Oct	London 29 Dec	148
Chaa-sze A Shewan	Canton 15 Aug	Anjer 17 Sep	London 15 Dec	122
Chrysolite T Roy	Whampoa 15 Aug	Anjer 27 Sep	Liverpool 28 Dec	135
Assyrian A Mearns	Shanghai 20 Aug	Anjer 29 Sep	London 29 Dec	131
Pegasus J Penrice	Shanghai 24 Aug		off Portland 23 Dec London 5 Jan	134
Ballarat H Jones	Shanghai 25 Aug	Anjer 30 Sep	London 29 Dec	126
Jubilee M A Jones	Shanghai 26 Aug	Anjer 4 Oct	London 1 Jan	128
Sir W F Williams D Rees	Shanghai 28 Aug	Anjer 2 Oct St H 13 Nov	London 30 Dec	124
Northfleet B Freeman	Whampoa 4 Sep Macao 7 Sep	Anjer 2 Oct St H 13 Nov	London 29 Dec	116
Ocean Mail Banks	Shanghai 12 Sep		London 30 Dec	109
Beemah T Johnson	Foochow 21 Sep		London 27 Jan	128
Weymouth Norris	Foochow 22 Sep	Anjer 29 Oct St H 26 Dec	London 10 Feb	141
Solent Passmore	Shanghai 14 Oct	Anjer 8 Nov	London 3 Feb	112
Lammermuir J Stewart	Foochow 21 Oct		London 6 Feb	108
Polmaise Carter	Foochow 2 Nov Sourabaya 26 Jan	in collision off Java Head	London 2 Jun	212
Gauntlet Welch	Whampoa 5 Nov		London 24 Feb	111
Dunmail Dinley	Whampoa 5 Nov	Anjer 26 Nov	London 7 Mar	122
Fairlight Kemball	Macao 8 Nov		London 2 Mar	114
Spirit of the Deep J Hewitt	Hong Kong 15 Nov	Anjer 28 Nov	Liverpool 5 Mar	110
Mirage J Roberts	Hong Kong 15 Nov	Anjer 1 Dec	London 9 Mar	114
Queen of Nations T Mitchell	Shanghai 28 Nov	Anjer 19 Dec	London 30 Mar	122
Harwood Forsyth	Shanghai 13 Dec	Anjer 30 Dec	London 17 Apr	125
Crest of the Wave J Steele	Shanghai 29 Dec	Anjer 12 Jan	Liverpool 16 Apr	108
Juanpore M King	Shanghai 8 Jan		Liverpool 24 Apr	106
Stornoway Clarke	Shanghai 21 Jan		Liverpool 31 May	130
Spirit of the North Steel	Shanghai 23 Jan	Anjer 17 Feb	off Kinsale 18 May Liverpool 25 May	122
Kate Carnie P Logan	Foochow 26 Jan	Anjer 12 Feb	London 29 May	123
Robert Henderson P Logan	Shanghai 27 Jan	Anjer 17 Feb	London 27 May	120
Red Riding Hood A Nicholson	Foochow 21 Feb		London 9 Jun	108
Leichardt T Clark	Shanghai 10 Mar	Anjer 8 Apr	off Falmouth 29 Jul (for London)	141
Lauderdale Hutchings	Canton 28 Mar	Anjer 23 Apr	London 29 Jul	123
Vanguard (1857) A Scott	Shanghai 31 Mar	Anjer 8 Apr St H 15 Jun	London 31 Jul	122

Ship/Master	Sailed	Passed	Arrived	Days
TEA SEASON 1863–64				
Fiery Cross / R Robinson	Foochow 27 May		London 7 Sep	103
Falcon / J Keay	Foochow 28 May		off Plymouth 2 Oct / London 4 Oct	129
Min / John Smith	Foochow 28 May		London 4 Oct	129
Flying Spur / J Ryrie	Foochow 1 Jun		London 4 Oct	125
Ellen Rodger / Mackinnon	Foochow 3 Jun		London 4 Oct	123
Robin Hood / J Mann	Foochow 4 Jun		London 4 Oct	122
Ziba / Jones	Foochow 5 Jun		Liverpool 19 Sep	106
Highflyer / A Enright	Foochow 8 Jun		London 19 Oct	133
Challenger / T Macey	Hankow 14 Jun / off Woosung –		off Falmouth 10 Oct / London 20 Oct	128
Coulnakyle / A Morrison	Shanghai 20 Jun		London 29 Oct	131
Silver Eagle / Longman	Shanghai 22 Jun	St H 16 Sep	London 30 Oct	130
Glenaros / W P Buckham	Shanghai 22 Jun		London 31 Oct	131
Chaa-sze / A Shewan	Shanghai 22 Jun		London 5 Nov	136
Valdivia / J Billington	Canton 25 Jun	Anjer 28 Jul	London 2 Nov	130
Kelso / Coulson	Whampoa 27 Jun	Anjer 28 Jul	London 23 Oct	118
Guinevere / McLean	Shanghai 27 Jun		London 28 Oct	123
Scawfell / R Thomson	Shanghai 2 Jul		London 30 Oct	120
Banian / Masters	Canton 5 Jul	Anjer 21 Aug	London 17 Nov	135
Whiteadder / F Bowers	Woosung 17 Jul		London 7 Nov	113
Chrysolite / Varian	Hong Kong 17 Jul	Anjer 21 Aug	London 14 Nov	120
Veronica / Douglas	Foochow 17 Jul		London 19 Dec	155
Aerolite / E Alleyne	Shanghai 20 Jul		London 16 Nov	119
Pegasus / J Penrice	Shanghai 21 Jul		London 21 Nov	123
Friar Tuck / Tierney	Foochow 23 Jul		wrecked Scilly 27 Nov	127
Whinfell / Whereat	Foochow 26 Jul		Deal 26 Nov / London 27 Nov	124
Assyrian / A Mearns	Shanghai 30 Jul	St H 28 Oct	Folkestone 5 Dec / London 28 Dec	151
Corea / J Gray	Foochow 2 Aug		London 23 Nov	113
Northfleet / W Symington	Canton 22 Aug	Anjer 28 Sep / St H 19 Nov	London 31 Dec	131
Strathmore / C Gale	Shanghai 24 Aug	Anjer 1 Oct / CGH 8 Nov	London 28 Dec	126
Spray of the Ocean / Slaughter	Foochow 25 Aug	dep Table Bay 9 Dec	London 5 Feb	164
Sir W F Williams / Corbel	Shanghai 25 Aug		London 16 Feb	174
Patna / Paul	Canton 27 Aug	Anjer 26 Sep	Liverpool 25 Dec	120
Solent / Passmore	Shanghai 1 Sep	Anjer 19 Oct	London 20 Jan	141
Jubilee / Grant	Shanghai 2 Sep	Anjer 20 Oct	off Plymouth 9 Feb / London 14 Feb	165
John Lidgett / Gamble	Hong Kong 16 Sep	Anjer 19 Oct / CGH 6 Dec	London 3 Feb	140
Gauntlet / Welch	Shanghai 26 Sep	Anjer 27 Oct	London 3 Feb	130
Queen of Nations / T Mitchell	Shanghai 2 Oct		London 9 Feb	130
Beemah / T Johnson	Foochow 8 Oct	Anjer 3 Nov	London 3 Feb	118
Julia / Bird	Shanghai 8 Oct	Anjer 7 Nov	London 2 Mar	146
Mimosa / Johnson	Foochow 24 Oct	Anjer 3 Nov / St H 9 Jan	London 3 Mar	131
Mirage / J Roberts	Shanghai 27 Oct	Anjer 20 Nov	off Scilly 19 Feb / London 2 Mar	127
Spirit of the Deep / J Hewitt	Shanghai 2 Nov	Anjer 23 Nov	London 7 Mar	126
Dunmail / Dinley	Canton 11 Nov	Anjer 29 Nov	London 9 Mar	118
Star of the North / Patterson	Shanghai 18 Nov	Anjer 7 Dec	Liverpool 12 Mar	115
Helen Nicholson / Halliday	Foochow 1 Dec		New York 15 Mar	104
Lammermuir / Jones	Woosung 17 Dec		wrecked 31 Dec (for London)	–
Young England (A) / Smith	Shanghai 18 Dec	Anjer 2 Jan	Liverpool 17 Mar	90
Nonpareil (A) / E W Smith	Shanghai 19 Dec	Anjer 1 Jan	Liverpool 15 Mar	87
Zingra / W Gould	Shanghai 26 Dec	Anjer 31 Dec (?)	Liverpool 20 Mar	85
Juanpore / Brown	Hong Kong 2 Jan		Liverpool 13 Apr	102
Kate Carnie / Brockenridge	Shanghai 14 Jan		New York 27 Apr	104
Weymouth / Norris	Foochow 15 Jan		Portland 8 May / London 12 May	118
Pak Wan / Wawn	Foochow 25 Jan / over Bar 31 Jan	St H 26 Mar	Deal 10 May / London 12 May	108
Queensberry / Dunne	Shanghai 29 Jan	Anjer 13 Feb	off R Mersey 9 May / Liverpool 11 May	103
Stornoway / Tomlins	Shanghai 11 Feb		Deal 20 Jun / London 22 Jun	132
Polmaise / C Butler	Shanghai 24 Feb		Liverpool 20 Jun	117
Crest of the Wave / Ellis	Hong Kong 27 Feb		Liverpool 19 Jun	113
Robert Henderson / P Logan	Foochow 6 Mar		Deal 20 Jun / London 21 Jun	107
Vanguard (1857) / A Scott	Hong Kong 11 Mar		London 26 Jun	107
Black Prince / W Inglis	Hong Kong 23 Mar		Liverpool 24 Jun	93
Spirit of the North / Halliday	Shanghai 24 Mar	Anjer 13 May	Queenstown 30 Aug (for Liverpool)	159
Lauderdale / Hutchings	Shanghai 6 Apr	Anjer 14 May	Liverpool 10 Aug	126
Elizabeth Nicholson / Ewart	Shanghai 18 May		Liverpool 23 Sep	128
TEA SEASON 1864–65				
Fiery Cross / R Robinson	Foochow 29 May		Deal 19 Sep / London 20 Sep	114
Flying Spur / Gunn	Foochow 1 Jun		off Penzance 1 Oct / London 13 Oct	134
Serica / G Innes	Foochow 2 Jun	Anjer 4 Jul	Deal 18 Sep / London 19 Sep	109
Belted Will / Graham	Hong Kong 3 Jun		London 20 Sep	109
Young Lochinvar / R Glass	Foochow 4 Jun	Ascension 28 Aug	off Plymouth 2 Oct / London 8 Oct	126
Robin Hood / J Darlington	Foochow 6 Jun		off Seaford 2 Oct / London 6 Oct	122
Scawfell / R Thomson	Whampoa 7 Jun	Anjer 14 Jul	off Penzance 7 Oct / London 13 Oct	128

Ship/Master	Sailed	Passed	Arrived	Days
Min / John Smith	Foochow 11 Jun		London 14 Oct	125
Eliza Shaw / J Steele	Shanghai 14 Jun	Anjer 25 Jul	London 21 Oct	129
Ziba / Jones	Foochow 14 Jun		Liverpool 13 Oct	121
Challenger / T Macey	Hankow 17 Jun / Kiukiang 20 Jun		London 25 Oct	130
Guinevere / McLean	Shanghai 17 Jun		London 20 Oct	125
Yang-tsze / W Billing	Foochow 17 Jun		London 22 Oct	127
Ellen Rodger / E Cobbett	Foochow 19 Jun		London 21 Oct	124
Falcon / J Keay	Woosung 20 Jun (dep Hankow 10 Jun)		Start Pt 11 Oct / London 14 Oct	116
Glenaros / W P Buckham	Macao 25 Jun	Anjer 26 Jul	London 20 Oct	117
Kelso / Coulson	Hong Kong 25 Jun		London 24 Oct	121
Whinfell / Whereat	Foochow 30 Jun		London 15 Nov	138
Silver Eagle / Longman	Shanghai 8 Jul	St H 30 Sep	London 11 Nov	126
Pegasus / J Penrice	Shanghai 8 Jul		London 14 Nov	129
Whitadder / Bell	Shanghai 8 Jul		London 17 Nov	132
Childers / A Enright	Foochow 9 Jul	Anjer 12 Aug	London 21 Oct	104
Highflyer / Smith	Shanghai 11 Jul		London 17 Nov	129
Fychow / Mathers	Shanghai 12 Jul		London 17 Nov	128
Banian / Masters	Whampoa 14 Jul	Anjer 15 Aug / St H 25 Sep	London 15 Nov	124
Red Riding Hood / A Nicholson	Foochow 17 Jul	Anjer 16 Aug	off Falmouth 9 Nov / London 14 Nov	120
Assyrian / A Mearns	Shanghai 2 Aug	Anjer 14 Sep	London 7 Dec	127
Chaa-sze / A Shewan	Hong Kong 6 Aug		Liverpool 6 Dec	122
Valdivia / J Billington	Canton 9 Aug		London 8 Dec	121
Solent / Paige	Shanghai 22 Aug		London 28 Dec	128
Wild Deer / G Cobb	Shanghai 24 Aug	Anjer 25 Sep	London 4 Dec	102
Everest / Curwen	Whampoa 17 Sep	Anjer 16 Oct	Liverpool 5 Jan	110
Coulnakyle / A Morrison	Hong Kong 28 Sep	Anjer 27 Oct	London 18 Jan	112
Veronica / Douglas	Foochow 28 Sep	Anjer 29 Oct	Liverpool 3 Feb	128
Patna / Lewis	Shanghai 30 Sep	Anjer 29 Oct	Liverpool 3 Feb	126
Leichardt / R Getting	Shanghai 3 Oct		London 4 Feb	124
Queen of Nations / T Mitchell	Shanghai 6 Oct		London 31 Jan	117
Taeping / MacKinnon	Amoy 8 Oct	Anjer 25 Oct	Deal 4 Jan / London 5 Jan	89
Gauntlet / Hudson	Foochow 21 Oct		London 2 Feb	104
Beemah / T Johnson	Shanghai 27 Oct		Deal 2 Feb / London 3 Feb	99
Aerolite / E Alleyne	Shanghai 17 Nov		Liverpool 23 Feb	98
Juanpore / Wilson	Macao 24 Dec	St H 3 Mar	London 3 May	130
Star of the North / Patterson	Foochow 2 Jan		London 4 May	122
Spirit of the Deep / J Hewitt	Shanghai 6 Jan	Anjer 22 Jan / St H 17 Mar	London 5 May	119
Jubilee / Grant	Shanghai 18 Jan		London 8 Jun	141
Queensberry / R Binnie	Shanghai 16 Mar	Anjer 6 Apr	Liverpool 16 Jul	122
Vanguard (1857) / A Scott	Shanghai 8 Apr		London 29 Aug	143
Sir W F Williams / E Wilson	Zebu 10 Apr		London 8 Aug	120
Mirage / J Campbell	Shanghai 22 May	dep Simons Bay 27 Aug	London 21 Oct	152

TEA SEASON 1865–66

Ship/Master	Sailed	Passed	Arrived	Days
Yang-tsze / Kemball	Foochow 26 May		off Plymouth 5 Oct / London 9 Oct	136
Ziba / Jones	Foochow 27 May		London 7 Oct	133
Fiery Cross / R Robinson	Foochow 28 May	Anjer 22 Jun	Isle of Wight 10 Sep / London 11 Sep	106
Serica / G Innes	Foochow 28 May	Anjer 22 Jun	Isle of Wight 10 Sep / London 11 Sep	106
Childers / A Enright	Foochow 30 May		wrecked 30 May (for London)	–
Flying Spur / J Ryrie	Foochow 31 May		off Penzance 4 Oct / London 8 Oct	130
Belted Will / A Locke	Macao 5 Jun		off Plymouth 4 Oct / London 8 Oct	125
Black Prince / W Inglis	Macao 5 Jun	Anjer 10 Jul / St H 22 Aug	Falmouth 5 Oct / London 9 Oct	126
Min / John Smith	Foochow 8 Jun	Anjer 8 Jul	London 9 Oct	123
Young Lochinvar / R Glass	Foochow 9 Jun	Anjer 8 Jul	London 7 Oct	120
Silver Eagle / Longman	Hankow 9 Jun	St H 4 Sep	Deal 11 Oct / London 14 Oct	127
Eliza Shaw / J Steele	Woosung 11 Jun (dep Hankow 6 Jun)		off Plymouth 3 Oct / London 7 Oct	118
Pak Wan / Wawn	Macao 14 Jun	Anjer 20 Jul	off Lizard 4 Oct / London 8 Oct	116
Guinevere / McLean	Shanghai 24 Jun	St H 29 Sep	London 16 Nov	145
Challenger / H W Browne	Woosung 28 Jun (dep Hankow 24 Jun)	Lombok 3 Aug	Start Pt 14 Oct / London 17 Oct	111
Taeping / MacKinnon	Shanghai 29 Jun		Downs 9 Oct / London 11 Oct	104
Northfleet / W Symington	Macao 2 Jul	Anjer 6 Aug / St H 12 Sep	London 27 Oct	117
Highflyer / Shutter	Shanghai 5 Jul	St H 11 Oct	London 20 Nov	138
Lauderdale / Hutchings	Foochow 6 Jul		London 20 Nov	137
Pegasus / J Penrice	Hankow 15 Jul		London 8 Dec	146
Weymouth / Norris	Shanghai 21 Jul	St H 22 Oct	London 7 Dec	139
Ethiopian / W Edwards	Shanghai 22 Jul		London 21 Nov	122
Valdivia / J Skelly	Canton 23 Jul		London 8 Dec	138
Dunmail / Birkett	Foochow 24 Jul		London 19 Dec	148
Elizabeth Nicholson / Crosbie	Shanghai 29 Jul		London 8 Dec	132
Golden Spur / Le Lacheur	Shanghai 31 Jul		London 9 Dec	131
Chaa-sze / A Shewan	Foochow 1 Aug	Anjer 10 Sep	London 18 Dec	139
Everest / Clarke	Foochow 5 Aug	Anjer 11 Sep	Liverpool 8 Dec	125
Whinfell / Whereat	Foochow 7 Aug	St H 25 Nov	London 23 Dec	138

Ship/Master	Sailed	Passed	Arrived	Days
Ellen Rodger / Tompkins	Shanghai 9 Aug	Anjer 14 Oct / St H 11 Dec	London 22 Jan	166
John Lidgett / Robertson	Hong Kong 19 Aug / Singapore 25 Oct (after repairs)	Ascension 13 Jan	Singapore 6 Sep / off Isle of Wight 26 Feb	18 / 126
Fychow / Mathers	Hankow 29 Aug	Anjer 11 Oct / St H 21 Nov	London 27 Dec	120
Kelso / Black	Shanghai 1 Sep		London 20 Jan	141
Scawfell / R Thomson	Hong Kong 3 Sep	St H 20 Nov	London 27 Dec	115
Veronica / Douglas	Hong Kong 15 Sep		Liverpool 21 Jan	128
Douglas Castle / McRitchie	Foochow 2 Oct		New York – Jan	–
Glenaros / W P Buckham	Foochow 4 Oct	Anjer 30 Oct	New York 17 Jan	105
Polmaise / C Butler	Shanghai 24 Oct		Deal 4 Feb / London 7 Feb	106
Chrysolite / Varian	Hong Kong 27 Oct	Ascension 22 Jan	London 23 Mar	147
Patna / Lewis?	Shanghai 27 Oct	Anjer 25 Nov	Liverpool 24 Mar	148
Wild Deer / G Cobb	Shanghai 28 Oct		London 3 Feb	98
Banian / Shiell	Amoy 28 Oct		London 15 Feb	110
Helen Nicholson / Halliday	Shanghai 1 Nov	Anjer 21 Nov	Deal 4 Feb / London 7 Feb	98
Beemah / T Johnson	Foochow 20 Nov	Anjer 5 Jan / St H 22 Jan	Deal 13 Mar / London 15 Mar	116
Invincible / Tallentyre	Shanghai 20 Nov	Anjer 10 Dec	Deal 13 Mar / London 15 Mar	116
Corea / J Garry	Foochow 23 Nov	Anjer 11 Dec	London 21 Mar	119
Juanpore / Wilson	Foochow 7 Dec		London 25 Mar	108
Assyrian / A Mearns	Foochow 28 Dec	Anjer 14 Jan	off Falmouth 3 Apr / London 14 Apr	107
Peter Denny / G Adams	Shanghai 2 Jan		London 14 May	114
Aerolite / E Alleyne	Shanghai 12 Feb	Anjer 17 Mar	Liverpool 19 Jun	127
Jubilee / Grant	Shanghai 6 Mar	Anjer 11 Apr	London 21 Jul	137
Vanguard (1857) / A Scott	Shanghai 2 May	Anjer 2 Jun	London 11 Sep	132

TEA SEASON 1866–67

Ship/Master	Sailed	Passed	Arrived	Days
Ariel / J Keay	Foochow 28 May / over Bar 30 May	Anjer 20 Jun / St H 29 Jul	Downs 6 Sep / London 6 Sep	101
Fiery Cross / R Robinson	Foochow 29 May / over Bar 29 May	Anjer 18 Jun / St H 28 Jul	Downs 7 Sep / London 8 Sep	102
Serica / G Innes	Foochow 30 May / over Bar 30 May	Anjer 22 Jun / St H 29 Jul	Downs 6 Sep / London 6 Sep	99
Taeping / MacKinnon	Foochow 30 May / over Bar 30 May	Anjer 20 Jun / St H 27 Jul	Downs 6 Sep / London 6 Sep	99
Taitsing / D Nutsford	Foochow 31 May	Anjer 26 Jun / St H 5 Aug	Downs 9 Sep / London 9 Sep	101
Ziba / G Bowes	Foochow 2 Jun	Anjer 29 Jun	Liverpool 25 Sep	115
Black Prince / W Inglis	Foochow 3 Jun	Anjer 3 Jul	London 20 Sep	109
Guinevere / McLean	Hankow 3 Jun		wrecked 4 Jun (for London)	–
Chinaman / Downie	Foochow 5 Jun		London 2 Oct	119
Flying Spur / J Ryrie	Foochow 5 Jun	Anjer 13 Jul	off Penzance 29 Sep / London 5 Oct	122
Ada / Jones	Foochow 6 Jun	Anjer 11 Jul	off Penzance 29 Sep / London 4 Oct	120
Falcon / J J Gunn	Foochow 7 Jun		Deal 3 Oct / London 4 Oct	119
Belted Will / A Locke	Hong Kong 9 Jun		off Falmouth 24 Sep / London 26 Sep	109
Min / John Smith	Hankow 9 Jun		London 15 Oct	128
Yang-tsze / Kemball	Foochow 12 Jun		off Scilly 10 Oct / London 17 Oct	127
Eliza Shaw / J Steele	Hankow 13 Jun		London 15 Oct	124
Ethiopian / W Edwards	Shanghai 20 Jun / Woosung 21 Jun	St H 4 Sep / Fayal 29 Sep	Start Pt 15 Oct / London 18 Oct	120
Lennox Castle / Dobbie	Hankow 27 Jun	St H 22 Sep	London 5 Nov	131
Sir Lancelot / McDougall	Shanghai 2 Jul	via Eastern Route	London 5 Nov	126
John R Worcester / W Brown	Shanghai 9 Jul		London 31 Oct	114
Pak Wan / Wawn	Shanghai 9 Jul		London 16 Nov	130
Maitland / Coulson	Foochow 11 Jul		London 23 Oct	104
Highflyer / Clayton	Shanghai 13 Jul (dep Hankow 10 Jun) Capt Shutter died at Shanghai	Got ashore in Yangtsze R	London 16 Nov	126
Coulnakyle / A Morrison	Shanghai 16 Jul	via Hong Kong	London 15 Nov	122
Fusi Yama / G F Thomson	Shanghai 17 Jul		London 21 Nov	127
Everest / Clarke	Foochow 18 Jul	Anjer 20 Aug	Liverpool 4 Nov	109
Lauderdale / Hutchings	Shanghai 21 Jul	Anjer 12 Sep	London 28 Nov	130
Coral Nymph / Winchester	Shanghai 23 Jul / pilot left 29 Jul	via Lombok Strt / CGH 9 Oct	Dungeness 18 Nov / London 21 Nov	121
Challenger / H W Browne	Shanghai 3 Aug		London 13 Dec	132
Valdivia / J Clements	Canton 7 Aug	Anjer 12 Sep	London 10 Dec	125
Ellen Rodger / E Corbett	Foochow 24 Aug		wrecked 20 Sep (for London)	–
Veronica / Brown	Foochow 26 Aug		Liverpool 22 Jan	149
Wild Deer / G Cobb	Shanghai 7 Sep	Anjer 14 Oct	London 28 Dec	112
Polmaise / C Butler	Shanghai 19 Sep	Ascension 11 Dec	London 28 Jan	131
Northfleet / W Symington	Hong Kong 25 Sep	St H 15 Dec	London 28 Jan	125
Kelso / Black	Canton 27 Sep		London 28 Jan	123
Helen Nicholson / Halliday	Hankow 29 Sep		Downs 9 Jan / London 10 Jan	103
Solent / Passmore	Hong Kong 30 Sep	Anjer 30 Oct / St H 20 Dec	London 1 Feb	124
Scawfell / R Thomson	Foochow 7 Oct		Deal 12 Jan / London 15 Jan	100
Sir W F Williams / E Wilson	Shanghai 13 Oct	Repairing at CGH 15 Dec to 11 Jan	London 25 Mar	163
Juanpore / Wilson	Shanghai 17 Oct	St H 11 Jan	London 26 Feb	132
Dunmail / P Thompson	Foochow 24 Oct	Anjer 28 Nov	Downs 2 Feb / London 4 Feb	103
Gauntlet / Hudson	Foochow 1 Nov	Anjer 3 Dec / St H 26 Jan	Scilly 18 Mar / London 27 Mar	146
John Bunyan / Allan	Nagasaki 7 Nov		London 25 Mar	138
Banian / Chase	Hong Kong 20 Nov	Anjer 10 Dec	London 25 Mar	125
Elizabeth Nicholson / Crosbie	Shanghai 23 Nov		London 9 Mar	106
Douglas Castle / McRitchie	Singapore 26 Nov	Anjer 2 Dec	London 26 Mar	120

Ship/Master	Sailed	Passed	Arrived	Days
Kate Carnie Brockenridge	Foochow 10 Dec		New York 7 Apr	118
Weymouth Norris	Foochow 12 Dec		Downs 25 Mar London 26 Mar	104
Assyrian A Mearns	Shanghai 14 Dec		New York 9 Apr	116
Harlaw Phillips	Shanghai 17 Dec	Anjer 30 Dec	Falmouth 21 Mar London 25 Mar	98
John Lidgett Polson	Foochow 5 Jan	St H 14 Mar	London 27 Apr	112
Beemah E W Hawkins	Shanghai 9 Jan	Anjer 1 Feb	Isle of Wight 13 May London 30 May	141
Dilpussund Jones	Hong Kong 25 Jan		London 17 May	112
Stornoway Tomlins	Hong Kong 2 Feb	Anjer 13 Mar	London 27 May	114
Red Riding Hood Henderson	Foochow 12 Feb	Anjer 25 Feb	London 28 May	105
Vanguard (1857) A Scott	Shanghai 16 Apr	Anjer 20 May	London 2 Sep	139

TEA SEASON 1867–68

Ship/Master	Sailed	Passed	Arrived	Days
Maitland Coulson	Foochow 1 Jun		Downs 23 Sep London 24 Sep	115
Serica G Innes	Foochow 1 Jun over Bar 2 Jun		London 28 Sep	119
Belted Will A Locke	Macao 2 Jun	Anjer 1 Jul St H 18 Aug	London 24 Sep	114
Taeping J Dowdy	Foochow 3 Jun over Bar 4 Jun	Anjer 27 Jun	London 14 Sep	103
Fiery Cross Kirkup	Foochow 4 Jun over Bar 5 Jun	Anjer 1 Jul	London 23 Sep	111
Whiteadder F W Moore	Foochow 6 Jun	Anjer 1 Jul	London 7 Oct	123
Min Sargent	Whampoa 7 Jun	Anjer 12 Jul CGH 14 Aug	Deal 7 Oct London 8 Oct	123
Flying Spur J Ryrie	Foochow 8 Jun	Ascension 26 Aug	London 2 Oct	116
Ziba G Bowes	Foochow 8 Jun		London 7 Oct	121
Taitsing D Nutsford	Foochow 9 Jun	Anjer 14 Jul	London 7 Oct	120
Black Prince W Inglis	Foochow 10 Jun	Anjer 14 Jul	London 7 Oct	119
John R Worcester Wawn	Shanghai 10 Jun		London 12 Oct	124
Yang-tsze Kemball	Foochow 12 Jun	Anjer 14 Jul	off Lizard 3 Oct London 7 Oct	117
Ariel J Keay	Foochow 12 Jun over Bar 13 Jun	Anjer 9 Jul St H 18 Aug	off Lizard 21 Sep London 23 Sep	103
Chinaman Downie	Foochow 14 Jun	Anjer 18 Jul	London 7 Oct	115
Sir Lancelot R Robinson	Shanghai 15 Jun Woosung 16 Jun	via Eastern Route	Mizen Head 19 Sep London 23 Sep	100
Eliza Shaw J Steele	Woosung 15 Jun (dep Hankow 11 Jun)		London 11 Oct	118
Challenger H W Browne	Woosung 17 Jun (dep Hankow 14 Jun)	Anjer 12 Aug	Deal 18 Oct London 19 Oct	124
Golden Spur Le Lacheur	Foochow 18 Jun		London 15 Oct	119
Ada Jones	Hankow 19 Jun		Deal 18 Oct London 19 Oct	122
Whinfell Jones	Shanghai 21 Jun		London 9 Nov	141
Everest Clarke	Foochow 25 Jun	Anjer 12 Aug St H 6 Sep	Liverpool 30 Oct	127
Silver Eagle Case	Shanghai 3 Jul		London 12 Dec	162
Coulnakyle A Morrison	Shanghai 7 Jul		London 10 Dec	156
Falcon J J Gunn	Canton 8 Jul	Anjer 12 Aug	London 31 Oct	115

Ship/Master	Sailed	Passed	Arrived	Days
Argonaut A Nicholson	Foochow 10 Jul	Anjer 18 Aug	London 29 Oct	111
Lennox Castle Brunton	Shanghai 10 Jul	Anjer 30 Sep	London 2 Dec	145
Peter Denny G Adams	Shanghai 16 Jul		London 10 Dec	147
Coral Nymph Winchester	Shanghai 30 Jul		London 17 Dec	140
Dunmail P Thompson	Shanghai 3 Aug		London 27 Dec	146
Helen Nicholson Halliday	Shanghai 7 Aug	St H 13 Nov	London 27 Dec	142
Pegasus J Penrice	Shanghai 8 Aug	St H 26 Nov	London 14 Jan	159
Wild Deer Ganzwyk	Shanghai 13 Aug	Anjer 22 Oct	London 15 Jan	155
Fusi Yama G F Thomson	Shanghai 14 Aug	Anjer 17 Oct	London 18 Jan	157
Invincible Beeching	Shanghai 19 Aug	dep Mauritius 26 Oct	London 13 Jan	147
Pak Wan Shiell	Foochow 22 Aug	Anjer 5 Oct	off Scilly 29 Dec London 7 Jan	138
Scawfell R Thomson	Foochow 27 Aug	Anjer 28 Sep	London 28 Dec	123
Jubilee P Kerr	Shanghai 27 Aug	Anjer 4 Oct	off Penzance 9 Jan London 13 Jan	139
Titania R Deas	Shanghai 2 Sep	Anjer 9 Oct	London 26 Dec	115
Juanpore Phillips	Shanghai 4 Sep		London 22 Feb	171
Douglas Castle McRitchie	Shanghai 12 Oct	Anjer 12 Nov	London 6 Feb	117
Weymouth Norris	Shanghai 13 Oct	Anjer 13 Nov	London 18 Feb	128
Veronica Brown	Canton 22 Oct	Anjer 9 Nov	Liverpool 17 Feb	118
Kelso Barnet	Hong Kong 23 Oct		London 20 Feb	120
Ethiopian Faulkner	Shanghai 27 Oct	Anjer 1 Dec	London 4 Mar	129
Cleta Middleton	Hong Kong 31 Oct		New York 6 Mar	127
Polmaise C Butler	Hong Kong 7 Nov	Anjer 25 Nov	London 17 Feb	102
Banian Chase	Amoy 11 Nov		New York –	–
Solent Nixon	Foochow 16 Nov		New York 16 Feb	92
Dilpussund Jones	Shanghai 16 Nov		London 10 Mar	115
Corea R Carr	Canton 23 Nov	Ascension 30 Jan	London 10 Mar	108
John Lidgett Polson	Shanghai 25 Nov	Anjer 16 Dec	London 15 Mar	111
Lauderdale G Moodie	Foochow 27 Nov		London 5 Mar	99
Elizabeth Nicholson Crosbie	Foochow 14 Dec	Anjer 26 Dec	London 15 Mar	92
Glenaros Roberts	Shanghai 22 Dec	Anjer 13 Jan	London 22 Apr	122
Patna Jones	Foochow 26 Dec	Anjer 11 Jan St H 16 Mar	London 13 May	139
Harlaw Phillips	Shanghai 7 Jan	Anjer 16 Jan	London 20 Apr	104
Beemah Wakeham	Foochow 17 Jan	Anjer 31 Jan St H 17 Mar	London 29 Apr	103
Assyrian A Mearns	Shanghai 13 Mar		London 20 Jul	129
Chaa-sze A Shewan	Macao 2 Apr	Anjer 23 Apr	London 3 Aug	123

Ship/Master	Sailed	Passed	Arrived	Days
TEA SEASON 1868–69				
Belted Will A Locke	Macao 25 May	Anjer 22 Jun	off Falmouth 3 Sep / London 8 Sep	106
Ariel J Keay	Foochow 28 May	Anjer 22 Jun	off Falmouth 31 Aug / London 2 Sep	97
Sir Lancelot R Robinson	Foochow 28 May	Anjer 22 Jun	Deal 2 Sep / London 3 Sep	98
Taeping J Dowdy	Foochow 28 May	Anjer 22 Jun / CGH 20 Jul	Land's End 2 Sep / London 7 Sep	102
Spindrift G Innes	Foochow 29 May	Anjer 23 Jun	Isle of Wight 1 Sep / London 3 Sep	97
Lahloo John Smith	Foochow 30 May	Anjer 23 Jun	off Lizard 3 Sep / London 8 Sep	101
Undine Scott	Canton 30 May		off Needles 9 Sep / London 11 Sep	104
Black Prince W Inglis	Foochow 31 May	Anjer 28 Jun	Deal 30 Sep / London 1 Oct	123
Serica Middleton	Foochow 1 Jun	Anjer 29 Jun	London 22 Sep	113
Fiery Cross Beckett	Foochow 2 Jun	St H 19 Aug	London 1 Oct	121
Ziba G Bowes	Foochow 3 Jun		London 8 Oct	127
Chinaman Downie	Foochow 4 Jun	Anjer 9 Jul / St H 23 Aug	London 30 Sep	118
Min Melville	Shanghai 7 Jun		London 23 Oct	138
Yang-tsze Kemball	Foochow 7 Jun		London 8 Oct	123
Leander Petherick	Shanghai 13 Jun	Anjer 10 Jul	Deal 29 Sep / London 30 Sep	109
Forward Ho! Hossack	Shanghai 13 Jun		Deal 16 Oct / London 17 Oct	126
Titania R Deas	Shanghai 13 Jun	St H 5 Sep	off Scilly 13 Oct / London 17 Oct	126
Everest Clarke	Foochow 14 Jun	St H 6 Sep	Liverpool 17 Oct	125
Taitsing Nutsford	Shanghai 15 Jun	St H 10 Sep	London 19 Oct	126
Eliza Shaw G Gaye	Woosung 16 Jun (dep Hankow 11 Jun)		London 19 Oct	125
Falcon J J Gunn	Macao 18 Jun (dep Canton 13 Jun)	Anjer 19 Jul	London 19 Oct	123
Golden Spur Ronald	Macao 20 Jun		London 2 Nov	135
Whinfell Jones	Shanghai 24 Jun		London 4 Nov	133
Ada Jones	Foochow 22 Jun		London 26 Oct	126
Whiteadder F W Moore	Shanghai 24 Jun		London 2 Nov	131
Challenger H W Browne	Woosung 24 Jun (dep Hankow 20 Jun)	St H 28 Sep	London 19 Nov	148
Lennox Castle McQueen	Shanghai 3 Jul		London 2 Nov	122
Flying Spur Atkinson	Foochow 4 Jul		London 4 Nov	123
Coral Nymph Winchester	Shanghai 8 Jul		London 9 Dec	154
Helen Nicholson Halliday	Shanghai 9 Jul	Anjer 13 Aug	London 4 Nov	118
John R Worcester Wawn	Foochow 10 Jul		London 2 Nov	115
Argonaut A Nicholson	Shanghai 13 Jul		London 3 Nov	113
Douglas Castle McRitchie	Shanghai 22 Jul		London 23 Nov	124
Wild Deer James Smith	Shanghai 26 July		off Scilly 16 Nov / London 23 Nov	120
Scawfell R Thomson	Foochow 26 Jul	Anjer 3 Sep	London 26 Nov	123
Dunmail P Thompson	Macao 29 Jul	Anjer 1 Sep	London 23 Nov	117
Peter Denny G Adams	Foochow 31 Jul		London 23 Nov	115
Vanguard (1857) T Hunter	Foochow 6 Aug	Anjer 21 Oct	London 16 Jan	163
Weymouth Gibson	Shanghai 16 Aug		London 30 Dec	136
Fusi Yama M C Borup	Hong Kong 17 Aug		Deal 22 Dec / London 23 Dec	128
Red Riding Hood Henderson	Foochow 22 Aug	Anjer 9 Oct / St H 25 Nov	London 7 Jan	138
Coulnaykyle A Morrison	Foochow 26 Aug	Anjer 15 Oct / Ascension 7 Dec	London 14 Jan	141
Jubilee P Kerr	Foochow 28 Aug	Anjer 6 Oct	London 28 Dec	122
Valdivia Sennett	Shanghai 30 Aug	Anjer 7 Oct	London 28 Dec	122
Pegasus Mackay	Shanghai 30 Aug	Anjer 6 Oct / St H 23 Nov	London 30 Dec	122
Juanpore Brown	Shanghai 30 Aug	Anjer 15 Oct	London 22 Jan	144
Maitland Coulson	Shanghai 8 Oct	Anjer 3 Nov / St H 19 Dec	London 25 Jan	109
Pak Wan Shiell	Shanghai 20 Oct		Deal 5 Feb / London 6 Feb	109
Dilpussund Jones	Shanghai 2 Nov	Anjer 16 Nov	New York 12 Feb	102
Corea R Carr	Macao 2 Nov	Anjer 27 Nov / Ascension 14 Jan	London 18 Feb	108
Ethiopian Faulkner	Shanghai 2 Nov	Anjer 5 Dec	London 1 Mar	119
Veronica Halden	Foochow 4 Nov	Anjer 5 Dec / St H 26 Jan	Liverpool 12 Mar	128
Polmaise C Butler	Woosung 14 Nov	Anjer 7 Dec / St H 23 Jan	Prawle Pt 1 Mar / London 5 Mar	111
Banian Chase	Shanghai 20 Nov		New York 24 Mar	124
John Lidgett Polson	Macao 27 Nov	St H 8 Feb	London 27 Mar	120
Elizabeth Nicholson Crosbie	Foochow 14 Dec		New York 31 Mar	107
Lauderdale G Moodie	Foochow 24 Dec		New York 12 Apr	109
Kelso M Vowell	Macao 8 Jan	Anjer 20 Jan / CGH 21 Feb	Deal 16 Apr / London 19 Apr	101
Glenaros Roberts	Foochow 9 Jan	Anjer 25 Jan	New York 20 Apr	101
Cleta Middleton	Foochow 9 Jan		New York 23 Apr	104
Harlaw Phillips	Shanghai 11 Jan	St H 25 Mar	Deal 16 Apr	95
Beemah Wakeham	Foochow 11 Jan	St H 25 Mar	London 6 May	115
Omba G F Thomson	Whampoa 3 Feb	Anjer 15 Feb / St H 19 Apr	Deal 2 Jun / London 3 Jun	120
Assyrian A Mearns	Shanghai 14 Feb	Anjer 7 Mar	London 17 Jun	123
Everest Clarke	Shanghai 2 Apr		London 28 Jul	117
Undine Scott	Shanghai 2 Apr		London 2 Aug	122
Chinaman J Downie	Shanghai 5 Apr		New York 5 Aug	122
TEA SEASON 1869–70				
Forward Ho! Hossack	Shanghai 12 Jun	Anjer 20 Jul	London 2 Oct	112
Eliza Shaw G Gaye	Woosung 13 Jun (dep Hankow 9 Jun)	Eastern Route	Deal 13 Oct / London 14 Oct	123
Titania W H Burgoyne	Shanghai 16 Jun / Woosung 17 Jun	Anjer 15 Jul	Deal 21 Sep / London 22 Sep	98

237

Ship/Master	Sailed	Passed	Arrived	Days
Taitsing / H Bloomfield	Woosung 23 Jun		London 14 Oct	113
Lennox Castle / Talbot	Woosung 23 Jun (from Hankow)		Deal 6 Nov / London 6 Nov	136
Whinfell / Jones	Woosung 26 Jun		London 3 Nov	130
Helen Nicholson / Halliday	Woosung 28 Jun		Deal 6 Nov	131
Ariel / Courtenay	Foochow 1 Jul	via Eastern Route	off Plymouth 9 Oct / London 12 Oct	103
Leander / Petherick	Foochow 1 Jul	Anjer 27 Jul	off Scilly 7 Oct / London 12 Oct	103
Argonaut / A Nicholson	Shanghai 2 Jul	Anjer 3 Aug	Dover 19 Oct	109
Thermopylae / Kemball	Foochow 3 Jul	Anjer 27 Jul / C Agulhas 21 Aug	off Lizard 30 Sep / London 2 Oct	91
Lahloo / John Smith	Foochow 3 Jul	via Eastern Route	off Eddystone 9 Oct / London 12 Oct	101
Spindrift / G Innes	Foochow 5 Jul	via Eastern Route	London 18 Oct	105
Deerhound / Carlin	Canton 6 Jul		Downs 15 Oct	101
Golden Spur / Ronald	Shanghai 7 Jul		London 15 Nov	131
Whiteadder / F W Moore	Shanghai 9 Jul		Deal 7 Nov	121
Taeping / J Dowdy	Foochow 13 Jul		Deal 23 Oct	102
Ziba / G Bowes	Foochow 13 Jul		Deal 6 Nov	116
Belted Will / A Locke	Macao 15 Jul (dep Canton 9 Jul)	Anjer 30 Jul	Dover 19 Oct	96
Douglas Castle / McRitchie	Hong Kong 16 Jul	Anjer 15 Aug	London 30 Oct	106
Sir Lancelot / R Robinson	Foochow 17 Jul	Anjer 7 Aug / St H 11 Sep	off Lizard 10 Oct / London 14 Oct	89
Kaisow / J Anderson	Foochow 18 Jul	Anjer 23 Aug	London 8 Nov	113
Weymouth / S W Gibson	Shanghai 19 Jul		Downs 29 Nov	133
Black Prince / W Inglis	Foochow 20 Jul	via Ombay / St H 7 Oct	Deal 15 Nov / London 16 Nov	119
Windhover / Nutsford	Foochow 22 Jul		London 8 Nov	109
Serica / Watt	Foochow 24 Jul		London 15 Nov	114
Juanpore / Brown	Shanghai 24 Jul	Anjer 29 Sep	Deal 31 Dec	160
Falcon / J L Dunn	Foochow 27 Jul	St H 11 Oct	London 15 Nov	111
Wild Deer / James Smith	Shanghai 28 Jul	St H 17 Oct (master dead)	London 29 Nov	124
Maitland / Coulson	Hong Kong 29 Jul	Anjer 23 Aug	Deal 6 Nov / London 8 Nov	102
Guinevere / Spowatt	Hong Kong 3 Aug (dep Shanghai 16 Jul)		London 15 Nov	104
John R Worcester / T Cawse	Shanghai 5 Aug		London 13 Dec	130
Dunmail / P Thomson	Hong Kong 6 Aug	Anjer 7 Sep / St H 18 Oct	Downs 29 Nov	115
Min / Melville	Foochow 7 Aug		London 14 Dec	129
Silver Eagle / Case	Foochow 12 Aug		Deal 20 Dec	130
Yang-tsze / W Smith	Foochow 19 Aug	St H 21 Nov	London 27 Dec	130
Scawfell / R Thomson	Canton 20 Aug	Anjer 18 Sep	London 13 Dec	115
Flying Spur / Beckett	Foochow 27 Aug		Deal 22 Dec	117
Vanguard (1857) / T Hunter	Hong Kong 1 Sep	Anjer 28 Sep	London 16 Dec	106

Ship/Master	Sailed	Passed	Arrived	Days
Veronica / Haldine	Canton 1 Sep	Anjer 30 Sep	Liverpool 25 Dec	115
Pegasus / A Mackey	Shanghai 16 Sep	Anjer 23 Oct	off Falmouth 25 Jan (for London?)	131
Fiery Cross / Middleton	Shanghai 24 Sep		London 7 Jan	105
Ada / Jones	Foochow 3 Oct		New York 9 Jan	98
Invincible / Beeching	Hong Kong 7 Oct	Anjer 27 Oct	off Scilly 18 Jan / London 27 Jan	112
Wylo / H W Browne	Shanghai 22 Oct		London 31 Jan	101
Gauntlet / Sutherland	Hong Kong 23 Oct		London 22 Feb	122
Pak Wan / Shiell	Hong Kong 14 Nov		London 28 Feb	106
Dilpussund / Jones	Shanghai 22 Nov		New York 16 Mar	114
John Lidgett / Polson	Shanghai 23 Nov		London 25 Mar	122
Corea / Carr	Shanghai 28 Nov		London 10 Apr	133
Beemah / Wakeham	Foochow 9 Dec		London 25 Mar	106
Elizabeth Nicholson / Crosbie	Shanghai 1 Jan	Anjer 14 Jan	New York 8 Apr	97
Omba / G F Thomson	Shanghai 6 Jan	Anjer 23 Jan	London 13 May	127
Red Riding Hood / Henderson	Foochow 14 Jan		Deal 12 May	118
Fusi Yama / M C Borup	Singapore 20 Jan	Anjer 27 Jan	Boston 21 Apr	91
Coulnakyle / A Morrison	Foochow 20 Jan		Deal 12 May	112
Crest of the Wave / Crombie	Yokohama 1 Feb	via Formosa / Anjer 27 Feb	New York 24 May	112
Harlaw / Phillips	Shanghai 24 Feb	Anjer 18 Mar / CGH 14 Apr	New York 24 May	89
Solent / Meldrum	Hong Kong 2 Mar		London 3 Jun	93
Banian / Shore	Shanghai 10 Mar	St H 17 Jun	New York 2 Aug	145

TEA SEASON 1870–71

Ship/Master	Sailed	Passed	Arrived	Days
Taeping / J Dowdy	Canton 5 Jun	Anjer 7 Jul	off Scilly 24 Sep / London 28 Sep	115
Deerhound / Carlin	Canton 16 Jun		Deal 13 Oct	119
Titania / W H Burgoyne	Woosung 18 Jun (dep Hankow 13 Jun)		off Scilly 5 Oct / London 8 Oct	112
Cutty Sark / G Moodie	Shanghai 25 Jun / Woosung 27 Jun	Anjer 2 Aug	Downs 12 Oct / London 13 Oct	110
Serica / A Sproule	Shanghai 28 Jun		Deal 22 Oct / London 24 Oct	118
Forward Ho! / Hossack	Shanghai 28 Jun		London 25 Oct	119
Ethiopian / Faulkner	Shanghai 1 Jul		London 12 Nov	134
John R Worcester / T Cawse	Shanghai 5 Jul		Deal 7 Nov / London 8 Nov	126
Lauderdale / J J Smith	Shanghai 5 Jul	Anjer 31 Aug	Portsmouth 29 Nov	147
Weymouth / S W Gibson	Shanghai 6 Jul		off Scilly 10 Dec (for London)	157
Whinfell / Jones	Shanghai 7 Jul		Deal 11 Nov	127
Argonaut / A Nicholson	Shanghai 8 Jul		London 15 Nov	130
Eliza Shaw / G Gaye	Shanghai 13 Jul		London 16 Nov	126
Belted Will / A Locke	Hong Kong 16 Jul	Anjer 12 Aug / CGH 9 Sep	Deal 23 Oct / London 25 Oct	101

Ship/Master	Sailed	Passed	Arrived	Days
Duke of Abercorn Dalrymple	Shanghai 19 Jul	Pitts Passage 14 Aug	off Scilly 9 Nov / London 14 Nov	118
Ambassador P Duggan	Foochow 25 Jul	Pitts Passage 24 Aug	Deal 15 Nov	113
Thermopylae Kemball	Shanghai 30 Jul	Anjer 28 Aug	Downs 11 Nov / London 12 Nov	105
Undine Scott	Shanghai 1 Aug		Cape Clear 5 Nov / London 14 Nov	105
Sir Lancelot Edmonds	Foochow 2 Aug	Anjer 4 Sep	Downs 12 Nov / London 14 Nov	104
Norman Court A Shewan	Foochow 3 Aug	Anjer 3 Sep	Start Pt 12 Nov / London 16 Nov	105
Thyatira J Ross	Shanghai 3 Aug		off Plymouth 1 Dec / London 8 Dec	127
Eme Gunn	Foochow 4 Aug		went ashore at Dungeness 11 Dec	129
Kelso M Vowell	Amoy 6 Aug	Anjer 21 Sep	New York 8 Dec	124
Golden Spur Ronald	Shanghai 15 Aug		Deal 3 Jan	141
Norham Castle A Marshall	Singapore 16 Aug		Liverpool 23 Nov	99
Wylo H W Browne	Foochow 18 Aug	Anjer 27 Sep	London 11 Dec	115
Everest Clarke	Foochow 27 Aug	Anjer 25 Sep	London 10 Dec	105
Chinaman McKenzie	Foochow 27 Aug	Anjer 25 Sep	London 12 Dec	107
Windhover Orr	Foochow 31 Aug	Anjer 26 Sep	Downs 7 Dec / London 8 Dec	99
Miako W Anderson	Canton ?		Buenos Aires 20 Nov	–
Wild Deer Cameron	Shanghai 1 Sep	Anjer 9 Oct	London 3 Jan	124
Ariel Courtenay	Yokohama 1 Sep	Diego Ramirez 22 Nov	New York 15 Jan	136
Falcon J L Dunn	Foochow 2 Sep		Deal 19 Dec / London 20 Dec	109
Maitland Hunter	Foochow 10 Sep	Anjer 6 Oct	London 30 Dec	111
Fiery Cross Murray	Canton 16 Sep		Deal 9 Jan / London 10 Jan	116
Yang-tsze W Smith	Foochow 19 Sep	Anjer 24 Oct	New York 10 Jan	113
Juanpore Haldane	Foochow 21 Sep		Deal 4 Mar	164
Flying Spur Barnett	Foochow 22 Sep	Anjer 21 Oct	London 19 Jan	119
Lufra J Hodge	Macao 30 Sep	Anjer 28 Oct	New York 14 Jan	106
Black Prince W Inglis	Yokohama 30 Sep	Anjer 3 Nov	New York 30 Jan	122
Lennox Castle Talbot	Foochow 3 Oct		Mount's Bay 30 Jan / London 3 Feb	127
Veronica Evans	Shanghai 8 Oct		London 10 Feb	125
Lahloo John Smith	Foochow 12 Oct		Deal 17 Jan / London 18 Jan	98
Leander Petherick	Foochow 12 Oct		Deal 17 Jan / London 18 Jan	98
Kaisow J Anderson	Foochow 22 Oct		Deal 1 Feb / London 3 Feb	100
Dilpussund Jones	Shanghai 23 Oct	Anjer 14 Nov	New York 4 Feb	104
Douglas Castle McRitchie	Foochow 29 Oct	Anjer 20 Nov	London 21 Feb	115
Guinevere Spowatt	Foochow 2 Nov		Deal 17 Feb	107
Taitsing H Bloomfield (dep Foochow 3 Nov)	Amoy 7 Nov	Anjer 24 Nov	St Catherine's 2 Mar / London 4 Mar	117
Whiteadder W E Tiptaft	Foochow 9 Nov		London 18 Feb	101
Min Melville	Yokohama 11 Nov		New York 16 Feb	97
Cleta Middleton	Canton 18 Nov	Anjer 10 Dec	New York 12 Mar	114
John Lidgett Sleigh	Canton 24 Nov		off Scilly 2 Mar / London 27 Mar	125
The Caliph Ritson	Foochow 6 Dec	Anjer 17 Dec	New York 3 Mar	87
Corea Carr	Canton 24 Dec		London 17 Apr	114
Kate Carnie R Lowe	Canton 25 Dec		London 17 Apr	113
Beemah J Waking (?Wakenham)	Foochow 4 Jan		London 20 Apr	106
Ada Jones	Foochow 16 Jan	Anjer 29 Jan	New York 20 Apr	94
Coulnakyle J Japp	Yokohama 20 Jan	Anjer 16 Feb	New York 11 May	111
Solent Meldrum	Yokohama 6 Feb	Anjer 27 Feb	New York 27 Jul	171
Elizabeth Nicholson Crosbie	Foochow 7 Feb	Anjer 23 Feb	New York 19 May	101
Omba G F Thomson	Foochow 8 Feb		Deal 8 Jun	120
Pegasus Mackey (?Mackay)	Hiogo 18 Feb	via Nagasaki CGH 15 May	London 16 Oct	240
Lothair E Peacock	Yokohama 23 Mar	Anjer 16 Apr CGH 15 May	New York 1 Jul	100
Vanguard (1857) Green	Shanghai 30 Mar		London 22 Aug	145
Osaka J L Leslie	Hong Kong 31 Mar	CGH 1 Jun St H 16 Jun	New York 17 Jul	108

TEA SEASON 1871–72

Ship/Master	Sailed	Passed	Arrived	Days
Forward Ho! Hossack	Shanghai 24 Jun	Pitts Passage 18 July	London 19 Oct	117
Thermopylae Kemball	Shanghai 25 Jun	Anjer 22 Jul	London 6 Oct	103
Undine Scott	Shanghai 28 Jun		London 16 Oct	110
Titania J Dowdy	Foochow 1 Jul	Anjer 26 Jul	London 2 Oct	93
Ziba G Bowes	Foochow 4 Jul		London 6 Nov	125
Harlaw Phillips	Foochow 7 Jul	Anjer 5 Aug	London 7 Nov	123
Maitland Reid	Foochow 8 Jul		London 8 Nov	123
Whinfell Jones	Shanghai 8 Jul		Deal 23 Nov / London 25 Nov	140
Argonaut A Nicholson	Shanghai 15 Jul	Anjer 21 Aug	London 8 Nov	116
Sir Lancelot Edmonds	Foochow 17 Jul		New York 16 Nov	122
Norman Court A Shewan	Hong Kong 19 Jul	Anjer 8 Aug	Deal 3 Nov	107
Duke of Abercorn Dalrymple	Foochow 23 Jul		Prawle Pt 9 Nov / London 11 Nov	111
Weymouth Gibson	Shanghai 26 Jul		London 22 Nov	120
Lahloo John Smith	Foochow 27 Jul	Anjer 2 Sep	London 15 Nov	111
Leander Knight	Amoy 3 Aug		New York 20 Nov	109
Deerhound Carlin	Canton 9 Aug		Deal 15 Nov	98
Eliza Shaw G Gaye	Shanghai 9 Aug		Beachy Head 25 Dec / London 29 Dec	142
Everest Owen	Shanghai 16 Aug	St H 16 Nov	off Swanage 20 Dec / London 23 Dec	129
Lauderdale Low	Foochow 17 Aug		London 31 Dec	136
John R Worcester T Cawse	Shanghai 18 Aug		off Dartmouth 21 Dec / London 23 Dec	127

Ship/Master	Sailed	Passed	Arrived	Days
Ambassador P Duggan	Canton 30 Aug	Anjer 2 Oct	London 1 Jan	124
Golden Spur Farvel	Hong Kong –		Buenos Aires 7 Nov	–
Cutty Sark G Moodie	Shanghai 2 Sep Woosung 3 Sep	Anjer 6 Oct St H 16 Nov	Start Pt 19 Dec London 21 Dec	110
Ariel Talbot	Shanghai 4 Sep		London 27 Dec	114
Taeping Gissing	Amoy 8 Sep		wrecked 22 Sep (for New York)	–
Serica G Innes	Shanghai 12 Sep		New York 28 Dec	107
Flying Spur Barnett	Yokohama 18 Sep		New York 23 Jan	127
Guinevere Spowatt	Shanghai 23 Sep		London 25 Jan	124
Kelso M Vowell	Foochow 25 Sep		New York 27 Jan	124
Yang-tsze W Smith	Foochow 29 Sep		wrecked 2 Oct (for New York)	–
Thyatira McKay	Foochow 30 Sep		off Plymouth 14 Jan London 16 Jan	108
Fiery Cross Murray	Yokohama 4 Oct		New York 26 Jan	114
Black Prince W Inglis	Yokohama 18 Oct		New York 6 Feb	111
Taitsing H Bloomfield	Shanghai 22 Oct		New York 7 Feb	108
Corea Carr	Macao 4 Nov		London 29 Feb	117
Crest of the Wave Harris	Canton 21 Nov		London 28 Feb	99
Beemah Wakeham	Foochow 29 Nov		London 11 Mar	103
Cleta Middleton	Shanghai 2 Dec		New York –	–
Miako W Anderson	Shanghai 17 Dec	Anjer 1 Jan St H 28 Feb	New York 10 Apr	115
Omba G F Thomson	Shanghai 28 Dec	Anjer 11 Jan St H 2 Mar	New York 11 Apr	105
Borealis Beard	Shanghai –		New York –	–
Ada Jones	Yokohama 30 Jan		New York 14 May	105
Coulnakyle J Japp	Yokohama 7 Feb		New York 22 May	105
Dilpussund Gray	Foochow 13 Feb		New York 1 Jun	109
Ethiopian Faulkner	Shanghai 28 Feb		New York 9 Jun	102

TEA SEASON 1872–73

Ship/Master	Sailed	Passed	Arrived	Days
Titania L Dowdy	Macao 25 May		London 19 Sep	117
Vanguard (1857) Luckes	Hong Kong 13 Jun?		London 8 Jan	209?
Duke of Abercorn Dalrymple	Foochow 18 Jun		London 10 Oct	114
Thermopylae Kemball	Shanghai 18 Jun	Anjer 19 Jul St H 4 Sep	London 11 Oct	115
Cutty Sark G Moodie	Shanghai 18 Jun	Anjer 19 Jul St H 9 Sep	off Portland 16 Oct London 18 Oct	122
Undine Shearer	Shanghai 24 Jun		Prawle Pt 15 Oct London 17 Oct	115
Blackadder F W Moore	Foochow 28 Jun		Deal 26 Oct London 27 Oct	121
Northfleet Oates	Foochow 29 Jun		London 19 Nov	143
Lahloo John Smith	Shanghai 30 Jun		wrecked 31 Jul (for London)	–
Argonaut A Nicholson	Shanghai 3 Jul		London 26 Oct	115
Sir Lancelot Edmonds	Foochow 7 Jul		London 6 Nov	122

Ship/Master	Sailed	Passed	Arrived	Days
Eliza Shaw G Gaye	Shanghai 11 Jul		London 6 Nov	118
Maitland Reid	Foochow 19 Jul		London 6 Nov	110
Ambassador Gray	Macao 23 Jul		Deal 7 Nov	108
Chinaman McKenzie	Shanghai 1 Aug	Anjer 17 Sep	New York 8 Dec	130
Deerhound Carlin	Foochow 2 Aug	Anjer 8 Sep	New York 25 Nov	115
Harlaw Phillips	Foochow 3 Aug	Anjer 8 Sep	St Catherine's 20 Nov London 21 Nov	110
Falcon J L Dunn	Hong Kong 4 Aug	Anjer 6 Sep	London 21 Nov	109
Taitsing H Bloomfield	Shanghai 8 Aug		London 30 Nov	114
Weymouth Gibson	Shanghai 16 Aug		London 17 Dec	123
Kaisow J Anderson	Shanghai 17 Aug Woosung 21 Aug	Anjer 17 Sep	New York 6 Dec	111
Everest Owen	Foochow 30 Aug		London 18 Dec	110
Norman Court A Shewan	Macao 14 Sep	Anjer 5 Oct	off Lizard 17 Dec London 19 Dec	96
Leander M J Knight	Yokohama 22 Sep	Anjer 25 Oct	New York 2 Jan	102
Beemah Wakeham	Hong Kong –		New York abt 4 Jan	–
Eme Sproule	Foochow 4 Oct	Anjer 26 Oct	London 14 Jan	102
Ziba Green	Foochow 4 Oct		London 15 Jan	103
Whiteadder Harris	Hiogo 20 Oct		Falmouth for orders 16 Feb (for Rotterdam)	119
Serica G Innes	Hong Kong 2 Nov		wrecked 3 Nov (for Montevideo)	–
Corea Carr	Canton 2 Nov		London 27 Feb	117
Flying Spur Barnett	Foochow 18 Nov		London 3 Apr	136
Fiery Cross Murray	Shanghai 4 Dec		London 2 Apr	119
Elizabeth Nicholson Webster	Foochow 6 Dec	Anjer 19 Dec	New York 16 Mar	100
Black Prince W Inglis	Foochow 7 Dec	Anjer 21 Dec	New York 18 Mar	101
Lothair E Peacock	Kobe 15 Dec	Anjer 12 Jan CGH 17 Feb	New York 9 Apr	115
Kate Carnie R Lowe	Foochow 17 Dec		Philadelphia 17 Jul	212
John R Worcester T Cawse	Amoy 19 Dec	Anjer 30 Dec	off Bar 17 Mar New York 18 Mar	89
Whinfell Jones	Foochow 3 Jan	Anjer 16 Jan	New York 10 Apr	97
Cleta Middleton	Yokohama 4 Jan		New York abt 5 May	–
Borealis R Beard	Woosung 7 Jan (dep Shanghai 31 Dec)	Anjer 21 Jan CGH 17 Feb	New York 10 Apr	93
Omba G F Thomson	Shanghai 25 Jan	Anjer 8 Feb St H 31 Mar	New York 17 May	112
Miako W Anderson	Yokohama 5 Mar	Anjer 1 Apr	New York 27 Jun	114

TEA SEASON 1873–74

Ship/Master	Sailed	Passed	Arrived	Days
Norham Castle A Marshall	Shanghai 21 Jun (from Hankow)	Anjer 18 Jul	London 27 Oct	128
Sir Lancelot Edmonds	Shanghai 28 Jun		London 1 Nov	126
Cutty Sark W E Tiptaft	Shanghai 9 Jul	Anjer 20 Aug	Deal 2 Nov London 3 Nov	117

Ship/Master	Sailed	Passed	Arrived	Days
Maitland Reid	Foochow 10 Jul		London 3 Nov	116
Thermopylae Kemball	Foochow 11 Jul	Anjer 8 Aug	off Lizard 16 Oct / London 19 Oct	100
Undine M Vowell	Foochow 16 Jul		Downs 24 Nov / London 26 Nov	133
Forward Ho! Wade	Shanghai 25 Jul		off Plymouth 20 Nov / London 1 Dec	129
Titania Hunt	Shanghai 25 Jul	Anjer 17 Sep	off Scilly 12 Dec / London 18 Dec	146
Norman Court A Shewan Jnr	Foochow 4 Aug	Anjer 5 Sep	London 28 Nov	116
Kaisow J Anderson	Shanghai 9 Aug		Deal 1 Dec / London 2 Dec	115
Argonaut A Nicholson	Foochow 11 Aug	Anjer 14 Sep	London 28 Nov	109
Duke of Abercorn Dalrymple	Foochow 25 Aug	Anjer 29 Sep	off Lizard 12 Dec / London 17 Dec	114
Deerhound Carlin	Canton 27 Aug		Deal 16 Dec	111
Eliza Shaw G Gaye	Yokohama 30 Aug		New York 28 Dec	103
Ambassador Gray	Foochow 23 Sep	Anjer 24 Oct	London 15 Jan	114
Chinaman McKenzie	Hong Kong 25 Sep	Anjer 23 Oct	New York 14 Feb	142
John R Worcester T Cawse	Shanghai 30 Sep	Anjer 23 Oct	New York 8 Jan	100
Taitsing H Bloomfield	Hiogo 1 Oct	Anjer 7 Nov	off Lizard 2 Feb / London 7 Feb	129
Ziba Richard	Hiogo 20 Oct		Falmouth for orders 16 Feb / Dordt 24 Feb	127
Harlaw Phillips	Shanghai 23 Oct / Woosung 24 Oct	CGH 18 Nov / Equator 7 Dec	New York 5 Feb	105
Falcon J L Dunn	Canton 27 Oct / Macao 28 Oct		New York 31 Jan	96
Leander Knight	Shanghai 28 Oct / Woosung 29 Oct	Anjer 17 Nov / CGH 19 Dec	New York 2 Feb	97
Hallowe'en J Watt	Shanghai 17 Nov / N Saddle 19 Nov	Anjer 5 Dec / St H 13 Jan	Downs 16 Feb / London 17 Feb	92
Black Prince W Inglis	Shanghai 10 Dec	Anjer 1 Jan	New York 1 Apr	112
Lothair B Orchard	Hong Kong 11 Dec (dep Macao 7 Dec)	Anjer 16 Dec / Azores 26 Feb	off Scilly 4 Mar / London 10 Mar	89
Miako W Anderson	Manilla 30 Mar		New York 18 Jul	110

TEA SEASON 1874–75

Ship/Master	Sailed	Passed	Arrived	Days
Osaka R Lowe	Hong Kong 6 Jun	Anjer 3 Jul	Prawle Pt 30 Sep / London 2 Oct	118
Ada J Asals	Hankow 7 Jun / Woosung ?30 Jun		London 22 Oct	137
Cutty Sark W E Tiptaft	Woosung 24 Jun (dep Hankow 12 Jun)	via Eastern Route	London 21 Oct	119
Deerhound Shearer	Canton 4 Jul		London 25 Oct	113
Thermopylae Kemball	Shanghai 15 Jul / Woosung 17 Jul	Anjer 14 Aug	London 27 Oct	104
Kate Carnie Wilson	Whampoa 15 Jul	St H 12 Oct	New York 28 Nov	136
Sir Lancelot Felgate	Foochow 18 Jul		London 19 Nov	124
Derwent J Gadd	Manilla 18 Jul	Anjer 1 Sep	New York 3 Dec	138
Norman Court A Shewan Jnr	Foochow 26 Jul	Anjer 30 Aug	London 18 Nov	115
Forward Ho! Wade	Foochow 4 Aug		London 13 Dec	131
Red Riding Hood Robertson	Shanghai 5 Aug		London 1 Jan	148
Lauderdale True	Shanghai 10 Aug		Deal 14 Jan	156
Kaisow J Anderson	Shanghai 18 Aug	Anjer 30 Sep	London 27 Dec	131
Norham Castle R H Carey	Shanghai 18 Aug		London 4 Jan	139
Lothair B Orchard	Shanghai 22 Aug	Anjer 4 Oct	Prawle Pt 24 Dec / London 28 Dec	128
Wylo H W Browne	Shanghai 31 Aug	Anjer 12 Oct	London 5 Jan	127
Undine M Vowell	Foochow 12 Sep		London 3 Jan	113
Borealis R Beard	Shanghai 15 Sep	Anjer 25 Oct	London 6 Jan	113
Duke of Abercorn Dalrymple	Shanghai 17 Sep	Anjer 23 Oct	London 6 Jan	111
Eliza Shaw G Gaye	Foochow 17 Sep	Anjer 20 Oct	Dover 18 Jan	123
John R Worcester T Cawse	Shanghai 22 Sep	Anjer 1 Nov	New York 14 Jan	114
Ambassador Prehn	Hiogo 28 Sep / Yokohama 30 Sep	Anjer 8 Nov / CGH 5 Dec	New York 19 Jan	113
Argonaut Cameron	Foochow 28 Sep		Deal 3 Feb	128
Hallowe'en J Watt	Shanghai 21 Oct	Anjer 10 Nov / CGH 8 Dec	Start Pt 18 Jan / London 20 Jan	91
Coulnakyle Gordon	Shanghai 2 Nov		off Penzance 4 Mar (for London)	122
Leander M J Knight	Shanghai 8 Nov / Woosung 10 Nov	Anjer 27 Nov / CGH 4 Jan	New York 19 Feb	103
Falcon Shiell	Hong Kong 13 Nov		Start Pt 21 Mar (for London)	128
Harlaw Phillips	Foochow 25 Nov		London 12 Mar	107
Taitsing Richard	Foochow 6 Dec		New York 17 Mar	101
Chinaman McKenzie	Hong Kong 15 Jan		New York 10 May	115
Titania W England	Hong Kong 4 Feb		Isle of Wight 10 May / London 11 May	96
Omba G F Thomson	Shanghai 18 Mar	St H 1 Jun	London 15 Jul	119
Sir Lancelot Felgate	Shanghai 6 May	Anjer 9 Jun / CGH 11 Jul	New York 20 Aug	106

TEA SEASON 1875–76

Ship/Master	Sailed	Passed	Arrived	Days
Cutty Sark W E Tiptaft	Shanghai 21 Jun	via Eastern Route	Deal 21 Oct / London 22 Oct	123
Thermopylae Matheson	Foochow 11 Jul		St Catherine's 29 Oct / London 31 Oct	112
Blackadder J Whyte	Woosung 19 Jul		London 20 Nov	124
Black Prince W Inglis	Foochow 20 Jul		Falmouth 7 Dec / London 12 Dec	145
Forward Ho! Wade	Foochow 26 Jul		London 16 Nov	113
Deerhound Shearer	Shanghai 5 Aug		wrecked 30 Aug (for London)	–
Fiery Cross Bates	Foochow 6 Aug		London 2 Mar	209
Osaka R Lowe	Hong Kong 9 Aug	Anjer 5 Sep	Falmouth 27 Nov / London 12 Dec	125
Undine E R Fawkner	Shanghai 23 Aug		London 17 Dec	116
Norman Court A Shewan Jnr	Shanghai 2 Sep	Anjer 10 Oct	Downs 31 Dec / London 2 Jan	122
Min Peters	Foochow 10 Sep		Plymouth 11 Feb / London 15 Feb	158
Lothair B Orchard	Yokohama 29 Sep	Anjer 2 Nov / CGH 12 Dec	New York 2 Jan	119
Ada J Asals	Hong Kong 3 Oct		London 27 Jan	116

Ship/Master	Sailed	Passed	Arrived	Days
Whiteadder Betham	Foochow 3 Oct		London 21 Feb	141
Wylo H W Browne	Shanghai 12 Oct	Anjer 5 Nov CGH 9 Dec	New York 21 Jan	101
Solent Meldrum	Hong Kong 21 Oct		Cowes for orders 1 Feb (arr Hamburg 15 Feb)	103
Ambassador Prehn	Yokohama 1 Nov		New York 7 Feb	98
Miako H Cape	Amoy 8 Nov	Anjer 21 Nov CGH 29 Dec	New York 12 Feb	96
Hallowe'en Watt (Fowler after St H)	Woosung 23 Nov	Anjer 8 Dec St H 15 Jan (Watt died there 17 Jan)	Downs 23 Feb London 24 Feb	93
Leander M J Knight	Amoy 25 Nov	Anjer 9 Dec CGH 11 Jan	C Hatteras 17 Feb New York 26 Feb	93
Coulnakyle Gordon	Hiogo 6 Dec	Anjer 21 Dec	London 25 Mar	110
Duke of Abercorn Dalrymple	Amoy 11 Dec	Anjer 21 Dec CGH 28 Jan	New York 13 Mar	93
Harlaw Stephens	Shanghai 18 Dec Woosung 19 Dec	Anjer 4 Jan CGH 8 Feb	New York 27 Mar	100
Borealis R Beard	Amoy 29 Dec	CGH 8 Feb	New York 27 Mar	89
Ethiopian Faulkner	Shanghai 8 Jan		London 21 Apr	103
Guinevere Mooney	Bangkok 15 Jan		London 20 Apr	96
Falcon Westrup	Shanghai 12 Feb		New York 10 Jun	119
Titania W England	Shanghai 27 Mar		New York 4 Aug	130
Flying Spur Croat	Nagasaki 29 Mar		Isle of Wight 21 Aug	145
Eliza Shaw J Hall	Manilla 8 May		London 7 Sep	122

TEA SEASON 1876–77

Ship/Master	Sailed	Passed	Arrived	Days
Cutty Sark W E Tiptaft	Woosung 9 Jun (dep Hankow 4 Jun)	Anjer 15 Jul St H 19 Aug	Start Pt 25 Sep London 26 Sep	109
Windhover Findlay	Shanghai 20 Jul		London 25 Nov	128
Thermopylae Matheson	Foochow 29 Jul	Anjer 4 Sep	off Scilly 21 Nov London 24 Nov	118
Blackadder J Whyte	Woosung 5 Aug		London 8 Dec	125
Sir Lancelot Hepburn	Yokohama 23 Aug		Plymouth for orders 28 Dec (for St Nazaire)	128
Kaisow J Gadd	Manilla 28 Aug	Anjer 25 Sep CGH 31 Oct	New York 20 Dec	114
Osaka R Lowe	Hiogo 3 Sep	Anjer 16 Oct St H 7 Dec	London 14 Jan	133
Undine Faulkner	Shanghai 7 Sep	Anjer 10 Oct	off Lizard 21 Dec London 27 Dec	111
Miako W Knight	Samarang 1 Oct		Falmouth for orders 1 Mar (arr Havre 10 Mar)	97
Wylo H W Browne	Manilla 19 Oct	Anjer 12 Nov	Boston 15 Feb	119
Ambassador Prehn	Yokohama 4 Nov	Anjer 8 Dec CGH 12 Jan	C Hatteras 22 Feb New York 26 Feb	114
Hallowe'en Fowler	Woosung 9 Nov (dep Shanghai 31 Oct)		London 23 Feb	106
Queensberry T Herring	Hong Kong 11 Nov		New York 16 Mar	126
Lothair B Orchard	Yokohama 12 Nov	Anjer 7 Dec CGH 10 Jan	New York 2 Mar	110

Ship/Master	Sailed	Passed	Arrived	Days
Elizabeth Nicholson Grierson	Manilla 12 Nov		Liverpool 4 Mar	112
Black Prince W Inglis	Shanghai 28 Nov		London 14 Mar	106
Salamis Phillips	Hong Kong 29 Nov		London 28 Mar	119
Borealis R Beard	Shanghai 26 Dec	Anjer 8 Jan St H 6 Mar	London 21 Apr	116
Leander M J Knight	Woosung 11 Jan		New York 20 Apr	99
Norman Court A Shewan Jnr	Shanghai 30 Jan		Start Pt 17 May (for London)	107
Eliza Shaw J Hall	Shanghai 14 Apr		London 29 Jul	106
Omba G F Thomson	Manilla	Anjer 15 May	Falmouth for orders 28 Aug (arr Liverpool 7 Sep)	129

TEA SEASON 1877–78

Ship/Master	Sailed	Passed	Arrived	Days
John R Worcester J Cawse	Woosung 4 Jun		London 24 Oct	142
Cutty Sark W E Tiptaft	Woosung 6 Jun (dep Hankow 2 Jun)		off Scilly 6 Oct London 11 Oct	127
Windhover W Findlay	Shanghai 26 Jun		London 23 Oct	119
Thermopylae Matheson	Shanghai 8 Jul		Lizard 18 Oct London 20 Oct	104
Forward Ho! E Wade	Shanghai 30 Jul	Anjer 29 Aug	London 16 Nov	109
Serapis J E Ilberry	Shanghai 29 Aug		New York 15 Jan	139
Blackadder J Whyte	Shanghai 26 Oct	Anjer 17 Nov	London 16 Feb	113
Wylo H W Browne	Foochow 30 Oct	Anjer 20 Nov St H 10 Jan	off Scilly 15 Feb London 18 Feb	111
Miako W Knight	Manilla 31 Oct	Anjer 20 Nov	London 19 Feb	111
Osaka R Lowe	Amoy 21 Nov	Anjer 8 Dec CGH 13 Jan	New York 3 Mar	102
Sir Lancelot Hepburn	Shanghai 28 Dec	Anjer 15 Jan CGH 17 Feb	New York 2 Apr	95
Hallowe'en Fowler	Shanghai 7 Jan		London 16 Apr	99
Lothair B Orchard	Amoy 8 Jan	Anjer 19 Jan CGH 12 Feb	New York 2 Apr	84
Leander M J Knight	Shanghai 12 Feb (?dep Woosung 22 Feb)		New York 26 May	103

TEA SEASON 1878–79

Ship/Master	Sailed	Passed	Arrived	Days
Coriolanus McLauchlan	Shanghai 28 Jun		London 30 Nov	150
Ambassador Gray	Shanghai 18 Aug	Anjer 25 Oct St H 23 Nov	London 30 Dec	134
Eme J Asals	Foochow 28 Aug		London 14 Jan	139
Windhover Findlay	Shanghai 1 Sep	Anjer 7 Oct	London 30 Dec	120
Omba J Hall	Cebu 3 Sep (Philippines)	St H 6 Dec	New York 18 Jan	137
Serapis Parkhurst	Shanghai 19 Sep Woosung 22 Sep	Anjer 7 Nov	Liverpool 8 Feb	142
Titania W England	Shanghai 22 Sep	Anjer 25 Oct	London 30 Dec	99
Wylo H W Browne	Foochow 24 Sep	Anjer 22 Oct St H 6 Dec	London 15 Jan	113
Taitsing Johnston	Shanghai 3 Oct	Anjer 6 Nov	Portland 28 Jan London 1 Feb	121
Eliza Shaw Cooper	Foochow 6 Nov		London 30 Mar	144

Ship/Master	Sailed	Passed	Arrived	Days	Ship/Master	Sailed	Passed	Arrived	Days
Thermopylae Matheson	Shanghai 27 Nov	Anjer 19 Dec	London 17 Mar	110	*Cutty Sark* Wallace	Manilla 23 Sep	CGH 25 Nov	New York 12 Jan	111
Osaka R Lowe	Singapore 18 Feb		Marseilles 3 Jun	105	*Hallowe'en* R W Fowler	Shanghai 24 Sep	CGH 19 Dec St H 27 Dec	London 6 Feb	135
Miako W Knight	Cheribon 20 Mar (Java)	Anjer 3 Apr	Liverpool 20 Jul	122	*Leander* Hamilton	Shanghai 29 Sep Woosung 1 Oct	Anjer 2 Nov St H 27 Dec	London 6 Feb	130
Kaisow J Gadd	Manilla 3 Apr	Anjer 8 May St H 4 Jul	London 18 Aug	137	*Taitsing* Bloomfield	Shanghai 3 Oct		Portland 25 Jan (for London)	114
					Norman Court A Shewan Jnr	Foochow 8 Oct	Anjer 2 Nov	London 4 Feb	119
TEA SEASON 1879-80					*Sir Lancelot* Brockenshaw	Foochow 22 Oct		London 27 Feb	128
Undine E Fawkner	Foochow 12 Aug	Anjer 30 Sep St H 20 Nov	London 4 Jan	145	*Ambassador* R H Bidwall	Manilla 23 Oct		London 29 Feb	129
Lothair T O Boulton	Cebu 21 Aug		New York 30 Nov	101	*Titania* Townsend	Manilla 25 Oct	Anjer 20 Nov CGH 27 Dec	New York 14 Feb	112
Windhover W Findlay	Shanghai 3 Sep	CGH 25 Nov St H 6 Dec	London 26 Jan	145	*Wylo* H W Browne	Kobe 25 Oct	Anjer 20 Nov CGH 27 Dec	New York 14 Feb	112

APPENDIX III
THE FASTEST PASSAGES MADE TO AND FROM CHINA

CHINA TO ENGLAND DURING THE SOUTH-WEST MONSOON

Shanghai to London   **98 days**
Titania (W H Burgoyne). Left Shanghai 16 June 1869, passed Woosung 17 June but was held up near the Saddles until 20 June. She passed Anjer 15 July and arrived off Deal 21 September, 93 days from the coast of China and 96 from Woosung, docking in London the next day.

Shanghai to London   **100 days**
Sir Lancelot (R Robinson). Left Shanghai 15 June 1867, passed Woosung 16 June, and going by the long Eastern route reached Dungeness 22 September, 98 days from Woosung, and docked the next day. She was said at the time to have taken 96 days, land to land.

Foochow to London   **89 days**
Sir Lancelot (R Robinson). Unmoored at 7.0 am on 17 July 1869, passed the White Dogs 18 July and Anjer 7 August. She was off the Lizard 10 October, 84 days after leaving the river Min, passed Dungeness 12 October with a 'foul baffling wind' and reached Gravesend 13 October at 2.0 pm, docking in London next day, 89 days out.

Foochow to London   **91 days**
Thermopylae (Kemball). Left Foochow 3 July 1869, passed Anjer 27 July, was off the Lizard 30 September, 89 days out, and docked on 2 October.

Foochow to London   **93 days**
Titania (J Dowdy). Left Foochow 1 July 1871, passed Anjer 26 July and reached London 2 October.

Macao to London   **96 days**
Norman Court (A Shewan Snr). Left Macao 14 September 1872, passed Anjer 21 days later, was off the Lizard on 17 December, 94 days out, and docked on 19 December.

Macao to Dover   **96 days**
Belted Will (A Locke). Left Macao 15 July 1869, passed Anjer 15 days later and reached Dover 19 October. She had unmoored at Canton on 6 July.

CHINA TO ENGLAND DURING THE NORTH-EAST MONSOON

Shanghai to Liverpool   **85 days**
Zingra (W Gould). Left Shanghai 26 December 1863, and reached Liverpool 20 March 1864, 85 days out.

Shanghai to Liverpool   **87 days**
Nonpareil (E W Smith). Left Shanghai 19 December 1863, passed Anjer 1 January 1864 and reached Liverpool 15 March. (American-built.)

Shanghai to Liverpool   **90 days**
Young England ex-Oracle (Smith). Left Shanghai 18 December 1863, passed Anjer 2 January 1864 and reached Liverpool 17 March. (American-built.)

Shanghai to London   **90 days**
Lord of the Isles (W Jamieson). Left Shanghai 29 November 1858, lost sight of coast the next day, passed the Lizard 25 February 1859, 87 days out land to land, reached Dover 26 February and docked the next day.

Shanghai to Beachy Head (for London)   **89 days**
Golden Gate (Dewing). Left Shanghai 25 November 1854 but was run into by barque *Homer* when 9 days out, and was obliged to put into Batavia to repair damage. She remained there 4 days, but no actual dates are available. She passed Anjer 10 December and was off Beachy Head on 23 February 1855, 89 days out after leaving Shanghai but only 86 days at sea. (American-built.)

Shanghai to London   **91 days**
Hallowe'en (J Watt). Left Shanghai 21 October, 1874, was off Start Point 89 days out, and docked on 20 January 1875.

Shanghai to London   **94 days**
Nightingale (S W Mather). Left Shanghai 16 February 1855, was off Beachy Head on 18 May, 91 days out, and docked 3 days later. (American-built.)

Foochow to London   **92 days**
Elizabeth Nicholson (Crosbie). Left Foochow 14 December 1867, reached Anjer 12 days later and London on 15 March 1868.

Amoy to London   **89 Days**
Taeping (MacKinnon). Left Amoy 8 October 1864, after being dismasted in July in a typhoon, passed Anjer 25 October, reached Deal 88 days out on 4 January 1865, and docked next day.

Whampoa to Liverpool   **88 days**
Scawfell (R Thomson). Left Whampoa 13 January 1861, and the Canton river 14 January, was off Anjer 25 January, picked up her pilot off Point Lynas at daybreak on 11 April and was in dock by noon the same day. Her master claimed his time as 84½ days, possibly pilot to pilot. (See *Sea Breezes*, Vol VI, 1924, p250).

Whampoa to London   **92 days**
Witch of the Wave (J H Millett). Left Whampoa 5 January 1852 and picked up her pilot off Dungeness 4 April, 90 days out, and docked 2 days later. (American-built.)

Whampoa to London   **93 days**
Cairngorm (J Ryrie). Left Whampoa 5 November 1858, left Macao 6 November passed Anjer 22 November, was off Deal 5 February 1859, 91 days from Macao, and docked the next day.

Hong Kong to London   **89 days**
Lothair (Orchard). Left Hong Kong 11 December 1873, passed Anjer 5 days later and the Scillies when 83 days out. She was off Prawle Point on 6 March 1874, and Deal on 9 March, 88 days out, and docked the next day. She sailed from Macao on 7 December.

CHINA TO AMERICA

Shanghai to New York   **81 days**
Swordfish (J W Crocker). Left Shanghai 12 December 1859 and reached New York 2 March 1860. (American-built.) During the north-east monsoon, the American ships *N B Palmer* and *Surprise* both took 82 days on this route; *Panama* took 85 days; *Eagle Wing* and *Kathaya* both took 86 days.

Shanghai to New York   **89 days**
Harlaw (Phillips). Left Shanghai 24 February 1870, had light winds in the China Sea, passed Anjer 18 March, had S and SW winds to the Cape, 14 April, and reached New York 24 May. Was 87 days between her pilots.

Foochow to New York   **87 days**
The Caliph (Ritson). Left Foochow 6 December 1870, dropped her pilot off Sharp Peak 7 December, passed Anjer 10 days later, took her pilot on 2 March 1871, 85 days between her pilots, and docked the next day.

Amoy to New York   **84 days**
Lothair (B Orchard). Left Amoy on 8 January 1878, passed Anjer 19 January and the Cape of Good Hope on 12 February, and reached New York on 2 April.

Amoy to New York   **89 days**
Borealis (R Beard). Left Amoy on 29 December 1875, passed the Cape of Good Hope on 8 February 1876, and reached New York 27 March.

Hong Kong to New York   **75 days**
Sea Witch (R H Waterman). Left Hong Kong 9 January 1849, passed Anjer 6 days later on 15 January, and reached New York on 25 March, 74 days 14 hours out. (American-built.)
     Also during the north-east monsoon, this ship took 77 days in 1847–48 and 81 days in 1847. Other American ships to make fast runs between these same ports, and all during the north-east monsoon, were: *Natchez* 78 days in 1845; *Sea Serpent* 79 days in 1856; and *Rainbow* 79 days in 1846.

CHINA TO ANJER DURING THE SOUTH-WEST MONSOON

Shanghai to Anjer   **27 days**
Leander (Petherick). Left 13 June 1868, and arrived 10 July.

Shanghai to Anjer   **27 days**
Thermopylae (Kemball). Left 25 June 1871, and arrived 22 July.

Foochow to Anjer   **20 days**
Fiery Cross (J Dallas). Left 9 August 1857, and arrived 29 August.

Foochow to Anjer   **20 days**
Fiery Cross (R Robinson). Left 29 May 1866, and arrived 18 June.

Macao to Anjer   **15 days**
Belted Will (A Locke). Left 15 July 1869, and arrived 30 July.

CHINA TO ANJER DURING THE NORTH-EAST MONSOON

Shanghai to Anjer   **9 days**
Harlaw (Phillips). Left 7 January 1868, and arrived 16 January.

Shanghai to Anjer   **13 days**
Elizabeth Nicholson in 1870, *Harlaw* in 1866 and *Spray of the Ocean* in 1859–60 all took 13 days.

Shanghai to Anjer   **5 days**
Zingra (W Gould) claimed a time of 5 days, 26 to 31 December 1863. Over a distance of about 3000 miles this means an average of 500 miles per day! So the time of passing Anjer must be incorrect. Two other ships sailing about this time made unusually fast passages, so *Zingra*'s departure and arrival dates are probably not at fault.

Foochow to Anjer   **7 days**
Spirit of the North (E Martin). Left 19 January 1858, and arrived 26 January.

Foochow to Anjer   **10 days**
Mirage (J Roberts). Left 27 November 1861, and arrived 7 December.

Whampoa to Anjer   **6 days**
Gauntlet (W Inglis). Left 23 October 1856, and arrived 29 October.

Whampoa to Anjer   **6 days**
Heroes of Alma (B Freeman). Left 27 November 1855, and arrived 3 December.

Macao to Anjer   **5 days**
Lothair (Orchard). Left 11 December 1873, and arrived 16 December.

ANJER TO ENGLAND

Anjer to London   **63 days**
Lennox Castle (Brunton). Left Anjer 30 September 1867 and reached London 2 December. Had left Shanghai on 10 July 1867 and so had taken 82 days to get to Anjer.

Anjer to Deal   **63 days**
Kelso (Coulson). Passed Anjer 30 October 1860, and was off Deal 1 January 1861, reaching London two days later.

Anjer to London   **65 days**
Titania (J Dowdy). Passed Anjer 26 July 1871, and reached London 20 October.

Anjer to Lizard   **64 days**
In 1869, *Sir Lancelot* and *Thermopylae* each took 64 days between these points, London being reached a few days later. (See CHINA TO ENGLAND DURING SOUTH-WEST MONSOON).

ENGLAND TO CHINA DURING THE NORTH-EAST MONSOON

London to Shanghai   **92 days**
Fiery Cross (R Robinson). Left London 8 November 1863, and reached Shanghai 8 February 1864.

Deal to Shanghai   **95 days**
Blackadder (F W Moore). Left Deal 3 January 1872, was off Dartmouth 5 January, passed Anjer 23 March and reached Shanghai 7 April, 93 days from Dartmouth.

London to Hong Kong   **83 days**
Ariel (J Keay). Left London 14 October 1866, passed Start Point 15 October with a fresh breeze, dropped her pilot at noon on 17 October, passed through Gillolo Passage 23 December, took her pilot at 9.0 am on 5 January 1867, 79 days 21 hours between her pilots, and anchored at Hong Kong at 11.0 pm on 5 January.

London to Hong Kong   **90 days**
Fiery Cross (R Robinson). Left London 1 November 1862, and reached Hong Kong 30 January 1863. Two years later *Fiery Cross* was 88 days between her pilots and 92 port to port.

ENGLAND TO CHINA DURING THE SOUTH-WEST MONSOON

London to Shanghai   **88 days**
Ocean Mail (Linklater). Left London 9 February 1863, and reached Shanghai 8 May.

The Downs to Shanghai   **93 days**
Assyrian (A Mearns). Left the Downs 4 February 1863, and reached Shanghai 8 May.

London to Hong Kong   **77 days**
Cairngorm (J Robertson). Left London 24 March 1853, but put into Lisbon 29 March partially dismasted. Left Lisbon 1 May and reached Hong Kong 12 July, 72 days from Lisbon and 77 days at sea from London or 110 days after first leaving London.

Sunderland to Hong Kong   **87 days**
Maitland (Coulson). Left Sunderland 24 February 1866, passed Anjer 25 April and reached Hong Kong 22 May.

Liverpool to Hong Kong   **84 days**
Comet (E C Gardner). Left Liverpool 17 June 1854 at 12.30 am and reached Hong Kong 9 September 1854 at 4.30 am. These times given by Cutler in *Five Hundred Sailing Records*, p83, give a passage of 84 days 4 hours, not 83 days 21 hours. Cutler states departure as '12.30 midnight' which presumably means 12.30 am. (American-built in 1851 but never carried tea to England).

Liverpool to Hong Kong   **87 days**
Chrysolite (A Enright). Left Liverpool 16 April 1853 but spent 6 days beating out of the Channel; reached Hong Kong 12 July.

London to Hong Kong **89 days**
Pride of the Ocean ex-Pride of America (J Kyle). Left London 11 May 1857 and reached Hong Kong 8 August. The passage has been claimed as 69 days or 79 days, and it could have been the latter from Land's End or between pilots, but there is no evidence to substantiate this.

MISCELLANEOUS PASSAGES TO AND FROM CHINA

Singapore to Hong Kong **7 days**
Annandale (S Crockett). Left 6 September 1856, and arrived 13 September. Wind SW. Had two royal stunsails and main skysail set for several days.

Melbourne to Hong Kong **31 days**
Annandale (S Crockett). Left 11 May 1856 and arrived 11 June.

Sydney to Hong Kong **22 days**
Lord Macaulay (Care). Left 9 August 1863 and arrived 31 August.

Sydney to Shanghai **32 days**
Highflyer (A Enright). Left 17 April 1861 and arrived 19 May.

Newcastle NSW to Shanghai **31 days**
Thermopylae (Kemball). Left 10 February 1869, took her pilot on 10 March off Video, 28 days out and reached Shanghai 13 March.

Dunedin to Shanghai **41 days**
Robert Henderson (P Logan). Left 27 September 1862, in ballast, and arrived 7 November.

Sydney to Yokohama **39 days**
Kaisow (J Gadd). Left 17 June 1880 and reached Yokohama Bay 26 July.

Shanghai to Victoria (Vancouver Island) **34 days**
Kaisow (J Gadd). Left Shanghai 26 March 1878 in ballast and arrived 29 April.

Shanghai to San Francisco **30 days**
Ringleader (J Bray). Left 2 July 1878 and arrived 1 August. (American-built.)

San Francisco to Shanghai **33 days**
Swordfish (C Collins). Left San Francisco 16 June 1853, dropped pilot 17 June at 2 pm, and anchored off Gutzlaff Island 19 July at 11 pm. (American-built.)

San Francisco to Hong Kong **31 days**
Pampero (C Coggins). Left 18 February 1854 and arrived 21 March. (American-built).

Bombay to Hong Kong **29 days**
Cairngorm (Irvine). Left 19 May 1856, and arrived 17 June.

Calcutta to Hong Kong **32 days**
Stornoway (H L Hart). Left 7 June 1854, and arrived 9 July.

Woosung to Azores (for London) **80 days**
Abergeldie (L Wilson). Left 30 November 1851, passed Mauritius 24 days out and was off the Azores 18 February 1852.

Hong Kong to Scillies **83 days**
Lothair (Orchard). Left Hong Kong 11 December 1873, passed Anjer five days later and was off Scilly 4 March, 1874. She had left Macao on 7 December and reached London on 10 March.

APPENDIX IV
SPAR DIMENSIONS OF *STORNOWAY, FALCON, ARIEL AND MAITLAND*

The spar dimensions of *Falcon* and *Ariel* were taken from a very comprehensive table published in a *Report made to the Committee of Lloyd's Register of British and Foreign Shipping by the Society's Chief Surveyor and his Assistants concerning the Dismasting of Large Iron Sailing Ships* and was printed in 1874 and again in 1886. *Maitland*'s dimensions were taken from the figures appearing on the draught of her spar plan, a photograph of which appears on page 162. The spar dimensions of *Stornoway* were supplied by the Director of the Science Museum, London, from a list sent to the Museum by her builder, Alexander Hall. The dimensions are in feet. The figures in brackets are the lengths of the arms of the yards.

SPARS	Stornoway	Falcon	Ariel	Maitland
Bowsprit				
Extreme length	—	35	35	—
Outside figurehead	5	—	—	—
Outside knightheads	—	25	25	22
Outside knightheads (dia)	—	—	2½	—
Jibboom, outside cap	28	—	—	—
Inner jibboom, outside cap	—	22	22	17
Outer jibboom	—	13½	13½	15
Flying jibboom, outside sheave	11	—	—	—
Pole	—	—	3	1
Foremast				
Lower mast, extreme length	—	75	76½	—
Lower mast, deck to hounds	36½	41	41	43
Lower mast, head	10½	12	14	15
Lower mast (dia)	—	—	2½	—
Topmast, extreme length	36	43	42	43
Topmast, head	6½	7	7½	8
Topgallant mast, extreme length	18	23	24	26
Royal mast	13	14	15	18
Royal mast, head	—	—	4½	—
Skysail mast	9	—	—	12
Skysail mast, head	—	—	—	6
Foreyard, extreme length	58	64 (3)	71 (3)	73 (3½)
Lower topsail yard, extreme length	single topsail	single topsail	62 (1⅙)	65 (2)
Upper topsail yard, extreme length	47	51 (3)	58 (3)	60 (3)
Topgallant yard, extreme length	32	38 (2)	44 (2½)	48 (2½)
Royal yard, extreme length	25	27 (1)	33 (1½)	37 (2)
Skysail yard, extreme length	skysail	—	—	28 (1)
Mainmast				
Lower mast, extreme length	—	79	79	—
Lower mast, deck to hounds	40	46	44½	47
Lower mast, head	11	12	14½	15

Lower mast (dia)	—	—	2½	—
Topmast, extreme length	36	43	42	43
Topmast, head	6½	7	7½	8
Topgallant mast, extreme length	18	23	24	26
Royal mast	13	14	15	18
Royal mast, head	—	—	4½	—
Skysail mast	9	skysail	skysail	12
Skysail mast, head	—	—	—	6
Mainyard, extreme length	61	70 (3)	75 (3)	73 (3½)
Lower topsail yard, extreme length	single topsail	single topsail	65 (1⅛)	65 (2)
Upper topsail yard, extreme length	50	57 (3)	61 (3)	60 (3)
Topgallant yard, extreme length	35	43 (2)	47 (2½)	48 (2½)
Royal yard, extreme length	25	31 (1)	36 (1½)	37 (2)
Skysail yard, extreme length	21	skysail	skysail	28 (1)
Spencer gaff, extreme length	22	—	—	—
Mizen mast				
Lower mast, extreme length	—	72	71	—
Lower mast, deck to hounds	35½	40½	39	42½

Lower mast, head	8½	11	12	12½
Lower mast (dia)	—	—	2½	—
Topmast, extreme length	30	35	37	37
Topmast, head	5	6	6	7
Topgallant mast, extreme length	15	18	20	20
Royal mast	10	11	12	14
Royal mast, head	—	—	4	—
Skysail mast	—	—	—	10
Skysail mast, head	—	—	—	6
Crossjack yard, extreme length	50	57 (2)	61 (2½)	57 (3)
Lower topsail yard, extreme length	single topsail	single topsail	52 (1)	50 (2)
Upper topsail yard, extreme length	40	45 (2)	48 (2½)	46 (3)
Topgallant yard, extreme length	26	33 (1¼)	35 (1½)	36 (2¼)
Royal yard, extreme length	20	24 (1)	26 (1)	28 (1¾)
Skysail yard, extreme length	—	—	—	22 (1)
Spanker room, extreme length	42	43	48	50 (1½)
Spanker gaff, extreme length	30	29	35	36 (4)

APPENDIX V
COMPARATIVE TABLE OF COEFFICIENTS OF UNDER DECK TONNAGE

The value and use of these coefficients has been discussed in Chapter Six, and although they are given in the various biographies, a tabulated list representing some of the better known ships affords an easier comparison. They are arranged in relative order of sharpness, beginning with the sharpest, *Leander*.

Leander	0.54	*Kelso* (1861)	0.60
Chaa-sze	0.55	*Miako*	0.60
Cutty Sark	0.55	*Sir Lancelot*	0.60
Crest of the Wave	0.55	*Undine*	0.60
Hallowe'en	0.55	*Fiery Cross* (1860)	0.61
The Caliph	0.56	*Norman Court*	0.61
Friar Tuck	0.57	*Wylo*	0.61
Julia	0.57	*Black Prince*	0.62
Scawfell	0.57	*Kaisow*	0.62
Serica	0.57	*Strathmore*	0.62
Spindrift	0.57	*Windhover*	0.62
Gauntlet	0.58	*Cleta*	0.63
Jubilee	0.58	*Lothair*	0.63
Thermopylae	0.58	*Taeping*	0.63
Titania	0.58	*Norham Castle*	0.65
Belted Will	0.59	*Red Riding Hood*	0.66
Falcon (1859)	0.59	*Horsa*	0.67
Ariel	0.60	*Argonaut*	0.69
Invincible	0.60		

APPENDIX VI
RULES FOR THE MEASUREMENT OF TONNAGE

Three different types of measurement have been referred to in the text: the Old Measurement, enacted in 1773 as the first general rule applying to all merchant ships; the New Measurement which lasted from 1836 to 1854; and the rule embodied in the Merchant Shipping Act of 1854, as formulated by George Moorsom. The results accruing from the method of measuring ships to determine their tonnage under these laws have been mentioned in the text, but nothing has been said about how the measuring was to be carried out. It is proposed, therefore, to quote the essentials of each rule as they applied to the hulls of sailing vessels.

The first two quotations, describing how ships were measured under the Old and New Measurements, were taken from a book written by George Moorsom and published in 1852, entitled *A Brief Review and Analyses of the Laws for the Admeasurement of Tonnage, etc.*, together with the mode he proposed.

1773

The length shall be taken on a straight Line along the Rabbet of the Keel of the Ship, from the Back of the Main sternpost to a perpendicular Line from the Forepart of the Main Stem under the Bowsprit, from which subtracting Three-fifths of the Breadth, the Remainder shall be esteemed the just Length of the Keel to find the Tonnage; and the Breadth shall be taken from the outside of the outside Plank in the broadest Place in the Ship, be it either above or below the Main Wales, exclusive of all manner of doubling Planks that may be wrought upon the Sides of the Ship; then multiplying the Length of the Keel by the Breadth so taken, and that Product by Half the Breadth, and dividing the whole by Ninety-four, the Quotient shall be deemed the true Contents of the Tonnage. (13 Geo III, c 74)

1836

Divide the length of the upper deck, between the after part of the stem and the fore part of the sternpost, into six equal parts.

Depths. At the foremost, the middle, and the aftermost of these points of division, measure in feet and decimals the depths from the underside of the upper deck to the ceiling at the limber strake.

In the case of a break in the upper deck, the depths are to be measured from a line stretched in a continuation of the deck.

Breadths. Divide each of these three depths into five equal parts, and measure the inside breadths at the following points, viz, at one-fifth and at four-fifths from the upper deck of the foremost and aftermost depths, and at two-fifths and four-fifths of the midship depth.

Length. At half the midship depth measure the length of the vessel from the after part of the stem to the fore part of the sternpost.

Then to twice the midship depth add the foremost and the aftermost depths, for the *sum of the depths.*

Add together the upper and lower breadths at the foremost division, three times the upper breadth and the lower breadth at the midship division, and the upper and twice the lower breadth at the after division, for the *sum of the breadths.*

Then multiply the sum of the depths by the sum of the breadths, and this product by the length, and divide the final product by 3500, which will give the number of tons for register.

If the vessel have a poop or half-deck, or a break in the upper deck, measure the inside mean length, breadth, and height of such part thereof as may be included within the bulkhead; multiply these three measurements together, and, dividing the product by 92.4, the quotient will be the number of tons to be added to the result as above found.

In order to ascertain the tonnage of open vessels, the depths are to be measured from the upper edge of the upper strake.

If it be required to find the real capacity of a vessel, multiply the total register tonnage by 92.4, which will give the contents in cubic feet. (5 and 6 Wm IV, c 56)

The third quotation is taken from *The Stowage of Ships and their Cargoes* by R W Stevens (1869 edition).

1854

Measure the length in a straight line along the upper side of the Tonnage Deck, from the inside of the inner plank (average thickness) at the side of the stem, to the inside of the midship-stern timber or plank there, as the case may be (average thickness) deducting from this length what is due to the rake of the bow, in the thickness of the deck, and what is due to the rake of the stern timber, in the thickness of the deck, and also what is due to the rake of the stern timber, in one-third of the round of the beam; divide this length into the number of equal parts required by the following table, according to the class in such table to which the ship belongs.

Class 1: Ships, of which the Tonnage Deck is, according to the above measurement, 50ft long or under, into 4 equal parts.
Class 2: Ships 50ft long and not exceeding 120ft, into 6 equal parts.
Class 3. Above 120ft and not exceeding 180ft, 8 equal parts.
Class 4. Above 180ft and not exceeding 225ft, 10 equal parts.
Class 5. Ships, of which the Tonnage Deck is, according to the above measurement, above 225ft long, into 12 equal parts.

Then, the hold being first sufficiently cleared, find the transverse area of such ship, at each point of the length, as follows: Measure the depth at each point of division, from a point at a distance of one-third of the round of the beam below such deck – or, in a case of a break, below a line stretched in continuation thereof, to the upper side of the floor timber at the inside of the limber strake, after deducting the average thickness of the ceiling which is between the bilge planks and limber strake; then, if the depth at the midship division of the length do not exceed sixteen feet; divide each depth into four equal parts; then measure the inside horizontal breadth at each of the three points of division, and also at the upper and lower points of the depth, extending each measurement to the average thickness of that part of the ceiling which is between the points of measurement; number these breadths from above (ie, numbering the upper breadth one, and so on down to the lowest breadth); multiply the second and fourth by four, and the third by two; add these products together, and to the sum, add the first breadth and the fifth; multiply the quantity thus obtained, by one-third of the common interval between the breadths, and the product is deemed the transverse area; but if the midship depth exceed sixteen feet, divide each depth into six equal parts instead of four, and measure as before directed, the horizontal breadth at the five points of division, and also at the upper and lower points of the depth; number them from above as before; multiply the second, fourth and sixth, by four, and the third and fifth by two; add these products together, and to the sum, add to the first breadth and the seventh; multiply the quantity thus obtained, by one-third of the common interval between the breadths, and the product is deemed the *transverse area.*

Having thus ascertained the transverse area of each point of division of the length of the ship, as required by the above table, proceed to ascertain the register tonnage as follows: number the areas successively, 1, 2 3, etc, no 1 being at the extreme limit of the length at the bow, and the last number at the extreme limit of the length at the stern; then, whether the length be divided according to the table into four or twelve parts, as in Classes 1 and 5, or any intermediate number, as in Classes 2, 3 and 4, multiply the second and every even numbered area by four, and the third and every odd numbered area (except the first and last) by two; add these products together, and to the sum, add the first and last, if they yield anything; multiply the quantity thus obtained by one-third of the common interval between the areas, and the product will be the cubical contents of the space under the tonnage deck; divide this product by 100, and the quotient being the tonnage under the tonnage deck, is deemed to be the register tonnage, subject to the additions and deductions herein after-mentioned. (17 and 18 Vict, c 104, sec 20–29)

Then followed the method of measuring all closed-in spaces on the tonnage deck, and also the spar deck, if there was one. All this, together with the above quotation, was contained in Rule 1. Rule 2 described how ships with cargo on board were to be measured. Rule 3 outlined the allowances to be made for the propelling power in steam ships; whilst Rule 4 applied to open vessels.

The adjacent diagrams indicate the parts of the hull which were measured to calculate tonnage.

APPENDIX VII
TEA CLIPPERS BUILT BY ROBERT STEELE & CO

Date	Name	Under deck tons	Coeff. of UD tons	Managing owners	Material	Register dimensions (ft)
*1855	*Kate Carnie*	573.69		A Rodger	wood	148.4 × 26.0 × 19.0
1858	*Ellen Rodger*	554.93	0.62	A Rodger	wood	155.8 × 29.4 × 19.5
*1859	*Falcon*	729.41	0.59	Phillips, Shaw & Lowther	wood	191.4 × 32.2 × 20.0
1861	*Min*	594.99		A Rodger	wood	174.5 × 29.8 × 19.3
1862	*Guinevere*	603.33	0.58	J MacCunn	wood	174.5 × 30.1 × 19.8
1862	*King Arthur*	654.47		J MacCunn	iron	175.0 × 31.7 × 20.0
1863	*Serica*	652.44	0.57	J Findlay	wood	185.9 × 31.1 × 19.6
*1863	*Taeping*	723.85	0.63	A Rodger	comp	183.7 × 31.1 × 19.9
1863	*Young Lochinvar*	680.41	0.61	McDiarmid & Greenshields	wood	181.7 × 31.1 × 19.8
1865	*Chinaman*	628.93		Park Bros	comp	171.0 × 31.1 × 19.1
*1865	*Ariel*	852.87	0.60	Shaw, Lowther & Maxton	comp	197.4 × 33.9 × 21.0
*1865	*Sir Lancelot*	847.04	0.60	J MacCunn	comp	197.6 × 33.7 × 21.0
*1866	*Titania*	879.45	0.58	Shaw, Lowther & Maxton	comp	200.0 × 36.0 × 21.0
*1867	*Lahloo*	756.54	0.60	A Rodger	comp	191.6 × 32.9 × 19.9
1868	*Kaisow*	767.19	0.62	A Rodger	comp	193.2 × 32.0 × 20.3
*1869	*Wylo*	766.67	0.61	Killick, Martin	comp	192.9 × 32.1 × 20.2

*plans or models known to exist.

BIBLIOGRAPHY
AND NOTES ON SOURCES

Almost all the newspapers listed here have been examined in the British Museum Newspaper Library. Many of the files, especially those published in China, have several numbers missing and sometimes whole years are omitted. In such cases the *London and China Telegraph* has proved of inestimable value.

MANUSCRIPTS AND PLANS
Barclay, Curle & Co. Original plans inspected in their shipyard. Now housed at National Maritime Museum.

Baring Brothers. Documents relating to *Falcon*, *Black Prince* and *Norman Court*.

Daniel R Bolt. His personal collection of ships' data in Tower Hamlets Central Library (formerly Poplar).

Mr and Mrs C A Bull.

Ryrie Letters: letters from Phineas Ryrie in Hong Kong written c1848–72.

Howard I Chapelle. Various plans; lines taken off half-models.

Dr & Mrs Donald. Log-books and letters of Captain Thomas Mitchell.

Glasgow Museum of Transport. Half-models from yards of A Hall & Sons and John Reid.

James Henderson Collection. Cost accounts of ships built by Alexander Hall & Sons; reconstructed plans of Aberdeen ships; ship models.

Jardine, Matheson & Co. Documents and letters at Cambridge University Library.

Killick, Martin & Co. Documents relating to their ships.

J Kennedy Mann. Log of the barque *Strathmore*.

Merseyside Maritime Museum, Liverpool. Plans of ships built by T & J Brocklebank and shipyard list; papers and models in Kellock Collection; records compiled by Arthur C Wardle.

National Maritime Museum. Plans of merchant ships; Admiralty draughts; Lubbock Collection; Lloyd's Register Survey Reports.

B E Nicholson. Half-models of ships built at Annan; account books.

Science Museum, London. Models; sail plans drawn by G C Watson.

James Steele. Half-models; shipyard list of Robert Steele & Co.

Sunderland Museum. Half-models.

Alexander Stephen & Sons. Original plans and half-models inspected in their shipyard (now deposited at National Maritime Museum); diaries kept by Alexander Stephen Jnr from 1856 onwards; letter-books (both now deposited at Department of Economic History, Glasgow University).

Author's Collection. Plans drawn from take-offs of models or traced from originals; shipyard list of vessels built by William Pile, beginning at no 52.

NEWSPAPERS
Aberdeen Herald
Greenock Advertiser
Illustrated London News (London, since 1841)
Liverpool Albion
Lloyd's List (London)
London and China Express (London, since 1859)
London and China Telegraph (London, since 1859)
Mitchell's Maritime Register (London 1856–84).
After 1884 it became *Lloyd's Weekly Summary*
The Times (London)
New York Herald
Adelaide Times (Adelaide, since 1848)
Sydney Morning Herald
Canton Press (Canton, since 1835)

China Mail (Hong Kong, since 1845)
Daily Shipping and Commercial News (Shanghai, since *c*1856)
Argus (Melbourne)
North-China Herald (Shanghai, since *c*1850)
Overland China Mail (Hong Kong, 1846–61)
Overland Register and Price Current (Hong Kong, 1846–61)

PERIODICALS
The American Neptune (Salem, since 1941)
Blue Peter (London 1921–39)
The Mariner's Mirror (London, since 1912)
Mercantile Marine Magazine and Nautical Record (London 1854–74)
Sea Breezes (Liverpool, since 1919)
Ships and Ship Models (London 1931–40)
Trident (London, since 1938)

BOOKS
ABELL, SIR WESTCOTT *The Shipwright's Trade* (Cambridge 1948)
ADMIRALTY *The China Sea Directory* (London 1894, 3rd ed, 4 vols)
ANSTED, A *A Dictionary of Sea Terms* (Glasgow 1933)
BLOCKSIDE, ERNEST W *Hints on the Register Tonnage of Merchant Ships* (Liverpool 1942, 2nd edition)
BOWEN, FRANK C *The Golden Age of Sail* (London 1925)
BOWEN, FRANK C *The Sea: Its History and Romance* (London vol 4)
BOWEN, FRANK C *Sailing Ships of the London River* (London)
BOWEN, FRANK C *The Flag of the Southern Cross: The History of the Shaw, Savill & Albion Co Ltd, 1858–1939* (London 1939)
BRETT, SIR HENRY *White Wings* (Auckland, 1924, 1928, 2 vols)
BRETTLE, ROBERT E *The 'Cutty Sark', Her Designer and Builder, Hercules Linton* (Cambridge 1969)
CABLE, BOYD 'The World's First Clipper', *The Mariner's Mirror* (Vol 29, 1943, pp66–91)
CARR, FRANK G G 'The Restoration of the *Cutty Sark*', *Transactions of the Royal Institution of Naval Architects* (1966, Vol 108, pp193–216)
CHAPELLE, HOWARD I *The Baltimore Clipper* (Salem 1930)
CHAPELLE, HOWARD I *The History of American Sailing Ships* (New York 1935)
CHAPELLE, HOWARD I *The Search for Speed under Sail* (New York 1967)
CHAPMAN, CHARLES *All About Ships* (London *c*1869)
CLARKE, ARTHUR H *The Clipper Ship Era* (New York 1910)
'Clipper Ships', *Naval Science* (July 1873, Vol II, pp265 *et seq*)
COATES, LT W H, RNR *The Good Old Days of Shipping* (Bombay 1900)
COLLIS, MAURICE *Foreign Mud* (London 1946)
CUTLER, CARL C *Greyhounds of the Sea* (New York 1930)
DERBY, W L A *The Tall Ships Pass* (London 1937)
DULLIES, FOSTER R *The Old China Trade* (Cambridge USA 1930)
FLETCHER, R A *In the Days of the Tall Ships* (London 1928)
FOX SMITH C *Ocean Racers* (London 1931)
GRAHAM, GERALD S 'The Ascendancy of the Sailing Ship 1850–85', *Economic History Review* (Vol IX, no 1, pp74–78)
HIDY, R W *The House of Baring in American Trade and Finance 1763–1861* (Harvard 1949)
HOWE, OCTAVUS T and FREDERICK C MATTHEWS, *American Clipper Ships 1833–1858* (Salem 1926–27, 2 vols)
JOHNSON, J *The Oriental Voyager, or . . . Remarks on a Voyage to India and China in HMS Caroline . . . in 1803–06* (London 1807)
KIPPING, ROBERT *The Elements of Sailmaking* (London 1851, 2nd ed)
LINDSAY, W S *History of Merchant Shipping 1816–74* (London, *c*1874, 2 vols)
LLOYD'S REGISTER *Lloyd's Register of British and Foreign Shipping* (London, annually since 1834)
LLOYD'S REGISTER *Report made to the Committee of Lloyd's Register of British and Foreign Shipping by the Society's Chief Surveyor and his Assistants, concerning the Dismasting of Large Iron Sailing Ships* (London 1886)
LONGRIDGE, C NEPEAN *The 'Cutty Sark'* (London 1949, 2 vols)
LUBBOCK, BASIL *The China Clippers* (Glasgow 1922, 5th ed)
LUBBOCK, BASIL *The Log of the 'Cutty Sark'* (Glasgow 1924)
LUBBOCK, BASIL *The Colonial Clippers* (Glasgow 1924)
LUBBOCK, BASIL *The Opium Clippers* (Glasgow 1931)
LUBBOCK, BASIL *The Last of the Windjammers* (Glasgow 1935, 2nd ed, 2 vols)
LYMAN, JOHN, 'Register Tonnage and its Measurement', *The American Neptune* (1945, Vol V, pp223–33 and 311–25)
LYMAN, JOHN, 'The Cutter Brig', *The Mariner's Mirror* (1969, Vol 55, pp17–21)
MACGREGOR, DAVID R *The China Bird* (London 1961)
MACGREGOR, DAVID R *Fast Sailing Ships, their Design and Construction 1775–1875* (Lymington 1973)
MACGREGOR, DAVID R 'Tendering and Contract Procedure in Merchant Shipyards in the Middle of the Nineteenth Century', *The Mariner's Mirror*, (1962, Vol 48, pp241–64.)
MCCULLOCH, J R A *Dictionary . . . of Commerce and Commercial Navigation* (London 1854)
MARRYAT, CAPTAIN, RN *The Universal Code of Signals for the Mercantile Marine of All Nations* (London, various eds 1820–69)
MAURY, MATTHEWS F *Explanations and Sailing Directions to Accompany the Wind and Current Charts* (New York 1859, 8th ed, 2 vols)
MOORSOM, GEORGE *A Brief Review and Analyses of the Laws for the Admeasurement of Tonnage* (London 1852)
PARKINSON, C NORTHCOTE *Trade in the Eastern Seas* (Cambridge 1937)
PARLIAMENTARY PAPERS *First to Fifth Reports from the Select Committee on Navigation Laws* (26 March to 17 July 1847)
PIDDINGTON, HENRY *The Sailor's Horn Book for the Law of Storms* (London 1855, 2nd ed)
REGISTRAR GENERAL OF SHIPPING AND SEAMEN *The Mercantile Navy List* (London, annually since before 1851)
RUSSELL, JOHN SCOTT *The Modern System of Naval Architecture* (London 1865, 3 vols)
SALISBURY, W 'Hollow Water-lines and Early Clippers', *The Mariner's Mirror* (1946, Vol 32, pp237–41)
SHEWAN, CAPTAIN ANDREW *The Great Days of Sail* (London 1927)
SMITH, J W and T S HOLDEN *Where Ships are Born: Sunderland, 1346–1946* (Sunderland 1947)
SPURLING, J and BASIL LUBBOCK *Sail* (London 1927, 1932, 1936, 3 vols)
STEEL, DAVID *The Elements and Practice of Rigging and Seamanship* (London 1794, 2 vols)
[STEPHEN, SIR A MURRAY] *A Shipbuilding History 1750–1932* (Glasgow *c*1932). Includes list of ships built by A Stephen and Sons
STEVENS, ROBERT W *On the Stowage of Ships and their Cargoes* (London 1869, 5th ed)
SYMONDSON, F W H *Two Years Abaft the Mast* (Edinburgh 1876).
TWEEDIE, FRANCIS 'The Era of Shipbuilding at Annan', (*The Mariner's Mirror* 1951, Vol 37, pp128–32)
UNDERHILL, HAROLD A *Masting and Rigging, the Clipper Ship and Ocean Carrier* (Glasgow 1946)
UNDERHILL, HAROLD A *Deep-Water Sail* (Glasgow 1952)
UNDERWRITERS' REGISTRY *Underwriters' List of Iron Vessels* (Liverpool, annually since 1862). Incorporated with Lloyd's Register, 1885
UKERS, W H *All About Tea* (New York 1935, 2 vols)
WINCHESTER, CLARENCE (Editor) *Shipping Wonders of the World* (London 1937, 2 vols)
WISE, HENRY *An Analysis of One Hundred Voyages to and from India, China, etc, performed by Ships in the Hon'ble East India Company's Service* (London 1839)
YOUNG, C F T *Fouling and Corrosion of Iron Ships* (London 1867)

INDEX

The numerals in bold type denote the page numbers of ships receiving biographies. The letter (A) after a ship's name indicates that she was built in the United States of America.